THE ELGAR COMPANION TO ECONOMICS
AND PHILOSOPHY

The Elgar Companion to Economics and Philosophy

Edited by

John B. Davis

University of Amsterdam, The Netherlands and Marquette University, US

Alain Marciano

University of Reims Champagne Ardenne (OMI-EDJ), Centre National de la Recherche Scientifique (GREQAM – Aix Marseille) and Institut d'Economie Publique, France

Jochen Runde

The Judge Institute of Management, University of Cambridge, UK

Edward Elgar

Cheltenham, UK • Northampton, MA, USA

Published by
Edward Elgar Publishing Limited
Glensanda House
Montpellier Parade
Cheltenham
Glos GL50 1UA
UK

Edward Elgar Publishing, Inc.
136 West Street
Suite 202
Northampton
Massachusetts 01060
USA

A catalogue record for this book
is available from the British Library

Library of Congress Cataloguing in Publication Data
The Elgar companion to economics and philosophy / edited by John B. Davis, Alain
    Marciano, Jochen Runde.
        p. cm.— (Elgar original reference)
    Includes index.
        1. Economics—Philosophy. 2. Economics—History. 3. Economics—
    Methodology. I. Title: Economics and philosophy. II. Davis, John Bryan. III.
    Marciano, Alain. IV. Series.

HB72.E44 2004
330'.01—dc22
                                                                        2004047145

ISBN   1 84064 964 X (cased)

Printed and bound in Great Britain by MPG Books Ltd, Bodmin, Cornwall

Contents

PART III   SOCIAL ONTOLOGY AND THE ONTOLOGY OF
           ECONOMICS

Contributors

Roger E. Backhouse is Professor of the History and Philosophy of Economics at Birmingham University. He is author of *The Penguin History of Economics/ The Ordinary Business of Life* (Penguin, 2002) and an editor (with Andrea Salanti) of *Macroeconomics and the Real World* (Oxford, 2000). He is an editor of the *Journal of Economic Methodology*.

Drucilla K. Barker is Professor of Economics and Women's Studies at Hollins University. She is a founding member of the International Association for Feminist Economics. Her research interests are in the areas of feminist philosophy and economic methodology. She is the co-editor of *Toward a Feminist Philosophy of Economics* (Routledge, 2003) and the co-author of *Liberating Economics: Feminist Perspectives on Gender and the Economy* (University of Michigan Press, forthcoming).

Matthias Benz is Research Assistant and Lecturer at the Institute for Empirical Research in Economics, University of Zurich. He has authored several papers in the fields of public choice, labour economics, and economics and psychology.

Marcel Boumans is Associate Professor of Methodology and History of Economics at the University of Amsterdam. His domain of research is marked by three M's: Model, Measurement and Mathematics. Last year he finished a book manuscript on measurement in economics, *How Economists Model the World into Numbers*. His current research explores a methodology of models that function as instruments in social science.

José Luís Cardoso is Professor at the Institute of Economics and Management (ISEG) of the Technical University of Lisbon. His main areas of research and teaching are the methodology, sociology and history of economics. He is the author of several books and articles on the history of economics, focusing particularly on a comparative approach to Portuguese economic thought between the seventeenth and the twentieth centuries, and is co-founder and co-editor of *The European Journal of the History of Economic Thought*.

John B. Davis is Professor of History and Philosophy of Economics, University of Amsterdam and Professor of Economics, Marquette University. He is the author of *Keynes's Philosophical Development* (Cambridge, 1994) and *The Theory of the Individual in Economics* (Routledge, 2003), co-editor with Wade

Hands and Uskali Mäki of *The Handbook of Economic Methodology* (Elgar, 1998) and a co-editor with Warren Samuels and Jeff Biddle of *The Blackwell Companion to the History of Economic Thought* (Blackwell, 2003). He is a past President of the History of Economics Society, current Chair of the International Network for Economic Method, and the editor of the *Review of Social Economy*.

Philip Faulkner is a Research Associate in the Department of Applied Economics at the University of Cambridge and College Lecturer in Economics at St. Catharine's College, Cambridge. His main research interests are the treatment of human agency in economics and economic methodology. He has published papers in the *Cambridge Journal of Economics* and the *Journal of Economic Methodology*.

Marc Fleurbaey is Professor of Economics at the University of Pau, France. Many of his publications deal with normative issues: theory of fairness, equality of opportunities, distributive justice and tax policies. In his work he has repeatedly tried to show how the analytical concepts of economics can be useful in studying philosophical issues of distributive justice. He is currently working on a new approach connecting the theory of social choice and the theory of fairness. This approach produces fair social preferences that are helpful in analysing public policies, including in a second best context. He has been an editor of *Economics and Philosophy* and is an editor of *Social Choice and Welfare*, and has set up the *Equality Exchange* website.

Bruno S. Frey is a Professor of Economics at the University of Zurich. He is the recipient of honorary doctorates in economics from the University of St. Gallen and the University of Goeteborg. He is the author of numerous articles in professional journals and books, including *Not Just for the Money* (Edward Elgar, 1997*)*, *Economics as a Science of Human Behaviour* (Kluwer, 1999*)*, *The New Democratic Federalism for Europe* (Elgar 999), *Arts & Economics* (Springer, 2000*)*, *Inspiring Economics* (Elgar, 2001), *Successful Management by Motivation* (Springer, 2001) and *Happiness and Economics* (Princeton, 2002).

Edward Fullbrook is a member of the School of Economics at the University of the West of England, the founder/editor of the *Post-Autistic Economics Review*, the editor of *Intersubjectivity in Economics* (Routledge, 2002), *The Crisis in Economics* (Routledge, 2003) and the author of numerous economics papers. He also maintains a strong research presence in the field of phenomenological and existential philosophy in which he has published many essays and authored two books (with Kate Fullbrook). He is a co-editor of *Cinquantenaire du Deuxième sexe* (2002).

Robert F. Garnett Jr. is Assistant Professor of Economics at Texas Christian University. His research examines the role of (and alternatives to) modernism in economic analysis, philosophy, and pedagogy. He is Secretary of the International Confederation of Associations for Pluralism in Economics (ICAPE) and Associate Editor of the University of Michigan Press book series, Advances in Heterodox Economics. He is editor of *What Do Economists Know?* (Routledge, 1999) and co-editor of *The Future of Heterodox Economics* (University of Michigan Press, forthcoming), and is currently working on a textbook with Arjo Klamer and Deirdre McCloskey, *An Introduction to the Economic Conversation* (Routledge, forthcoming).

D. Wade Hands is Professor of Economics at the University of Puget Sound in Tacoma WA. He has written on a number of topics in the history and philosophy of economics. He is the author of *Reflection Without Rules: Economic Methodology and Contemporary Science Theory* (Cambridge, 2001), and one of the editors, along with John Davis and Uskali Mäki, of *The Handbook of Economic Methodology* (Edward Elgar, 1998). His most recent book is *Introductory Mathematical Economics*, 2nd edition (Oxford, 2004).

Shaun P. Hargreaves Heap teaches economics at the University of East Anglia. His current research is on rationality in a social and historical context, inequality and the economics of public service broadcasting. His publications include *Rationality in Economics* (Basil Blackwell, 1989), *The New Keynesian Macroeconomics* (Edward Elgar, 1992), *Game Theory: a critical introduction* (with Y. Varoufakis, Rouledge, 1995) and several journal articles, most recently 'Some experimental evidence on the evolution of discrimination, cooperation and the perception of fairness' (with Y. Varoufakis) *Economic Journal*, July 2002. He is working on a book about public service broadcasting.

Geoffrey M. Hodgson is Research Professor at the Business School, University of Hertfordshire, Hatfield, UK, and was formerly Reader in Institutional and Evolutionary Economics at the University of Cambridge. He is the author of *The Evolution of Institutional Economics* (Routledge, 2004), *How Economics Forgot History* (Routledge, 2001), *Economics and Utopia* (Routledge, 1999), *Evolution and Institutions* (Elgar, 1999), *Economics and Evolution* (Polity, 1993), *After Marx and Sraffa* (Macmillan, 1991), *Economics and Institutions* (Polity, 1988), *The Democratic Economy* (Pelican, 1984), over 80 articles in academic journals, and over 70 articles in academic books. He is listed in *Who's Who in Economics* (4th edn., Elgar, 2003). His research interests are principally in the methodology of economics, institutional economics and evolutionary economics.

Geoffrey Ingham is Fellow and Director of Studies in Social and Political Sciences, Christ's College, Cambridge, and since 1995 has taught political economy and sociology in the Faculty of Social and Political Sciences.

Between 1971 and 1995, he taught sociology in the Faculty of Economics and Politics. These experiences have resulted in a profound dissatisfaction with the increasingly sharp separation of mainstream economics from the other social sciences. He has published widely on the social and political construction and production of money over the past decade and his *The Nature of Money* was published by Polity in early 2004.

Peter Kesting wrote his Ph.D. thesis at the University of Hamburg on the work of Joseph A. Schumpeter fro m a methodological perspective. He is currently Assistant Professor at the department for microeconomics of Leipzig Graduate School of Management. The focus of his present research is on the fundamentals of company dynamics and economic development, with particular emphasis of bounded rationality.

Harold Kincaid recieved his Ph.D from Indiana University in 1983 and is the author of *Philosophical Foundations in the Social Sciences: Analyzing Controversies in Social Science* (Cambridge, 1996) and *Individualism and the Unity of Science* (Rowman and Littlefield, 1997).

Tony Lawson is Reader in Economics at the Faculty of Economics and Politics, Cambridge. He has published numerous articles on philosophical issues in economics and is the author of *Economics and Reality* (Routledge, 1997) and *Reorienting Economics* (Routledge, 2003). He sits on various editorial boards of journals and is the general editor of the Routledge series 'Economics and Social Theory'.

Paul A. Lewis was educated at Peterhouse, Cambridge, and Christ Church, Oxford, before becoming a Research Fellow of Emmanuel College, Cambridge. He is currently a Newton Trust Lecturer in the Faculty of Economics and Politics, and the Faculty of Social and Political Sciences, Cambridge University, and a Fellow of Selwyn College. His research interests include the philosophy of the social sciences, social theory, the Austrian school of economics, and economic sociology.

Alain Leroux is Professor of Economics at the University of Aix-Marseille, where he manages the doctoral program of economic philosophy. He is the author of ten of books, which deal with two major topics: the role of ideology in social science and the elaboration of a renewed *personalism*. He is the editor of the *Revue de Philosophie Economique*.

Alain Marciano is Assistant Professor at the University of Reims Champagne Ardenne. He is the author of two books in economics and philosophy and has published various papers in law and economics, and public choice theory. His research interests include the nature of institutions, in particular, democracy and the normativity of rules.

Charles R. McCann, Jr. is a Research Associate in the Department of Economics at the University of Pittsburgh. Author of *Probability Foundations of Economic Theory* (Routledge, 1994), he is currently writing on issues in political and social philosophy and the history of economic thought.

Stephen Pratten is Lecturer in Economics at the Management Centre, King's College London. His main research area is the methodology of economics, focusing particularly on issues related to social ontology and realist theorising. He is an Editor of the *Cambridge Journal of Economics*.

Jochen Runde is Senior Lecturer in Economics at the Judge Institute of Management Cambridge, Director of Graduate Programmes, the Cambridge-Massachusetts Institute (CMI), and Fellow and Graduate Tutor (Arts) at Girton College, Cambridge. He is a coeditor of the *Cambridge Journal of Economics* and, with Sohei Mizuhara, of *The Philosophy of Keynes's Economics* (Routledge, 2003). His current research is on the development and commercialisation of digital technologies.

Arnis Vilks is Professor of Microeconomics and Dean of Leipzig Graduate School of Management. He is the author of two books on aggregation in a general equilibrium context, and on the foundations of equilibrium economics, respectively. His research interests include methodological issues in economics, modeling of knowledge and belief, and formal logic approaches to game theory.

Jack J. Vromen is Associate Professor at the Faculty of Philosophy of Erasmus University Rotterdam, where he teaches philosophical aspects of economics. He is also Managing Director and member of the teaching staff of the Erasmus Institute for Philosophy and Economics. His main interests are the relations between economic and evolutionary theorizing broadly conceived, and particularly the ontological presuppositions, key concepts and modes of explanation of evolutionary economics, (new) institutional economics, and evolutionary game-theoretic analyses of conventions. His recent publications include 'Ontological Commitments of Evolutionary Economics', in *The Economic World View* (Cambridge, 2001, ed. by Uskali Mäki), 'Stone Age Minds and Group Selection – What difference do they make?', in *Constitutional Political Economy* (2002), and 'Collective Intentionality, Evolutionary Biology and Social Reality', in *Philosophical Explorations* (2003).

Introduction

John Davis, Alain Marciano and Jochen Runde

The closing decades of the twentieth century saw a dramatic increase in interest in the role of philosophical ideas in economics. The period also saw a significant expansion in scholarly investigation into the different connections between economics and philosophy, as seen in the emergence of new journals, professional associations, conferences, seminar series, websites, research networks, teaching methods, and interdisciplinary collaboration. One of the results of this set of developments has been a remarkable distillation in thinking about philosophy and economics around a number of key subjects and themes. The goal of this *Companion to Economics and Philosophy* is to exhibit and explore a number of these areas of convergence. The volume is accordingly divided into three parts, each of which highlights a leading area of scholarly concern. They are: political economy conceived as political philosophy, the methodology and epistemology of economics, and social ontology and the ontology of economics. The authors of the chapters in the volume were chosen on the basis of their having made distinctive and innovative contributions to their respective areas of expertise. In addition, authors were asked to not only survey the state of the field as they saw it, but also provide statements of their own positions and their perspectives on the field in question and its possible direction of development in the future. We thus hope this volume will serve not only as an introduction to the field, but also stimulate further work and thinking concerning the questions it investigates.

Political economy conceived as political philosophy

The essays in the first part of this *Companion* investigate the idea of economics or political economy as political philosophy. This last term should not to be understood in the pejoratively restrictive sense of Rosenberg's (1992) definition of economics as mathematical political science. Rather, it should be taken to refer to the use of specific (namely economic) tools to understand the conditions of social order. This perspective harks back to the founders of economics and their conception of the discipline. Of course some would argue that more than two hundred years of scientific research have carried the discipline away from this conception. In fact, however, and as the issues discussed in the chapters in this section show, the distance that separates political economy in its recent developments from its origins is not that large.

Regarding political economy as a form of political philosophy is not to deny its existence as a self-standing scientific discipline. Political economy is indeed a separate science in its own right and, in the opening chapter on 'Natural Law, Natural History and the Foundations of Political Economy', José Luìs Cardoso shows how it came to be so. Cardoso's argument proceeds in two stages that correspond to two distinct but complementary developments in the eighteenth century. The first of these was the identification of an object interesting and important enough to require analysis over and above that already provided within the framework of the philosophy of natural law. Social and economic organisation thus came to be viewed as parts of the natural order. The second development was a recognition of the need for some form of scientific method in terms of which the analysis would be conducted. Here, according to Cardoso, political economy was deeply influenced by the growing stature of sciences that aimed to uncover the laws that governed the functioning of the natural world. Natural history, the most authoritative field of knowledge in the eighteenth century, along with the conceptual constructions of the natural sciences, accordingly came to provide the tools with which political economy was able to establish itself as a science.

The three chapters that follow, by Alain Marciano, Shaun Hargreaves Heap and Bruno Frey and Mathias Benz respectively, discuss the virtues and limitations of the mainstream (neoclassical) economic model of the human agent, and the potential fruitfulness of a more refined representation. The objective is not, as Hargeaves Heap makes clear, to suggest that people never act in accordance with the assumptions of mainstream rational choice theory. Rather, it is to show that the highly stripped down psychology of the standard model of the economic agent is too thin to give an adequate account of people's actions in all possible walks of life. As Frey and Benz explain, this model is a relatively recent consequence of economists' efforts to rid the discipline of all traces of psychology, a contention well supported by Marciano's demonstration that the conception of economic man adopted by the founding fathers of political economy was indeed considerably richer than it is now. As Marciano describes it, the rejection of Cartesian rationalism in favour of empiricism by Scottish Enlightenment authors such as Hume and Smith, led naturally to a theory of man limited in his cognitive abilities, whose knowledge would always be highly subjective and situation-dependent.

The central message in Hargreaves Heap's chapter on 'Economic rationality' is the need to pay attention to intersubjectively shared beliefs, particularly when attempting to understand behaviour that seems resistant to the standard model of economic agency. In many situations, according to Hargreaves Heap, individual agents are not driven solely by instrumental reason and the direct satisfaction they might derive from the outcome of any action, but also by the sense of self-respect they achieve from knowing that their actions reflect well upon them. The difficulty this raises is that even if the desire for self-respect is regarded as a kind of preference, self-respect does not fit into the analytical framework of the standard rational choice model. This is because people's judgements regarding what actions reflect well on them cannot be decided in isolation, namely without reference to the beliefs and values of other members of the community. And if so, it then it becomes necessary to analyse how individuals acquire and share beliefs about what is worthy. Obviously, these questions go beyond the boundaries of the rational choice model, and require input from other disciplines. Hargreaves Heap points out that psychology offers some relevant insights here, especially about cognitive dissonance and intrinsic/ extrinsic motivation.

Frey and Benz, in their essay 'From Imperialism to Inspiration: A Survey of Economics and Psychology', also argue that economists can no longer rely only on an approach to human behaviour based on the model of the 'homunculus economicus'. They too observe that there are many forms of human behaviour that are in conflict with the assumptions of, and therefore incomprehensible within, the framework of the standard model. In particular, Frey and Benz point out that, in contrast to the standard model, people face cognitive limits and are emotionally constrained, are not systematically egoistic in their behaviour, and are not committed to acting under the constraints of the material elements of their material utility function. The suggested remedy is that economists might draw on psychology to 'inspire' them out of the current impasse. But again, Frey and Benz are not proposing that economics be replaced by psychology. They continue to regard the standard model of the rational economic agent as a consistent general framework against which the insights of psychology, which 'consists of a large number of partial theories and special effects, which are more or less isolated from each other', may be thrown into sharper relief.

A more refined, 'inspired' conception of economic man necessarily leads to normative implications in relation to the nature, the scope and the role of institutions. For example, in his essay entitled 'The historical and philosophical foundations of *new* political economy', Marciano shows that sympathy is a necessary condition for successful co-ordination, although not sufficient to order large and open societies. Therefore, even if spontaneously emerging conventions play an important role in allowing successful coordination, there is also a place for consciously designed institutions in overcoming the natural limits of sympathy. Hargreaves Heap, for his part, stresses the necessity of deriving prescriptive consequences from the expressive conception of rationality he proposes. In particular, from his perspective, it is important to take seriously the role institutions play in shaping, and contributing to the sharing of beliefs. Societies need institutions that allow people to participate in the discussion of shared beliefs, and which give them scope to express those beliefs in action, in Hargreaves Heap's view, much in the way suggested by Habermas.

Geoffrey Hodgson's chapter, 'Institutional Economics: From Menger and Veblen to Coase and North', surveys the commonalities and differences between the 'old' and the 'new' institutionalist schools, as well as some differences between individual members of each camp. Like many of his co-contributors, Hodgson is interested in competing theoretical conceptions of the economic actor. On this front, in his view, the new institutionalism represents a step backwards in that its commitment to the standard model of rational agency has obscured various key insights of the older institutionalists. But Hodgson's main concern is with the related idea that individual action and institutions bear on each other in a reciprocal way, i.e., that while individual action presupposes institutions (or rules), institutions are at the same time affected, indeed reproduced, by the total of individual action. Hodgson argues that this mutual dependence is recognised in the writings of the old institutionalist school, which is therefore not restricted to the doctrine that all human behaviour is socially or institutionally determined. For example, he demonstrates that both Veblen and Commons see the interactions between individuals and institutions as a top-down and a bottom-up process of reciprocal influences. But Hodgson recognises that the different ways in which institutions affect peoples' behaviour remain underdeveloped in the old institutional economics, and suggests that this issue therefore provides fertile ground for further work.

As Hodgson notes, one way to proceed here is to adopt an evolutionary approach to the study of institutions. Veblen's attempt to harness some of Darwin's ideas as a basis for an evolutionary economic science provides an early example here, and there is of course something of a tradition in economics of authors advocating evolutionary approaches of various kinds. Jack Vromen's chapter, 'Taking evolution seriously: what difference does it make for economics?' is essentially a survey of this tradition, and provides the valuable service of providing a coherent overview of what is by any measure a pretty disparate literature. Vromen's organising principle is the extent to which the introduction of evolutionary thinking is seen to affect standard methods, and he provides a revealing grouping of various commentators under the following three headings: the 'revolutionaries', like Veblen, who believe that taking evolution seriously requires profound changes to standard economic theory; the 'conservatives', like Alchian, Friedman and Becker, who believe it possible to accommodate evolutionary economic processes within standard economic theory; and 'revisionists' like Robert Frank, who claim that evolutionary themes can be accommodated by revising or amending parts of standard economic theory while leaving its essential elements unchanged.

We have noted Hargreaves Heap's emphasis on specifically rational, private deliberation in the process of individual preference formation, but other writers have focused instead on public deliberation. Indeed economists, political scientists, and political philosophers, who have devoted their attention to the role that deliberation could or should play in our societies, have in some instances even gone so far as to propose public deliberation as a means of producing a definition of social justice. However, while it may be convenient to allow normative economics and political philosophy to be guided by the standards of public deliberation, this falls well short of what is required for a serious investigation of the foundations of ethical principles. Indeed, as Marc Fleurbaey notes in his essay 'Normative economics and theories of distributive justice', too often ordinary thinking about moral principles is guided by pragmatic considerations and unexamined moral intuitions, when what is needed is that precise criteria be developed and analysed to produce theories that are complex enough to address the normative problems society encounters. As a step towards this end, Fleurbaey provides a careful survey of the various approaches to the problem of defining social justice that have been developed by economic theorists and philosophers over the last fifty years. From the Pareto criterion and its limits to the theories of fairness and equality of resources, and including discussion of libertarian views and social contract theories, Fleurbaey provides a detailed and comprehensive analysis of the normative economics literature that has assumed increasing importance in economic analysis.

The final chapter in this part of the Companion, Alain Leroux's 'Ideology: an economic point of view', returns to the themes explored in Cardoso's opening essay regarding the possibility of separating science from ideology. Leroux begins with the standard interpretation of ideology offered by Karl Marx. According to Marx, ideology is an inferior form of discourse that offers a distorted and coerced representation of the social order – as distinct from science, the domain of an objective, non-distorted and unconstrained knowledge. Leroux explains how Marx's approach leads to a vicious circle, namely that it is impossible to maintain that any discourse is not spoiled by ideological bias while at the same time maintaining the possibility of developing an alternative discourse free from any ideology. This logical trap is known as the Mannheim Paradox and Joseph A. Schumpeter is one of its most famous victims. In the face of the impossibility of eliminating ideology from economic discourse, Leroux proposes instead to put ideology, science, and even philosophy on the same footing. He does so by presenting them as *cognitive strategies* or *pure forms of thought* that are interdependent and simultaneously active. From this perspective, science, philosophy and ideology allow us to identify the major form of thought that characterises a discourse, rather than the objective quality of the knowledge that is produced.

The methodology and epistemology of economics
The chapters in the second section of this *Companion* tackle various issues that have been extensively discussed by methodologists and philosophers of economics since Thomas Kuhn's *The Structure of Scientific Revolutions* (1962).

Indeed the field of economic methodology as a separate field basically dates from this period, since practising economists addressed philosophical and methodological issues in economics prior to Kuhn's book but mostly left the field to specialists thereafter. One consequence of this development was an increasingly sharp division between economists and methodologists regarding epistemological matters in economics. While economists remained attached to traditional logical positivist methods and the empirical verification of theories, economic methodologists almost universally rejected them. At the same time, by the 1980s there were a number of quite different, competing approaches pursued by economic methodologists. For a brief time, Karl Popper and Imre Lakatos's views held centre stage, but since then economic methodology has developed multiple currents. The chapters in Part II are accordingly meant to introduce some of the ideas and themes that have preoccupied economic methodologists in recent decades.

The first chapter addresses Lakatos' methodology of scientific research programmes (MSRP), which in important respects was a development and reformulation of Popper's thinking, and was the last approach enjoying a degree of consensus among methodologists. Roger Backhouse charts the rise and fall of the MSRP, explaining its appeal and subsequent doubts. The reason for the latter was less second thoughts regarding the fruitfulness of the MSRP approach and more a growing interest in a whole variety of new ways of looking at methodological questions in economics: rhetoric and discourse analysis, sociology of scientific knowledge, the re-discovery of J.S. Mill, etc. In effect, methodological thinking was becoming increasingly sophisticated, and this introduced new subtleties into debate among methodologists. The MSRP, which offered a broad, comprehensive view of the growth and development of research programmes began to be perceived as 'thin', because it ignored many issues that had previously been perceived as peripheral. Backhouse's own discussion reflects this, as he goes beyond the question that long preoccupied methodologists in connection with the MSRP – whether it offered an adequate account of how economists adopted and abandoned research programmes – to examine Lakatos's own history before his arrival in Britain, and how this contributed to the development of his thinking.

Backhouse's discussion leads naturally to the second chapter in Part II, Wade Hands' 'Constructivism: the social construction of scientific knowledge', on the sociology of scientific knowledge (SSK). Whereas the type of question methodologists and philosophers had once asked concerned the nature of scientific knowledge, social constructivists rather asked how scientists came to hold their theories and beliefs. That is, SSK investigated the determination of scientists' beliefs. This focus led to many new ideas (for example, pragmatism, hermeneutics, postmodernism, and feminism) that significantly expanded the scope of economic methodology substantially beyond its original confines. It also raised difficult philosophical issues, such as what was meant by saying a theory was true when social factors could be shown to have led to its adoption. Hands surveys the debates within SSK, and then looks at their application to, first, economic methodology and, second, the history of economic thought. The former involves a reflexive exercise in which methodologists ask how their own beliefs are determined. The latter concerns how economists' beliefs are determined. Here we ask need to ask ourselves about social factors that influence the adoption of beliefs by economists.

One such factor, until recently much under-appreciated, is gender. Historically economists have generally ignored gender in their explanations of markets and individual decision-making. How, then, might economics be different were this particular factor given attention? Drucilla Barker's chapter in this section, 'From feminist empiricism to feminist poststructuralism: philosophical questions in feminist economics', surveys the evolution in thinking on the part of feminist philosophers, methodologists, and economists since the 1980s, in the process distinguishing feminist empiricism, feminist standpoint theory, feminist poststructuralism, and feminist postmodernism. She explains how this development has raised fundamental epistemological and other philosophical issues, and how these issues have generated debates over objectivity of science, the tension between facts and values, and the relation between science and advocacy. Barker emphasises a key perspective on this discussion in her emphasis on epistemological communities, the feminist one in particular. Feminist economics is a relatively late arrival in professional economics, and this had led its proponents to work more closely together to ensure its progress, reinforcing its character as a community. Like Hands in his treatment of SSK, then, Barker also makes economic methodology reflexive: or something that applies to those who develop it as well as to practising economists.

Rob Garnett provides the next contribution to this general discussion in his 'Rhetoric and postmodernism in economics'. Another of the important pathways away from methodologists' early Popper–Lakatos focus concerns the role of discourse, language, and rhetoric in economic explanation and argument. Deirdre McCloskey's work originated much of this literature, and she made a case for rhetoric as the method of economics by directly contesting traditional economic methodology – logical positivism, behaviourism, operationalism, and the hypothetico-deductive model of explanation – as all part of a modernist intellectual culture. In contrast, a postmodernist economic methodology rejects foundationalist epistemologies and the search for Truth with a capital-T. Like SSK and feminist economic methodology, postmodernism examines how scientific communities operate. One significant theme that arises in this regard is the extent of pluralism in economics. McCloskey thus not only rejects modernist economic methodology, but also illiberal and authoritarian practices on the part of economists who foster it. Economics and economic methodology, in her view, ought rather to be modelled on the idea of an open conversation that is inclusive rather than exclusive in nature.

The remaining chapters in Part II address particular problems and issues in economic methodology that cut across the recent development of the field. Jointly they provide a sample of the diversity in themes that have come to reflect the rapid expansion of methodological thinking in the last two decades. They also point us towards the first and third parts of this *Companion*, since they have also been of interest to philosophers of economics investigating political economy as political philosophy and the ontology of economics.

Marcel Boumans, in 'Models in economics', addresses the practice of economics in the development of modelling. Traditionally the poles of economic practice have been thought of as theory and empirical analysis. But economists generally reason in terms of models, which lie intermediate between theory and empirical analysis. What does economic methodology then have to tell us about models in economics? Because models simplify what they represent they are necessarily unrealistic. This has led some philosophers of science to argue that models are not representations of the world, but rather instruments of investigation used to interact with the world (Morgan and Morrison 1999). To bring out these issues, Boumans traces the evolution in methodological thinking about models and modelling from arguments developed in physics to the early thinking about the nature of macro-econometric models on the part of Jan Tinbergen for the League of Nations. This history is then linked to current debates in philosophy of science and a discussion of model-building practices in economics. A surprising result is the variety of different types of elements that go into models. Models emerge out of a process analogous to baking: separate ingredients are blended and ultimately combined into the final product.

A related topic is the role and nature of mathematics in economics. Peter Kesting and Arnis Vilks examine this in their chapter 'Formalism'. One obstacle to understanding formalism in economics is the many ways in which the term is used. Kesting and Vilks consequently begin by explaining formalism broadly as any approach to theorising that aims at making explicit the logical structure of a theory, and then distinguish formal systems from set-theoretic formalism. One of the remarkable developments in economics in the last half century is general acceptance of set-theoretic formalism. While it is true that most of present-day mathematics is derived from set theory, this does not imply that this is the only or even necessarily the best basis for connecting formal models and reality. The set-theoretic approach owes much of its influence to Bourbaki-influenced Gerard Debreu's axiomatic account *Theory of Value* (1959). But as many commentators have noted, the rigor of formal models often comes with a relatively loose interpretation of those same models. Kesting and Vilks pursue this tension through the recent history of development of formal models in economics, noting how parables, tacit knowledge, and 'as if' assumptions play a role in the justification of accepted formalist strategies.

The final chapter in this section, Harold Kincaid's 'Methodological individualism and economics', turns us to a perennial issue in the methodology of economics: the extent to which explanations can and ought to be cast in terms of the behavior of individuals. For some, economics is identified with individualism. But close examination of the underlying claims making such explanations raise a number of difficult philosophical issues. One of the most challenging concerns the requirements for reducing statements about social phenomena to statements about individuals. In the philosophy of science reductionist arguments have been examined in connection with the question of whether all science is ultimately physics. Another fundamental issue involves what constitutes the 'best' explanation in science or in economics. These more philosophical questions return us to economic methodology's epistemological concerns, but no less important are the ontological ones the topic of individualism raises. When we privilege individualist explanations in economics, do we believe that only individuals exist? That society itself does not exist? Kincaid argues that many of these questions cannot be solved in an a priori manner apart from attention to concrete empirical inquiry. But few economists, he notes, are prepared to accept this conclusion.

Social ontology and the ontology of economics

The chapters in the third and final part of this *Companion* concentrate on questions of ontology, that is, questions regarding existence or being and, in particular, the nature and structure of the socio-economic realm.[1] Some of the authors represented here analyse particular aspects of the social world in a direct fashion, addressing things such as the relationship between agency and structure, the nature of probability, and the nature of money. Others take a more indirect route, starting off with particular theories or modelling tools adopted by economists, and then asking what these theories or tools presuppose about the nature and structure of the social world that they are applied to.

The first three chapters are contributions to critical realism, an important stream in the literature on ontological issues in economics that has been developing over the last fifteen years or so (see Fleetwood 1999, Lawson 1997, 2003). One of the hallmarks of critical realism is a view of the social world as structured and open,[2] and the broad strategy employed in much of this literature is to use this view of the world as a benchmark against which to assess the extent to which different methods are likely to bear fruit in social research. This strategy is both described and put to work in the first chapter in Part III, Tony Lawson's 'philosophical underlabouring'. Following Locke, Lawson argues that the appropriate role of the philosopher of science is not to do science or even to attempt to provide general methodological rules for scientists to follow, but rather to engage in what he calls 'ground clearing' or removing the 'rubbish that lies in the way to knowledge' in any particular discipline. Lawson identifies three broad ways in which philosophical ground clearing might be useful, in what he calls its demystifying, informing and method-facilitating functions.

In Lawson's view, academic economics is currently in particularly urgent need of ground clearing, and that the rubbish to be removed is the dogma that the only legitimate mode of economics analysis is mathematical and/or statistical modelling. The starting point of his argument is the observation that any specific set of research practices and procedures presuppose particular (usually implicit) conceptions of the nature and structure of reality. This is where ontology comes in, according to Lawson, and why it is so important. He then goes on to argue that the mathematical and statistical tools of mainstream economics presuppose a world that 'everywhere comprises (closed) systems of isolated atoms', in sharp contrast to the image of the structured and open social world associated with critical realism (and which he subsequently goes on to outline). The implication is that, if the social world is indeed as described in critical realism, then there is a fundamental mismatch between the tools of mainstream economics and the social material that those tools are applied to. But Lawson's arguments here are not only destructive in intent. He also demonstrates different ways in which his preferred social ontology may aid social research, by way of providing a categorical grammar that may help to sharpen substantive social theoretical conceptions and distinctions, by suggesting a distinctive theory of rationality that is rather different from the model standardly employed in economics, as well as by providing directionality to research in various ways.

The two chapters that follow, by Steve Pratten and Paul Lewis respectively, provide good illustrations of different ways in which some of the lessons of critical realism may be put to work. Pratten's chapter is devoted to the New Institutional Economics, focusing particularly on the transactions costs approach associated with the work of Oliver Williamson (1985, 1989, 1991). Pratten's point of departure is the often-noted 'gap' between modern economic theory and the socio-economic reality that it purports to be about. Like Lawson, Pratten attributes this gap to the profession's a priori commitment to mathematical modelling and the preoccupation with the analysis of fictitious model 'worlds' that this commitment seems invariably to entail. Indeed, as Pratten sees it, the need that many economists feel to conduct research that bears the mathematical imprimatur of 'serious' economic analysis is fundamentally at odds with moving toward a more realistic and relevant economics. The thing that particularly interests Pratten about the New Institutional Economics is that this is an area in which he sees this tension as being especially apparent. For despite criticising mainstream economics for being unrealistic and promoting their project as one aimed at greater realisticness and relevance, proponents of the New Institutional Economics tend ultimately to retain a strong commitment to formalism. Of course it is possible to maintain that this tension is an illusion on the grounds that that the particular formalisms employed so far simply haven't been the right ones. However, and drawing on the ontological insights of critical realism, Pratten argues that so long as the assumptions underpinning mathematical methods conflict with the constitution of social reality, the mismatch between method and material will persist and the various resulting tensions and compromises that he identifies will remain.

Paul Lewis tackles the relationship between human agency and social structure, a perennial theme in social theory, by way of comparing how this relationship is dealt with in contemporary Austrian economics on the one hand and in critical realism on the other. In recent years, members of the radical subjectivist wing of the Austrian school rejected the atomistic conception of the economic actor and have emphasised instead the virtues of portraying people as social beings embedded within networks of shared meanings and interpretive traditions (e.g. Boettke 1990, 1998; Boettke and Storr 2002; Prychitko 1994a; Vaughn, 1994). On this view, as Lewis puts it, traditions and people are mutually constitutive, 'with the former being both an ever-present condition for the possibility of socio-economic activity and also a continually reproduced outcome of the latter' and that the social sciences deal 'with a pre-interpreted world, where the creation and reproduction of meaning-frames is an (ontological) condition of that which it seeks to analyse, namely human conduct'. These phrases are reminiscent of the so-called transformational model of social activity associated with critical realism, according to which agency and structure presuppose each other, and the hermeneutic moment. Lewis points out various points of overlap with the Austrian position. But there remain significant differences between the two, and Lewis emphasises in particular that the Austrian view of the 'socio-economic world as an intersubjective fabric spun from shared meanings that persist or change as people negotiate interpretations of events and states of affairs, the radical subjectivists run the risk of failing to do justice to the importance of the non-discursive (material) aspects of social structure – vested interested and power distributions'.

The subject of intersubjectivism leads on neatly to the next two chapters by John Davis and Edward Fullbrook who tackle the theme of collective or shared intentionality. Davis proposes 'collective intentionality analysis' as a prospective theoretical framework suited to addressing what he calls 'complex' economic behaviour. By complex behaviour Davis means behaviour that is not amenable to a single explanatory framework such as the mainstream model of instrumental economic rationality. Collective intentionality analysis involves a distinct approach to rationality in the form of a deontological or principle-based type rationality that is appropriate to explaining individual interaction in social groups. If we suppose individuals are both members of social groups and also have occasion to act in relative isolation, then their behaviour needs to be explained in terms of both sorts of rationality principles, giving rise to its characterisation as complex.

The rationale for employing collective intentionality analysis as an additional account of economic behaviour is that economic agents appear to behave differently in organisational, group, and institutional contexts. For example, it is often noted that trust relationships based on shared intentions emerge in markets characterised by repeated exchange, whereas spot markets with little repeated contact tend to be characterised by instrumentally rational behaviour. Here, the relevant model involves instrumental and collective rationality operating 'side-by-side' in proportion to the extent that individuals act socially or in a more autonomous manner. Further, social groups and organisations differ according to how they delegate independent action to individuals. When individuals have considerable autonomy and discretion, this may be due to shared intentions having created a platform for a circumscribed instrumentally rational behaviour. That is, instrumentally rational behaviour is embedded in collectively intentional behaviour. An opposite sort of case involves deceit, deception, and fraud. Individuals may claim to share intentions while yet acting in a self-serving manner. Davis points, then, that the possibility that economic behaviour may be complex implies that the policy value space may itself be complex. Moving from an exclusive reliance on the instrumental model of economic rationality also entails moving from an exclusive reliance on efficiency criteria in normative economics towards complex accounts of valuation and recommendation which combine efficiency as a value with such values as justice and fairness.

The theme of collective intentionality is continued in the chapter by Edward Fullbrook, a prominent proponent of intersubjectivism in economic analysis (Fullbrook 1996, 1997). The guiding idea on the intersubjectivist approach is that human consciousnesses are constitutionally interdependent, that human subjects form and reform themselves, not in isolation, but rather in relation to and under the influence of other human subjects and institutions. As Fullbrook points out, given how commonsensical this idea is, it is an interesting question why it had so little impact on modern philosophy until the last century, and, until recently, in mediating in social theory between holistic and radically individualistic explanations. Even more significantly, from the viewpoint of this collection, it is an interesting question why intersubjectivism continues to remain banished from mainstream economics. Fullbrook attempts to answer these questions by drawing on the histories of modern philosophy and social theory and their relations to economics. The first two-thirds of his chapter explore the Cartesian philosophy from which the atomistic conception of the standard model of the economic actor derives, and the development of intersubjective philosophy and social theory over the last century. The final section considers the case of economics. Here Fullbrook argues that, in turning its back on all economic phenomena that do not conform to its Cartesian metaphysic, economics not only neglected awkward but central empirical realities but also became wedded to a spurious naturalism and the unarticulated but culturally powerful line of racism and sexism that this entails.

Philip Faulkner and Jochen Runde devote their chapter to how the standard model of the economic actor employed in mainstream microeconomics has limited the way in which it approaches information, knowledge and the related issues of ignorance and uncertainty. The first half of the chapter is devoted to an overview of kind of assumptions typically made in respect of economic actors' knowledge in mainstream economic models. This is achieved by way of a detailed exposition of a representative mainstream model, in this case a simple one-shot Cournot duopoly game under conditions of both complete and incomplete information. It is shown that even where the model is extended to the case of incomplete information, a move intended explicitly to highlight the effects of imperfections and asymmetries in actors' knowledge, the degree to which the complexities of human knowledge are reflected remains severely limited.

The second half of the chapter is devoted to three aspects of human agency that are neglected by the mainstream approach: non-probabilistic forms of uncertainty and ignorance, the subjectivity of knowledge, and tacit knowledge. Faulkner and Runde conclude that the much vaunted information theoretic revolution in economics (Stiglitz 2000) represents only a first step towards incorporating the effects of factors such as uncertainty, ignorance and subjectivity into economics. For instance, by virtue of the commitment to expected utility models of decision-making, the actors within mainstream microeconomic models inevitably suffer only certain forms of uncertainty. There is no scope in these models for actors to be affected by ignorance of the full set of possible eventualities that might result from their actions (or indeed the options open to them), or to alter their behaviour as a result of being unable to state precise probabilities. Categories such as surprise and novelty, which are closely associated with uncertainty and ignorance, consequently remain outside the scope of mainstream economics.

The theme of uncertainty and ignorance is also taken up in the chapter by Chuck McCann, who surveys the major competing interpretations of probability and how these have emerged in and coloured different parts of economic theory (note that McCann's focus is on knowledge and belief, and the way in which probability theorists have attempted to model them, rather than on probability as it is employed in statistics and econometrics). After two brief preliminary sections on knowledge and belief and the axiomatic structure of probability, McCann introduces the key ontological distinction on which his presentation turns, between aleatory conceptions of probability on the one hand and epistemic conceptions on the other. On the aleatory conception, probability is taken to be a property or feature of the external world (e.g. the frequency of a particular kind of realisation within a class of otherwise similar realisations). On the epistemic conception, in contrast, probability is taken to be a feature of how we think about the world (e.g. your subjective degree of belief in there being rain tomorrow). This distinction is then deployed as organising principle in McCann's review of the major interpretations of probability – classical, frequentist, logical and personalist – as well as forming the basis for his subsequent elucidation of the distinction between risk and uncertainty. McCann closes by touching briefly on some areas in economics in which probability and uncertainty have come to the fore: (post)Keynesianism, Rational Expectations and Austrianism.

The final chapter in this collection is Geoff Ingham's wide-ranging study of various views on the nature of money that have been propounded in different parts of the discipline. The first part of the chapter deals with the commodity-exchange theory that has come to dominate mainstream economic theory, and the associated conception of money as a neutral veil over what is fundamentally a barter economy. Ingham raises various criticisms of this account, chief of which is that its emphasis on money as a device to overcome the problem of a double coincidence of wants in a pure barter economy, has led to a misunderstanding and neglect of *money of account*. This then leads to a long section on heterodox conceptions of money that theorise money as abstract value and token credit. The central idea here is that money is constituted, not simply by some commodity that becomes accepted as a medium of exchange, but by social relations. Among the figures considered are Knapp, Simmel, Keynes and Weber, and Ingham shows how the kinds of ideas expressed by these authors emerge in recent debates on endogenous money, the theory of the 'money circuit' and modern neochartelism.

Ingham outlines his own position in a closing section on 'the fundamentals of a theory of money', focusing on three questions: what is money?; how is it produced?; and how does it obtain, retain or lose its value? Here Ingham sides with the heterodox tradition and its emphasis on money being constituted by social relations. Some of the key ontological themes developed here are that money is uniquely specified as a measure of abstract value and a means of transporting this abstract value, that money cannot be created without simultaneous creation of debt, indeed that 'vast dense networks of overlapping and interconnected bilateral credit–debt relations constitute money', and that the abstract idea of money is a prerequisite for the things that represent money (cash, cheques, credit cards, magnetic traces on a computer disk, and so on) to work as money. In an unusual and refreshing touch, Ingham makes various telling points about how these seemingly abstruse and often-dismissed considerations can illuminate various recent events on monetary history.

Economics and philosophy
What does the future hold for economics and philosophy? On the one hand, as readers will see from the chapters included in this volume, philosophical

questions have a surprisingly natural place in economics, since so many issues fundamental to the latter find clear and immediate expression when re-presented in philosophical terms. No doubt many find this an unexpected development, since for many years economics was widely thought to be a relatively separate science (Hausman 1992). This view, however, has come into question in light of the influence that formal mathematical methods have had on economics over the last half century, and so it is not unreasonable to suppose that economics will be further changed in the future by growing awareness of and sensitivity to its philosophical dimensions. On the other hand, the way forward for economics and philosophy is difficult to predict. Whereas the application of mathematics to economics generally presupposes a pre-existing set of problems in economics which it is typically hoped may be illuminated by mathematics, combining philosophy and economics often involves re-considering one's very starting points. Thus not only is there always the potential for fundamental redirection of economics in light of new philosophical entry points, but it is not easy to predict what sources of philosophical inspiration might be important to economists in the future.

However, one possible guide to the future role of philosophy in economics might be found in the broad philosophical issues afoot in society today regarding such fundamental issues as the relation between society and nature, the effects of technological change, the place of moral values in the world, the future of humanity, and so on. For many years, academic economics has held little interest for most people. But the now wider place of economics in higher level education and the greater influence economics seems to have today on people's everyday lives appears to have changed this, such that it is no longer unusual for people from across society to have both some understanding of economics and opinions about it. Then, on the assumption that peoples' different views of the world and the society they live in depends upon their various philosophical presuppositions, however well articulated or ill-formed these may be, it might well be the case that these deep-seated views will re-emerge as issues discussed in the domain of economics and philosophy. But whatever their origin, philosophical concerns now appear to be well-embedded in economics, and not likely to drift off into the background again where they once resided.

Notes
1. Recent years have seen a growing interest in ontological issues in economics (see for example Mäki 1998, 2000, 2001; Lawson 1997, 2003).
2. By the world being structured we mean that it comprises not only events and states of affairs (the actual) and our experiences of them, but also of an 'underlying' and often unobservable reality of capacities, powers, structures and mechanisms that, once triggered or being otherwise in play, give rise to and govern those events and states of affairs. By the world being open we mean that the actual could always have been other than it was.

References

Boettke, Peter (1990), 'Individuals and institutions', *Critical Review*, **4**, 10–26.

Boettke, Peter (1998), 'Rational choice and human agency in economics and sociology: exploring the Weber–Austrian Connection', in H. Giersch (ed.), *Merits and Limits of Markets*. Berlin: Springer-Verlag.

Boettke, Peter and V. H. Storr (2002) 'Post-classical political economy: polity, society and economy in Weber, Mises and Hayek', *American Journal of Economics and Sociology* **61**, 161–91.

Fleetwood, Stephen (ed.), (1999) *Critical Realism in Economics: Development and Debate*, London and New York: Routledge.

Fullbrook, Edward (1996), 'The metaphysics of consumer desire and the French intersubjectivists', *International Advances in Economic Research*, **2**, 287–94.

Fullbrook, Edward (1997), 'Post-modernising *homo economicus*', in S. Earnshaw (ed.), *Just Postmodernism*. Amsterdam: Rodopi.

Hausman, Daniel (1992), *The Inexact and Separate Science of Economics*, Cambridge: Cambridge University Press.

Kuhn, Thomas (1962), *The Structure of Scientific Revolutions*, Chicago: University of Chicago Press.

Lawson, Tony (1997), *Economics and Reality*, London and New York: Routledge.

Lawson, Tony (2003), *Reclaiming Reality*, London and New York: Routledge.

Mäki, Uskali (1998), 'Aspects of realism about economics', *Theoria*, **13**, 301–19.

Mäki, Uskali (2000), 'Reclaiming relevant realism', *Journal of Economic Methodology* **7**, 109–25.

Mäki, Uskali (ed.) (2001), *The Economic Worldview: Studies in the Ontology of Economics*, Cambridge: Cambridge University Press.

Morgan, Mary and Margaret Morrison (1999), *Models as Mediators: Perspectives on Natural and Social Science*, Cambridge: Cambridge University Press.

Prychitko, David L. (1994a), 'Ludwig Lachmann and the interpretive turn in economics: a critical inquiry into the hermeneutics of the plan', *Advances in Austrian Economics*, **1**, 303–19.

Rosenberg, Alexander (1992), 'Economic theory as political philosophy', *Social Science Journal*, **36** (4), 575–87.

Stiglitz, Joseph E. (2000), 'The contributions of the economics of information to twentieth century economics', *Quarterly Journal of Economics*, **115**, 1441–78.

Vaughn, Karen I. (1994), *Austrian Economics in America: The Migration of a Tradition*, Cambridge: Cambridge University Press.

Williamson, Oliver E. (1985), *The Economic Institutions of Captialism*, New York: Free Press.

Williamson, Oliver E. (1989), 'Transaction Cost Economics' in R. Schmalensee and R.D. Willig, *Handbook of Industrial Organization*, Amsterdam: North Holland.

Williamson, Oliver E. (1991), 'The Logic of Economic Organization' in Oliver E. Williamson and Sydney Winter (eds), *The Nature of the Firm: Origins, Evolution and Development*, Oxford: Oxford University Press.

PART I

POLITICAL ECONOMY AS POLITICAL PHILOSOPHY

1 Natural law, natural history and the foundations of political economy

José Luís Cardoso

Introduction

The emergence of political economy as an autonomous scientific discourse was a complex process, not a fixed moment in a diary of events. Investigating its origins or roots therefore requires consideration of the multiple of factors involved, and lends itself to multiple interpretations and provides a variety of research orientations. Even if, in order to fit in with conventional wisdom, it is accepted that 1776 represented the year of grace, the road that made it possible to announce the good news brought by the science that deals with the wealth of nations proved to be a long one.

First of all, it was necessary for economic phenomena and problems to become established as an everyday reality that required attention, understanding and mastery. In other words, it was necessary to isolate and identify a subject that came to represent a permanent motive for constructed knowledge. This condition was met from the late fifteenth century onwards, when the western economic world underwent gradual yet profound changes and suffered a series of convulsions that led to the production of an abundant economic literature. Such writings were not only intended to justify new forms for the political reconciliation of the interests of different social groups connected with the revival of mercantile activities, but also sought to explain the theoretical, technical and practical problems arising from these same activities, such as: variations in the balance of trade, oscillations in prices and their relationship with specie flows, the fiscal and political instruments used for reinforcing trade and fostering the development of manufacturing, or the strategies that were best suited to achieving economic and financial hegemony at the world level. That is to say, the formation of political economy as a science was largely the result of the advances brought about by the mercantilist economic literature written in the sixteenth and seventeenth centuries and the first half of the eighteenth century. This particular avenue has already been suitably explored and will not be pursued here.[1]

These economic transformations also gave rise to different perceptions of a reality that was now being understood through numbers, calculations, measurements, statistical information and political arithmetic. The development of double-entry bookkeeping suggested the acceptance of the principles of

3

methodological exactitude, precision, credibility and accuracy that represented the essence of the 'modern fact', all of which structured the innovative modes of reasoning used by the emergent sciences of wealth and society (Poovey 1998). Practical knowledge and the instruments and processes used for capturing the empirical world consequently represented the accumulated capital of a cognitive experience that was essential for the improvement of political economy. I shall touch on this subject again later on.[2]

Discussion of the foundations of modern political economy also inevitably implies making close contact with the developments of seventeenth and eighteenth-century European philosophical thought from Bacon to Hume. This theme has been the subject of regular investigation, not only from the point of view of the genealogy of the inductive and deductive methods of political economy and the processes involved in the construction of knowledge within this scientific environment (Redman 1997), but also in terms of the more general acceptance of the identification of the empirical and rational elements inherent in the formation of economic discourse (Coleman 1995). I believe that this is a crucial matter for explaining the philosophical foundations of political economy. Although I shall not discuss this matter in the way that is normally suggested, I shall nonetheless return to it when explaining the main argument that is to be developed in this text.

My argument consists in establishing the close connection between the formation of political economy as a science that sought to explain the logic whereby the market operated, and the understanding of this same market as the natural order of things. In order to explain this argument, two distinct but complementary paths must be followed in showing how the intelligibility of the natural order was constituted until the mid-eighteenth century.

The first path – which will be explored in section 2 – directs us towards the framework provided by the philosophy of natural law for interpreting the foundations of social and economic organisation. The existence of universally accepted natural laws that are inherent in human nature, the belief in a natural spontaneous, harmonious and self-regulating order, were all crucial elements for explaining the economic order of the market and were consequently inseparable from the discourse of the science that sought to elucidate the mechanisms to which this same order was subject.

Another possible interpretation of the expression 'natural order' – dealt with in section 3 – refers to the physical world of material nature described by the so-called natural and exact sciences. In the second half of the eighteenth century, the term *natural history* was the one that was most frequently used and which best expressed the concerns related to this subject of study. Such is also the acceptance that is given here to the notion of natural order, which shows itself to be just as important for understanding the formation of economic science as is traditionally believed to have been the case of the philosophy of natural law. This is a research avenue that has been marginalised by conventional historiography, but which is considered to be particularly pertinent for reordering the methodological framework within which the history of economic science has traditionally operated. In section 4, some concluding remarks will be presented, in an attempt to explain the complementary nature of the two paths proposed earlier.

Natural law, sciences of society and political economy

The study of the relationship between natural law and political economy is almost unavoidable in any analysis concerning the process by which political economy emerged as a social science in its own right. Among the many authors who could be quoted to illustrate this issue, it is worth singling out J.A. Schumpeter, for whom the extent and importance of the study of natural law goes far beyond the limited scope of economic science:

> The first discovery of every science is the discovery of itself. Awareness of the presence of a set of interrelated phenomena that give rise to 'problems' is evidently the prerequisite of all analytical effort. And in the case of the social sciences, this awareness shaped itself in the concept of natural law. (1954, p. 107)

The existence of multiple languages and discourses in those social sciences which have, today, acquired a status of autonomy, makes us think about Schumpeter's suggestion and leads us to reflect upon the initial stage of evolution of such sciences. In other words, it leads us to reflect on the moment in which 'a set of interrelated phenomena give rise to "problems"'. And this is also the point at which one may achieve 'awareness of its presence', thanks to the enlightening function Schumpeter grants to the concept of natural law.

The natural law roots of the social sciences are grounded on the idea that, irrespective of any concrete, positive legislation, there exists a system of natural law made up of universally accepted and applicable rules and norms, resulting from the attributes of human nature and the needs of the collective social organism. Such attributes and needs in turn arise from the 'instinctive conviction'[3] that there exists a natural harmony which excludes any type of arbitrariness and transcendent design, and which enables man to simultaneously become aware of the order that governs him and make himself responsible for his own destiny. Natural order and natural law become essential factors in the development of a new scientific spirit, in the urgent desire to establish a science which 'was not just a means (to move things, mash things, make things) but the ultimate demonstration of human rationality, the proof that a single individual could discover the workings of the universe itself' (Solomon 1986, p. 12).

There thus develops a new cognitive attitude wherein man ceases to be thought of in one single dimension. The plurality of modes of being of the natural individual involves a multiplicity of research interests with regard to man, who, as a private person, tries to achieve his objectives that are peculiar to an individual in possession of natural rights, and who, as a member of a given community, achieves and promotes objectives of a social nature. Human action, considered in its different manifestations, becomes the object of specific though fragmented investigation, thus producing the conditions required to break down a large-scale knowledge into the multiple autonomous areas of learning which are the *raison d'être* of the variety of scientific fields claiming to promote the study of man and society.

But despite these different conceptual arrangements, the separate destinies are tied together by their obedience to the cohesive nucleus of natural law metaphysics. Discovery of the cognitive possibilities afforded by the man–nature binomial, materialisation of this relationship in the concept of human nature and identification of its own attributes and (natural) laws revealed through reason, the configuration of a natural order that presupposes and legitimises the coherence and harmony of the social entity as a whole, in short, all these ingredients of the philosophy of natural law have made it possible for the study of individual and collective human action to assume much greater or at least substantially different importance.[4]

We may therefore conclude that one of the merits of natural law – particularly through the developments, sometimes complementary, sometimes contradictory,[5] introduced by Grotius, Hobbes, Locke and Pufendorf – lies in the fact that it placed natural man at the centre of philosophical speculation and thus paved the way for 'a process of "secularisation" [which] manifested itself most significantly through the emergence of differentiated intellectual disciplines, each with its own expertise and, in time, with its own special experts' (Viner 1978, p. 115). However, it was also this process of secularisation[6] that led to a process of autonomy and self-fulfilment of natural man, thus introducing the principle of the rational search for specific ends, including economic ones, which also represents an implicit acknowledgement of the economic dimension of individual activities.

The paths of research suggested by Jacob Viner are directed towards demonstrating that the natural law tradition renewed by Grotius goes back to the civic humanist-inspired juridical and political literature produced between the eleventh and the fifteenth centuries, which developed alongside the scholastic tradition of natural law prevalent at the time. According to Viner: 'It was in jurisprudence and political philosophy, rather than in metaphysics, moral philosophy, economics, or even natural science, that "human reason" first gained a large measure of autonomy from theology and the effective exercise of ecclesiastical authority' (1978, p. 117). The same line of argument is consistently followed by Nuccio (1986).

This kind of approach is a convincing alternative to the vision presented by Schumpeter, according to which it was an 'illusory notion that the work of the seventeenth-century philosophers of natural law spelled a violent break with scholastic analysis' (1954, p. 141). For Schumpeter, the Aristotelian–Thomistic tradition (centred on the concept of 'naturally just') extended as far as the late seventeenth century, and in his opinion 'these facts teach a lesson of continuity in development' (ibid. p. 141).

In favouring such continuity, Schumpeter warns us (albeit implicitly) of the problem of preserving the elements of divine nature throughout the process of establishing natural and social laws advocated by 'modern' natural law apologists. In fact, the medieval concept of natural law, strongly marked by the idea that there exists a supreme divine legislator whose directives determine the regularities observed in nature and society, was to persist throughout the seventeenth and eighteenth centuries. This issue is equally important in so far as it enables us to understand the extent to which the setting-up or discovery through reason of the laws governing the (natural) social order remains imbued with a sense of moral value that causes such laws to be, above all, compulsory rules for social conduct.[7]

However a different view is given by Pocock (1975), who follows a line of reasoning similar to Viner's. In fact, Pocock sets out to define an alternative paradigm based on the tradition of civic humanism dating from the Renaissance era. According to Pocock, this tradition considerably influenced the shaping of eighteenth-century political, social and economic thought, particularly through the authors of the Scottish Enlightenment, independently of the influence that may have been exerted by the natural law tradition. The fundamental features of the civic humanism paradigm are to be found in the recognition of the fact that the individual has an ideal of citizenship displayed through responsible, active and committed participation, where the spirit of virtue inherent in individual behaviour implies the subordination of self-interest to the imperatives of the public good.[8]

Pocock's thesis has given rise to a broad range of studies and debates,[9] which are far from being concluded. And, should it be true that this thesis did a great deal to form a critical alternative to the view presented and developed by Schumpeter, it is also true that the approach based on the 'scholastic thought – modern natural law – modern social sciences' continuity, still has its unwavering supporters.[10]

The dilemma between continuity and change, as applied to the study of the origins and sources of modern social thought, is to some extent expressed by J.M. Keynes in one of his most brilliant, persuasive essays:

> At the end of the seventeenth century the divine right of monarchs gave place to natural liberty and to the compact, and the divine right of the church to the principle

of toleration, and to the view that a church is 'a voluntary society of men', coming together, in a way which is 'absolutely free and spontaneous'. Fifty years later the divine origin and absolute voice of duty gave place to the calculations of utility. In the hands of Locke and Hume these doctrines founded individualism. The compact presumed rights in the individual; the new ethics, being no more than a scientific study of the consequences of rational self-love, placed the individual at the centre. (Keynes 1926, p. 272)

Through the words of Keynes, we may take up the theme of natural law once more, not, however, from the standpoint of its importance in obtaining an overall understanding of the birth of new ways of perceiving the features of human nature and human actions, but rather with regard to its specific relationship with the ways of understanding economic life or, in other words, the relationship between natural law and political economy.

According to the natural law doctrines developed in the seventeenth century, the fulfilment of individual natural rights implies the satisfaction of economic interests and objectives, which, as well as ensuring individual survival, contribute to the harmony and well-being of the entire society.

We are thus led to isolate the economic dimension of a natural man who struggles to satisfy his immediate, fundamental interests and who rationally premeditates the most efficient means to obtain expected goals. As, in order to survive, he/she must produce and exchange, and since the meaning each individual attributes to his/her action encounters either convergent or different meanings, complex economic relations are inevitably established, requiring an explanation or, paraphrasing Schumpeter once more, the phenomena give rise to problems of which an awareness must be formed. The possibility that political economy develops its conceptual corpus autonomously is therefore the first meaning one may draw from this process of emergence of a science shaped from its early origins by the philosophy of natural law.

Another meaning to be borne in mind relates to the doctrinal burden associated to the idea that self-interest spontaneously favours the achievement of social welfare. Self-interest and social welfare are not to be regarded as two distinct, incompatible endeavours. First and foremost stands the individual, and it is precisely free, spontaneous, individual action that is felt to automatically produce social harmony in society. More than 'that which it is', social order is considered from the standpoint of 'that which it should be' as opposed to that which one did not want it to be. Belief in a spontaneous social order is the expression of the desire and will to overcome the obstacles preventing the full exercise of individual economic activity. In this sense, the individualist ingredient of natural law acquires the status of a supreme value, which commands the analytical efforts of the rising economic science.[11]

The combination of these two meanings requires further attention with regard to the relationship between natural law and political economy. And the new issue that arises is this: given the fact that the creation of conditions favourable to the formation of an autonomous scientific explanation brings about reinforcement of the doctrinal and ideological nature of this very same explanation, how is it possible to build up a minimum conceptual apparatus, i.e. to warrant the scientific citizenship of economic discourse?

The phrase from Keynes quoted above is not a satisfactory answer to the problem, although it does suggest an initial rough idea. Let us dwell on the meaning of his explicit message by considering the following issue: the triumph of economic individualism implies the possibility that individual economic agents (or economic agents acting as a group) may rid themselves, in a first phase, of the moral and religious power and authority of the Church, which imposed strict norms of behaviour, and, later, of the political power and authority of the State, whose interventionist propensity prevented the natural order of things from acting for itself; in this case, it is the mercantilist economic practices and doctrines that yield before the accusing judgement of the supporters of a broader economic freedom. As a conclusion to all this, it may be said that the main outcome of a belief in the virtual capacities of human nature – materialised in the rational activity of the economic agents – is the autonomous creation of an economic object, free of any religious, moral and political interference.[12]

This does not mean that economic discourse has ceased to be impregnated with value judgements of an ethical nature and norms of a political kind. It is precisely the presence of these apparently external interferences, during different phases of the development of political economy, that lies at the heart of the problem under scrutiny here.

The emphasis given to justify a spontaneous process of socialisation, founded on the interaction of multiple agents, becomes clearer with the increasing acceptance of the formula laissez-faire, laissez-passer. This expression succinctly throws into relief the involvement and economic consequences of the role played by individuals, and it is through such a formula that there takes shape a new mode of understanding and of being aware of the phenomena and problems associated with private or public economic life. Individualism and laissez-faire therefore become the key elements of an economic doctrine that is nourished by the legacy of the philosophy of natural law.

However, it should be noted that the impact of such ideas on economic literature begins to come to light in some writings of the sixteenth and seventeenth centuries, produced at the height of the mercantilist era. This means that it is not only the renewed philosophy of natural law that provides a doctrinal framework conducive to the triumph of individualism. Moreover, in allowing for individual economic agents whose contribution to mercantile activities becomes more and more significant, the constantly changing economic world itself gives rise to the formation of a critical outlook vis-à-vis the extra-economic factors that determine their actions.[13]

Thus, the increasing assimilation of an individualist credo and the acceptance of the laissez-faire ideology is especially important in shaping political economy as a science in its own right, as they act as a counterweight to, and internal criticism of, the basic arguments of mercantilist-type discourse, which corresponds to a sharp governmental economic intervention. Henceforth there is nothing to disprove the presence of political interference: however, its presence is subsequently to assume another meaning, as will be argued in the remaining paragraphs of this section.

The emergence of an autonomous discourse, which treats the economic dimension of human action as a proper category of analysis, is related, up to a certain point, to a belief in a spontaneous economic and social order. This belief, in turn, implied less State intervention in the economic sphere. Herein lies the different attitude of authors who broke free from mercantilist tradition. However the harmony of civil society may not prove to be an immediately attainable objective, which is why it would be advisable to accept the intervention of a correcting force in the natural order. In other words, the State – though not an integral part of the spontaneous natural order – is trusted with the supreme task of preserving its stability.

It was for this reason that authors who were acknowledged or regarded themselves as champions of individualism and laissez-faire, voluntarily or otherwise, upheld the role of guardian of the temple, which the State should rightfully perform. In fact, and contrary to what over-simple analyses may lead us to believe, it should be borne in mind that 'more profoundly than the physiocrats, also more deeply than his friend Hume, Smith was especially aware that calling for government to end regulation of economic activity was not the same thing as calling for government to abdicate all its power in the economic realm' (Teichgraeber 1986, p. 5).

Finally, it is worth highlighting the essence of the question addressed: adherence to the principles of economic individualism and laissez-faire (cast in the natural law tradition) is a doctrinal and dogmatic commitment which contributed to the autonomy of an economic object as a category of analysis, but did not, by itself, establish the specific analytical procedures of a science aspiring to build up its own identity.

The problem at issue is, once again, how to account for the way in which the satisfaction of self-interest becomes the realisation of social welfare, how to account for the way in which private vices become public virtues, how, in short, to account for spontaneous social harmony.

A number of different reasons have been offered to explain these issues in the course of the seventeenth and eighteenth centuries: prospects that were somewhat catastrophic, an absence of faith in the socially constructive nature of individual passions and interests, which led to an appeal for the submission of civil society before a powerful State; more optimistic standpoints related to the benevolence inherent in human nature, which would act as a kind of preventive, controlling force before possible individual excesses; standpoints which endeavoured to understand social order as subject to a moral attraction similar to that of gravitation, as observed in the physical world. However, in each case, we are confronted with (political, psychological or philosophical) explanations, in which the answer to the problem of the harmony between private interests and public benefits is provided by exogenous forces.[14]

Political economy still remained in a state of expectation, awaiting the moment when the actual economic explanation to the problem could be found. As conventional wisdom has it, this moment finally arrived in the second half of the eighteenth century: partly with the French physiocrats and decisively with Adam Smith.

The privilege granted to the physiocrats and to Smith does not imply a disregard for the scattered analytical contributions made by their predecessors. Obviously, neither Quesnay nor Smith developed a conceptual apparatus from scratch. One may even add that they said nothing that had not been formulated beforehand. But what is significant is that they did so differently, in a way that enabled one to explain the relationship between self-interest and social welfare endogenously.

In the case of Quesnay and physiocracy – not to ignore the inheritance received from Boisguilbert and Cantillon – their merit lies in what Schumpeter calls the 'method that visualised the (stationary) economic process as a circuit flow that in each period returns upon itself' (1954, p. 243). The relations between the different classes are presented in the form of a circuit wherein landowners, producers and consumers cross one another's paths, a circuit, which also serves to quantify output produced in a given period of time, and which ensures the reproduction of economic activity in the following period. The idea that immediately arises in Quesnay's *Tableau Economique* is one of equilibrium and harmony of the economic and social universe as a whole. As it is economic, such an equilibrium is described through the economic relations binding the autonomous interests of different groups and actors to a common project.

Despite its internal coherence, the physiocratic scheme of a circular flow contains a significant restriction that reduces the analytical range of its message: the *Tableau Economique* refers to a hypothetical rather than real situation, and is meant as a simplified representation of reality. It is Quesnay himself who openly admits this in his texts, when he considers the following restrictions:

> Let us assume, then, a large kingdom whose territory, fully cultivated by the best possible methods, yields every year a reproduction to the value of *five milliards*; and in which the permanent maintenance of this value is ensured by the constant prices which are current among trading nations, in a situation where there is unremitting free competition in trade and complete security of property in the wealth employed in agriculture. (Quesnay 1766, p. 210; Meek 1962, p. 151, original emphasis)

The hypotheses the author builds up are a clear sign of the limitations arising from the construction of a model which presupposes: (1) efficient and optimal allocation of resources and factors in agriculture, with access to and use of the best techniques; (2) constant prices and neutrality of money; (3) internal economic freedom and free trade, and (4) absolute security of private property. In this sense, the harmonious functioning of the circular flow and the supposed natural order of things are founded on rational arguments which are not only economic, but owe a great deal to a set of institutional and political restrictions.

It is in this context that the basic principles of the doctrine of legal despotism make themselves felt. According to this doctrine the political government of the *royaume agricole* assumes a key mission, 'so that the sovereign authority, always guided by what is self-evident, should institute the best laws and cause them to be scrupulously observed, in order to provide for the security of all and attain to the greatest degree of prosperity possible for the society' (Quesnay 1767, p. 236; Meek 1962, p. 231).

We may therefore conclude that the contribution of Quesnay and the physiocrats to the development of economic analysis was a theoretical effort, which only partially contributed to the constitution of an autonomous scientific programme.[15] The emphasis placed on the natural order inherent in the circular flow does not prevent the sovereign, invested with absolute authority, from directing the workings of this order when the results differ from those expected.[16]

The limitations of the physiocrats[17] were overcome by Adam Smith, who was left with the task of unravelling ambiguities that continued to persist as to the best way of conducting the *economic* analysis of the individual-society relationship. This is not, however, the theme that concerns us at present. Its meaning is well grasped and summarised by Hirschman: 'The main impact of the *Wealth of Nations* was to establish a powerful *economic* justification for the untrammelled pursuit of individual self-interest, whereas in the earlier literature the stress was on the political effects of this pursuit' (1977, p. 100). This does not mean that non-economic factors lost their determining influence.[18] But, once again, they did so in a different way.

Natural order, sciences of nature and political economy
Let us now direct our attention towards one of the most widely recognised and distinctive characteristics of the Enlightenment, namely the growing interest in the development of sciences that explained the material functioning of the natural order. Such interest presupposes a different attitude on the part of man towards the natural world that surrounds him, particularly with regard to a never-ending search for details recorded through meticulous observation, which to a large extent was made easier by the process of secularisation mentioned in the previous section. One of the main consequences of the attraction exercised

by natural history was that of substantially enlarging the audience of people interested in knowing the natural order of things, without requiring advanced preparation as in the frequently inaccessible fields of moral philosophy.

In effect, in dealing with subjects that aroused curiosity and provoked fascination, natural history ensured that a non-specialist audience became both witness and accomplice to an expanded process for the formation and sharing of knowledge about the natural bases of the surrounding world. The consumption of novelties from natural history might become transformed into a mere demonstration of taste and fashion, but, even if reduced to this limited scope, it would still represent yet another reason for the restricted universe of professional scientists to be greatly exceeded.

However, contact with the knowledge built up in the fields of botany, zoology and mineralogy served much vaster purposes, for it also involved the acquisition of additional education and self-development that would influence the understanding of how human intelligence itself was improved. Natural history was therefore a key to the understanding of the very evolution of human nature, in both its physical and moral aspects. In the words of E. Spary:

> Natural historical knowledge was considered a valuable means of self-improvement because its very acquisition repeated the steps of self-development judged necessary for the enlightened individual. One made the transition from natural (the brute) to social (member of polite society) by recapitulating the Adamic process of generating order from an initial perceptual chaos. Here, the trajectory of the individual confronted with nature mirrored that conceptual shift. (1999, p. 295)

This modern scientific discourse was extremely well received amongst the educated public in the eighteenth century. The spread of new knowledge was consequently greatly facilitated by the favourable climate for understanding the laws that governed the organisation of the natural world, which called for the incessant observation and classification of phenomena. This idea was neatly summarised by Charlton as follows: 'The motto for eighteenth-century science was "observation for observation's sake", but what matters here is that the outcome was a tremendous extension in people's awareness of the range, the marvels and the beauties of the phenomena of the natural world' (1984, p. 71).

Amongst the various fields of knowledge that prospered in the eighteenth century, natural history was perhaps the one that attracted most followers. It is therefore not surprising that in the 500 eighteenth-century library catalogues studied by D. Mornet, the most commonly found titles were Buffon's *Histoire Naturelle* (220 mentions) and Pluche's *Spectacle de la Nature* (206 mentions), which appeared far more frequently than Voltaire's *Nouvelle Héloise* (165 mentions) and Rousseau's *Discours sur l'Inégalité* (77 mentions) (Mornet 1911 [2001], pp. 248–49). Natural history acquired the status of fashion and played a privileged role in the organisation of erudite societies and scientific academies, which had intense and innovative activity in the production and spread of new knowledge.

The progressive abandonment of Latin as the language of communication also favoured the greater spread and circulation of knowledge beyond the traditionally restricted community of scholars. Excessively technical vocabularies were transposed into more accessible languages that made it possible to foresee the utilitarian and pragmatic sense of scientific discourse. Science was made in order to be useful, as well as to permit applications that corroborated the service that it provided to ordinary mortals in the course of their everyday business. Popular encyclopaedias proliferated, as did practical dictionaries, systematic manuals and textbooks, journals and reviews and the treatises that transmitted the good scientific news (Mornet 1911 [2001], pp. 173–91).

Signs of growing scientific interest could also be detected in the development of a spirit of curiosity and an appetite for collection at both a private and public level. Herbariums, fossils, experimental laboratories, reading rooms, botanical gardens, astronomical observatories and museums, all became important instruments in registering and cataloguing the advances being made in scientific knowledge, besides expressing the delight and fascination caused by nature being lived with such intensity. Natural history conquered salons, cafés, academies and universities. Naturalists persisted in their desire to enlarge their audiences and widen their networks of influence.

The growing disinterest in theological obstinacy and the replacement of belief, fantasy and mysticism by controlled observation and methodical experiment gave natural pastimes a new and surprising dimension marked by the rigour of scientific method. Initial admiration was followed by verification through empirical processes. Observed and tested phenomena represented the final step of the scientist's work in search of stable truths.

Thus, natural history became a space for the convergence of multiple directions and orientations, most notably: the attraction for curiosities and scientific work based on rigorous observations and processes of experimentation; the taste for the sublime and the extraordinary; the simple aim of establishing factual truth; the desire both to dare to know and to oblige reason to speculate; as well as the purpose of serving the public with useful practical knowledge (Roche 1996, p. 130).

In short, there were various reasons and factors that help us to understand both the erudite and popular attraction for natural history. But the main motivation for the growing interest aroused by the sciences of the natural world was the usefulness associated with the applications of the diverse fields of knowledge to the concrete problems of real life. It is precisely this latter situation that defines the scope of natural history as a founding element for reflections in the field of political economy.

Research undertaken in the field of natural history and applied to the resources of a territory or kingdom was designed to improve the processes for their respective allocation, as well as to improve the physical and social conditions of the population. The involvement of both people and institutions in finding remedies for the ills that were diagnosed clearly reveals the social functions that the science of the natural world was now exercising. As E. Spary notes:

> Improvement became immensely popular in the latter half of the eighteenth century, as Europe's monarchs and ministers came to see natural history and the introduction of new species of plants and animals as a certain way to increase national revenues and private wealth. (1999, p. 179)

The basic idea that should be remembered is that the knowledge attained in the various branches of natural history was of an eminently practical and applied nature. This was the reason for the close relationship between the natural order and the economic order, which leads us to the conclusion that one could not exist without the other. In other words, natural history would have remained sterile and inconsequential if not seen in relation to its economic applications; political economy would not have achieved the status of a science if not based on knowledge that had already been consolidated by natural history.[19]

In this way, it is possible to understand that the importance of natural history as a discipline did not derive only from its contribution to the formation of a new and more extensive scientific knowledge. We must not overlook the institutional and political significance acquired by the work of eighteenth-century naturalists in terms of regulating the social and economic order. The strategy of reforming and improving natural resources and, generally speaking, all discourse that was centred on the problems of regenerating the natural order, indicated a broader strategy dictated by motivations of a political nature. Naturalists set up networks of influences – mainly, but not exclusively, through scientific academies – that expanded the scope of the practices that had already given them fame and prestige.[20]

The public recognition afforded to natural history meant that, by the mid-eighteenth century, this discipline had established itself as a field of research and inquiry that was not restricted to merely describing the surrounding world such as it existed. The development of natural history corresponded to a new 'epistemological imperative' (Gusdorf 1972, p. 262), which not only involved elite scholars and scientists, but also the more enlightened public opinion prepared to recognise that the natural world could be conceived of in a rational way. It was believed to be possible to create a universal and rigorous language, as well as descriptive and classificatory systems, in which the specificity and individuality of each species, in each kingdom, only made sense as characteristics of elements that belonged to the natural world as a whole.

We have already seen that in this world uncovered by natural history, the objects that were observed were not only of interest as a pretext for satisfying curiosity or fascination. Nor were utilitarian criteria the ones that exclusively concerned naturalists. Minerals, plants and animals represented separate forms of existence giving rise to the formation of an organised knowledge that allowed for a better understanding of the functioning of the natural world within which humankind operated. Attention was not only centred on curiosities, attractive or useful things. Naturalists made inventories of natural productions in a rigorous and systematic manner, which involved processes of description, comparison and classification, or, in other words, the construction of ordered systems of knowledge that formed the basis for the development of modern science (Guntau 1996).

In their work, naturalists were confronted with stability – but also with change – which occurred in the natural world, most particularly in terms of the capacity that species have for perpetuating themselves infinitely through successive generations. The diversity, complexity and interdependence evident in nature not only lent themselves to contemplation. They were also characteristics of a complex system equipped with self-sustaining regenerative capacity.

This is a decisive matter for clarifying the question announced as the main issue to be investigated in this section, i.e. the influence exercised by conceptual constructions in the fields of the natural sciences on the formation of the science of political economy, particularly as far as the notions of order, equilibrium and regulation are concerned. In fact, one of the most notable aspects of the post-Newtonian scientific environment was the development of a conception of the natural world in which the attributes that were responsible for its transformation and dynamic evolution also included the achievement of equilibrium and harmony in the sphere of economic organisation.

Let us take as an illustrative example, the clearly visible relationships of similarity between the works of Newton and Smith, which have not escaped the attention of specialists (Hetherington 1993). Newton's grand design, which consisted of discovering great mathematical principles for determining the general laws of natural philosophy, set in motion a vast movement seeking to discover the principles that governed the various fields of knowledge, naturally including the study of economic phenomena. As far as Smith was concerned, his adherence to the Newtonian universe was expressed not only in his works on the history of astronomy in which he made direct use of the teachings of the author of the *Principia*. At countless points throughout the *Wealth of Nations*, Smith incorporated Newton's overall conception of the invisible chains and relationships that gave coherence to scattered objects by integrating them into an order governed by general principles that were induced through observation and experimentation. Or, in other words, the visible order is explained by an invisible structure that organises the observed facts of real life.[21] One of the most frequently quoted examples is that of the implicit recourse to the law of gravitation to explain how the market price gravitates around the natural price of a certain good. Although he did not succeed in turning political economy into an abstract science immune to the deliberate intervention of man, which would call for an alteration of the conditions for the existence of certain laws, there is no doubt that Smith sought to maintain some obedience to the criteria arising from the philosophical and scientific system introduced and developed by Newton.[22]

Nonetheless, this type of approach shows itself to be even more significant when applied to the study of physiocracy, in view of the way in which physical nature presents itself as a model for explaining the economic organism. The economic theory of production and the exclusive productivity of agriculture, as well as the circular flow of wealth described in Quesnay's famous *Tableau Economique*, were based on a vision of the economy as something that functioned in a similar way to the physiological processes conceived of as an explanation for the natural world. As Paul Christensen neatly summarised this idea:

> From Hobbes to Quesnay, the dominant set of metaphors shaping the conceptual structure of the economic theory of production and exchange were drawn from physiology and the comparison of the economy to the living body (and the larger economy of nature). (1994, p. 249)

In analysing the net product created exclusively in agriculture, nature is given prime responsibility for explaining its source or origin. In effect, it was the powers and properties of the natural world, existing before human labour and the means used by this for the transformation thereof, that produced the gift in terms of natural energy that was transmitted to the products created by the earth. This in turn gave rise to the very particular attention given to the material and physical order of the natural world, which physiocrats sought to explain economically, since it is nature itself that represents the motive force behind the processes of production and circulation of the net product.[23]

Concluding remarks

The economic discourse of the late eighteenth century based its premises and foundations on the characteristic order of the natural world. The natural laws that regulated economic life were given characteristics that were identical to those attributed to the laws governing the spontaneous organisation of nature.

Natural history occupied a crucial position in the genesis of political economy, in so far as it constituted a duly established and cultivated field of knowledge providing links and heuristic connections that consolidated the discourse of the new science, not only in relation to the procedures involved in the formation of knowledge (observation and experimentation), but also in relation to the definition of fundamental interpretative principles (order, equilibrium, stability, harmony). Thus, natural history was a factor that legitimated a discourse that proclaimed the providential nature of some categories referring to economic processes (the concept of the market, for example), which were considered reflections of the natural order of things.

The naturalisation of some concepts was a popular procedure amongst both the physiocrats and Adam Smith who sought to reinforce the idea of the normality and inevitability of the economic processes that they described. It was almost always conceptual abstractions (the *natural* division of labour, the *natural* order of the market, or the system of *natural* liberty, to mention just some of the best known and most obvious examples to be found in Smith's work) that represented an indispensable requirement for understanding the different facts and occurrences to which they referred. By way of example, it should be said that what matters is not to describe the series of interacting operations involved in the production taking place at a pin factory, but to understand that the process described embodies a series of attributes and advantages that make the division of labour a *natural* process guaranteeing an increase in the productive power of labour.

Consequently, the nature that was captured by political economy was not limited to a mere empirical description of individual facts, without any connections between them. The natural world is the one understood by the natural philosophers through the formation of a systematic knowledge based on clearly defined analytical categories and produced in clearly identified and well-known historical and institutional contexts.[24]

But the natural order is also the one that results from the understanding elaborated through the philosophy of natural law, especially through the identification of the characteristics, regularities and permanencies of universal human nature. Understanding the behaviour of men in society (namely their economic behaviour) presupposes a knowledge of human nature, which, in turn, calls for a capacity for understanding the laws that regulate and govern it. As I sought to demonstrate in the first part of this chapter, it is precisely these laws that have determined the framework for the possibility of discovering the motivation and economic sense of human action. It should also be stressed that the natural law approach, with its insistence on the secularisation process, paves the way for the natural history approach. In both cases, man is at the centre of the enquiry concerning the functioning of the natural order.

For all these reasons, the process involved in the emergence of political economy in the second half of the eighteenth century benefited greatly from the support provided by the attributes of the natural order that were revealed simultaneously, in a distinct but complementary manner, by natural history and the philosophy of natural law. This was the fabric within which political economy wove its object and method, and which ended up guaranteeing it its own citizenship and disciplinary autonomy.

Notes

1. See Letwin (1963) and Appleby (1978). For a systematic presentation of the similarities of goals and methods among seventeenth century English economic writers, see Finkelstein (2000). For a modern neoclassical interpretation of mercantilism as a system and process of rent seeking and economic regulation and control, see Ekelund and Tollison (1997). For an overall consideration of the most immediate antecedents of the formation of political economy, it is always useful to recall the neat synthesis offered by Winch (1973).
2. In addition to the study by Poovey (1998) already mentioned, see also Perrot (1992), which develops a similar line of argument about the importance of the way in which the perception and knowledge of the empirical world evolved towards the formation of the modern discourse of political economy. The search for an objective language that emphasised numbers, was of a considerable importance for the emergence of models of reasoning which were particularly relevant to the development of economics as a discipline, namely the balance of trade model, the circulatory model and the national accounting model. On this topic see Finkelstein (2000).
3. The concept is borrowed from Whitehead (1926, especially Chs. I and III), where the author discusses the importance of an instinctive conviction in the order of nature for the development of economic science.
4. On the political aims contained in this conceptualisation and the dimension of natural law as a historical category, see Knight (1944, pp. 312–57).
5. It is not my purpose to analyse here the original sources nor to discuss the different approaches and theories of natural law. Nevertheless, it should be remembered that the broader picture presented here does not ignore nor forget the existence of continuities and discontinuities within the systems of natural law. For a general account of the specificities of the leading natural law theorists, see Tuck (1979), Buckle (1991) and Haakonssen (1996). A brief outline of the principal distinctions, in which particular attention is paid to the economic implications of natural law theories, is provided by Hont and Ignatieff (1983b, pp. 26–44).
6. For Viner (1978), secularisation consists fundamentally of reducing the influence of the ecclesiastical authority and traditional creeds of the church on ethical, political and economic thought, and of shifting the emphasis from transcendental values to temporal values.
7. On this theme, see Brown (1984, Introduction).
8. For a summary of this approach, see Pocock (1983) and Robertson (1983).
9. The most important of these are collected in Hont and Ignatieff (1983a), and Geuna and Pesante (1992).
10. Such is the case with Young and Gordon, who consider that 'Scholastic economic analysis as may have come to influence Adam Smith was almost certainly derived chiefly from that which was taken up in the Protestant natural law tradition [Grotius and Pufendorf]' (1992, p. 6).
11. It should be borne in mind that the founding or constituent relationship that natural law shares with political economy sometimes serves as an excuse to justify the characteristic presumption of contemporary economics, whereby there exists a natural, positive determination of the observed uniformities and regularities of social life. In other words, economic theory ceases to concern itself with determining factors of a social or historical nature and is interested only in the definition of supposed natural laws that regulate economic phenomena. For a critical analysis of this type of argument, see Clark (1992).
12. See Dumont (1977, pp. 43–9) and Vidonne (1986, pp. 73–86).
13. On these issues, see Chalk (1951), Grampp (1952), Viner (1959), Horne (1978) and, above all, Appleby (1978).
14. For a detailed characterisation of these explanatory types, see Myers (1983, pp. 11–89). Somewhat different, though to some extent complementary, standpoints are to be found in Hirschman (1977) and Teichgraeber (1986). The refutation of the idea – supported by Myers – that those new conceptions were designed 'as a reaction to the extreme reductionist view of human nature advanced by Hobbes', is briefly but pertinently presented in Moss (1991).
15. Some authors uphold the absolute merit of the physiocrats in relation to this subject, and consider them responsible for actually founding the science of political economy. This is the thesis defended – although not in a very convincing way – by Larrère (1992).

16. On the problem of the political regulation of economic harmony in physiocratic thought, see Fox-Genovese (1976, pp. 100–133).
17. One author who is particularly aware of these limitations, as well as of other supposed manifestations of a spontaneous, self-regulating kind, is Polanyi (1944). See also Hont (1989, p. 127) and Herlitz (1997).
18. On this point, see Haakonssen (1981, especially pp. 178–89).
19. A good example of this symbiosis is given by both the work and activities undertaken by Linnaeus in Sweden, combining his talents as a naturalist with his qualities as an adviser in matters of economic policy. For some considerations about the significance of his work, see Koerner (1999).
20. For an analysis of different approaches to the question of how natural history can provide models for the interpretation and functioning of the moral and political order of human society, see Jardine et al. (1996).
21. With regard to the relationship between visible and invisible order in Smith's work, see Rothschild (2001). See also Fiori (2001), whose main argument is summarised as follows: 'The notion of the "invisible hand" is the core of political economy, and not merely an evocative metaphor: the actions of individuals are visible, but the way in which they achieve co-ordination must be explained by invisible principles which reveal the hidden organisation of the system' (p. 443).
22. On this subject, see Cohen (1993), and, in particular, Redman, who summarises the importance of Newton's legacy for the formation of a social science, as follows: 'After Newton had founded order and harmony in the physical universe by discovering the laws that govern its movements, philosophers reasoned that disorder must be man-made and could be averted by studying human nature and ascertaining the natural laws or connecting principles that govern society. The existence of guiding social principles was taken for granted; the search for them than became a primary goal. The scholars of this age were convinced that immutable laws such as those reigning in the physical universe existed in society and in mental states of human beings' (Redman 1997, p. 111).
23. As Banzhaf summarised this idea: 'Nature, rather than being merely decorative, is this crucial source. It is a kind of "deism" ex machina ushered in to regulate the system. And the net product is the quantitative measure of this motive force; it is the gift of motion from nature, while subsequent economic activity only traces this motion through its pathway and on to consumption' (2000, p. 547).
24. In this way, it is possible to understand the constructivist character of scientific knowledge, in the sense that was given to this expression by Golinski, or, in other words, an acceptance 'which regards scientific knowledge primarily as a human product, made with locally situated cultural and material resources, rather than as simply the revelation of a pre-given order of nature' (1998, p. ix).

References

Appleby, Joyce O. (1978), *Economic Thought and Ideology in Seventeenth-Century England*, Princeton, NJ: Princeton University Press.
Banzhaf, H. Spencer (2000), 'Productive nature and the net product: Quesnay's economies animal and political', *History of Political Economy*, **32** (3), 517–51.
Brown, Robert (1984), *The Nature of Social Laws: Machiavelli to Mill*, Cambridge and New York: Cambridge University Press.
Buckle, Stephen (1991), *Natural Law and the Theory of Property, Grotius to Hume*, Oxford: Clarendon Press.
Chalk, Alfred (1951), 'Natural law and the rise of economic individualism in England', *Journal of Political Economy*, **59** (3), 330–47.
Charlton, D.G. (1984), *New Images of the Natural in France. A Study in European Cultural History, 1750–1800*, Cambridge and New York: Cambridge University Press.
Christensen, Paul P. (1994), 'Fire, motion and productivity: the proto-energetics of nature and economy in François Quesnay', in Philip Mirowski, (ed.), *Natural Images in Economic Thought*.

'Markets Read in Tooth and Claw', Cambridge and New York: Cambridge University Press, pp. 249–88.

Clark, Charles M.A. (1992), *Economic Theory and Natural Philosophy: the Search for the Natural Laws of the Economy*, Aldershot, UK and Brookfield, US: Edward Elgar.

Cohen, I. Bernard (1993), 'The *Principia*, the Newtonian style, and the Newtonian revolution in science', in Paul Theerman and Adele F. Seeff (eds), *Action and Reaction. Proceedings of a Symposium to Commemorate the Tercentenary of Newton's 'Principia'*, Newark: University of Delaware Press, pp. 61–104.

Coleman, William O. (1995), *Rationalism and Anti-rationalism in the Origins of Economics. The Philosophical Roots of 18th Century Economic Thought*, Aldershot, UK and Brookfield, US: Edward Elgar.

Dumont, Louis (1977), *Homo Aequalis: Genèse et Epanouissement de l'Idéologie Economique*, Paris: Gallimard.

Ekelund, Robert B., and Robert D. Tollison (1997), *Politicized Economies. Monarchy, Monopoly and Mercantilism*, College Station: Texas A&M University Press.

Finkelstein, Andrea (2000), *Harmony and the Balance. An Intellectual History of Seventeenth-Century English Economic Thought*, Ann Arbor: University of Michigan Press.

Fiori, Stefano (2001), 'Visible and invisible order: the theoretical duality of Smith's political economy', *European Journal of the History of Economic Thought*, **8** (4), 429–48.

Fox-Genovese, Elisabeth (1976), *The Origins of Physiocracy: Economic Revolution and Social Order in Eighteenth-Century France*, Ithaca, NY: Cornell University Press.

Geuna, Marco, and Maria Luisa, Pesante (eds), (1992), *Passioni, Interessi, Convenzioni: Discussioni Settecentesche su Virtù e Civiltà*, Milan: Franco Angeli.

Golinski, Jan (1998), *Making Natural Knowledge: Constructivism and the History of Science*, Cambridge and New York: Cambridge University Press.

Grampp, William D. (1952), 'The liberal element in English mercantilism', *Quarterly Journal of Economics*, **66** (4), 465–501.

Guntau, Martin (1996), 'The natural history of the earth', in N. Jardine, J.A. Secord and E.C. Spary (eds), *Cultures of Natural History*, Cambridge and New York: Cambridge University Press, pp. 211–29.

Gusdorf, Georges (1972), *Dieu, la Nature, l'Homme au Siècle des Lumières*, Paris: Payot.

Haakonssen, Knud (1981), *The Science of a Legislator. The Natural Jurisprudence of David Hume and Adam Smith*, Cambridge and New York: Cambridge University Press.

Haakonssen, Knud (1996), *Natural Law and Moral Philosophy. From Grotius to the Scottish Enlightenment*, Cambridge and New York: Cambridge University Press.

Herlitz, Lars (1997), 'Art and nature in pre-classical economics of the seventeenth and eighteenth centuries', in Mikulás Teich, Roy Porter and Bo Gustafsson (eds), *Nature and Society in Historical Context*, Cambridge and New York: Cambridge University Press, pp. 163–75.

Hetherington, Norriss S. (1993), 'Isaac Newton and Adam Smith: intellectual links between natural science and economics', in Paul Theerman and Adele Seeff (eds), *Action and Reaction. Proceedings of a Symposium to Commemorate the Tercentenary of Newton's 'Principia'*, Newark: University of Delaware Press, pp. 277–91.

Hirschman, Albert O. (1977), *The Passions and the Interests: Political Arguments for Capitalism Before its Triumph*, Princeton, NJ: Princeton University Press.

Hont, Istvan (1989), 'The political economy of the "unnatural and retrograde" order: Adam Smith and natural liberty', in Maxime Berg et al. (eds), *Französische Revolution und Politische Ökonomie*, Trier: Schriften aus dem Karl-Marx-Haus, pp. 122–49.

Hont, Istvan, and Michael, Ignatieff (eds), (1983a), *Wealth and Virtue: the Shaping of Political Economy in the Scottish Enlightenment*, Cambridge and New York: Cambridge University Press.

Hont, Istvan, and Michael, Ignatieff (1983b), 'Needs and justice in the *Wealth of Nations*: an introductory essay', in Istvan Hont and Michael Ignatieff (eds), *Wealth and Virtue: the Shaping of Political Economy in the Scottish Enlightenment*, Cambridge and New York: Cambridge University Press, pp. 1–44.

Horne, Thomas (1978), *The Social Thought of Bernard de Mandeville: Virtue and Commerce in Early Eighteenth-Century England*, New York: Columbia University Press.

Jardine, N., J.A. Secord and E.C. Spary (eds), (1996), *Cultures of Natural History*, Cambridge and New York: Cambridge University Press.

Keynes, John M. (1926 [1972]), 'The end of laissez-faire', reprinted in: *The Collected Writings of John Maynard Keynes, Vol. IX: Essays in Persuasion*, edited by E. Johnson and D. Moggridge, London: Macmillan.

Knight, Frank (1944 [1982]), 'The rights of man and natural law', reprinted in: F.H. Knight, *Freedom and Reform: Essays in Economics and Social Philosophy*, Indianapolis: Liberty Press.

Koerner, Lisbet (1999), *Linnaeus: Nature and Nation*, Cambridge, MA and London: Harvard University Press.

Larrère, Catherine (1992), *Du Droit Naturel à la Physiocratie: L'Invention de l'Economie au XVIIIe Siècle*, Paris: Presses Universitaires de France.

Letwin, William (1963), *The Origins of Scientific Economics*, London: Methuen and Co.

Meek, Ronald (1962), *The Economics of Physiocracy: Essays and Translations*, London: George Allen and Unwin.

Mornet, D. (1911 [2001]), *Les Sciences de la Nature en France, au XVIIIe Siècle*, Geneva: Slatkine Reprints.

Moss, Laurence S. (1991), 'Thomas Hobbes's influence on David Hume: the emergence of a public choice tradition', *History of Political Economy*, **23** (4), 587–612.

Myers, Milton (1983), *The Soul of Modern Economic Man. Ideas of Self Interest: Thomas Hobbes to Adam Smith*, Chicago and London: University of Chicago Press.

Nuccio, Oscar (1986), 'Epistemologia economica: il ruolo dei concetti di "natura" e di "diritto naturale" nelle genese dell'economia politica', *Rivista di Politica Economica*, **76** (VII), 974–1023.

Perrot, Jean-Claude (1992), *Une Histoire Intellectuelle de l'Economie Politique (XVIIe–XVIIIe Siècle)*, Paris: Editions de l'EHESS.

Pocock, J.G.A. (1975), *The Machiavellian Moment: Florentine Political Thought and the Atlantic Republic Tradition*, Princeton, NJ: Princeton University Press.

Pocock, J.G.A. (1983), 'Cambridge paradigms and Scottish philosophers: a study of the relations between the civic humanist and the civil jurisprudential interpretation of eighteenth-century social thought', in Istvan Hont, and Michael Ignatieff (eds), *Wealth and Virtue: the Shaping of Political Economy in the Scottish Enlightenment*, Cambridge and New York: Cambridge University Press, pp. 235–52.

Polanyi, Karl (1944), *The Great Transformation*, New York: Farrar and Rinehart, (new edition, 1978), Boston: Beacon Press.

Poovey, Mary (1998), *A History of the Modern Fact: Problems of Knowledge in the Sciences of Wealth and Society*, Chicago and London: University of Chicago Press.

Quesnay, François (1766 [1991]), 'Analyse de la formule arithmétique du *Tableau Economique* de la distribution des dépenses annuelles d'une nation agricole', reprinted in F. Quesnay, *Physiocratie: Droit naturel, Tableau Économique et Autres Textes*, edited by Jean Cartelier, Paris: Flammarion, pp. 207–33.

Quesnay, François (1767 [1991]), 'Maximes générales du gouvernement économique d'un royaume agricole', reprinted in F. Quesnay, *Physiocratie: Droit naturel, Tableau Economique et Autres Textes*, edited by Jean Cartelier, Paris: Flammarion, pp. 235–67.

Redman, Deborah A. (1997), *The Rise of Political Economy as a Science: Methodology and the Classical Economists*, Cambridge, MA and London: MIT Press.

Robertson, John (1983), 'The Scottish Enlightenment at the limits of the civic tradition', in Istvan Hont and Michael Ignatieff (eds), *Wealth and Virtue: the Shaping of Political Economy in the Scottish Enlightenment*, Cambridge and New York: Cambridge University Press, pp. 137–78.

Roche, Daniel (1996), 'Natural history in the academies', in N. Jardine, J.A. Secord and E.C. Spary (eds), *Cultures of Natural History*, Cambridge and New York: Cambridge University Press, pp. 127–44.

Rothschild, Emma (2001), *Economic Sentiments. Adam Smith, Condorcet and the Enlightenment*, Cambridge, MA and London: Harvard University Press.

Schumpeter, Joseph A. (1954), *History of Economic Analysis*, Oxford: Oxford University Press.

Solomon, Robert (1986), *History and Human Nature: a Philosophical Review of European Philosophy and Culture, 1750–1850*, New York: Harcourt Brace Jovanovich.

Spary, E.C. (1999), 'The "Nature" of Enlightenment', in, William Clark, Jan Golonski and Simon Schaffer (eds), *The Sciences in Enlightened Europe*, Chicago and London: University of Chicago Press, pp. 272–304.

Spary, E.C. (2000), *Utopia's Garden. French Natural History from Old Regime to Revolution*, Chicago and London: University of Chicago Press.

Teichgraeber, Richard (1986), *'Free Trade' and Moral Philosophy: Rethinking the Sources of Adam Smith's Wealth of Nations*, Durham, NC: Duke University Press.

Tuck, Richard (1979), *Natural Rights Theories: Their Origin and Development*, Cambridge and New York: Cambridge University Press.

Vidonne, Paul (1986), *La Formation de la Pensée Economique*, Paris: Economica.

Viner, Jacob (1959), 'The Wabash Lectures: five lectures on economics and freedom', reprinted in Jacob Viner, *Essays on the Intellectual History of Economics*, edited by Douglas A. Irwin, Princeton, NJ: Princeton University Press, pp. 37–81.

Viner, Jacob (1978), *Religious Thought and Economic Society: Four Chapters of an Unfinished Work*, edited by J. Melitz and D. Winch, Durham: Duke University Press.

Whitehead, Alfred (1926), *Science and the Modern World*, Cambridge and New York: Cambridge University Press.

Winch, Donald (1973), 'The emergence of economics as a science, 1750–1870', in Carlo M. Cipolla (ed.), *The Fontana Economic History of Europe. The Industrial Revolution*, Glasgow: Fontana/Collins, pp. 507–73.

Young, Jeffrey T., and Barry Gordon (1992), 'Economic justice in the natural law tradition: Thomas Aquinas to Francis Hutcheson', *Journal of the History of Economic Thought*, **14** (1), 1–17.

2   The historical and philosophical foundations of *new* political economy

Alain Marciano

Introduction

Since the 1950s, economists have shown an increasing recognition that 'institutions matter' (Frey 1990), and have worked to develop economic analyses of institutions and rules, analysing their origins and how they shape and influence individual behaviour. These contributions have subsequently led to the suggestion that the analyses of institutions in question – such as public choice, law and economics and, later, constitutional political economy – might form a *new* political economy reviving the spirit of the founders of classical political economy, Hume and Smith among others (Atkinson and Stiglitz 1980; Inman 1987; Hirshleifer 1982; Johnson 1991). While the various branches of the *new* political economy differ in many respects, they can nevertheless be captured in two broad categories. On the one hand, a contractualist (constructivist) approach considers that institutions are explicitly built from a state of nature characterised by the absence of any rule. On the other hand, a spontaneous order approach argues that institutions are not created or designed by human beings but emerge through a market process. Now, these two approaches claim to descend from the same ancestors, namely the classical political economists. In fact, and it is the argument that we develop in this chapter, neither can legitimately claim their heritage.

With regard to contractualist new political economy, the alleged classical political economy heritage is a consequence of the fact that it emerged and developed at a time of economic imperialism, when economists were trying to demonstrate that their models were relevant to explaining, in particular, political phenomena. To legitimise the new approach, therefore, some of its proponents were keen to show that the classical political economists were themselves 'the first imperialists'.[1] More precisely, as Brennan puts it, 'the enterprise of attempting to erect a single unified theory of social phenomena on rational-actor foundations should not surprise us. It is, after all, by no means a new enterprise. It was specifically, an important part of the Enlightenment project from which economics as a discipline emerged' (1992, p. 15). Now, such an assumption is linked to the assumption that individuals are self-interested and that their behaviour is guided by rational deliberation. Buchanan, a well-known contractualist, is worth quoting here. Launching constitutional economics, he states that the 'foundational position [of constitutional economics] is summarised in *methodological individualism*' and 'the concomitant ... postulate of rational choice' (1990, pp. 13–14). He then quotes Hume in support: 'each man ought to be supposed a knave, and to have no other end, in his actions, than private interest' (Hume 1741 [1992, pp. 117–118], in Buchanan 1987, p. 587). Even if, as Salmon writes, 'economists have always known that to assume rationality is a research strategy for the purpose of modelling interesting mechanisms rather than a descriptive assertion about reality' (2001, p. 453; see also 2000), it remains that assuming rationality and self-interest nonetheless influences the way institutions are analysed. Indeed, it implies that rules and institutions are to be tailored to control the potential opportunism of these rational self-interested and non-benevolent ('knaves') individuals. The social contract is then considered as the only institutional form that has the capacity to reach this objective.

Now, in contrast to what is put forward by modern contractualists, the classical political economists did not actually conceive of individual actors as rational beings. Rather, they developed a theory of human nature, whose major characteristic is not only the subjectivist dimension of human cognition but essentially the weakness, or the limitations of human rationality. The latter point has been stressed by the advocates of a theory of spontaneous order. Criticising the top-down contractualist approach to the study of institutions, the spontaneous order theorists have defended a bottom-up line of reasoning in which institutions are assumed to emerge from the repetition of interactions between individuals. Hayek, among others, is well known for having both rejected the rationalist constructivism of social contract theories and having claimed the heritage of Hume or Smith. The argument then goes on to show that spontaneously emerging institutions are likely to generalise and to govern large and open societies. However, if one accepts Hume's or Smith's theory of human nature, one has also to accept the fact that spontaneous orders depend upon and therefore are limited by the existence of sympathy between individuals. In other words, it is not possible to envisage an unlimited generalisation of emerging rules without more formal rules.

Therefore, a genuine new political economy should really elaborate upon the non-rationalist conception of man proposed by Hume and Smith. The goal of this chapter is thus to explore this theory of human nature and its consequences in terms of rules and institutions. We shall distinguish between formal and informal rules, and show that they are complementary rather than competing and that they serve to highlight the crucial role of sentiments in the emergence of institutions.

Interestingly, our perspective overlaps with that of 'inspired economics' (Frey and Stutzer 2001, see also Frey and Benz, this volume), which builds upon the necessity of going 'beyond *homo œconomicus*' (see Anderson 2000) and moving 'from *homo œconomicus* to *homo sapiens*' (Thaler 2000). Various behavioural anomalies and irrational behaviours that have come to light – especially thanks to experiments performed by psychologists or even by economists[2] – suggest that 'humans do not act rationally in the sense of following the von Neumann/ Morgenstern axioms' (Frey and Stutzer 2001, p. 9). Of course, reference to the classical political economists has disappeared in this work – implicitly confirming that economists' attempts to analyse rules and institutions with the help of the assumption of rational individual behaviours was indeed a legacy of the origins of the discipline. To be inspired, economics could no longer refer to economists who were used by imperialistic economics. As a consequence, inspiration could not but come from other social sciences. In this respect, while a large literature was devoted to understand the implications of abandoning the assumption of rational behaviour, many attempts were also made to incorporate the insights of other social sciences into the economic models of institutions (for instance, see Frey 1997; Frey and Stutzer 2001; Mueller 2001). Thus, it was proposed to develop *behavioural* political economy, such as behavioural law and economics (see Jolls et al. 1998) and behavioural public choice (Ostrom 1998). Now, since Hume or Smith do not defend the assumption of rationality, it appears that inspiration could come from within rather from outside the discipline after all. Economists could be inspired by the founders of political economy.

The chapter is organised as follows. First, we analyse the theory of human nature proposed by Hume, Smith and other classical political economists. In particular, we show that human reason played a less powerful role here than is usually assumed in modern economics (section 1). As a consequence, the problems of co-ordination which result from the older conception of human beings cannot be solved by institutions. Therefore, successful co-ordination requires information on the behaviour of others and institutions cannot be considered as a means to convey information (section 2). In fact, focusing exclusively on institutions throws into relief the logical aspect of co-ordination and co-operation, at the expense of the psychological dimension of the problem. It is therefore necessary to understand how individual beliefs about others are formed, independently from institutions. Sympathy plays a crucial role here, delineating the domain in which institutions can emerge (section 3). Thus, the core argument of this chapter is that, in contrast to standard analyses, sympathy is a necessary condition for successful co-ordination, and institutions complement sympathy.

Human nature: from sensualism to associationism

'Inspired economics' has insisted on the necessity, usefulness and innovation of looking towards psychology to understand and model human behaviour. This insistence is all the more interesting in view of the fact that the founders of political economy had themselves already based their analysis upon psychology, namely associationist psychology, whose origins can be traced back to the publication in 1749 of David Hartley's *Observations on Man, his Frame, his Duty and his Expectations*.[3] Thus, as noted by Young, 'the association of ideas was also a basic assumption of the epistemology and psychology of David Hume and had continental parallels in the work and influence of Condillac' (1985, p. 65). More precisely, Hume as well as Condillac do not investigate the physical origins of association, but address the question from a philosophical point of view. As philosophers, the classical political economists, included Condillac, belong to the philosophical movement of the Scottish Enlightenment. In fact, associationist psychology and the philosophy of the Scottish Enlightenment are closely intertwined because of the emphasis put on the role of the senses in the perception of the world and the building of human knowledge. The Scottish Enlightenment, as opposed to the Continental version of the *Siècle des Lumières*, rejected Cartesian dualism and the corresponding rationalist conception of human behaviour. As a consequence, the problem that has necessarily to be dealt with is that of explaining how a mind can know an external object. More precisely, challenging Cartesian dualism not only raises the question of the origins of human faculties, capacities and knowledge, it also implies locating the origin of human knowledge within the object rather than within the knowing mind. This is the reason why associationism cannot be understood without reference to the process through which knowledge results from sensory perception. Conversely, to insist on the role of senses – rather than on that of reason – in the relation between human beings and their environment, necessarily leads to an associationist conception of human cognition. Associationism, in psychology, and sensualism, in philosophy, are the two sides of the same theory of human nature.

Sensualism and the weakness of human reason
Let us begin with sensualism. Hume, Smith and other Scottish scholars, such as Ferguson or Stewart, are praised for having proposed a *sensualist* theory of human nature. Sensualism is a philosophy of the mind that considers man as a tabula rasa upon which impressions received *through the senses* from the external world progressively gather and draw the shape of an individual. To illustrate this assumption of a tabula rasa, the French philosopher Condillac imagined, not unlike the way social contract theorists envisage the fiction of a state of nature, the fiction of a marble statue that, although having the same internal organisation as a man, has none of the five senses that characterise human beings. Condillac builds his demonstration around describing how the statue becomes a man when senses give him access to the world, that is, how senses allow the statue to perceive the world. The lesson that Condillac draws is

simple: without sensory perception, man is nothing more than a marble statue. In his own 'version' of the statue, Hume writes that 'When my perceptions are remov'd for any time, as by sound sleep; so long am I insensible to myself, and may truly be said not exist' (1739 [1992], p. 252). Thus, the basic, and also the smallest, unit that constitutes human beings is a perception of the world. As Hume writes, 'for any part, when I enter most intimately into what I call myself, I always stumble on some particular perception or another, of heat, cold, light or shade, love or hatred, pain or pleasures. I can never catch myself without a perception' (Hume 1739 [1992], p. 252). More precisely, there are two forms of perceptions, impressions and ideas: 'All the perception of the human mind resolve themselves into two distinct kinds, which I shall call IMPRESSIONS and IDEAS' (Hume 1739 [1992], p. 1). This is an interesting classification of perceptions for it already reveals that ideas also have their origins in the external world as well as within the mind. Furthermore, the difference between impressions and ideas, as it is indeed put forward by Hume, is solely a matter of 'force and liveliness', the 'force and liveliness with which they strike upon the mind, and make their way into our thought or consciousness' (ibid.). In this comparison between these two forms of perceptions, impressions dominate ideas:

> Those perceptions which enter with most fort and violence, we may name impressions; and under this name I Comprehend all our sensations, passions and emotions, as they make their first appearance in the soul. By ideas I mean the faint images of these in thinking and reasoning. (ibid.)

Therefore, not only do ideas have their origin in the world, but they are also solely images of impressions. As Hume repeatedly remarks, ideas are only *copied* or *derived* from impressions. The hierarchy that Hume establishes between ideas and impressions is clearly in favour of the latter: 'our impressions are the causes of our ideas, not our ideas of our impressions' (1739 [1992], p. 5), and 'all our simple ideas proceed either mediately or immediately from their correspondent impressions' (ibid., p. 7). Therefore, everything proceeds from the senses, and nothing exists in the mind that has not been first experienced, that is perceived through the senses.

At this first stage of reasoning, the human being is left as a sum or more precisely a 'chaos' (Renault 1989) of impressions received from the environment. To propose a complete analysis of human cognition, sensualism has to deal with the need to explain how the ongoing information that is transmitted to the mind is stored (memorised), processed (impressions transformed into ideas) and utilised. What does the mental activity of human beings, which organises impressions into structured and meaningful knowledge, consist of? From the perspective of a comparison with a rational conception of man, the role and nature of human reason have to be investigated. The description of the rationalist view on human cognition will help us to see why sensualism cannot but imply that human rationality is bounded.

Rationalism, particularly as expressed by Descartes, assumes the existence of a specific human capacity, namely reason or, more precisely, rational reason. Reason, which distinguishes man from animals, goes far beyond the simple capacity to compute data: it not only organises the impressions that are received from the environment but also allows human beings to identify the false information conveyed by the senses as well as speculate about facts and events that have not been experienced. Rationalism thus develops a 'central planning view of brain function' (Gifford 1996). This perspective is in total contradiction to the Scottish Enlightenment philosophy. Indeed, interpreted within the sensualist framework, rational reason should be considered as an impression and, moreover, should be defined as a specific impression, standing above all other impressions, granted with stability and permanence to which other impressions would be referred. Now, as Hume points it out; 'there is no impression constant and invariable' (1739 [1992], p. 251). Therefore, reason does not exist as a central and organising capacity. Furthermore, it is not solely the absence of a rational reason that is at stake. Hume's conception of man conveys the more general absence of a central organising function in the mind which, beside unifying impressions, would define goals and means, and would check upon their execution. Absence of rational reason also precludes men from introspection, and does not allow self-awareness. Hume thus writes that 'It cannot, therefore, be from any of these impressions, of from any other, that the idea of the self is deriv'd; and consequently there is no such idea' (1739 [1992], p. 252).

Therefore, what sensualism denies is that individuals possess rational reason, viewed as a cause of knowledge and the origin of behaviour, a capacity very close to what mainstream economic theorists assume of the rational economic agents. Nevertheless, the existence of reason is acknowledged as 'a heap or collection of different perceptions' (Hume 1739 [1992], p. 207).[4] Reason is not a capacity for organising knowledge. Rather than being a cause, reason is a consequence – the unintended consequence of the accumulation of impressions. Thus, even if reason exists, it cannot but be a far more limited capacity than rationalism assumes. That is to say, human beings cannot but be labouring under bounded rationality.

Rules of association
Having rejected what may be regarded as a constructivist approach to human mental activity or human cognition, Hume develops a spontaneous order theory based on rules or principles of association. More precisely, having identified the basic units of knowledge transmitted to the mind by the senses, and having

rejected reason as an organising capacity, Hume proposes that these units cannot but spontaneously organise into structured and meaningful knowledge.

In a nutshell, the process breaks down into three major parts. First, the structure of knowledge is influenced by the exercise of two important faculties, memory and imagination: memory stores and 'repeat impressions in the first manner' (1739 [1992], p. 8) while imagination separates ideas and unites 'them again in what form it pleases' (ibid., p. 10), thus creating new and perfect ideas. Imagination thus has a clear speculative and forward-looking role to play. Once this role has been played, impressions become structured in meaningful way by virtue of a 'gentle force' (ibid.), a 'kind of ATTRACTION, which in the mental world will be found to have as extraordinary effects as in the natural, and to show itself in as many as various forms' (ibid., p. 13). Impressions are joined, united and associated according to three 'qualities', 'RESEMBLANCE, CONTIGUITY in time and place, and CAUSE and EFFECT'. (ibid., p. 11). Hume then sums up human cognition as follows: 'These are therefore the principles of union or cohesion among our simple ideas, and in the imagination supply the place of that inseparable connection, by which they are united in our memory' (ibid., p. 12). These are the principles or rules of association among impressions which are at the basis of human cognition.

Human cognition is thus depicted as a process through which impressions are associated and connected into networks and groups of networks or, more exactly, classes: 'sensory perception' is thus what Hayek has described as 'an act of classification' (1952, p. 142). Indeed, the formation of classes reduces the costs of cognition in separating out the important and ongoing stream of impressions that are received. The idea that human beings are able to identify each received bit of information assumes cognitive abilities that far exceed the effective capacities of human beings. Perception is therefore not a passive act but an act of interpretation which consists in assigning the incoming data to the already existing classes: 'External objects ... become present to the mind [when] they acquire such a relation to a connected heap of perceptions, as to influence them very considerably in augmenting their number by present reflections and passions, and in storing the memory with ideas' (Hume 1739 [1992], p. 207). Thus, the human mind always selectively utilises information, classifies and re-classifies perceived stimuli and frames them within existing patterns according to a 'winner-take-all' strategy (Gifford 1996). Either an impression can be recognised, that is can be identified as belonging to an existing class, or it is rejected. As a consequence, a phenomenon or an event is perceived because the impression related to this event or phenomenon is associated with an impression related to past events or phenomena. If the impression is rejected, therefore the event is not 'perceptible' (Hayek 1952, pp. 142–3). Data are thus received only if they are consistent with other beliefs. This conception of human cognition explains the phenomenon known as the curse of knowledge – once an individual knows something, he cannot imagine thinking otherwise. Put in different terms, it means that the perception of an event is path-dependent. Indeed, it depends on the already accumulated knowledge and, subsequently, is driven by our tacit expectations about this event. As Kuran, among many others, puts it, individuals 'perceive selectively, noticing facts consistent with our beliefs more readily. This bias imparts resistance to our beliefs by shielding them from counter-evidence' (1995, p. 173). Now, psychologists and economists as well (Rosenberg 1999; Rabin 1998; Witt 1998, 1999; Rizzelo and Turvani 2000) have insisted on the role of 'perception-filters', 'preconceptions' and even prejudices in how individuals perceive and organise the data 'received' from their environment. This has also been utilised to demonstrate the limitations of human reason.

The conception of man developed by the sensualist–associationist approach of the classical political economist fathers of political economy, contrasts with the traditional model of man that is utilised by economic analysis. For the sensualist-associationist approach acknowledges that reason is not as powerful as is suggested by standard economic analysis. Besides, the process of knowledge acquisition depicted above not only conveys the image that the human mind functions as a screening device or a 'filter of experience' (Lachmann 1975, p. 9, quoted by O'Driscoll 1977) but also that 'each individual's filter is different from every other filter' (ibid.). Indeed, each individual is a unique example of a human being because his cognitive history is unique. This insight implies a subjective appraisal of the environment and a subjective elaboration of the individual plans of actions that govern behaviour. The subjective nature of human cognition therefore reveals that, within this framework, co-ordination among individual actions is an issue of the utmost importance. The nature of the problems raised by subjectivity and the role of institutions with regard to these difficulties are analysed in the next section.

Subjectivism, expectations and induction

There are at least two important sources of inconsistency that stem from the theory of human nature we have just decribed. First, as we have seen, perception, which is an act of classification, involves interpretation (selection) and imagination (speculation) as essential aspects of human cognition. Thus, because of the role of imagination in the elaboration of individuals' plans of action, inconsistencies may arise because each individual forms his own image of the future.[5] Besides possibly diverging expectations about the future, a second but not unrelated problem results from the fact that individuals' plans of actions depend on expectations about others' behaviours. Indeed, the differing and subjective nature of individual plans of action can be carried out successfully only if expectations converge and, in particular, if individuals are able to co-ordinate with others. Now, individuals' capacity and willingness to co-operate with others is related to the possibility of gathering information about others in order to identify reliable and trustworthy partners. The problem is made all the more complex in view of the fact that individuals' expectations are not about others' behaviour but about their expectations. Therefore, in such a theory of human nature, co-ordination depends on the possibility of gathering information about others' intentions and actions that would stop an infinite regress of reciprocally conditioned expectations. One could imagine that discrete mental experiments allow each of us to assess the subjective preferences of every individual we meet. This is probably a psychological impossibility. Moreover, the associated transaction costs would be prohibitively high and prevent any interaction. What is needed to elicit information about others is a framework in which it is possible to make stable and reliable expectations.

Undoubtedly, rules and institutions, either formal or informal, explicit or tacit, written or unwritten, do enable large numbers of individuals to co-ordinate their actions, locking their expectations into a self-consistent pattern. The point has been heavily emphasised that tacit norms or rules of law guide peoples' actions in order to give birth to stable and consistent expectations about each others' behaviour. However, although true, the statement that institutions serve to co-ordinate the actions of millions of individuals is only partial because it assumes the solution without explaining how the problem is solved.[6] The hypothesis that institutions exist leaves unanswered the question of the origins of institutions. In a rationalist, Cartesian or Hobbesian (namely, contractualist), setting, it is possible to envisage the explicit and constructivist design of institutions that generate ordered and co-ordinated behaviours. However, the assumption that rationality is an act of classification, depending on the accumulation of experiences, rather than an act of creation, makes it difficult to accept the idea of a social contract, at least in its Hobbesian form. Sensualist rationality, does not allow individual to create institutions that never existed. The question about the mutual consistency of individuals' plans of action thus echoes the individual problem of the origin of knowledge and of the internal consistency of perceptions: since individuals cannot create rules that they have not yet experienced and in the absence of a central planner, institutions have to be considered as the result of a decentralised process of repetition of interactions. That is to say, the theory of human nature developed by the classical political economists does not support a social contract approach of institution but legitimates a theory of spontaneous order. Institutions emerge as the result of the repetition of interactions; even Smith and Hume emphasised that individuals learn from their experiences of repeated interactions. Conditions are nonetheless required for institutions to emerge.

First, individuals have to initiate interactions. Why should they choose to do so? The many game-theoretical models that, since the pioneering work of

Axelrod (see, for example, 1984), have been developed to analyse the emergence of rules mostly focus upon the logical aspect of the co-ordination problem: once individuals have agreed to participate in interaction, one can expect that they will end up in co-ordinating with one another. However, a necessary condition for repeated interactions is the a priori existence of reciprocity. For instance, when Parisi writes that 'the principle of reciprocity serves as a crucial pillar for the process of law formation' (1998, p. 575), he means that reciprocity is a causal mechanism which explains the origins of institutions. In the same vein, when Hayek writes that 'wherever the use of competition can be rationally justified, it is on the ground that we do not know in advance the facts that determine the actions of competitors' (1978, p. 179), the problem is just that we do not know *in advance the facts that determine the actions of competitors*. Put differently, individuals engage in repeated interactions because they anticipate the repetition of interactions, and thus because they already display some willingness to co-operate. Therefore, the hypothesis that institutions exist assumes the existence of reciprocity and that individuals already have stable expectations, but it does not provide an answer to the question of the consistency of expectations. The problem remains: one has to explain the consistency of expectations and the existence of trust towards others to understand why individuals initiate and then repeat interactions. Therefore, rules must exist to inform individuals about the behaviour of others but these rules cannot exist without their having such information, expectations or beliefs about others.

Second, suppose that actors nonetheless enter an interaction without having the required knowledge of each others' characteristics. The next question concerns the possibility of learning from repeated interactions. If one returns to the process of human cognition, we see that knowledge acquisition about others' characteristics – in order to know whether they are reliable partners or not – as well as knowledge about facts or events, is also a matter of inductive inference. As Hayek put it, 'one person's *actions* are the other person's *data*' (1952, emphasis added), echoing Smith's affirmation that rules emerge from 'our continual observation upon the *conduct* of others' (1759 [1976], p. 139; emphasis added). What is important in these two sentences is that the focus is on actions rather than on intentions. In a sensualist–associationist process of knowledge acquisition, we have no access to the motives and intentions of others. Thus, information about others' characteristics is acquired only by observing others' behaviours. However, to learn about others by observing their behaviour is tricky. As we have demonstrated elsewhere (Josselin and Marciano 2000), building upon the reasoning of Hempel (1943) and Goodman (1983), observing the behaviour of another person might inform us that this individual follows a rule but does not tell anything about the rule he follows. Now, the reasons that motivate an individual to act in a specific way are diverse and may be based on grounds quite different from what the observer expects. Obviously, this informal way of communicating allows individuals to co-ordinate without knowing each others' intentions. However, because different persons may be interested in different aspects of a similar problem, and because intentions to act remain hidden, there is no way to have reliable information about others' characteristics. In particular, observing behaviour does not always allow us to separate cheaters and potential defectors from reliable partners. Indeed, cheaters and defectors can imitate the signs that we use for identifying reliable trading partners (Frank 2001).

Of course it is not totally true that observation fails to provide the observer with any information whatsoever. Indeed, an inductive learning process systematically relies on prior beliefs about the behaviour of those being observed – pure induction does not exist. In the same way that perception is always an act of interpretation, which consists in classifying impressions, the behaviour of others is always interpreted through the cognitive history of the spectator. Therefore, our perception of the behaviour of others is driven by our expectations about this behaviour. The behaviour of others is understandable (and then understood) only if it fits coherently with our other beliefs. Then, while observing behaviours does not inform us about the intentions of others, it can confirm our own expectations; this is a typical illustration of the 'curse of knowledge' applied to expectations about others and to the way one learns from the observation of the conduct of others. Two consequences follow. First, successful co-ordination requires a correct interpretation of the behaviours of others – mutual understanding is necessary for us to co-ordinate with others; if these reciprocally conditioned expectations diverge co-ordination is unlikely. Second, to explain successful co-ordination, one must, in the first place, explain why and how stable and consistent expectations are possible.

Let us sum up our line of reasoning. Co-ordination is possible if mutual expectations about each others' behaviour are consistent, that is, if individuals have information about each others' characteristics. Thus, to enter into an interaction, an individual also needs information about others party to that interaction. Furthermore, these expectations cannot result from observation of the actions of other persons alone, since these observations do not teach us more that what we expect to learn. Therefore, it is necessary to understand how our beliefs about others are formed, if it is not from the repetition of interactions.

Sympathy and spontaneous co-ordination: necessary but not sufficient
The Scottish Enlightenment scholars were convinced that co-ordination and co-operation could not be analysed solely as logical problems. For instance, Hume was aware of the necessity to understand individual psychological motives to explain why people could be led to follow a particular convention. This is the reason why he emphasised sympathy as a means by which individuals are able recognise people who are predisposed to co-operate. From this perspective,

as Vanderschraaf (1998) shows, Hume anticipated the modern account of co-ordination given by Lewis (1969) and Schelling (1960). The latter demonstrated that co-ordination requires the existence of a 'common background': behaviours co-ordinate *because* expectations about one another's behaviour are consistent. Their argument presupposes that the reliability of partners has to be known before the interaction takes place – more precisely, the interaction takes place because partners have been identified as being trustworthy. The willingness or propensity to co-operate must therefore precede co-operation. Thus, sympathy can be used as a psychological justification for the spontaneous propensity to co-operate identified by Schelling and can be used to explain how it functions. Put differently, the formation of beliefs about others' behaviours depend on sympathy and thus grounds a spontaneous co-ordination. However, sympathy is also a relatively limited 'quality'. Thus, its limits the domain of spontaneous orders.

Sympathetic identification and communication with others
The crucial role played by sympathy stems from its role as a communication mechanism, which allows tacit communication among individuals. Thus, Hume considers that 'no quality of human nature is more remarkable in itself and its consequences, than the propensity we have to sympathise with others, and to receive by communication their inclinations and sentiments, however different from, and even contrary to our own' (1739–40 [1992], p. 316). And he adds: 'The minds of all men are similar in their feelings and operations, nor can any one be actuated by any affection, of which all others are not in some degree susceptible. As in strings equally wound up, the motion of one communicates itself to the rest; so all affections readily pass from one person to another, and beget correspondent movements in every human creature' (ibid., pp. 575–6). Here, Hume insists on the fact that an individual who feels sympathy towards others, participates in the same experiences. Therefore, because of sympathy, knowledge is not restricted to one individual but is shared by all the individuals feeling sympathy towards one another. Sympathy extends individual knowledge beyond the limits of personal experience, by providing information about experiences that have not yet been experienced but that have been experienced by others and, further, by providing information about others' feelings and behaviours. Thus, one cannot dissociate the two aspects, individual and social, of cognition. Sympathy not only explains communication, it also explains the origins and existence of social beliefs about one another's behaviour. Sympathy explains why, 'although subjective in nature, the individual's cognitive development ... is moulded in social process' (Witt 1999, p. 102).

The reason that sympathy facilitates communication is that it rests on identification with others (Fontaine 1997). Thus, 'sharing another's feelings cannot be regarded as mere contagion or infection, but rather as the outcome of an act of imagination, whereby the spectator tries to figure out what it is like to be the other person in his or her circumstances' (1997, p. 265). Human beings are able to communicate and to co-ordinate their actions because they are capable, not only of imagining themselves in the same circumstances with others, but also of imagining oneself as being another person: when I sympathise, 'I consider what I should suffer if I was really you, and I not only change circumstances with you, but I change persons and characters' (Smith 1759 [1976], p. 317). Further, sympathy differs from another, narrower form of identification with others, namely empathy. While empathetic identification consists solely in the simple imaginary change of positions with others, sympathy implies concern for others' welfare. Smith was clear about this (see Fontaine 1997). Because of sympathetic identification, individual behaviour is not motivated by self-interest and the search for personal advantage. Therefore, sympathy not only explains the possibility of communication; it also exemplifies the normative value of behaviour. In societies shaped by sympathy, free-riding disappears and individuals no longer behave as knaves.

Sympathy thus becomes a principle of communication which allows, through identification with others and because of concern for their welfare, spontaneous co-ordination among individuals. Sympathy is a precondition for human interactions. It creates the common background or tacit commonalities that are necessary to repeat interactions, and which allows for the emergence of rules. As Frank puts it, 'emotional commitment' is a necessary condition for co-operation (2001).

The scarcity of sympathy and the limits of spontaneous order
Sympathy can thus be regarded as the characteristic of human nature that explains individuals' willingness to co-operate. At the same time, even if sympathy is a universal characteristic, in the sense that all human beings, as well as animals, 'possess' such a 'quality', this does not imply that every one must feel sympathy towards anyone else in particular. Sympathy indeed depends on the psychological and physical distance (where distance is expressed in psychological as well in physical terms) that separates individuals. As Hume puts it, 'Nothing is more certain, than that men are, in a great measure govern'd by interest, and that even when they extend their concern beyond themselves, 'tis not to a great distance; nor is it usual for them, in common life, to look farther than their nearest friends and acquaintance' (1739 [1992], p. 534). More precisely, sympathy decreases when distance between individuals increases: 'sympathy, we shall allow, is much fainter than our concern for ourselves, and sympathy with persons remote from us, much fainter that with persons near or contiguous' (Hume 1739 [1992], p. 116). Sympathy can thus be considered as a 'scarce' feeling, being restricted to those groups of individuals who, having been able to repeat interactions, share rules and common beliefs. Because of

its scarcity, sympathy explains why spontaneous order societies are 'nearness societies' in the geographical space or in the space of preferences (Josselin and Marciano 2001). These societies consist as a sum of close-knit groups of 'nearest friends and acquaintances', in which interactions are sympathetic and thus possible. Therefore, sympathy not only defines the condition for co-operation but also explains its limits. Indeed, since reliable expectations about others remain limited to group members, the individuals with whom sympathetic links exist, there is a problem with interactions with outsiders, namely the individuals who belong to other groups, that is those individuals who have a different degree of sympathy. The problem is twofold.

The first difficulty concerns the arrival of newcomers who are supposedly attracted by efficient groups, which are groups assumed to rest upon efficient rules. An individual will choose to join a group, and to imitate other individuals, because he assumes that they have better information. Thus, the choice depends upon a comparison between the benefits and costs of joining the group. In this respect, threshold or bandwagon models (Schelling 1978; Granovetter 1978) or models of informational cascade (Barnejee 1992; Bikhchandani et al. 1992, 2000), that implicitly relate efficiency and the size of the group, link the cost of joining a group and the number of people who are already members of the group. Furthermore, when a newcomer enters a group, he or she cannot know the rule that guides the behaviours of the group members. They can only observe group members' behaviour and infer from these observations the rules the members follow. Thus, an individual entering a new group, because he or she only imitates behaviours and does not sympathise with other members, will fail to gather information about reliable partners and will be unable to co-ordinate with them. Put differently, he or she may face induction problems because they are unable to know positively the meaning another person gives to the rules or to infer this meaning from the observation of the member's behaviour (Josselin and Marciano 1995).

Second, problems may arise due to the differences – differences revealed by free-riding and opportunistic behaviours – that exist between individuals' degree of sympathy. These differences affect interactions between individuals from different groups, as seen in the preceding paragraph. These differences may also appear within a given group when the size of the group in which interactions take place increases. Indeed, the greater the number of individuals involved, the higher the probability of meeting individuals characterised by a different degree of sympathy, that is by a willingness to co-operate. Here, the problem is not only that it is difficult to know the rules that these individuals follow. Rather, the difficulty consists in identifying these individuals as reliable. Therefore, when the size of the group increases, non co-operative behaviours are likely to emerge and to persist, whether or not the game is repeated (Witt 1989). Moreover, it is possible to show that interactions between players characterised by different degrees of sympathy lead to exploitation (Buchanan 1975; Stark 1989). Costs are thus imposed on group members. Of course, one can argue, thanks to evolutionary models, that homogeneous groups composed by individuals with a high willingness to co-operate can resist the invasion of individuals less prone to co-operate. However, the problem does not disappear but rather is only moved one step further. Indeed, in this type of situation, conflicts among groups, and especially border conflicts, are likely to occur. These possible conflictual outcomes increase the costs of spontaneous order and therefore reinforce and strengthen the respective limits of the groups.

As a consequence, although sympathy is a necessary condition for co-ordination, it is not sufficient in large and open societies. On the contrary, rules that emerge from repeated interactions tend to remain limited to the group of individuals that took part in interaction with one another. Thus, emerging rules cannot be considered general rules (Josselin and Marciano 1999). Beyond the frontiers of the original group or as the number of individuals increase, egoism and self-interest tend to replace sympathy. Interactions are no longer peaceful and cooperative. Then, emerging rules have to be sustained by 'human conventions' as Hume (1739 [1992], p. 483) himself insisted. Even if such conventions do not resemble to a Hobbesian social contract, their purpose is nonetheless of the same nature: to extend identification with others beyond the limits of sympathy.

Conclusion

The first works in the new political economy that has been developing in recent years, have assumed that rules are tailored to rational individuals – an assumption presented as a heritage of the classical political economists, the founders of the discipline. Now that the necessity of going beyond homo oeconomicus is admitted, this link to the origins of political economy has been abandoned. In this chapter, we have tried to show why reference to these early findings about human nature nonetheless remains important. Rather than the 'first imperialist' economists, it is Hume and Smith who should be regarded as the true forefathers of 'inspired' economists. Their contribution rests in the 'complete' theory of human nature that they propose, linking associationism, bounded rationality and identification with others – and moral sentiments – as a condition for co-operation. Two final points are thus worth noting. First, a political economy approach towards institutions cannot neglect the possibility of spontaneous orders which are restricted to spheres characterised by sympathetic identification. Thus, a covenant remains necessary to order large societies. Second, institutions must be built upon sympathy and must not oppose these moral sentiments on pain of threatening the areas in which it already exists.

Acknowledgements

An earlier version of this text has been presented in a seminar held at the Chaire Hoover (June 2003). I thank Albena Azmanova, Axel Gosseries, Myron Frankman, Hervé Pourtois, Philippe van Parijs, Michel de Vroey for their comments. I also thank John Davis and Jochen Runde for very helpful remarks.

Notes

1. Here, we paraphrase Anderson who, analysing Adam Smith's 'economics of religion', argues that 'Smith was probably the first "economic imperialist"' (1988, p. 1067).
2. Among others, one can quote Kahneman et al. (1982), Arkes and Hammond (1986), Dawes (1988), Schoemaker (1982), Hogarth and Reder (1987), Thaler (1992).
3. Hayek is often rightly presented as one of the first and rare twentieth century economists having attempted to understand how the mind of human beings functions, trying also to link the mechanics of the human mind with individual behaviour and the rules. His 1952 *Sensory Order* is then put forward as a work of a great importance, a book where Hayek develops a theory according to which the mind functions on an associative basis (see among others Tuerck 1995; Rizzelo and Turvani 2000). Interestingly, it appears that Hayek's argument reflects an old tradition.
4. The entire sentence is as follows 'we may observe, that what we call a *mind*, is nothing but a heap or collection of different perceptions, united together by certain relations, and suppos'd, tho' falsely, to be endow'd with a perfect simplicity and identity'.
5. Once again it is interesting to parallel Hume with Lachmann who writes that 'the formation of expectations is an act of our mind by means of which we try to catch a glimpse of the unknown. Each one of us catches a different glimpse' (1976, p. 59).
6. As does Lachmann: 'In a complex society such as our own, in which the success of our plans indirectly depends on the actions of millions of other people, how can our orientation scheme provide us with firm guidance? The answer has to be sought in the existence, nature and functions of institutions' (1971, p. 49). Bianchi notes the same problem about Hayek: 'Hayek does more to pinpoint the problem of arriving at social order than he does to solve it' (1993, p. 209). These two economists illustrate a more general problem of Austrian economics about institutions (see Gloria 1999).

References

Anderson, Elisabeth (2000), 'Beyond homo œconomicus: new developments in theories of social norms', *Philosophy and Public Affairs*, **29** (2), 170–200.

Anderson, Gary (1988), 'Mr Smith and the preachers: the economics of religion in the *Wealth of Nations*', *Journal of Political Economy*, **96** (5), 1066–88.

Arkes, Hal R., and Kenneth R. Hammond (eds) (1986), *Judgement and Decision-making: An Interdisciplinary Reader*, Cambridge: Cambridge University Press.

Atkinson, A.B., and Joseph E. Stiglitz (1980), *Lectures in Public Economics*, New York, McGraw Hill.

Axelrod, Robert (1984), *The Evolution of Co-operation*, New York, Basic Books.

Barnejee, A.V (1992), 'A simple model of herd behaviour', *Quarterly Journal of Economics*, **107** (3), 797–818.

Bianchi, Marina (1993), 'How to learn sociability: true and false solutions to Mandeville's problem', *History of Political Economy*, **25** (2), 209–40.

Bikhchandani, S., David Hirshleifer and Ivo Welch (1992), 'A theory of fads, fashion, custom, and cultural change as informational cascades', *Journal of Political Economy*, **100** (5), 992–1026.

Bikhchandani, S., David Hirshleifer and Ivo Welch (2000), 'Informational cascades and rational herding: an annotated bibliography', www.welch.som.vale.edu/cascades.

Brennan, Geoffrey (1992), 'Taking political economy seriously', *Methodus*, **4** (1), pp. 11–15.

Buchanan, James M. (1975), 'The Samaritan's dilemma', in E.S. Phelps (ed.), *Altruism, Morality and Economic Theory*, New York, Sage Foundation, pp. 71–85.

Buchanan, James M. (1987), 'Constitutional economics', *The New Palgrave*, London: Macmillan, pp. 585–8.

Dawes, Robyn M. (1988), *Rational Choice in an Uncertain World*, San Diego and New York: Harcourt, Brace, Jovanovich.

Debreu, Gerard (1959), *Theory of Value: An Axiomatic Analysis of Economic Equilibrium*, New Haven and London: Yale University Press.

Fontaine, Philippe (1997), 'Identification and economic behaviour: sympathy and empathy in historical perspective', *Economics and Philosophy*, **13** (2), 261–80.

Frank, Robert (2001), 'Cooperation through emotional commitment', mimeo.

Frey, Bruno S. (1990), 'Institutions matter', *European Economic Review*, **34**, 443–9.

Frey, Bruno S. (1997), 'A constitution for knaves crowds civic virtues', *Economic Journal*, **107**, 1043–53.

Frey, Bruno S. and Alois Stutzer (2001), 'Economics and psychology: from imperialistic to inspired economics', *Revue de Philosophie Economique*, **2** (2), 5–22.

Gifford, Adam Jr. (1996), 'Subjectivity, bounded rationality, and rule following behavior', mimeo, Department of Economics, California State University.

Gloria, Sandye (1999), 'An Austrian dilemma: necessity and impossibility of a theory of institutions', *Review of Austrian Economics*, **11** (1/2), 31–45.

Goodman, Nelson (1954 [1983]), *Fact, Fiction and Forecast*, 4th edn, Cambridge, MA: Harvard University Press.

Goodman, N. (1964), *Fact, Fiction and Forecast*, Cambridge, MA: Harvard University Press.

Granovetter, Mark (1978), 'Thresholds models of collective behavior', *American Journal of Sociology*, **83**, 1420–43.

Hayek, Friedrich (1952), *The Sensory Order. An Inquiry into the Foundations of Theoretical Psychology*, London: Routledge and Kegan Paul.

Hayek, Friedrich (1978), *New Studies in Philosophy, Politics, Economics and the History of Ideas*, Chicago: Chicago University Press.

Hempel, Carl Gustav (1943), 'A purely syntactical definition of confirmation', *Journal of Symbolic Logic*, **8**, 122–43.

Hirshleifer, Jack (1982), 'Evolutionary models in economics and law: co-operation versus conflict strategies', *Research in Law and Economics*, **4** (1), 1–60.

Hogarth, Robin M., and Melvin W. Reder (eds) (1987), *Rational Choice*, Chicago: University of Chicago Press.

Hume, David (1739–40 [1992]), *Treatise of Human Nature*, Buffalo, NY: Prometheus.

Inman, Robert P (1987), 'Markets, governments and the "new" political economy' in A.J. Auerbach and Martin S. Feldstein (eds), *Handbook of Public Economics*, Elsevier, pp. 647–777.

Johnson, D.B. (1991), *Public Choice: An Introduction to the New political Economy*, Mountain View, CA: Mayfield Publishing.

Jolls, C., Cass Sunstein and Richard H. Thaler (1998), 'A behavioral approach to law and economics', *Stanford Law Review*, **50**, 1471–1550.

Josselin, Jean-Michel, and Alain Marciano (1995), 'Constitutionalism and common knowledge: assessment and application to a future European constitution', *Public Choice*, **85** (3/4), 173–88.

Josselin, Jean-Michel and Alain Marciano (1999), 'General norms and customs', in Juergen G. Backhaus (ed.), *The Elgar Companion to Law and Economics*, Cheltenham: Edward Elgar, pp. 115-20.

Josselin, Jean-Michel, and Alain Marciano (2000). 'L'efficacité du droit coutumier: une evaluation microéconomique', *Revue Internationale de Droit Economique*, **2**, 351–63.

Josselin, Jean-Michel, and Alain Marciano (2001), 'Public decisions in the Scottish Enlightenment tradition', *Journal of Economic Studies*, **27** (6), 5–13.

Kahneman, Daniel, Paul Slovic and Amos Tversky (eds) (1982), *Judgement under Uncertainty: Heuristics and Biases*, Cambridge: Cambridge University Press.

Kuran, Timur (1995), *Private Truths, Public Lies. The Social Consequences of Preference Falsification*, Cambridge, MA: Harvard University Press.

Lachmann, Ludwig (1971), *The Legacy of Max Weber*, London: Heinemann.
Lachmann, Ludwig (1975), 'Reflections on Hayekian capital theory', mimeo.
Lachmann, Ludwig (1976), 'From Mises to Shackle: an essay in Austrian Economics and the Kaleidic Society', *Journal of Economic Literature*, **14**, 54–62.
Lewis, David K (1969), *Convention: A Philosophical Study*, Oxford: Oxford University Press.
Marciano, Alain, and Maud Pélissier (2000), 'Altruistic preferences and social cooperation within an heterogeneous population', mimeo, working paper, GREQAM.
McDonald, D.N., J.H. Kagel and R.C. Battalio (1991), 'Animals' choices under uncertain outcomes: further experimental results', *Economic Journal*, **101**, 1067–84.
Mueller, Dennis C. (2001), 'Public choice after 50 Years, Bruno Frey after 60', *Kyklos*, **54** (2/3), 334–54.
O'Driscoll Jr., Gerald P. (1977), 'Spontaneous order and the coordination of economic activities', *Journal of Libertarian Studies*, **1** (2), 137–51.
Ostrom, Elineor (1998), 'A behavioral approach to the rational choice theory of collective action', *American Political Science Review*, **92** (1), 1–22.
Parisi, Francesco (1998), 'Customary law', in Peter Newman (ed.), *The New Palgrave Dictionary of Economics and the Law*, London: Macmillan, pp. 572–8.
Pinker, Steven (1994), *The Language Instinct*, New York: W. Morrow.
Rabin, Matthew (1998), 'Psychology and economics', *Journal of Economic Literature*, **36**, 11–46.
Renault, Alain (1989), *L'ère de l'individu*, Paris: Gallimard.
Rizzelo, Salvatore, and Margherita Turvani (2000), 'Institutions meet mind: the way out of an impasse', *Constitutional Political Economy*, **11**, 165–80.
Rosenberg, Shawn W. (1991), 'Rationality, markets, and political analysis: a social psychological critique of neoclassical political economy', in: Kristen R. Monroe (ed.), *The Economic Approach to Politics: A Critical Reassessment of the Theory of Rational Action*, New York: HarperCollins, pp. 386–404.
Salmon, Pierre (2000), 'Modèles et mécanismes en économie: essai de clarification de leurs relations', *Revue de Philosophie Economique*, **1**, 105–26.
Salmon, Pierre (2001), 'Thinking about something else: a rationality-compatible mechanism with macroscopic consequences', *Kyklos*, **54** (2/3), 453–64.
Schelling, Thomas (1960), *The Strategy of Conflict*, Cambridge, MA: Harvard University Press.
Schelling, Thomas (1978), *Micromotives and Macro Behavior*, New York: Norton.
Schoemaker, Paul J. (1982), 'The expected utility model: its variants, purposes, evidence and limitations', *Journal of Economic Literature*, **20** (June), 529–63.
Smith, Adam (1759 [1976]), *The Theory of Moral Sentiments*, Indianapolis: Liberty Press.
Stark, Oded (1989), 'Altruism and the quality of life', *American Economic Review*, **79**, 86–90.
Thaler, Richard H. (1992), *The Winner's Curse. Paradoxes and Anomalies of Economic Life*, New York: Free Press.
Thaler, Richard H. (2000), 'From Homo oeconomicus to homo sapiens', *Journal of Economic Perspectives*, **14** (1), 133–41.
Tuerck, David G, (1995), 'Economics as a mechanism: the mind as a machine in Hayek's Sensory Order', *Constitutional Political Economy*, **6** (3), 281–92.
Vanderschraaf, Peter (1998), 'The informal game theory in Hume's account of convention', *Economics and Philosophy*, **14**, 215–47.
Witt, Ulrich (1989), 'The evolution of economic institutions as a propagation process', *Public Choice*, **62**, 155–72.
Witt, Ulrich (1998), 'Imagination and leadership – the neglected dimension of an evolutionary theory of the firm', *Journal of Economic Behaviour and Organisation*, **35**, 161–77.
Witt, Ulrich (1999), 'Do Entrepreneurs need firms? A contribution to a missing chapter in Austrian economics', *The Review of Austrian Economics*, **11** (1/2), 99–109.
Young, Robert M. (1985), *Darwin's Metaphor: Nature's Place in Victorian Culture*, Cambridge and New York: Cambridge University Press.

3 Economic rationality

Shaun P. Hargreaves Heap

Introduction

The dominant model of individual agency in economics has individuals acting to best satisfy their preferences. This is an instrumental conception of rational action where reason is concerned, not with the ends pursued, but with calculating the action that will best achieve those ends. Its philosophical roots prominently go back to Hume who cast 'reason as the slave of the passions' and it quite naturally sits within the wider tradition in political theory of liberal individualism by providing a clear account of what individual qua individual action might consist of. It is also commonly known as either the rational choice or the economic model of action. I discuss this model in the second section.

Few would doubt that many actions are well described by this model, but there are real questions over whether *all* action is captured by it. In particular, there are doubts over whether this model can be used to explain what is perhaps best described as the institutional or normative side of life. There are two aspects to this problem. The first is whether one can account for the origin of institutions using this model. The second is whether the model is sufficiently complex in a psychological sense to allow for how action is connected to self-respect (or other related psychological motivations, see below). People often reflect on their actions and when they find them worthy, they derive a sense of self-worth. It is an anthropological commonplace that such feelings (or their reverse when one experiences guilt, shame or embarrassment) affect behaviour and the question is whether this influence can be accommodated within the instrumental model.

The two weaknesses are related because self-respect often comes from acting in accordance with norms of behaviour which specify what is 'right', 'honourable', 'just', etc. and such norms are the lifeblood of institutions, broadly understood. Indeed they are two sides of the same coin: how institutions, or rule-following, play a part in the individual's psychological world. I consider this weakness in section III and point to the new models of action that have recently been developed in response (e.g. models of 'team thinking' and expressive reason). Normative beliefs play an important role in these new theories and I examine some of what is known from the psychology literature on norm formation in Section IV.

Models of individual action are important not just for explanation but also for prescription and I turn in the final section to consider how the explanatory weaknesses of the instrumental model discussed earlier produce deficiencies in prescriptive analysis. These are sometimes referred to as the problems of 'economic rationalism': these are the problems that arise when individuals are construed exclusively as preference satisfiers and so enter into social life only because it promotes the better satisfaction of their preferences. Social life is simply an exchange relationship on this account and, as a consequence, it becomes natural to assess and prescribe institutions for social life according to how well they promote efficiency in these exchanges. If, however, individuals are something more than preference satisfiers, then this focus on efficiency in institutional design is potentially misleading and I turn to this critique of 'economic rationalism' in the last section.

A final word in this introduction is in order. I am concerned here with action that can be explained through an appeal to some form of reason. As a result, I shall not be explicitly considering habitual types of behaviour and the related but separate issue of tacit knowledge. This may seem unfortunate as habit plainly explains much human activity. However some habits have a rational core in the sense that they can be rationally reconstructed and so the analysis here may still be relevant to such cases, albeit at one stage removed, so to speak. For instance, it is often argued when people follow simple rules of thumb that this is boundedly rational in an instrumental sense if the rules are updated in the light of experience of how well they serve the individual's interests. This is the kind of evolutionary spin on the ubiquitous use of rules in decision making which yields the interpretation that people behave 'as if' they were instrumentally rational. I touch on this approach in section III.

Instrumental rationality: the rational choice model

There are two ways in which the instrumental or rational choice model is presented. One has an explicit psychology with individuals acting so as to best satisfy their preferences. Preferences are represented via a utility function and the individual chooses the action that maximises their utility. Some care is required not to confuse this with utilitarianism: the 'utility' function for this purpose is simply a mathematical device whereby outcome 'a' is given a higher number than 'b' when 'a' is preferred to 'b'. Thus when the individual maximises their utility function (by selecting the action that yields the outcome with the highest number) they are taking the action which by definition best satisfies their preferences.

The other presentation of the model dispenses with an explicit psychology and associates rational action with action that satisfies certain requirements (e.g. transitivity, completeness, etc.). These requirements form the axioms of rational choice and it can be shown that when an individual's actions satisfy them, it is 'as if' they had preferences which could be represented by a utility function and they acted so as to maximise their utility/expected utility (see, for example, Green 1971).

It is sometimes claimed that the axiomatic version is to be preferred to the explicitly psychological one because it deals only in observable behaviour and does not require a commitment to any psychology (see, for example, Binmore 1994). This is a version of the (old) argument found in the social sciences for a behaviourism that eschews theories which deal in unobservables (e.g. the state of people's minds). Like those arguments, it is far from persuasive. For example, the utility maximising version also yields predictions for behaviour without the need to give details of the underlying utility function (e.g. see the prediction with respect to the substitution effect in consumer theory that underpins the 'law of demand' and which depends only on people having well-defined preferences). So it is not clear that the axiomatic version is superior in this respect. Likewise, it is not obvious why these axioms should characterise 'rational' behaviour (i.e. why one should imagine that they will apply to the actions of rational people) unless there is some connection between them and an underlying rational psychology. Not unsurprisingly given the formal equivalence between the two approaches, the most plausible explanation of why the axioms constitute rationality involve appeals to the instrumental conception of reason.[1] Indeed, it is often argued (e.g. Davidson 1980) that the point of the axioms is not to undo the need for a psychology of choice rather they give substance to what an instrumental psychology is.

There is a final difficulty with the behaviourist interpretation of the axiomatic approach that is worth mentioning now because it will surface again later, albeit in a different form. It arises whenever outcomes need to be distinguished according not just to their physical and temporal/spatial characteristics but also with respect to their symbolic properties (as when an outcome is deemed 'good', 'bad', 'fair' or some such). In these cases behaviour cannot be defined independently of an account of how the mind attaches terms like 'good' and 'bad' to particular kinds of behaviour; so one cannot escape the need for an account of what is going on in the mind.

The rational choice model yields a variety of predictions in consumer/ decision theory in non-interactive settings that have been extensively tested in laboratory experiments. It is probably fair to say that while the model can account for a large part of people's behaviour in these circumstances it also fails in a number of cases (see Starmer 2000, for a survey of the laboratory evidence). For example, it seems that when people face choices characterised by risk they frequently attach excessive significance to extreme events (like nuclear accidents or winning the lottery). Similarly they judge outcomes not in some absolute way but with respect to a reference point where gains and losses are evaluated asymmetrically (with losses weighing more heavily than similar gains).

The model is also a building block in the game-theoretic analysis of interactive decision making. Here the assumption that people are rational in the rational choice sense, that they have common knowledge of this rationality and they hold common priors, yields the prediction that people will take actions which form a Nash equilibrium. This is an equilibrium where the strategies are best replies to each other. In many forms of collective action (e.g. joining a union or a lobbying organisation, or subscribing to a public good, like street lighting, the police force and the army), this application of the rational choice model yields a very precise prediction because the interaction takes the form of prisoner's dilemma/free-rider game and there is only one Nash equilibrium.

Thus to take a famous example, consider the choice each individual might face in a state of nature over whether to pay for the institutions of law and order. The individual might plausibly reason in the following way. Suppose everyone else contributes to these institutions. Then since my subscription is small relative to everyone else, there will be a system of law and order whether I subscribe or not, and since it costs me to subscribe, I am best served by not subscribing. Suppose alternatively that no one else subscribes. Then again since my subscription is small relative to the whole population, there will be no system of law and order whether I subscribe or not; and since it costs me to subscribe, I am best served by not subscribing. Hence whether I expect others to subscribe or not, my best action is not to. If everyone reasons in the same way, no one subscribes and there is no system of law and order. Yet again quite plausibly, the position where there is law and order and everyone pays for it may be preferred by everyone to the outcome where there is no system and no one pays for it. Thus when each decides quite rationally what to do for the best, the result is collectively self-defeating.

This is the paradox of rational choice in these settings and it famously forms the basis for the Hobbesian argument for the creation of the State. To obtain the superior outcome where there is a system of law and order, we have to give up the freedom to contract in or out. We simply have to accept the authority of the State and surrender some of the freedom that we would otherwise enjoy.

It is a testament to the power of the rational choice model that this problem will be familiar to anyone who has tried to organise a form of collective action. Nevertheless, the existence of many voluntary organisations that engage in collective action, from The National Rifle Association to Greenpeace, also points to a weakness with this model. Indeed in laboratory experiments with free-rider games, it is common to find that around 40 per cent do make a voluntary contribution (see Dawes and Thaler 1988).

The rational choice model has also been applied with interesting effect to other issues outside the usual domain of economics. Becker's work is an outstanding example, particularly his work on the family (see, for example, Becker 1991). The economics of law paradigm and the work of Public Choice theorists like Buchanan (1974) are further examples. Thus Public Choice theorists have assumed that politicians are rational choice people concerned to maximise their chances of re-election facing a population of rational choice electors who are not fully informed as information is costly to acquire. They then predict that governments will have a tendency to grow in size and run deficits. Again this will both strike a chord with many and yet leave a feeling that, like the laboratory experiments in non-interactive and interactive settings, the rational choice model only tells part of the story as there is more to politics than simple vote seeking.

As a prelude to the next section, which considers what might be missing from the rational choice model, it is worth noting in conclusion here that there are many interactive settings where the model itself appears formally incomplete as an account of action. Many games have multiple Nash equilibria, so a theory which predicts that rational people will choose actions that form a Nash equilibrium is not very useful since it begs a question about which one should be chosen. For example imagine a simple interaction where two people are walking towards each other on a collision course and each has a choice between veering to the left or veering to the right. [left, left] is one Nash equilibrium as veering to the left is better for each person than veering to the right when the other person is veering to the left because it avoids a collision, but so is [right, right] on the same grounds. So knowing that rational players will select actions which form a Nash equilibrium is not very helpful to an individual in these circumstances as it has not narrowed the choice of action down at all. What is required in addition is a theory of equilibrium selection. Although there have been attempts to develop such theories none either commands wholesale allegiance or is clearly connected to the rational choice model itself (see Hargreaves Heap and Varoufakis 1995, for a discussion; Schelling 1960, supplies a pioneering account of equilibrium selection which dispenses with rationality and deals in 'salience').

Filling the gaps in the rational choice model with other accounts of rationality

Even when the rational choice model successfully predicts behaviour, there is a complaint that it takes too much for granted. Where do preferences and the institutions which frame actions come from? Actions, for instance, only have clear outcomes that can be ranked when property rights are well defined, so where do property rights come from? In this section, I suggest that the failure always to predict action in games with multiple Nash equilibria, as noted above, is linked to this further complaint.

To take the question of where institutions come from first, one obvious rejoinder by the rational choice camp treats institution formation as itself the product of some earlier set of interactions between rational choice agents. So, for example, one could argue along the Hobbesian lines sketched earlier that rational agents would agree to give up some of their freedom in order to have an enforceable set of property rights. The institutions of 'law and order' thus emerge from an agreement between rational choice agents.

The difficulty with this argument is that, although it is possible to show with the aid of the free-rider game that all will gain from law and order in this sense because without it life is 'nasty, brutish and short', there are typically, on closer inspection, more than one set of property rights which would deliver an improvement. Consider the following case. Suppose there is some contested resource that A and B are disputing. Both are better off if they can agree to share rather than fight over it, but it could be shared in any manner of ways. In the language of game theory, a game is formed by the choice that A and B have over how much of the resource to claim and it has several Nash equilibria. For instance, where the figures refer respectively to the share claimed by A and B, there are (10%, 90%), (20%, 80%), (30%, 70%)....(50%, 50%).....(90%, 10%), to pick up on just a few on the continuum moving from B's advantage to A's.

In this way, the problem of the indeterminacy of rational choice action in games with multiple Nash equilibria referred to above applies to the attempt to explain the origin of property institutions as deposits from some previous set of interactions between rational choice agents. Indeed the problem is likely to affect most accounts in this vein because most interactions are repeated indefinitely and indefinitely repeated games have multiple Nash equilibria even when a one-shot version of the interaction has a unique one (this is the so-called Folk theorem in game theory, see Hargreaves Heap and Varoufakis 1995).[2]

There is an approach that keeps a measure of faith with the rational choice model and which can explain equilibrium selection. It treats people as boundedly rational in the sense that while they still have preferences that they want to satisfy, they no longer calculate how best to do this before acting. Rather they adopt some action, see what the results are, compare them with the outcomes associated with other actions, adjust their future action accordingly and so on. In other words, they learn through trial and error how to act so as to satisfy best their preferences. This approach to modelling repeated interactions is sometimes called evolutionary game theory because of the similarity between the learning process behind action choice and the evolutionary process through which genes are selected (see Schotter 1981 and Sugden 1986). It makes the selection of an equilibrium highly sensitive to the initial actions selected by each individual and the precise learning mechanism that each employs. To see why, suppose A claims 80 per cent and B claims 50 per cent and A adjusts his or her claim downwards only very slowly when there is a disagreement while B has a fast rate of adjustment. They are then likely to converge on something like 75 per cent for A and 25 per cent for B; whereas if either A's initial claim had been smaller or his or her adjustment rate faster, then something closer to 50–50 would have been reached.

So, while the evolutionary approach supplies an account of equilibrium selection, it does so at some cost to the rational choice model because it makes the selection depend on factors which are strictly extraneous to the rational choice model. Nevertheless, this dependence offers an interesting way of making sense of how arbitrary beliefs can have a self-fulfilling characteristic and for history (in the sense of the details of how people have and adjust a particular set of beliefs) to be connected to rational choice explanations. For instance, it would be natural to suppose that the initial claims owe something to the background ideas regarding difference (again see Schelling 1960, on the idea of 'salience'). So suppose A is a young man and B is an old woman. If the dispute occurs in a society where there is the beginning of a gender distinction which favours men, then A is more likely to make a higher claim and B a lower claim than would be the case if the dispute occurred in a society where there was the beginning of an age distinction favouring the old. In turn, whichever the initial source of distinction is, it will be reinforced by the character of the subsequent equilibrium which is selected in this game. So history matters because arbitrary or entirely contingent beliefs have the scope for becoming self-fulfilling.

Even when history in this sense rescues the rational choice model, there is an aspect of institutions which remains unexplained. When people agree to, say, a 75–25 division of some disputed resource, it may be because they have inherited conventions which point to this division and they do not reflect beyond the appreciation they cannot do better by claiming more or less given the other's claim. However, it is more common to find that people reflect in another respect on the arrangement: they find that it is 'fair' or 'right' in some sense. In short, it is not merely self-enforcing, but also supported by a set of normative beliefs. This is what lies at the heart of the distinction between a convention and an institution. Both embody rules but when people follow a convention, it is because this is the sensible course of action given that others use the rule; whereas the rules of an institution command a deeper allegiance. People follow them not just because others do, but also because it is the 'just' or 'good' or 'honourable' etc thing to do.

The question then is how to make psychological sense of the way that these beliefs might motivate people to act or follow a shared rule and so turn it into an institution. I have argued elsewhere (following a line which goes back at least to Smith 1759) that the key to understanding this type of behaviour turns on recognising that people are concerned with self-respect (see, for example, Hargreaves Heap 1989, 2001). People do not always simply act because the action satisfies some preference or other, they sometimes act because the act reflects well upon them and they derive a sense of self-worth from knowing this. Or to put this round the other way, people experience feelings like guilt, shame and embarrassment through reflecting on the worth of their actions and the anticipation of such feelings can affect people's choice of actions.

So much is self-evident from any anthropological study (see, for example, Douglas 1978), I need to do two things with it in the context of the argument of this chapter. First I need to show that behaving in this way marks a departure from the instrumental model. The second is that such behaviour depends on the existence of norms and so is connected to the earlier observation regarding the failure of the instrumental model to account for institution formation.

With respect to the first of these, it is tempting for the instrumental model to respond to the anthropological point by turning self-respect into one of the preferences that people attempt to satisfy. In this way, action that is motivated by self-respect presents no problem for the instrumental model. Indeed, since the model is commendably quiet about the nature of a person's preferences (all that is required is that they are coherent in the sense that the person has a well-defined preference ordering), this seems a particularly easy move to make. A difficulty arises, however, because one frequently seems to gain this sense of self-respect from acting 'honourably', 'ethically', or 'justly' and what makes an action 'honourable', 'good' or 'right' is often that it is distinct from what one would otherwise have done. Gauthier (1986) is rare exception where what is moral is also turned into what is instrumentally rational and the argument is controversial for exactly that reason. After all, if what one would have done in the absence of a moral sense is always exactly what one does with a moral sense, then actions simply fail to instantiate anything that is distinctly moral.

The language of preference satisfaction can be stretched to cover self-respect in these circumstances by distinguishing between two kinds of preferences. Suppose a person has ordinary, selfish preferences and in addition a preference for self-respect which is 'satisfied' by reflecting on how some standard of 'honour', 'ethics' or 'justice' judges actions in the particular circumstances of his or her and other people's ordinary, selfish preferences. In this way, a person can act morally or honourably in support of self-respect because this differs from what would be dictated by his or her ordinary, selfish preferences. Yet one can preserve the model of preference satisfaction because self-respect is still a kind of preference, albeit of a different kind to the ordinary ones one might have for food, warmth, shelter and the like.

Such two-tier structures for preferences are now to be found in the economics literature. For example, Rabin (1993) introduces a new category of 'psychological pay-offs', in part to explain the apparently anomalous co-operative behaviour observed in one-shot prisoner's dilemma games. These new pay-offs are not explicitly connected to a sense of self-worth in his model but they amount to the same analytic extension of the basic rational choice model. Thus 'psychological pay-offs' are additional to the 'material', selfish ones which are depicted in the usual game-theoretic representation of an interaction and people experience them when their actions conform to a particular belief about what 'kindness' requires. The particular belief judges kindness by the extent to which one forgoes satisfaction of the 'material', selfish pay-offs and it has to be reciprocated. So Rabin might say that people co-operate in prisoner's dilemma games because they value reciprocal kindness, while I might say they co-operate because this gives them a sense of self-worth, but the basic idea is the same. People are motivated by two kinds of preferences and the second, new addition to the rational choice model depends on the symbolic properties of people's actions (i.e. what they mean to the actors).

Likewise, other economists have argued that there are 'team preferences' which can motivate (see Bacharach 1999 and Sugden 2000; and see Chapter 19 by John Davis in this volume for a different account of collective intentionality). 'Team preferences' are similar analytically in the sense that they are again transformations of the underlying individual (or 'material') preferences which encode the shared values of the 'team' and they come into play when people belong to the same 'team'. Thus two people who belonged to the same group might play the prisoner's dilemma game differently from two people who did not. The 'team's preferences' over outcomes might be derived, for instance, through a simple addition of each individual's material pay-offs and in this way a pair of 'team' players might choose mutual co-operation while non-team members choose mutual defection.

Both Rabin's and the 'team preference' extensions to the rational choice model make the sharing of the relevant belief about the symbolic properties of action crucial. This is a feature of those theories by construction and it marks an important difference from earlier ways of explaining why, for instance, people might co-operate in a prisoner's dilemma game by introducing an altruistic preference (see, for example, Elster 1989). When altruism is introduced to explain co-operative behaviour the altruist's inclination to co-operate is not affected by the motives of the other player; whereas with Rabin (and the team preference version), the intention of the other players matters and it is the prospect of reciprocal kindness that produces the symbolic pay-offs which can tip the balance towards co-operation. I turn now to consider why sharing the relevant belief might matter for behaviour.

For this purpose it helps to have the explicit psychology of self-respect in play because a standard for judging action has to be external to the individual if it is to contribute to that person's sense of self-worth. This is for the simple psychological (but more complicated philosophical) reason that a purely personal standard is likely to become self-serving and so defeat the object of providing a sense of self-worth. One simply cannot at the same time be in charge of the standard and derive a particular sense of worth from behaving in accordance with that standard. The potential for bad faith is just too transparent. Of course, there is scope for some self-deception in this matter but it does not extend wholesale. Instead it is the judgement of others which comes from sharing beliefs about what is worthy which gives substance to a standard for behaviour.

Here is the connection, then, to the earlier discussion of the gap in the rational choice account of institutions. I argued earlier that the evolutionary version of the rational choice model might (with the help of an historical dimension) account for the choice of conventions, but that institutions are more than this. They typically have a normative structure: that is people believe that following the rule is the 'good or honourable or just, etc., thing' to do. To begin to make sense of how institutions go beyond mere convention through this additional type of legitimacy, one needs a model of individual agency where *shared* normative beliefs play a part. The amended rational choice model with a two-tier structure of preferences at least fits that bill and once in place it may actually help with the original problem of equilibrium selection which beset the rational choice account of institution formation.

To see how this might work, consider the earlier example of multiple equilibria in the resource sharing game where there were a range of Nash equilibria from B receiving 90 per cent and A 10 per cent to B receiving 10 per cent and A 90 per cent. It seems entirely possible that people sharing normative beliefs will have beliefs regarding what is 'just' that will distinguish between the various possible outcomes in ways that all will agree. Hence what looks like a game with multiple equilibria when played by rational choice agents is transformed into one with a unique equilibrium when the players share normative beliefs and derive a sense of self-worth from acting in accordance with them. In so far as a shared set of normative beliefs did explain equilibrium selection in this way, then there would be no need to rely on evolutionary versions of the rational choice model to do this. But this would not necessarily mean that the 'historical' dimension encouraged by that the evolutionary approach disappears. There would remain a question concerning the origin of these shared normative beliefs; and I turn to this in the next section.

I conclude this section by reflecting on the change that is brought by recognising the motivating power of normative beliefs. The two-tier structure of the amended rational choice model may appear, by preserving the language of preference satisfaction, to save the generality of the rational choice model. However, the two-tier structure actually marks a significant change in the underlying model of motivation. One way of drawing out this change is to note that beliefs have migrated from Hume's 'slave of the passions' to a constitutive part of the 'passions' and so it might be more natural to think of action expressing beliefs now rather than satisfying some antecedent set of desires. This may seem like a semantic quibble but preferences or desires are primitives in the simple rational choice model and that is no longer the case once beliefs play this constituting role. For the contribution of beliefs cannot necessarily be fixed in advance just through simply knowing antecedently that people, say, believe that 'reciprocated kindness' is a good thing.

To see this in more detail, suppose in the prisoner's dilemma game the players are motivated by psychological pay-offs that come from reciprocated kindness. It follows that if each expects the other to cooperate, they may each instrumentally decide to cooperate because they each obtain a 'psychological' pay-off from the reciprocated kindness that comes from cooperative play when each holds these beliefs. Alternatively each could expect that the other will defect and decide instrumentally to defect on instrumental grounds because no one expects any reciprocation of kindness. Notice in both cases the beliefs are in equilibrium in the sense that kindness was expected and it was delivered in the first case while it was not expected and not produced in the second. So one cannot appeal to the concept of equilibrium to choose between which set of beliefs will prevail. What is at issue here is not whether people are motivated by psychological pay-offs per se. In both cases they are so motivated. The difference lies in whether there are any psychological pay-offs to be had and not whether one is susceptible to them. In other words, it is whether they expect each other actually to follow the norm of reciprocated kindness. Once it is known that they will follow the norm, then the character of their beliefs can be fixed and it becomes instrumentally rational to decide to cooperate. But since the moment it is known that they are following the norm of reciprocated kindness, their actions are also known, the gain from putting a spin of instrumental reason on the choice of the action begins to seem rather obscure.

For these reasons I prefer to think of norm-guided action as 'expressively rational' rather than instrumentally so. But I do not wish to press the change in terminology. The key point is that the two-tier version of the rational choice model marks a shift in the underlying model of motivation. Beliefs move centre stage: they help to constitute preferences when they are shared and this gives a social and plastic character to preferences in the amended rational choice model.

To summarise, I began this section with a complaint that the rational choice model assumes too much. It takes institutions for granted and says nothing about the origin of the preferences which do all the work. I have focused on the first of these, arguing that what is missing from the rational choice model is the psychological space for individuals to value what they do. Once this is opened up and the crucial part played by shared beliefs in people's assessment of worth is recognised, then not only is there the material for understanding how institutions command loyalty or legitimacy, there is also a powerful complementary resource to the rational choice model for explaining equilibrium selection. Both points turn on the fact that institutions often encode shared beliefs. This emendation of the rational choice model also provides a partial redress to the second complaint. The part played by shared normative beliefs marks a social influence on preferences. It leaves open, however, the big question of how shared beliefs actually shift and change and this is the topic I turn to in the next section.

How do shared beliefs emerge and change?

There are two aspects to this question. The first relates to how the individual acquires or changes beliefs about what is worthy and the second concerns how individual beliefs come to be shared. There is much that might be said on both aspects. In the space available I concentrate on what feeds into the discussion of prescription in the final section.

Plainly the various processes through which children are socialised provides part of the answer to both questions (and would connect in a full account with an analysis of habit and tacit knowledge). In addition, there are a variety of institutions in society where the ideas with respect to what is worthy are either explicitly or implicitly discussed. For instance, organised religions and political parties are important sources for advice and discussion of ideas about what makes a life worthy. Likewise, the mass media supply explicit comment on behaviour through editorials and frequently engage, implicitly, in debate over people's behaviour in the drama and soap operas on television and radio. So people's participation in these institutions helps answer both questions too.

In addition, if the earlier argument is correct and people's actions frequently express ideas about what is worthy, then one might expect that behaviour outside these explicitly normative institutions could also be a source of shared idea formation. It is in this context that the psychological literatures on cognitive dissonance and 'extrinsic' and 'intrinsic' reason also supply some guidance.

There are two key ideas in these literatures which are helpful (see Chapter by Frey and Benz in this collection for more details). One is that people explain their action in terms of two distinct types of reason: 'intrinsic' and 'extrinsic'. An action may be taken either because it is 'intrinsically' the right thing to do or because it just happens to be the right thing to do in the circumstances (i.e. 'the price was right', so as to speak, and this supplies an 'extrinsic' reason). The contrast may seem rather strange to rational choice theorists where every choice involves how best to satisfy preferences given the circumstantial constraints and so seems to entail both an intrinsic and an extrinsic aspect. But the distinction makes much greater sense once the rational choice model is amended to take account of a two-tier structure of preferences. Extrinsic reasons plausibly map on to the calculative, instrumental reasons associated with satisfying ordinary preferences; whereas intrinsic reasons are the ones that motivate expressive actions in support of self-worth.

The second idea is that people like to be able to rationalise their action through reference to one or other of the two types of reason. They like to have clear reason for their actions and will adjust their beliefs about the intrinsic worth of any action accordingly. Thus if a person finds they are taking an action for which there are both extrinsic and intrinsic reasons, then there is an excess or ambiguity of 'reason' and they will adjust their beliefs so that its intrinsic value falls, leaving extrinsic reason solely in charge. Alternatively, if the person finds that they are taking an action for which there are neither extrinsic nor intrinsic reasons, they will adjust their beliefs so that its intrinsic value rises.

In this way, the literature explains how individuals adjust their beliefs about what is worthwhile by appeals to a well-established psychological mechanism of cognitive dissonance avoidance. The adjustment of the belief avoids the cognitive dissonance that would otherwise arise when there is either too much or too little reason for an action. This is helpful for our purpose, for example, because it would explain why people who follow a convention seek out normative reasons for their behaviour and so turn the convention into an institution enjoying legitimacy. In other words, it is precisely when there are gaps in the simple rational choice model that people seek out other ('intrinsic') reasons for their action through developing their beliefs (see Hargreaves Heap and Varoufakis 2002, for an experiment where this seems to occur).

Likewise, it supplies an insight into why the introduction of 'payments by results' frequently fails to produce the expected improved performance (see Frey 1997a). If the discretion that existed before such payment systems had actually permitted a norm of professional good performance to develop and guide action on intrinsic grounds, then the introduction of an extrinsic reason for good performance in the form of a system of payments by results would merely substitute one reason for good performance for another. This might not only yield little change in the area covered by the new payment system, but it would tend to undermine the norm more generally as people adjusted their beliefs to the excess of reason for good performance. In turn, this could impair performance in areas that had been covered by the norm but which were not covered by the new payment system and so worsen performance overall.[3]

Prescriptions

The argument so far has been concerned with how the explanation of institutions and their legitimacy requires an expanded, norm-based conception of rational action. In this section I turn to the issue of how the introduction of such an expanded conception of rational agency might affect prescriptions in economics. In this context it helps to begin with a sketch of how the rational choice model is usually employed to make prescriptions in economics.

Since rational choice theorists depict individuals exclusively as preference satisfiers, it is natural to think of them entering into social relations for the purpose of increasing preference satisfaction. Social life amounts to a relationship of exchange for mutual benefit. Not unsurprisingly, the prescriptions based on this model are then primarily concerned with the institutions that promote efficient exchange. The analysis of the circumstances under which the market operates efficiently is a case in point; and there is a voluminous literature on market failure in this sense and how to remedy it. The transactions cost approach to the boundary between the firm and the market and the assignment of property rights are others. The use of cost-benefit analysis to decide on what public projects should be undertaken and the public choice proposals for constraining government follow likewise from a concern to promote efficiency (see Mueller 2001, for a recent survey and suggestions for the development of public choice insights based on the psychology literature regarding the failures of rational choice).

So the question in this section becomes: to what extent would the introduction of an expressive conception of rationality create further criteria for judging institutions or public interventions and how do such criteria relate to that of efficiency?

The short answer to the first part of this question is that societies need institutions where people can participate in the discussion of shared beliefs and which give them scope to express those beliefs in action. This follows directly from the argument in the previous sections. People want to make sense of their lives. They don't just want to achieve something through their actions, they also want to feel that what they have achieved is worthy. Shared ideas about what is worthy are crucial in this. This is so, incidentally, even if one supposes that, in significant respects, what makes life worthy is the pursuit of one's own preference satisfaction in the simple rational choice sense. This may not be obvious to those who naturalise the rational choice model. But even if preference satisfaction was what made life worthy, then it would do so in virtue of some justificatory idea about the value of preference satisfaction, it would not follow from the mere fact that we were preference satisfiers. Justifications deal in ideas not preferences and so belief formation is crucial.

In order to express such ideas in action, people both need to participate in the institutions where such ideas are discussed and debated to have access to the ideas in the first place and they need the scope to instantiate the ideas in their actions. The last condition is not trivial. When a decision can be made solely with reference to the logic of simple rational choice calculations, there is no scope for action to be guided by justificatory ideas. Of course, the action might still be consistent with what some justificatory idea would suggest, but the action would no longer express this idea distinctly because the action could have equally followed from instrumental calculation. This is not merely a problem in the sense that the action would contain a mixed message, it is also a problem because of what is known from the literature on cognitive dissonance. These are exactly the circumstances when the intrinsic reason for action is likely to disappear (see Frey 1997b for application of this idea to constitution design).

This line of argument suggests an answer to the second part of the question. It seems that the writ of the rational choice model and the associated criteria of efficiency need to be constrained when designing institutions. Otherwise, there will be no scope for people to express their shared beliefs in action.

There is another reason for such a design constraint. It comes from considering the actual institutions where ideas are discussed and debated (i.e. political parties, churches, the mass media and so on) because these institutions tend not to function discursively if they become arenas where people pursue their simple rational choice interests by other means. This is perhaps clearest if one considers an institution like the judiciary which is similar in the sense that, in seeking the truth surrounding alleged crimes, it too is not to be judged according to how well it promotes the preference satisfaction of those who are involved with it.

Most people do not commit crimes on the basis of a simple calculation of rational choice type costs and benefits. They do not commit crime because, in upholding the law, they are embracing an idea about the way that a society ought to be organised. This includes ideas that relate specifically to the judiciary, like the equal treatment of all before the law, that guilt and innocence should be determined by the facts, tempered by the concept of reasonable doubt, and so on. The moment the judiciary itself seemed to be guided simply by people pursuing their own interests, then upholding the law in this sense would no longer command people's allegiance. It would simply mean that disputes were resolved, as they are in a market when two people want the same thing, by who is willing to pay the most; and the allure of following the law would be lost.

The point is entirely general and applies not just to the legal system. Society has institutions that orchestrate discussion and decide on what is the proper object of exchange: that is, what can be bought and sold. We draw the line at humans, body parts and not just the legal system. Furthermore, the boundary is always under negotiation as for instance in the contemporary debate over the environment and genetic material. Again these institutions must be something other than vehicles for the pursuit of individual interest by other means because the moment they become dominated by the principle of unfettered individual exchange, the ability to draw the boundary would rather obviously have been lost.

This is a bit like another version of the Gresham's Law in the psychological literature where 'extrinsic' reason drives out the 'intrinsic' type; and it is not difficult to see why. Shared ideas have to transcend individual interest if they are to be genuinely shared and valued. Or to put this slightly differently, an idea may serve a particular individual's interest but this could never in itself be the general basis that made it attractive to all individuals. This would make it attractive to that particular individual but the appeal to others would have to come, in so far as it did, from some other reason relating to why an individual of that kind should have their interest favoured. In other words, it would have to move beyond the currency of individual preference satisfaction.

It is easy for these reasons to see why a society's institutions of debate and discussion cannot be simply regulated by the criteria of efficiency with respect to the satisfaction of the preferences of those who participate in them. Otherwise they fail to provide the frameworks within which exchange relations prosper (for example, the judiciary or more generally the institutions which enable rational choice calculations to be made because they help avoid difficulties like multiple Nash equilibria). It is much more difficult, however, to specify how they should be guided. It may be self-evident that jurors or witnesses should not accept payment, say, from a newspaper which is interested in a story. But it is much more difficult to devise payment packages for the members of these institutions that encourage performance without eroding the values of the institution. Equally it is difficult to judge the extent to which the output of the industries of television, film and radio drama are affected by operating in a market environment and so need to be constrained in one way or another.

The nub of the matter is to devise an alternative criterion to the one of efficient preference satisfaction for judging performance in these institutions. Once this has been articulated, there are some suggestions as to how to encourage performance by the employees of these institutions without eroding its values. For instance, it has been argued that institutions can, by paying more attention to the remuneration package offered to potential employees, select those who intrinsically share the values of the organisation. In this way the gap between the 'principal' and the 'agent's' interests, that systems of payments by results are designed to close, would not arise in the first place (see Brennan 1996). Equally once these alternative criteria have been articulated one can begin to analyse the extent to which the way that a discursive institution rubs up against the world where rational choice considerations dominate will affect their performance.

The argument, then, in this section is that we need public institutions: that is, institutions which give scope for discussion and deliberation (see Habermas 1985/6 and Buchanan 1974, for contrasting approaches which come to the same conclusion). It is an argument in a long tradition. It connects with more narrow arguments for deliberative democracy (see, for example, Miller 1992) and goes back at least to Smith(1776 [1999]) who was concerned with the way that the growth of an anonymous urban, industrial society would undermine the capacity for ordinary people to form sympathetic judgements. Such judgements, Smith thought, depended on shared moral codes of conduct of a community and were crucial to a person's sense of self-worth (or 'self-love' as Smith called it).

> While he remains in a country village his conduct may be attended to, and he may be obliged to attend to it himself. In this situation, and in this situation only, he may have what is called a character to lose. But as soon as he comes into a great city he is sunk in obscurity and darkness. His conduct is observed and attended to by nobody and he is therefore very likely to neglect it himself, and to abandon himself to every sort of low profligacy and vice. (p. 383)

He goes on to argue that ordinary people in the city are drawn to religious sects: 'He never emerges so effectually from this obscurity ....as by his becoming a member of a small religious sect'. The problem which Smith diagnoses, however, is that the 'morals of those little sects have ... frequently been rather disagreeably rigorous and unsocial' (p. 383). His proposal to combat this is twofold.

> The first of those remedies is the study of science and philosophy ... science is the great antidote to the poison of enthusiasm and superstition. ... The second of those remedies is the frequency and gaiety of public diversions. The state by encouraging that is by giving entire liberty to all those who for their own interest would attempt ... to amuse and divert the people by painting, poetry, music, dancing; by all sorts of dramatic representations and exhibitions would easily dissipate ... that melancholy and gloomy humour which is almost always the nurse of popular superstition and enthusiasm. (p. 384)

Unfortunately this takes us no further than the recognition that we need public institutions in this sense and I have no answers to offer to the important question of what the alternative criteria for judging the performance of these discursive public institutions should be. This seems to me to be part of a pressing research programme, but one which will only feature significantly on the research agenda of economics if something other than the simple rational choice model becomes a part of the mainstream. If it doesn't then the rational choice model will continue to sweep all before it, its insights will inform all policy, the resources for holding shared ideas will gradually disappear; and we will all be the worse off for this.

Conclusion

It is important to put the arguments of this chapter in perspective. There are many settings in which the simple rational choice model is perfectly adequate. Whenever we attend to the price of a commodity or consider the opportunity cost of an action, it is likely that instrumental reason is at work.

The point of the argument of this chapter, then, is *not* that we should dispense with the rational choice model. Rather it is that there are other sources of rational action which fill the *significant* gaps left by the instrumental model with respect to the normative/institutional aspects of agency. Economics needs to understand better these other sources of motivation both for explanation and prescription. This is happening with respect to explanation through the development of various models of, broadly understood, norm-guided action. However, there is rather less progress with respect to prescription where there is a need, in effect if one preserves the language of preference satisfaction, for criteria for judging the institutions that are responsible for preference formation. It will be rather obvious that a criterion of efficient preference satisfaction, which comes from the rational choice model, cannot be used in such cases.

Acknowledgement

My thanks go to the editors for many helpful comments on an earlier draft.

Notes

1. For example, the axiom of transitivity is often justified through an appeal to a money pump argument. This is an argument when you prefer A to B and B to C, but intransitively prefer C to A, that someone could trade you into poverty. To see this, suppose you begin with A, then you would pay to trade it for C, pay again to trade C for B and then pay again to trade B for A. So you would end up holding A again, having paid for the privilege at each stage, ready to trade through the same cycle again and again until the onset of poverty. What seems wrong to many people about being money pumped in this way (and hence the underlying intransitive preferences) is that it seems inconsistent with the idea that person has objectives which they pursue through their actions.
2. It is perhaps worth noting that the 'transactions cost' approach, which also makes institutional selection depend on considerations of efficiency (see Williamson 1975), also suffers from this problem. Thus to take a canonical example, the 'firm' may be a more efficient than the 'market' for organising a particular transaction because the transaction is repeated and involves transaction specific investments, but the benefits can be distributed in a variety of ways within the firm. In other words, there can be a variety of different kinds of firm which show advantages over the market and, just as Hobbes's account shows the advantage of a system of property rights without pointing to any particular set, so the transactions cost approach cannot explain the selection of a particular kind of firm.
3. This section is necessarily brief. It may help to notice that socialisation supplies, to use Elster's (1983) classification, a 'causal' explanation of these beliefs, while those that come from explicit discussion are 'intentionally' generated and the ones that shift through the mechanism of cognitive dissonance removal are 'sub-intentional causally' explained.

References

Bacharach, M. (1999) 'Interactive team reasoning: a contribution to the theory of cooperation', *Research in economics*, **53**, 117–47.

Becker, Gary S. (1991), *A Treatise on the Family*, Cambridge, MA: Harvard University Press.

Binmore, Ken (1994), *Game Theory and the Social Contract:* vol. 1, *Playing Fair*, Cambridge, MA: MIT Press.

Brennan, Goeffrey (1996), 'Selection and the currency of reward' in R. Goodin (ed.), *The Theory of Institutional Design*, Cambridge: Cambridge University Press.

Buchanan, James M. (1974), *The Limits of Liberty: Between Anarchy and the Leviathan*, Chicago: Chicago University Press.

Davidson, Donald (1980), 'Psychology as philosophy', in *Essays on Actions and Events*, Oxford: Clarendon Press.

Dawes, Robert and Richard Thaler (1988), 'Anomalies: cooperation', *Journal of Economic Perspectives*, **2**, 187–97.

Douglas, M. (1978), *Cultural Bias*, London: Royal Anthropological Society.

Elster, Jon (1983), *Explaining Technological Change*, Cambridge: Cambridge University Press.

Elster, Jon (1989), *The Cement of Society*, Cambridge: Cambridge University Press.

Frey, Bruno S. (1997a), *Not Just for the Money*, Cheltenham, UK and Lyme USA: Edward Elgar.

Frey, Bruno S. (1997b), 'A constitution for knaves crowds out our civic virtues', *Economic Journal*, **107**, 1043–53.
Gauthier, David (1986), *Morals by Agreement*, Oxford: Clarendon Press.
Green, H. (1971), *Consumer Theory*, Harmonsworth: Penguin.
Habermas, Jürgen (1985/6), *The Theory of Communicative Action*, Cambridge: Polity Press.
Hargreaves Heap, Shaun (1989), *Rationality in Economics*, Oxford: Basil Blackwell.
Hargreaves Heap, Shaun (2001), 'Is self worth just another kind of preference?' in Uskali Mäki (ed.), *The Economic World View: Studies in the Ontology of Economics*, Cambridge: Cambridge University Press, pp. 98–113.
Hargreaves Heap, Shaun, and Yanis Varoufakis (1995), *Game Theory: a Critical Introduction*, London: Routledge.
Hargreaves Heap, Shaun, and Yanis Varoufakis (2002), 'Some experimental evidence on the evolution of discrimination, co-operation and fairness', *Economic Journal*, **112**, July, 679–703.
Miller, D. (1992), 'Deliberative democracy and social choice', *Political Studies*, XL special, 54–67.
Mueller, Dennis (2001), 'Public choice after 50 years, Bruno Frey after 60 years', *Kyklos*, **54**, 343–53.
Rabin, Matthew (1993), 'Incorporating fairness into economics and game theory', *American Economic Review*, **83**, 1281–302.
Schelling, Thomas (1960), *The Strategy of Conflict*, Cambridge, MA: Harvard University Press.
Schotter, Andrew (1981), *The Economic Theory of Social Institutions*, Cambridge: Cambridge University Press.
Smith, Adam (1759 [1976]), *The Theory of Moral Sentiments*, edited D. Raphael and A. Macfie, Oxford: Clarendon Press.
Smith, Adam (1776 [1999]), *The Wealth of Nations*, Harmondsworth: Penguin.
Starmer, C. (2000), 'Developments in non-expected utility theory; the hunt for a descriptive theory of choice under risk', *Journal of Economic Literature*, **XXXVIII**, 332–82.
Sugden, Robert (1986), *The Economics of Rights, Co-operation and Welfare*, Oxford: Basil Blackwell.
Sugden, Robert (2000), 'Team preferences', *Economics and Philosophy*, **16**, 175–204.
Williamson, Oliver (1975), *Markets and Hierarchies*, New York: Free Press.

4 From imperialism to inspiration: a survey of economics and psychology

Bruno S. Frey and Matthias Benz

Introduction

Modern economics and psychology are both sciences of human behaviour. Although they have a common theme, their relationship still swings between pure co-existence and selective interaction. Starting from the analysis of human behaviour on markets, modern economics has developed a behavioural model which disregards psychological factors almost completely. The 'homo oeconomicus' takes decisions in a rational and emotionless manner. He or she compares the expected costs and utilities of the different alternatives at hand, and finally selects the one that benefits him or her the most. Decisions are assumed to have a high degree of rationality (cognitive limitations resulting in systematically suboptimal decisions are disregarded); they are based on unlimited willpower (self-control problems and emotions do not play a role); and actions are solely guided by self-interest (the homo oeconomicus does not have pro-social preferences, i.e. the utility of other individuals does not enter into his decision calculus). Homo oeconomicus, however, reacts to changes in his possibility space in a systematic and therefore predictable way: when the relative price (or the opportunity cost) of a good or an activity increases, the demand for the respective good will fall, and the respective activity will be carried out less ('law of demand'). This economic approach to human behaviour has been successfully applied to areas outside of the economy. Often termed 'economic imperialism', the economic approach has produced fruitful insights in such areas as politics ('Public Choice'), law ('Law and Economics'), history ('New Economic History'), the arts ('Cultural Economics'), or family ('Economics of the Family').

Economics has not always been so distant from psychology, however, as the concept of the homo oeconomicus suggests. In the beginnings of economics, economists like Smith, Bentham, Edgeworth, Marshall and many others were aware of, and even analysed, the psychological foundations of preferences and beliefs, and acknowledged them as important determinants of human behaviour. Psychological considerations in economics were lost when neoclassical economics started its triumphant progress within the field of economics throughout the twentieth century. In the second section of this chapter, we briefly describe this historical process. Then we give a detailed account of the concept of homo oeconomicus, show the strengths of this approach in explaining (market) behaviour, and argue that the approach offers important insights for psychology and other social sciences.

In the decades since 1980, the neoclassical assumptions underlying the concept of homo oeconomicus have been increasingly criticised. In many cases, empirical studies have produced results conflicting with economic predictions. This has led to the development of a 'Behavioural Economics', which has successfully adapted the economic approach by incorporating psychological aspects into the model of human behaviour. At the same time, the usefulness of the traditional economic model for understanding the workings of the economy has been reconsidered, and its implications for practical economic policy have been revised. We demonstrate this new relationship between psychology and economics for three major areas. Section three is concerned with the limitations of the traditional economic approach resulting from the *bounded rationality* of individuals. Numerous *anomalies* have been identified, indicating that behaviour can systematically deviate from a fully rational model of decision making. We discuss the often divergent ways by which these anomalies have been incorporated into economic theory. Section four deals with the limitations of the economic approach resulting from *bounded self-interest*. Individuals have been found to behave in a non-selfish way in many situations, which has implications for economic theory in three respects. First, experimental economics has shown that pro-social preferences play a major role in human behaviour: individuals often follow *social norms,* like fairness or reciprocity. Second, the economic approach does not take sufficiently into account that individuals do many things out of *intrinsic motivation,* or because it corresponds to their self-image (*identity*). Third, non-selfish behaviour is crucial when *market failure* occurs and certain public goods are not, or only insufficiently, produced. Many areas of public and economic life are characterised by social dilemma situations, and non-selfish behaviour is a necessary precondition to overcome them (given that they cannot be regulated by the state). Section five treats the limitations of the economic approach resulting from its *bounded utility concept.* Neoclassical economics has constructed a utility concept completely deprived of any hedonic content. Utility can only be observed and assessed indirectly by looking at the revealed behaviour of individuals. In contrast, psychology treats utility as directly observable: utility can be assessed using measures of reported subjective well-being (or *happiness*), which are regularly assessed in surveys. By using happiness as an alternative measure of welfare, and studying its economic and institutional determinants, new insights about the impact of economic and political choices on human welfare can be gained.

Imperialistic economics drives out psychology

Economics is considered to be 'the Queen of the Social Sciences' by its proponents and to be 'an Imperialistic Science' by its critics. Both characterisations of economics are due to the development toward a fully rational model of economic decision-making, which represents the core of the generally accepted and rigorous neoclassical economics. The analytical strengths of the neoclassical assumptions have made it possible to apply the economic approach not only to questions traditionally within the scope of economics (market behaviour), but also to many non-market situations traditionally studied in psychology. Both aspects of this imperialistic programme are illustrated in this section. After an outline of the historical development of economic theory, the economic approach to human behaviour is presented in detail. We discuss its strengths and successes, and its importance for psychology and other social sciences.

The loss of psychology in economics

Within today's mainstream economics, the relationship between economics and psychology can best be described as imperialistic on the part of economics. In the course of developing neoclassical economic theory, the psychological content (which still existed in the work of economic precursors) was totally squeezed out. Many classical economists (those living in the eighteenth and nineteenth centuries) carefully considered psychological reasoning when debating preferences and beliefs. Developments in economic science after 1930 have led to a loss of psychological content (Lewin 1996). This can best be shown with the concept of utility. Using the concept of utility as an illustration is also useful because the assumption that individuals maximise expected utility is at the core of neoclassical theory.

The Utilitarians, such as Bentham (1789 [1948]), had very broad views on utility and were convinced that utility could be measured. Their extensive reflections on human utility started from the view that human experiences had a hedonic quality. Bentham, for example, distinguished no less than fourteen different components of utility. His 'pleasures' and 'pains' contained many hedonic experiences resulting from tangible, but also intangible goods, such as 'pleasure of sense, wealth, skill, amity, a good name, power, piety, benevolence, malevolence, memory, imagination, expectation, relief and the pleasures dependent on association' (Bentham 1789 [1996], S. 34–35). Edgeworth (1881) even wanted to measure utility using a 'hedonometer', assuming that utility had a cardinal quality.

The 1930s witnessed a revolutionary change in the concept of utility. Robbins (1932) questioned the existence of a cardinally measurable utility function based on subjective experiences, and therewith declared a direct assessment of utility to be impossible. An ordinal concept of utility gained ground. It requires that utility only be indirectly inferred from actual choices made. Utility is only reflected in the 'revealed behaviour' of individuals. One can also speak of 'decision utility' in the sense of an ordinal preference index indicating whether good A is preferred over good B, whether the opposite holds, or whether individuals are indifferent. Utility thus just becomes a number without any further substantive meaning whatsoever, and it only serves to explain the choices made by individuals between various goods. After World War II, these views have become enshrined in myriads of theoretical treatises and textbooks as the mainstream 'New Welfare Economics'. The switch from the idea of measurable cardinal utility to a preference index of ordinal utility – graphically represented by the consumer indifference curves – was successful in economics for two good reasons. First, states of minds, such as how much satisfaction or pleasure a good yields, are indeed inherently difficult to measure. Economists endeavouring a scientific approach to their discipline are therefore still deeply sceptical about being able to measure utility. Second, cardinal utility is not necessary for economic theory. As Hicks (1934) and Allen (1934) have shown, demand theory can be entirely grounded in ordinal utility in the form of a preference index. Samuelson (1938) then formulated the general behavioural foundations of the still widely accepted standard theory. It attributes utility solely to actual choices. Revealed behaviour is the only way to find out about individuals' utility. This also means that no empirical knowledge of persons' emotional states or opinions about their utility is needed to explain the choices individuals make between goods in markets.

For utility to be properly reflected in actual choices, individuals have to meet some important requirements when making their decisions: they have to be well (or even perfectly) informed about the alternatives; they have to build correct expectations about the consequences of their choices; and they have to pursue their wishes – and only their own wishes – in a logically consistent way. These assumptions are at the core of neoclassical economics and reflected in other theoretical cornerstones of economics: the theory of expected utility maximisation (based on the von Neumann/Morgenstern axioms, see, for example, Schoemaker 1982; Machina 1987), the theory of rational expectations (Muth 1961; Lucas and Prescott 1971), and game theory (e.g. Gibbons 1992). These theories have been cleared of any psychological content in a similar way to that illustrated for the concept of utility. The 'homo oeconomicus', which is at the centre of the next subsection, is built around these behavioural assumptions of rational and selfish behaviour.

The economic approach to human behaviour (homo oeconomicus)
The homo oeconomicus stands for a behavioural model which is grounded in the analysis of human behaviour on markets. Understood as a general social science paradigm, however, it is in principle applicable to all areas of human

behaviour (see Becker 1976, 1996; Becker and Murphy 2000; Frey 1999). Human action can be analysed with the help of five principles.

Individuals act   What happens on the social level is explained by the behaviour of persons (methodological individualism). This does not mean at all that human beings are considered isolated; rather, their behaviour can only be understood as the result of interactions with their surroundings, other people and institutions.

This approach differs fundamentally from theories in which collectivities act on their own, as is assumed, for example, in the organic conception of the state. No further distinctions are made below the level of the individual. This distinguishes the economic approach from several variants of psychology where split personalities are studied, and also from sociobiology where there genes are a level below the individual person.

To take the individualistic stand also means that a person's evaluations and normative views are accepted. Statements such as 'something is socially desirable' are taken to be meaningless because 'society' is not a behavioural unit which could proffer an evaluation. What counts is how people in society evaluate the various possibilities open to them.

Incentives determine behaviour   People do not act randomly but react systematically and predictably to incentives. Incentives signal which possibilities for action are more advantageous or more disadvantageous. Individuals compare the advantages and disadvantages of the actions available to them in an implicit and sometimes explicit way. They thereby also form expectations about the future. Homo economicus needs not to be fully informed, but he will seek and find solutions, learn and invent, and extend his limited knowledge if found worthwhile.

Incentives are structured by preferences and constraints which are strictly distinguished   Changes in human behaviour are attributed (as far as possible) to observable and measurable changes of the opportunity set determined by the constraints. The most important constraints individuals face are: (1) disposable income (including wealth and the possibility of getting credit); (2) the relative prices for goods and services (in case goods are traded on markets), or in a more general sense, the implicit prices of the different choice alternatives (opportunity costs); and (3) the time required for consuming and acting. The first two conditions define a person's disposable real income, which is important for economic analysis. The more general point is, however, that people's possibilities for action are always constrained, and therefore there is a constant necessity to trade off between different alternatives. Moreover, constraints need not solely be monetary or of time, but can also consist of physical or psychological limitations. This potentially opens the economic approach to the incorporation of psychological effects, as will be shown in sections three to five.

Individuals pursue their own interests and generally behave in a selfish way   This assumption about preferences seems at first sight to represent a negative evaluation of man: an egoist is not likeable. This is, however, a misunderstanding. Selfish behaviour means that it cannot be assumed that every person acts magnanimously towards others – this would certainly be unrealistic. Nor does it mean that every person always endeavours to harm others. Selfish behaviour takes a middle position. Most people are neither saints nor devils. Selfish behaviour can be relied on, especially when human interaction takes place on anonymous markets. In the economic realm, it can generally be expected that people act to their own advantage. Whether this assumption also holds for situations with smaller social distance is discussed in section 4.

On the basis of these five principles of the economic model of human behaviour, it is possible to derive a central law for economics – the generalised *law of demand*. Suitably applied, it allows us to theoretically and empirically explain how people act.

The law of demand states: if the price (or cost) of a good or activity rises in comparison to other goods or activities (i.e. if the relative price rises), the particular good is demanded less and the particular activity is pursued less.

This central law is based on the principle of *marginal substitution*. A relative price rise does not provoke a total or abrupt change in behaviour but rather a more or less strong adjustment to changing scarcities. The law only applies provided other influences stay constant (this is the *ceteris paribus* assumption). The influence of other factors on demand (especially of changes in income) must be taken into account separately.

An important property of the law of demand is that the direction of the expected change in behaviour is well determined. The relatively more expensive activity is undertaken to a lesser extent, and the relatively *more expensive* good is purchased and consumed *less*, and vice versa. This property does not normally obtain for other influences on demand. In particular, no general theoretical hypotheses exist about whether higher income raises or lowers demand. The demand for larger cars may increase with rising income, the demand for ordinary foodstuffs may decrease. Theoretically, however, the direction of the influence of a higher income is uncertain; it can only be determined by empirical observation.

The importance of the economic approach for psychology (and other social sciences)
For psychology (and other social sciences), the significance of the economic approach to human behaviour lies mainly in its coherence and universal validity

and that this approach offers clear predictions for behaviour. Psychology, in contrast, does not have a general model of behaviour, but consists of a large number of partial theories and special effects, which are more or less isolated from each other. The differences become clear when the economic approach is compared to models of behaviour in social psychology, which are also based on the hypotheses that individuals behave in such a way as to maximise their own utility (for example, Ajzen 1988; Fishbein and Ajzen 1975). According to these latter models, social attitudes are the central determinants of behaviour. Attitudes are defined as a propensity to judge an object as positive or negative. It is taken as being self-evident that a tendency towards positive judgement is followed by corresponding behaviour; that, for example, citizens vote for politicians whom they value, and that they buy goods they think are good. Economists do not say that behaviour can be predicted on the basis of preferences, a concept that is related to attitudes in psychology. Some economists (in particular Stigler and Becker 1977) have even argued that changes in human behaviour can and should only be explained by changes in constraints. The reason is that it is difficult to empirically capture and separate changes in preferences from the change in behaviour that is to be explained. In contrast, changes in constraints are observable and mostly exogenous. In particular, changes in the prices of goods and services, which are central for economic analysis, are easy to observe and quantify. They are, moreover, independent from preference changes of single individuals, and therefore empirically distinguishable from the latter.

This methodological strategy is not confined to market behaviour. The economic approach treats 'prices' very extensively: the concept includes not only monetary prices (such as the price of goods) or monetary burdens (such as taxes), but all costs which arise when undertaking an action (opportunity costs). Changes in prices or opportunity costs can be identified also in non-market settings when constraints are broadly understood as all forms of *institutions* shaping and coordinating human behaviour (North 1990).

There are many examples of the successful application of this modern view of economics, in particular in areas of human life that are traditionally linked with psychology. Important examples are the family: marriage, children, divorce, suicide (Becker 1971, 1981), including the determinants of abortion (Medoff 1988); drug addiction (Winston 1980; Becker and Murphy 1988); religious practices (Ehrenberg 1977; Iannacone 1991, 1998); criminal behaviour (Becker 1968; Cameron 1988; Freeman 1999); and social segregation and norms (Becker and Murphy 2000). Introductory surveys to this literature are given, for example, in Becker (1976), Frey (1999) and Lazear (2000).

The economic approach is moreover important for psychology and other social sciences because it takes a completely different view of the possibilities of influencing human behaviour. The aim of scientific research should not only be to make sound positive analyses, it should also be to offer advice on possible welfare improvements. Economics is able to derive well-defined policy implications from the general law of demand. The starting point for inducing behavioural changes are the incentives. Prices for unwanted activities should be raised in order to lower demand for such activities, and vice versa. In environmental economics, for example, it is stipulated that a price should be put on the use of the environment by introducing pollution taxes. Empirical observation shows that such policies are often effective. In contrast, psychology generally focuses on people's preferences when behaviour should be changed. Influencing people's preferences, however, is normally much more difficult than applying the price mechanism, and the direction of behavioural change often remains unpredictable. For these reasons, it is in many instances easier to achieve changes in behaviour by relying on the incentive instruments proposed by economic theory than by trying to change people's attitudes and values.

The return of psychology
The application of the economic approach to other areas of life has also made the weaknesses of homo economicus more obvious. There are signs that the easy gains in insight achieved when the paradigm was applied to new areas are diminishing (Hirshleifer 1985; Frey 2001). The diminishing marginal returns of the 'imperialist programmes' of economics suggest that the time has come for a change in direction: in the future, the main emphasis should not lie in exporting economics but rather in *importing* aspects and insights from other social sciences, like psychology. What is needed is an effort to overcome the model of 'homunculus economicus', who is at all times in full control of his or her emotions, who does not have any cognitive limitations, who is not embedded in a personal network, who is only extrinsically motivated and whose individual preferences are not distinguished from his or her individual happiness. There is already a considerable amount of literature pointing the way this future development may go, and there are a great number of ideas from psychology which have been fruitfully introduced into economics (for other surveys see Earl 1990; Rabin 1998; 2002 or Mullainathan and Thaler 2000). Today's behavioural economics not only builds on the work of precursors like Simon (1978), Katona (1975), Leibenstein (1976), and Scitovsky (1976), but also on German speaking economists like Schmölders (1962) and Jöhr (1972). Later, authors like Akerlof (1984), Kahneman and Tversky (1984), Frank (1985, 1988), and Thaler (1992) contributed important insights. In the next three sections, we shall discuss several areas in which social psychology has proved to enlighten economics.

Limits of homo oeconomicus: bounded rationality
Homo oeconomicus is based on the theory of expected utility maximisation, which builds on logically consistent and rational propositions on how humans

make decisions (the von Neumann/Morgenstern axioms). These propositions are generally seen as reasonable, and therefore it was taken as plausible for quite some time that individuals behave according to them. Over the last two decades, however, a large literature has accumulated that shows both experimentally and theoretically that the theory of expected utility maximisation can explain only a limited part of observed behaviour. This is so because individuals face *cognitive and emotional constraints*, which are discussed in this section three.

Behavioural anomalies
Evidence on behavioural anomalies was published early on in economics journals. The Allais paradox (1953) and the anomalies found by Ellsberg (1961) regarding individuals' treatment of small probabilities were well-known and fundamental, but were not taken seriously. It needed further experiments by psychologists (see Tverksy and Kahneman 1974; Kahneman and Tversky, 1979; Kahneman et al. 1982; Arkes and Hammond 1986; Dawes 1988) and by economists (see Schoemaker 1982; Hogarth and Reder 1987; Thaler 1992) for behavioural anomalies to be recognised. These experiments revealed overwhelming evidence that humans, as well as animals (McDonald et al. 1991), do not act rationally in the sense of following the von Neumann/Morgenstern axioms. Violations of expected utility maximisation were found to be not random but systematic. Important anomalies for economics include (for more complete accounts see Starmer 2000; Rabin 1998; Frey and Eichenberger 2001): sunk costs (people tend to take forgone costs into account in their decisions, although they should only evaluate future costs and utilities); opportunity cost effect (out-of-pocket monetary costs are given greater weight in the decision calculus than opportunity costs of the same size); endowment effect (goods in a person's endowment are valued more highly than those not held in the endowment); and preference reversal (when choosing between two lotteries, individuals once choose the first and once choose the second lottery when the decision context is logically completely identical, but framed differently). Moreover, anomalies well known in social psychology like availability bias, anchoring, certainty effect, reference point effect and especially framing can be relevant for economic contexts. All these anomalies show that expected utility maximisation theory does not fully describe individual behaviour under risk and uncertainty. What the consequences are for economic theory is thus an important question.

Orthodox economists often advance the argument that anomalies might be relevant at the individual level, but that they are not important for aggregate markets. The more complete and efficient a market is, so goes the standard counter-argument, the more 'irrational' agents are driven from the market, and the less anomalies are observed. Individuals prone to anomalies lose money, which allows rational agents to take over wealth and dominate the overall market. Even if a substantial number of individuals are prone to anomalies, market forces provide strong monetary incentives for rational decisions. For market outcomes to be efficient, moreover, it is sufficient if only some 'marginal' agents act rationally and exploit arbitrage possibilities. Empirical tests of the hypothesis that markets are efficient are therefore a crucial means for evaluating the relevance of psychological factors for economic theory. In recent years, many such studies have been conducted for *financial markets*, because they come the closest to the ideal of a perfect market. Two studies are summarised as an example (based on Mullainathan and Thaler 2000; see Shleifer 2000 for a more detailed account of this literature).

The study by De Bondt and Thaler (1985) is explicitly motivated by the psychological finding that people overreact to new information and underweight more distant information when taking decisions. Given that investors on stock markets behave accordingly, it can be expected that stocks which have performed well over a period of time will be overvalued. Individuals who overreact to good news drive the prices of these stocks too high. Similarly, stocks which had performed badly for some time should be undervalued. From this, DeBondt and Thaler derive the hypothesis that past 'winners' should have lower future returns than the average market, while past 'losers' should outperform the market. Using data from the New York Stock Exchange, they are able to corroborate this hypothesis: the 35 stocks which had performed the worst over the past five years yielded above-average returns over the next five years, while the 35 biggest winners subsequently underperformed. Thus, bounded rationality (in the sense of limited cognitive information processing abilities) plays a role in investor decisions, and the anomaly is evident even at the aggregate market level.

Odean (1998) investigates whether investors are subject to loss aversion, i.e. whether they weight losses more heavily than gains. This is the case, for example, if investors are more reluctant to realise capital losses than to realise capital gains. Odean's empirical study finds exactly this behaviour: around 15 per cent of all gains are realised by investors, but only 10 per cent of all losses. This behaviour, however, comes at an economic cost and is surprising in so far that investors face strong monetary incentives to make rational decisions.

A host of other studies have identified anomalies in financial markets. A recent overview of the by-now substantial literature is given by Shleifer (2000); see also the more popular book by Shiller (2000).

Self-control problems
Individuals are also boundedly rational because they are often not able to stick to their long-term goals, but succumb to the temptation of immediate gratification. Human beings have limited will-power. An obvious example is smokers who want to quit in the interests of better long-term health, but repeatedly fail to refrain from the immediate pleasure of smoking a cigarette. Such 'self-control problems' are also relevant for economic contexts. Banks et al. (1998), for

example, show that people's consumption expenditures fall sharply when they retire and their incomes drop. This is against their long-term preferences, because most people would like to maintain their standard of living even after retirement. But individuals simply seem unable to save enough for retirement. One reason for this is that individuals' short-term and long-term preferences often conflict with each other: saving more money would be in their long-term interests, but the 'short-term selves' of people often choose the immediate gratification of spending the money. As this behaviour violates intertemporal utility maximisation, the phenomenon is also called 'time-inconsistent preferences' or 'hyperbolic discounting' (Laibson 1997; O'Donoghue and Rabin 1999; for a critical evaluation see Frederick et al. 2002). Self-control problems have been identified for a wide range of consumer decisions (Angeletos et al. 2001; Mullainathan and Gruber 2002). However, the existence of self-control problems does not mean that the rational choice approach has to be completely relinquished. One of the defining characteristics of human beings is that they are able to recognise their weaknesses and to overcome them (at least partly). A much-discussed way to circumvent anomalies, or to reduce the cost incurred when falling prey to them, is to establish rules of self-commitment. Probably more importantly, individuals resort to social institutions in order to get help when struggling to overcome their weaknesses (Frey and Eichenberger 2001). For example, individuals who know that they are unable to resist the temptation of consuming more and faster than they wish, have an incentive to support political actions forcing them to plan more for their future, e.g., by introducing an obligatory old age pension scheme run by the state.

Emotions

Apart from cognitive limitations, human decisions can also be constrained by emotions. This seems clear: everybody is aware of situations where strong emotions have precluded a rational decision. In recent years, the role of emotions in human decision making has been studied mainly by psychologists (for a survey see Loewenstein and Lerner 2001). The mostly experimental studies have identified numerous effects of emotions on behaviour. Nevertheless, the relevance of emotions for a general model of (market) behaviour is not very clear (Elster 1998). First, there are hardly any empirical studies which try to isolate emotional effects in economically relevant contexts. The investigations of self-control problems illustrated in the previous subsection come closest. Second, in many situations it is difficult to distinguish 'good' and 'bad' influences of emotions. The view that all emotions are irrational is not supported by current research (Loewenstein and Lerner 2001, p. 38). Whereas emotions may lead to suboptimal decisions in some situations, the absence or deliberate oppression of emotions can substantially harm the *ability* of individuals to make a decision at all (Damasio 1994). Third, further investigation is needed to establish the extent to which emotions change market outcomes. If positive and negative emotions are distributed randomly across market participants, for example, the (potential) behavioural effects tend to average out in the aggregate.

Limits of homo oeconomicus: bounded self-interest

The economic approach starts from the assumption that people are selfish. It has been repeatedly shown that in many situations, especially when individuals act in markets, this is a powerful approximation to actual behaviour (Smith 1962; Becker 1976). Over the last ten years, however, experimental economists and other social scientists have collected unambiguous evidence that individuals are often *boundedly selfish*. This finding is important for many economically relevant situations of exchange between individuals that do not correspond to the traditional view of a perfectly functioning market. In this section, three applications are discussed: (1) the role of pro-social preferences, like norms of fairness and reciprocity, in shaping human behaviour and market outcomes; (2) the role of intrinsic motivation and identity for economics; and (3) the role of non-selfish behaviour for overcoming social dilemmas (i.e. when markets fail).

Pro-social preferences
The assumption of rational self-interest has been tested intensively over the last few years, and the introduction of experimental techniques into economic science has played a major role in this regard. Economic experiments are different from experiments undertaken by other social scientists (like, for example, psychologists) mainly because individuals are paid to participate in the experiment. This makes it possible to derive game theoretic predictions about how a homo economicus would act in a given experiment. The predictions can then be compared to actual behaviour.

A large number of experiments have now been conducted, showing that individuals often do not act like complete egoists (for surveys see Fehr und Gächter 2000; Fehr and Schmidt, 2003). The observed behaviour can only be explained by other-regarding, pro-social preferences: individuals follow social norms like fairness, reciprocity, or altruism. By fairness it is meant that people want to achieve an equitable distribution of resources between the parties involved in an exchange relationship. Reciprocity means that individuals reward kind actions of others by acting kindly as well, and punish unkind actions by responding in a hostile manner, even if this comes at a (monetary) cost. Both types of behaviour are not compatible with homo economicus, as well as a third type of pro-social preference often observed which consists of unconditional, pure altruism (Andreoni 1989; Frey and Meier 2004).

The existence of pro-social preferences has hardly any consequences for aggregate outcomes on markets if exchanges are perfectly contractible. On *incomplete markets*, however, they can substantially alter market outcomes. An impressive example is given by Bewley (1999) who conducted an extensive survey of American personnel managers during the recession of the early 1990s. Asked why firms did not cut their workers' pay (although that is what economics would expect firms to do in a recession, because of the difficult market situation, and because rising unemployment allows them to do so), personnel managers answered: pay cuts would be perceived as unfair, and workers would react negatively to them by lowering their work morale. This surprising result is based on the fact that labour contracts are incomplete: because not all aspects of a job can be contracted upon ex ante, workers are given some discretion. Obviously, when workers decide to use their discretion in the interests of the firm (high work morale) or not (low work morale), preferences for fairness seem to play a major role. High work morale can thus be maintained by not cutting pay. But these fairness considerations also come at an economic cost. Because they lead to downward wage rigidities (which have been observed for many industrialized countries), workers are laid off rather than average wages of the workforce lowered. This causes higher unemployment than would be observed on a perfectly functioning labour market. Pro-social preferences are also of some importance for consumer decisions. As has been shown in surveys for the US (Kahneman et al. 1986) and for Europe (Frey 1999, Chapter 10), consumers judge the prices set by companies mainly by their fairness.

Intrinsic motivation and identity
Economic analysis is based on the idea that individuals respond systematically to changes in relative prices. *Incentives* set from outside motivate people to act in a predictable way. This view disregards that there are other motivating forces, like intrinsic motivation or individuals' self-image (identity). They can systematically affect market outcomes or the effectiveness of incentive instruments, as will be shown in this subsection.

Psychologists generally distinguish between two kinds of motivation: *extrinsic* motivation, induced by manipulations of rewards or sanctions from the outside (the economist's relative prices), and *intrinsic* motivation, where people perform an activity for its own sake or because of reasons lying within their own person (DeCharms 1968; Deci 1971). Intrinsically motivated behaviour is relevant in many areas of economic and political life; examples are work morale, voluntary compliance with social norms, civic virtue, or tax morale. For economic theory, intrinsic motivation is of special importance because it cannot be simply treated as a constant. There is a systematic dynamic interaction between extrinsic and intrinsic motivation. Experimental research in psychology has shown that, under identifiable conditions, external interventions affect people's sense of self-determination, self-perception and their feeling of justice, which in turn influences intrinsic motivation (e.g. Deci and Ryan 1985). Among psychologists, much attention has been paid to the 'hidden costs of reward' (see Lepper and

Greene 1978), stating that introducing a reward into a situation where people already have a high interest in an activity results in a decrease in their intrinsic motivation (see Deci et al. 1999 for a survey). This finding has been introduced into economic theory as the 'crowding-out effect of intrinsic motivation' and has been applied to many economically relevant contexts (for surveys see Frey, 1997; Frey and Osterloh 2001; Frey and Jegen 2001). The damage done to intrinsic motivation by changing external instruments helps explain why pricing (monetary rewards) and regulating (the use of punishment) under identifiable conditions prove to have little or sometimes even counterproductive effects. For example, work incentives in the form of pay for performance can undermine work morale if they are perceived as controlling (in the sense that the workers' voluntary efforts are not acknowledged), and therefore often do not lead to increases in work effort. The crowding out effect suggests that economic incentives and the price mechanism more generally should only be used with caution if individuals have some intrinsic motivation to undertake an activity.

Identity (an individual's self-image) can also lead to decisions that conflict with rational self-interest. A strong identity can undermine the workings of economic incentives if people derive utility from behaving according to their self-image. Akerlof and Kranton (2000) show that this is relevant in many economic areas. For example, the still very unequal distribution of the sexes across different jobs is difficult to reconcile with economically rational decisions of men and women. It can be explained, however, if individuals derive utility from conforming with a (socially predetermined) gender identity. Identities are supposed to influence economic decisions in areas like consumption, savings, education, work relations, or donations, although there is not yet much rigorous empirical evidence on these topics.

Market failure and social dilemmas
Markets generally fail in the production of public goods: if no one can be excluded from the consumption of a good and therefore does not have to pay a price for it, these public goods are either not produced or only suboptimally produced in the market, although their existence would be desirable from a societal point of view. Because in these situations, individual and collective rationality diverge, they are also called social dilemmas. Social dilemmas exist in a considerable number of economic and political contexts: e.g. environmental protection, a functioning legal system, national defence, the formation of political interest groups, unionisation, teamwork in firms, and functioning cartels, all advance the welfare of the respective group or even of society as a whole. But everyone can profit from these public goods, even if he or she has not incurred costs to facilitate their production. Traditional economics offers two solutions: the structure of the problem can be changed by defining property rights, so that individually rational behaviour again leads to socially desirable

outcomes. This approach is often advanced, for example, in environmental economics with the claim that environmental certificates (pollution rights) should be introduced. Alternatively, public goods can be produced by the state (via tax financing), which is, for example, the case in national defence or the provision of a legal system.

These solution concepts disregard, however, that they possibly start from wrong premises. As has been shown in the subsection on 'pro-social preferences', individuals do not always act selfishly, but are often willing to cooperate. Social dilemmas thus can also be solved by providing an institutional environment that enables and encourages cooperation. This is especially important for social dilemma situations that are confined to relatively small groups of people, i.e. where government interventions do not make much sense and it is not possible to define property rights. Examples are common pool resources with respect to the environment and, for the economic realm, firm-specific pool resources (e.g. a firm's reputation, accumulated firm-specific knowledge, or core competences). Ostrom (1990, 2000) shows that common pool resources are governed efficiently when social sanctioning mechanisms can come into play through the possibility of self-organisation and self-regulation. Thus, non-selfish behaviour is often a valuable, if not necessary, precondition to overcome social dilemma situations and mitigate the consequences of market failure. The traditional economic approach systematically disregards such possibilities.

Beyond a bounded utility concept: economics and happiness
Over the past few years, economists have become increasingly interested in happiness or subjective well-being (surveys are given by Frey and Stutzer 2002a, 2002b). This area has long been the province of psychologists (see, for example, Kahneman et al. 1999). It has become clear, however, that the concept of happiness is able to offer new insights on issues which so far have been treated lightly or been totally neglected by neoclassical economics. First, happiness research helps to identify the determinants of individual well-being. Happiness can thus serve as an alternative measure for welfare. A considerable number of economists have become convinced that utility should be given content in terms of happiness, and that it can, and should, be measured. Subjective well-being is assessed in surveys on individuals' happiness or life satisfaction. It is a straightforward strategy to ask individuals directly about their well-being, and it corresponds to a good tradition in economics: as people are supposed to be the best judges of the overall quality of their own lives, one should rely on their individual judgements. Second, happiness research offers new possibilities for testing economic theories and discriminating between theoretical answers on empirical phenomena. Some of the results clearly contradict the standard assumptions of economics as used in most models, but others support the conventional economic views. By way of example, this inspiration of economic

research is discussed with respect to four different issues: (1) Does money (in the form of higher income) buy happiness? (2) Are people in poor countries happier than people in rich countries? (3) Do people get accustomed to higher income? (4) How does unemployment affect happiness?

(1)   25 years ago, Easterlin (1974) asked the question whether higher income would lead to greater happiness (i.e. that, corresponding to the economic view, more money would result in more utility). Easterlin's research received some attention, but only towards the end of the 1990s did economists begin to conduct large-scale empirical analyses of the relationship between income and subjective well-being (see, for example, Di Tella et al. 2001). It is a stable result of all these studies that richer people are on average happier than poorer people. But the studies also show that income does not have much effect on happiness; other factors like health or having a job are equally or more important. Research has also addressed the question of causality: does a higher income lead to happiness, or do happier people simply earn more money? Using exogenous life events like winning the lottery, it can be established that causality indeed runs from more money to more happiness. Income, moreover, seems to have decreasing marginal utility: for low-income persons, an improvement in the income level raises happiness substantially, while for high-income persons, this is not the case. These results give support to traditional economic views, while others are contradictory. For example, one reason for the limited effect of income on happiness is that individuals evaluate their income not so much in absolute terms, but with respect to other people (relative income hypothesis). The importance of relative income can explain why, on average, richer people are happier in a country at a certain point in time, but why raising average incomes does not increase the average happiness of the population over time.

(2)   Sometimes it is questioned whether people living in richer countries are any happier than people living in poor countries. A number of studies have shown, however, that this is not the case (for example Diener et al. 1995, and Inglehart 1990). Corresponding to conventional economic views, welfare is positively connected with economic development. On average, persons living in countries with a higher GDP per capita are happier than those living in poor countries. The differences in income between the countries are measured by using exchange rates, as well as purchasing power parities, in order to control for the international differences in the cost of living. However, there again seems to be decreasing marginal utility of money. While in poor countries economic growth is able to raise happiness, GDP becomes less important for more developed countries. This suggests that additional factors are important to explain differences in reported subjective

well-being between countries. The evidence nevertheless indicates that the notion that people in poor countries are happier because they live under more 'natural' and less stressful conditions is a myth.

(3) For many countries, however, a striking and curious result has been found: whereas per capita income has risen sharply over past decades, average happiness has stayed constant, or has even declined over the same period (e.g. Blanchflower and Oswald 2000). In the United States, for example, real per capita income has risen from US$ 11 000 in 1946 to US$ 27 000 in 1991, i.e. by a factor of 2.5, but average life satisfaction has fallen from 2.4 to 2.2 (on a three-point scale). Obviously, people adapt to raising incomes over time. This might have to do with the notion that relative income matters: if everyone gets richer, overall happiness is not affected. Alternatively, people might adjust their aspirations over time. Initially, higher income causes a rise in happiness, but then one gets used to the higher income level and happiness adjusts downwards (for psychological theories of adaptation see Helson 1964, or Frederick and Loewenstein 1999). This phenomenon suggests that happiness is importantly influenced by the difference between aspiration levels and the things already achieved (e.g. Inglehart 1990, chap. 7). It also explains why most people feel less happy in the present than they think they were in the past, but expect to become happier in the future (Easterlin 2001).

(4) Most economists see unemployment as an unfortunate event to be avoided as much as possible. To become unemployed is considered to be burdensome and, above all, involuntary. But there are also economists who hold a quite different view. Following the 'new classical macroeconomics', unemployment is voluntary. People choose to go out of employment because they find the burden of work and the wages paid unattractive compared to being unemployed and getting unemployment benefits. Involuntary unemployment is a disequilibrium phenomenon and exists only in the short run until individuals and firms have adjusted. The issue of whether, and to what extent, the unemployed are dissatisfied is therefore unresolved. Happiness research on unemployment is able to offer important insights on this topic.

How particular people are affected when they become unemployed can be analysed with the help of individual micro-level data. The studies conducted have consistently documented a detrimental effect of unemployment on psychological well-being (see Darity and Goldsmith 1996 for a survey from the economic perspective). Based on their study for Britain, Clark and Oswald (1994) state that 'joblessness depresses well-being more than any other single characteristic (including important negative ones such as divorce and separation)' (p. 655). Using panel data for Germany, Winkelmann and Winkelmann (1998) show that the effect of unemployment on happiness is in fact causal. It is not due to unobserved individual specific characteristics which might affect the likelihood of becoming unemployed and happiness simultaneously. In the same vein, all the studies control for losses in income or other indirect effects which might depress the happiness of the unemployed. Still, they find a large, negative 'pure' effect of being unemployed on happiness.

People may be unhappy about unemployment even if they are themselves not put out of work. They may feel bad about the unfortunate fate of those unemployed, and they may also feel there are repercussions on the economy and society as a whole. They may dislike the increase in unemployment contributions and taxes likely to happen in the future, they may fear that crime and social tension will increase, and they may even see the threat of violent protests and uprisings. A study of 12 European countries over the period 1975–91 (Di Tella et al. 2001) indeed finds that an increase in the general rate of unemployment reduces reported life satisfaction considerably.

Concluding remarks

The relationship between economics and psychology is characterised by a phase of economic imperialism and a phase of psychological inspiration. After World War II, the development towards the neoclassical standard model has squeezed almost all psychological content out of economics. The resulting economic model of human behaviour has been successfully applied to other areas outside the economy, some of them traditionally studied by psychology.

In recent years, economics has been inspired more and more by psychology. As behavioural anomalies were increasingly recognised, and more attention paid to the role of self-control problems and emotions in individual decision-making, a 'behavioural economics' gained ground. Today, it is on the way to being accepted even by mainstream economists. It is no longer taken for granted in economics that individuals always act as rational selfish maximisers. It is now seen as important that people have pro-social preferences, that extrinsic incentives may harm intrinsic motivation, that people act according to their identities, and that non-selfish behaviour is essential for overcoming social dilemma situations. It does not seem to be an irrational expectation to us that in the future, many other concepts and ideas will be fruitfully borrowed from psychology in order to make economics a more inspiring science.

Acknowledgement
The authors wish to thank Alois Stutzer and Reto Jegen for helpful comments.

References
Ajzen, I. (1988), *Attitudes, Personality, and Behaviour*, Milton Keynes: Open University Press.

Akerlof, G.A. (1984), *An Economic Theorist's Book of Tales*, Cambridge: Cambridge University Press.

Akerlof, G., and R. Kranton (2000), 'Economics and identity', *Quarterly Journal of Economics*, **115** (3), 715–53.

Allais, M. (1953), 'Le comportement de l'homme rationnel devant de risque: Critique des postulats et axiomes de l'école Americaine', *Econometrica*, **21**, 503–46.

Allen, R.G.D. (1934), 'A reconsideration of the theory of value', II. *Economica*, **1**, 196–219.

Andreoni, J. (1989), 'Giving with impure altruism: applications to charity and Ricardian equivalence', *Journal of Political Economy*, **97**, 1447–58.

Angeletos, G., D. Laibson, A., Repetto, J., Tobacman and S. Weinberg (2001), 'The hyperbolic consumption model: calibration, simulation and empirical evaluation', *Journal of Economic Perspectives*, **15** (3), 47–68.

Arkes, H.R., and K.R. Hammond (eds) (1986), *Judgement and Decision-making: An Interdisciplinary Reader*, Cambridge: Cambridge University Press.

Banks, J., R. Blundell and S. Tanner (1998), 'Is there a retirement-savings puzzle?', *American Economic Review*, **88** (4), 769–88.

Becker, G.S. (1962), 'Irrational behavior and economic theory', *Journal of Political Economy*, **70** (1), 1–13.

Becker, G.S. (1968), 'Crime and punishment: an economic approach', *Journal of Political Economy*, **76** 169–217.

Becker, G.S. (1971), *The Economics of Discrimination*, 2nd edn, Chicago: University of Chicago Press.

Becker, G.S. (1976), *The Economic Approach to Human Behavior*, Chicago: Chicago University Press.

Becker, G.S. (1981), *A Treatise on the Family*, Cambridge, MA: Harvard University Press.

Becker, G.S. (1996), *Accounting for Tastes*, Cambridge, MA: Harvard University Press.

Becker, G.S., and K.M. Murphy (1988), 'A Theory of rational addiction', *Journal of Political Economy*, **96**, 675–700.

Becker, G.S., and K.M. Murphy (2000), *Social Economics. Market Behavior in a Social Environment*, Cambridge, MA: Belknap Press.

Bentham, J. (1789 [1948]), *An Introduction to the Principles of Morals and Legislation*, Oxford: Blackwell.

Bewley, T. (1999), *Why Wages Don't Fall During a Recession*, Cambridge, MA: Harvard University Press.

Blanchflower, D.G., and A.J. Oswald (2000), 'Wellbeing over time in Britain and the USA', NBER working paper no. 7487, Cambridge, MA: National Bureau of Economic Research.

Cameron, S. (1988), 'The economics of crime deterrence: a survey of theory and evidence', *Kyklos*, **41**, 301–23.

Clark, A.E., and A.J. Oswald (1994), 'Unhappiness and unemployment', *Economic Journal*, **104** (424), 648–59.

Damasio, A. (1994), *Descartes' Error*, New York: Putnam.

Darity, W., and A. Goldsmith (1996), 'Social psychology, unemployment and macroeconomics', *Journal of Economic Perspectives*, **10** (1), 121–40.

Dawes, R.M. (1988), *Rational Choice in an Uncertain World*, San Diego and New York: Harcourt, Brace, Jovanovich.

De Bondt, W. and R. Thaler (1985), 'Does the stockmarket overreact?', *Journal of Finance*, **40** (3), 793–805.

DeCharms, R. (1968), *Personal Causation: The Internal Affective Determinants of Behavior*, New York: Academic Press.

Deci, E.L. (1971), 'Effects of externally mediated rewards on intrinsic motivation', *Journal of Personality and Social Psychology*, **18**, 105–15.

Deci, E.L., and Ryan, R.M. (1985), *Intrinsic Motivation and Self-Determination in Human Behavior*, New York: Plenum Press.

Deci, E.L., R. Koestner and R.M. Ryan (1999), 'A meta-analytic review of experiments examining the effects of extrinsic rewards on intrinsic motivation', *Psychological Bulletin*, **125** (6), 627–68.

Diener, E., E.M. Suh, H. Smith and L. Shao (1995), 'National differences in the pooled subjective wellbeing: why do they occur?' *Social Indicators Research*, **34** (1) 7–32.

Di Tella, R., R.J. MacCulloch and A.J. Oswald (2001), 'Preferences over inflation and unemployment: evidence from surveys of happiness', *American Economic Review*, **91** (1), 335–41.

Earl, P.E. (1990), 'Economics and psychology: a survey', *Economic Journal*, 100, 718–55.

Easterlin, R.A. (1974), 'Does economic growth improve the human lot? Some empirical evidence', in P.A. David and M.W. Reder (eds), *Nations and Households in Economic Growth: Essays in Honor of Moses Abramowitz*, New York: Academic Press, pp. 89–125.

Easterlin, R.A. (2001), 'Income and happiness: towards a unified theory', *Economic Journal*, **111** (473), 465–84.

Edgeworth, F.Y. (1881), *Mathematical Psychics: An Essay on the Application of Mathematics to the Moral Sciences*, London: Kegan Paul.

Ehrenberg, R.G. (1977), 'Household allocation of time and religiosity: replication and extension', *Journal of Political Economy*, 85, 415–23.

Ellsberg, D. (1961), 'Risk, ambiguity, and the savage axioms', *Quarterly Journal of Economics*, **75**, 643–69.

Elster, J. (1998), 'Emotions and economic theory', *Journal of Economic Literature*, **36** (1), 47–74.

Fehr, E., and S. Gächter (2000), 'Fairness and retaliation: the economics of reciprocity', *Journal of Economic Perspectives*, **14** (3), 159–81.

Fehr, E., and K. Schmidt (2003), 'Theories of fairness and reciprocity – evidence and economic applications', in Matthias Dewatripont et al. (eds), *Advances in Economic Theory*, Eighth World Congress of the Econometric Society, Cambridge: Cambridge University Press.

Fishbein, M., and I. Ajzen (1975), *Belief, Attitude, Intention, and Behavior: An Introduction to Theory and Research*, Reading, MA: Addison-Wesley.

Frank, R.H. (1985), *Choosing the Right Pond*, New York: Oxford University Press.

Frank, R.H. (1988), *Passions within Reason. The Strategic Role of the Emotions,* New York: Norton.

Frederick, S., and G. Loewenstein (1999), 'Hedonic adaptation', in D. Kahneman, E. Diener and N. Schwarz (eds), *Well-Being: The Foundations of Hedonic Psychology*, New York: Russell Sage Foundation, pp. 302–29.

Frederick, S., G. Loewenstein and T. O'Donoghue (2002), 'Time discounting and time preference: a critical review', *Journal of Economic Literature*, **40** (2), 351–401.

Freeman, R. (1999), 'The economics of crime', in O. Ashenfelter and D. Card (eds), *Handbook of Labor Economics*, vol. 3C, Amsterdam; New York and Oxford: Elsevier Science, North-Holland, pp. 3529–71.

Frey, B.S. (1997), *Not Just for the Money. An Economic Theory of Personal Motivation*, Cheltenham, UK and Lyme, USA: Edward Elgar.

Frey, B.S. (1999), *Economics as a Science of Human Behaviour*, extended 2nd edn, Dordrecht: Kluwer.

Frey, B.S. (2001) *Inspiring Economics. Human Motivation in Political Economy*, Cheltenham, UK and Northampton, MA, USA: Edward Elgar.

Frey, B.S., and A. Stutzer (2002a), *Happiness and Economics: How the Economy and Institutions Affect Human Well-Being*, Princeton, NJ: Princeton University Press.

Frey, B.S., and A. Stutzer (2002b), 'What can economists learn from happiness research?', *Journal of Economic Literature*, **40** (2), 402–35.

Frey, B.S., and R. Eichenberger (2001), 'Economic incentives transform psychological anomalies', in B.S. Frey, *Inspiring Economics. Human Motivation in Political Economy*, Cheltenham, UK and Northampton, USA: Edward Elgar.

Frey, B.S., and R. Jegen (2001), 'Motivation crowding theory: a survey of the empirical evidence', *Journal of Economic Surveys*, **15** (5), 589–611.

Frey, B.S., and S. Meier (2004), 'Pro-social behaviour, in a natural setting', *Journal of Economic Behavior and Organization*, **54** (1), 65–88.

Frey, B.S., and M. Osterloh (eds) (2001), *Successful Management by Motivation. Balancing Intrinsic and Extrinsic Incentives*, Berlin: Springer.

Furnham, A., and A. Lewis (1986), *The Economic Mind. The Social Psychology of Economic Behaviour*, Baltimore and Brighton: Wheatsheaf Books, Harvester Press.

Gibbons, R. (1992), *A Primer in Game Theory*, New York: Harvester Wheatsheaf.

Helson, H. (1964), *Adaptation-Level Theory: An Experimental and Systematic Approach to Behaviour*, New York: Harper and Row.

Hicks, J.R. (1934), 'A reconsideration of the theory of value', *Economica*, **1**, 52–75.

Hirshleifer, J. (1985), 'The expanding domain of economics', *American Economic Review*, **75**, 53–68.

Hogarth, R.M. and M.W. Reder (eds) (1987), *Rational Choice*, Chicago: University of Chicago Press.

Iannacone, L.R. (1991), 'The consequences of religions market structure: Adam Smith and the economics of religion', *Rationality and Society*, **2**, 156–77.

Iannacone, L.R. (1998), 'Introduction to the economics of religion', *Journal of Economic Literature*, **36** (4), 1465–96.

Inglehart, R.F. (1990), *Culture Shift in Advanced Industrial Society*, Princeton, NJ: Princeton University Press.

Jöhr, W.A. (1972), 'Zur Rolle des psychologischen Faktors in der Konjunkturtheorie', *Ifo-Studien*, **18**, 157–84.

Kahneman, D., and A. Tversky (1979), 'Prospect theory: an analysis of decision under risk', *Econometrica*, **47** (2), 263–91.

Kahneman, D., and A. Tversky (1984), 'Choices, values, and frames', *American Psychologist*, **39**, 341–50.

Kahneman, D., E. Diener and N. Schwartz (eds) (1999), '*Well-being, the Foundation of Hedonic Psychology*', New York: Russell Sage Foundation.

Kahneman, D., J. Knetsch and R. Thaler (1986), 'Fairness as a constraint on profit seeking: entitlements in the market', *American Economic Review*, **76** (3), 728–41.

Kahneman, D., P. Slovic and A. Tversky (eds) (1982), *Judgement under Uncertainty: Heuristics and Biases*, Cambridge: Cambridge University Press.

Katona, G. (1975), *Psychological Economics*, Amsterdam: Elsevier.
Laibson, D. (1997), 'Golden eggs and hyperbolic discounting', *Quarterly Journal of Economics*, **112** (2), 443–77.
Lazear, E.P. (2000), 'Economic imperialism', *Quarterly Journal of Economics*, **115** (1), 99–146.
Lea, S., R. Tarpy and P. Webley (1987), *The Individual and the Economy. A Survey of Economic Psychology*, Cambridge: Cambridge University Press.
Leibenstein, Harvey (1976), *Beyond Economic Man. A New Foundation for Microeconomics*, Cambridge, MA: Harvard University Press.
Lepper, M.R., and D. Greene (eds) (1978), *The Hidden Costs of Reward: New Perspectives on the Psychology of Human Motivation*, New York: Erlbaum.
Lewin, S. (1996), 'Economics and psychology: lessons for our own day from the early twentieth century', *Journal of Economic Literature*, **34** (3), 1293–323.
Loewenstein, G., and J. Lerner (2001), 'The role of affect in decision making', in Richard Davidson et al. (eds), *The Handbook of Affective Science*, Oxford: Oxford University Press.
Lucas, R., and E. Prescott (1971), 'Investment under uncertainty', *Econometrica*, **39**, 659–81.
MacFadyen, A., and H. MacFadyen (eds) (1987), *Economic Psychology: Intersections in Theory and Application*, Amsterdam: North-Holland.
Machina, M.J. (1987), 'Choice under uncertainty: problems solved and unsolved', *Journal of Economic Perspectives*, **1**, 121–54.
McDonald, D.N., H.J. Kagel and R.C. Battalio (1991), 'Animals choice under uncertain outcomes: further experimental results', *The Economic Journal*, 101, 1067–84.
Medoff, M.H. (1988), 'Constituencies, ideology, and the demand for abortion legalisation', *Public Choice*, **60**, 185–91.
Mullainathan, S., and Gruber, J. (2002), 'Do cigarette taxes make smokers happier?', NBER working paper no. 8872.
Mullainathan, S., and R. Thaler (2000), 'Behavioural economics', MIT working paper no. 00–27, Cambridge, MA.
Muth, J. (1961), 'Rational expectations and the theory of price movements', *Econometrica*, **29**, 315–35.
North, D.C. (1990), *Institutions, Institutional Change and Economic Performance*, Cambridge: Cambridge University Press.
Odean, T. (1998), 'Are investors reluctant to realize their losses?', *Journal of Finance*, **53** (5), 1775–98.
O'Donoghue, T., and M. Rabin (1999), 'Doing it now or later', *American Economic Review*, **89** (1), 103–24.
Ostrom, E. (1990), *Governing the Commons. The Evolution of Institutions for Collective Action*, Cambridge: Cambridge University Press.
Ostrom, E. (2000), 'Collective action and the evolution of social norms', *Journal of Economics Perspectives*, **13** (4), 137–58.
Ostrom, E., T. Dietz, N. Dolsak, P.C. Stern, S. Stonich and E. Weber (eds) (2002), *The Drama of The Commons*, Washington: National Academy Press.
Pittman, T.S. and J.F. Heller (1987), 'Social motivation', *Annual Review of Psychology*, **38**, 461–89.
Rabin, M. (1998), 'Psychology and economics', *Journal of Economic Literature*, **36** (1), 11–46.
Rabin, M. (2002), 'A perspective on psychology and economics', *European Economic Review*, **46** (4–5), 657–85.

Robbins, L.C. (1932), *An Essay on the Nature and Significance of Economic Science*, London: Macmillan, selections reprinted in Daniel M. Hausman (ed.), (1984), *The Philosophy of Economics: An Anthology*, New York: Cambridge University Press.

Samuelson, P. (1938), 'The numerical representation of ordered classifications and the concept of utility', *Review of Economic Studies*, **6** (1), 65–70.

Schmölders, G. (1962), *Volkswirtschaftslehre und Psychologie*, Reinbek: Berlin.

Schoemaker, P.J. (1982), 'The expected utility model: its variants, purposes, evidence and limitations', *Journal of Economic Literature*, **20**, 529–63.

Scitovsky, T. (1976), *The Joyless Economy: An Inquiry into Human Satisfaction and Dissatisfaction*, Oxford: Oxford University Press.

Shiller, R.J. (2000), *Irrational Exuberance*, Princeton, NJ: Princeton University Press.

Shleifer, A. (2000), *Inefficient Markets: An Introduction to Behavioural Finance*, Clarendon Lectures, New York: Oxford University Press.

Simon, H.A. (1978), 'Rationality as a process and product of thought', *American Economic Review*, **68** (2), 1–16.

Smith, V. L. (1962), 'An experimental study of competitive market behaviour', *Journal of Political Economy*, **70**, 111–37.

Starmer, C. (2000), 'Developments in non-expected utility: the hunt for a descriptive theory of choice under risk', *Journal of Economic Literature*, **38** (2), 332–82

Stigler, G.J. and G.S. Becker (1977), 'De gustibus non est disputandum', *American Economic Review*, **67**, 76–90.

Thaler, R.H. (1992), *The Winner's Curse. Paradoxes and Anomalies of Economic Life*, New York: Free Press.

Tversky, A., and D. Kahneman (1974), 'Judgement under uncertainty: heuristics and biases', *Science*, **185**, 1124–31.

Van Raaij, W.F., G. van Veldhoven and K. Waerneryd (eds) (1988), *Handbook of Economic Psychology*, Dordrecht: Kluwer.

Winkelmann, L., and R. Winkelmann (1998), 'Why are the unemployed so unhappy? Evidence from panel data', *Economica*, **65** (257), 1–15.

Winston, G. C. (1980), 'Addiction and backsliding: a theory of compulsive consumption', *Journal of Economic Behaviour and Organization*, **1**, 295–324.

5 Institutional economics: from Menger and Veblen to Coase and North

Geoffrey M. Hodgson

Introduction

Institutional economics is now a major subdiscipline, with important applications to studies of business, developing economies, transitional economies, property rights and much else. Prominent names in this 'new institutional economics' include the Nobel Laureates Ronald Coase and Douglass North, as well as Oliver Williamson – the most highly cited economist of all time. In some respects their work continues a tradition which can be traced back to Carl Menger in the nineteenth century. Modern 'new institutional economics' was also preceded in America in the interwar period by another tradition of 'institutional economics', inspired by Thorstein Veblen, Wesley Mitchell and John Commons. For a time this was pervasive in leading American universities and research institutes.

This entry surveys both the 'new' and the 'old' institutional economics, with a focus on some important theoretical and philosophical issues. Foremost among these are the questions of methodological individualism, the depicted relationship between individuals and institutions, and the nature of institutions themselves. These issues tie in closely with the question of the relationship between agency and structure, which is central to the philosophy of the social sciences.

It is proposed here that there are distinguishing and characteristic theoretical approaches within both the 'old' and the 'new' institutionalism, and hence in some respects the two traditions contrast with each other. However, it is important to emphasize that there are not only important theoretical and philosophical differences *between* each camp, but also *within* each camp. Furthermore, these internal differences are no less great if we turn to matters of policy and politics. It is possible to find conservative defenders of capitalism, institutional reformers, critics of unrestrained markets, and advocates of socialism or planning that are prominent in *both* the old and the new institutional economics. The two schools are not readily distinguishable in terms of ideology. In any case, our fundamental concern here is not with matters of policy but with the theoretical and philosophical foundations of each school.

Three sections follow. The first discusses an essential characteristic of the old institutional economics and identifies some of the problems involved. The second examines the central theoretical project of the new institutionalism and some of the recent criticisms of its plausibility. The third and final section discusses some of the recent partial convergences between the old and the new institutionalism and the agenda for further enquiry. It is argued that a reformulated institutionalist project is beginning to emerge.

A central theme of the 'old' institutional economics

A common theme pervades institutionalism, from the writings of Veblen in the 1890s to those of John Kenneth Galbraith in more recent decades. A notion that the individual is not given, but can be reconstituted by institutions, pervades that tradition. For instance, in 1909 Veblen (1919, pp. 242–3) wrote:

> The wants and desires, the end and the aim, the ways and the means, the amplitude and drift of the individual's conduct are functions of an institutional variable that is of a highly complex and wholly unstable character.

Likewise, writing in 1899, Commons (1965, p. 3) saw institutions as 'shaping each individual'. Commons (1934, p. 73–4) made it clear that 'the individual with whom we are dealing is the Institutionalized Mind. ... Individuals ... meet each other ... prepared more or less by habit, induced by the pressure of custom'. Mitchell (1910, p. 203) made a similar point:

> Social concepts are the core of social institutions. The latter are but prevalent habits of thought which have gained general acceptance as norms for guiding conduct. In this form the social concepts attain a certain prescriptive authority over the individual. The daily use by all members of a social group unremittingly molds those individuals into common patterns without their knowledge, and occasionally interposes definite obstacles in the path of men who wish to act in original ways.

In his study of the evolution of money as an institution, Mitchell (1937, p. 371) emphasized how it changed human mentality and nature:

> Now the money economy ... is in fact one of the most potent institutions in our whole culture. In sober truth it stamps its pattern upon wayward human nature, makes us all react in standard ways to the standard stimuli it offers, and affects our very ideals of what is good, beautiful and true.

Similarly, Clarence Ayres (1944, p. 84) explained:

> 'wants' are not primary. They are not inborn physical mechanisms and they are certainly not spiritual attributes. They are social habits. For every individual their point of origin is in the mores of his community; and even these traditions have a natural history and are subject to modification in the general process of social change.

The idea that individual tastes are not given, but are shaped by institutional circumstances and by particular influences such as advertising, is a major theme in the writings of Galbraith. For instance, Galbraith (1969, p. 152) insisted that individual 'wants can be synthesized by advertising, catalysed by salesmanship, and shaped by the discreet manipulations of the persuaders'. The theme persists throughout his writings. Indeed, no author has brought these ideas to the attention of the modern reader more clearly and resolutely than Galbraith. His analysis puts particular emphasis on the effects of advertising on individual wants. This is one version of the core institutionalist story. More generally, institutionalists recognize the potential influence of many institutions on individual habits, conceptions, and preferences.

Such ideas permeate and endure through the 'old' institutionalism as a whole. The 'old' institutionalism is distinguished from both mainstream economics and the 'new institutional economics' precisely for the reason that it does not assume a given individual, with given purposes or preference functions. Instead of a bedrock of given individuals, presumed by the mainstream and new institutional economics, the old institutionalism holds to the idea of interactive and partially malleable agents, mutually entwined in a web of partially durable and self-reinforcing institutions. No other criterion demarcates so clearly the old institutional economics, on the one hand, from new institutional and mainstream economics on the other (Hodgson 1988, 2004).

Note that the acceptance of the institutionalized individual does not immediately rule out the possibility that institutionalism and neoclassical economics may be complementary. Although Veblen wished to purge economics of classical and neoclassical errors, other institutionalists searched for some complementarity between neoclassical and institutional economics. This group included leading institutionalists such as Commons, Mitchell, John Maurice Clark and Arthur F. Burns. They all saw institutionalism as compatible with aspects of Marshallian price theory. This is a controversial position. But the complete exclusion of any element of neoclassical economics from institutionalism would rule out Commons and several others from the institutionalist canon.

Having identified the most important common theme in old institutionalism, it is necessary to enquire more deeply into its meaning. Several versions of this doctrine have surfaced over the years. It is also necessary to deal with some potential misunderstandings and rebuttals. Perhaps the most frequent attack on the notion that individual tastes and preferences are moulded by circumstances is the criticism that this leads to some kind of structural or cultural determinism. The individual, it is said, is made a puppet of social or cultural circumstances.

Admittedly, some old institutionalists have promoted such a view. When Ayres (1961, p. 175) wrote that 'there is no such thing as an individual' he was giving succour to such ideas (Rutherford 1994, pp. 40–41). The danger is to see social order as *exclusively* a 'top down' process in which individuals are formed and cajoled by institutions, with a neglect of individual autonomy and agency.

·The Ayresian version of the old institutionalism has been so prominent in the post-1945 era that many commentators wrongly take it to be representative of institutionalism as a whole.

However, such exclusively 'top down' versions of the core institutionalist idea are not common to all old institutionalists. This is clearly the case with both Veblen and Commons. For instance, Veblen (1919, p. 243) argues that institutions are the outcome of individual behaviour and habituation, as well as institutions affecting individuals:

> The growth and mutations of the institutional fabric are an outcome of the conduct of the individual members of the group, since it is out of the experience of the individuals, through the habituation of individuals, that institutions arise; and it is in this same experience that these institutions act to direct and define the aims and end of conduct.

Writing in 1899, Commons (1965, pp. 6–8) wrote similarly of the dependence of institutions upon beliefs:

> Social beliefs ... furnish the basis in the affections of each person which alone makes possible his responsiveness to the appeals of those with whom he must coöperate. The institution in which he finds himself is both the cause and effect of his beliefs. ... Common beliefs and desires are the vitalizing, active force within the institution.

These statements show a valid recognition of both the dependence of institutions upon individuals and the moulding of individuals by institutions. In the writings of Veblen and Commons there is both upward and downward causation; individuals create and change institutions, just as institutions mould and constrain individuals. Institutionalism is not necessarily confined to the 'top down' cultural and institutional determinism with which it is sometimes associated.

A merit of the institutionalist idea that institutions shape individual behaviour is that it admits an enhanced concept of power into economic analysis. Power is not simply coercion. For Steven Lukes (1974), the over-emphasis on the coercive aspect of power ignores the way that it is often exercised more subtly – and often without overt conflict. He points out that supreme power is exercised by orchestrating the thoughts and desires of others. These considerations are absent from mainstream economics. Preference functions are not subject to 'reconstitutive downward causation' from institutions to individuals (Hodgson 2002, 2004).

Learning typically takes place through and within social structures, and at least in this sense it is an important case of reconstitutive downward causation. Neoclassical economics has difficulty accommodating the notion of learning because the very idea of 'rational learning' is problematic. It treats learning as the cumulative discovery of pre-existing 'blueprint' information, as stimulus and response, or as the Bayesian updating of subjective probability estimates in the light of incoming data. However, instead of the mere input of 'facts' to given individuals, learning is a developmental and reconstitutive process. Learning involves adaptation to changing circumstances, and such adaptations mean the reconstitution of the individuals involved. Furthermore, institutions and cultures play a vital role in establishing the concepts and norms of the learning process (Hodgson 1988).

The single most important characteristic of institutionalism is the idea that the individual is socially and institutionally constituted. The argument here is that all the old institutional economists, from Veblen to Galbraith, embrace the notion that the individual is moulded by cultural or institutional circumstances. Within institutionalism, there are many variants of this view.

By adopting this approach, conceptions of social power and learning are placed at the centre of economic analysis. This means that institutionalism is more able to address questions of structural change and long-term economic development, including the problems of less-developed economies and the transformation processes in the former Soviet bloc countries. On the other hand, the analysis becomes much more complicated and less open to formal modelling. In normative terms, the individual is no longer taken as the best judge of his or her welfare. This opens up the difficult question of the discernment and evaluation of human needs.

In mainstream economics, it is partly because of perceived difficulties of analytical tractability that individuals are often taken as given. To assume otherwise would seem to make things much too complicated. The old institutionalist ideas might seem reasonable (as long as exclusively 'top down' approaches are avoided and an explanatory role for the individual is retained), but their theoretical application may seem to encounter insurmountable problems of analytical tractability.

The classic 'new' institutionalist project
By contrast, a unifying theoretical project in the 'new institutional economics' is to explain the existence of political, legal, or social, institutions by reference to a model of given, individual behaviour, tracing out its consequences in terms of human interactions. The explanatory movement is from individuals to institutions, taking individuals as primary and given. An initial institution-free 'state of nature' is typically assumed.

For example, in a book first published in German in 1871, Carl Menger (1871 [1981]) pioneered a basic analysis of how institutions evolve. He saw many institutions emanating in an unplanned and unforeseen process, from the rational decisions and interactions of individual agents. His chosen example was the institution of money. Menger saw money as emanating in an undesigned manner from the interactions of individual agents. He started with a barter economy and its well-known problem of a lack of a general 'double coincidence of wants'. To deal with this problem, traders look for a convenient and frequently exchanged commodity to use in their exchanges with others. Once such usages become prominent, a circular process of institutional self-reinforcement takes place. Emerging to overcome the difficulties of barter, a prototypical money is chosen because it is a frequently-used commodity, and its use becomes all the more frequent because it is chosen. Money is chosen because it is convenient, and it is convenient because it is chosen. This circular positive feedback leads to the emergence of the institution of money.

Once convenient regularities emerge, a circular process of institutional self-reinforcement takes place. Apart from the emergence of money, other examples in this literature include driving on one side of the road and traffic conventions at road junctions (Elster 1989; Schotter 1981; Sugden 1986; Ullmann-Margalit 1977; Young 1996). For instance, once the convention of driving on the left of the road is established in a country, it is clearly rational for all drivers to follow the same rule.

In the above cases, the typical starting point is a set of given individuals. Although in many cases it is not strictly a theoretically necessary starting point, it is often asserted as necessary or desirable. The injunction that institutions should be explained entirely in terms of given individuals, perhaps including some assumptions as to how they are related together, is a version of methodological individualism. This term is used in several different ways, but one strong and prominent usage is the doctrine that all social phenomena should be explained solely in terms of the properties of, intentions of, and relations between, given individuals.

This focus on individuals as the ultimate elements in the explanation is clearly evident, for example, in North's (1981) theory of the development of capitalism, Coase's (1937) and Williamson's (1975, 1985) transaction cost analysis of the firm, and Schotter's (1981) general game-theoretic analysis of institutions. In all these cases, the proposal is to start with given individuals and their interactions, and from that starting point to move on to explain institutions.

The value of this work should not be denied. Substantial heuristic insights about the development of institutions and conventions have been gained on the basis of the assumption of given, rational individuals. The main problem addressed here is the inherent incompleteness of the research programme in its attempt to provide a general theory of the emergence and evolution of institutions.

A fundamental criticism has been advanced by Alexander Field (1979, 1981, 1984). In attempting to explain the origin of social institutions, the new institutional economics has to presume given individuals acting in a certain context. Along with the assumption of given individuals, is the assumption of given rules of behaviour governing their interaction. What is forgotten is that in the original, hypothetical, 'state of nature' from which institutions are seen to have emerged, a number of weighty rules, institutions and cultural and social norms have already been presumed. Arguably, these original institutions, roles and norms are unavoidable: even in an unreal 'thought experiment' we can never properly envisage an original 'state of nature' without them.

For example, game theorists such as Schotter (1981) take the individual 'for granted', as an agent unambiguously maximizing his or her expected payoff. Further, in attempting to explain the origin of institutions through game theory, Field points out that certain norms and rules must inevitably be presumed at the start. There can be no games without rules, and thus game theory can never explain the elemental rules themselves. As Field (1984, p. 703) argues:

> Game theorists sometimes become so enamored of the mechanics of the theory and the single-minded determination of their players to win that they lose sight of what any game-theoretic problem presupposes: the arena in which the players are to compete or cooperate. ... it is theoretically possible to develop for the game of chess ... a theory that would predict what actions a rational opponent interested in winning would undertake given the layout of the board and the next move one makes. But one will not obtain ... an explanation for why knights move in an L-shaped pattern or bishops move diagonally. Similarly, although one can investigate with game theory the dilemmas possibly faced by two prisoners, one should not expect from such a theory an explanation for why escape or insurrection is not part of the strategy space.

Even in a sequence of repeated games, or of games about other (nested) games, at least one game or meta-game, with a structure and payoffs, must be assumed at the outset. Any such attempt to deal with history in terms of sequential or nested games is thus involved in a problem of infinite regress: even with games about games about games to the nth degree there is still one preceding game left to be explained.

As another example, Williamson's transaction cost theory of the firm takes its original state of nature as the market. He writes that 'in the beginning there were markets' (Williamson 1975, p. 20; 1985, p. 143). This starting point is characteristic of his approach. From this original context, some individuals go on to create firms and hierarchies. He argues that these endure if they involve lower transaction costs.

However, the market itself is an institution. The market involves social norms and customs, instituted exchange relations, and – sometimes consciously organized – information networks that themselves have to be explained (Hodgson 1988, 1998a). Market and exchange relations themselves involve complex rules.

Markets are not an institution-free beginning. Hence Williamson fails to explain the firm from an institution-free 'state of nature'. In a type of comparative static approach, he assumes one institutional framework and derives another.

Accordingly, the 'new' institutionalist project of starting simply from given individuals is abandoned.

In particular, the institution of private property itself requires explanation. Williamson addressed the latter problem in an excursion into legal theory, arguing that property can emerge through 'private ordering', that is, individual-to-individual transactions, without state legislation or interference (Williamson 1983).

The possibility of property and contract without any role for the state has been challenged (Sened 1997; Mantzavinos 2001, ch. 8). However, there is another fundamental objection. Even if the state is absent, individuals rely on customs, norms, and, most emphatically, the institution of language, in order to interact. Interpersonal communication, which is essential to all stories of institutional emergence, itself depends on linguistic and other rules and norms.

For instance, the shared concept of individual property requires some means of communication using common concepts and norms, both before and after explicit or tacit recognition of property rights can be established. Even if the state can be absent from these processes, some prior institutions are still required.

There are good reasons why the starting point of a given individual is generally misconceived. Choosing requires a conceptual framework to make sense of the world. The reception of information by individuals in the new institutionalist explanatory project requires a paradigm or cognitive frame to process and make sense of that information. Further, our interaction with others requires the use of language. Language itself is an institution. We cannot understand the world without concepts and we cannot communicate without some form of language. As the old institutionalists argue, the transmission of information from institution to individual is impossible without a coextensive process of *enculturation*, in which the individual learns the meaning and value of the sense-data that is communicated. The transmission of information between agents *always and necessarily* involves such a process of enculturation. In general, the new institutional economists have devoted insufficient attention to this point.

In the old institutional economics, cognition and habit have a prior and central place in the story. This may be expected from a school of thought that insists that 'institutions are an outgrowth of habit' (Veblen 1919, p. 241). Knowledge and learning are stressed. But the crucial difference is the insistence that the perception of information is not possible without prior habits of thought to endow it with meaning. Without such habits, agents cannot perceive or make use of the data received by their senses. Habits thus have a crucial cognitive role. As Veblen (1914, p. 53) put it: 'All facts of observation are necessarily seen in the light of the observer's habits of thought'. Furthermore, acquired habits and conceptual frameworks are seen to reflect culturally-based social norms and rules.

What is being contested here is the possibility of using given individuals as the institution-free starting point in the explanation. Institutions are structures which at least constrain and influence individuals. Accordingly, if there are institutional influences on individuals and their goals, then these are worthy of explanation. In turn, the explanation of those may be in terms of other purposeful individuals. But where should the analysis stop? The purposes of an individual could be partly explained by relevant institutions, culture and so on. These, in their turn, would be partly explained in terms of other individuals. But these individual purposes and actions could then be partly explained by cultural and institutional factors, and so on, indefinitely. We are involved in an apparently infinite regress, similar to the puzzle 'which came first, the chicken or the egg?' Such an analysis never reaches an end point. It is simply arbitrary to stop at one particular stage in the explanation and say 'it is all reducible to individuals' just as much as to say it is 'all social and institutional'. As Robert Nozick (1977, p.359) remarks in his critique of methodological individualism: 'In this apparent chicken and egg situation, why aren't we equally methodological institutionalists?' The key point is that in this infinite regress, neither individual nor institutional factors have legitimate explanatory primacy. The idea that all explanations have ultimately to be in terms of individuals (or institutions) is thus unfounded.

There is thus an unbreakable circle of determination. This does not mean, however, that institutions and individuals have equivalent ontological and explanatory status. Clearly, they have different characteristics. Individuals are purposeful, whereas institutions are not, at least not in the same sense. Institutions have different lifespans from individuals, sometimes enduring the passing of the individuals they contain. Their mechanisms of reproduction and procreation are very different.

All theories must first build from elements which are taken as given. However, the particular problem of infinite regress identified here undermines any 'new institutionalist' claim that the explanation of the emergence of institutions can start from some kind of institution-free ensemble of (rational) individuals in which there is supposedly no rule or institution to be explained. At the very minimum, new institutionalist stories of the development of institutions depend upon interpersonal communication of information. And the communication of information itself requires shared conventions, rules, routines and norms. These, in turn, have to be explained. Consequently, the new institutionalist project to explain the emergence of institutions on the basis of given individuals runs into difficulties, particularly with regard to the conceptualization of the initial state from which institutions are supposed to emerge.

This does not mean that new institutionalist research is without value, but it suggests that the starting point of explanations cannot be institution-free: the main project has to be reformulated as just a part of a wider theoretical analysis of institutions. The reformulated project would stress the evolution of institutions, in part from other institutions, rather than from a hypothetical, institution-free 'state of nature'. It is not suggested that there is a ready-made answer. It simply means that the question of how institutions emerge from an imaginary and original world with individuals but without institutions is misconceived. What is required is a theory of process, development and learning, rather than a theory that proceeds from an original 'state of nature' that is both artificial and untenable.

Abandoning the classic new institutionalist project does not mean that all of the insights of the new institutional economics have to be abandoned. Many of these are of lasting importance. The contribution of transaction cost analysis can be singled out for mention here. Building on the earlier work of Coase, Williamson (1975, 1985) has made a major contribution to the analysis of the nature, boundaries and structure of the firm, by use of the concept of transaction costs. In particular, Williamson significantly extended Coase's analysis by applying the transaction cost analysis to the internal structure of the firm. What is relatively unexplored, however, is the extent to which a transaction cost explanation may complement rather than displace other explanations of phenomena related to the firm (Hodgson 1998b). Transaction costs also play a major role in the work of North (1981, 1990). However, North (1990) departs from Williamson in stressing the path dependence and possible suboptimality of some institutional outcomes. Overall, transaction cost analysis is a major achievement of the new institutional economics.

Recent developments and convergences
The 'old' institutional economics had strong evolutionary overtones. One of the reasons for the rehabilitation of 'evolutionary' thinking in economics since the early 1980s has been an attempt to break the constraints of the 'comparative statics' mode of explanation with its two fixed end-points. Accordingly, moves away from comparative statics and towards a more evolutionary and open-ended framework of analysis, within what is regarded as the new institutionalism, have unwittingly led to a degree of convergence with the evolutionary and open-ended ideas of the old institutionalists. This is apparent in the later works of Hayek (1982, 1988) and the more recent writings of North (1990, 1994). We are reminded of Veblen's (1919, p. 37) search for 'a theory of the process of consecutive change, realized to be self-continuing or self-propagating and to have no final term'.

A reformulated institutionalist project would stress the evolution of institutions, in part from other institutions, rather than from a hypothetical, institution-free 'state of nature'. Notably, in recent years, a number of significant studies have developed in this direction. Accordingly, Jack Knight (1992) criticizes much of the new institutionalist literature for neglecting the importance of distributional and power considerations in the emergence and development of institutions. Even more clearly, Masahiko Aoki (2001) identifies the problem of infinite regress in much of the former literature and develops a novel approach. He not only takes individuals as given, but also a historically bestowed set of institutions. With these materials, he explores the evolution of further institutions, using game theory. The next step, which Aoki recognizes but does not fully complete, is to develop a more evolutionary and open-ended framework of analysis. Instead of focusing on just two points in time – the given starting point and the evolved outcome – the next step is to develop an evolutionary approach, in which the emphasis is on the ongoing process of change.

Once we take a step in the direction of a more open-ended evolutionary approach, another question is raised. If in principle every component in the system can evolve, then so too can individual preferences. Of course, most economists recognize that preferences are malleable in the real world. But they have often taken the assumption of fixed preferences as a reasonable, simplifying assumption. In contrast, the possibility is raised here that some malleability of preferences may be necessary to explain fully the evolution and stability of institutions.

What is proposed here is a contingent and tentative hypothesis. We may briefly sketch out a possible argument along the following lines. The institutional*izing* function of institutions means that a degree of order and relative stability can be reinforced despite variety and diversity at the microeconomic level. Institutions involve rules, constraints, practices and ideas that can – through psychological and social mechanisms that have to be specified – sometimes mould individual purposes and preferences in some way. This preference malleability could improve the possibility and stability of an emergent institution and overcome difficulties in some cases where institutions fail to emerge.

As noted above, such intuitions can be found in the writings of the neglected tradition of 'old' institutionalism. However, what is lacking in much of this literature is a clear exposition of the causal processes involved. It is one thing to claim that institutions affect individuals in a process of downward causation. It is another to explain in detail the causes and effects. The most satisfactory explanation of the relevant processes in the writings of the 'old' institutionalists was in the writings of Veblen (1899, p. 190), who wrote: 'The situation of today shapes the institutions of tomorrow through a selective, coercive process, by acting upon men's habitual view of things'.

From this viewpoint, inspired by pragmatist philosophy and habit–instinct psychology, the key element in this process is habit. Habits themselves are formed through repetition of action or thought. They are influenced by prior activity and have durable, self-sustaining qualities. However, within this paradigm, and contrary to some popular formulations, habit does not mean behaviour. According to many authors writing broadly in this tradition since William James and John

Dewey, it is a *propensity* to behave in particular ways in a particular class of situations (Camic 1986; Margolis 1994; Murphy 1994). Crucially, we may have habits that lie unused for a long time. A habit may exist even if it is not manifest in behaviour. Habits are submerged repertoires of potential behaviour; they can be triggered by an appropriate stimulus or context.

Our habits help to make up our preferences and dispositions. When new habits are acquired or existing habits change, then our preferences alter. Dewey (1922, p. 40) thus wrote of 'the cumulative effect of insensible modifications worked by a particular habit in the body of preferences'. Crucially, institutional changes and constraints can cause changes in habits of thought and behaviour. Institutions constrain our behaviour and develop our habits in specific ways. What does happen is that the framing, shifting and constraining capacities of social institutions give rise to new perceptions and dispositions within individuals.

Institutions are enduring systems of socially ingrained rules. They channel and constrain behaviour so that individuals form new habits as a result. At the level of the human agent, there are no mysterious 'social forces' controlling individuals, other than those affecting the actions and communications of human actors. People do not develop new preferences, wants or purposes simply because 'values' or 'social forces' control them. What does happen is that the framing, shifting and constraining capacities of social institutions give rise to new perceptions and dispositions within individuals. Upon new habits of thought and behaviour, new preferences and intentions emerge.

As above, this process of habit formation, resulting from institutional channels and constraints, is described above as 'reconstitutive downward causation'. The crucial point in the argument here is to recognize the significance of reconstitutive downward causation on *habits*, rather than merely on behaviour, intentions or beliefs. Clearly, the definitional distinction between habit (as a propensity or disposition) and behaviour (or action) is essential to make sense of this statement. Once habits become established they become a potential basis for new intentions or beliefs. As a result, shared habits are the constitutive material of institutions, providing them with enhanced durability, power and normative authority.

A pressing issue for future research is the extent to which these mechanisms of habituation play a role in different cases of institutional evolution. What is being proposed here is; first, the possibility of a viable causal mechanism by which institutions can lead to changes in individual purposes and preferences; second, the possibility that such mechanisms may lead to some degree of conformity; and third, the possibility that such conformism may help to strengthen and sustain the institution in question.

To recapitulate, two important and connected issues have been raised here as part of a future research agenda. The first is the possibility of institutions having a reconstitutive effect on the preferences of individual actors. The second is the key element in the mechanism of reconstitution: the formation of habits through the operation of institutional channels and constraints.

The rediscovery of the role of habit in human behaviour and the realization of the powerful role of institutional constraints, together point to the development of a research agenda focused on the reconstitutive effects of institutions on individuals, and on the degree to which institutional evolution may depend on the formation of concordant habits.

Clearly, there are many different types of institution and they can emerge and evolve in different ways. Some institutions – such as language – appear and develop with little planning or state interference. A question of importance is: what other institutions can emerge in a similarly spontaneous manner? Alternatively, is the assistance of a powerful, pre-existing institution required to create or sustain some other institutions? As well as language, we here consider two more examples: the institutions of money and of contract.

In the earlier versions of his theory of the evolution of money, Menger saw the emerging monetary unit as homogeneous and invariant. In this case there is no possibility of quality variation, debasement or forgery. In contrast, with potential quality variation, the purity and value of the emerging monetary unit may be in doubt. Some actors may notice the high frequency of the trade in a particular commodity, but regard the commodity in question as unreliable and thereby avoid it as a medium of exchange.

In later discussions, Menger did raise the question of potential and covert quality variation of money. In his article on 'Geld', Menger recognized that the problem of potential quality variation could be so serious that the state had to play a role. Menger (1909 [1936], p. 42) thus wrote: 'Only the state has the power to protect effectively the coins and other means of exchange which are circulated, against the issue of false coins, illegal reductions of weight and other violations that impede trade'. Nevertheless, Menger applied this argument to a 'developed economy' only. He was reluctant to admit that the state was necessary to protect the integrity of the monetary unit at earlier stages of economic development, and he still clung to his view that, in essence, money was a phenomenon independent of the state. Arguably, however, debasement is a potential problem at the inception of money, not merely at its developed stage.

Of course, another strong institution, or coalition of traders, may be able to overcome some of these problems, as an alternative to the state. However, there is a particular reason why the state is more likely to take this role. While Menger was right to emphasize that many social institutions emerge and develop without a conscious plan, it is often the case that an institution reaches an important stage of development when it becomes consciously recognized and legitimated by other institutions. Symbol and ceremony have an important part here. Money has self-regulating and spontaneous properties, but typically it is also endorsed by another powerful socio-economic institution. Although state decree alone is far from sufficient to create money, as a commanding social institution at the apex of the legal system, the state is well positioned to take on this declaratory and legitimizing role. In legitimating a monetary unit and helping to engender trust in it, the state relies on its crucial symbolic as well as its legislative powers. Menger's original account of the origin of money as a purely spontaneous process downplays these declaratory aspects and their symbolic representations. This argument does not imply that the state is necessarily the best or more efficient solution. It suggests that the state is well-positioned to take a regulatory role.

If legal or state instruments are necessary to some degree for the full development of money, then these elements could reasonably account for part of the essence of money itself: they are more than mere accidental, historical appearances. As a result, Menger's argument against the 'state theory of money' – as promoted by the German historical school and others – would lose some of its impact. Furthermore, if the state and other institutions are necessary at the very point of conception of money, then they, along with individuals, have to enter as elements in the explanation of its emergence and development (Bell 2001; Ingham 2000; Wray 2000).

It is reasonable to ask the question why the evolution of the institution of money may require some state involvement but, in contrast, institutions such as language may emerge spontaneously. It has been argued elsewhere (Hodgson 1993, 2004) that a crucial difference is whether or not an institution has intrinsic error-correcting or self-policing mechanisms. For example, individuals have an incentive to make their words clear. As an essential condition of communication, the coding itself (the signifier) must be unmistakable, even if the meaning (the signified) remains partly ambiguous. In communication we have strong incentives and inclinations to use words and sounds in a way that conforms as closely as possible to the perceived norm. Although languages do change through time, there are incentives to conform to, and thus reinforce, the linguistic norms in the given region or context. Norms of language and pronunciation are thus largely self-policing.

Similarly, some legal rules have a strong self-policing element. For example, there are obvious incentives to stop at red traffic lights and to drive on the same side of the road as others. Although infringements will occur, these particular laws can be partly enforced by motorists themselves. However, things are very different with many other laws and institutions. Laws that restrict behaviour, where there are substantial, perceived net advantages to transgression, are the ones that require the most policing. Hence people frequently evade tax payments or break speed limits.

Any self-policing mechanisms can be undermined if there is the possibility of undetected variation from the norm and there is sufficient incentive to exert such variations. Language and money differ in this respect. The argument for the intervention and policing of the state is thus much stronger in the case of money and some laws, than in the case of language.

Another recent development in the new institutional economics also brings the state back into the analysis. In his analysis of contract and private property, the institutional economist Itai Sened (1995, 1997) has challenged the notion of property without the state. Sened (1995, p. 162) notes:

> Like traditional economists, most game theorists systematically overlook the role of law enforcement. ... Many important social institutions do not emerge as equilibria in games among equal agents, but as equilibria in games among agents who control old institutions and agents who challenge such institutions with new demands. In particular, governments play a crucial role in the evolution of institutions that protect individual rights.

In his extended critique of the notion of property without law, Sened (1997) argues that true individual rights are established only when a territorial institution establishes its monopoly over the use of force. Sened's argument departs significantly from that of Robert Sugden (1986, p. 5) and others, who argue that legal codes 'merely formalize ... conventions of behaviour' that have evolved out of individual interactions. However, to accept the role of the state in the evolution of property and contract is not to romanticize this institution. Sened sees the state not as a benevolent and disinterested legislator but as an institution whose members pursue their own interests.

Sened develops something redolent of the Hobbesian 'social contract'. This 'social contract' is not just between individuals in agreeing laws and rights, but also between the individuals and the state. For Sened, governments weight the benefits of granting rights against the cost of enforcement. He writes:

> Governments do not erect such structures out of benevolence or moral concern. They grant and protect rights in order to promote their own interests. But in doing so, they fulfil two crucial social functions. The function of maintaining law and order that is a necessary condition for economic growth and affluence, and the function of arbitrage between conflicting interests. (Sened, 1997, p. 123)

In addition, Sened shows the limitations of the aforementioned type of game-theoretical model involving a few agents. With a larger number of players it is more difficult for individuals to establish mutual and reciprocal arrangements that ensure contract compliance. If trading coalitions do emerge, then these themselves take upon state-like qualities to enforce agreements and protect property. In a world of incomplete and imperfect information, high transaction costs, asymmetrically powerful relations and agents with limited insight, powerful institutions are necessary to enforce rights. These institutions result from a complex bargaining process. Sened uses an n-person prisoner's dilemma to show that the introduction of a government, enforcing rights, can often improve on a sub-optimal outcome.

It is an open question as to whether another strong institution, apart from the state, could fulfil this necessary role. However, it is not to endorse or glorify the state if we start analytically from the likelihood and reality that a state will emerge and analyse its possible role on the process of establishment of property.

Individual property is not mere possession; it involves socially acknowledged and enforced rights. Individual property, therefore, is not a purely individual matter. It is not simply a relation between an individual and an object. It requires a powerful, customary and legal apparatus of recognition, adjudication and enforcement. Such legal systems make their first substantial appearance within the state apparatuses of ancient civilization. Since that time, states have played a major role in the establishment, enforcement and adjudication of property rights.

At the same time, the development of any state apparatus carries the omnipresent danger that individual private property would be wilfully appropriated by the state, perhaps using the ancient norms and precedents of communal tenure. The state has the capacity to appropriate, as well as to protect, private property. For private property to be relatively secure, a particular form of state had to emerge, countered by powerful and multiple interest groups in civil society. This meant a pluralistic state with some separation of powers, backed up by a plurality of group interests in the community at large. With such a balance of power, a framework of constitutional law could be established, in which the interests of both the state and the citizenry could be protected to some degree. According to this line of argument, the emergence of a powerful institution like the state is a necessary but not a sufficient condition for the protection of property and other individual rights.

Conclusion

In conclusion, this survey of issues that are current in both the old and new institutionalism shows that there is a growing overlap in areas of research and the possibility of fruitful dialogue between the two schools. The extreme individualism of the new institutional economics in its earlier forms is being challenged from inside as well as outside that school. What emerges as 'institutional economics' in the next few decades may turn out to be very different from what was prominent in the 1980s and 1990s, and it may trace its genealogy from the old as well as the new institutionalism.

Acknowledgement

The author is very grateful to John Davis, Alain Marciano and Jochen Runde for helpful comments on an earlier version of this chapter.

References

Aoki, Masahiko (2001), *Toward a Comparative Institutional Analysis,* Cambridge, MA: MIT Press.

Ayres, Clarence E. (1944), *The Theory of Economic Progress,* 1st edn, Chapel Hill, NC: University of North Carolina Press.

Ayres, Clarence E. (1961), *Toward a Reasonable Society: The Values of Industrial Civilization,* Austin, TX: University of Texas Press.

Bell, Stephanie A. (2001), 'The role of the state and the hierarchy of money', *Cambridge Journal of Economics,* **25** (2), March, 149–63.

Camic, Charles (1986), 'The matter of habit', *American Journal of Sociology,* **91** (5), 1039–87.

Coase, Ronald H. (1937), 'The nature of the firm', *Economica,* **4**, November, 386–405.

Commons, John R. (1934), *Institutional Economics – Its Place in Political Economy,* New York: Macmillan.

Commons, John R. (1965), *A Sociological View of Sovereignty,* reprinted from the *American Journal of Sociology* (1899–1900) and edited with an introduction by Joseph Dorfman, New York: Augustus Kelley.

Dewey, John (1922), *Human Nature and Conduct: An Introduction to Social Psychology,* 1st edn, New York: Holt.

Elster, Jon (1989), *Nuts and Bolts for the Social Sciences,* Cambridge: Cambridge University Press.

Field, Alexander J. (1979), 'On the explanation of rules using rational choice models', *Journal of Economic Issues,* **13** (1), March, 49–72.

Field, Alexander J. (1981), 'The problem with neoclassical institutional economics: a critique with special reference to the North/Thomas model of pre-1500 Europe', *Explorations in Economic History,* **18** (2), April, 174–98.

Field, Alexander J. (1984), 'Microeconomics, norms and rationality', *Economic Development and Cultural Change,* **32** (4), July, 683–711.

Galbraith, John Kenneth (1969), *The New Industrial State,* Harmondsworth: Penguin.

Hayek, Friedrich A. (1982), *Law, Legislation and Liberty,* 3-volume combined edn, London: Routledge and Kegan Paul.

Hayek, Friedrich A. (1988), *The Fatal Conceit: The Errors of Socialism. The Collected Works of Friedrich August Hayek, Vol. I,* edited by William W. Bartley III, London: Routledge.

Hodgson, Geoffrey M. (1988), *Economics and Institutions: A Manifesto for a Modern Institutional Economics,* Cambridge and Philadelphia: Polity Press and University of Pennsylvania Press.

Hodgson, Geoffrey M. (1993), *Economics and Evolution: Bringing Life Back Into Economics,* Cambridge, and Ann Arbor, MI: Polity Press and University of Michigan Press.

Hodgson, Geoffrey M. (1998a), 'The approach of institutional economics', *Journal of Economic Literature,* **36** (1), March, 166–92.

Hodgson, Geoffrey M. (1998b), 'Competence and contract in the theory of the firm', *Journal of Economic Behavior and Organization,* **35** (2), April, 179–201.

Hodgson, Geoffrey M. (2002), 'Reconstitutive downward causation: social structure and the development of individual agency', in Edward Fullbrook (ed.), *Intersubjectivity in Economics: Agents and Structures,* London and New York: Routledge, pp. 159–80.

Hodgson, Geoffrey M. (2004), *The Evolution of Institutional Economics: Agency, Structure and Darwinism in American Institutionalism,* London and New York: Routledge.

Ingham, Geoffrey (2000), ' "Babylonian madness": on the historical and sociological origins of money' in John Smithin (ed.), *What is Money?,* London: Routledge, pp. 16–41.

Knight, Jack (1992), *Institutions and Social Conflict,* Cambridge: Cambridge University Press.

Lukes, Steven (1974), *Power: A Radical View,* London: Macmillan.

Mantzavinos, C. (2001), *Individuals, Institutions and Markets,* Cambridge and New York: Cambridge University Press.

Margolis, Howard (1994), *Paradigms and Barriers: How Habits of Mind Govern Scientific Beliefs,* Chicago: University of Chicago Press.

Menger, Carl (1909), 'Geld', reprinted in *The Collected Works of Carl Menger,* vol. IV, *Schriften über Geldtheorie und Währungspolitik,* 1936, London: London School of Economics, pp. 1–116.

Menger, Carl (1981), *Principles of Economics*, edited by J. Dingwall and translated by B. F. Hoselitz from the German edition of 1871, New York: New York University Press.

Mitchell, Wesley C. (1910), 'The rationality of economic activity', *Journal of Political Economy*, **18** (2–3), parts I and II, February–March, 97–113; 197–216.

Mitchell, Wesley C. (1937), *The Backward Art of Spending Money and Other Essays*, New York: McGraw-Hill.

Murphy, James Bernard (1994), 'The kinds of order in society', in Philip Mirowski (ed.), *Natural Images in Economic Thought: 'Markets Read in Tooth and Claw'*, Cambridge and New York: Cambridge University Press, pp. 536–82.

North, Douglass C. (1981), *Structure and Change in Economic History*, New York: Norton.

North, Douglass C. (1990), *Institutions, Institutional Change and Economic Performance*, Cambridge: Cambridge University Press.

North, Douglass C. (1994), 'Economic performance through time', *American Economic Review*, **84** (3), June, 359–67.

Nozick, Robert (1977), 'On Austrian methodology', *Synthèse*, **36**, 353–92.

Rutherford, Malcolm H. (1994), *Institutions in Economics: The Old and the New Institutionalism*, Cambridge: Cambridge University Press.

Schotter, Andrew R. (1981), *The Economic Theory of Social Institutions*, Cambridge: Cambridge University Press.

Sened, Itai (1995), 'The emergence of individual rights', in Jack Knight and Itai Sened (eds), *Explaining Social Institutions*, Ann Arbor MI: University of Michigan Press, pp. 161–88.

Sened, Itai (1997), *The Political Institution of Private Property*, Cambridge: Cambridge University Press.

Sugden, Robert (1986), *The Economics of Rights, Co-operation and Welfare*, Oxford: Basil Blackwell.

Ullmann-Margalit, Edna (1977), *The Emergence of Norms*, Oxford: Oxford University Press.

Veblen, Thorstein B. (1899), *The Theory of the Leisure Class: An Economic Study in the Evolution of Institutions*, New York: Macmillan.

Veblen, Thorstein B. (1914), *The Instinct of Workmanship, and the State of the Industrial Arts*, New York: Macmillan.

Veblen, Thorstein B. (1919), *The Place of Science in Modern Civilization and Other Essays*, New York: Huebsch.

Williamson, Oliver E. (1975), *Markets and Hierarchies: Analysis and Anti-Trust Implications: A Study in the Economics of Internal Organization*, New York: Free Press.

Williamson, Oliver E. (1983), 'Credible commitments: using hostages to support exchange', *American Economic Review*, **74** (3), September, 519–40.

Williamson, Oliver E. (1985), *The Economic Institutions of Capitalism: Firms, Markets, Relational Contracting*, London: Macmillan.

Wray, L. Randall (2000), 'Modern money' in John Smithin (ed.), *What is Money?*, London and New York: Routledge, pp. 42–66.

Young, H. Peyton (1996), 'The economics of convention', *Journal of Economic Perspectives*, **10** (2), Spring, 105–22.

6 Taking evolution seriously: what difference does it make for economics?

Jack J. Vromen

Introduction

The issue what relevance (if any) the theme of evolution has for economics can be tackled from several vantage points. One could start with a discussion of 'evolution', pin down its meaning (or possible meanings), for example, and then continue to flesh out its normative implications for doing economics. The focus would then be on the issue of what consequences some prior notion of evolution would (or should) have for the study of economics. Alternatively, one could start with looking at how economists treat the theme of evolution and how they see its relevance for economics. In this chapter I opt for the second approach. I mainly discuss economists who want to take (or who have taken) evolution seriously (whatever that implies) in practising their own discipline.

Economists who want to take evolution seriously: who are they? What distinguishes economists who do so from economists who do not? Perhaps it can be argued that the majority of economists still simply ignore evolution (but see, for example, the *Symposium* devoted to *Evolutionary Economics* in *The Journal of Economic Perspectives,* 2002). These economists seem to be perfect candidates for economists who do *not* take evolution seriously. It seems that they can be safely ignored for the purpose of this chapter. But we have to be careful here. We should not rule out the possibility from the outset that some of these economists do not spend a word on 'evolution' and related notions for good reasons. Perhaps they neglect evolution because they have come to the conclusion, after having had a look at evolutionary theory and after having carefully thought things over, that nothing valuable for economics is in the offing from looking more closely at evolution. They then at least took the trouble of contemplating whether or not something could be learnt by economists about their own discipline from thinking about evolution. So 'revealed disregard' of the theme of evolution in the writings of economists cannot be taken as evidence that these economists do not want to take the theme seriously. In this chapter, I will simply evade these problems by taking 'economists who want to take evolution seriously' to mean economists who have taken the trouble to think about the subject *and* who explicitly state that new insights for or about economic theorising result from doing so. This implies that I neglect economists who neglect evolution in their writings.

By invoking 'seriously', I do not want to single out economists who in my opinion really understand what evolution is all about and really know what conclusions with respect to economics to draw from it. Although I do have my own predilections, I do not want to prejudge issues from the outset by confining my attention to economists who in my opinion display a profound and accurate understanding of evolution (if there are any such at all). There appear to be many different ways in which economists take evolution seriously. In my discussion I include several sorts of economists of different stripes and persuasions who, each in their own way, try to come to grips with evolution and who try to draw some lessons from it. Part of the exercise here is exactly to find out what it means for different economists to take evolution seriously. How do they understand evolution and what implications do they think this understanding has for economics?

As there are many different ways in which economists take evolution seriously some principle is called for to structure the discussion. The organising principle opted for here is how economists position evolution, evolutionary theory and evolutionary arguments vis-à-vis standard economic theory. Three categories of economists are distinguished: the conservatives, the revisionists and the revolutionaries.[1] Roughly speaking, conservatives believe that taking evolution seriously does not necessitate making any change in standard economic theory. Revisionists hold that taking evolution seriously leaves standard economic theory's basic structure largely intact, but has consequences for how the structure's slots are filled in; consequences that that may run counter to how they are traditionally filled in. Revolutionaries, finally, are convinced that standard economic theory should be completely superseded if evolution is taken seriously.

The three categories of economists are internally divided. Each of them hosts economists who may not have anything in common with each other but a shared overall theoretical and meta-theoretical attitude towards standard economic theory. Indeed, as we shall see, in each category differences between groups of economists belonging to the category are manifold. Part of the discussion below will be devoted to explicating the several dimensions in which the one group of economists differs from others. It is pointed out, for example, that within the categories there are different ideas about what 'evolution' stands for. We shall see that some put some force similar to natural selection centre stage, whereas others stress the importance of other evolutionary forces. A general issue that pops up here is whether economic evolution should be conceived of along the lines of the (neo)Darwinian theory of biological evolution or of some generalisation thereof. Furthermore, some seem to envisage primarily remnants of evolutionary processes that took place in the distant past, while others seem to have ongoing evolutionary economic processes in mind. Some engage in attempts to model evolutionary processes explicitly, whereas others draw upon modelling efforts done by others. Finally, some situate evolutionary processes at the level of individual human beings, while others deal with the evolution of firm and industry behaviour.

The conservatives: evolution coming to the rescue of standard economic theorising?

The central idea of the conservatives is that acknowledging the actual existence of evolutionary economic processes is perfectly reconcilable with accepting standard economic theory. The idea has two crucial parts. One is that there are actually significant evolutionary economic processes going on. This, in turn, can be unpacked in two parts. One is that ongoing economic processes are truly evolutionary in kind. And the other is that recognising their evolutionary nature is essential for a proper understanding of ongoing economic processes and their outcomes. The second crucial part of the conservatives' central idea is that standard economic theory accurately describes outcomes of such evolutionary economic processes. Taken together, what is implied is that standard economic theory accurately describes what remains after some sort of evolutionary economic process has come to an end.

Giving concrete examples may help in bringing home the point. In the middle of the last century Alchian (1950), Friedman (1953) and Becker (1962) put forward their *selection arguments*. They did so in the heat of the so-called marginalism controversy. What was at stake in the marginalism controversy was whether marginalism in general, and the neoclassical theory of the firm in particular, could be upheld in the face of seemingly disconfirming empirical evidence. The empirical evidence at stake, gathered by Hall and Hitch and Lester, suggested that no entrepreneur based his decisions on marginalist considerations. This, anti-marginalists believed, was ample reason to reject the neoclassical theory of the firm *tout court*. Clearly, since one of this theory's crucial assumptions is that marginalist considerations underlie entrepreneurial decisions, massive evidence disconfirming the assumption effectively undermines the whole theory?

Not so, argued Alchian (1950), Friedman (1953) and Becker (1962). Even if the alleged disconfirming empirical evidence were reliable, they argued, the neoclassical theory of the firm can still be defended. Alchian, Friedman and Becker posited that a force or mechanism similar to natural selection, competitive or market selection, is working in competitive markets. This force favours firms that happen to make positive profits over those that fail to do so. As a consequence, they argued, only those firms that behave approximately as the neoclassical theory of the firm assumes all firms do will after a while stay in business. For example, consider what happens if real wages rise (*ceteris paribus*). Even if individual firms do not change their production techniques, if there is variation then firms with a relatively capital-intensive technique will outperform those with a relatively labour-intensive technique. Eventually the first group of firms will dominate the industry. This outcome is roughly the same as what would have happened if all firms were to base their decisions on marginalist considerations. So despite the (alleged) 'fact' that entrepreneurs are not as rational (or not as prescient) as the neoclassical theory of the firm assumes they are, in the end competitive selection will see to it that the predictions (or theorems) of the theory about industry behaviour will be borne out by the facts.[2]

What notion of evolution is involved here? In the selection arguments a selection mechanism akin to natural selection, competitive selection, is believed to operate in competitive markets. What is allegedly going on in competitive markets is likened to what Darwinian evolutionary theory says is going on in evolutionary processes. It is clear that the competitive selection mechanism or force is believed to favour profitable firms and to punish unprofitable ones. But beyond this much is left somewhat unclear. By virtue of what features do some firms make profits whereas others suffer losses, for example? What distinguishing features do surviving firms have? In standard (neo-)Darwinian theory of biological evolution ultimately genes are selected. Genes in the one generation are inherited by offspring in subsequent generations. At the population level, when going from the one generation to the next gene frequencies in the gene pool will change as a result of different organisms in the earlier generation having different reproductive success. Such selection effects are only forthcoming if there is phenotypic variation (at the level of the organism) that is grounded in genetic variation. If only selection were to work, this variation would be reduced in due time. But there are also countervailing forces operating in evolution that create new variation. Mutation is a prime example of such a force. In standard (neo-)Darwinian theory variation-enhancing mechanisms like mutation are assumed to work independently from the selection mechanism. Thus whether new variation is produced is assumed not to depend on whether, given prevailing selection pressure, it is badly needed. There is no presumption that new variants arrive on the scene that are better adapted to the prevailing selection pressure than the already existing variants. In this sense variation is taken to be 'blind' (Cziko 1995).

What is the relation between this more elaborate and articulate depiction of evolution in the (neo-)Darwinian theory and evolutionary economic processes as portrayed by the proponents of the selection arguments? It seems far-fetched to argue that something similar to genetic inheritance is going on in selection processes in competitive markets. Firms do not leave offspring. But still, are there comparable, or analogous counterparts of genes in economic 'natural selection', units that have some durability and that are at least partly responsible for the success or failure of firms having them? If not, how then do the alleged selection processes in competitive markets unfold? Furthermore, how does new variation in economic evolution come about and what are the mechanisms behind it? Are such processes 'blind' also in economic evolution? Or does the ability of entrepreneurs, managers and other business men to foresee and anticipate future developments make such processes goal-directed rather than blind?

The proponents of the selection arguments are not very outspoken on these issues. This does not mean, however, that we cannot discern the broad contours of what they have in mind. Since Alchian's argument is relatively speaking the most elaborated and articulated one, it is perhaps best to concentrate on his argument. As a matter of fact, Alchian advances not one but two evolutionary 'tales'. In the first and most simple one the driving force is the competitive environment that 'adopts' which firms are viable. In this tale it is assumed that firms do not try to adjust to the environment that they are confronted with. Those profitable variants survive that happen to be available. In the second, more sophisticated tale, it is no longer assumed that firms passively undergo selection processes. They actively try to adapt to the prevailing circumstances. Firms are assumed to engage in some 'trial and error' search process. Here new variants appear on the scene as a consequence of conscious, deliberate attempts of firms to cope with their environment. It is clear that Alchian takes the second tale to be much more realistic than the first one. But it is also clear that the overarching point Alchian is trying to make is that it does not matter how smart entrepreneurs are, in the end only firms survive that make the highest profits. What counts in evolutionary processes are not deliberations and intended outcomes, but actual, realised outcomes. Especially if there is pervasive uncertainty, deliberate, smart attempts of firms to adjust to their environment do not guarantee success. In this sense, there is 'blindness' in both tales.

Evolutionary reinterpretations of rational choice theory

Arguments similar to those of Alchian *cum suis* have been advanced in game theory. The central solution concept in traditional, 'rationalistic' or 'eductive' (non-cooperative) game theory is Nash equilibrium. Crudely put, some combination of actions (or strategies) is in Nash equilibrium if no one can be better off by unilaterally deviating from the combination. It may be tempting to think that fully rational players, which are all endowed with common knowledge of rationality, should have no problem with reasoning their ways to Nash equilibria. But perhaps surprisingly convergence of such super-rational creatures on some Nash equilibrium is by no means guaranteed (Hargreaves Heap and Varoufakis 1995). Many games have multiple Nash equilibria. And in a game with several equilibria super-rational players may fail to reach any of these.

Paradoxically, it turns out that the centrality of the notion of Nash equilibrium in game theory can be justified better if we assume that players go through some evolutionary process. That is, we can show more easily that there is a tendency towards some Nash equilibrium if individuals, which are *not* fully or perfectly, but boundedly rational at most, undergo some evolutionary process. Here we enter the province of *evolutionary* (or 'evolutive', Binmore 1987) *game theory*. Within evolutionary game theory we again (as was also the case with Alchian 1950) have several scenarios. The most basic and crude scenario was pioneered by the evolutionary biologist John Maynard Smith (1982). In his most simple models Maynard Smith assumes (among other things) that all individuals in some population are of a fixed strategic type: they are genetically pre-programmed to play some fixed strategy. This in effect means that there is nothing for individuals to choose. They are simply stuck with whatever strategy 'nature' has endowed them with. So at the level of the individual there is no evolutionary change.[3] But if natural selection holds sway there can nevertheless be evolutionary change at the level of the population. Individuals of some particular strategic type can leave more offspring than individuals of another type simply by virtue of obtaining higher payoffs (in terms of fitness). In order to find out how this could work out, Maynard Smith made several additional simplifying assumptions. One of them is that there is asexual reproduction (so that *like begets like*: individuals leave offspring of exactly the same strategic type).[4]

The static solution concept that Maynard Smith introduces, that of an evolutionarily stable strategy (ESS), can be seen as a refinement of 'Nash equilibrium'. If an ESS is established in a population, then it is resistant to invasion by mutants. No single mutant then can get a foothold in the population: if a single mutant appears in the population, it cannot proliferate in the population through natural selection. What this already indicates is that natural selection is the sole (or at least predominant) force driving evolution here. Genes are the replicators and asexual reproduction is assumed to be the simple inheritance mechanism. Gene mutations are assumed occasionally to take care of blind variation. But it can be argued that they play a role only in conditional and hypothetical reasoning. One of the leading questions, as we have seen, is: is there is strategy (within some antecedently specified strategy set) such that if all individuals in the population play this strategy, no single mutant can invade the population by means of natural selection? It is furthermore assumed that all single mutants considered fall within the antecedently specified strategy set. In this sense, genuinely new variants (that would enlarge the strategy set) are not taken into consideration.[5]

Later on it was pointed out that under such restrictive conditions evolutionary processes tend to converge on Nash equilibria in a fairly wide class of situations (van Damme 1994). This then seemed to provide a more solid justification of the central place that the notion of Nash equilibrium has acquired in applied game theory than the traditional rationalistic (or 'eductive') one. But if this is so, does this not call for a reinterpretation of 'Nash equilibrium' and, even more generally, of (applied) game theory (Aumann 1997)? If it turns out to be hard to show that super-rational creatures co-ordinate on Nash equilibria, whereas it is much easier to show that less-than-(fully) rational creatures that go through some evolutionary process converge on Nash equilibria, then why keep to the idea that 'Nash equilibrium' designates a state on which super-rational individuals co-ordinate? Why not reinterpret it as a state on which boundedly rational individuals converge in due time, after having gone through some evolutionary process?[6] More generally, why not replace the idea that (applied) game theory is about solutions that super-rational creatures, endowed with common knowledge of rationality, immediately and infallibly reach with the idea that (applied) game theory is about outcomes that evolutionary processes eventually converge on?

Such a reinterpretation is in line with what Satz and Ferejohn (1994) plead for with respect to rational choice theory *tout court*. Satz and Ferejohn notice that rational choice theory is successful mainly if not only in situations in which there are tight environmental pressures on individuals, forcing them to behave rationally. Only if there is a tight environmental pressure, Satz and Ferejohn argue, can we expect to have 'surviving' individuals in due time that behave in a way that is rationally responsive to the environmental pressures. But if this is so, they go on to argue, there are no longer good reasons to stick to the standard individualistic and psychological-internalist interpretation of rational choice theory. If the predictions of rational choice theory come true, this is not because of the mental states of the individuals involved. Predictions of rational choice theory do not hold because they are the intended outcomes of the fully rational behaviour of the individuals involved. They hold because external, non-individualistic environmental pressures make them behave in certain ways. What is doing the real explanatory work here are not the mental states of individuals, but the external environmental pressures. And if that is so, it does not make sense to insist that rational choice theory is about desires (preferences) and beliefs (expectations) of individuals leading to certain social phenomena. It makes more sense to conclude that rational choice theory is about tight, constraining environmental pressures.

On Satz and Ferejohn's radical reinterpretation, rational choice theory is much closer to functionalism and structuralism in social theorising than traditionally assumed. Traditionally it is assumed that rational choice theory on the one hand and functionalism and structuralism on the other present two opposites in social theorising. While the one stresses the wilful creation of social processes and phenomena by 'autonomous' individuals (unaffected by the society in which they live), the other emphasises the way in which society at large is organised, how its interconnected parts work together in the smooth functioning of society and how the social roles available in it affect the behaviour of individuals. But if Satz and Ferejohn are right, the applicability of rational choice theory depends more on how society at large is organised than on the properties and powers of individuals. On Satz and Ferejohn's account the scope of rational choice theory is limited to societies in which there are tight environmental pressures (of a particular kind).

For all of its attractive features, one of the apparent weaknesses of Satz and Ferejohn's proposal is that it seems to be based on a confusion between the delineation of the proper domain of applicability of rational choice theory and its proper interpretation. The observation that rational choice theory performs best when individuals are confronted with tight environmental pressures does not imply that rational choice theory essentially refers to properties of the environment that individuals find themselves in rather than to properties of the individuals themselves. On the other hand, the merit of Satz and Ferejohn's proposal is that it draws our attention to the fact that to the extent that it performs satisfactorily, rational choice theory need not do so because individuals do have the 'hyperrational' properties and do not go through the deliberations and calculations that the theory attributes to them. Rational choice theory's success may be due to altogether different evolutionary processes and mechanisms.

What we have seen so far are attempts of economists to show that standard economic predictions, notions and even whole theories that have been developed without paying attention to possibly ongoing evolutionary processes can be retained as useful tools of analysis if attention is paid to evolutionary processes. What is argued is that evolutionary processes terminate in exactly the outcomes that standard economic theory predicts.[7] Sometimes the argument advanced is sketchy and informal. At other times it is precise and formal. But in neither case is the argument meant to point out what is wrong with or missing in standard economic theory and to indicate how a superior, truly non-standard evolutionary economics could look like. On the contrary, the argument is meant to demonstrate that nothing serious is amiss with standard economic theorising and that, therefore, there is no need to engage in non-standard economic theorising. In some cases, as in the case of 'Nash equilibrium' in game theory, the evolutionary defence or justification given seems to be superior to traditional non-standard justifications. This has inspired some to plead for a radical evolutionary reinterpretation of standard economic theory. The message here again is the same: taking evolution seriously does not in any way diminish the usefulness of standard economic theory. Taking evolution seriously does not necessitate any repair, revision or modification of standard economic theory.[8] Exactly the opposite is true: taking evolution seriously only strengthens the confidence those conservatives had in standard economic theory anyway.

The revisionists: evolutionary theory calls for a friendly amendment of standard economic theory

Conservatives hold that standard economic theory is not jeopardised by taking evolution seriously. They argue that standard economic theory aptly and succinctly summarises the outcomes of evolutionary processes. This means that their plea for retaining standard economic theory is based on *instrumental* reasons. Their acceptance of standard economic theory is not grounded in their belief that standard economic theory, when taken at face value, realistically and adequately depicts underlying causal processes and mechanisms. This is different for revisionists. Revisionists typically argue that taking evolution calls for an amendment of standard economic theory. It is not that the whole edifice of standard economic theory has to crumble to pieces, however. Large parts of it can be held upright. Indeed, it can be argued that revisionists hold that the most essential parts of standard economic theory are unchallenged, if not vindicated by evolutionary theory. The meta-theoretic stance motivating this stance is not any form of instrumentalism. No, revisionists accept the constrained maximisation framework of standard economic theory because they believe that this framework gets roughly right how individuals actually choose.

Note that the issue what implications evolution has for standard economic theory tacitly transforms here into the issue what implications evolutionary *theory* has for standard economic theory. This is quite telling for revisionists. Revisionists do not pose the question whether *ongoing* evolutionary processes tend to produce results that standard economic theory predicts, as conservatives do. The question typically posed by revisionists is whether what we can learn from evolutionary theory about the results of *past* evolutionary processes can help us understand better present phenomena that are puzzling from the perspective of current standard economic theory. The issue what consequences this has for standard economic theory, albeit not unimportant, is of secondary importance. Thus three differences with the conservatives stand out immediately. First, unlike conservatives, revisionists do not come up with speculations, stories, arguments or models of evolutionary processes of their own making. Revisionists rather take contemporary evolutionary theory as an authoritative source of knowledge about evolutionary processes. Second, the evolutionary processes that revisionists take to be relevant for understanding present economic phenomena are processes that took place a long time ago. When conservatives talk of evolution they have ongoing evolutionary processes in mind. Third, whereas conservatives seem to be mainly if not solely interested in how much of standard economic theory can be rescued, revisionists are primarily interested in understanding phenomena better that hitherto we have understood only dimly at most.

At a more concrete level, what revisionists take as a starting point is the belief that individual human beings are evolved creatures. Put more precisely, individual human beings belong to the evolved species *homo sapiens sapiens*. As such they share a common heritage with each other. In particular, current individuals still display characteristics that bear the mark of the phylogenetic history of their species. This by itself is not controversial. Many would readily agree that we can learn from the phylogenetic history of our species why we have the anatomical and morphological characteristics that we have. What is controversial is that revisionists hold that we can also learn from our evolutionary past what *behavioural* characteristics (or at least behavioural dispositions) we currently have. In particular, revisionists argue that evolutionary theory can tell us what basic preferences we have. Evolutionary theory, revisionists argue, enables economists to identify in a non-arbitrary way what basic preferences individuals have. The specific evolutionary theories economists have in mind here go under the names of sociobiology and evolutionary psychology.

Early attempts to relate sociobiology to economic theory are Becker (1976) and Hirshleifer (1976, 1977, 1978, 1982). Sociobiology assumes that natural selection is the dominant force driving evolution. In the sociobiologist's scheme of things, this implies that only those behavioural traits and dispositions can have survived that have conferred a greater reproductive success (fitness) to their carriers than extant alternative traits have conferred to their carriers. Now it may seem to be almost a truism to say that natural selection favours selfish organisms, organisms promoting their own fitness (at the expense of the fitness of others), over non-selfish ones. Yet examples of self-sacrificing altruistic behaviour seem to abound in nature. Just think of colonies of ants and beehives. This then poses the central problem for sociobiology: '… how can altruism, which by definition reduces personal fitness, possibly evolve by natural selection?' (Wilson 1975, p. 3). This challenge is taken up by Becker (1976). Becker takes standard economic theory to task in arguing that genuine altruism can evolve.[9] What Becker shows more precisely is that altruistic *Big Daddy* does not only derive subjective satisfaction from transferring part of the family money to selfish *Rotten Kid*, but that *Big Daddy's* objective income is also enhanced if *Rotten Kid* anticipates *Big Daddy's* behaviour correctly. For correct anticipation of *Big Daddy's* behaviour makes *Rotten Kid* behave in a co-operative way. *Big Daddy's* altruism then induces *Rotten Kid* to behave as if it too were altruistic.

Standard economic theory is applied here to solve sociobiology's central problem.[10] Conversely, however, can sociobiology's insights be taken up by standard economic theory. In particular, if it can be pointed out conclusively that genuine altruistic dispositions or inclinations could have evolved by natural selection (as Becker believes could happen), then there is no longer good reason not to include altruism as a term in the utility function. Note that inclusion of altruism in the utility function does not call for a wholesale revolution in economic theory. The fact that altruism traditionally is not taken up in the utility function de facto does not imply that standard economic theory cannot make room for it *in principle*. Ever since Robbins (1932), many economists have argued that economic theory does not (or at least need not) prejudge the issue of what preferences individuals have. In principle these could be anything: preferences for material goods and wealth, or preferences for immaterial things; and preferences for one's own welfare or for that of others. Robbins thought that psychology was to be the supplier of knowledge about what preference people actually have. In a sense, what Becker *cum suis* argue is that sociobiology should take the place of psychology. They hold that the blank in utility functions are to be filled in by evolutionary theory.

Thus, Becker *cum suis* believes that accommodating the insights of sociobiology in particular and evolutionary theory in general does not necessitate a drastic change in, let alone a rejection of standard economic theory. Quite the contrary: the idea is that the backbone of standard economic theory stands unaffected. The alleged insight that our current behavioural dispositions are remnants from the evolutionary past of our species, imprinted by the incessant working of natural selection, does not in any way undermine the applicability of the constrained maximisation framework, in which it is assumed that individuals maximise utility functions subject to constraints. This reconciliatory view, that taking evolution seriously supplements rather than contradicts standard economic analysis, can also be found in Ben-Ner and Putterman (1998, 2000).

An evolutionary rationale for genuine altruism
In the so-called indirect evolutionary approach (IEA), pioneered by Güth and Yaari (1991), it is also maintained that taking insights from evolutionary modelling on board does not invalidate the constrained maximisation framework of standard economic theory. Again the presumption is that what studying evolution and evolutionary processes can contribute to economic theory is that it allows economists to identify in an informed and non-arbitrary way what basic preferences real people have. But acknowledging that real people are stuck with evolved basic preferences (whether they like it or not), proponents of the IEA argue, does not prevent people from making flexible, rational choices on the basis of them. This is where the IEA parts ways with direct evolutionary approaches such as evolutionary game theory. In evolutionary game theory individuals are assumed to be the vehicles or executors of fixed, pre-programmed strategies (or algorithms). There is nothing more to behaviour than whatever it is that their strategies make individuals do. In the IEA, only basic preferences are fixed and pre-programmed. How individuals behave does not depend solely on their preferences, but also on the prevailing circumstances. Retrospectively, this had also repercussions for what preferences evolved. The IEA's basic logic, as Huck puts it succinctly, is that '... preferences guide behavior, behavior determines fitness and fitness drives the evolution of preferences' (Huck 1997,

p. 773). Thus in the IEA's scheme of things preferences influence evolutionary success indirectly. And, conversely, evolution affects behaviour indirectly (see Vromen 2003a for further discussion).

Interesting results obtain if not all individuals in some population pursue maximum material payoffs for themselves (which is taken to be a 'proxy' for fitness). Güth and Yaari (1991), for example, show that individuals that are genetically disposed to reciprocate 'nasty' behaviour by others, even if that brings high personal costs with it, may well realise higher material payoffs than individuals that do the seemingly rational thing: yielding to nasty behaviour by others. This will happen only if others know that individuals of the reciprocating type are determined to reciprocate.[11] As Güth and Kliemt (1998) notice, this line of argument is similar to the one followed by Frank (1988). Frank also argues that 'irrational' behaviour can be favoured by natural selection over 'rational' behaviour. People who are emotionally disposed to cooperate no matter what the other does in a prisoner's dilemma can obtain higher material payoffs than rational opportunists who do whatever is in their own interest, Frank argues. Frank recognises that this scenario can only work if cooperators can choose to interact only with other cooperators and if the costs of screening types are not prohibitively high.

Just how much revision of standard economic theory does it need to accommodate Frank's ideas? Frank himself argues that his commitment model only calls for a *friendly amendment* of standard economic theory (Frank 1988, p. 258).[12] What he means is that his own commitment model accepts the same 'basic materialist framework' that standard economic theory is also wedded to. Both theories (or models) assume that only those things can be sustained that perform (or have performed) relatively well in terms of material payoffs. Only those commitments, emotions and moral sentiments had survival value, for example, that, when acted upon, yielded superior material results. This should not be taken to imply, however, that the emotionally committed individuals figuring in Frank's commitment model choose to have and display the emotions that bring them maximum material payoffs.[13] Either some emotion and the associated behavioural response are triggered in a particular situation or they are not, whether the individual in question likes it or not. Whether or not Frank's individuals are endowed with emotional commitments to act in certain ways is due to a complex interplay between processes of biological and cultural evolution. In Frank's evolutionary scenario, material rewards are *ultimate*, not *proximate* causes of behaviour (Mayr 1961). Material rewards in the past determined what behavioural dispositions survived processes of biological and cultural evolution. The surviving behavioural dispositions are proximate causes of behaviour. They determine how individuals behave today. Frank's emotionally committed individuals cooperate, for example, not because they expect to be best off (in terms of material payoffs) by doing so. They are committed to cooperate because they feel that this is the right or appropriate thing to do.

As Frank (1999) himself acknowledges, his line of reasoning is similar to that of evolutionary psychology. Evolutionary psychology tries to identify psychological mechanisms in individuals by looking at ancient evolutionary problems that these mechanisms purportedly solve (for extended discussions, see Vromen 2002, 2003a). Cosmides and Tooby (1992) argue that people have an evolved mechanism that is specifically dedicated to detect cheaters in cooperative endeavours, for example. This mechanism still helps people to uphold otherwise fragile cooperative arrangements. Gintis (2000) and Fehr and Gächter (2002) similarly argue that people tend to display behavioural patterns of *strong reciprocity*. It is not just that people have a keen eye for spotting cheaters, they also are willing to incur personal costs to punish cheaters single-handedly even in situations in which there is not the slightest chance of future personal benefits.

The guiding idea of revisionists, to recapitulate, is not that the main or basic determinants of human behaviour are undergoing evolutionary changes all the time. The guiding idea is rather that current human behaviour is the outcome of individuals with evolved invariant behavioural characteristics responding to prevailing and possibly changing environmental circumstances. What revisionists fulminate against thus is not so much the notion of a fixed, invariant human nature. On the contrary, it can be argued that revisionists resuscitate this notion. Revisionists hold that for the time horizon relevant for economic and social studies, it can safely be assumed that the mental mechanisms underlying human behaviour are immutable. More specifically, the basic preferences (or, more generally, the motivational repertoire) that individuals are endowed with can be assumed to be given for these purposes.[14] This is not to deny that under different cultural and other environmental influences basic proclivities and preferences may translate into different 'superficial' preferences for consumption bundles, however. So even if we assume stable underlying basic preferences, if we are interested in consumption patterns, for example, the importance of ongoing processes of ontogenetic development and of cultural evolution cannot be belittled.[15]

The revolutionaries: evolutionary theorising should supersede standard economic theorising

Although some minor modifications may be necessary, revisionists hold that the overall framework of standard economic theory can be retained. To be more precise, revisionists hold that taking evolution seriously does not undermine the constrained maximisation framework of standard economic theory. The revision that it implies at most is that the terms in the utility function are identified in a non-arbitrary way and that this identification differs from the one many economists traditionally (but not necessarily) give. Revolutionaries believe that taking evolution seriously implies that more drastic changes in standard economic theory are needed. Indeed it can be argued that revolutionaries hold that standard economic theory is to be discarded altogether and that it has to give way to a radically different non-standard way of economic theorising. Perhaps surprisingly the reason for revolutionaries holding this belief is not always that standard economic theory has got its subject matter all wrong. Some revolutionaries believe that standard economic theory has got it partially right in at least some cases. They nevertheless think that standard economic theory has to be superseded by an altogether different approach.

Different groups of revolutionaries have different reasons for developing a non-standard economic theory. The revolutionaries are themselves internally divided in this respect. Not all revolutionaries share the same meta-theoretical stance, for example. Those old and (neo-)institutionalists who follow Veblen (1898) in aspiring for a full-blown evolutionary economic theory strongly dislike standard economic theory's alleged over-emphasis on theoretical virtues such as parsimony and formal rigour, precision and tractability. They favour a clearly distinct type of economic theorising.[16] By contrast, it can be argued that evolutionary game theorists engage in the same type of theorising, displaying the same theoretical virtues, as standard economic theorists. Some other revolutionaries, especially those of the so-called ABC group, go along with the revisionists in arguing that evolution primarily bears on economic theorising via the products that evolutionary processes long ago have endowed us with and that still influence our current behaviour. It is just that revolutionaries argue that these products are of such a kind that considerably more than mere minor modifications of standard economic theory are needed. Yet other revolutionaries, evolutionary economists, focus on ongoing evolutionary processes. They argue that these, rather than static equilibrium notions, should be studied by economists. Yet another disagreement among revolutionaries pertains to the level of analysis chosen. Some argue that populations of individual human beings should be studied, while proponents of evolutionary economics argue that industries and firms are the proper units of analysis.

Evolutionary game theory
Evolutionary game theory we have already encountered under the heading of *the conservatives*. The reason why it reappears here is that some argue that rather than a justification or reinterpretation of standard 'rationalistic' game theory's key notion, the Nash equilibrium, evolutionary game theory is a theory in its own right that is different from standard 'rationalistic' game theory. What is more, some argue that there are good reasons to stop doing standard game theory and to turn to evolutionary game theory.

One reason is that standard 'rationalistic' game theory ran into several problems that it was unable to solve. The so-called *equilibrium selection problem* is perhaps the most nagging one. In games with multiple equilibria, standard game theory was unable to single out what equilibrium, if any, players converge on. Evolutionary game theory holds out the hope of solving this problem (Binmore 1995; Alexander 2002). Another reason for replacing standard game theory by evolutionary game theory is that standard game theory is felt to assume an unrealistically high degree of rationality on the part of players. Players are assumed to be hyperrational. Not only is it assumed that players reason their ways to equilibria instantaneously and effortlessly (without incurring deliberation costs, for example), there is also the assumption of common knowledge of rationality. The latter in effect means that every single relevant feature of each player (their payoffs measured in utilities and their full rationality, for example) is transparent to all. Evolutionary game theory relaxes these heroic assumptions. Individuals are assumed to be boundedly rational at most. Yet another reason is that it has turned out that not all results in standard game theory are reproduced in evolutionary game theory. Evolutionary game theory does not underpin the elimination of weakly dominated strategies, for example (Samuelson 1993). If it is believed, as it often is, that evolutionary game theory more realistically depicts the 'nuts and bolts' of social interaction than standard game theory, then this provides all the more reason for game theorists to revert to evolutionary game theory.

Current work at the frontiers of evolutionary game theory is miles away from the basic scenario Maynard Smith (1982) started out with. Maynard Smith's scenario was one in which populations of genetically programmed individuals are subject to natural selection. Nowadays the type of 'evolution' mostly modelled in evolutionary game theory is of quite a different type: changes in population characteristics because of individually and socially learning individuals. The degree of sophistication in the assumed learning abilities varies a lot. It ranges from very simple-minded and myopic behaviourist operant conditioning over purposeful 'trial and error' learning to the quite sophisticated updating of beliefs under the stimulus of new empirical evidence (best-reply dynamics, see Young 1998). The one thing that they have in common, it seems, is that they all fall short of perfectly rational Bayesian learning. Rather than being implicitly assumed, the dynamics in question is modelled explicitly here. Initially it was often assumed that the *replicator dynamics* that was introduced to analyse processes of biological evolution by natural selection also aptly describes processes of individual and social learning. But increasingly other types of dynamics, also non-monotonic ones,[17] are also explored (see, for example, Vega-Redondo 1996 and Samuelson 1997).

Evolutionary game theory has also been increasingly used to study social or cultural evolution (Schotter 1981; Sugden 1986; Bicchieri 1993; Binmore and

Samuelson 1994; Skyrms 1996; Young 1998). The leading idea here is that it is possible to show that stable, self-sustaining social (or aggregate) patterns of behaviour can emerge spontaneously, that is without being designed by some authority and without being the result of concerted action. Exercises in evolutionary game theoretic modelling are presented here as formalisations of intuitions that can be found in Hayek's notion of the spontaneous evolution of social order and Menger's notion of the organic origin of institutions and even further back in David Hume's notion of conventions and in Adam Smith's notions of unintended consequences and the invisible hand.[18] These attempts are very much in line with memetics, the particular take on cultural evolution already discussed briefly in the previous section: Universal Darwinism applied to cultural evolution. The central tenets of Universal Darwinism, blind variation and selective retention, are quite easily discernible here. Individuals making mistakes or experimenting with new lines of behaviour provide blind variation. Formally, these are treated as random shocks. The learning algorithms assumed determine whether or not some already tried line of behaviour will be retained. Furthermore, there is one more distinguishing feature of memetics that is clearly present in these applications of evolutionary game theory: unlike the other approaches to cultural evolution discussed in section II, no explicit links are forged between the processes of cultural evolution studied and processes of biological evolution and outcomes thereof. Cultural evolution is studied as if it is fully cut loose from any other evolutionary process.

Evolutionary game theory is radically different from standard economic theory in that it explicitly models dynamic processes and that it dispenses with the assumption of fully rational individual behaviour (see Vromen 2001b for a further discussion of the ontological commitments of evolutionary game theory). As indicated earlier, it is not radically different in other respects, however. With standard economic theory it shares a preference for a certain type of theorising. Keywords here are theoretical parsimony and mathematical rigour, precision and tractability. Sugden (2001) observes the apparent ease with which game theorists give up elements (such as perfect individual rationality and market equilibrium) that many took to be definitive for standard economic theory. Sugden goes on to argue that this suggests where their real commitments lie: economists are willing to abandon core elements of their theory if this forestalls engaging themselves seriously with potentially devastating empirical research and its findings. This 'contempt' or fear for empirical research then is the continuity that Sugden sees in the transition from standard to evolutionary theorising in economics. But perhaps Sugden is too pessimistic here. There are interesting new connections in the offing between evolutionary game theory and experimental economics, as witnessed by the newly emerging field of behavioural game theory (Camerer 2003).

The ABC group

The basic ideas of the ABC group (The Center for Adaptive Behavior and Cognition group) have a lot in common with those of evolutionary psychology. This is recognised by proponents of both groups (Cosmides and Tooby 1996 and Todd and Gigerenzer 2000). Where evolutionary psychologists argue that biological evolution has endowed us with a multitude of special-purpose psychological modules, members of the ABC group argue that biological evolution has equipped us with an adaptive toolbox of fast and frugal heuristics. Here is a succinct synopsis of the gist of 'the adaptive toolbox': '... the collection of specialized cognitive mechanisms that evolution has built into the human mind for specific domains of inference and reasoning, including fast and frugal heuristics' (Todd and Gigerenzer 2000, p. 740). The notion of 'fast and frugal heuristics' is coined primarily to bring out that they economise on search and deliberation efforts:

> fast and frugal heuristics employ a minimum of time, knowledge, and computation to make adaptive choices in real environments ... the purest form of bounded rationality is to be found in fast and frugal heuristics, which employ limited search through objects (in satisficing) or cues and exploit environmental structures to yield adaptive decisions. (Todd and Gigerenzer 2000, p. 731)

It is precisely because fast and frugal heuristics save on search and deliberation costs that biological evolution has equipped us with a toolbox full of them rather than with some general-purpose intelligence that is bound to investigate all options and their expected consequences indiscriminately in each separate case.

Members of the ABC group oppose the main thrust of the so-called 'Heuristics and Biases Program' associated with Kahneman and Tversky (Kahneman and Tversky 2000). These authors and their followers have conducted many experiments in which a multitude of anomalies in expected utility theory have been identified. The conclusion that proponents of the Heuristics and Biases Program tend to draw from this is that carefully observed actual behaviour of 'real people' systematically violate expected utility theory and that, therefore, expected utility theory is refuted empirically. Proponents of the ABC group find fault in this reasoning mainly for two reasons. They first call the experimental setups deviced by Kahneman and Tversky et al. in question. What they argue in particular is that in the experiments deviced by Kahneman and Tversky et al., subjects are placed in artificially created environments to which they are not adapted. Symptomatic in this regard is Gigerenzer (1996). Gigerenzer argues that in the experiments run by Kahneman and Tversky, people only appear as poor statisticians because the statistical problems are put in terms of point estimates. Gigerenzer points out that people do much better if the problems are put in frequentist terms. This should not come as a surprise, Gigerenzer goes on to argue, because our hominid ancestors were faced with statistical problems in frequentist terms rather than in terms of point estimates. This then is the main difference between the general thrust of the Heuristics and Biases Program and that of the ABC group: whereas proponents of the Heuristics and Biases Program emphasise the irrationality of actual human behaviour, proponents of the ABC group tend to stress its adaptedness.[19]

The second reason why proponents of the ABC group disagree with Kahneman and Tversky et al. is that in attributing deviations from expected utility theory to biases and in calling actual human behaviour irrational, Kahneman and Tversky et al. implicitly subscribe to the notion of rationality-as-constrained-maximisation inherent in expected utility theory. Unintendedly Kahneman and Tversky et al. herewith even help to reinforce the dominance of this notion in economics. Proponents of the ABC group want to dispense with this notion. Prima facie it may seem that the ABC group sides with standard economic theory on the issue of the rationality of human behaviour. But this impression is wrong. It is true that proponents of the ABC group emphasise that experimental results that blatantly seem to disconfirm standard economic theory, tend to vanish if problems are framed in ways that people are used to and if all costs of time- and energy-consuming search and deliberation are factored in. But that does not mean that members of the ABC group subscribe to the maximisation under constraints notion of rational behaviour. Members of the ABC group put forward their own, qualitatively different notion of *ecological rationality*.

What is stressed in 'ecological rationality' is that the degree of sophistication needed for some search heuristic to produce adapted behaviour very much depends on the structure of the environment. As a rule fast and frugal search heuristics are not very sophisticated. But often this does not prevent them from producing adapted behaviour in the environments in which they evolved. The fact that the heuristics reflect limited knowledge at most does not yet warrant the conclusion that they are irrational. It is at this point, proponents of the ABC group argue, that 'ecological rationality' differs from 'rationality-as-constrained-maximisation'. Proponents of the ABC group acknowledge that it is possible to incorporate search and deliberation costs in the 'rationality-as-constrained-maximisation' framework. But they point out that in this framework it is tacitly assumed that individuals avail of unlimited time and knowledge to evaluate the costs and benefits of further 'limited search'. This is clearly an unrealistic assumption. Worse, it is further assumed that if individuals were to avail of limited time and knowledge only, their behaviour would fall short of attaining the normative ideal of rationality. Given that proponents of 'ecological rationality' stress that limited fast and frugal heuristics can be adapted to the structure of the environment, they fulminate against calling acting with limited time and knowledge irrational. The flaw here is not in the behaviour displayed, proponents of 'ecological rationality' argue, but in sticking to the normative ideal of unlimited time and knowledge. The normative ideal inherent in 'ecological rationality' is of a relative rather than absolute nature. The key question here is how well the structure of heuristics matches with the structure of the environment.

Proponents of the ABC group see their own notion of ecological rationality as an elaboration of Herbert Simon's 'bounded rationality'. They acknowledge that the textual evidence in Simon's writings on 'bounded rationality' warrant alternative elaborations. Their own elaboration goes back mainly to Simon (1956) where it is stressed that the cognitive machinery of organisms need not be very sophisticated to survive. Organisms can acquire the resources necessary for their survival, for example, if only they succeed in exploiting environmental clues to their own advantage. Better known among economists is Simon (1955).[20] There Simon argues that individuals do not go to great lengths to find best solutions. Instead they settle with the first alternative found that yields satisfactory results. If they happen to find such a satisfactory alternative relatively fast and effortlessly, they tend to adjust their aspiration level in an upward direction; if they do not succeed in finding such an alternative even after many time and energy-consuming attempts, they tend to adjust their aspiration level in a downward direction. This approach is further worked out in, for example, Selten (2002). Proponents of the ABC group thus do not rule out that there may be other faithful and fruitful elaborations of 'bounded rationality'. But they do argue that it goes against Simon's original views to call observed violations of expected utility theory irrational, as proponents of the Heuristics and Biases Program in experimental psychology do. The interesting thing, however, is that the proponents of this Program believe that their work is very much in the spirit of Herbert Simon's original views on 'bounded rationality'. Indeed, several movements with different theses and claims present themselves as the true heirs of Herbert Simon. In this sense there is currently a debate going on about the legacy of Simon's ideas.

Evolutionary economics
The label 'evolutionary economics' will be reserved here for attempts to develop explicit evolutionary theories and models of economic change in a way that is reminiscent of Nelson and Winter (1982). Ever since Nelson and Winter's book appeared, a few evolutionary economists have distanced themselves from the alleged '*biological metaphor*' underlying the book (see, for example, Hodgson 2000; Foster 1999 and Witt 1993, 2003). At the end of the discussion I will briefly comment on these. But as Nelson and Winter (1982) has remained a more or less obligatory point of reference for any innovative move in evolutionary economics, the bulk of the discussion here will be devoted to their book. Evolutionary economists distance themselves quite conspicuously from mainstream economics (or from 'orthodox' economics, as they themselves often call it). What they discard in particular is mainstream economics' assumption

of rational individual behaviour and its typical static equilibrium approach. What evolutionary economists set out to do as an alternative to this is to develop theories and models about dynamic processes that travel almost always through non-equilibrium states and in which individuals are involved that are boundedly rational at most. Since this is believed to be radically different from the dominant way of theorising and modelling in mainstream economics, what evolutionary economists want to accomplish is nothing less than a revolution in economic theory.

Nelson and Winter (1982) go to great length in arguing that firms do not engage in the type of flexible decision-making that is assumed in mainstream economics. Firms are unable to change their operating characteristics overnight. In a more realistic depiction of firm behaviour, Nelson and Winter argue, firms appear as behavioural units that have built up their own specific *routines* for how to handle things. Routines embody accumulated tacit knowledge enabling firms to cope with familiar recurrent problems in a relatively effortless way. But the flip side of the coin is that routines can also constrain: when confronted with unprecedented problems, a firm's routines may stand in the way of making flexible and profitable adjustments. Thus there is a trade-off here. Routines economise on search and deliberation costs and allow for relatively effortless and reliable solutions for recurrent problems, but they incapacitate flexible responses to sudden environmental changes.[21] This implies that routines do better in stable environments and flexible decision-making does better in volatile environments. However, we should not expect flexible decision-making of firms to evolve in volatile environments, Nelson and Winter argue, because this type of behaviour is simply not available to firms. Routines also serve as some sort of organisational memory and as a truce in intra-organizational conflict that firms cannot do without. Whether firms like it or not, their behaviour will always be routinised to a large extent.

Nelson and Winter liken routines to genes. But they do not argue that the operating characteristics of firms are immutable. When some routines do not yield satisfactory results, firms will start searching for better ones. At the industry level such search efforts create new variation. This feature is one of the two reasons for Nelson and Winter to call their own evolutionary economic theory a distinctly Lamarckian one. The other reason is that in their own theory acquired characteristics are inherited. If firms find better routines during their search efforts, these better routines are retained in the next time interval. Both 'Lamarckian' features follow directly from Herbert Simon's notion of *satisficing* that Nelson and Winter take over. 'Satisficing' implies both that search efforts get started if results are not satisfactory (if they fall below some critical aspiration level) and that search efforts stop as soon as some option or alternative is found that does yield satisfactory results. As long as the option found yields satisfactory results, a satisficer will stick to it. The notion of satisficing that Nelson and

Winter adopt does not seem to sit easily with their overall account of routine firm behaviour. After all, 'satisficing' seems to presuppose someone who is in command of the choice of routines and who furthermore engages in deliberate choice of routines, whereas on Nelson and Winter's account of it routines are contrasted with deliberate choice. They try to resolve this tension within their theory following Cyert and March (1963), who argue that firms typically avail of a hierarchy of routines, where for example second-order routines guide the search for better first-order routines (operating characteristics).

In Nelson and Winter's evolutionary theory, satisficing is not the only mechanism driving economic change. Competitive (or market) selection is the other one. Nelson and Winter assume that in competitive markets only those firms that succeed in making positive profits can expand. Firms that suffer losses cannot but contract. The attentive reader will recognise certain elements of the selection arguments that were discussed in section I here. Nelson and Winter's theory seems to further elaborate and articulate especially Alchian's version, in which the twin working of competitive markets adopting certain firms and individual firms trying to adapt to prevailing circumstances via some trial-and-error process was envisioned. But note that Alchian *cum suis* were portrayed as conservatives, while Nelson and Winter are ranked among revolutionaries. What prompts Nelson and Winter to plead for a radical change in economic theorising and modelling, when the acknowledgement of roughly the same underlying evolutionary mechanisms lead Alchian *cum suis* to a defence of standard economic theorising? Nelson and Winter seem to have at least three reasons for going a radically different way.

The first reason is that they do not want to take the soundness of the selection arguments for granted. Something more than the wave of a hand is needed, Nelson and Winter argue, to establish that evolutionary processes in competitive markets lead to the results that are predicted by standard economic theorising. Rather than trusting on it that evolutionary mechanisms in competitive markets steer processes in the direction of standard economic theory's predictions, this has to be demonstrated. So one of the reasons that Nelson and Winter develop evolutionary economic models is to check whether they yield results that are consistent with those of standard economic theory. This had already started with Winter (1964) who showed with the aid of an explicit evolutionary model that the selection arguments hold water only under very restrictive conditions. Nelson and Winter's second reason for arguing that standard economic theory has to be superseded by evolutionary economic theory is that the scope of economic theorising will be extended by doing so. Issues such as the nature, the competencies, operating characteristics and the dynamics of organisations, technological change and economic growth, (radical) innovation and Schumpeterian competition that are treated niggardly if at all in standard economic theory are then put centre stage.

The third reason Nelson and Winter have for modelling evolutionary economic processes explicitly is more of a meta-theoretical or philosophical kind. It stems from a particular version of *realism*. This version holds that scientific theories and models should aim at uncovering and explicating causal mechanisms that underlie the 'behaviour' of the phenomena that we observe. If we relate this version of realism to the issue at stake here, what it implies is that if mechanisms such as competitive selection and satisficing are believed to guide the behaviour of market phenomena then an adequate economic theory or model specifies these mechanisms and their workings. In Nelson and Winter's own words, what is *appreciative theorising* only in standard economic theory should become *formal theorising* in their own evolutionary theory. The mechanisms should not be referred to in order to defend standard economic theory, they should rather be modelled explicitly in a truly evolutionary economic theory. This meta-theoretical argument is already to be found in Koopmans (1957), but it is given practical consequences in Nelson and Winter (1982). Note that this argument applies also if the selection arguments were to have been flawless. Even if it was to turn out that evolutionary economic processes as studied in evolutionary economic models lead to the results that standard economic theory predicts, there would still be sufficient reason to turn away from standard economic theory and to build evolutionary economic models instead. Indeed, one of the things Nelson and Winter (1982) set out to do is to show that their own evolutionary models can generate the same results in comparative statics as standard economic theory. Although their own evolutionary models cannot claim superiority on empirical grounds here, it can claim superiority on theoretical grounds: unlike those in standard economic theory, their own models study the workings of real underlying mechanisms.

Nelson and Winter devise several different evolutionary models to analyse processes of economic change. Part of their diagnosis of why appreciative 'evolutionary' theorising in 'orthodox' economics never made it to formal evolutionary theorising is that the modelling techniques necessary for formal evolutionary theorising were simply lacking at the time. But this has changed in the meantime. Nelson and Winter themselves employ the Markov chains modelling technique to analyse dynamic out-of-equilibrium processes. Other modelling techniques have become available that also have gained some popularity among evolutionary economists (Marengo and Willinger 1997). More recently other work, especially John Holland's genetic algorithms and classifier systems and Santa Fé-type complexity theory has drawn a lot of attention. Related are phenomena like path dependence and lock-in effects (David 1985 and Arthur 1989). These phenomena indicate that it may crucially depend on accidents and contingencies obtaining at the beginning of a dynamic process what path the process will follow later on. In such cases 'history matters'. It may happen that the path taken leads to some suboptimal or inefficient outcome that the process gets then stuck (or is 'locked-in') into. So wholeheartedly are these phenomena embraced in evolutionary economics that it seems that they are elevated to the status of a first principle (Nelson 1995).

Nelson and Winter's invocation of phrases as 'routines as genes' has led many commentators into thinking that Nelson and Winter are proposing a kind of evolutionary economics that is strictly analogous to evolutionary biology. Nelson and Winter make it perfectly clear, however, that they are not uncritically pursuing 'the biological metaphor'. They are looking for a better economic theory and selectively take over only some elements from biological evolutionary theory.[22] Many have nonetheless felt that Nelson and Winter's evolutionary theory is too much crafted on analogues of the notions of gene and natural selection adopted from evolutionary biology. Instead of putting 'genes' and 'natural selection' centre stage, some have suggested that processes of self-transformation and of the incessant endogenous creation of novelty more aptly characterise the peculiar nature of *economic* evolution (Witt 2003).

There are considerable differences between the three groups of revolutionaries discussed here. Evolutionary game theorists seem to be wedded much more strongly to the sort of theorising and modelling prevalent in standard mathematical economic theory than evolutionary economists, for example. But they both are unlike proponents of the ABC group in that they try to model ongoing evolutionary economic processes. Proponents of the ABC group are more interested in what decision-making machinery evolutionary processes in the past have endowed us with. When it comes to the level of organisation at which the revolutionaries analyse evolutionary processes and their effects, however, proponents of the ABC group and evolutionary game theorists are on one side and evolutionary economists on the other. Proponents of the ABC-group and evolutionary game theorists study evolutionary processes and their effects at the level of individuals and the populations they are part of, whereas evolutionary economists study evolutionary processes at the level of firms and the industries or markets in which they operate. Yet there are also striking similarities between all three groups. All revolutionaries hold that more realistic accounts of dynamic processes, whether these are situated at the individual, firm or market level, are badly needed. And whatever else this entails, it entails at any rate the acknowledgement that individuals are not perfectly rational, but boundedly rational at most.

Concluding remarks
The concluding discussion of the previous section shows that the stance towards standard economic theory is but one of the possible vantage points from which the available material can be ordered. Many more dimensions have been indicated in this chapter in which economists who take evolution seriously, vary. Rather than going once again through the distinguishing features

of conservatives, revisionists and revolutionaries, it may be more helpful to conclude with a brief overview of these other dimensions.

The core notion of *evolution* itself is understood in widely diverging ways. Both conservatives putting forward some version of the selection argument and Nelson and Winter type evolutionary economists conceive of evolution as a process at the industry or market level controlled predominantly by competitive market *selection*. Others rather seem to have processes of social or *cultural evolution* in mind in which certain ways of handling things change in populations or groups of individuals because these are transmitted from the one individual human being to others via non-genetic means (via imitation, for example). Yet others think of changes in individual behaviour due to processes of *individual learning*. What this shows is not only that evolution can take place at different levels of organisation (individual persons, groups, markets). It also suggests that there might be evolutionary processes going on simultaneously that are of interest to economics. Models of *co-evolution* might be needed to come to grips with such multi-level evolutionary processes and their interactions, but the complexity of such interactions may well be staggering (see Vromen 2002 and 2004 for a further discussion).

Another dimension pertains to the issue of whether the evolutionary processes at stake are ongoing or have been already completed in the past. The evolutionary processes envisaged by conservative proponents of the selection argument and most of the revolutionaries are ongoing ones. Revisionists by contrast envisage evolutionary processes that have come to an end a long time ago. They mainly have processes of the phylogenetic development of our species *homo sapiens* in mind that allegedly shaped what we now call human nature. What revisionists hold is that biological evolution has endowed us with our basic preferences and our capacity to choose flexibly and rationally. Given these endowments we can do (and actually do) what standard economic theory assumes we do: we engage in constrained maximisation. Thus revisionists in effect show that it is entirely possible that we human beings are the products of evolutionary processes in the past, but that currently there are no relevant evolutionary processes going on anymore. Arguing that ancient processes of biological evolution established our capacities once and for all does not necessarily imply that there are no more evolutionary processes going on that economic theory should pay attention to, however. On the basis of fixed, biologically evolved capacities there may still be significant processes of cultural evolution and ontogenetic development (and individual learning) going on. What is more, these biologically evolved capacities may not only facilitate these processes, they may also constrain and channel these processes. This is exactly the point where revisionists evolutionary psychology and the revolutionary ABC group part company. Where the revisionists tend to stress only the facilitating powers of the capabilities, the revolutionaries draw attention also to their constraining and channelling powers.

Yet another dimension on which there are differences that run through the different categories is whether economists engage in theorising about evolutionary processes themselves or consult theorising about evolutionary processes done by others. One might think that economists only feel competent to develop theories and models about *economic* evolution and that they would draw on the expertise of practitioners of other disciplines to obtain insights about non-economic evolutionary processes and their outcomes. But some economists have boldly developed theories and models of non-economic evolutionary models of their own. What is more, some of them have deployed standard economic theories and models to shed light on non-economic evolutionary processes and their outcomes. Although evolutionary processes undoubtedly are dynamic, theorising about evolutionary processes need not be explicitly dynamic. Some argue, for example, that although biological evolution is likely to have equipped us with brains that do not seem to match well with standard economic theory's depiction of human behaviour, standard economic theory can be profitable applied to enhance our understanding of the way our brain functions. There is no contradiction here. Using standard economic theory to better understand the functionings of our brains may well lead to the conclusion that standard economic theory (when taken literally) gives an utterly unrealistic depiction of our internal decision-making (or behaviour-generating) machinery.

Finally, however, there is also the meta-theoretical issue whether theorising and modelling should focus on the workings of the most important forces and mechanisms actually at work in evolutionary processes. Even if standard economic theory were to reliably predict the outcomes of evolutionary processes, if the actual forces and mechanisms driving these processes to their predicted outcomes are not constrained maximisers, then using standard economic theory to predict these outcomes is not acceptable. For that would not get it right (not even approximately) how these outcomes are actually produced. The issue of realism versus instrumentalism looms large here. Instrumentalists are to be found among conservatives, but not among revolutionaries. Revolutionaries tend to be realists, although the converse does not hold true. For revisionists also tend to be realists. Revisionists and revolutionaries alike argue that evolution is taken seriously only if this leads to a better causal understanding of ongoing economic processes.

Notes
* Parts of this chapter were prepared as a paper while the author was a Ludwig Lachmann Research Fellow at the London School of Economics
1. Associations with the political–ideological movements that go under these names should be suppressed. It is entirely possible, for example, that revolutionaries in this chapter are conservative in the political–ideological sense.

2. Similar selection arguments are also sometimes put forward to buttress claims and theses in new institutional economics. See Vromen (1995), Chapter 3, for a further discussion.

3. In more recent versions of evolutionary game theory boundedly rational individuals are assumed to be able to learn both individually and socially. See the further discussion of evolutionary game theory under the heading of 'Revolutionaries'.

4. Other additional simplifying assumptions are that the population is infinitely large and that interactions are pair-wise and not selective (or assortative).

5. Although it is to be noted that in one of Maynard Smith's most famous applications of evolutionary game theory, the explanation of the spontaneous evolution of de facto property rights, a new strategy (Bourgeois) is smuggled in in the original Hawk–Dove game. See Vromen (1995), Chapter 7, for a more extensive discussion.

6. It was John Nash himself who, in his doctoral dissertation, first drew attention to this interpretation of his own notion of Nash equilibrium. See Weibull (1995).

7. See also Robson (2001, 2002) who uses standard economic theory to point out why processes of biological evolution have endowed us with utility functions and with the capacity to act rationally upon them. Glimcher (2003) urges neuroscientists to use economic theory in studying brain processes.

8. Sometimes it is argued that standard economic theory's focus on equilibria may not be so ill-taken since equilibria also figure prominently in attempts of contemporary standard evolutionary biology to come to grips with processes of evolutionary change (see, for example, Krugman 1999). Note that what here is allegedly vindicated with recourse to evolutionary biology is not the substance of standard economic theory, but its theoretical approach (or analytical framework).

9. That is, Becker applies standard indifference curve analysis. The only difference with traditional applications is that preferences are not defined here over pairs of goods, but over pairs of incomes and that personal income is replaced by social income.

10. Note that this use of standard economic theory is in accordance with the take of 'conservatives' on the relation between evolution and economic theory. This is not surprising, since Becker (1962) himself was one of the first 'conservatives'.

11. In the literature on behavioural and experimental economics this is sometimes referred to as the *social preferences* hypothesis: next to a concern for their own material welfare, a concern for the wellbeing of others (altruism) or a 'taste' for fairness, equality and reciprocity are built in (as terms) in utility functions.

12. See also Nesse (2001) for further work on commitment in an evolutionary setting.

13. Frank himself can be blamed here for giving rise to misunderstanding, for he frequently writes as if individuals can choose their own preferences, goals and motives (Frank 1988, 2003).

14. It is not at all clear that evolutionary psychology really supports (or is even consistent with) the constrained maximisation framework of standard economic theory, however. A case can be made that the strict separation of affective (or motivational) and cognitive components that is implied in the constrained maximisation framework is inconsistent with evolutionary psychology's view on psychological mechanisms as the proximate causes of behaviour (see Vromen 2003a, 2003b; see also the discussion of the ABC group in the next section). See also the section on the 'revolutionary' ABC group.

15. To which can be added, however, that if we want to understand these processes of ontogenetic development and of cultural evolution, revisionists argue that we cannot ignore the biological heritage of our species.

16. In the remainder of this chapter I will be silent on these old and neo-institutionalists for the simple reason that they are dealt with in other contributions.

17. A dynamics is monotonic if the difference between the growth rates of the frequencies of any pair of strategies in some population has the same sign as the difference between their payoffs.

18. Hayek (1969) used to call Hume, Smith an other proponents of the Scottish Enlightenment 'Darwinians before Darwin' and urged social scientists interested in social evolution to orient themselves on these Darwinians before Darwin rather than on Darwin himself.

19. A question that one could pose here is: adapted to what? The 'logic' of the reasoning in both the ABC group and EP implies that the behaviour allegedly is adapted to ancestral circumstances.

But is the behaviour also adapted to present circumstances? Proponents of the ABC group tend to suggest that current actual behaviour is also adapted to present circumstances. Proponents of EP tend to follow suit (Cosmides and Tooby 1996), but no real arguments are given for this.

20. It is clear, however, that Simon himself considered the two to be the blades of a pair of scissors. Each of the approaches is incomplete and cannot work unless complemented by the other.

21. Note, however, that if routines have a conditional form, they generate different sorts of behaviour in different circumstances. Thus routines do not necessarily make for inert, rigid behaviour.

22. In this connection it is worth repeating that Nelson and Winter stress that their evolutionary theory is Lamarckian and not ('orthodox') Darwinian. For arguments that evolutionary economics is not and should not be committed to the view that individual behaviour is genetically prescribed, see Vromen (2001a).

References

Alchian, Armen A. (1950), 'Uncertainty, evolution and economic theory', *Journal of Political Economy*, **58**: 211–22.

Alexander, J. McKenzie (2002), 'Evolutionary Game Theory', *The Stanford Encyclopedia of Philosophy* Fall, Edward N. Zalta (ed.), URL = www://plato.stanford.edu/archives/fall2002/entries/game-evolutionary/.

Arthur, Brian (1989), 'Competing technologies, increasing returns and lock-in by historical events', *Economic Journal*, **99**, 116–31.

Aumann, R. (1997), 'On the state of the art in game theory: an interview with Robert Aumann (taken by Eric van Damme)', in W. Albers, W. Güth, P. Hammerstein, B. Moldovonu and E. van Damme (eds), *Understanding Strategic Interaction: Essays in Honor of Reinhard Selten*, Berlin: Springer Verlag, pp. 8–34.

Becker, Gary S. (1962), 'Irrational behavior and economic theory', *Journal of Political Economy*, **70**: 1–13.

Becker, Gary S. (1976), 'Altruism, egoism and genetic fitness: economics and sociobiology, *Journal of Economic Literature*, **14**, 817–26.

Ben-Ner, Avner, and Louis Putterman (1998), 'Values and institutions in economic analysis', in A. Ben-Ner and L. Putterman, *Economics, Values and Organization*, Cambridge: Cambridge University Press, pp. 3–69.

Ben-Ner, Avner, and Louis Putterman (2000), 'On some implications of evolutionary psychology for the study of preferences and institutions', *Journal of Economic Behavior and Organization*, **43**, 91–9.

Bicchieri, Christina (1993), *Rationality and Coordination,* Cambridge: Cambridge University Press.

Binmore, Ken (1987), 'Modelling rational players', part I, *Economics and Philosophy*, **3**, 179–214.

Binmore, Ken (1995), 'Foreword' in Jurgen W. Weibull, *Evolutionary Game Theory*, Cambridge, MA: MIT Press, pp. ix–xi.

Binmore, Ken and Larry Samuelson (1994), 'An economist's perspective on the evolution of norms', *Journal of Institutional and Theoretical Economics*, **150**, 45–63.

Camerer, Colin F. (2003), *Behavioral Game Theory: Experiments in Strategic Interaction*, New York: Russell Sage Foundation.

Cosmides, Leda, and J. Tooby (1992), 'Cognitive adaptations for social exchange', in J.H. Barkow, L. Cosmides and J. Tooby (eds), *The Adapted Mind*, Oxford: Oxford University Press, pp. 163–228.

Cosmides, Leda, and J. Tooby (1996), 'Are humans good intuitive statisticians after all? Rethinking some conclusions from the literature on judgment under uncertainty', *Cognition*, **58**, 1–73.

Cosmides, Leda, and J. Tooby (1999), 'Evolutionary psychology', in Robert A. Wilson and Frank C. Keil (eds), *MIT Encyclopedia of Cognitive Science*, Cambridge, MA: MIT Press, pp. 294–97.

Cyert, Richard M., and James G. March (1963), *A Behavioral Theory of the Firm*, Englewood Cliffs, NJ: Prentice-Hall.

Cziko, Gary (1995), *Without Miracles: Universal Selection Theory and the Second Darwinian Revolution*, Cambridge, MA: MIT Press.

David, Paul (1985), 'Clio and the economics of QWERTY', *American Economic Review Proceedings* **75**, 332–37.

Fehr, Ernst, and Simon Gächter (2002), 'Altruistic punishment in humans', *Nature* **415** (6868), 137–40.

Fodor, Jerry (1983), *The Modularity of Mind*, Cambridge, MA: MIT Press.

Foster, John (1999), 'The interaction of economic self-organisation and competitive processes', paper presented at workshop Progress in the Study of Economic Evolution, Ancona, 20–22 May 1999.

Frank, Robert H. (1988), *Passions within Reason*, New York: W.W. Norton.

Frank, Robert H. (1999), *Luxury Fever: Why Money Fails to Satisfy in an Era of Excess*, New York: Free Press.

Frank, Robert H. (2003), 'Adaptive rationality and the moral emotions', in R. Davidson, K. Scherer and H. Geldsmith (eds), *Handbook of Affective Sciences*, Oxford: Oxford University Press, pp. 891–6.

Friedman, Milton (1953), *Essays in Positive Economics*, Chicago: University of Chicago Press.

Gigerenzer, Gert (1996), 'On narrow norms and vague heuristics: a reply to Kahneman and Tversky', *Psychological Review*, **103**, 592–6.

Gintis, Herbert (2000), *Game Theory Evolving*, Princeton, NJ: Princeton University Press.

Glimcher, Paul M. (2003), *Decisions, Uncertainty, and the Brain: The Science of Neuroeconomics*, Cambridge, MA: MIT Press.

Güth, Werner, and H. Kliemt (1998), 'The indirect evolutionary approach: bridging the gap between rationality and adaptation', *Rationality and Society* **10** (3), 377–99.

Güth, Werner, and M.E. Yaari (1991), 'Explaining reciprocal behavior in simple strategic games: an evolutionary approach', in Ulrich Witt (ed.), *Explaining Process and Change: Approaches to Evolutionary Economics*, Ann Arbor, MI: University of Michigan, pp. 23–34.

Hargreaves Heap, Shaun, and Yanis Varoufakis (1995), *Game Theory: A Critical Introduction*, London: Routledge.

Hayek, Friedrich A. (1969), 'Dr. Bernhard Mandeville', in F.A. Hayek, *Freiburger Studien*, Tübingen: Mohr, pp. 126–43.

Hirshleifer, Jack (1976), 'Shakespeare vs. Becker on altruism: the importance of having the last word', *Journal of Economic Literature*, **14**, 500–502.

Hirshleifer, Jack (1977), 'Economics from a biological viewpoint', *Journal of Law and Economics*, **20**, 1–52.

Hirshleifer, Jack (1978), 'Competition, cooperation, and conflict in economics and biology', *American Economic Review (Papers and Proceedings)*, 68, 238–43.

Hirshleifer, Jack (1982), 'Evolutionary models in economics and law: cooperation versus conflict strategies', in R.O. Zerbe Jr. (ed.), *Research in Laws and Economics*, vol. 4, Greenwich, CT: JAI Press, pp. 1–60.

Hodgson, Geoffrey M. (2000), *Evolution and Institutions: On Evolutionary Economics and the Evolution of Economics*, Cheltenham, UK and Northampton, MA, USA: Edward Elgar.

Huck, S. (1997), 'Institutions and preferences: An evolutionary perspective', *Journal of Institutional and Theoretical Economics*, **153** (4), 771–9.

Kahneman, Daniel, and Amos Tversky (eds) (2000), *Choices, Values, and Frames*, Cambridge: Cambridge University Press.

Koopmans, Tjalling (1957), *Three Essays on the State of Economic Science*, New York: McGraw-Hill.

Krugman, Paul (1999), 'What economists can learn from evolutionary theorists – and vice versa', in J. Groenewegen and J. Vromen (eds), *Institutions and the Evolution of Capitalism: Implications of Evolutionary Economics*, Cheltenham, UK and Northampton, MA, USA: Edward Elgar, pp. 17–29.

Marengo, Luigi, and Marc Willinger (1997), 'Alternative methodologies for modelling evolutionary dynamics; Introduction', *Journal of Evolutionary Economics*, **7**, 331–8.

Maynard Smith, J. (1982), *Evolution and the Theory of Games*, Cambridge: Cambridge University Press.

Mayr, Ernst (1961), 'Cause and effect in biology', *Science*, **134**, 1501–6.
Nelson, Richard (1995), 'Recent evolutionary theorizing about economic change', *Journal of Economic Literature*, **39**, 48–90.
Nelson, Richard R., and Sidney Winter (1982), *An Evolutionary Theory of Economic Change*, Cambridge, MA: Harvard University Press.
Nesse, Randolph M. (ed.), (2001), *Evolution and the Capacity for Commitment*, New York: Russell Sage.
Robbins, Lionel (1932), *An Essay on the Nature and Significance of Economic Science*, London: Macmillan.
Robson, Arthur J. (2001), 'The biological basis of economic behavior', *Journal of Economic Literature*, **39**, 11–33.
Robson, Arthur J. (2002), 'Evolution and human nature', in *Journal of Economic Perspectives*, **16**, 89–106.
Samuels, Richard, Stephen Stich and Patrice D. Tremoulet (1999), 'Rethinking rationality: from bleak implications to Darwinian modules', in Ernest LePore and Zenon Pylyshyn (eds), *What is Cognitive Science*, Oxford: Blackwell, pp. 74–120.
Samuelson, Larry (1993), 'Does evolution eliminate dominated strategies?', in Ken Binmore, Alan Kirman and Pietro Tani (eds), *Frontiers of Game Theory*, Cambridge, MA: MIT Press, pp. 213–35.
Samuelson, Larry (1997), *Evolutionary Games and Equilibrium Selection*, Cambridge: MIT Press.
Satz, Debra, and John Ferejohn (1994), 'Rational choice and social theory', *Journal of Philosophy*, **91** (2), 71–87.
Schotter, Andrew (1981), *The Economic Theory of Social Institutions*, Cambridge: Cambridge University Press.
Selten, Reinhard (2002), 'What is bounded rationality?' in G. Gigerenzer and R. Selten (eds), *Bounded Rationality: The Adaptive Toolbox*, Cambridge, MA: MIT Press, pp. 13–36.
Simon, Herbert A. (1955), 'A behavioural model of rational choice', *Quarterly Journal of Economics*, **63**, 99–118.
Simon, Herbert A. (1956), 'Rational choice and the structure of the environment', *Psychological Review*, **63** (2), 128–38.
Skyrms, Brian (1996), *Evolution of the Social Contract*, Cambridge: Cambridge University Press.
Sperber, Dan (1996), *Explaining Culture: A Naturalistic Approach*, Oxford: Basil Blackwell.
Sperber, Dan (2001), 'An objection to the memetic approach to culture', in Robert Aunger (ed.), *Darwinizing Culture*, Oxford: Oxford University Press, pp. 163–73.
Sugden, Robert (1986), *The Economics of Rights, Cooperation, and Welfare*, Oxford: Basil Blackwell.
Sugden, Robert (2001), 'The evolutionary turn in game theory', *Journal of Economic Methodology*, **8**, 113–30.
Todd, Peter M., and Gerd Gigerenzer (2000), 'Précis of *Simple heuristics that make us smart*', *Behavioral and Brain Sciences* **23**, 727–80.
van Damme, Eric (1994), 'Evolutionary game theory', *European Economic Review*, **38**, 847–58.
Veblen, Thorstein (1898), 'Why is economics not an evolutionary science?', *Cambridge Journal of Economics*, **22** (4), 403
Vega-Redondo, Fernando (1996), *Evolution, Games, and Economic Behaviour*, Oxford: Oxford University Press.
Vromen, Jack J. (1995), *Economic Evolution: An Enquiry into the Foundations of New Institutional Economics*, London: Routledge.
Vromen, Jack J. (2001a), 'The human agent in evolutionary economics', in J. Laurent and J. Nightingale (eds), *Darwinism and Evolutionary Economics*, Cheltenham, UK and Northampton, MA, USA: Edward Elgar, 184–208.
Vromen, Jack J. (2001b), 'Ontological commitments of evolutionary economics', in Uskali Mäki (ed), *The Economic World View: Essays in the Ontology of Economics*, Cambridge: Cambridge University Press, pp. 189–224.

Vromen, Jack J. (2002), 'Stone Age minds and group selection – what difference do they make?', *Constitutional Political Economy*, **13**, 173–95.

Vromen, Jack J. (2003a), 'Cognitive science meets evolutionary theory – what implications does evolutionary psychology have for economic theorising?' in S. Rizzello (ed.), *Cognitive Developments in Economics*, London: Routledge, pp. 53–81.

Vromen, Jack J. (2003b), 'Why the economic conception of human behaviour might lack a biological basis', *Theoria*, **18** (48) 297–323.

Vromen, Jack J. (2004), 'Conjectural revisionary economic ontology: outline of an ambitious research agenda for evolutionary economics', *Journal of Economic Methodology*, **11**, 213–47.

Weibull, Jürgen W. (1995), *Evolutionary Game Theory*, Cambridge, MA: MIT Press.

Wilson, Edward O. (1975), *Sociobiology: The New Synthesis*, Cambridge, MA: Harvard University Press.

Winter, Sidney G. (1964), 'Economic "natural selection" and the theory of the firm', *Yale Economic Essays*, **4**, 225–72.

Witt, Ulrich (1993), 'Evolutionary economics: some principles', in Ulrich Witt (ed.), *Evolution in Markets and Institutions*, Berlin: Springer Verlag.

Witt, Ulrich (2003), *The Evolving Economy: Essays on the Evolutionary Approach to Economics*, Cheltenham, UK and Northampton, MA, USA: Edward Elgar.

Young, H. Peyton (1998), *Individual Strategy and Social Structure: An Evolutionary Theory of Institutions*, Princeton, NJ: Princeton University Press.

7 Normative economics and theories of distributive justice

Marc Fleurbaey

1. Introduction

The definition of what is good or just for society is not only important for political philosophy, it is also essential for economics insofar as the latter is involved in policy decision-making with consequences for the well-being of the population. The second half of the twentieth century witnessed an impressive joint effort in both disciplines to put some order into the various arguments and basic principles which may be relevant to the definition of a 'just' or a 'good' society, and to develop comprehensive doctrines and rigorous methods.

Three historical lines of thought about social justice provide the background of the more recent developments. The first is *utilitarianism*, a doctrine initiated by Jeremy Bentham, and oriented toward 'the greatest happiness of the greatest number', in its founder's words.[1] The utilitarian approach views *happiness* as the primary goal of human life, or at least as the goal which ought to be promoted by social and collective policies. The second pillar is *libertarianism*, whose core value is *freedom*, and focuses on individual *rights* rather than happiness. John Locke is commonly considered to be one of the first prominent authors in this line. The third historical pillar has been *egalitarianism*, the development of which can be traced back to Jean-Jacques Rousseau and Karl Marx, and which focused initially on the distribution of social advantage. Actually, utilitarianism and libertarianism have a significantly egalitarian flavor too, because utilitarianism is based on the principle that every individual should be given equal consideration in the global evaluation of total happiness, while libertarianism advocates an even distribution of basic rights and liberties.

In the last decades, the domination of utilitarianism (in the Anglo-Saxon world) and of Marxism (on the Continent) in political philosophy has been shaken by the surge of *liberal egalitarianism*, under the influence of John Rawls. Liberal egalitarianism combines features of libertarianism and egalitarianism. From the former it borrows a priority given to the respect of basic rights and the requirement that public policies should be neutral with respect to private goals that motivate individuals in their lives. But, out of egalitarian inspiration, it seeks a genuine equality in economic conditions by giving *priority to the worst-off*. This new brand of political philosophy has triggered a debate over what should be the proper focus of equalization: Equality of what? In particular, the key role of freedom and individual responsibility in this line of theory brings to the fore the distinction between legitimate and illegitimate inequalities.

The egalitarian features in Rawls' theory have led to a reaction from libertarian quarters, notably by Robert Nozick, who argued that a proper respect for freedom leaves no room for any kind of egalitarian redistribution. Discussions of the notion of *social contract* have also given way to other theories. But the attraction of a theory that gives priority to the worst-off has remained quite strong in spite of all criticisms, and egalitarian versions of utilitarianism and even of libertarianism have been elaborated, showing a kind of interesting convergence, even though many issues remain controversial.

In normative economics, things have taken a more dramatic turn. A traditional coexistence of advocates of the laissez-faire, such as Friedrich Hayek, with theorists of *welfare economics*, like Arthur Pigou, John Hicks or Paul Samuelson, has been troubled by a series of soul-searching developments in the latter field, ending up in its quasi disappearance from the mainstream of economic research.[2] The first event has been the realization that the interpersonal comparisons of utility needed in the traditional utilitarian calculus of total happiness could not be made on a purely empirical basis, and required value judgments for which no clear basis was available. This fact, vividly acknowledged by Lionel Robbins,[3] led to a growing resistance to the concept of utility itself, and to its replacement by the concept of preference in a stream of research that came to be known as 'New Welfare Economics'. The second event was the publication by Kenneth Arrow of an impossibility theorem which showed that no simple rule similar to majority voting could generate consistent social decisions on the basis of individual preferences. The third development was the emergence of a consensus, under the influence of Amartya Sen, that the only way to obtain a consistent criterion for social decisions was to resort to the kind of interpersonal utility comparisons which had been viewed as problematic decades earlier. At first glance, one could interpret this as meaning that welfare economics was back at square one.[4] And this might explain why most economists have deserted the field of normative thinking.

In the meantime, however, the theory of social choice had developed rigorous concepts about preference aggregation in general and interpersonal comparisons in particular. Moreover, the theory of bargaining, initiated by John Nash, had obtained an impressive array of results about solution concepts. Similarly, the theory of fair allocation, launched by Serge Kolm, Elisha Pazner, and others, had shown how important notions of fairness could be rigorously formulated in various economic models, and relied upon to single out satisfactory rules of allocation. These various theories provide valuable tools for new developments in welfare economics, and with them cross-fertilization with political philosophy is on more favorable ground than ever before.

The following sections present various approaches to defining social justice, and questions related to that issue. Developments belonging to economics and concepts from philosophical theories of justice are introduced according to their relevance to the topic of each section, and not by reference to a particular discipline, historical moment, or theory of justice. In this way, the focus is on issues and problems rather than on individual theories. The first concept to be discussed is Pareto efficiency, whose appeal and limitations pave the way for more refined developments, such as those inspired by the ideal of impartiality, from which authors like John Harsanyi and John Rawls have tried to derive ambitious conclusions. The libertarian reaction against such ambitious theories is the next considered, and its radical nature compared with more moderate theories of the social contract, such as David Gauthier's, which can be related to the economic theory of bargaining. With a richer set of ethical principles, the theory of social choice has provided invaluable analytical tools to describe a variety of social objectives, and one of the most interesting conceptual advances that followed its development has been the growing recognition that the ethics of interpersonal comparisons is not as subjective and arbitrary as was previously thought. In this respect the theory of fair allocation, and related theories of justice in terms of equality of resources, are quite interesting examples of how to deal with this issue in a tractable way, and, as will be explained below, much of the conventional wisdom on the difficulties of social choice has to be radically revised in this light. This chapter concludes with a brief description of other issues which challenge the main concepts and theories and suggest directions for future developments.

2.   The limits of Paretianism

Vilfredo Pareto noticed the conceptual significance of situations of *unanimous preference*. If the whole population prefers one alternative to another, this gives a strong argument in favor of this alternative. This notion can be used in particular in order to identify situations of *inefficiency*, where it is possible to make a move toward another situation which is better for some individuals and worse for none. In particular, the idea that competitive equilibria always produce efficient allocations has become a cornerstone of economics.

The attraction of the Pareto criterion is that it does not involve any interpersonal comparisons of utility, and does not convey any value judgment about the distribution. Because of this apparent ethical neutrality, it is tempting to try to make the most of this criterion. There have been many dubious uses of the Pareto criterion. The most common is the idea that, since any *Pareto improvement* (that is, any move to a situation preferred by some and less liked by no one) is a good thing, any identification of a Pareto-improving change should automatically lead to its implementation. This view implies a sanctification of the status quo, and this is even more dramatic in the attitude which makes some economists restrict their attention to reforms that are Pareto-improving.

One consequence of this kind of attitude is a general principled support for freedom of contract in economics, since free contractors never accept a deal unless it is good for both parties. Free trade is always Pareto-improving over autarky. This, however, neglects the fact that opening or deregulating a particular market has redistributive effects. Moreover, in situations of gross inequalities of initial endowments, the poorly endowed are easily willing to accept unfavorable transactions and terms of trade, even under competitive conditions. Freedom of contract is then a very questionable way to help improve their lot.

Paradoxically, when some welfare economists such as Nicholas Kaldor and John Hicks tried to get rid of the Pareto straitjacket in order to be able to defend policies that would hurt a well-to-do minority and benefit the rest of the population, they worsened the misuses of the Pareto principle. They argued that reforms that are not Pareto-improving but are such that the gainers could compensate the losers were almost as good as true Pareto improvements (Hicks 1939; Kaldor 1939). But the *potential* Pareto improvements epitomized in their *compensation tests* could not reasonably be considered as ethically significant as actual Pareto improvements. Moreover it was shown by Tibor Scitovsky and others that they lead to gross inconsistencies as soon as the price system is affected by the contemplated changes (Scitovsky).[5] Unfortunately, this approach has survived devastating criticism, under the guise of the *surplus criteria* (sum of compensating variations and sum of equivalent variations) which are still commonly used in some areas of economics (for a critical review, see Blackorby and Donaldson 1990). And, contrary to the initial intention, such criteria are usually biased in favor of the rich whenever there are income effects.

The only reasonable use of the Pareto principle consists in the identification of inefficient situations, which call for a change. But the direction of the change need not be dictated by the Pareto principle.[6]

Even under this cautious attitude, the application of the Pareto principle may still be problematic. Its *respect for individual preferences* (when they are unanimous) is appealing only when individual preferences are respectable, which is not always the case. Antisocial and obnoxious preferences are the most immediate example, but a more interesting problem occurs when uncertainty taints the contemplated options. Under uncertainty, individual preferences are based on tastes but also on beliefs about the probabilities of the states of nature, and when beliefs are heterogeneous in the population, spurious unanimity may come out as a result of a mixture of divergent tastes and opposite beliefs.[7]

3.   Impartiality and the veil of ignorance

All in all, the main limitation of the Pareto criterion is that it ignores distributional issues, and does not discriminate between situations of immense inequalities and more impartial situations. Introducing a requirement of impartiality is then a natural step at this stage. Impartiality is a concept which, like the Pareto criterion, can also be viewed as minimalist. It may be related to an attitude of equal respect, and does not immediately convey any strong preference for a pattern of distribution. In its now common definition, it just means that individuals' identities (names) are not a relevant characteristic in the evaluation of the distribution.[8]

But, once again, the temptation is to try to make the most of little, in order to avoid difficult value judgments. John Harsanyi has made an interesting attempt at deriving utilitarianism from impartiality. His *impartial observer* argument is based on the following story.[9] An impartial observer should decide for society as if she had an equal chance of becoming anyone in the considered population. Assuming that there are n individuals, and that the von Neumann/Morgenstern (VNM) utility for the observer to become individual i under policy x is $U(x, i)$, then her expected utility under policy x is computed as

$$\sum_{i=1}^{n} \frac{1}{n} U(x,i)$$

The similarity with the utilitarian criterion, which seeks to maximize the sum of individual utilities $U_i(x)$, is striking. In order to obtain a total congruence between the two formulae, it is enough to assume that $U(x, i) = U_i(x)$.

But this latter equality condition eludes any easy assessment. On the left-hand side, one has the observer's VNM utility, whereas the right-hand side features the individual utility as a utilitarian would like to measure it. It is not clear how the two concepts can be related, unless the observer is somehow supposed to be strongly influenced by utilitarianism. In other words, it is not so easy to obtain a thick criterion such as utilitarianism out of a thin requirement of impartiality.[10] This is hardly surprising.

Moreover, it is not even obvious that the character of the impartial observer really captures the content of impartiality. When the impartial observer decides that it is indifferent for her to experience one unit of VNM utility under the identity of i or of j, which are equiprobable, does this imply that the distribution of utility among individuals does not matter? The impartial observer is making trade-offs between alternative selves which are (equally) improbable, but social decisions have to do with conflicting interests of individuals who are all equally real and alive. It would be natural to find more egalitarianism in the latter context (see Kolm 1996, p. 191).

John Rawls has also tried to exploit the requirement of impartiality in an ambitious way.[11] He argued that the basic structure of society should be decided by a hypothetical assembly of individuals placed under a veil of ignorance hiding their identities and particular characteristics and goals. Since such ignorance deprives individuals of their personal traits, and places them all in an identical situation, called the 'original position', the setting is not so different from Harsanyi's impartial observer. But Rawls refused to rely on decision-making under uncertainty like Harsanyi,[12] and claimed that the uncertainty under which individuals consider their actual life in society from behind the veil of ignorance is so radical that their criterion should be the maximin, which gives absolute priority to the worst-off, rather than the expected utility. Moreover, he criticized the utility approach and argued that social justice has to do with allocating resources and rights, not utility, because individuals should at least assume responsibility for their ends, and, on grounds of justice, can only claim a fair share of resources. This ended in a complex architecture of principles, featuring equality of basic rights above equality of opportunity (careers open to talents), and the latter above the maximin applied to economic resources. It is impossible here to adequately describe the richness of Rawls' theory, whose impact on political philosophy and welfare economics has been profound and lasting. Even though many details of his theory have not survived decades of critical scrutiny, his defense of egalitarianism (represented by the maximin criterion) and his focus on resources rather than utility have influenced many authors and set the stage for many later developments.

Among them, it is worthwhile mentioning an original application of the veil of ignorance by Ronald Dworkin (1981, 2000). In order to define the fair allocation of resources among individuals, Dworkin proposes to refer to the ideal allocation that would result from a hypothetical insurance market, operating under the veil of ignorance, in which individuals would have equal budgets and would be allowed to buy insurance against unfavorable personal characteristics. The veil of ignorance would hide personal talents, but, contrary to Rawls' version, would let individuals remember their own goals and ambitions. As a consequence, for instance, someone with athletic ambitions could insure against physical disabilities, while someone with intellectual ambitions could insure against a low IQ. Once the veil of ignorance is lifted and talents are revealed, transfers would be operated in the form of indemnities toward those who would have insured against their bad draw. Dworkin suggests that the welfare state should be organized so as to mimic the result of such hypothetical indemnities as much as possible.

In view of the Harsanyi–Rawls opposition regarding the distributional criterion (sum or maximin), it is interesting to scrutinize Dworkin's proposal. If, on the hypothetical market, under the veil of ignorance, individuals maximize their expected utility, attributing equal probability to the possibility of ending up with any individual's talents, the final allocation will be closer to maximizing a sum of utilities than giving absolute priority to the worst-off. Equality of initial endowments on the hypothetical insurance market does little to avoid a utilitarian kind of outcome in the final allocation.[13]

4. The freedom flag

Utilitarianism as well as Rawlsian theories of justice generally advocate substantial redistribution, in favor of those who have greater needs (as measured by marginal utility of income, for utilitarianism, or by an inferior share of resources, for Rawlsian theories). In reaction to such support of the welfare state, Robert Nozick has tried to revive the libertarian ideal by delineating the constraints that an absolute priority of individual rights would impose on the scope of state intervention.[14]

The basic intuition on which the libertarian view is based is the following. If able and consenting adults engage in activities (such as production, exchange) that do not hurt third parties, there is no reason for the state to interfere and force them to relinquish part of their surplus. Taxing transactions and income is an intrusion into the individuals' sphere of freedom, and is therefore not so different from more violent kinds of oppression such as forced labor.

Now, the very protection of individual freedom, the guarantee of contracts, and the like, may require some state monitoring. As a consequence, Nozick allows for a minimal state with such basic functions, but other libertarians are more radical and would trust the market even in the presence of public good effects such as in law and order issues.

But the important conclusion derived by Nozick is that a proper respect for freedom of contract is totally incompatible with having the state maintain a pattern of income distribution, like those advocated by utilitarianism or egalitarianism. If individuals freely decide to pay a small fee to see a basketball star performing, this may create a situation in which one individual becomes extremely rich, in contradiction to any desirable pattern, but nothing can be done against such unintended but voluntary consequences of free exchange.

Needless to say, Nozick's plea has aroused a vivid rejoinder from egalitarian quarters. Nozick has been criticized in particular for his circular definition of freedom.[15] He defined freedom as the absence of any interference by others that violates individual rights. The latter clause about rights violation is needed because the minimal state, by protecting private property, may directly prevent individuals from certain actions (picking the neighbor's apples), and, in the libertarian creed, this is not a reduction of freedom. Since I have no right to my neighbor's apples, my being barred from his apples is not impinging on my freedom. But, in the libertarian approach, rights themselves are based on the guarantee of freedom, so that such notions seem indeed to be just tailored to defend private property. Egalitarians have rejuvenated the Marxian notion of real freedom in order to argue that, even if the minimal libertarian state may somehow maximize formal freedoms, what matters is the distribution of real freedom (see, in particular, Cohen 1995; van Parijs 1995). They have also argued that the basic institutions, including various sorts of state intervention, define what individuals are allowed to do in general, and that there is no prima facie reason for granting free exchange the sacred status it has in libertarianism.[16]

This latter argument is less convincing, and fails to see the attraction of the libertarian intuition as described above. When individuals spontaneously gather and strike a deal, it is certainly a burden for them to have to comply with a regulation of the terms of their contract or with an imposed obligation to pay part of their surplus to a third party. Even though this third party may happen to be the state and this payment may contribute to a better pattern of real freedom in society, the fact of the matter is that this is a burden they would, prima facie, rather do without. The massive reality of tax evasion proves this beyond doubt. A proper notion of real freedom should capture the need for minimizing state interference in daily life, including in transactions, and this, perhaps, would reconcile the libertarian intuition with the need for a comprehensive definition of freedom.

Variants of libertarianism have been proposed, which go a long way toward a wider acceptance of public assistance and redistribution. Nozick himself acknowledged that the minimal state was an ideal solution only for a perfect world with no anterior violations of rights. In the troubled history of mankind, violations of human rights and property have been so massive that it is impossible to defend the current distribution of property as an acceptable starting point for free transactions. A principle such as the Rawlsian maximin may, as Nozick admitted (1974, end of Ch. 7), be a better guide toward a reasonable solution in this imperfect context.

Nozick also insisted that the freedom of association requires, by its intrinsic logic, the acceptance of communities in which strong principles of solidarity and redistribution are enacted. The respect for freedom and individual rights does, however, require the possibility that any individual emigrate at little cost, and the availability of various kinds of communities with different life-styles and degrees of collective redistribution. In addition, Nozick also noticed that redistributive institutions may have an important symbolic utility for individuals who view such institutions as an expression of their own attitude and feelings toward others (Nozick 1974, 1989).[17]

Other authors have exploited another loophole in the libertarian theory. Before resources can be exploited and/or exchanged, they must be appropriated. This first appropriation cannot be justified by freedom of transaction, and requires a different principle. Locke himself, in the discussion of the American frontier, requested that 'enough and as good' should be left for others (Locke 1690), and Nozick transformed this proviso into the condition that no third party should be made worse-off by a first appropriation of some resource. Steiner has argued that the only way to implement this ideal condition is to put 'initially unowned resources' under a special status of common rights-holding, so that, even when they are privately managed, their use can benefit all mankind.[18] Concretely, this means that the rent from the use of such resources should be used for the general good, and distributed as equally as possible.

5.   Social contract and bargaining theory

The possibility for a group of individuals of any size, including the whole society, to decide freely on how to allocate the benefits of their mutual cooperation, suggests an extension of the notion of free contract epitomized in libertarianism. When the size of the group and the complexity of the matter make it impossible to let individuals themselves strike the deal, a fallback position is to devise a tacit agreement in the form of a 'social contract', that is, a contract that any individual, under ideal conditions, should reasonably accept. This line of thought leads back to considerations of social justice.

Brian Barry has opposed this approach, in which justice is viewed as based on mutual agreement, in favour of an approach based on impartial normative principles. And he has analysed in particular how Rawls' theory ambiguously toys with both approaches. The main difference lies in the fact that under the mutual agreement perspective, no attempt is made at compensating for initial inequalities that put some individuals in more favorable situations in the bargaining process (see Barry 1989, 1995).[19]

After long being dominated by Edgeworth's pessimistic conclusions about the impossibility of predicting where on the contract curve agents would make an agreement, the economic theory of bargaining was radically transformed by John Nash's introduction of the axiomatic method in order to pin down more precise solutions (Nash 1950).[20] The idea is that not all agreements are equally satisfactory, and in particular, that a good solution must be consistent over a whole class of conceivable bargaining problems.

In the two-agent case, Nash showed how to justify the agreement which maximizes

$$(U_1(x) - U_1(d)) (U_2(x) - U_2(d)),$$

where x denotes the agreement, d the disagreement point to which the agents would fall back in absence of a deal, and U_i is agent i's ($i = 1$ or 2) VNM utility function over all feasible alternatives. His axioms involved in particular a collective rationality condition (if the set of available options shrinks, no change is needed if the original agreement remains possible) and a scale invariance condition with respect to the choice of VNM functions (if one replaces a VNM function by another representing the same preferences, the agreement is not changed). But, more importantly, and questionably, he based his analysis on the *welfarist* principle that the agreement should only depend on the shape of the utility possibility set and not at all on other features pertaining to the structure of the alternatives or to the agents' preferences.[21]

Another prominent solution,[22] in the theory of bargaining, consists in equalizing the relative concession made by every agent:

$$\frac{\max_x U_1 - U_1(x)}{\max_x U_1 - U_1(d)} = \frac{\max_x U_2 - U_2(x)}{\max_x U_2 - U_2(d)},$$

where $\max_x U_i$ is the best utility agent i can reach on the set X of available alternatives x which are at least as good as d for both agents. This solution directly inspired David Gauthier's theory of justice (1986), in which the disagreement point is roughly defined as the libertarian laisser-faire situation, and in which the surplus from cooperation on public goods and externalities is divided so as to minimize the maximum relative concession made by individuals of the relevant population. This theory exemplifies the peculiar feature of the 'justice as mutual agreement' approach, namely, that no attempt is made to compensate for the disadvantage of those agents who are ill-endowed at the disagreement point and cannot offer much in the cooperation with others.[23]

6.   Social choice and social welfare
The mainstream of welfare economics accepted the need to develop concepts of the social good, or social justice, which combine basic Pareto and impartiality requirements with more explicit equity principles.

But one must first recall the alarming result which initially brought into question the mere possibility of combining Pareto and impartiality requirements. Kenneth Arrow, in a generalization of the problems encountered with the compensation tests of welfare economics[24] and of the paradoxes displayed by voting rules,[25] claimed to have uncovered a fundamental difficulty in defining 'social preferences' on the basis of individual preferences (see Arrow 1951). The object he submitted to axiomatic analysis was a function mapping the set of profiles of population preferences over a given set of alternatives into the set of complete preorders over that set. Such a function can be viewed as 'aggregating' individual preferences into a social relation of preferences.

The axioms imposed by Arrow on this function are the following. The Pareto principle requires that if all individuals strictly prefer one alternative to another, social preferences should exhibit the same ranking. Impartiality requires, at the very least, that no individual should be able, like a dictator, to impose his strict preference relation over the social preferences for all profiles of population preferences. In addition, Arrow introduced an axiom called 'Independence of Irrelevant Alternatives' (IIA), stipulating that the social ranking of two alternatives should only depend on individual pairwise preferences over these two alternatives, and not on any other feature of individual preferences.

Arrow's impossibility theorem states that there is no function satisfying these three conditions, when there are at least three alternatives, two individuals, and the domain of the function contains all conceivable profiles of individual preferences (in which every individual preference is a complete preorder).

Although Arrow's IIA axiom has been extensively commented upon and criticized after its introduction, it slowly came to be widely accepted, so that the theorem could be viewed as implying the devastating conclusion that even minimal formulations of Pareto and impartiality requirements were incompatible. At the beginning commentators actually could not agree on the relevance of this result for welfare economics, and the discussion erred for some time around the issue of whether one really needed to define social preferences for several population profiles.[26] It soon became clear that a similar result could be obtained even for a single profile of population preferences,[27] and it later also became transparent that Arrow's theorem could be rigorously reproduced in most economic models, which seemed to show its definite relevance (and destructive significance) for welfare economics.[28]

Under the influence of Amartya Sen in particular, the focus shifted to the limited informational basis imposed by Arrow's formulation in terms of individual non-comparable preferences.[29] If one had more information about individual well-being, allowing for instance the comparison of the levels of individuals' welfare in a particular alternative, could one escape the frightening impossibility? This question is based on the replacement of the function mapping population preferences into social preferences by a 'social welfare functional' mapping profiles of individual *utility functions* into social preferences (see d'Aspremont and Gevers (1977), Roberts (1980), Sen (1986, 1999)). In this extended setting, the Pareto and impartiality requirements can be retained unaltered. But the IIA axiom has been weakened into the condition that the social ranking of two alternatives should only depend on the *levels of utility* attained by individuals at these two alternatives (independently of utility levels at other alternatives). With this weakened version of IIA, the impossibility disappears, and is replaced by a flurry of possibilities, since any social welfare functional based on a traditional kind of social welfare function that is increasing and symmetrical will satisfy the three axioms. More precisely, let W be such a social welfare function, mapping any vector of utility levels $(u_1,\ldots,u_n)$ for the n individuals of the population into a real number $W(u_1,\ldots,u_n)$ measuring social welfare. One then simply has to define social preferences by stipulating that alternative x is weakly preferred to alternative y whenever

$$W\,(U_1(x),\ldots,U_n(x)) \geq W\,(U_1(y),\ldots,U_n(y)),$$

where $U_i(x)$ denotes individual i's utility level at alternative x.

Although this may have looked like a return to an antediluvian state of welfare economics, this re-introduction of social welfare functions was accompanied by several conceptual innovations. First, the availability of the axiomatic method made it possible to analyse with more precision the properties of the social welfare functionals, in particular those related to the shape of function *W*. And in the process it appeared that there was a relation between the degree of inequality aversion displayed by *W* and the kind of information about interpersonal utility comparisons one wants to rely upon.[30] At one extreme, the utilitarian social welfare function (with zero inequality aversion with respect to utilities)

$$W\left(u_1,...,u_n\right) = \sum_{i=1}^{n} u_i$$

is obtained if one wants to rely only on information about interpersonal comparisons of utility *differences*[31] whereas the maximin social welfare function (with infinite inequality aversion)

$$W\left(u_1,...,u_n\right) = \min_i u_i$$

obtains if one relies on interpersonal comparisons of *levels*. In between these two extremes, a social welfare function like the CES, with a finite degree of aversion to inequality ρ,

$$W\left(u_1,...,u_n\right) = \sum_{i=1}^{n} u_i^{1-\rho^{\frac{1}{1-\rho}}}$$

is related to the use of a more extensive information about levels, differences, and ratios of utility.[32]

A second difference between this approach and its pre-'new welfare economics' ancestor is that the difficulty of making interpersonal utility comparisons was now widely admitted, and was incorporated into a general philosophical questioning about how U_i should be conceived. The traditional approach in terms of subjective utility, dubbed 'welfarism', was submitted to intense criticism. The most influential criticism was probably the idea, already mentioned above, that subjective satisfaction belongs to the individual sphere of responsibility and that social justice has to do with the more limited issue of offering resources or opportunities see Rawls (1971, 1982), Dworkin (1981), Scanlon (1975) and Sen (1979, 1987).

At any rate, it became clear that the mathematical apparatus of social welfare functionals could be indifferently applied to any concept of individual well-being, including an objective view for which U_i is not individual i's personal characteristic but, rather, the ethical observer's (or the so-called 'social planner's') evaluation of i's value or importance for the achievement of social goals.[33] Following the line initiated by Rawls, Sen proposed defining U_i in terms of opportunities for a comprehensive list of individual beings and doings (including subjective and objective variables). The beings and doings he called *functionings,* and the opportunities for functionings were named *capabilities* (see Sen 1985, 1987).

Sen's approach is somewhat ecumenical as he does not make a very precise proposal about the relative importance of various functionings, though it has become usual, and convenient, to analyse the main theories of justice in terms of these two questions: (1) what is the shape of W (sum or maximin, most often)? (2) what is the definition of U_i? For instance, Rawls' theory can be summarized as being based on the *maximin* criterion applied to U_i defined by an objective index of the quantity of *primary goods* made available to the individual, where the notion of primary goods is meant to cover basic and all-purpose resources which are useful in any reasonable life-plan (the list of primary goods includes basic rights in addition to more ordinary economic resources).

The welfarist line has not been totally eclipsed by the new theories, but it is now widely accepted that individuals' ordinary preferences cannot be taken at face value. For many authors, anti-social preferences (sadism, jealousy, xenophobia) should not be allowed to influence the formation of social preferences, and it seems that even pro-social features such as altruism are problematic when they may lead to favoring the egoist at the expense of the altruist. Individual preferences should then be 'laundered' of all other-regarding traits, in order to retain only self-centered evaluations by individuals of their own personal situation. Impartial social preferences then have the task of comparing individual situations on the basis of individual self-centered preferences. Besides, individual welfare should presumably not be evaluated through the individuals' own immediate subjective impressions but on the basis of the best assessment they could reach in ideal conditions of deliberation and formation (see Harsanyi 1982; Goodin 1986).

7.   Theory of fairness and equality of resources

The theory of fair allocation emerged after the development of the Arrow–Debreu model of general equilibrium provided convenient representations of simple exchange and production economies, and was initially focused, in the seminal works of Serge Kolm, Hal Varian, among others, on the concept of '*envy*', which led to the definition of a fair allocation as one in which no agent would prefer consuming another's bundle (Kolm 1972; Varian 1974). The object that such a theory then started to look for was an *allocation rule,* namely, a function which selects a particular subset of feasible allocations (i.e. the subset of fair allocations) for every economy in a relevant domain of economies. The prominent allocation rule to which the no-envy criterion was related was the egalitarian competitive equilibrium, namely, the Walrasian equilibrium in which all agents have identical initial endowments.

On such a basis, the theory of fair allocation grew by borrowing the axiomatic method from the theory of bargaining, which has a similar solution concept in terms of a selection of a good subset of alternatives (as opposed to the theory of social choice which has the more ambitious goal of ranking all alternatives in a fine-grained way – on this difference, see below). The no-envy criterion can then provide an axiom requiring that any selected allocation be envy-free. The Pareto principle leads to an axiom requiring any selected allocation to be Pareto-efficient, etc. It soon appeared that the no-envy criterion was not the only notion of equity that could be formulated in this setting, and other concepts of equity were progressively introduced.[35] This was motivated in particular by difficulties with the no-envy criterion, which may lead to impossibilities, when agents have unequal production skills for instance. Consider an agent who is totally unproductive but has a very small labor disutility. In the presence of another agent who is productive but also more reluctant to work, a problem may occur because Pareto-efficiency requires that only the productive agent be at work. The trouble is that as soon as he is given a sufficient compensation in his own eyes, the unproductive but less labor-averse agent starts envying his labor-consumption bundle (see Pazner and Schmeidler (1974).

This problem is now understood to be traceable to a basic incompatibility between two requirements combined in the no-envy criterion when applied to such a setting (see Fleurbaey 1994; Fleurbaey and Maniquet 1996a). The first requirement is that agents who have identical preferences and differ only in their talents should end up with bundles they deem equivalent (on the same indifference curve). This can be motivated by the desire to neutralize the effect of differential talents, and may be related to a comprehensive *compensation principle* applied to all morally irrelevant individual characteristics (i.e. characteristics that cannot justify a more or a less favorable fate). The second requirement is that agents with identical talents who differ only in their preferences should not display envy, and this can be justified on the ground that they should have equal access to resources. Indeed, whenever agents get to choose their bundle in a common set, the resulting allocation is envy-free, as anyone could have chosen any other's bundle; conversely, any envy-free allocation could be obtained by letting every agent choose his bundle among the common set formed by the bundles currently consumed by the whole population. Giving equal resources to agents with identical talent can be related to a neutrality requirement of minimal interference. When talents (and more generally morally irrelevant characteristics) are identical there is no need for redistribution, and equally endowed the agents may obtain, with their morally relevant characteristics, whatever accrues to them.[36]

An interesting alternative to no-envy is the concept of egalitarian-equivalence, proposed by Elisha Pazner and David Schmeidler (1978), which concerns allocations in which every agent is indifferent between her current bundle and some reference bundle, the same for all agents. Allocation rules based on this concept have good properties in terms of solidarity. That is, they can guarantee that when the population size changes, for instance, all agents who are present before and after the change are all affected in the same direction (they all suffer or they all gain, according to their own preferences). Some of them also guarantee a similar solidarity when resources or the technology change and modify the set of feasible allocations. Such solidarity properties have been shown to be largely incompatible with the no-envy requirement. More precisely, they are not incompatible with the compensation principle; it is only the neutrality part of no-envy which raises a problem (see Moulin 1990; Fleurbaey and Maniquet 1996a).

There has been marked hesitation about how to relate the theory of fair allocation to philosophical theories of justice. One temptation is to restrict its scope to microeconomic problems with no bearing on general social justice. But authors like Kolm (1972, 1996) and Varian (1974) tried to relate the equity concept to Rawls' theory. After Dworkin's extensive use of the no-envy criterion (in 1981, 2000) in order to assess equality of resources, it has become clear that the main equity concepts of the theory of fair allocation are closely related to the idea of equalizing resources, as opposed to welfare. In particular, the informational setting that is common to all models in this theory displays only individual non-comparable preferences, and the equity requirements are all formulated in terms of individual preferences.

It is actually an interesting achievement of the theory of fair allocation to have explored the many facets of the idea of an equal sharing of resources. For instance, the requirement that every agent should be at least as well-off, according to her own preferences, as with an equal-split of the available resources, illustrates another possible formulation, different from no-envy. And it can be derived from the more general principle that all agents should benefit (or all should lose) from the fact that their preferences are heterogeneous (on this notion, see Moulin 1991). Similarly, the solidarity requirements with respect to population or resources also have to do with equal sharing.[37]

The relation between the theory of fair allocation and the theory of social choice also deserves some comment. There is a widespread consensus that their objects are different, because the theory of fair allocation focuses on selections of subsets of allocations, whereas the theory of social choice deals with social preferences. And actually, the early literature on fairness criticized the theory of social choice for being too ambitious in its goal of ranking all alternatives from the best to the worst, and the striking contrast between impossibility results in social choice and the many positive results in fair allocation is usually ascribed to this difference.[38] Later on, however, authors from the fairness field regretted their inability to say anything about imperfect allocations and second-best issues like optimal taxation. But the conventional idea is that this is the price to pay for positive results that do not involve interpersonally comparable utilities.[39]

It is very strange that such an explanation of the difference between the two theories may have been so successful in spite of its being so blatantly inaccurate. The theory of fair allocation and the theory of social choice both actually produce complete preorders on the set of alternatives. In fair allocation, attention is restricted to coarse preorders with only two classes, the good allocations and the bad ones. But a coarse ranking is still a ranking. This implies that the axioms of the theory of social choice can be directly called upon to see whether allocation rules satisfy them or not. And most interestingly, one can examine how allocation rules from the fairness side fare with respect to the axioms of Arrow's impossibility theorem. This only can provide the true explanation for the positive results in the theory of fair allocation.

The results of this examination are rather striking. The fair allocation rules fail to satisfy the IIA axiom, because they evaluate allocations on the basis of the agents' indifference curves at the allocations, whereas IIA forbids even the use of marginal rates of substitution in the analysis of allocations.[40] They do satisfy a weakened kind of independence axiom, according to which the social ranking of two allocations should only depend on the agents' indifference curves at these two allocations. For further reference, let this be called weak independence.[41]

Secondarily, the fair allocation rules also fail to satisfy the Pareto principle of Arrow's theorem, since they refuse to rank bad allocations, even when one is strictly preferred to another by the whole population. The question which arises at this stage is whether weak independence, instead of IIA, would make it possible to obtain fine-grained (i.e. Paretian) social preferences instead of coarse allocation rules. The answer is definitely positive. A trivial example was proposed long ago by Paul Samuelson and later refined by Elisha Pazner, and consists in applying a social criterion like the maximin to the fractions of total consumption to which individuals are indifferent with their current bundles. In other words, just ask every individual what fraction of the total consumption she would accept in exchange for her current consumption. Then use these fractions as numbers on which the maximin criterion can be applied (see Samuelson 1977; Pazner 1979).[42]

Not only is the answer positive, but the possibilities are so wide that the very weak impartiality condition posited in Arrow's theorem under the no-dictator heading can be supplemented by much more demanding equity principles borrowed from the theory of fair allocation. Social preferences are not only possible, they can be required to be substantially equitable.[43]

In other words, the theory of fair allocation contains an interesting solution to the problem of social choice, and the two theories can be merged to construct fair social preferences. This has far-reaching consequences, because it means that, without introducing interpersonally comparable utilities, it is possible to rank all allocations in a fine-grained way, on the basis of equity principles. Analysis of reforms in an imperfect world, cost–benefit analysis and optimal taxation are then open to the tools of this broadened theory of fair social choice.[44]

Let us compare this with the theory of social welfare functionals based on interpersonal comparisons of utility. The characteristic feature of the latter is that it depends on interpersonally comparable utility functions that must be provided from outside the theory, for instance by moral philosophy. In contrast, the theory of fair social choice does not require any further information about individuals than ordinal non-comparable preferences (and possibly other characteristics like productive talent, but nothing about utility), and is able to derive, on the basis of equity principles, how to evaluate a social situation. As the Samuelson–Pazner example mentioned above shows, such social preferences may actually rely on interpersonal comparisons[45] of some index of resources (like the fraction of total resources to which an agent is indifferent), which means that the formal description of the social preferences may not be so different from what is obtained in some versions of the social welfare functionals approach. More precisely, the theory of fair social choice may supplement the theory of social welfare functionals when the latter defines individual utility in terms of resources, by helping to construct the relevant index of individual resources. For instance, instead of letting Rawls' theory be poorly defined as the maximin applied to some unspecified index of primary goods, one can try to make it more precise by relying on the theory of fair social choice in order to justify, on axiomatic grounds, not only the maximin criterion, but also a precise formulation for the index of primary goods.

8.   Challenges

The theory of social welfare functionals and the theory of fair social choice, and their connections with recent philosophical theories of justice, allow us to be optimistic about our ever increasing ability to say more, and more relevant things, about the evaluation of social states of affairs. But there remain important challenges which will be briefly listed here.

A first difficulty has to do with the fact that economic models remain highly idealised, so that it is not easy to jump to practical conclusions. For instance, the theory of fair allocation, and by way of consequence the theory of fair social choice, is still unable to say anything of substance about equity in a general model with production of multiple private and public goods. The exploration of more concrete models seems a precondition for the ability to have more productive exchanges with philosophers who are concerned with institutions of the real world, and to gain more relevance in public debates. In absence of serious concepts from sound normative theories, the playing field is left entirely to untidy applications of dubious surplus criteria, GDP comparisons, fancy indices of human development, or ideological dogmatism based on ill-understood elementary economics.

Another challenge, also related to realism of the framework, has to do with time and uncertainty. The two always go hand in hand in practice, but they involve different conceptual difficulties. The difficulty with time is mostly about future generations. The period in which an individual lives is a morally irrelevant characteristic, and there is no reason to favor future generations or to impose time preference in social preferences, but applying a rough egalitarian approach to intergenerational allocation is likely to kill any possibility of growth, and this is usually criticized as morally counter-intuitive. This no-growth conclusion can however be avoided by giving some role to parental altruism, that is, by abandoning the principle that only self-centered individual preferences should serve for social evaluation. Uncertainty about the future may also help since guaranteeing an equal certainty-equivalent consumption for future generations requires granting them a growing expected consumption, since uncertainty is larger in a more remote future. But uncertainty itself raises difficult issues, and focusing on expected utility (or certainty-equivalent resources) leads to neglecting ex-post inequalities that may be produced by independent risk-taking decisions by the agents. It remains largely an open question how to consistently take account of ex ante prospects and of ex-post inequalities.[46]

The issue of future generations also raises the question of optimal demography. The size and composition of the future population is affected by our current decisions, and this seems to require a criterion of optimal population size. There is an opposition between criteria expressed in terms of total population welfare, which are biased in favor of large populations, and criteria in terms of average population welfare, which are biased in favor of small and affluent populations. The key concept is that of a critical level, which determines the threshold of individual welfare (or resources) such that the introduction of a new individual below the threshold is considered socially undesirable. No theory has yet proposed a precise way to define the level of this threshold.[47]

Similar but even more difficult problems arise in respect of populations of non-human species. Considering environmental and biodiversity issues purely in terms of public goods for humans is offensively anthropocentric, and defenders of animal rights and welfare have argued that impartiality requirements should apply beyond the limited circle of human beings. The definition of a fair adjudication of conflicting interests between humans and non-humans is for the moment quite out of the reach of the theory of social choice, and most theories of justice shun the issue altogether (see, for example, Singer 1986).

On purely human matters regarding the organization of society, another array of criticisms can be addressed at the reductionist anthropology on which economic models and Rawlsian theories of justice alike are based. It is often said that homo economicus is not a proper rendering of human motivations, but the problem lies much deeper than that, and Rawlsian theories cannot be accused of adopting such a narrow view of human activity. Moreover, it has been explained above that, from a normative standpoint, focusing on self-centered (which does not mean egoistic) preferences is justified in the name of impartiality. The problem is rather that these theories largely ignore the social nature of individual constitution. This has to do with the formation of preferences, and with the importance of social relations for individual welfare. Both issues are usually barely mentioned, and most of the attention is concentrated on trading-off the supposedly well-defined interests of individuals and on sharing resources as if every individual was afterward supposed to use such resources privately. Such an approach therefore ignores how deeply social relations shape individuals, their goals and the quality of their life (see, for example, Sandel 1982).[48]

For instance, the Marxian concept of domination has been abandoned to sociology and is seldom used in normative economics or in theories of justice, which are then blind to the fact that normally able adults, in particular social conditions, may consent to social relations which deprive them of their autonomy. The insistence on liberal neutrality, which prevents any discussion of public policies and social institutions from being based on a particular conception of the 'good life', assumes that individuals are autonomous enough to always remain the masters of their goals and views about the good life, and ignores the power of social convention which may bias individuals' perceptions about the goodness of things.[49] Aristotle and Locke were not shocked by slavery. What will our descendants think of our own complacency with current social relations?

A final challenge to be mentioned has to do with metaethics. The legitimacy of normative thinking and the relevance of theories of justice are recurrently questioned. Many economists are tempted by the apparently neutral view that justice is whatever the population wants, failing to see that this itself is controversial, and certainly quite meaningless when the population is not unanimous. It is convenient to defend normative economics and political philosophy as offering clarification and concepts for the public deliberation, but this does not really address the issue of the foundations of ethical principles. In this respect, Rawls' own evolution (between Rawls 1971 and 1993) from Kantian ambitions to a more modest goal of expressing and deciphering the common values of western societies, is a significant measure of the vulnerability of philosophical debates which too often appeal to immediate moral intuition through contrived examples. Fundamentally, one may ask whether our attraction toward ethical principles is not based primarily on pragmatic considerations about the viability of social arrangements,[50] or on a desire to cast in stone an expression of our mutual feelings, rather than on purely logical constraints imposed by the dry project of a peaceful coexistence of rational beings with separate aims. The repercussions of such questioning on the content of theories of justice and on the axiomatic routines of social choice have yet to be explored.

Acknowledgement

I am grateful to J. Davis and J. Runde for their helpful remarks. The usual disclaimer applies.

Notes

1. The idea of maximizing total happiness, or average happiness, or the number of happy people, had been circulating throughout the Enlightenment century among European thinkers. Bentham's (1789) formula is interestingly ambiguous.
2. As recently regretted in Atkinson (2001): 'the study of welfare judgments ... is no longer a mainstream subject and is not regarded as an essential part of the economics curriculum.' (p. 193) 'Just as one should be able to inspect estimated statistical relations, so too a well-trained economist should be able to scrutinize the moral underpinnings of a policy statement' (p. 204).
3. Robbins (1932). His intention was less to dismiss value judgments than to emphasize their separate but necessary role, as made clear in Robbins (1981).
4. Here is an example of a typical view on these matters: 'For many years, the majority of economists took the position that the making of interpersonal comparisons, if not impossible, was certainly no part of the economist's trade. In view of Arrow's theorem, such a view leaves very little for welfare economics to do, and much of the so-called new welfare economics of the 1940's and 1950's that embodied this position makes sterile reading by contemporary standards' (Deaton and Muellbauer 1980, p. 217).
5. Scitovsky (1941). A good synthesis on the Kaldor–Hicks–Scitovsky compensation tests is made in Boadway and Bruce (1984).
6. As an example, suppose that three distributions of wealth are possible, between two main subpopulations: $A = (1, 5)$, $B = (2, 6)$, and $C = (4, 4)$. Staying at A would be inefficient, because of the availability of B, but this docs not mean that if A is the status quo, moving to B should be the favored option. Moving to C is likely to be the best choice.
7. For instance, consider two policies, a risky x and a non-risky y, and two subpopulations. The outcome of y is the distribution $(3, 3)$. The outcome of x may be either $(4, 1)$ or $(1, 4)$. If the first subpopulation thinks that the outcome of x is more likely to be $(4, 1)$, it may prefer x. If the second subpopulation thinks that the outcome of x will be $(1, 4)$, it also prefers x. But, at the social level, it seems clear that y gives a better outcome. For a recent in-depth analysis of these matters, see Mongin (1995).
8. Interestingly, one may enlarge the list of irrelevant characteristics in order to strengthen the impartiality requirement. For instance, sex, social origin, ethnic descent may be declared irrelevant in a broader view of impartiality. The fact that such data are usually ignored in models of welfare economics reflects an implicit adoption of more stringent impartiality requirements than the restrictive definition in terms of anonymity that is made explicit.
9. See Harsanyi (1953). This paper and related ones are reprinted in Harsanyi (1976).
10. Recent discussions on the interpretation of Harsanyi's argument may be found in Weymark (1991), Fleurbaey (1996), Mongin (2001).
11. His major work is Rawls (1971), and important clarifications and revisions have been made in Rawls (1982, 1993).
12. This is discussed in Rawls (1974). See Harsanyi (1976) on this controversy.

13. This point was made by Roemer (1985), and recently developed in Fleurbaey (2002).
14. Nozick (1974). See also Friedman (1973), Rothbard (1973). Hayek's defense of the market economy is often compared to libertarianism, but is based on quite different grounds. Whereas libertarians base their argument on normative principles, Hayek mainly advocated the superiority of the market over other institutions on pragmatic grounds, especially the impossibility for the state to process as efficiently as the market, the complex information about the agents' characteristics and goals that is relevant to coordinating their activities (see, for example, Hayek 1960). Hayek's normative criteria were not much different from traditional utilitarianism. A similar assessment can be made about Buchanan (see Buchanan 1975, Brennan and Buchanan 1985), who questions Rawls' optimism about the possibility of redistributive policies, because individuals should be expected to display self-interested behavior in the political arena and not only in their economic decisions. Buchanan proposes to adopt a constitutional definition of property that incorporates some rules of transfer and support for the destitute, in order to avoid any need for further redistribution.
15. Nozick's (1969, 1974) moralized definition of coercion and freedom has triggered a huge literature. Among recent contributions, see Cohen (1995), Olsaretti (1998), Trebilcock (1993).
16. According to Cohen, for instance, 'the standard use of 'intervention' esteems the private property component in the liberal or social democratic settlement too highly, by associating that component too closely with freedom' (1995, p. 57). 'The general point is that incursions against private property which *reduce* owners' freedom by transferring rights over resources to non-owners thereby *increase* the latter's freedom. In advance of further argument, the net effect on freedom of the resource transfer is indeterminate' (ibid.).
17. The fact that private contracts may be supplemented by collective contracts around the provision of public goods (such as poverty reduction) has been emphasized by Kolm (1985, 1996), who extended that idea to tacit social contracts discussed in the next section.
18. In a fully appropriated world, each person's original right to an equal portion of initially unowned things amounts to a right to an equal share of their total *value*' Steiner (1994, p. 271).
19. Again, the temptation here is to derive a lot (social justice) from little (impartiality). In the strict sense of anonymity, theories of justice as mutual agreement are also fully impartial. Only a broader notion of impartiality (a more extensive list of irrelevant characteristics, although it remains quite vague) enables Barry to make the distinction.
20. For recent surveys on the theory of bargaining, see Peters (1992) and Thomson (1999).
21. Roemer (1990) shows that in absence of this welfarist principle, Nash's axioms lose all their power. Further, the welfarist principle is hardly acceptable. For instance, suppose that two agents have to bargain on the probability with which one of them will win in a lottery. The lottery may be exogenously biased in the sense that the prize given to the first agent if she wins may differ from the prize given to the second agent if he wins. Any welfarist solution that is impartial and satisfies the scale invariance axiom (such as the Nash solution) will invariably select the 50–50 deal, no matter how biased the lottery is. This is not reasonable: When the lottery is biased in favor of one agent, they may choose a probability that is more favorable to the other agent, in compensation. And they may do so independently of any utility information. A rejection of welfarism in experiments was presented by Yaari and Bar-Hillcl (1984). For a recent synthesis, see Schokkaert (1999).
22. This is due to Kalai and Smorodinsky (1975), who replace Nash's collective rationality axiom with a condition stipulating that a deformation of the utility possibility set in favor of one agent should not hurt this agent.
23. Ken Binmore (1994, 1998) relies on bargaining theory in an original way in order to address the problem of social justice. His theory mixes the maximin criterion, the Nash bargaining solution and laisser-faire. In the short run, the maximin criterion (over utilities) will apply as a consequence of the possibility that individuals appeal to a veil of ignorance argument. In the medium run, interpersonal utility comparisons are moulded so that the maximin coincides with the Nash bargaining solution. In the long run, individual preferences evolve so that all that boils down to the market competitive solution.
24. See Hicks (1939) and Kaldor (1939) and note 5 above.

25. The majority rule applied to pairs of alternatives may lead to intransitive rankings. Alternative *x* may beat alternative *y* with a majority, *y* may beat alternative *z*, and the latter may beat alternative *x*! This is known as the Condorcet paradox. Sec Young (1994) for a simple exposition of the issue and of an interesting solution, and Young (1988) for an in-depth analysis of Condorcet's views.
26. For a recent synthesis by one of the main early critics, see Samuelson (1987).
27. This was shown by Kemp and Ng (1976), who replaced the IIA axiom, which bears on the multi-profile setting, with a single-profile independence axiom stipulating that when two pairs of alternatives entail a similar pattern on individual preferences (whenever an individual prefers the first over the second in the first pair, the same occurs in the second pair), the two pairs should be identically ranked by social preferences. For an answer and a rebuttal of this axiom, see Samuelson (1977).
28. A short survey of social choice in economic environments appears in Le Breton (1997), and a very extensive one is provided by Le Breton and Weymark (2002).
29. Sen (1970) has been influential in attracting interest to the challenge raised by Arrow's theorem, and in orienting researches toward the re-introduction of utility functions. Sen (1977) argued that Arrow's framework was relevant to the aggregation of preferences, but not to the aggregation of economic interests (which, according to him, required interpersonally comparable utilities). For a recent synthesis, see Sen (1999).
30. There are many excellent surveys, such as d'Aspremont (1985), Sen (1986), Bossert and Weymark (1998).
31. An often ignored subtlety is that the mere knowledge of comparisons of utility differences may not be enough for the utilitarian criterion. For instance, with a population of three individuals, assume that

$$U_1(x) - U_1(y) > U_2(y) - U_2(x) > U_3(y) - U_3(x) > 0.$$

This information is insufficient to rank *x* and *y* with the utilitarian criterion. See Bossert (1991). The ratios of utility differences give sufficient information for the utilitarian criterion.
32. Notice that those social welfare functions do not actually *require* that much information. For instance, knowing how the sum $\Sigma_i u_i$ ranks all alternatives of a given set does not always enable one to say much about interpersonal comparisons of utility differences (when there are more than two individuals). The relation described in the text goes in the other way, that is: When the only information available is such or such, then the social preferences have to be such or such.
33. This view is applied for instance in Atkinson (1995).
34. Variants of welfarism are proposed in Griffin (1986) and Sumner (1996). Arneson (1989) defines justice as equality of *opportunity for* welfare. This remains welfarist but goes a long way toward the Rawlsian approach, insofar as opportunities for welfare are largely determined by available resources. Cohen (1989) advocates a similar (but less strictly welfarist) view, which comes very close to Sen's theory of capabilities.
35. For a recent survey, see Moulin and Thomson (1997). See also Moulin (1990).
36. On these notions, see Fleurbaey (1995, 1998), Fleurbaey and Maniquet (1999b).
37. True enough, solidarity requirements can be satisfied by quite inegalitarian allocation rules (for instance, the rule that gives everything to one agent), but the connection becomes more transparent under an impartiality constraint, since, for instance, solidarity with respect to changes in productive talents implies, for any impartial allocation rule, satisfaction of the compensation principle (give agents with equal preferences bundles they deem equivalent, i.e. on the same indifference curve). This is due to the fact that, because of solidarity, any selected allocation must be indifferent, for all individuals, to an allocation that would be selected in some virtual economy with identical talents. In the latter allocation, agents with identical preferences would then be fully identical, so that impartiality would require giving them bundles on the same indifference curve. See Fleurbaey and Maniquet (1999a).
38. This interpretation is proposed by Sen (1986) and Moulin and Thomson (1997) among others.

39. In Varian (1976), for instance, an effort is made at proposing fine-grained rankings of allocations based on the no-envy criterion, but they rely on interpersonally comparable utilities.
40. Let us consider the egalitarian Walrasian allocation rule, as an example, in a population with 20 agents. This allocation rule ranks all equal-budget Walrasian allocations above all other allocations. Consider two allocations x and y, such that all agents $i = 1,\ldots, 10$ prefer x and all agents $i = 11, \ldots,20$ prefer y. According to IIA, this should be enough information to rank x and y. But this is certainly not enough to know whether any one of these allocations is a Walrasian equilibrium (with equal budgets). For a criticism of Arrow's IIA along these lines, sec Pazner (1979), Samuelson (1987), Fleurbaey and Maniquet (1996b).
41. That is, if individual preferences change but indifference curves at x and y remain unaltered, then social preferences over x and y should not change. See Fleurbaey and Maniquet (1996b). This condition was already proposed by Pazner (1979) and, in a slightly different way, by Hansson (1973).
42. For other examples and a general method of construction of social preferences, see Fleurbaey and Maniquet (1996b).
43. Characterizations of social preferences on the basis of equity axioms are proposed in, for example, Fleurbaey and Maniquet (2000, 2001).
44. For an application to optimal taxation, see Fleurbaey and Maniquet (2002).
45. For a general analysis of interpersonal comparisons in the various approaches to social choice, see Fleurbaey and Hammond (2002).
46. Harsanyi's (1955) aggregation theorem states that under uncertainty (with objective probabilities), when individual preferences satisfy the expected utility hypothesis, and social preferences are based on the maximization of the expected value of social welfare, the Pareto principle (with respect to individual ex ante preferences over prospects) implies that social welfare must depend on a weighted sum of individual VNM utilities, which excludes any inequality aversion. In other words, maximizing the expected value of an inequality-averse social welfare function is incompatible with respecting individual preferences over risky prospects. Broome (1991) and Hammond (1996) propose to rely on a utilitarian social welfare function, but redefining individual well-being so as to take account of ex post inequalities. Other proposals may be found in Deschamps and Gevers (1979), Ben-Porath et al. (1997), Gajdos and Maurin (2002).
47. For a synthesis on this issue, see Blackorby et al. (1997).
48. A valuable collection on communitarianism has been edited by S. Avineri and A. de-Shalit (1992). Rawls (1993) addresses such criticism, but his rejoinder restricts the collective project to the peaceful and ordered coexistence of individuals in a just society. This cannot satisfy the critics who consider that the ethics of individual life is also permeated by a collective dimension.
49. On neutrality, see, for example, Dworkin (2000, Ch. 5). For a defense of a non-neutral promotion of autonomy, see, for example, Raz (1986) and Galston (1991).
50. This approach is articulated in Copp (1995). See also Binmore (1994, 1998).

References

Arneson, R.J. (1989), 'Equality and equal opportunity for welfare', *Philosophical Studies*, 56, 77–93.
Arrow, K.J. (1951), *Social Choice and Individual Values,* New York: Wiley.
Atkinson, A.B. (1995), *Public Economics in Action. The Basic Income/Flat Tax Proposal*, Oxford: Clarendon Press.
Atkinson, A.B. (2001), 'The strange disappearance of welfare economics', *Kyklos*, 54, 193–206.
Avineri, S. and A. de-Shalit (1992), *Communitarianism and Individualism*, Oxford: Oxford University Press.
Barry, B. (1989), *A Treatise on Social Justice, I. Theories of Justice*, Berkeley: University of California Press.
Barry, B. (1995), *A Treatise on Social Justice, II. Justice as Impartiality*, Oxford: Oxford University Press.

Ben Porath, E., I. Gilboa and D. Schmeidler (1997), 'On the measurement of inequality under uncertainty', *Journal of Economic Theory*, 75, 194–204.

Bentham, J. (1789 [1967]), *An Introduction to the Principles of Morals and Legislation*, Oxford: Basil Blackwell.

Binmore, K. (1994), *Game Theory and the Social Contract I. Playing Fair*, Cambridge, MA: MIT Press.

Binmore, K. (1998), *Game Theory and the Social Contract II. Just Playing*, Cambridge, MA: MIT Press.

Blackorby, C. and D. Donaldson (1990), 'A review article: the case against the use of the sum of compensating variations in cost–benefit analysis', *Canadian Journal of Economics*, 23, 471–94.

Blackorby, C., W. Bossert and D. Donaldson (1997), 'Critical-level utilitarianism and the population-ethics dilemma', *Economics and Philosophy*, 13, 197–230.

Boadway, R. and N. Bruce (1984), *Welfare Economics*, Oxford: Basil Blackwell.

Bossert, W. (1991), 'On intra- and interpersonal utility comparisons', *Social Choice and Welfare*, 8, 207–19.

Bossert, W. and J.A. Weymark (1998), 'Utility theory in social choice', forthcoming in S. Barbera, P.J. Hammond and C. Seidl (eds), *Handbook of Utility Theory*, vol.2, Dordrecht: Kluwer.

Brennan, G. and J. Buchanan (1985), *The Reason of Rules: Constitutional Political Economy*, Cambridge: Cambridge University Press.

Broome, J. (1991), *Weighing Goods*, Oxford: Basil Blackwell.

Buchanan, J. (1975), *The Limits of Liberty: Between Anarchy and Leviathan*, Chicago: University of Chicago Press.

Cohen, G.A. (1989), 'On the currency of egalitarian justice', *Ethics*, 99, 906–44.

Cohen, G.A. (1995), *Self-Ownership, Freedom and Equality*, Paris/Cambridge: Maison des Sciences de l'Homme: Cambridge University Press.

Copp, D. (1995), *Morality, Normativity, and Society*, Oxford: Oxford University Press.

d'Aspremont, C. (1985), 'Axioms for social welfare orderings', in L. Hurwicz, D. Schmeidler and H. Sonnenschein (eds), *Social Goals and Social Organization. Essays in Memory of Elisha Pazner*, Cambridge: Cambridge University Press.

d'Aspremont, C. and L. Gevers (1977), 'Equity and the informational basis of collective choice', *Review of Economic Studies*, 44, 199–209.

Deaton, A. and J. Muellbauer (1980), *Economics and Consumer Behaviour*, Cambridge: Cambridge University Press.

Deschamps, R. and L. Gevers (1979), 'Separability, risk-bearing, and social welfare judgments', in J.J. Laffont (ed.), *Aggregation and Revelation of Preferences*, Amsterdam: North-Holland.

Dworkin, R. (1981), 'What is equality? Part 1: equality of welfare; Part 2: equality of resources,' *Philosophy and Public Affairs*, 10, 185–246 and 283–345.

Dworkin, R. (2000), *Sovereign Virtue. The Theory and Practice of Equality*, Cambridge, MA: Harvard University Press.

Fleurbaey, M. (1994), 'On fair compensation', *Theory and Decision*, 36, 277–307.

Fleurbaey, M. (1995), 'Equality and responsibility', *European Economic Review*, 39, 683–9.

Fleurbaey, M. (1996), *Theories economiques de la justice*, Paris: Economica.

Fleurbaey, M. (1998), 'Equality among responsible individuals,' in J.F. Laslier, M. Fleurbaey, N. Gravel and A. Trannoy (eds), *Freedom in Economics*, London: Routledge.

Fleurbaey, M. (2002), 'Equality of resources revisited', *Ethics*, 113, 82–105.

Fleurbaey, M. and F. Maniquet (1996a), 'Fair allocation with unequal production skills: the no-envy approach to compensation', *Mathematical Social Sciences*, 32, 71–93.

Fleurbaey, M. and F. Maniquet (1996b), 'Utilitarianism versus fairness in welfare economics', forthcoming in M. Salles and J.A. Weymark (eds), *Justice, Political Liberalism and Utilitarianism: Themes from Harsanyi and Rawls*, Cambridge: Cambridge University Press.

Fleurbaey, M. and F. Maniquet (1999a), 'Fair allocation with unequal production skills: the solidarity approach to compensation', *Social Choice and Welfare*, 16, 569–83.

Fleurbaey, M. and F. Maniquet (1999b), 'Compensation and responsibility', forthcoming in K. J. Arrow, A.K. Sen and K. Suzumura (eds), *Handbook of Social Choice and Welfare*, vol. 2, Amsterdam: North-Holland.

Fleurbaey, M. and F. Maniquet (2000), 'Fair orderings with unequal production skills', Thema, 2000–2017.

Fleurbaey, M. and F. Maniquet (2001), 'Fair social orderings', mimeo, University of Pau and University of Namur.

Fleurbaey, M. and F. Maniquet (2002), 'Fair income tax', mimeo, University of Pau and Institute of Advanced Studies, Princeton.

Fleurbaey, M. and P.J. Hammond (2002), 'Interpersonally comparable utility', forthcoming in S. Barbera, P.J. Hammond and C. Seidl (eds), *Handbook of Utility Theory*, vol.2, Dordrecht: Kluwer.

Friedman, D. (1973), *The Machinery of Freedom*, New York: Arlington.

Gajdos, T. and E. Maurin (2002), 'Unequal uncertainties and uncertain inequalities', mimeo, CREST-INSEE.

Galston, W.A. (1991), *Liberal Purposes. Goods, Virtues, and Diversity in the Liberal State*, Cambridge: Cambridge University Press.

Gauthier, D. (1986), *Morals by Agreement*, Oxford: Clarendon.

Goodin, R.E. (1986), 'Laundering preferences,' in J. Elster and A. Hylland (eds), *Foundations of Social Choice Theory*, Cambridge: Cambridge University Press.

Griffin, J. (1986), *Well-Being. Its Meaning, Measurement and Moral Importance*, Oxford: Clarendon Press.

Hammond, P.J. (1996), 'Consequentialist decision theory and utilitarian ethics,' in F. Farina, F. Hahn and S. Vannucci (eds), *Ethics, Rationality, and Economic Behaviour*, Oxford: Clarendon Press.

Hansson, B. (1973), 'The independence condition in the theory of social choice', *Theory and Decision*, 4, 25–49.

Harsanyi, J.C. (1953), 'Cardinal utility in welfare economics and in the theory of risk-taking', *Journal of Political Economy*, 61, 434–5.

Harsanyi, J.C. (1955), 'Cardinal welfare, individualistic ethics, and interpersonal comparisons of utility', *Journal of Political Economy*, 63, 309–21.

Harsanyi, J.C. (1976), *Essays on Ethics, Social Behavior, and Scientific Explanation*, Dordrecht: Reidel.

Harsanyi, J.C. (1982), 'Morality and the theory of rational behavior', in A.K. Sen and B. Williams (eds), *Utilitarianism and Beyond*, Cambridge: Cambridge University Press.

Hayek, F. (1960), *The Constitution of Liberty*, Chicago: University of Chicago Press.

Hicks J. (1939), 'The foundations of welfare economics', *Economic Journal* 49, 696–712.

Kalai, E. and M. Smorodinsky (1975), 'Other solutions to Nash's bargaining problem', *Econometrica*, 43, 513–18.

Kaldor, N. (1939), 'Welfare propositions of economics and interpersonal comparisons of utility', *Economic Journal*, 49, 549–52.

Kemp, M.C. and Y.K. Ng (1976), 'On the existence of social welfare functions, social orderings and social decision functions', *Economica*, 43, 59–66.

Kolm, S.C. (1972), *Justice et équité*, Paris: Editions du CNRS, reprinted and translated as *Justice and Equity*, Cambridge, MA: MIT Press, 1999.

Kolm, S.C. (1985), *Le contrat social libéral. Théorie et pratique du libéralisme*, Paris: Presses Universitaires de France.

Kolm, S.C. (1996), *Modern Theories of Justice*, Cambridge, MA: MIT Press.

Le Breton, M. (1997), 'Arrovian social choice on economic domains', in K.J. Arrow, A.K. Sen and K. Suzumura (eds), *Social Choice Re-examined*, vol. 1, International Economic Association Conference volume, London and New York: Macmillan and St. Martin's Press.

Le Breton, M. and J.A. Weymark (2002), 'Arrovian social choice theory on economic domains,' forthcoming in K.J. Arrow, A.K. Sen and K. Suzumura (eds), *Handbook of Social Choice and Welfare*, vol. 2, Amsterdam: North-Holland.

Locke, J. (1690 [1947]), *Two Treatises of Government*, London: Macmillan.

Mongin, P. (1995), 'Consistent Bayesian aggregation', *Journal of Economic Theory*, 66, 313–51.

Mongin, P. (2001), 'The impartial observer theorem of social ethics', *Economics and Philosophy*, 17, 147–80.

Moulin, H. (1990), 'Fair division under joint ownership: recent results and open problems', *Social Choice and Welfare*, 7, 149–70.

Moulin, H. (1991), 'Welfare bounds in the fair division problem', *Journal of Economic Theory*, 54, 321–37.

Moulin, H. and Thomson W. (1997), 'Axiomatic analysis of resource allocation problems', in K.J. Arrow, A.K. Sen and K. Suzumura (eds), *Social Choice Re-examined*, vol. 1 International Economic Association Conference volume, London and New York: Macmillan and St. Martin's Press.

Nash, J. (1950), 'The bargaining problem', *Econometrica*, 18, 155–62.

Nozick, R. (1969), 'Coercion', in S. Morgenbesser, P. Suppes and M. White (eds), *Philosophy, Science and Method. Essays in Honor of Ernest Nagel*, New York: St. Martin's Press.

Nozick, R. (1974), *Anarchy, State and Utopia*, New York: Basic Books.

Nozick, R. (1989), *The Examined Life*, New York: Simon & Schuster.

Olsaretti, S. (1998), 'Freedom, force and choice: against the rights-based definition of voluntariness', *Journal of Political Philosophy*, 6, 53–78.

Pazner, E. (1979), 'Equity, nonfeasible alternatives and social choice: a reconsideration of the concept of social welfare', in J.J. Laffont (ed.), *Aggregation and Revelation of Preferences*, Amsterdam: North-Holland.

Pazner, E. and D. Schmeidler (1974), 'A difficulty in the concept of fairness', *Review of Economic Studies*, 41, 441–43.

Pazner, E. and D. Schmeidler (1978), 'Egalitarian equivalent allocations: a new concept of economic equity', *Quarterly Journal of Economics*, 92, 671–87.

Peters, H. (1992), *Axiomatic Bargaining Game Theory*, Dordrecht: Kluwer.

Rawls, J. (1971), *A Theory of Justice*, Cambridge, MA: Harvard University Press.

Rawls, J. (1974), 'Some reasons for the maximin criterion', *American Economic Review*, 64 (2), 141–6.

Rawls, J. (1982), 'Social unity and primary goods', in A.K. Sen and B. Williams (eds), *Utilitarianism and Beyond*, Cambridge: Cambridge University Press.

Rawls, J. (1993), *Political Liberalism*, New York: Columbia University Press.

Raz, J. (1986), *The Morality of Freedom*, Oxford: Clarendon Press.

Robbins, L. (1932), *An Essay on the Nature and Significance of Economic Science*, London: Macmillan.

Robbins, L. (1981), 'Economics and political economy', *American Economic Review, AEA Papers and Proceedings*, 71 (2), 1–10.

Roberts, K. (1980), 'Interpersonal comparability and social choice theory', *Review of Economic Studies*, 47, 421–39.

Roemer, J.E. (1985), 'Equality of talent', *Economics and Philosophy*, 1, 151–87.

Roemer, J.E. (1990), 'Welfarism and axiomatic bargaining theory', *Recherches Economiques de Louvain*, 56, 287–301.

Rothbard, M. (1973), *For A New Liberty*, New York: Macmillan.

Samuelson, P.A. (1977), 'Reaffirming the existence of "reasonable" Bergson–Samuelson social welfare functions', *Economica*, 44, 81–8.

Samuelson, P.A. (1987), 'Sparks from Arrow's anvil', in G.R. Feiwel (ed.), *Arrow and the Foundations of the Theory of Economic Policy*, New York: New York University Press.

Sandel, M. (1982), *Liberalism and the Limits of Justice*, Cambridge: Cambridge University Press.

Scanlon, T. (1975), 'Preference and urgency', *Journal of Philosophy*, 72, 655–70.

Schokkaert, E. (1999), 'M. Tout-le-monde est post-welfariste: opinions sur la justice redistributive', *Revue Economique*, 50, 811–32.

Scitovsky, T. (1941), 'A note on welfare propositions in economics', *Review of Economic Studies*, 9, 77–88.

Sen, A.K. (1970), *Collective Choice and Social Welfare*, San Francisco: Holden-Day.

Sen, A.K. (1977), 'Social choice theory: a re-examination', *Econometrica*, 45, 53–89.

Sen, A.K. (1979), 'Personal utilities and public judgments: or what's wrong with welfare economics', *Economic Journal*, 89, 537–58.

Sen, A.K. (1985), *Commodities and Capabilities*, Amsterdam: North-Holland.

Sen, A.K. (1986), 'Social choice theory', in K.J. Arrow and M.D. Intriligator (eds), *Handbook of Mathematical Economics*, vol. 3, Amsterdam: North-Holland.

Sen, A.K. (1987), *On Ethics and Economics*, Oxford: Basil Blackwell.

Sen, A.K. (1999), 'The possibility of social choice', *American Economic Review*, 89, 349–78.

Singer, P. (1986), 'All animals are equal', in P. Singer (ed.), *Applied Ethics*, Oxford: Oxford University Press.

Steiner, H. (1994), *An Essay on Rights*, Oxford: Blackwell.

Sumner, L.W. (1996), *Welfare, Happiness and Ethics*, Oxford: Oxford University Press.

Thomson, W. (1999), *Bargaining Theory: The Axiomatic Approach*, New York: Academic Press.

Trebilcock, M.J. (1993), *The Limits of Freedom of Contract*, Cambridge, MA: Harvard University Press.

van Parijs, P. (1995), *Real Freedom for All. What (if Anything) Can Justify Capitalism[1]?*, Oxford: Oxford University Press.

Varian, H. (1974), 'Equity, envy and efficiency', *Journal of Economic Theory*, 9, 63–91.

Varian, H. (1976), 'Two problems in the theory of fairness', *Journal of Public Economics*, 5, 249–60.

Weymark, J.A. (1991), 'A reconsideration of the Harsanyi–Sen debate on utilitarianism', in J. Elster and J.E. Roemer (eds), *Interpersonal Comparisons of Weil-Being*, Cambridge: Cambridge University Press.

Yaari M. and M. Bar-Hillel (1984), 'On dividing justly', *Social Choice and Welfare*, 1, 1–24.

Young, H.P. (1988), 'Condorcet's theory of voting', *American Political Science Review*, 82, 1231–44.

Young, H.P. (1994), *Equity. In Theory and Practice*, Princeton, NJ: Princeton University Press.

8　Ideology: an economic point of view

Alain Leroux

Introduction

Unlike their colleagues in sociology and philosophy, economists seldom address the question of ideology. This is an enigma for those who regard economics not only as a social science – probably the best elaborated of all – but also as a social philosophy. So why are questions of ideology ignored in economics, even though they can be considered to be a central part to social science and social philosophy more generally?

Economists not only have published little on the subject of ideology over the last half-century, but what has been published has also shown an astonishing lack of depth. It is true that the notion of ideology (or the concept – when pushed far enough) is partially linked to the unconscious, but this by itself does not mean that discussions of ideology are purely polemical or a simple exchange of unquestionable opinions. Yet economists who have engaged with this subject – even some of the best reputed – have not always been able to avoid falling into such a trap.

In breaking from the trivial treatment of ideology within economics, we shall attempt to develop an entirely conceptual approach of it. Thus, in this chapter, we are not trying to compose an anthology of the affirmations on ideology made by economists over the last fifty years. We rather propose a critical analysis with the aim of placing in perspective the two major kinds of negligence or lack of care made by economists when discussing this subject. The reasoning will proceed in three steps.

The first section highlights the assimilation that is often made of ideology and value judgements. This amalgamation causes the confusion of two dimensions of ideology that are nonetheless separate: folk ideology and learned ideology. Economists who avoid this confusion generally subscribe to the concept of ideology inherited from Marx. However, they then unfortunately tend to commit the logical error of using this concept for operative ends, without noticing the paradox that forbids such a use.

This gives rise to a second misconduct. In order to evaluate its implications, we will devote the second section to Marx's conception of ideology. But rather than presenting an exhaustive survey of the debates, amendments and improvements that this concept underwent during the course of the twentieth century, we will concentrate on its limits. The principal one, known for a long time but only clearly identified a few decades ago, is generally referred to as the 'Mannheim Paradox'. Schumpeter provides a major historical example of transgression of this limit.

The final section shows how the Mannheim Paradox is due to the self-referential structure of Marx's concept of ideology. Indeed, if we substitute Marx's sociological basis of ideology with a cognitive one, the paradoxical loop may be defused. We will thus propose a way of getting round the Mannheim Paradox by a slight shift in the concept of ideology. Its practical application will thus no longer be compromised in advance. It will be good, however, to put this re-established analytic power to the test. The best way to do so is perhaps to see how the rectified concept of ideology allows us to recognise the ideological or scientific nature of a particular discourse (an enterprise which is paradoxically impossible with Marx's concept). Consequently, we will indicate two possible modes of use that rely on the corpus economicus.

An analytical error: confusing ideology and value judgements

Economists are accustomed to reducing ideology to value judgements. In order not to burden the discussion, we will content ourselves with only one illustration of this practice, which is all the more demonstrative as it comes from a famous economist (Solow 1971). In a twice published article, although named 'Science and ideology in economics', Solow only discusses the position and role of value judgments in economics: 'value-free social science?'. The term 'ideology' never receives much attention. When Solow then casually uses the word or its derived epithet, it is most often in assertions whose simplicity sound deliberately trivial. Indeed, the word ideology remains undefined all through the article and, according to Solows's reasoning, the reader must even imperatively refuse to give to it any special content. He or she has just to accept the pejorative connotation that this term has in day-to-day language. Finally, ideology appears just as a verbal convenience, an indirect and vague means of designating the presence of value judgements. Examples of this nature are legion, and Katouzian (1980, p. 135) has already convincingly denounced the hasty amalgamation customary in our profession:

> Two distinct types of confusion are frequently met with respect to the twin concepts of value judgements and ideology: one is the total reduction of value judgements to ideology and vice versa – that is the (implicit) belief that these concepts are completely synonymous; the other is the confusion of the various meanings and implications of each concept taken separately.

It may seem strange that we do not pay as much attention to ideology as do the adjacent disciplines (those of philosophy of science and sociology) and we have to reflect on the reason why this is so. Two possible responses may be put forward. The first, rather speculative one, clarifies the foundations of this frequent assimilation of ideology and value judgements. The second one, historical in nature, illuminates the origin of this practice.

Weber's silence

Associating ideology and value judgements is in itself nothing less than normal. In all contexts, in any occasion, the halo of meanings that surround the word 'ideology' mobilises value judgements. What is strange however – and specific to our discipline – is to reduce the former to the latter and then to deprive the term ideology of its own identity. The first hypothesis is that such a tradition must be guaranteed by a very strong authority to resist the common practice of the other disciplines!

Actually, it might be said that we find in Weber the guardianship of our special use of ideology. As everyone knows, the father of the 'individualising method', better known as the methodological individualism popularised by Schumpeter, was an encyclopaedic thinker. In a major posthumous work [1971], Weber developed a methodological apparatus to which all necessary concepts in social scientific thought are consigned. But, throughout his whole intellectual endeavour, there is no trace of any discussion about ideology. This absence is particularly alarming given the fact that Weber lived at a time and a place where the ideological question stimulated all areas of political and intellectual life. To explain this manifest omission, we should only remember that Weber decisively addressed the problem of value judgements in the social sciences. So the explanation of his silence becomes simple: if Weber did not treat ideology, it is because his so minutely deepened question of value judgements constitutes the correct way to deal with the problem raised by ideology.

Such a conclusion rings as an exemplary, although unconscious, justification of the little attention paid to the ideological question in economics. But it is not sufficient. What actually matters is not to know the reasons why we neglect the ideological question, but whether we are right to do so. In other words, the right enquiry is not psychological in nature, but epistemological. What practice should we privilege: the frequent confusions of the economists who assimilate ideology and value judgements, or the efforts of the sociologist and philosopher who give a specific conceptual content to ideology?

One of the reasons why this alternative still seem open is the ambivalence of the term 'ideology', that, for the last hundred years, has lived an uneven double life: one foot in learned literature, the other in popular language. It is therefore useful to retrace, in a few lines, the well-known history of this term.

The history of a word

The neologism 'ideology' was forged at the very end of the eighteenth century. Its heritage comes from a group of French philosophers who were ardent defenders of the Republic and admirers of scientific thinking, such as it triumphed during that time. These avant-garde thinkers, all convinced materialists and declared adversaries of metaphysics, saw themselves as pioneers of a new science aiming to account to the productions of the human mind (ideas) as Newtonian science could account for the movement of the celestial bodies. This future science of ideas is precisely what they named 'ideology'.

Many other neologisms were created during that era and especially in France, such as 'biology' prophesied by Lamarck at the beginning of the nineteenth century, and 'sociology' envisioned by Comte a few decades later. But contrary to the science of life or the science of society, which rapidly and assuredly produced an embryo of content under their title, the science of ideas would remain empty. Logically, the word 'ideology', such as it had been conceived, fell into oblivion.

Yet before being totally eradicated from the learned vocabulary, the term ideology was propelled into common speech, despite the double handicap of its masterful phonetic and a rather obscure lexical construction for those who had not studied humanities. Indeed, the Emperor in person (helped by a few opportunists, such as Chateaubriand) took it upon himself to instruct the masses. The reason for all this linguistic fuss came down to the fact that the promoters of the dubious science of ideas were also men of action, driven by conviction and courage. The same republican ideal that had led these philosophers earlier to support Bonaparte would lead them now to oppose Napoleon. Certainly, it was a praiseworthy, yet unequal, combat. Those who had dreamed of becoming 'ideologists' were imperially treated as 'ideologues': a scornful expression indicating politicians who are devoid of any political sensibility, capable of assimilating dangerous and false ideas and who can even be suspected of manipulating the masses. Thanks to this actualisation of the term, the word ideology would penetrate everyday language with such a force that it was exported with this same meaning into all modern western languages. In this sense, ideology condescendingly designates a series of arbitrary and fragmented value judgements that contain no truth and do not respect any logical structure. This linguistic evolution therefore accredits the synonymy of ideology and value judgements. This is however what should be called 'folk' ideology, that which lies in everyday language and activates political debate.

But folk ideology is not the whole story of ideology. Stillborn into the scientific jargon for which it had been conceived, saved into common speech where it seems foreign, the term ideology resurfaced in learned language in the mid-nineteenth century. Here again, the biggest authorities participated in it. As was its introduction into everyday language due to Napoleon, so was its reintroduction into learned language due to Marx. Of course, Marx's concept of ideology splendidly ignores the original term intended by the 'ideologists'. What Marx rather designates by the terms is a particular form of learned discourse, characterised at the same time by an ambition to sum up (the whole of life in society is within its range) and an origin that is unconscious (the positioning within a class is its cause). Ideology, once again, definitely contains value judgements, but this time strongly structured thanks to a coherency obligation imposed by its totalling-up range. A famous economist, to whom we will return, fixes this holistic idea while speaking of 'vision'.

Thus, over the last two hundred years, the term 'ideology' has evolved through the filter of language in two clearly distinct directions. On the one hand, folk ideology, which is associated with a simple juxtaposition of moral or normative judgements (conscious and fragmented), on the other, learned ideology, which is associated with a coherent 'vision' (unconscious and total).

A correct distinction between ideology and value judgements
Returning now to the epistemological question asked by different disciplinary practices with regard to ideology: should we assimilate ideology into value judgements (as in contemporary economics) or is it more legitimate to provide it with a specific content (as is habitual in philosophy and sociology)? The answer to this question depends directly upon our perception of (mental) reality. If, beyond the simple accumulation of value judgements, we discern their emergence under the form of sufficiently stable regular and consistent arrangements, then it is useful to have a word to speak about such, and a concept to precise its extension. If we do not, it would be better to banish the term 'ideology' from our analytical vocabulary (as Weber does), or at least use ideology and value judgements as vague synonyms (as is frequent in our discipline).

The position that we defend here, and for which we will give an original argument in the last section, is that it is legitimate, in economics as in the neighbouring disciplines, to avoid reducing ideology to value judgements. It is then proper to operate a necessarily conventional conceptual distinction between one and the other. However, in order not to multiply terminological distinctions, it is reasonable to align this with the double linguistic evolution mentioned above – as it was done excellently by Katouzian (1980, p. 135):

> The distinction between the concepts of value judgements and ideology (we hope) will become clear (soon). But perhaps a few words on this subject may be helpful at the outset. Value judgement refer to *conscious* and *piecemeal* objective norms of subjective (moral predilections). On the other hand, ideology refers to an *unconscious*, or 'semi-conscious', and *total* 'world view'.

The distinction between value judgements and ideology in the above quotation explicitly links the weight of linguistic origin to the clarity of convention, since it rests on the distinction between folk ideology and learned ideology. But it still remains a difficulty. The learned ideology, which is taken into account, is clearly the conception inherited from Marx. Incentive is then given to adopt the Marxian version of ideology, without bringing any attention to the logical stumbling block inherent in the concept, yet well indicated today and known as the 'Mannheim paradox'.

A logical error: the Mannheim paradox

In a posthumously published book entitled *The German Ideology*, joint work written with Engels in 1845–1846, Marx reintroduced the term 'ideology' into learned debate. But he did not conduct his enterprise with the rigour that we could retrospectively expect from the author of *The Capital*. Was this deliberate, or a premonitory sign of the conceptual minefield that is Marx's view of ideology? Both interpretations are possible. True is that the Marxian concept of 'ideology' is double-edged and can be turn against Marx's work after all.

Extending its original target (the Hegelian philosophers), Marxists used soon the word 'ideology' to disqualify economic theories that were legitimising the new order that had established itself during the nineteenth century (which Marx himself named 'capitalism' for posterity). Contrary to the true economic science, of which Marx claims to be the promoter, the word 'ideology' serves to degrade the political economy of his era to an inferior form of learned discourse. But by making a sequential study of his work, the thinking of Marx can in turn be analysed in light of this opposition between ideology and science: on one hand, the works of young Marx, strongly marked by ideology, on the other, the mature productions, where the Marxist science takes shape. This epistemological rupture in Marx's work is nowadays well accepted even if the exact dating remains controversial: just before *The German Ideology* (as Althusser maintains) or just after (as Ricoeur thinks)?

Marx's conception of ideology
The main reason why the reintroduction of the term of 'ideology' into learned language first lacked precision is that Marx never gives a clear statement of it. Preferring the power of formulae to the precision of concepts, the eponymous work (*The German Ideology*) illustrates rather than define what ideology is. But the force of the expressions used by Marx, along with the ceaselessly reattempted exegeses by multiple Marxist schools, end up allowing some characteristic traits to emerge, which could validly serve as a definition of ideology, in Marx's sense of the word.

The best known and most commented-upon passage of *The German Ideology* is:

> The production of ideas, of conceptions, of consciousness, is at first directly interwoven with the material activity and the material intercourse of men, the language of real life. Conceiving, thinking, the mental intercourse of men appears at this stage as the direct efflux of their material behaviour. The same applies to mental production as expressed in the language of politics, laws, morality, religion, metaphysics, etc. of a people. Men are the producers of their conceptions, ideas, etc. – real, active men, as

they are conditioned by a definite development of their productive forces and of the intercourse corresponding to these, up to its furthest forms. Consciousness can never be anything else than conscious existence, and the existence of men is their actual life-process. If in all ideology men and their circumstances appear upside-down as in a *camera obscura*, this phenomenon arises just as much from their historical life-process as the inversion of objects on the retina does from their physical life-process.

In establishing (learned) ideology as a distorted representation of the social order, Marx and the tradition that he initiated connotes the concept negatively, just as the notion (folk ideology) was already, but for other reasons. This prejudice is certainly useful to immunate the learned concept against the influence of the popular notion. But in satisfying this criterion, the Marxist proposition exposes itself to an objection, or at least a question: how can the ideologue, as described by Marx, always be in error? As a matter of fact, it is no longer the same person as he who is stigmatised by the political accusation: a politician who offers no guarantee of clairvoyance, not even depth, whose sole enterprise of persuasion is shamelessly limited to the techniques of propaganda. No, the ideologue of whom Marx speaks is patently wise. A man immersed in the exercise of thought. Rigorous and knowledgeable, as all learned people, honest and circumspect, as they all should be. A thinker who obliges himself to produce a discourse as rational, conceptual and open to criticism as the rest; a man for whom the original emblematic figure for Marx was any Young Hegelian philosopher and will be soon the effigy of any classical economist that he qualifies 'vulgar', as he does with Say or Constant. Why is this learned man (the ideologue) condemned to error in principle, whereas the other (the scientist) is expected to move us endlessly towards the truth?

Ideology is a false discourse because it escapes the control of the person who uses it. Knowledgeable or ignorant, we are all spontaneously inclined to adhere to norms and values, interpretations and arguments that our social class needs to confront its role and legitimise its aspirations. Although collective, this unconscious is no less of a manipulator than the personal unconscious brought up by psychoanalysis a few decades later. As scholarly and honest as he may be, as rigorous and circumspect as he strives to be, the ideologue succumbs unknowingly to his class positioning.

If Marx stigmatises the false knowledge brought about by ideology, it is because he conceives of a way of telling the truth. For him, in effect, there is one and only one way of escaping the social determinism of thought, that is to commit oneself to the only art of reasoning capable of repulsing the error, as holy water is the only accessory capable of exorcising an evil spirit: science. By advancing this proposition, Marx is evidently thinking about real science, that of which he establishes the basis, which would be developed under the apocryphal name 'historical materialism'. Science (Marxist) has for objective an account of 'the process of real life' of which ideology only gives a false 'echo', rather like the brain has for function the redressing of the inverted image impressed upon the retina.

The visual metaphor of the camera obscura, at the same time physicalist and naturalist, would do more for the reintroduction of the concept of ideology than all the other developments in *The German Ideology*, a rather uneven work. In it we find the germ of the sextuplet predicate on which the contemporary learned community would base an extended form (lacking any autographic definition) that would become known as Marx's conception of ideology. As such: ideology is a form of learned discourse (1) that attempts to give a total representation of social life (2), yet only really offers (partially) false knowledge (3), because of its being unconsciously produced (4) by class positioning (5); opposed to which is the only form of learned discourse capable of attaining the truth: science (6).

With regard to the abundant literature produced on the subject of Marx's idea of ideology, the above extended definition may seem a bit terse. During the course of the last century, many philosophers (from Heidegger to Gramsci) and sociologists (from Geertz to Dumont) have modified and ordered these six properties differently. Nonetheless, the scientific *doxa* was hardly shaken by this. In effect, there has only been one addition, foreign and even literally contrary to the original expression offered by Marx that has been definitively incorporated into the concept. This decisive correction, proposed at the beginning of last century, is due to Mannheim.

The Mannheim paradox
When Mannheim published *Ideology and Utopia* (Ideology and Utopia) in 1929, positivism was challenging the possibility of adopting an abstract and general point of view. In this context, Mannheim stressed the need to study the relation between intellectual activity and social existence. Thought (ideas) should not only be observed from a logical and psychological perspective, but should also be the object of sociological study. Through him (and Scheler) the sociology of knowledge was born, aiming to establish the relation between the content of thought and its social and historical conditioning.

The concept of ideology proposed by Marx already contains the idea of the social determinism of thought. But, in the same movement, it postulated that the conditions of real life permitted only the dominant class to build a representation of the whole of society, thus imposing it upon the dominated class. This simplification was underpinned by Marx's prediction of a social dynamic that converges towards the bipolarisation of the bourgeoisie and the proletariat. Yet, the society that Mannheim observed during the first quarter of the twentieth century was more indicative of booming complexity in structure than of direct opposition. A society brought about by a multiplicity of different 'points of view' concerning the social order rather than by one thinking only. This perspectivism put forward by Mannheim confirmed the destruction of 'the ontological unity of the world'. However, to remain faithful to Marx's text, Mannheim kept the word 'ideology' for the representation that the dominant class produces, using the word 'utopia' to designate the representation secreted by each dominated class. Apart from remaining true to Marx, this conceptual split helped distinguish the conservative character of ideology from the progressivism of utopia. Ideology, fortified by the dominant class, tends in effect to mentally fix society in a stage that it has already historically passed. Conversely, utopias that are produced by dominated classes project society into an imaginary state that it will never know.

As far as this is concerned, the conceptual opposition proposed by Mannheim would not succeed in conquering minds. It is true to say that it is not habitual to thus compare ideology to utopia, since each usually belongs to separate intellectual universes: utopia coming from the literary genre and ideology from the learned genre. Also, more than an opposition, it is a similarity between the two that is brought to light: if the conservative representation generated by the dominant class is *already* (definitively) false while the progressivist representation produced by the dominated classes is *still* (and will *always* be) false, the main feature is that both are false and, beyond that, both conform to the six predicates that characterise Marx's concept of ideology. The two categories of representation distinguished by Mannheim are thus quickly confused. Posterity recognises in this author the merit of having opened Marx's concept to the multiplicity of ideologies, while Marx had arbitrarily fixed it in uniqueness.

This conceptual correction passed immediately as a substantial contribution, as it was consistent with the observation of present-day society. Yet, in the long run, this enrichment would soon be the revelation of the logical paradox that upholds Marx's concept of ideology: once a social thinking is situated, how is one to detect its ideological bias without being influenced by one's own social positioning? This is the content of what has been called the 'Mannheim paradox' for a few decades now. In attempting to overcome the dilemma, the most imaginative strategy has been to invoke an external, needless to say extraordinary, property: the existence of an intellectual practice adopting an external point of view on the world (Marx), the ability of the observer to penetrate his own unconscious conditioning (Myrdal), the convocation of incontestable presuppositions (Lacroix). All these attempts naturally failed, but at least they had the merit of looking beyond Marx's concept of ideology to a stable point from which to transcend the logical trap. Others have made totally endogenous attempts, committing the naïve mistake of thinking that Marx's concept of ideology possesses its own Archimedean point. They sought thus to use the concept itself as a means to untie the paradox that it contains, in the manner of a fireman seeking to extinguish a fire by playing with it. As fate would have it, the person who applied this naïve strategy with the most rigour is an economist. And, unfortunately, this economist is justifiably considered one of the best by the professional body: many recognise him as having effectively contributed to the orientation of our discipline towards what we today call the neoclassical economic science. This master who (mis)conceived of ideology, and whose responsibility is considerable in our lack of interest in the ideological question, is Joseph Schumpeter.

Schumpeter's (bad) example
In a famous and short article, 'Science and Ideology' (1949), Schumpeter proposes to solve the problem of the relation between science and ideology in economic discourse through an examination of the work of Smith, Marx and Keynes. In doing this, he takes into account two forms of learned discourse (scientific and ideological), as originally done by Marx. But he adopts a more subtle position than his precursor, without realising that this refinement cannot satisfy Marx's concept of ideology. Marx, in effect, had reintroduced the term ideology into learned language by opposing it to that which science should be. He thus postulates that science would at once permit liberation from ideological illusions. In order to support this proposition, ideology could be valuably described with the help of the six above-mentioned predicates, of which two stipulate that ideological representation is unconsciously determined by the social positioning of the subject. But these two predicates contain the seed of the paradigm with which Scheler and Mannheim would equip the sociology of knowledge at the beginning of the twentieth century: knowledge, even the learned variety, can never be a pure exercise of the intellect because it is always socially conditioned. Yet if we adopt their paradigm, it becomes difficult to accept the Marxist postulate according to which science (Marxist or otherwise) immediately escapes this existential determinism.

Schumpeter obviously knows this and recalls it in his article. By doing so, he wants to grab the Marxist bull by the horns, taking charge of both his concept of ideology and the paradigm of the sociology of knowledge that is derived from it. Like Marx, Schumpeter accepts by definition (i.e. Marx's conception of ideology) to carry the weight of the social determinism of thought onto ideology and then declares in his turn that science is free from such unconscious factors. But in contrast to Marx, he goes by the principle (i.e. the paradigm of the sociology of knowledge) that the idea of learned knowledge cannot be scientific right away (or *ex ante*), since all thought supports the weight of an unconscious social determinism. And to escape to the contradiction, he postulates that it is possible to subsequently (or *ex post*) separate that which comes from science (free from unconscious conditioning) and that which emanates from ideology (given away by social determinism). To do this, he introduces his famous conceptual distinction between 'vision' and 'model':

So soon as we have realized the possibility of ideological bias, it is not difficult to locate it. All we have to do for this purpose is to scrutinize scientific procedure. It starts from the perception of a set of related phenomena, which we wish to analyse and ends up – for the time being – with a scientific model in which these phenomena are conceptualised and the relations between them explicitly formulated as assumptions or as propositions (theorems). ... First that perception of a set of related phenomena is a prescientific act. ... But though prescientific, it is not preanalytic. It does not simply consist in perceiving facts by one or more of our senses. These facts must be recognized as having some meaning or relevance. ... The mixture of perceptions and prescientific analysis we shall call the research worker's Vision or Intuition. (Schumpeter 1949, p. 348)

This distinction between 'vision' and 'model' allows the fixing of ideology: 'The original vision *is* ideology by nature'. With this it becomes possible to envisage a critical work that has for objective eliminating, in the 'model', the ideological dross of the 'vision', in order to obtain a purified scientific thinking *ex post*. Nonetheless, if the conceptual distinction between 'vision' and 'model' allows the theoretical isolation of the good seed from the bad, the practical method of discarding ideological adherences from learned thought remains to be shown.

As for the practical method, Schumpeter finds it once again in Marx's concept of ideology, to which he attributes a new aim. The concept no longer designates only a synthetic category of thought (ideology), but also an analytic principle of reasoning (to evacuate the ideology from an author's work), 'Proceeding on the Marxist principle we shall look to his social location, that is, to his personal and ancestral class affiliations and in addition to the class connotation of the influences that may have formed or may have helped to form what we called his vision'.

On first reading, Schumpeter's position appears to be more coherent than that of Marx, whose pretension of being situated outside worldly contingency (via the Marxist science) has something of a messianic element to it. However, if Schumpeter admits that the ideological bias blurs all human thinking (the paradigm of the sociology of knowledge), how can he determine that which he truly gets out of the 'vision' of Smith, Marx and Keynes? That which Schumpeter puts forward in his article is only the 'point of view' of Schumpeter on a reality lived by others, who were neither from his class, nor his times, nor his culture... His appreciation of the 'visions' of these three authors is therefore undermined by all manner of possible ideological distortions: the Mannheim paradox closes in on his analysis.

Despite the logical error in his reasoning, Schumpeter's argumentation convinced most economists. Some, notably Heilbronner, took up his conception of 'vision'. Others, such as Hutchinson, thought of Schumpeter as the economist who had best dealt with the question of ideology. Many in turn revisited Marx's concept of ideology (Elster, Fine, Robinson, Ryan, van Parijs and so on) and an overwhelming majority of the profession thought the question of ideology had been definitively resolved. A large consensus thus gradually emerged in the economics community, so deeply rooted in our collective unconscious that the question hardly ever arises in our professional discussions any more. This consensus upholds the Schumpeterian conclusion of the distinction between science and ideology, and replaces only the practical method that Schumpeter suggests ('Proceeding on the Marxist principle...') by the work practice put in place systematically during the second half of the twentieth century. As such all economic theory is, today, under fire from the critique of the scientific community. And, unless we suppose that all economists represent the same class, this critical work should normally succeed in removing the ideologically loaded 'original visions' in scientific 'models'. However, the robustness of this silent and unconscious *aggiornamento* depends on the solidity of the Schumpeterian argument on which it relies. Unfortunately, as we saw, the Schumpeterian argument is not immune to the Mannheim paradox, of which Schumpeter described certainly all the springs but without seeing the mechanism.

'Each ideology is the expression of a class, the false conscience that it has of itself, the mythical whole of its options, the symbolic appeasing of its desires and fundamental warlike cunning to devalue the enemy classes'. This definition given by Sartre (during the course of a novel *L'idiot de la famille*) in an out-of-fashion Marxian–Freudian register, speaks volumes for the doubly-specified theoretical universe that gives full sense to Marx's conception of ideology: the class struggle in the social sciences, and the pre-eminence of the unconscious in the philosophy of mind. However, the dominant intellectual context has substantially evolved over the last decades. In the social sciences, and particularly in our discipline, the approach in terms of class struggle is marginalised. At the same time, the philosophy of mind has returned to think of consciousness in positivist terms, promising the abandoning to the unconscious of only the remainder of that which still temporarily escapes its explanation. This intellectual shift should logically put an end to the virtues that were formerly spontaneously granted onto Marx's conception of ideology. What is more, the Mannheim paradox is today sufficiently well recognised such that we can no longer entertain any illusions about its operative range. But despite this loss of theoretical environment and the vanity of any analytic use, Marx's conception of ideology still holds sway over learned minds. Although attempts have been made to substitute it for another conception of ideology, both from eminent sociologists (like Boudon) and philosophers (Habermas), the Marxian conception of ideology remains the reference, probably because it is difficult to liberate a tradition of thinking when its object is regularly and explicitly discussed, as is the case for philosophy and sociology.

If this is the reason for Marx's conception of ideology being such a surprisingly robust yet disputed concept, economics could be a more favourable field in which to approach it in a novel manner, as the discipline shows such little interest in the question! The next section reviews the possible routes of such an attempt.

Ideology: a cognitive approach

Whoever refuses to take into account Marx's conception of ideology confronts a wall of incomprehension, given the profound appropriation of the concept by the learned community. Conversely, whoever accepts Marx's conception of ideology becomes the prisoner of the logical circle of Mannheim's paradox. In all evidence, the self-referential structure of this paradox comes from the joint nature postulated by the two faces of ideology: that which it points out and that which specifies it. As such, in Marx's version, ideology is simultaneously an interpretation and a product of society. Being the interpretative reflection of that which causes it, ideology functions necessarily in a self-justifying way, with all the fantastic risks this entails. For those in the specular process, ideology is invisible. For the external observer, it is blinding. 'Ideology is the thinking of the other person' mocks Aron through a psychological indication of the operational inability, which inflicts Marx's conception of ideology.

Relying on this assertion, the concept of ideology that we are going to present is achieved by shifting the formula proposed by Marx, intending to conserve its ability to describe a reality that everyone feels, while avoiding the paradox that spoils it. To keep the positive elements of Marx's sense, we will employ the same denotation: ideology will continue to identify a particular type of learned discourse, a holistic vision of the life of man in society. But, in order to escape the logical closure of the Mannheim paradox, we will change its specification. For the concept of ideology inherited from Marx, that which specifies ideology in learned discourse is sociological in nature (since ideology is the unconscious product of a given social situation). For us, however, that which specifies it is of cognitive making (ideology is the matter of a particular form of thought).

The pure forms of thought

Since Marx, ideology has been constantly opposed to science. From time to time, it is even seen as contrary to philosophy. Then, if there is to be an immediate and shared perception of the singularity of ideology, it has to be cognitive in nature since it would be perceived in opposition of two standard forms of contemporary learned thought: science and (to a lesser extent) philosophy. Nonetheless, it is not for the field of cognition that its specification was originally intended. In holding that ideology is an unconscious product of class positioning, Marx had effectively placed the analysis in the field of sociology. Yet the over-determination of the cognitive singularity of ideology (spontaneously perceived) by this (at the very least speculative) sociological causality entails the Mannheim paradox. But this famous paradox disappears if the specification of ideology is no longer attempted in the field of sociology. It is also difficult to understand why the learned community continues to follow Marx on hardly consolidated ground when it seems natural to specify ideology in a field where it springs immediately to attention: that of cognition.

Of course, the cognitive specification of ideology is difficult because it imposes, in one way or another, a distinction between the major forms of learned knowledge. In doing this however, it is not necessary to adopt a 'spatial' approach and to partition the field of knowledge by delineating exclusive territories, each one separately: science here, philosophy over there, ideology elsewhere, utopia or other types of knowledge even further off. It is possible to prefer another posture that we will call 'temporal', suggesting the philosophical reference that guides us (Bergson).

From this perspective, what interests us is the process of thought more so than its final expression. The hypothesis is no longer that each type of knowledge extracted from the objective world of reviews and learned books is to be localised into different provinces of knowledge, each one isolated from the others by as many Rubicons as the epistemologist may have in his jurisdiction: science or metaphysics (Popper), philosophy or ideology (Granger)… It is supposed rather that there are multiple cognitive strategies, never isolated and always simultaneously active, developing in flurries through all learned discourse. None among them can serve to objectively delineate a zone of knowledge, as they are never alone in burgeoning, but taken together they all permit the subjective appreciation of a particular discourse, intervening each time by varying arrangements.

Henceforth we will call these strategies of knowledge *pure forms of thought*. And in order to be in harmony with the spontaneous perception of learned works, we will immediately postulate the existence of at least three types: the scientific form (which we will admit as having become the matrix of reference for all learned knowledge), the philosophical form (that also had its heyday and conserves a certain aura) and the ideological form (which at first glance could be considered a perversion of learned cognition). From this epistemological posture, it is still legitimate to speak of science, philosophy and ideology. No longer does it express a specific quality of the targeted knowledge types, but only indicates the pure form of thought that principally impregnates the discourse that produces them.

Obviously, it is out of the question to 'define' these pure forms of thought, as they need to be understood as simple bearings or 'tendencies' of the learned mind, and not as explicit and well-formed schemas of thought. Contrary to the demarcationist (or spatialised) approach that has to define the categories of knowledge in order to force unanimity of classification, this tendency (or temporal) approach only targets the standardising of the evaluation procedure. By constraining the epistemologist to reveal the hierarchy of knowledge strategies put in place and by forcing him to recommence his analysis of each new discourse placed under examination, the judgement must necessarily be well weighted, communicable and criticisable, concentrated upon the thing being judged. And if appreciation can still vary, from one evaluator to another, the elements taken into consideration are the same for all.

This epistemological position ('by tendencies') however, contends that one can see the pure forms of thought at work. In particular, it is proper to agree upon the means of detecting the ideological pure form of thought. In order to do this, we will start by indicating the major trait that opposes it to the two forms of reference. Then we will specify that which it shares with the two other pure forms of thought. The first feature prevents the confusion of the ideological pure form of thought with the two others, while the second feature explains why it can never be separated from them.

Characteristics of the ideological pure form of thought
It has become habitual to repeat Plato's formula and to say of all knowledge that it is 'justified true belief'. Without entering into an exploration of this definition (thus risking getting lost in its abysses), we can rely upon it to validly distinguish the ideological pure form of thought from the scientific and philosophical pure forms of thought. We are more particularly interested in the relationship between 'true belief' on the one hand, and its 'justification' on the other.

This relationship permits us to qualify the immediate perception of what we call science or philosophy: the scientific and philosophical forms of thought make of the acceptance (or refusal) of the justification the necessary and sufficient condition of the constituting (or abandoning) of a belief. In other words, if its justification reveals a vice in form or does not succeed in forcing the judgement the scientist or philosopher must (ideally) forget about the belief. Conversely, the same relationship allows us to oppose to these two noble forms of thought with a third one (the ideological pure form of thought), that one is quick to judge ignoble because it works in exactly the opposite way: if its argument reveals itself as incorrect or insufficient, the ideologue keeps his belief... and seeks for another justification!

This proposition, in the form of an opposition, can thus be condensed: in the philosophical and scientific pure forms of thought, justification is logically primary, the belief being simply its correlate. For the ideological pure form of thought, the belief is (psycho)logically primary, the justification merely opportune.

The main characteristic that prevents a confusion between the ideological pure form of thought and the two forms of reference (scientific and philosophical) shows through this difference in the attitude of the learned person: over here riddled with doubt, over there fired up with certainty. This opposition however, as simple as it may be, cannot easily be grasped, as it is psychological in nature and can be effortlessly masked by the rhetoric of discourse. The risk of confusion is thus certain. But it is especially unavoidable if only due to the fact that the ideological pure form of thought is not in all respects contradictory to the other two pure forms of thought. Notably, all three share a founding element without which learned social knowledge could not be possible: a primary non-justified belief (and often even non-explicit) about the life of man in society.

In order to speak of man in society, our analytic thought is only in effect capable of distinguishing two separate entities, man **M** and society **S**, that reflect however inseparable empirical realities: that all human society is made up of men is a truism, but to say that men generally live in society is an irrefutable statement. The conceptual distinction between humans and society therefore leads to an old unsolvable riddle: which came first, the chicken or the egg? In order to link in reasoning that which analysis forces the unlinking, there has to be an articulation between **M** and **S**. Alas, nothing offers itself as obvious. Should we rather lean towards a schema of the type '**M** makes **S**', due to the undeniable fact that human society is at each instant only that which man makes up? Or is it better to privilege the inverse link, '**S** makes **M**', remarking that society is already there when we arrive in the world? Or can one, faced with the perplexity that these two contrary truths arouse, come round to a partial and mutual determination of **M** and **S**?

Since the dividing line between **M** and **S** is not empirically decidable, an argument to authority is needed to split these incompatible alternatives and give social thought an assured line of conduct. Only an ontological principle, deciding once and for all the essential articulation between man and society responds to this necessity of thought. But things are not as simple as that, as the necessary choice of an articulation between the two poles of reasoning, artificially separated by analysis, falls upon the supposed nature of man and society. According to whether man is seen as the author of society or its table companion, the same essential qualities cannot be present. Similarly, granting society an existence of its own or conceiving of it as the result of human action does not mean attributing it the same contours. All ontological principles linking **M** and **S** are necessarily accompanied by a primitive anthropology and an immediate sociology, specifying man's character and the characteristics of society that make their possible coupling particular.

We have called the necessary analytical base for seating all learned social thought 'ontological presupposition'. Whether it is conscious or not, conventional or not, deserves without a doubt to be debated case by case. Whether it is indispensable to the development of learned thought is not up for discussion: this is the common trait that prevents the categorical separation of the different pure forms of thought being considered.

Nevertheless, the relation between the ontological presupposition and the learned discourse can be more or less relaxed according to the dominant tone of the remark (just think of the cries of indignation of Weber and Durkheim when accused of ontologism!). Also, even if it is an affair of degree and not nature, it is still possible to find a means of disclosing the action of the ideological pure form of thought, inasmuch as its particularity is to be situated at one end of the spectrum. We have in effect remarked that what clearly opposes this form of thought to the forms of reference, is the inversion of the logical relation that unites true beliefs and their justification. In the ideological pure form of thought, beliefs are primary, their justifications opportune. Yet ideologies are totalising discourses that target the whole of life in society, mobilising vast groups of beliefs that bear on realities of very different nature: politics, economics, morals, culture and so on. How can a set of already formulated beliefs bearing on heterogeneous domains be coherent without a meta-belief, or first principle, from which all its ideological assertions can derive? And if this first principle exists, what can it be other than one of these ontological presuppositions that serve as the apodictic link between **M** and **S**?

This hypothesis has obviously to be argued for. This is made easy by showing that the main constitutive beliefs of the major ideologies (regrouped around vague headings but sufficiently laden to orientate a large patch of literature in economics: liberalism, socialism, personalism, communitarianism…) logically find themselves each time such a presupposition is made, according to the different modes of questioning (ethical, methodological, political) and the different subjects treated (Leroux 1995).

Here are the two traits of the ideological pure form of thought: that which distinguishes the forms of reference, and that which brings it closer. The first is a reminder that the cognitive process accords primacy to the true belief over its justification, while the scientific pure form of thought does the opposite. The second indicates that the ideological pure form of thought operates, more than any other, with a strict respect for an ontological presupposition, articulating two analytically separated polar entities: man and society. The first characteristic is therefore of *local* order, as it is active at every ideological proposition: it puts forward the psychological posture of the ideologue (certitude), opposed to that which the scientific and philosophical forms of thought require (doubt). The second characteristic is of *global* order, since it is the source of the internal coherence of the set of knowledge types produced by this sort of cognitive process.

Once the characteristics are recognised, it becomes possible to validate some procedures that permit a distinction of the influence of the ideological pure form of thought in such and such a learned discourse, as is shown by the following examples.

Applications in economic literature

Of the two characteristics of the ideological pure form of thought that have been called local and global, the most discriminatory is the first. However, the psychological opposition between doubt and certitude is dodged by the organisation of the learned discourse. Bearing in mind the superiority granted to science (and to a lesser extent to philosophy), the ideological belief is always camouflaged as a proposition of scientific (or philosophical) nature. In economics, this systematic travesty of learned discourse has been largely recognised today, thanks to the pioneering work of D.M. McCloskey. The analysis of economic rhetoric, adapted to the epistemological 'tendency' approach proposed here, should lead to the validation of useful techniques in detecting the ideological pure form of thought found in a learned text. In the meantime, it is even possible to mobilise the local characteristic of the ideological pure form of thought, as shown by the following procedure.

The two constituents of knowledge ('true belief' on one hand, and 'justification' on the other) are each in close connection with one of the extremities of learned reasoning, respectively: its conclusions and its premises. From the disposition of one or the other, can we hope to find revelatory signs of the psychological posture of the learned person: doubt or certitude? Such is the content of the following proposition, baptised in self-derision as the 'theorem of the fixed idea': if a learned work, spreading out over decades and crossing various historical contexts, draws attention to itself by the steadiness of its conclusions and the variation of the premises that support the argument, the sign of a preponderant ideological influence can be retained. Inversely, if the work makes a remarkable consistency apparent in the hands of its premises and a considerable extension in the domain of the validity of its conclusions, then it is all the better to think of a predominant influence of the scientific tendency (or philosophical, with a few compromises).

The authors who are open to this detection are only small in number, but exist nonetheless. The work of Hayek and Schumpeter, for example, clearly conform to the two opposing requisites of the theorem of the fixed idea (Leroux 1999a). The evident limit to this procedure is the fact that it only indirectly seeks to reveal the presence of doubt or certitude, that which constrains it to embrace a considerable mass of information (a work spreading out over decades). The study of economic rhetoric should here be an obvious contribution, authorising a direct examination of the discursive technique that allows the learned person to misrepresent (consciously or not) his ideological beliefs as scientific or philosophical. The greater the extent to which economic rhetoric is studied, the greater the extent to which it will be possible to validate the detection procedures of the ideological pure form of thought, while mobilising the local characteristic, but requiring a lesser quantity of information: a book, an article, a proposition.

The global characteristic, that demands the close dependence of ideological beliefs on the given ontological presupposition, permits another kind of investigation. What matters is the exhibition of the primary belief that makes a set of propositions coherent. This study can be transversally executed, questioning a particular field, or longitudinally, inspecting a specific work (for example, Marciano 1999; Quiquerez 2000; Leroux et al. 2001). But, beyond the evaluation, this global characteristic of the ideological pure form of thought can equally serve the production of learned discourse. The first step consists in making the ontological presupposition explicit. In the second step, the concrete questions relating to the social link are tallied one by one, whatever their nature (economic, political, moral, cultural and so on). This way, the ontological presupposition is therefore not only made explicit, but used as a guide in the formulation of 'beliefs'. More than just heuristic, it is a method of thought that, for being dominantly ideological in construction, should sufficiently gain in dignity and no longer be purely and simply rejected by the learned community for being contrary to good character (Leroux 1999b).

Concluding remarks

Plagiarizing Jankélévitch, there is some epistemological interest in considering the following three expressions of the same kind: to demonstrate, to convince and to persuade. Between demonstration (that would be ideal for a rational mind) and persuasion (that appears as the perverted form) there is a lot a space for convincing. Yet, in our discipline, only the axiomatic approach to 'pure' economy allows for the possibility of demonstration. As for the rest, and thus the essential, the economist can prove nothing, neither in positive nor normative economics. Nevertheless, we can give some credit to the economist, as he does not only seek to persuade. His discursive project is there to convince, and to do this he mobilizes all the strategies of knowledge that are at his disposition, as much those that one appreciates highly (science and philosophy) as those one recognizes as ideology. Such is the posture suggested by an epistemology 'by tendencies' in Bergson's manner. If this is admitted, the place held by ideology in economics remains problematic. But at least one thing becomes certain: we can do better than satisfy ourselves with the falsely innocent silences of Weber (that encourage a confusion of ideology and value judgements) or the truly misleading writings of Schumpeter (that make-believe ideology is eliminable).

Acknowledgement

Many thanks to Lloyd Alexander Bottomley and Miriam Teschl for their precious help in presenting this chapter.

References

Katouzian, Homar (1980), *Ideology and Method in Economics*, London: Macmillan.
Leroux, Alain (1995), *Retour à l'idéologie*, Paris: Presses Universitaires de France.

Leroux, Alain (1999a), 'Idéologie et science', in Alain Leroux and Alain Marciano (eds), *Traité de philosophie économique*, Brussels: De Boeck.

Leroux, Alain (1999b), *Une société à vivre*, Paris: Presses Universitaires de France.

Leroux, Alain, Guillaume Quiquerez and Gilbert Tosi (2001), *Idéologies et doctrines en économie*, Paris: Economica.

Mannheim, Karl (1929 [1970]), *Ideology and Utopia*, taken from the French translation (1956), Paris: Librairie Marcel Rivière, reprinted New York: Harcourt Brace.

Marciano, Alain (1999), *Ethiques de l'économie*, Brussels: De Boeck.

Marx, Karl and Friedrich Engels (1846 [1998]), *The German Ideology*, taken from the French translation (1992), Paris, Editions ouvrières, reprinted Buffalo, NY: Prometheus Books.

Quiquerez, Guillaume (2000), 'Le rôle des a priori cognitifs en économie', doctoral thesis, Université d'Aix-Marseille.

Schumpeter, Joseph (1949), 'Science and ideology', *American Economic Review*, **34** (2) 345–59.

Solow, Robert (1971 [1994]), 'Science and ideology in economics', reprinted in Daniel Hausman (ed.), *The Philosophy of Economics – An Anthology*, Cambridge: Cambridge University Press.

Weber, Max (1911–1920 [1971]), *Economie et société*, Paris: Plon.

PART II

THE METHODOLOGY AND EPISTEMOLOGY OF ECONOMICS

9 The methodology of scientific research programmes

Roger E. Backhouse

MSRP and economic methodology

Economic methodology emerged as an identifiable field at the boundaries of economics and philosophy in the early 1980s. Lakatos's methodology of scientific research programmes (MSRP) played an important role in this process. *Method and Appraisal in Economics* (Latsis 1976), edited by one of Lakatos's students, contained detailed case studies in which the MSRP was applied to economics. Partly because the contributors included distinguished economists (John Hicks, Herbert Simon and Axel Leijonhufvud) as well as established historians of economic thought (Terence Hutchison, Mark Blaug, Bob Coats, Neil de Marchi) this book obtained a wide readership. It encouraged younger scholars (such as Bruce Caldwell) to take methodology seriously. Shortly afterwards, Mark Blaug's *Methodology of Economics* (1980 [1992]), dominated by Popperian and Lakatosian philosophy, provided a survey of the field, a textbook and a provocative thesis about economics: it became the standard target at which those wanting to make a name for themselves could and did take aim. During the 1980s, it is arguable that the MSRP provided the dominant approach to economic methodology.

There were several reasons why the MSRP proved attractive to those turning to economic methodology. It held out the hope of providing a rigorous conceptual framework within which to analyse episodes in the history of economics (many of those who turned to it were historians). Its combination of history with appraisal seemed superior to Thomas Kuhn's *Structure of Scientific Revolutions* (1970), with which it had much in common. It also offered a framework within which it might be possible to solve long-standing puzzles, such as why the Keynesian revolution took place. It also appeared to offer an appraisal criterion that was less harsh than Popper's falsificationism, yet rigorous enough to be able to distinguish between good and bad economics. It had the further advantage, given that the history of economic thought was well established as a field within economics, of its historiographic orientation. There was a resonance between MSRP and some of the issues with which historians of economics were already familiar.

Towards the end of the 1980s, however, the tide turned. The application of MSRP to economics was found to be much harder, and the results of such applications less promising, than had been first anticipated. The main reason, however, was growing interest in other ways of viewing developments within economics. The analysis of rhetoric, discourse and the sociology of scientific knowledge came to be seen as offering a more fruitful approach. MSRP came to be equated with a 'thin' and dated Popperianism that methodologists felt they had outgrown (a clear example was Weintraub 1988). This shift in attitudes was clearly illustrated in a conference held in Capri in 1989. Despite including many of those who had been responsible for the surge of interest in Lakatos, the mood was overall one of great hostility, captured in Mark Blaug conclusions to the volume that emerged from the conference (de Marchi and Blaug 1991). MSRP was also strongly criticised by Hausman (1992), whose revived Millian methodology was one of the most widely discussed approaches to the subject during the 1990s. MSRP came to be seen as part of the older Popperian tradition, beyond which economic methodology had progressed.

MSRP and the Popperian tradition
The MSRP can be seen as an outgrowth of the Popperian tradition in the philosophy of science. Though he developed and qualified his ideas over time, the essence of Popper's view of science was always that scientific theories should be subject to severe criticism, notably empirical testing. Theories could never be proven to be true, but testing could eliminate false theories and the ability to survive such tests served to corroborate those that remained. In its simplest form, this was falsificationism: the idea that science progresses by the elimination of false theories. The moral was that scientists should propose theories that could conceivably be falsified and that they should attempt to falsify them. According to Lakatos's interpretation, Popper started out a naïve falsificationist, stressing the asymmetry between confirmation and refutation of a theory (one observation is sufficient to refute a theory whereas no finite number of observations can confirm it with complete certainty). In response to the problems inherent in naive falsificationism, however, Popper moved on to a sophisticated methodological falsificationism. (Lakatos 1970) presented his MSRP as an extension of this programme – as a type of 'sophisticated methodological falsificationism'.

Lakatos parted company with Popper in two ways. First, the unit of appraisal became the 'scientific research programme' rather than the individual theory. Second, the appraisal criterion was not falsificationism but the prediction of novel facts. Lakatos defined a scientific research programme as a set of rules, or heuristics, governing research within the programme. These fall into two categories. On the one hand, 'negative heuristics' direct researchers not to question the *hard core* of the programme – the set of assumptions regarded as irrefutable by anyone working within the programme. Thus in the Newtonian research programme, the negative heuristics would include 'Do not question Newton's laws of motion or the law of gravity'. In economics, comparable heuristics might be 'Do not construct theories in which irrational behaviour plays a significant role', which would protect a hard-core assumption that 'Agents optimize subject to constraints'. 'Positive heuristics', on the other hand, provide rules by which research is to be conducted. These rules lay out the strategy by which anomalies are to be dealt with, and how the research programme is to be developed. They are concerned with the programme's 'protective belt': the assumptions and procedures which are needed in order to apply the hard-core assumptions to specific problems, but which can be modified without calling the programme into question. Thus Newtonian astronomy starts by modelling planets as point-masses, then as spheres and then as spheres that are distorted by their rotation. When the theory fails to predict correctly, such assumptions can be modified without threatening anything that is fundamental to the programme. In economics, such positive heuristics might include 'Explain Pareto-inefficient allocations of resources by finding missing markets', or 'Start by assuming identical agents and full information, dropping these assumptions when necessary'.

Though research programmes involve an invariant hard core, these changes in the protective belt mean that research programmes are not static. New facts are discovered, new problems emerge, and as a result modifications have to be made. Lakatos, therefore, argued that it was inappropriate to appraise individual theories. What mattered was not individual theories but the way in which a research programme evolved over time. If the modifications made to a programme did no more than explain away new evidence, he described the programme as 'degenerating'. If, on the other hand, modifications not only explained anomalies but also led to the prediction of new facts – facts the modifications were not designed to explain – Lakatos called the programme 'progressive'. It was 'theoretically progressive' if new facts were predicted. It was 'empirically progressive' if those new facts were corroborated.

Whereas Kuhn saw that one paradigm would typically displace another, Lakatos emphasised that there would usually exist competing research programmes. Appraisal, therefore, involved not just deciding for or against a particular research programme, but choosing between competing ones. Lakatos proposed that scientists should abandon degenerating research programmes in favour of progressive ones. The typical pattern, he claimed, was for a research programme to start out as progressive – predicting or corroborating novel facts. It would, however, end up explaining facts only by increasing use of ad hoc expedients that increased the complexity of the theory faster than it provided satisfactory explanations of the phenomena it was trying to explain. However, though this criterion has attractions, and is arguably superior to naïve falsificationism, it is problematic. Research programmes may go through progressive and degenerating phases. A programme may degenerate for a while but then become progressive. This means that it may sometimes not be rational to abandon a degenerating research programme. Rational scientists need to be forward-looking, and the fact that a programme is less progressive than a rival does not mean that it will continue to be so in future. It may be rational to allow fledgling research programmes time to develop.

Popper's methodology suffered from two related weaknesses. As Kuhn (1970) showed, scientists did not follow Popperian rules. They clung to refuted theories, worked with ones that were unfalsifiable and frequently applied scientific theories without criticising them. This was related to the second weakness – that Popper could not provide evidence that following his methodological rules would lead to greater success in science. Lakatos's response to these two problems was his 'methodology of historical research programmes' (MHRP) (Lakatos 1971). His contention was that 'a rationality theory – or demarcation criterion – is to be rejected if it is inconsistent with an accepted "basic value judgement" of the scientific community' (1971, p. 124). There was, he claimed, considerable agreement over whether specific cases were examples of good or bad science. For example, there was no serious dispute about the success of Newtonian mechanics or Lavoisier's chemistry. Any theory of scientific rationality, including his own, should therefore be rejected if it failed to portray these moves as rational. Lakatos went on to propose that this way of appraising the MSRP could be implemented by a particular approach to the history of science. This involved reconstructing the history of science as if it had developed in accordance with the MSRP. Footnotes would then document points where the actual history failed to correspond with its rational reconstruction. If the footnotes were substantial, it would be evidence against the MSRP.

Lakatos's MSRP lay squarely in the Popperian tradition, to the extent that, when compared with certain of Popper's writings (for example Popper 1972, pp. 240–48), Lakatos seems hardly to go beyond him. The MSRP appears to represent a minor variation on what Lakatos termed Popper's sophisticated methodological falsificationism, distinguished from the latter as much by Lakatos's new terminology as by its content. Lakatos, however, altered the emphasis is some key respects. Notably, his concept of a research programme involves placing certain assumptions (the hard core) beyond criticism. Though Popper saw the heuristic power of metaphysical hypotheses, and even wrote about metaphysical research programmes (Popper 1983, pp. 189–93), to place anything beyond criticism was very un-Popperian (though critics have argued that he made an exception of his own theories). Furthermore, though Lakatos thought of empirical content in a Popperian way, as the set of potential falsifiers, he placed greater emphasis on corroboration than on falsification. Progressive research programmes were ones whose predictions are corroborated. There is thus an element of inductivism in the MSRP. Lakatos also went beyond Popper in proposing a criterion by which to judge whether his methodology was consistent with the historical record and whether his rationality criterion made sense of the best moves in science. However, his approach could be seen as thoroughly Popperian in its inspiration. Popper had argued that any scientific theory should be potentially falsifiable and that scientists should specify the conditions under which they would be prepared to abandon it. Lakatos proposed conditions under which he would be prepared to abandon the MSRP: if it failed to reconstruct the best moves in science as rational, it should be abandoned.

MSRP and the Lakatosian tradition

Though Lakatos's MSRP clearly fitted into the Popperian tradition, it draws on elements from outside that tradition. It can be understood only by being placed in the context of Lakatos's own intellectual development. The immediate context was his work on the philosophy of mathematics, notably his PhD dissertation (Lakatos 1967), submitted to the University of Cambridge in 1961, where he studied from his departure from Hungary in 1956 till his appointment as LSE in 1960. His target in this thesis was the 'Euclidian' view of mathematics that sought to provide secure foundations for mathematical truth. According to this view, mathematical knowledge was justified by showing how it could be deduced from self-evidently true statements made up of only perfectly clear terms. Lakatos claimed that this certainty was an illusion. It was impossible ever to define terms perfectly clearly – all that could be done was to define terms using other terms, which led to a problem of infinite regress (Lakatos 1978, II, pp. 3–23). Meaning and truth, he claimed, could only be transferred, not established. The reason the situation appeared otherwise was that terms were stretched so as to ensure success.

Lakatos provided an illustration of this using the history of the Descartes–Euler conjecture: that, for a polyhedron, $V - E + F = 2$, where V is the number of vertices, E the number of edges and F the number of faces. The conventional account of this story held that the theorem had been proved with ever-greater rigour. Lakatos showed that this had been achieved only through stretching and changing the concept of a polyhedron. It began by being a solid (that could have a physical form) the faces of which were polygons. As proofs of the conjecture were refined, it became a surface that could be stretched and a network of edges and vertices. The theorem eventually became a theorem in matrix algebra. Several aspects of this process are important. Progress involved the production of counter-examples and the analysis of proofs to establish how these counter-examples could arise and to point out new proofs. Proofs were therefore never final. Counter-examples would result in proof-analysis and revisions to the original proof. Even more important, narrowing or broadening the definitions of concepts could make theorems true or false. Lakatos was therefore led to write of the content-decreasing power of rigour.

The impossibility of defining terms with perfect clarity meant that an important role was played by the mathematician's intuition. In the case of the Descartes–Euler conjecture, mathematicians had to decide whether proposed objects (such as a cube with a hole in the middle, or a picture frame) were real polyhedra or were monsters – pathological cases that could be ignored. This decision would depend on intuitive ideas about what a polyhedron was. This intuition might in turn be changed by exposure to theorems and counter-examples. The role of intuition meant that mathematics was inherently informal, and that the boundary between discovery and justification was blurred. Mathematicians could imply otherwise only through surreptitious shifts in the meaning of the word mathematics – sometimes using it to refer to formal systems and at other times using it to refer to mathematics in the ordinary sense.

Before his arrival in Britain, Lakatos had been active in the Hungarian Communist Party (see Kadvany 2001, Chapter 12, for the argument on which this and the following paragraph are based). The Soviet Union had taken over Hungary in 1945 and by 1949 had transformed it into a Stalinist state in which the Party had dictatorial powers. For the present argument, the important feature of this is that it was achieved not only by the systematic use of violence, but also through changing ideas of truth and falsehood. Show trials were orchestrated to eliminate people thought dangerous to the regime. Statistics were altered to conceal economic failures. The Party was deemed infallible and history was rewritten accordingly. People lived a life of lies in politics, culture, business, and everyday life. These lies were justified through a Marxist rhetoric of dialectical materialism, 'producing a terror state through a parody of Hegelian-Marxist epistemology' (Kadvany 2001, p. 269). Lakatos, though he became a victim of this regime, was a Party intellectual, thoroughly implicated in these practices, where 'falsification' was standard practice. He lived a life where the rhetoric of Hegelian-Marxism was used to blur the boundaries between truth and falsehood.

Lakatos graduated in 1947, having written a dissertation, 'On the sociology of concept building in the natural sciences', which used external economic and social factors to explain scientific change. He became an ardent supporter of the Communist regime, actively working against those who wanted a more liberal regime, spying and informing on others for the political police. Despite a period in a labour camp, it was not until 1956 that he changed his views, turning against the regime. Self-criticism was an essential element in this process, both under the Stalinist regime and in the process of rejecting it. This background is relevant for his later philosophical work in several ways. Throughout his career, historiography is central: history cannot be written independently of normative considerations, and multiple histories are possible. Falsification of a rationally reconstructed history parallels what Hungarian intellectuals tried to achieve in 1956 (see Kadvany 2001, pp. 294–316 for a more detailed elaboration of these arguments). There are also parallels in the role of elites in the Stalinist regime and in MSRP. Perhaps most important, self-criticism provides the basis for rationality.

> Lakatos's work, therefore, is a complete historical philosophy of science, mathematics, and criticism that answers, in the Hegelian-Marxist tradition, philosophical problems raised by Hungarian Stalinism and the 1956 Revolution. (Kadvany 2001, p. 300)

The unifying theme in Lakatos's work, from his life as a Hegelian-Communist in Hungary before 1956, through his work as a philosopher of mathematics to his MSRP, is Pyrrhonian scepticism, as mediated by Hegelian dialectics. The essence of Pyrrhonian scepticism is to take one's opponent's argument and to turn it against itself. The point about scepticism is not that we can know nothing but that it provides a method for questioning everything. It is not a doctrine about cognition but a way to undermine any claim to certain knowledge, based on the premise that any criterion for absolute truth is either dogmatically imposed or refers to some other criterion, leading to a potential infinite regress. The Pyrrhonian method lies at the heart of Hegelian dialectics, where the arising of the antithesis out of the thesis can be seen as a sceptical turning of the thesis against itself, to produce a new synthesis. This is clearly the method of *Proofs and Refutations* (1967). Proof analysis involves turning a mathematical proof against itself – using the proof to inspire a counter-example that then leads to a reformulation of the problem and hence a new proof. With his MSRP, the sceptical method was applied to the methodology of science.

Popper has emphasised that all knowledge was uncertain (one of the criticisms of Popper is that he goes too far in this direction). Lakatos agreed with this but took the argument a stage further, thereby turning Popper's methodology against itself. Popper had argued that the hallmark of a scientific theory was specifying the conditions under which the theory would have to be abandoned. Lakatos retorted that this should apply to *theories of* science (including Popper's falsificationism) as well as to scientific theories themselves. The criterion Lakatos adopted was that a methodology should be abandoned if it was inconsistent with the value judgements of the relevant scientific elite. In this way, falsificationism would be made falsifiable.

Lakatos's methodology of *historical* research programmes involved exposing the MSRP to criticism in exactly this way. The historian/philosopher should rationally reconstruct the history of important episodes in science: telling the story as if it had developed in accordance with the MSRP. This rational reconstruction could be seen as what MSRP predicted should happen. Divergences of the actual history from the rational reconstruction should be noted in footnotes. If the MSRP were correct, these footnotes would not be very substantial, showing that the actual story was close to that predicted by MSRP. On the other hand, if the footnotes were substantial, it meant that the rational reconstruction was inadequate as an account of the actual history – that the MSRP could not predict correctly. Judging the MSRP by its success in predicting the history of science amounted to turning the MSRP against itself. This was important for Lakatos because it provided him with a source of rationality in a world where nothing is certain. The sceptical method of self-criticism provided a source of rationality in a world of falsehoods. His willingness to make this step differentiated his views from those of Paul Feyerabend, also a sceptic, but not willing to see the method of scepticism as the basis for a rationalist philosophy.

It is, therefore, possible to construct multiple histories of the MSRP. The conventional one locates MSRP firmly in the Popperian tradition, as a modification – even a softening – of Popper's falsificationism. The less familiar story relates MSRP to the journey Lakatos made, applying a Pyrrhonian/Hegelian scepticism first to provide a source of rationality in Stalinist Hungary; then to the philosophy of mathematics; and finally to scientific theories and scientific methodology. In all three situations, the elimination of error though sceptical methods provided a source of rationality in a world where it was possible to rely on nothing. In the second history, Lakatos is a covert Hegelian, undermining Popperian methodology by subjecting it to falsificationist criticism. MSRP is a historicisation of Popper, an approach that can be placed in the Hegelian–Marxist tradition represented by Lukács.

The application of MSRP to economics
The first application of MSRP to economics was by Latsis (in 1976). He argued that 'situational determinism' was the dominant research programme in neoclassical microeconomic theory. Focusing on approaches that determined decisions uniquely, he claimed that it was characterised by the following heuristic.

> Look at the situational constraints and the preferences of the actor in question. Look at the institutional, technological or structural obstacles, given his goal. Given that the actor correctly perceives all these, they will uniquely determine his course of action. Then, using the rationality principle as the trivial animating law, you will be led to an explanatory argument which suggests why the actor in question did x rather than *not* x. (Latsis 1976, p. 21)

Using this framework, Latsis was able to reinterpret incidents in the history of economics. 'Monopolistic competition' no longer appeared as a revolution but became a problem shift within the same research programme.

In the same volume, others applied MSRP to economics and psychology (Coats), the Keynesian revolution (Leijonhufvud), the theory of international trade (de Marchi), and alternative forms of rationality (Simon). Blaug, Hicks and Hutchison provided more wide-ranging appraisals of MSRP. The overall message of the book is probably fairly summed up as one of guarded optimism regarding MSRP as a tool for analysing economics. None of the essays could be described as offering a simple, mechanical application of the method. Coats (Latsis 1976, pp. 60–61) offered a good summary.

> MSRP must be applied to economics with due caution. Much depends on how literally it is interpreted. … MSRP is a valuable tool for analysing the methods by which an established research programme or scientific tradition is preserved, and the changes it undergoes at the hands of its proponents. … To the historian, MSRP is essentially a practical tool which will ultimately be judged by its results. At this early stage of its application it seems to possess considerable promise.

Coats's essay identified two issues that were to recur throughout the ensuing literature. One was the related problems that clear-cut examples of progressiveness and degeneration were hard to find, and that progress or degeneration did not appear to explain the adoption and abandoning of research programmes. Economists frequently continued with degenerating programmes. They also readily adopted and casually abandoned new ones. Consistent with Lakatos's MSRP, Coats did not draw the conclusion that MSRP was wrong, but that it needed time to develop. The other problem was whether economics should be viewed as one massive research programme (perhaps dating from Adam Smith) or a series of much smaller ones. There were arguments in favour of both. It was to address this problem that Remenyi (1979) proposed complicating Lakatos's framework by distinguishing between programmes and sub-programmes, with cores and demi-cores. This, he maintained, provided a framework that might be usable to analyse the complex interrelations between theories that MSRP on its own could not.

During the following decade or so, many economists applied MSRP to economics (see de Marchi and Blaug 1991, pp. 29–30 for a list). The literature sought to identify both 'large-scale' and 'small-scale' research programmes. The former included Smithian, Ricardian, Marxian, Keynesian, neoclassical, behavioural and Austrian research programmes; the latter included demand theory, production theory, human capital theory and the economics of the family. Two points are worth making about this list. Most of the 'large-scale' research programme candidates involve using MSRP to reinterpret approaches to economics that had previously been identified as methodologically distinctive and were well explored by historians. In contrast, the 'small-scale' case studies, most of which were in (Blaug 1980 [1992]) dealt with fields within modern economics that had previously been unanalysed and were being investigated for their methodological rather than historical lessons. The other point is that comparatively few of these studies explicitly characterised their candidate programme's hard core, its heuristics and empirically assessed it. Many did no more than one or two of these.

One of the studies that did all three of these things was Weintraub's attempt (Weintraub 1985) to characterise a neo-Walrasian research programme. Given the influence of this study, his definition of the hard core and heuristics merit citing in full.

HC1   There exist economic agents.

HC2   Agents have preferences over outcomes.

HC3   Agents independently optimise subject to constraints.

HC4   Choices are made in interrelated markets.

HC5   Agents have full relevant knowledge.

HC6   Observable economic outcomes are co-ordinated, so they must be discussed with reference to equilibrium states.

PH1   Go forth and construct theories in which agents optimise.

PH2   Construct theories that make predictions about equilibrium states.

NH1   Do not construct theories in which irrational behaviour plays any role.

NH2   Do not construct theories in which equilibrium has no meaning.

NH3   Do not test hard-core propositions.

He argued that this defined a research programme, at the heart of which lay general equilibrium analysis. It served to define a role for general equilibrium analysis, something that methodologists had previously failed to do. General equilibrium analysis, by which Weintraub meant the literature on the existence of general equilibrium, served to 'harden the hard core of the neo-Walrasian research programme' (Weintraub 1985, p. 112). Some elements of the hard core go back to Walras and others to economists such as Cassel. However, Weintraub (1985, p. 113) concluded:

> The hard core as presented can be said to have existed only as early as the early 1950s. The recognition that Arrow, Debreu, and McKenzie had accomplished a major feat was precisely the recognition that the hard core of the neo-Walrasian program was, by their work, no longer problematic.

This characterisation of the role of general equilibrium analysis within the neo-Walrasian programme can be questioned (c.f. Backhouse 1993). However, it was a framework that could be extended, with extremely minor modifications to the specification of the programme, to encompass episodes in the history of economics that Weintraub had not intended to explain. The neo-Walrasian research programme can be used to explain why economists used it in macroeconomics in the 1970s – it was progressive, predicting novel facts (Backhouse, in de Marchi and Blaug 1991). Weintraub's neo-Walrasian research programme was arguably the most detailed and most successful application of MSRP to economics.

Economic methodologists' disillusion with MSRP

By the end of the 1980s, there were many applications of MSRP to economics. MSRP had made sense of important phenomena in the history of economics and had stimulated methodological investigation of problems and episodes that otherwise might not have been investigated. However, the results were ambiguous. The problems raised by Coats, concerning the level at which MSRP should be applied and how the failure of economists to follow Lakatos's criteria for adopting and abandoning programmes should be interpreted, were no nearer resolution (this account draws on the discussions of Lakatos in Backhouse 1997, 1998a). Economic methodologists found two main problems.

Lakatos's definition of a research programme in terms of an invariant hard core is too narrow. Research programmes need to be characterised in more complex ways in order to capture their evolution over time. For example, Hoover (in de Marchi and Blaug 1991) argued that the new classical macroeconomics, perceived by most economists to be a coherent, well-defined programme, could not be described in terms of an invariant set of hard-core assumptions. Even the neo-Walrasian research programme identified by Weintraub (1985), one of the most persuasive applications of MSRP, is defined by heuristics and assumptions that are primarily methodological. It is a programme held together by a modelling strategy rather than by anything else. It is thus thought to be different from research programmes identified in physics or chemistry where the hard core was believed to include substantive assumptions about the subject matter under analysis.

Lakatos's appraisal criterion is linked to Popper's attempt to solve the problem of induction (see Hands in de Marchi and Blaug 1991). The justification for the prediction of novel facts as an appraisal criterion is that applying it should result in increases in the truth content of the theories concerned. However, Popper's theory of verisimilitude has serious flaws and, without it, Lakatos's appraisal criterion was considered to have lost its rationale.

Such doubts were reinforced by broader doubts about the Popperian tradition of which MSRP formed a part. Mäki (1990) and de Marchi (1992) were among those arguing that the Popperian tradition, with its emphasis on rules governing the growth of scientific knowledge, focused attention on a range of issues that was much too narrow. For example, by distinguishing sharply between the context of discovery and the context of justification, with the former dismissed as irrelevant to the truth of scientific knowledge, it distracted attention from the many philosophical problems associated with the social context out of which scientific ideas arise.

At the same time, there was growing scepticism about the role of general philosophical frameworks – grand theories or visions as their critics often referred to them – and increasing concern with the peculiarities of economics as a discipline. The most influential expression of these views was McCloskey's article, 'The rhetoric of economics' in the *Journal of Economic Literature* (McCloskey 1983), shortly followed by a book of the same title (McCloskey 1986). McCloskey's target was the collection of ideas he discussed under the label of 'modernism', one of which was 'Rule-Bound Methodology'. Such methodological rules, he contended, were narrowing and bore little relation to the way science actually worked or even ways in which it could work. They should therefore be abandoned. Lakatos was not McCloskey's main target. However, Lakatos's MSRP was clearly what he had in mind when he included Lakatos among those he termed 'methodological authoritarians', who dismissed even moderately argued cases for wider notions of rationality, such as those of Stephen Toulmin or Paul Feyerabend, as 'irrationalism' (McCloskey 1985, p. 36).

Though his arguments were the most widely cited, McCloskey was far from alone. Klamer 1984) had independently come to similar conclusions. More important, they reflected a much more widespread philosophical movement, the character of which is best illustrated with some examples. Rorty (1980) sought to undermine the idea that philosophy could underwrite or debunk claims to knowledge made in other fields: there was no privileged position from which such judgements could be made. Through focusing on what he called the conversation of mankind, he moved towards a social view of knowledge. This was taken even further in the literature on the sociology of knowledge (for overviews, see Hands 2001; Sent 1999) where knowledge was analysed as a social construct. Though most of those engaged in the sociology of scientific knowledge did not go this far, it was possible to draw from this literature the conclusion that notions such as objectivity, truth and scientific rationality should be abandoned. Against this background, Lakatos's MSRP seemed distinctly problematic.

The change in attitude towards MSRP is well illustrated by the contrast between the conferences reported in de Marchi (1988) and de Marchi and Blaug (1991). In the first, in 1985, Popperian methodology was subject to severe criticism, but it was actively defended. McCloskey and Klamer proposed discourse analysis as an alternative. However, their approaches were generally considered novel but insufficiently developed for it to be possible to determine whether they should displace more traditional philosophical analysis. The second conference, in 1989, included in its aims the promotion of case studies in MSRP and re-examination of the relevance of MSRP to economics. Despite this, there was what Blaug described as 'a generally dismissive, if not hostile, reaction to Lakatos's MSRP' (de Marchi and Blaug 1991, p.500). The main factor underlying this change was much greater sympathy towards arguments about the social construction of knowledge. The clearest representative of the transition that had taken place is Roy Weintraub. In 1985 he was using Lakatos's MSRP to interpret modern economics. His contribution to the 1989 conference argued that, not only was the Lakatosian framework one perspective among many, but it was not a particularly interesting one. The reason he gave was that it involved reconstructing history as rational. Pointing to the parallels between his view and that of the sociologist, Knorr Cetina (1991), he proposed an alternative perspective in which meaning and knowledge are the outcome of a social process of negotiation and argument. Taken together with the problems involved in applying Lakatos's framework to economics – it was hard to identify research programmes in a convincing way and economists did not behave as the methodology suggested they should – this convinced many that MSRP was not the way forward.

What is left of Lakatos's MSRP?
Amongst specialists in economic methodology, Lakatos's MSRP is widely discredited. It forms part of a Popperian tradition that is considered philosophically flawed and it is perceived to involve forcing economics into a mould into which it does not fit and for which there is little justification. However, there are several reasons for not dismissing it so easily.

The first reason is that MSRP appeals to economists. Prediction of novel facts is an appraisal criterion that resonates with the way many economists see their work. For example, Friedman and Schwartz, echoing Friedman (1953), have written, referring to the work of David Hendry and Neil Ericsson (1991) on the UK demand for money:

> A persuasive test of their results must be based on data not used in the derivation of their equations. This might mean using their equations to predict some kind of phenomena for other countries, or for a future or earlier period for the United Kingdom, or deriving testable implications for other variables. ... Similarly, that is the only kind of evidence that we would regard as persuasive with respect to the validity of our own results. (Friedman and Schwartz 1991, p.47)

Hendry's concern with developing a progressive research programme is very much in the Lakatosian tradition (see, for example, Hendry and Mizon 1990; Gilbert 1986). Prediction of novel facts is favoured as a realistic, yet demanding appraisal criterion by economists who are committed to testing theories against data. On top of this, it is natural for economists to think in terms of research programmes. One need think no further than the persistent appeal of terms such as Keynesianism, monetarism, the new classical macroeconomics, real business cycle theory, and so on. The rise and decline of research programmes is clearly a major issue, and Lakatos's methodology provides an attractive starting point for analysing it. This is why economists continue to use it, despite the philosophical problems it has encountered.

A second reason is that the place of MSRP can be seen as having provided economic methodology with an important stepping stone on the way from the comparatively arid logical empiricism that dominated methodological discussions in the 1950s and 1960s to the much broader questions that are being explored today. By focusing on research programmes, it directed attention, even more clearly than had Popper, away from evaluating the logical status of individual theories. From MSRP, with its emphasis on heuristics and decisions of scientific communities, it was but a short step towards a richer view of economics. For example, (Hausman 1992) could be seen as having articulated a heuristic, or set of rules, underlying contemporary mainstream microeconomics. Though he presented his work as an alternative to Lakatos, his work could have been presented as an exercise in the spirit of Lakatos. In addition, MSRP was important in linking methodology of economics to the history of economics, a link that is widely considered to be very important. With this link, the sociological dimensions of economics were almost inevitably brought in. Lakatos's MSRP captures the important tension between positive and normative methodology with its insistence that methodology can be judged only in relation to scientists' practices.

MSRP does not have to be seen as part of the Popperian tradition. It can equally be seen as arising from a tradition that goes back, through Hegel, to the ancient sceptics. In this tradition, the meaning of terms is forever being questioned. If viewed against the background of Lakatos's philosophy of mathematics, which focuses on the continual reassessment of the meaning of terms, MSRP appears in a much more positive light (see Backhouse 1997, chapter 10; and 1998b) and arguably less dependent on Popperian ideas such as verisimilitude. The way in which the meaning of economic concepts, even 'fundamental' ones such as agents, markets, competition, as well as more specialised ones such as unemployment, has changed has not been sufficiently explored and Lakatos's ideas on the changing meaning of mathematical concepts provide a possible way forward. MSRP, if taken together, as it should be, with Lakatos's MHRP, directs attention not simply to the rational elements in science, but to the non-rational. Why do research programmes degenerate? Why do economists hang on to ideas even when there is evidence against them? We are directed towards historical accounts in which positive and normative issues are intertwined. Used like this, MSRP may still be useful in resolving historical puzzles. It certainly cannot successfully be applied to economics, or any other science, in a mechanical way and to use Lakatosian ideas today may require going beyond MSRP. However, it remains an important starting point and source of ideas.

References

Backhouse, Roger E. (1993), 'Lakatosian perspectives on general equilibrium analysis', *Economics and Philosophy*, **9** (2), 271–82.

Backhouse, Roger E. (1997), *Truth and Progress in Economic Knowledge*, Cheltenham, UK and Lyme, USA, Edward Elgar.

Backhouse, Roger E. (1998a), *Explorations in Economic Methodology: From Lakatos to Empirical Philosophy of Science*, London and New York, Routledge.

Backhouse, Roger E. (1998b), 'If mathematics is informal, then perhaps we should accept that economics must be informal too', *Economic Journal*, **108** (451), 1848–58.

Blaug, Mark (1980 [1992]), *The Methodology of Economics: How Economists Explain*, Cambridge: Cambridge University Press.

Coats, A.W. (1976), 'Economics and psychology: the death and resurrection of a research programme', in Spiro J. Latsis (ed.), *Method and Appraisal in Economics*, Cambridge: Cambridge University Press, pp. 42–64.

de Marchi Neil (ed.), (1988), *The Popperian Legacy in Economics*, Cambridge: Cambridge University Press.

de Marchi, Neil, and Mark Blaug (eds) (1991), *Appraising Economic Theories: Studies in the Methodology of Research Programmes*, Aldershot, UK and Brookfield US: Edward Elgar.

de Marchi, Neil (1992), *Post-Popperian Methodology of Economics: Recovering Practice*, Boston, Dordrecht and London: Kluwer Academic Publishers.

Friedman, Milton (1953), 'The methodology of positive economics', in *Essays in Positive Economics*, Chicago: Chicago University Press, pp. 3–43.

Friedman, Milton, and Anna J. Schwartz (1991), 'Alternative approaches to analyzing economic data', *American Economic Review*, **81** (1), 39–49.

Gilbert, C.L. (1986 [1990]), 'Professor Hendry's econometric methodology', *Oxford Bulletin of Economics and Statistics*, **48** (3), 283–307, reprinted in C.W.J. Granger (ed.), *Modelling Economic Series*, Oxford: Clarendon Press.

Hands, D. Wade (2001), *Reflection Without Rules: Economic Methodology and Contemporary Science Theory*, Cambridge: Cambridge University Press.

Hausman, Daniel M. (1992), *The Inexact and Separate Science of Economics*, Cambridge: Cambridge University Press.

Hendry, D.F., and N. Ericsson (1991), 'An econometric analysis of U.K. money demand in Monetary Trends in the United States and the United Kingdom by Milton Friedman and Anna J. Schwartz', *American Economic Review*, **81** (1), 8–38.

Hendry, D.F., and G. Mizon (1990), 'Procrustean econometrics: or stretching and squeezing data', in in C.W.J. Granger (ed.), *Modelling Economic Series*, Oxford: Clarendon Press, pp. 121–36.

Hoover, Kevin D. (1991), 'Scientific research program or tribe? A joint appraisal of Latkos and the new classical macroeconomics, in Neil DeMarchi and Mark Blaug (eds), *Appraising Economic Theories: Studies in the Methodology of Research Programmes*, Aldershot, UK: Edward Elgar, pp. 364–94.

Kadvany, J. (2001), *Imre Lakatos and the Guises of Reason*, Durham, NC: Duke University Press.

Klamer, Arjo (1984), *The New Classical Macroeconomics: Conversations with New Classical Macroeconomists and their Opponents*, Brighton: Harvester Press.

Knorr Cetina, Karen (1991), 'Epistemic cultures: forms of reason in science', *History of Political Economy*, **23** (1), 105–22.

Krugman, Paul (1996), 'How to be a crazy economist', in Steve G. Medema and Warren J. Samuels (eds), *Foundations of Research in Economics: How Do Economists do Economics?* Cheltenham, UK and Brookfield, US: Edward Elgar.

Kuhn, Thomas S. (1970), *The Structure of Scientific Revolutions*, Chicago: University of Chicago Press.

Lakatos, Imre (1967), *Proofs and Refutations*, Cambridge: Cambridge University Press.

Lakatos, Imre (1970), 'Falsification and the methodology of scientific research programmes', in Imre Lakatos and A. Musgrave (eds), *Criticism and the Growth of Knowledge,* Cambridge: Cambridge University Press, reprinted in Imre Lakatos (1978), *The Methodology of Scientific Research Programmes: Philosophical Papers*, vol. I, Cambridge: Cambridge University Press.

Lakatos, Imre (1971), 'History of science and its rational reconstructions', in R.C. Buck and R.S. Cohen (eds), *PSA 1970*, *Boston Studies in the Philosophy of Science*, **8**, 91–135, reprinted in Imre Lakatos (1978), *The Methodology of Scientific Research Programmes: Philosophical Papers*, vol. I, Cambridge: Cambridge University Press.

Lakatos, Imre (1978), *The Methodology of Scientific Research Programmes: Philosophical Papers*, vol. I, Cambridge: Cambridge University Press.

Lakatos, Imre (1978), *The Methodology of Scientific Research Programmes: Philosophical Papers*, vol. II 'Mathematics, science and epistemology', Cambridge: Cambridge University Press.

Latsis, Spiro J. (1976), 'A research program in economics', in Spiro J. Latsis (ed.), *Method and Appraisal in Economics*, Cambridge, Cambridge University Press, pp. 1–41.

Latsis, S.J., (ed.), (1976), *Method and Appraisal in Economics*, Cambridge, Cambridge University Press.

Mäki, Uskali (1990), 'Methodology of economics: complaints and guidelines', *Finnish Economic Papers*, **3** (1), 77–84.

McCloskey, Donald (now Deirdre N.) (1983), 'The rhetoric of economics', *Journal of Economic Literature*, **21**, 481–517.

McCloskey, Donald (now Deirdre N.) (1986), *The Rhetoric of Economics*, Brighton: Wheatsheaf Books.

Popper, Karl R. (1972), *Conjectures and Refutations: The Growth of Scientific Knowledge*, London: Routledge and Kegan Paul.

Popper, Karl R. (1983), *Realism and the Aim of Science*, London: Hutchinson.

Remenyi, J.V. (1979), 'Core-demi-core interaction: towards a general theory of disciplinary and sub-disciplinary growth', *History of Political Economy*, **11**, 30–63.

Rorty, Richard (1980), *Philosophy and the Mirror of Nature*, Oxford: Basil Blackwell.

Sent, Esther-Mirjam (1999), 'Economics of science: survey and suggestions', *Journal of Economic Methodology*, **6** (1), 95–124.

Weintraub, E. Roy (1985), *General Equilibrium Analysis: Studies in Appraisal*, Cambridge: Cambridge University Press.

Weintraub, E. Roy (1988), 'The neo-Walrasian research program is empirically progressive', in Neil de Marchi (ed.), *The Popperian Legacy in Economics*, Cambridge: Cambridge University Press.

10 Constructivism: the social construction of scientific knowledge

D. Wade Hands

Introduction

Philosophers have traditionally approached the subject of scientific knowledge from the 'What is ____?' perspective. 'Scientific Knowledge' of course fills the blank in the most general case, but a variety of more specific expressions have been inserted to cover various special topics that have been of interest to philosophers of science: 'explanation', 'testing', 'scientific inference', etc. This approach to science, scientific knowledge, and related topics, of course reflects the way that philosophers have traditionally approached most subjects of inquiry: 'What is Truth?', 'What is Beauty?', 'What is the Good?' ... While this approach to scientific knowledge is part of a grand philosophical heritage, and perhaps even has a certain edictal charm, it frankly makes it rather difficult to understand much of the work that goes on within contemporary science theory: particularly the work informed by social constructivism and its cognates.

The social constructivist view of scientific knowledge is much easier to understand if we begin with a different question than the standard philosophical point of embarkation. Rather than asking 'What is scientific knowledge?', it is more useful to begin an inquiry into the social construction of scientific knowledge by asking the question 'What determines scientific beliefs?' Scientists, qua scientists, clearly hold a wide array of different scientific beliefs. Some of these beliefs are rather mundane and are widely accepted outside of the scientific community (like the belief that the melting point of copper is 1083°C, or that the speed of light is 186000 miles per second), while others may be shared by almost every contemporary scientist and yet remain controversial within certain segments of the wider social community (like the belief in the Big Bang as the origin of the universe, or Darwinian random variation and selective retention as the explanation for the particular characteristics of homo sapiens). In addition to these widely held scientific beliefs, scientists also hold other beliefs that are much more local in nature; some of these are exclusive to members of a particular scientific group who share a common research program (punctuated equilibrium theory for example), while others are shared by almost no one outside of a specific research community (cold fusion for example). The best way to understand the social constructivist view of scientific knowledge is to start with the question of what determines such beliefs.

Notice how different the question 'What determines scientific beliefs?' is from the question 'What is scientific knowledge?' First of all, the traditional philosophical question begs for an essentialist answer: 'What is scientific knowledge essentially (i.e. really)?' Like the question 'What is Truth?' or 'What is the Good?' the standard philosophical approach to scientific knowledge begs for an answer in terms of the underlying *essential nature* of the subject matter in question. The modus operandi for answering such philosophical questions has traditionally been the method of conceptual analysis: the method of rational (armchair) philosophical speculation. The question 'What determines scientific knowledge?' elicits a more *naturalistic* response. It is more like the question 'What determines a solar eclipse?' or 'What determines the scents of various orchids?' or 'What determines the rate of inflation?', than the question 'What is Truth?' Although certain variants of scientific realism would link the answers to such naturalistic questions to the underlying essential nature of the objects of inquiry, it is no more necessary to forge such linkage in this case (scientific knowledge in general) than it is in the context of any more specific scientific investigation.

Second, notice that the constructivist question shifts the responsibility for what counts as 'scientific' onto the relevant (in this case scientific) agents. For the traditional approach, the domain of inquiry is circumscribed by the (philosophical) inquirer; in the constructivist framework the domain of inquiry is circumscribed by the subjects themselves (the scientists). Of course in order to conduct such an investigation one must still establish who counts as a 'scientist' before their beliefs can become the subject of inquiry, but this is fairly easy to establish since both the scientists and those conducting the inquiry are members of a wider social community where there is general agreement about who does and does not count as a 'scientist.' This is of course not the case for the traditional philosophical approach, since the very purpose of such an inquiry is to delineate the 'scientific' in a (philosophical) way that is *different* from the way that is accepted by non-philosophers and others within the wider social community. One does not need philosophers of science to establish the essential character of the 'scientific' designator, when its only purpose is to designate the professional beliefs of those who everyone agrees are 'scientists.'

The constructivist literature discussed in this chapter draws on resources from a wide variety of earlier and ongoing intellectual traditions. Some of these resources are also shared by those working in contemporary philosophy of natural science, but many are unique to the social constructivist approach. The Mertonian literature on the 'sociology of science' – beginning with Robert K. Merton's 1935 doctoral dissertation (Merton 1970), and continuing to the present day by sociologists of science guided by Mertonian functionalism – is certainly one of the approaches that has significantly influenced the constructivist literature on scientific knowledge. A second important influence was the 'sociology of knowledge' associated with the work of Karl Mannheim (1936) and others in the late 1930s. A third set of influential ideas involves the so-called Bernalist literature associated with the work of John Desmond Bernal (1939) and other (primarily British) Marxist historians of science during the 1940s and 1950s. Finally, but perhaps most importantly, Thomas Kuhn's *Structure of Scientific Revolutions* (1970) not only had a profound impact on the development of the constructivist literature, but also on the history and philosophy of natural science more generally: 'After Kuhn, philosophy of science would never be the same' (Callebaut 1993, p. 12). While Kuhn was clearly not the first to note that science in general, and specific scientific communities in particular, are actually *social communities* and that the social character of these communities conditions the observations, theorizing, and day-to-day practices of the scientists within them, his work was crucial to the spread of such ideas among contemporary science theorists. Now almost everyone writing in science theory agrees that science is fundamentally social and that understanding the character of that sociality is essential to understanding scientific knowledge.

While these, and a variety of other ideas (pragmatism, hermeneutics, postmodernism, feminism, ...) have influenced the constructivist literature on scientific knowledge, no attempt will be made to review these ideas in the following discussion. Doing justice to any of these topics is clearly beyond the scope of the current project and detailed discussions of each, and the impact of each on the constructivist approach, are available within the existing literature (see for example Barnes 1982; Barnes et al. 1996; Biagioli 1999; Collins and Restivo 1983; Golinski 1998, Hands 1997a, 2001a; Jasanoff et al. 1995; Pickering 1992, 1995; or Shapin 1982, 1988, 1992). The following discussion will focus on the social constructivist literature itself – or more realistically a small, but defining, portion of the constructivist literature – and how that work relates to disciplinary economics.

So what is this social constructivist literature? And who exactly is, and is not, a social constructivist? Given that social constructivism emerged out of the fusion of various aspects of so many different sets of ideas and approaches, it might seem a bit presumptuous to even attempt to identify a particular body of research that constituted the 'origin' of what is now called the social constructivist approach to scientific knowledge. Nonetheless, that is exactly what I would like to do. If constructivism has a point of origin, it is clearly the early work of the *Strong Program* (or Edinburgh School), particularly the contributions of Barry Barnes (1977, 1982) and David Bloor (1976/1991, 1983) in the late 1970s and early 1980s. Intellectual material came from a vast array of different sources, and the constructivist genesis spawned innumerable (and often rather contemptuous) offspring, but the Strong Program nonetheless represents the obligatory passage point for all the ideas that funneled into, and ultimately came out of, the social constructivist approach to scientific knowledge. The next section will examine the Strong Program in some detail and also briefly indicate some of the vast and varied constructivist literature that has appeared in the decades since the first work of the Strong Program. The second section will examine the numerous points of contact between these various social constructivisms and economics.

Belief, knowledge and social construction

Let us begin by returning to the question of what determines the beliefs of scientists. Talking about the 'beliefs of scientists' is of course *not* the way that philosophers of science would frame the subject of 'scientific knowledge.' But suppose they did. In other words, suppose one could somehow persuade philosophers of science to reformulate what they have traditionally said about scientific knowledge as an answer to the question of what determines the beliefs of scientists. What would they say? The answer would probably come in two parts; the first part would involve the *scientific method* and the second would involve *nature*. The story would be that *if* the scientific method is properly followed, then *nature* will determine the beliefs of scientists. In fact, the scientific method is nothing more than a particular set of procedures that allows scientists to see/hear objective nature in a way that other human procedures (prayer, poetry, auto-mechanics, Hegelian philosophy, karaoke, ...) do not allow the practitioners of those methods to see/hear objective nature. According to traditional philosophy of science (and the scientists themselves) *nature determines the beliefs of scientists*, or at least the beliefs of scientists who have correctly applied the scientific method.

The traditional belief-determination-by-objective-nature story itself actually comes in two different versions: realism and instrumentalism. The scientific realist version is most familiar; scientists believe in electrons and genes because *there are* electrons and genes, and the scientific method makes it possible for these existent things to be discovered. According to scientific realism, objective nature not only determines the beliefs of scientists, the theoretical beliefs of successful scientists are successful precisely because they are in fact true of nature. The instrumentalist version also has nature determining the beliefs of scientists, but at a slight remove; scientific beliefs facilitate the efficient organization and categorization of empirical evidence – the observational signals received from nature. The scientific method allows scientists to construct theories that organize and classify nature's signals – save the phenomena – in predictively efficient ways. In either case objective nature is ultimately the cause of scientific beliefs, it is just that in one case the beliefs are about the way that nature really is, while in the other case the beliefs only help organize the observational evidence that nature conjures up. In either case *if* the beliefs of scientists are determined by *social* factors – social interests, social forces, social conditioning, etc. – then they are not truly scientific beliefs. Some scientists have allowed their beliefs to be determined by social forces rather than objective nature – Nazi eugenicists, Lysenkoists in Soviet biology, and those extolling Creation science, for example – but these are paradigm cases of erroneous (or non-)science. According to the traditional philosophical view, proper scientific beliefs are determined by nature; if social conditioning plays a role then the resulting scientific beliefs are either wrong, or simply not science at all.

The Strong Program and other social constructivists turn this traditiónal argument on its head. If one were studying the beliefs of a particular premodern culture – say the belief that the god Zarwa causes the crops to grow – one would never consider the possibility that the reason people in the society believe such things is because in fact Zarwa *does* cause the crops to grow (or sends off observational signals to that effect). One would explain such beliefs in *social terms* – perhaps in terms of the function that such beliefs serve in reinforcing solidarity within the society, or the perpetuation of the social interests that are served by such beliefs, or in some other fundamentally social way: but in any case the beliefs would be socially determined, not determined by the actions of the posited deity. Now suppose the culture under investigation is not in an isolated jungle, or in history, but exists within a modern scientific laboratory. Why should the explanatory strategy be any different? Why should sociologists stop seeking social explanations just because the society under investigation moves from the jungle to the science building of a modern university? When social scientists study the determination of the beliefs of any set of acculturated individuals – and since Kuhn's work, most studies of science definitely treat scientists as products of scientific, or a scientific paradigm-specific, acculturation – the resulting explanation of those beliefs is entirely in terms of social forces. Of course if the beliefs of scientists are explained socially, then they are *not* being explained in the way that philosophers of science, scientists themselves, and the (scientifically educated) general public explain them: that is by nature. In the words of one critical philosopher, this means that for social constructivists 'inputs from nature are impotent' (Kitcher 1993, p. 164).

This was essentially the position of the original Strong Program sociologists, and it continues to be a defining insight for much of the social constructivist literature. Scientific beliefs, like the beliefs of any other social agents, are socially constructed; they are the products of the particular social conditions, interests, influences, structures, and so forth, that are at work within (and around) the scientific community. While the social determination of scientific beliefs is a characteristic feature of constructivist science studies, there is much less agreement on exactly how this 'social construction' takes place. Is it class interest that determines scientific beliefs? Or professional interests? Or individual career goals? Or the structure of the operative social institutions?

Or the existing conditions of social power and domination? Or the function that such beliefs play in the overall reproduction of social life? Or ... It seems that there are as many possible stories about exactly *how* scientific beliefs get socially determined as there are different approaches to social explanation in general. According to the Strong Program, scientific beliefs are explained by *social interests* – the scientists' place in the overall pattern of social relations – but other constructivist approaches employ different explanatory frameworks. For the Strong Program, this type of science studies – explaining scientific beliefs on the basis of social interests – is not an epistemologically radical approach to inquiry. It is just the application of relatively standard techniques from social science to a particular domain of social inquiry: natural science. In David Bloor's words, the 'search for laws and theories in the sociology of science is absolutely identical in its procedure with that of any other science' (Bloor 1991, p. 21). Of course, not every constructivist sees the social study of science as simply the application of the scientific method to the subject of scientific knowledge, but that has remained the main focus of the Strong Program.

The body of literature produced by such sociological-based studies of scientific knowledge has come to be called the sociology of scientific knowledge (SSK), and the Strong Program is just one example, though perhaps the most influential example, of this sociological literature. For many, SSK is simply the application of science to the study of science, but even for those who are less scientistic (and perhaps more radical) SSK is simply the application of familiar explanatory strategies from social and human inquiry to the particular question of explaining the beliefs of natural scientists. While such constructivist approaches do *not* necessarily exclude the possibility of other, non-social, perhaps even natural, factors also playing a role in the determination of scientific beliefs – Bloor is quite explicit about the non-exclusivity of the social component: 'It does not say that it is the only component, or that it is the component that must necessarily be located as the trigger of any and every change; it can be a background condition' (Bloor 1991, p. 166) – they are frequently interpreted to be saying that scientific beliefs are socially determined *without remainder* (i.e. without nature playing any role). Some of the responsibility for this 'nature has nothing to do with science' interpretation of SSK should be assigned to the more radical authors within SSK, many of whom *do* in fact want to argue that nature has nothing to do with science; some of the responsibility should be assigned to less radical authors (like those in the Strong Program) for neglecting to emphasize the non-exclusivity of their social explanations; and finally, some of the responsibility should also be assigned to critics who choose the most extreme readings because they are the easiest to attack. In any case, regardless of how one assigns responsibility, the fact is that SSK is often characterized as claiming that *only* social forces have *any* role in the determination of scientific beliefs. That is not the view of the Strong Program, but nonetheless it has become a standard interpretation of the SSK position (and in some cases it is accurate).

Returning specifically to the Strong Program, suppose that one were to undertake an investigation into the social forces determining certain beliefs held by a particular group of scientists. What methodological rules would be most appropriate for such an investigation? First, it seems that one would need to commit to providing a *causal explanation* of the relevant beliefs; one would want to explain the cause of the particular scientific beliefs. Let's call such a maxim *causality*. Second, since one desires a social explanation of such beliefs, one would require *impartiality* about whether the beliefs are true or false, rational or irrational, etc. Going back to the case of the god Zarwa, one would want the social explanation of such a belief – an explanation in terms of the role that such a belief plays in the overall pattern of social relationships – to be the same whether there is in fact a god Zarwa or not. Third, not only should those engaged in SSK be impartial between the social explanation of true and false beliefs, the resulting social explanations should be *symmetric*; the same type of causes (social interests, factors, conditions, relationships, etc.) should be at work in the explanation of true and false beliefs. The discovery that Zarwa actually exists should leave unscathed the sociologist's explanation of the social role of Zarwa-belief within the community of Zarwa-believers. So too for similar discoveries within the community electron-believers, gene-believers, or utility function-believers. Finally, since the social scientists doing the SSK are themselves scientists – albeit social, not natural, scientists – the explanations offered for scientific beliefs should be *reflexive*; they should apply equally well to those who are actually doing SSK.

According to David Bloor's influential statement of the Strong Program, *Knowledge and Social Imagery*, these four tenets – causality, impartiality, symmetry, and reflexivity – essentially *define* the program's approach to the study of scientific knowledge (Bloor 1991, p. 7). Although recent restatements of the Strong Program – (Barnes et al. 1996 in particular) – have criticized the 'methodological idealism' of contemporary SSK, and have intentionally reopened the door for nature (or at least our experiences of nature) to play a significant role in the determination of scientific beliefs, Bloor's original goal of providing causal, impartial, symmetric, and reflexive explanations for the *social determination of scientific beliefs* remains the defining strategy of the Strong Program and many other approaches within the sociology of scientific knowledge.

While the Strong Program may have been the first systematic and self-conscious research program within SSK, it did not remain alone for very long. Beginning in the late 1970s, the SSK literature, as well as the science studies literature in general (where science studies is a broader category that includes a vast array of different approaches that draw inspiration from discourse theory, cultural studies, classical rhetoric, neopragmatism, feminism, and a host of other traditions, in addition to the primarily sociology-based SSK) has exploded onto the intellectual landscape. In addition to the constructivist research that appeared as an immediate response to the original Strong Program (for example Collins 1985; Knorr Cetina 1981; Latour and Woolgar 1979/1986; and Latour 1987) and the work of later Strong Program-inspired authors (MacKenzie 1990, 1998, 2001; Shapin and Schaffer 1985, and Shapin 1994 for example), the field has also been populated by a number of different approaches that, while clearly inspired by social constructivism, also deviate from it in sufficient ways to warrant their own individual labels. These literatures include the reflexive school (Ashmore 1989 and Woolgar, 1988 for example), Actor Network Theory (Callon et al. 1986 and Latour 1993, 1999, for example), the mangle of practice (Pickering 1995), the rhetoric of science (Gross 1990 and Gross and Keith 1997, for example), science as discourse (Gilbert and Mulkay 1984 and Lynch 1985, for example), certain types of feminist science studies (Haraway 1991, for example), as well as some of the literature emphasizing the role of instruments and technical equipment in science (Galison 1987 and 1997, for example). Perhaps it goes without saying that social constructivism has also generated an extensive critical literature, most of it written by philosophers of science, but even some practicing scientists have joined the fray (Gross and Levitt 1994 and Gross et al. 1996 for example). While each of these various constructivist literatures is interesting and important enough to warrant a detailed discussion, I will not provide it here (a number of detailed sources were cited above). At this point I will leave the reader to their own investigation of the various renditions of social constructivism (and its critics), and turn to the question of the relationship between the constructivist literature and the particular science of economics.

The discussion of SSK and economics will be divided into two parts. The first part will briefly note a few of the many indirect points of contact between the two literatures. The second set of topics involves more direct, self-conscious, contact and will be examined in more detail.

Economics, the history of economic thought, and social construction

One area of indirect contact between economics and social constructivism concerns the role of 'the economy' in constructivist histories of science: the constructivist-based literature in the history of natural science that emphasizes the relationship between the ideas and values of the scientific community and the surrounding (or underlying) economic conditions. Of course it is always dangerous to try to draw a very crisp line between 'the economy' and 'disciplinary economics'. Is 'the British economy in the 1840s' something totally separate from 'Ricardian economics'? Or is the 'New Deal' totally independent of Keynesian and/or Institutionalist economic theory? Of course not. But even though the economy and the associated economic ideas involve deep and fundamental interdependencies, they can often be separated for the purpose of certain types of analysis; if the subject is the work of Charles Dickens, the emphasis is 'more' on the economy (than Ricardian economics), and if the subject is the work of William Whewell it is 'more' on Ricardian economics (than the economy). So too for the impact of 'the economy' and 'disciplinary economics' on the construction of scientific knowledge. The impact of economic conditions on the development of science was of course the main subject for the Marxist historians of science like J.D. Bernal (1939) and Boris Hessen (1931), but there is also an extensive contemporary literature that links various aspects of science and the scientific community to particular economic, actually political economic, conditions. This literature draws inspiration from a vast array of sources, and elaborates a wide range of different connections, but they all in some way link the emergence of scientific knowledge (or particular forms of scientific knowledge) to particular economic conditions. Examples of such work include Hadden (1994); Poovey (1998); Smith and Wise (1989); and to a lesser extent Shapin and Schaffer (1985) and Shapin (1994).

Another point of indirect contact stems from the fact that much of the 'social analysis' employed within the SSK literature looks, prima facie, more like economic analysis than sociological theory. Sometimes the particular economics involved in SSK is heterodox in orientation (particularly Marxist), and sometimes it looks a lot more neoclassical or rational choice-theoretic, but in either case, some version of (disciplinary) economics informs (implicitly or explicitly) much of the work of those writing within SSK. Numerous authors have examined this connection in detail (Mäki 1992; McClellan 1996, and Mirowski and Sent 2002 among others), and I have discussed it in a number of previous works (Hands 1994, 1997a, 2001a and 2002).

The final indirect connection, concerns economic methodology. While SSK is only one of many forces that contributed to the demise of the Received View within mainstream philosophy of science, it was certainly an important factor. Given the profound impact that the demise of the Received View (and the associated falsificationist version of Popper's philosophy) has had on the literature in economic methodology during the last thirty or so years, SSK's role in that demise certainly suggests that SSK has also had a significant impact (at least indirectly) on the complexion of recent methodological writing about economics. Once one is exposed to the SSK literature, it is very difficult to accept the standard philosophical vision – the view that the philosophy of natural science provides the *rules* for the proper conduct of scientific inquiry (rules that are relatively simple, universal, and provide adequate epistemological grounding for the resulting science) – as the only game in town for understanding the character of scientific knowledge: natural or economic. This is also a topic examined in more detail in Hands (2001a).

In addition to these, and perhaps other, relatively indirect contacts, there seem to be two areas where the intellectual border crossing has worn a much deeper trail. The first is the literature on the 'Economics of Scientific Knowledge' (ESK) and second involves using SSK as a resource for the history of economic thought. Let us consider ESK first.

If science is fundamentally social and should be understood as such, then why not employ the resources of the social science of economics rather than functionalism, interests sociology, social psychology, or one of the other sociological approaches employed in SSK? In many respects economics seems to be a 'natural' for the job. On one hand, economists are particularly ambitious (some would say aggressive or imperialistic) in their efforts to apply economic analysis to various social phenomena outside their traditional subject domain of prices, markets, consumers, and firms. The literature on the economics of the family, law and economics, and public choice theory, are just a few of the many examples of this general – let's see if we can explain it as the equilibrium outcome of the actions of rational agents with well-ordered preferences – approach to various social phenomena. Why not the economics of science? Since this literature touches on a number of substantive philosophical issues, I previously (Hands 1994) emphasized the distinction between the 'economics of science' (analogous to Mertonian sociology of science) and a more philosophically engaged 'economics of scientific knowledge' or ESK (analogous to SSK), and while this is a useful distinction for many investigations, it does not seem to be necessary to pursue it in the current context. Here I will use the term ESK for both, with the only relevant distinction being the difference between the minimally philosophical literature produced by economists, and the more self-consciously philosophical literature written by philosophers of science. See Dasgupta and David (1994); Diamond (1996); Mirowski and Sent (2002); Sent (1999); Shi (2002); Stephan (1996); and Wible (1998) for a range of different perspectives on the economist-produced side of this rapidly growing literature.

The main focus of the philosophers doing work that might be labeled ESK, has been to recruit economics into the battle against the relativism, particularly SSK-inspired relativism, of recent science theory. One of the main themes of the later SSK literature has been to undermine or 'debunk' the traditional philosophical (and scientists' own) view of the epistemic and/or cognitive privilege of science. If science is social all the way down, then it is literally 'just like' other aspects of social life, and is thus denied the special epistemic place that it has traditionally been assigned within the post-Enlightenment world. This role of SSK – essentially kicking the epistemic pedestal out from underneath natural science – has not been (surprise, surprise) particularly well-received by either philosophers of science or by the scientists themselves. Philosophers of science were relatively quick to notice that economics might be an effective tool for mounting a response to this debunking and relativist aspect of the SSK literature.

Even if one accepts that science is social, and that scientists do not actually follow the methodological rules set down by positivist or Popperian philosophers of science, the lesson one gets from economics is that the resulting scientific knowledge may still be (epistemically) just fine. The professional reputation of the economics has been built on the construction of economic models, often intimidatingly mathematical models, that show how it is possible for the right stuff (economic efficiency, Pareto optimality, social welfare ...) to emerge from the actions of self-interested individuals with even the worst of motives. This seems to be the perfect counter to the potential relativism of SSK; accept along with Kuhn and others that science is fundamentally social and that scientists do not follow 'the' scientific method, but then show the social institutions of science are such that these sullied activities produce legitimate scientific knowledge (cognitive efficiency) anyway. As Philip Kitcher, a philosopher of science who has employed economic resources in this way, summarizes his argument:

> Much thinking about the growth of science is permeated by the thought that once scientists are shown to be motivated by various types of social concerns, something epistemically dreadful has been established. On the contrary, as I shall repeatedly emphasize, particular kinds of social arrangements make good epistemic use of the grubbiest motives. (Kitcher 1993, p. 305)

While a substantial critical response to this anti-debunking philosophical literature has been offered by both economists and philosophers (see, for example, Downes 2001; Fuller 1994; Hands 1995, 1997b, 2001b; Kincaid 1997; Mirowski 1995, 1996; Roorda 1997; Solomon 1995; and Wray 2000, 2001), all that can be said at this point is that the debate remains open regarding the success of these endeavors to recruit economics into the philosophical fight against the relativist implications (most philosophers would say corrosive implications) of SSK. Regardless of how it turns out, the fact is that it represents a body of literature that combines ideas from economics and SSK in a number of new and substantive ways; and yet unlike most of the ESK literature produced by economists, this philosophical literature drops economics squarely into the center of the fray within contemporary science theory.

The second significant point of contact involves the use of SSK, or SSK-inspired historical approaches, in the history of economic thought. Since SSK has been so influential in the recent literature on the history of science – changing both the standard interpretation of major episodes within the history of science, and also shifting the historical focus away from such major episodes and more toward smaller scale, more situated, and more contingent sites of scientific activity – then why not apply a similar approach to the history of economic science? A number of those writing in the history of economic thought have begun to do precisely that; the relevant papers are too numerous to list (see Hands 2001a, p. 211 for a partial listing), but book-length studies include Klein 1997; Mirowski 1989, 2002; Sent 1998; Weintraub 1991, 2002; and Yonay 1998. There seem to be a number of reasons why such approaches might be, and have been, well-received among historians of economic thought.

For one thing, the whole idea that knowledge is socially constructed seems to be far less radical in a social science like economics than in a natural science like physics. To say that physicists' beliefs about electrons are socially determined is to not only to say something contrary to the view of most philosophers of natural science, it is also at odds with how the general public and physicists themselves view the determination of such physical beliefs. This is less the case in economics. Of course economists' beliefs about, say inflation, are socially determined; even if an economist strictly adheres to the scientific method as laid down by positivism or falsificationism, it is still the case that the numbers involved in the proper scientific determination of such beliefs are *constructed* by human agents to serve human purposes. Even in the (epistemically) best case the source of economists' beliefs come from society (not nature), the relevant empirical evidence is constructed not given, and no such beliefs (about say inflation) would exist at all if it had not been recognized as a substantive social problem about which theories, evidence, and social action were required. Of course economics is social: no society, no economics. Now this still leaves open the question of *proper* versus *improper* social determination – having one's beliefs about inflation socially determined by the (socially constructed) CPI is proper, while having them determined by the political party that paid for the study is not – but the general notion that the beliefs of economists are socially determined is hardly a radical idea.

For another thing, there is a grand tradition within the history of economic thought regarding the impact of social conditions (separate from the social character of the empirical *facts*) on the history of economic thought. How would one tell the story of Ricardo's *Principles* in the absence of the associated (social) story about the class structure of early nineteenth century England and the debate over the Corn Laws? How does one tell the story of the Keynesian revolution without the great depression? Given the proto-constructivist character of so much of the traditional literature within the history of economic thought, the two main changes initiated by the recent spate of SSK-informed studies have been simply to narrow the focus of the subject matter (moving away from the study of major 'revolutions' in economic thought), and to look seriously at the history of twentieth-century, and thus highly mathematical, economic theory (a previously rather Whiggish subject).

Finally, it seems that historians of economic thought might turn to SSK because the philosophy of science and traditional economic methodology has been so trenchantly unhelpful. The relationship between the history of economic thought and economic methodology is certainly very complex, but the bottom line is that while historians have often looked to philosophy of science (through the conduit of traditional economic methodology) for guidance regarding the character of scientific knowledge, they have seldom been the recipient of anything very useful; the philosophical programs of positivism and falsificationism have provided almost no help on the type of questions that interest historians of economics. These traditional approaches boil the whole continuum of questions about scientific knowledge down to a few simple methodological rules – like 'make bold conjectures and subject them to severe empirical tests' – and such rules offer little help to the historian, whether they have actually been followed by the relevant economists or not. The consensus among economic methodologists is of course that such rules have not generally been obeyed, but for a moment suppose they were. What would the historian do with such information? Such rules, if actually met, would *exhaust* the reasons for why a particular theory was accepted or rejected, leaving nothing else to say about the episode in question – nothing about the relevant personal lives; nothing about the political, social, or even economic context; in essence nothing historical at all. Now suppose that it is discovered (as it usually is in methodological studies) that a 'successful' economic theory did not follow the strict rules laid down by some particular philosopher of natural science. What would be the response in this case? If one remains within the traditional philosophical context all one can do is to reprimand the economists in question for not being 'scientific'; and once the complaint is filed, there is nothing else much to say. Again there is no real reason to do the history of economic thought. On the traditional view, if economists did not follow the rules of the scientific method then the results were not legitimate economic science, and while an investigation into the causes of such erroneous beliefs might be of interest to the social or political historian, they have no place within the history of scientific economics. In either case, whether the rules are, or are not, followed, there seems to be little to guide, or even any particular need for, the history of economic thought. On the other hand, SSK starts with precisely the question of the complex and contingent social determination of the beliefs of (even proper) scientists. It thus seems to be a far more useful framework for understanding the historical development of various economic fields than the framework provided by traditional economic methodology.

To conclude, I have discussed three indirect connections between economics and the social constructivist literature (the role of the economy in the history of natural science, the role of economic analysis within the social studies of science, and SSK's role in helping to undermine rules-based philosophy of science), and also two connections that are more direct, and perhaps more substantive (ESK, and SSK in the history of economic thought). While there are undoubtedly many other points of contact between SSK and economics, these five subjects certainly cover a large portion of the rapidly growing literature connecting these two overlapping domains of inquiry. Of course the next development, or the next connection, between these two fields is yet to be determined. What is clear, is that there has already been a substantial amount of fertile interaction, and that the interaction will continue to produce interesting and important results for a long time to come.

References
Ashmore, Malcolm (1989), *The Reflexive Thesis: Writing the Sociology of Knowledge*, Chicago: University of Chicago Press.
Barnes, Barry (1977), *Interests and the Growth of Knowledge*, London: Routledge.
Barnes, Barry (1982), *Thomas Kuhn and Social Science*, New York: Columbia University Press.
Barnes, Barry, David Bloor and John Henry (1996), *Scientific Knowledge: A Sociological Analysis*, Chicago: University of Chicago Press.
Bernal, John Desmond (1939), *The Social Function of Science*, London: Routledge.
Biagioli, Mario (ed.), (1999), *The Science Studies Reader*, London: Routledge.
Bloor, David (1976), *Knowledge and Social Imagery*, London: Routledge.
Bloor, David (1983), *Wittgenstein: A Social Theory of Knowledge*, New York: Columbia University Press.
Bloor, David (1991), *Knowledge and Social Imagery*, 2nd edn, Chicago: University of Chicago Press.
Callebaut, Werner (1993), *Taking the Naturalistic Turn*, Chicago: University of Chicago Press.
Callon, Michael, John Law and Arie Rip (eds) (1986), *Mapping the Dynamics of Science and Technology: Sociology of Science in the Real World*, London: Macmillian.
Collins, Harry M. (1985), *Changing Order: Replication and Induction in Scientific Practice*, Beverly Hills, CA: Sage.
Collins, Randall, and Sal Restivo (1983), 'Development, diversity, and conflict in the sociology of science', *The Sociological Quarterly*, **24**, 185–200.
Dasgupta, Partha and Paul A. David (1994), 'Toward a new economics of science', *Research Policy*, **23**, 487–521.
Diamond, Arthur M. Jr. (1996), 'The economics of science', *Knowledge and Policy: The International Journal of Knowledge Transfer and Utilization*, **9**, 6–49.
Downes, Stephen M. (2001), 'Agents and norms in the new economics of science', *Philosophy of the Social Sciences*, **31**, 224-38.
Fuller, Steve (1994), 'Mortgaging the farm to save the (sacred) cow', *Studies in History and Philosophy of Science*, **25**, 251–61.
Galison, Peter (1987), *How Experiments End*, Chicago: University of Chicago Press.
Galison, Peter (1997), *Image and Logic: A Material Culture of Microphysics*, Chicago: University of Chicago Press.
Gilbert, G. Nigel, and Michael Mulkay (1984), *Opening Pandora's Box: A Sociological Analysis of Scientists' Discourse*, Cambridge: Cambridge University Press.
Golinski, Jan (1998), *Making Natural Knowledge: Constructivism and the History of Science*, Cambridge: Cambridge University Press.
Gross, Alan G. (1990), *The Rhetoric of Science*, Cambridge, MA: Harvard University Press.
Gross, Alan G., and William M. Keith (eds) (1997), *Rhetorical Hermeneutics: Invention and Interpretation in the Age of Science*, Albany: State University of New York Press.
Gross, Paul R. and Norman Levitt (1994), *Higher Superstition: The Academic Left and Its Quarrels with Science*, Baltimore, MD: Johns Hopkins University Press.
Gross, Paul R., Norman Levitt and Martin W. Lewis (eds) (1996), *The Flight From Science and Reason*, New York: New York Academy of Sciences.
Hadden, Richard W. (1994), *On the Shoulders of Merchants: Exchange and the Mathematical Conception of Nature in Early Modern Europe*, Albany: State University of New York.

Hands, D. Wade (1994), 'The sociology of scientific knowledge: some thoughts on the possibilities', Roger E. Backhouse (ed.), *New Directions in Economic Methodology*, London: Routledge, pp. 75–106 (reprinted in Philip Mirowski and Esther-Mirjam Sent (eds), 2002, *Science Bought and Sold*, Chicago: University of Chicago Press.

Hands, D. Wade (1995), 'Social epistemology meets the invisible hand: kitcher on the advancement of science', *Dialogue*, **34**, 605–21.

Hands, D. Wade (1997a), 'Conjectures and reputations: the sociology of scientific knowledge and the history of economic thought', *History of Political Economy*, **29**, 695–739.

Hands, D. Wade (1997b), 'Caveat emptor: economics and contemporary philosophy of science', *Philosophy of Science*, **64** (proceedings), S107–16.

Hands, D. Wade (2001a), *Reflection Without Rules: Economic Methodology and Contemporary Science Theory*, Cambridge: Cambridge University Press.

Hands, D. Wade (2001b), 'Relativism, rationality, and economics: instrumental rationality and contemporary science theory', paper presented of a conference on 'Science, Philosophy and Democracy: A Contemporary Debate', University of Catania, Italy, October 2001.

Hands, D. Wade (2002), 'The more things change, the more they stay the same: social realism in contemporary science studies', in *Fact and Fiction in Economics*, (ed.), Uskali Mäki, Cambridge: Cambridge University Press, pp. 341–55.

Haraway, Donna J. (1991), *Simians, Cyborgs, and Women: The Reinvention of Nature*, New York: Routledge.

Hessen, Boris (1931), 'The social and economic roots of newton's "principia"', in N. Bukharin et al. (eds), *Science at the Crossroads*, London: Frank Cass and Co., pp. 151–211.

Jasanoff, Sheila, Gerald Markle, James Petersen and Trevor Pinch (1995), *Handbook of Science and Technology Studies*, Thousand Oaks, CA: Sage.

Kincaid, Harold (1997), 'Individualism and rationality', in Harold Kincaid (ed.), *Individualism and the Unity of Science*, Lanham, MD: Roman and Littlefield, pp. 119–42.

Kitcher, Philip (1993), *The Advancement of Science: Science Without Legend, Objectivity Without Illusions*, Oxford: Oxford University Press.

Klein, Judy L. (1997), *Statistical Visions in Time: A History of Time Series Analysis 1662–1938*, Cambridge: Cambridge University Press.

Knorr Cetina, Karin (1981), *The Manufacture of Knowledge: An Essay on the Constructivist and Contextual Nature of Science*, New York: Pergamon.

Kuhn, Thomas S. (1970), *The Structure of Scientific Revolutions*, 2nd edn, Chicago: University of Chicago Press.

Latour, Bruno (1987), *Science in Action*, Cambridge, MA: Harvard University Press.

Latour, Bruno (1993), *We Have Never Been Modern*, Cambridge, MA: Harvard University Press.

Latour, Bruno (1999), *Pandora's Hope: Essays on the Reality of Science Studies*, Cambridge, MA: Harvard University Press.

Latour, Bruno, and Steve Woolgar (1979), *Laboratory Life: The Construction of Scientific Facts*, Beverly Hills, CA: Sage.

Latour, Bruno, and Steve Woolgar (1986), *Laboratory Life: The Construction of Scientific Facts*, 2nd edn, Princeton, NJ: Princeton University Press.

Lynch, Michael (1985), *Art and Artifact in Laboratory Science: A Study of Shop Work and Shop Talk in a Research Laboratory*, London: Routledge.

MacKenzie, Donald (1990), *Inventing Accuracy: A Historical Sociology of Nuclear Missile Guidance*, Cambridge, MA: MIT Press.

MacKenzie, Donald (1998), *Knowing Machines: Essays on Technical Change*, Cambridge, MA: MIT Press.

MacKenzie, Donald (2001), *Mechanizing Proof: Computing, Risk, and Trust*, Cambridge, MA: MIT Press.

Mäki, Uskali (1992), 'Social Conditioning in Economics', in Neil De Marchi (ed.), *Post-Popperian Methodology of Economics*, Boston: Kluwer, pp. 65–104.

Mannheim, Karl (1936), *Ideology and Utopia: An Introduction to the Sociology of Knowledge*, San Diego, CA: Harcourt Brace Jovanovich.

McClellan, Chris (1996), 'The economic consequences of Bruno Latour', *Social Epistemology*, **10**, 193–208.

Merton, Robert K. (1970), *Science, Technology and Society in Seventeenth-Century England*, New York: Harper and Row (originally published in *Osiris* in 1938).

Mirowski, Philip (1989), *More Heat Than Light: Economics As Social Physics: Physics as Nature's Economics*, Cambridge: Cambridge University Press.

Mirowski, Philip (1995), 'Philip Kitcher's *Advancement of Science*: a review article', *Review of Political Economy*, **7**, 227–41.

Mirowski, Philip (1996), 'The economic consequences of Philip Kitcher', *Social Epistemology*, **10**, 153–69.

Mirowski, Philip (2002), *Machine Dreams: Economics Becomes a Cyborg Science*, Cambridge: Cambridge University Press.

Mirowski, Philip, and Sent, Esther-Mirjam (eds) (2002), *Science Bought and Sold*, Chicago: University of Chicago Press.

Pickering, Andrew (ed.) (1992), *Science as Practice and Culture*, Chicago: University of Chicago Press.

Pickering, Andrew (1995), *The Mangle of Practice: Time, Agency, and Science*, Chicago: University of Chicago Press.

Poovey, Mary (1998), *A History of the Modern Fact: Problems of Knowledge in the Sciences of Wealth and Society*, Chicago: University of Chicago Press.

Roorda, Jonathan (1997), 'Kitcher on theory choice', *Erkenntnis*, **46**, 215–39.

Sent, Esther-Mirjam (1998), *The Evolving Rationality of Rational Expectations*, Cambridge: Cambridge University Press.

Sent, Esther-Mirjam (1999), 'Economics of science: survey and suggestions', *Journal of Economic Methodology*, **6**, 95–124.

Shapin, Steven (1982), 'History of science and its sociological reconstructions', *History of Science*, **20**, 157–211.

Shapin, Steven (1988), 'Understanding the Merton thesis', *Isis*, **79**, 594–605.

Shapin, Steven (1992), 'Discipline and bounding: the history and sociology of science as seen through the externalism–internalism debate', *History of Science*, **30**, 333–69.

Shapin, Steven (1994), *A Social History of Truth: Civility and Science in Seventeenth-Century England*, Chicago: University of Chicago Press.

Shapin, Steven, and Simon Schaffer (1985), *Leviathan and the Air-Pump: Hobbes, Boyle, and the Experimental Life*, Princeton, NJ: Princeton University Press.

Shi, Yanfei (2002), *The Economics of Scientific Knowledge: A Rational Choice Institutionalist Theory of Science*, Cheltenham, UK and Northampton, MA, USA: Edward Elgar.

Smith, Crosbie, and M. Norton Wise (1989), *Energy and Empire: A Biographical Study of Lord Kelvin*, Cambridge: Cambridge University Press.

Solomon, Miriam (1995), 'Legend Naturalism and scientific progress: an essay on Philip Kitcher's *The Advancement of Science*', *Studies in History and Philosophy of Science*, **26**, 205–18.

Stephan, Paula E. (1996), 'The economics of science', *Journal of Economic Literature*, **34**, 1199–235.

Weintraub, E. Roy (1991), *Stabilizing Dynamics: Constructing Economic Knowledge*, Cambridge: Cambridge University Press.

Weintraub, E. Roy (2002), *How Economics Became a Mathematical Science*, Durham, NC: Duke University Press.

Wible, James R. (1998), *The Economics of Science: Methodology and Epistemology as if Economics Really Mattered*, London: Routledge.

Woolgar, Steve (ed.), (1988), *Knowledge and Reflexivity*, London: Sage.

Wray, K. Brad (2000), 'Invisible hands and the success of science', *Philosophy of Science*, **67**, 163–75.

Wray, K. Brad (2001), 'Science, biases, and the treat of global pessimism', *Philosophy of Science*, **68** (Proceedings), S467–78.

Yonay, Youval P. (1998), *The Struggle Over the Soul of Economics: Institutionalist and Neoclassical Economists in America Between the Wars*, Princeton, NJ: Princeton University Press.

11 From feminist empiricism to feminist poststructuralism: philosophical questions in feminist economics

Drucilla K. Barker

Introduction

Feminist economics, a dynamic field of intellectual inquiry that has emerged over the last ten years, is uniquely situated at the intersection of economics, feminism, and methodology. Feminist economists observe that much of economics relies on highly gendered and raced metaphors, and that it fails to adequately account for a wide variety of factors particularly germane to women's lives such as women's labor force participation, the wage gap, and the value of household labor. It was not that these topics had not been studied before. They had, but not from a feminist perspective. They were not feminist because they did not question the gender division of labor and did not employ gender as a category of analysis. Using gender as an analytical category, feminist economists showed that unquestioned and unexamined masculinist values were deeply embedded in the theoretical and empirical analyses of economic issues associated with women.

Feminist economics is developing during a period of interesting transformations in epistemology and the philosophy of science. The works of V.O. Quine and Thomas Kuhn are particularly significant to framing these changes and to casting doubt on the claims of foundationalist epistemologies underlying mainstream economics (Kuhn 1962; Quine 1953). Kuhn's contribution was to show that observations are always theory laden: the data used to test theories and hypotheses are seen through the lens of the theories that are supposed to refute or support scientific hypotheses. Quine showed that theories are always underdetermined by the evidence. Since statements about the world face the tribunal of evidence not in isolation but as part of a larger belief system, the same evidence can support a variety of theories. Feminist empiricism is one of the epistemologies that emerges out these insights.

Feminist empiricism, as a type of feminist practice, has its origins in the work of feminist scholars in biology and related life sciences who recognized that standard answers to many questions involving sex and gender reflected a distinct androcentric and/or sexist bias (Harding 1986). According to this early research, the problem was not the scientific method, but rather, the problem was that researchers were not following it. Androcentric bias could be eliminated by rigorously following the norms of existing scientific methodology. The inclusion of women is necessary to this endeavor because they are the ones most likely to notice sexist and androcentric bias in posing research questions, proposing hypotheses, and collecting data (Tuana 1992). Thus the inclusion of women in science was necessary for good scientific practice. Similarly, in feminist economics scholars recognized that the inclusion of women in the profession was necessary to expose and eliminate androcentric bias in economics (Ferber and Nelson 1993).

Feminist empiricism, as an epistemology, soon transcended these neat boundaries. As philosophers of science and epistemologists worked in this area, the concept expanded to include a discussion of the social nature of scientific knowledge, the nature of the knowing subject, and the relationships between science and politics. Similarly, feminist economists began to question the ways in which the composition of the economics community – mainly men, nearly all white, and almost all affluent – came to name what could legitimately count as 'economics' (Strassmann 1993b). The role of personal, social, and political values, as well as power relations, in constructing economic knowledge were also examined (Barker 1995; Grapard 1995; Nelson 1993). Using gender, as well as other categories of difference such as race, nation, and sexual orientation, as legitimate categories of analysis, enabled feminist economists to enlarge the domain of economic inquiry and expand the variety of economic explanations offered. Relationships predicated on dependency rather than contract, the paradox posed by caring labor, and the role of social reproduction in both micro and macroeconomic outcomes, are all now part of the established lexicon of feminist economics (Jacobsen 2003). This phenomenon is an instance of feminist empiricism in practice in the sense that as a community of scholars began to question the biases and implicit assumptions in economics they began to transform their understandings of the discipline. And like feminist empiricism as epistemology, feminist economics soon escaped its boundaries. As feminist economists questioned the wide disparity between the prestige of neoclassical economics and its obvious shortcomings as an empirical science, the relationships between meaning, power, and knowledge came to the fore. These questions are addressed most effectively within feminist poststructuralism and feminist postmodernism.

This is not to deny the influence on feminist economics of other important intellectual currents, especially in economic methodology. The rhetorical turn of Deirdre (formerly Donald) McCloskey and the realist approach associated with Tony Lawson and Uskali Mäki have both been important to the development of feminist economic thought. The rhetorical approach, characterized by its commitment to examining the role of rhetoric and persuasion in economic arguments, conceives of economics as an ongoing conversation that uses metaphors, analogies, and other literary devices (Mäki 1993; McCloskey 1985; Lawson 1997). This approach has facilitated an analysis of the patriarchal and racist underpinnings associated with various economics stories (Strassmann 1993a; Grapard 1995 and Williams 1993). Mäki's articulation of realism anchors economic discourse to truth with claims about how the world really is (Peter 2003a, 2003b). Lawson's critical realism understands the social world as structured. Social structures can be changed by human beings who act intentionally and exercise choice, and the ability for intentional agency in turn depends upon social structures, creating the possibility of emancipatory projects in economics.

Although rhetoric and realism have made an extremely important contribution to both economic methodology and to the development of feminist economics, neither rhetoric or realism alone is sufficient for the feminist economics project. McCloskey's work is not a critique of economics; rather it is a different way of conceptualizing its persuasiveness. As scholars have pointed out, McCloskey does not examine the significance of economics as a closed intellectual community and thus she does not question the shared implicit assumptions of that community (Peter 2003a, 2003b; Waller and Robertson 1990). Likewise, realism, with its emphasis on ontology rather than epistemology, does not seem to accommodate many of the questions and issues that are of concern to feminist economists (Barker 2003; Harding 1999; Peter 2003a, 2003b). Feminist economics, like other feminist science projects, requires an epistemology that facilitates critical evaluations of the affects of social, cultural, and political values on knowledge production. Feminist empiricism does precisely this.

Feminist empiricism examined
The term, feminist empiricism, was originally coined by Sandra Harding, who defined it in contrast to feminist standpoint theory and postmodern feminism (Harding 1986). Harding recognized that the epistemological problem for feminism was to show how feminist inquiry, which is necessarily value-laden, actually increases objectivity. The solution for feminist empiricists was to argue that feminism actually requires stricter adherence to existing methodological norms. Examining scientific methods through the lens of feminism reveals androcentric bias, and women scientists are more likely than men to notice such bias. Harding went on to argue that the strength of this strategy was that it appeared as though it did not challenge established methodological norms. This meant that feminists could identify bad science as the problem, not 'science-as-usual' (ibid., p. 25). The problem with this strategy, according to Harding, was that the feminist empiricism undermines empiricism. According to traditional empiricism, the identity of the researcher is considered irrelevant to research results. Objective, unbiased research results from following appropriate

scientific methods, regardless of the particular social location of the scientist. This seems to contradict the notion that women are more likely than men to notice and correct for androcentric bias.

Commitment to the empiricist notion that the social location of the scientist is irrelevant implies that feminist empiricism will be unable to address some of the pressing concerns such as the relationship between science and politics, as well as the role of race, class, and culture in constituting women as the subjects of knowledge. Women are more likely than men to notice androcentric bias, just as racially marginalized groups are more likely to notice racial bias, because in their absence the homogeneity of science communities allows shared assumptions and values within that community to go unquestioned. Hence doing better science, science less biased and less false, requires diversity in scientific communities. Thus, according to Harding, feminist empiricism must exist in creative tension with the two other more radical schools of feminist epistemology, feminist standpoint theory and feminist postmodernism.

Briefly, feminist standpoint epistemology draws on the Marxist notion that material conditions structure the way we apprehend the world, and in social systems based on hierarchy and domination, the visions of the privileged will be partial and distorted. The sexual division of labor structures men's lives differently from women's lives and forms the basis for a feminist standpoint, one that offers a more humane vision of social relations (Harding 1986; Hartsock 1983). Postmodern feminist epistemologies, on the other hand, hold that both the feminist standpoint of epistemology and feminist empiricism are flawed because they require an appropriation of Enlightenment ideals (Flax 1992; and Haraway 1990). Postmodern feminists contest notions of rationality, universality, and singular conceptions of truth, and foreground the relationship between knowledge and power. According to Harding, all three epistemologies have important roles to play in feminist science projects. They are however incommensurate, in her view, and the relation between them has to be one of creative tension.

Harding's tripartite classification has become deeply embedded in feminist scholarship. According to the feminist epistemologist, Nancy Tuana, however, the incommensurability between the three epistemologies is only an apparent one (Tuana 1992). The contradiction between the empiricist notion that the social location of the researcher is irrelevant and the feminist claim that diverse science communities are necessary for better science can be resolved by reconsidering the nature of the knowing subject. The radically revised feminist empiricism articulated by Nelson (1990) resolves the contradiction in this fashion, and hence provides a lens for seeing the ways that the three feminist epistemologies complement one another (Tuana 1992). Nelson's work may be characterized as a neo-Quinian version of feminist epistemology.

Epistemological communities

According to Tuana, Nelson's version of feminist epistemology addresses three important tensions in the relationship between feminism and empiricism (Nelson 1990; Tuana 1992). They are the tension discussed above between the empiricist view that scientists are objective observers and the feminist view that the gender (or race, class, nationality, or sexual identity) of the scientist matters; the tension between the notion that science and values are radically separate and the feminist emphasis on advocacy and engagement; and finally the tension between the notion that institutions are irrelevant to the practice of good science with the feminist insight that gendered institutions matter to science.

Conceptualizing the nature of the scientific 'knower' is central to Nelson's strategy. She argues that the knower in foundationalist accounts of knowledge developed by philosophers such as Descartes and Hume was an isolated, passive recipient of knowledge. That is to say, the specific social relations and context in which knowers were situated was completely irrelevant to their knowing. She labels this view epistemological individualism. Rejecting the epistemological individualism of foundationalist accounts, in favour of an account of epistemological communities as agents of knowledge, is central to reconciling the tensions between feminism and empiricism.

Her rejection of the solitary, solipsistic knower is informed by the Quinian insight that experience and knowledge are made possible and shaped by public conceptual schemes. Like Quine, she holds that our experiences of the world are sensory experiences and all evidence for science is sensory experience. Sensory experiences, however, cannot be foundational because they are only made coherent by theories which are themselves embodied in language, a necessarily public phenomenon. Thus all evidence, according to Nelson, is fundamentally communal. It is communities, not individuals, which acquire and construct knowledge. They are the primary epistemological agents. Of course individuals 'know'. But their knowing is derivative in that it depends on the community of which they are a part. It is the epistemological community that constructs and shares knowledge and standards of evidence. These communities are not collections of knowing individuals, but are 'epistemologically prior to individuals who know' (Nelson 1990: 124).

Nelson goes on to argue that a feminist epistemology that recognizes communities as the primary agents of knowledge must be a naturalized epistemology. That is to say, it would involve constructing accounts of how we actually go about building knowledge and the evidence we use to do this. A naturalized epistemology assumes that we do in fact know, and that such knowledge is justified to the extent that is allows us to make sense of and explain experience. Naturalized epistemology is, however, distinct from other postfoundationalist epistemologies such as the Strong Program in sociology of science in that it is not merely descriptive. Rather, naturalized epistemology is evaluative in nature. This entails providing accounts of how knowledge is constructed and evidence used, and evaluating knowledge claims in terms of the processes and arrangements through which such claims are generated. This does not mean that evidence is irrelevant. Nelson's commitment to empiricism is most evident in the claim, 'knowledge is socially constructed *and* constrained by evidence' (Nelson 1990, p. 129 emphasis in the original).

A feminist naturalized epistemology would appeal to feminist experience and knowledge. Now this may seem circular, but only if one is still searching for a foundationalist account of epistemology. A naturalized account recognizes the radical interdependence between epistemology and other knowledge projects. As scholars articulate the standards and conventions by which knowledge is constructed within particular communities, these standards may be revised or even rejected. In this story the relationship between epistemologists and scientists is dialectical rather than hierarchical. These accounts entail examining the histories, social relationships, and practices of scientific communities within which standards of evidence are adopted and theories are evaluated (Nelson 1990). Although there are no extratheoretic standards brought to bear, feminist naturalized epistemology allows us to examine and evaluate the methodologies and knowledge claims of one community in light of other such communities. Nelson advocates the coherence theory as the appropriate evaluative criterion: theories should be evaluated by how well they cohere within a web of other theories, evidence, politics, ethics, culture, and so forth. Included in these normative criteria must be an acknowledgment of the explanatory success of science.

Facts and values
In Nelson's neo-Quinian conception of feminist empiricism, as in most feminist philosophy of science, the fact/value distinction no longer makes sense. The primary reason for the fact/value distinction in positivist epistemologies is to insure that science produces knowledge that is untainted by special interests or political ideologies. In this account, if science is to produce unbiased accounts of the natural or social world it must be value-neutral. Of course it is not denied that values play a role in deciding which questions to ask and which phenomena to study. Once these judgments are made, however, theories must be tested according to the scientific method with its strictly prescribed rules and goal of value neutrality. The only values permissible are those constitutive of the modern science project, for example, accuracy, simplicity, and robustness. Contextual values, on the other hand, are values that reflect particular economic, social, and cultural locations. They are considered antithetical to the scientific method because they introduce bias into scientific results.

The goal of value neutrality has been contested by a variety of scholars who argue that it masks the influence of contextual values on scientific inquiry.

Sandra Harding has argued that value neutrality weakens standards for maximizing objectivity because it precludes actively seeking socially marginalized viewpoints from which to critically examine common cultural assumptions (Harding 1995). When culturally specific values and interests shape research projects, the neutrality ideal legitimates the institutions and practices through which distortions and their exploitative consequences are generated because it allows the objections of marginalized groups to be dismissed as 'special' interests. The neutrality ideal does not allow for a close examination of the ways in which contextual values impinge on any science, including economics.

The feminist philosopher of science, Helen Longino, makes an important contribution to our understanding of the relationship between science and values (Longino 1997). Longino's analysis starts from the Quinian underdetermination thesis: any theory can be protected from empirical evidence that would refute it because no theory is ever tested in isolation. Empirical testing requires that a number of assumptions and judgments be made about the evidence, the type of tests, *ceteris paribus* conditions, and so forth. So it is never clear whether contradictory evidence refutes the theory or whether the problem is with some other prior condition not being met (Hands 2001). Hence theories are neither proved nor disproved purely on the basis of empirical evidence. The familiar social science dilemma between correlation and causation is a good example of underdetermination. According to Longino, one of the strategies developed to minimize the threat that the underdetermination thesis poses to aspirations to scientific knowledge is to invoke additional criteria from a pool of cognitive or theoretical values. These values – simplicity, accuracy, generality, and so forth – are used to support judgments about the worth of particular models, theories and hypotheses.

In her view, which she calls contextual empiricism, data are the least defeasible grounds for theory assessment, but theories, models and hypotheses are always underdetermined by the evidence. Thus the relationship between theory and evidence is secured in context, by background assumptions. The question that follows is, of course, what controls background assumptions? Are theories merely subjective? Her answer is that intersubjective interaction, diverse knowledge communities if you will, is necessary to mitigate the influence of subjective preferences on background assumptions and theory choice. While such subjective interactions are necessary, not just any interaction will suffice. They must constitute genuine and mutual checks. This can be accomplished by a knowledge community that will 'facilitate transformative criticism and enable a consensus to qualify as knowledge' (Longino 1997, p. 40). Among the features that are necessary for such knowledge communities is the existence of publicly recognized standards by reference to which theories, hypotheses, and observational practices are evaluated. 'Such standards serve as ideals regulating normative discourse in a community' (ibid., p. 40). In her early work she argued that such standards contained cognitive values, those values constitutive of modern science, as well a non-cognitive values that reflected a society's social and political commitments. In her later work, however, she questions the distinction between the two.

Cognitive values are values that are supposed to guide scientific inquiry and, according to Kuhn (1977), constitute objective grounds for theory choice. Longino discusses the virtues enumerated by Kuhn – accuracy, consistency, simplicity, breadth of scope, and fruitfulness – and argues that these virtues are generally considered the constitutive values of science. She argues that while these values have epistemic worth, they are not independent of particular contexts. She then lists a set of feminist theoretical values or virtues: empirical adequacy, novelty, ontological heterogeneity (see below), and so on. These feminist theoretical virtues are desirable qualities of theories and model that guide feminist judgments. Her purpose in contrasting them with a more traditional set of desiderata is not to show that we have two competing sets of values, but rather to show that all values import significant socio-political values into the context of scientific judgemnts. There are no value-neutral grounds for judgment. The question she poses is:

> If the cognitive virtues, that is the standards that regulate discursive interaction in a scientific community, lose their context-independent, universalist status, as I have been advocating, then what is left to adjudicate scientific disputes? If underdetermination undermines even empirical adequacy's ability to put definitive, uninterested, end to disputes, are we not faced with either anarchy or the rule of the powerful – a tyranny of the majority? (Longino 1997, p. 54)

Part of her answer is that to the extent that cognitive anarchy does emerge, it will be global rather than local. Scientific communities will adopt standards that reflect their aspirations. But these aspirations and standards are provisional and may be modified as a result of interactions with other communities. I now turn to an examination of feminist economics as an epistemological community, and articulate some of the values that regulate discourse within that community.

Feminist economics as epistemological community
Feminist economics is a relative newcomer to the profession. Although women had been members of the economics profession for a good while, and the Committee for the Status of Women in Economics (CSWEP) has been in existence since 1971, a uniquely feminist community of economists did not emerge until the early 1990s. The International Association for Feminist Economics (IAFFE) was officially recognized by the Allied Social Science Association in 1992, and the first volume of the journal, *Feminist Economics*, was published in 1995. The intellectual impetus behind the emergence of feminist economics can be explained by the fact that the women who were being trained in traditional

economics, both neoclassical and heterodox, did not live in isolation from the general intellectual currents around them, especially feminism. By the time feminist economics was officially 'named,' feminism had made significant transformative contributions to other social sciences, such as anthropology and sociology, as well as to many disciplines within the humanities such as philosophy and literary criticism. As economists noticed the huge discrepancy between the treatment of gender inequality in these other disciplines and their own, they began to question and transform the assumptions and methods of economics. Feminist economics provided an epistemic community where this could occur.

The intellectual groundwork for a uniquely feminist community of economists was laid by pioneering work done by scholars like Barbara Bergmann, Francine Blau, Marianne Ferber, and Myra Strober. Working mainly in the neoclassical and institutionalist traditions, they demonstrated that the mainstream treatment of so-called women's issues such as women's labor force participation, the wage gap, and occupational segregation reflected a distinct androcentric bias (Bergmann 1986; Blau and Ferber 1986; Strober 1982). Similarly, scholars working in the Marxist political economy tradition such as Lourdes Benería, Nancy Folbre, Heidi Hartmann, Susan Himmelweit, Simon Mohun, and Gita Sen offered explicitly feminist analyses of the sexual division of labor and the connections between patriarchy and capitalism (Benería and Sen 1981, Folbre 1982, Hartmann 1981, Himmelweit and Mohun 1977).

As feminist economics coalesced as an intellectual community in the 1990s, a consensus emerged around the nature of economics. Economics was not the value-free, objective, scientific enterprise that its practitioners claimed it to be. Instead it was deeply imbued with values that reflected an elite masculine worldview, which one would expect. After all, as Strassmann (1993b) argues, economics is an interpretive community whose members are socialized not to question the overarching values of the profession, values that are partly a reflection of the demographic characteristics of the profession: relatively prosperous, male, and white.

Most immediately apparent was the fact that much of neoclassical economics relies on highly gendered and raced metaphors, the most famous of which is homo economicus, or the rational economic agent, a conception of human agency that reflects a privileged, male worldview (Nelson 1993; Strassmann 1993a; Grapard 1995). Rational agents have no necessary obligations or responsibilities and interact contractually with others only when it is in their best interest to do so. Also apparent was the fact that neoclassical economics is defined by its method of analysis rather than by its domain of study. Conventional economic accounts generally admit only explanations based on self-interested exchange between rational economic agents and therefore fail to adequately account for a wide variety of factors germane to women's (and men's) lives. For example, the gendered and raced division of labor is explained in terms of the individual choices of rational agents. The provision of non-market, caring labor (such as parenting, caring for the sick, housework, and so forth) is either largely ignored or analysed in the same terms as the provision of paid labor, and the gendered and raced effects of globalization are explained as the natural consequences of differing endowments of skills, technology, and resources. Feminist economists seek to do better by questioning implicit assumptions about traditional gender roles as well as race, class and national hierarchies, thus revealing the biases and distortions in masculinist views of the economy. Feminist economists also seek to increase the variety of explanations that can count as economics, thus freeing economics from the straightjacket of constrained optimization and formal mathematical modeling. For many feminist economists, this does not mean giving up on the idea of economics as a science, but rather on doing better science.

Feminist economic practice
One way of thinking about what constitutes better science is to reconceptualize science. Instead of thinking of science as a way of representing the world, science may be thought of as a method of inquiry or set of practices. The implications for epistemology are that scientific practices can then be evaluated in terms of what their goals are and how well they achieve them (Harding 2003), and this means that scientific practices may be contested in on democratic and ethical grounds (Peter 2003b). As Harding points out, this is particularly relevant to feminist economics because it explicitly aims toward improving the well-being of women, children, and marginalized social groups.

Helen Longino's list of feminist theoretical virtues – empirical adequacy, novelty, ontological heterogeneity, mutuality of interaction, applicability to human needs, and diffusion of power – are particularly useful for articulating the theoretical, empirical, and ethical criteria that inform feminist economic practice. First, empirical adequacy, both a Kuhnian and a feminist virtue, requires that the observational content of a theory should be in agreement with the data. Clearly this virtue has particular import for feminist economists, as they, along with many other heterodox economists, recognize that mainstream economics has well known and serious problems with empirical fidelity in general and with the estimation of economic relationships in particular. For feminist economics, empirical adequacy entails developing new methodologies, informed by the specifically feminist theoretical virtues, which ameliorate the biases and incompleteness of conventional accounts.

Novelty, as a theoretical virtue, entails privileging theories that postulate different entities, adopt different principles of explanation, or investigate what traditional scientific inquiry has not. For feminists, the issue is that traditional frameworks rationalize alleged male superiority. This is clearly seen in economics in the ways that conventional economic explanations based on contractual exchange between self-interested individuals naturalize the gender division of labor and treat instances of gender discrimination as the result of rational choices on the part of women. Feminist economists admit other types of explanations, based on social norms such as reciprocity and responsibility, and so they come to quite different conclusions. Most feminist economic accounts employ novel approaches to traditional issues. Two examples are offered here.

First, consider the work on engendering macroeconomic modeling. This novel approach to macroeconomics accounts for the relationship between the economy of monetized production and the non-monetized economy of reproductive labor. Scholarship in this area by Diane Elson, Caren Grown, Nilfur Catagay, Lourdes Benería, and many others, has shown that making unpaid domestic labor visible and treating labor as a produced input fundamentally reshapes our understanding of the paid, market economy (Grown et al. 2000; Benería 1992).

For a microeconomic example, consider the work by Bina Argawal on household bargaining models. Argawal (1997) characterizes her work on bargaining and gender relations within the household as 'analytical description,' a method of spelling out the qualitative and quantitative factors of interest to the researcher. This analytical approach allows her to examine the role of social norms in intra-household bargaining, the coexistence of self-interest and altruism, and the role of the household in wider social institutions.

Ontological heterogeneity as a virtue entails favoring theories that grant parity to different kinds of entities. This is in contrast to theories that posit abstract, paradigmatic entities-- ontological homogeneity. As Longino points out, all scientific theories posit an ontology, either explicitly or implicitly, which characterizes what is considered real or causally efficacious. Heterogeneity is a feminist virtue because accounts in which one type is shown as the standard are inherently hierarchical. Different types are considered as departures from the norm and as such are considered inferior. In neoclassical economics ontological homogeneity is the rule. Economic agents are rational, self-interested individuals, a description that applies only to self-sufficient adults. Feminist economists, on the other hand, incorporate other visions of agency and may allow for agents who act for motivations other than self-interest or altruism. The work on 'caring labor,' pioneered by Nancy Folbre (1995, 2001) is a good example here. Caring labor is labor, both paid and unpaid, that is often undertaken out of affection or a sense of responsibility for other people, a motivation generally at odds with the notion of rational self-interest.

In addition to favoring theories that are pluralist with respect to entities, Longino argues that mutuality of interaction is another feminist virtue. This entails valuing theories that posit relationships between entities and processes that are mutual rather than unidirectional and involve multiple factors. In feminist economics this entails a more nuanced examination of the ways that economic and social relationships are constructed. For example, in debates over whether the gender wage gap is caused by human capital differences or by discrimination, Jane Humphries examines the impacts of discrimination on human capital differences (Humphries 1995). Likewise, Deborah M. Figart, Ellen Mutari, and Marilyn Power, interrogate the neoclassical notion of wages as price and through careful historical analyses show that wage setting has always been embedded in larger social institutions and norms (Figart et al. 2002).

Applicability to current human needs is an explicitly ethical virtue. It implies that scientific inquiry that is directed at meeting human needs and protecting the environment should be preferred over knowledge that is directed toward political domination or knowledge for its own sake. Its centrality in feminist economics is illustrated by Julie Nelson's suggestion that instead of conceptualizing economics as a theory of choice, it should be conceptualized as a theory of provisioning (Nelson 1996). This conception of economics directs attention away from the theoretical modeling of preferences to an examination of ways to improve peoples' material well-being, and allows both needs and wants to be included in economic analysis. Randy Albelda's and Chris Tilley's work on poverty and welfare, which privileges questions about the economic well-being of women and children, exemplifies this idea (Albelda and Tilley 1997).

Finally, consider the diffusion of power virtue. This virtue privileges research programs that do not require arcane expertise, or otherwise unnecessarily limit access to participation. For feminist economists, this requires an examination of the manner in which abstract mathematical and statistical techniques unnecessarily limit peoples' participation in economics and shield it from effective and meaningful public scrutiny. It also entails facilitating fuller participation in economics by the people whose lives are affected by economic policy, but who are generally not privileged to participate in either the construction of economic knowledge, or in economic policy making. Ironically, however, this particular epistemological virtue creates its own set of problems as the community of feminist economists is itself a relatively homogenous, prosperous, and privileged group. Feminist economists work to address this issue in a variety of ways by ranging from publishing work directed at a general audience (Folbre 2001; Albelda and Tilley 1997), to expanding research methods to include ethnography, oral history, and other qualitative research techniques (Berik 1997; Olmsted 1997; van Stavern 1997).

Of course, all the work discussed in these examples could easily illustrate several of Longino's feminist theoretical virtues because these virtues generally work together rather than in isolation. Empirical adequacy, for one, is a virtue common to all of them. The important point is to say that as feminist economics develops as a new field, new criteria, informed by feminist philosophy of science, are emerging for critically evaluating feminist economic practices.

It is also important to realize that feminist economics, as an epistemological community, exists in relationship with other such communities and is affected by them. Thus, the questions and issues posed by poststructuralism, such as the relationships between power and knowledge, theory and practice, and identity and difference, surface on the margins of the community. While deeply influential in other fields such as feminist political science or sociology, poststructuralism remains deeply suspect among feminist economists. This is partly because of the challenges it poses to the humanist project in which both economics and feminism are deeply embedded.

Poststructuralist feminist economics
Feminist economists are well aware of the tendencies of a universalized economic discourse to obliterate the economic realities of women, children, and other disempowered groups. Poststructuralist feminist economists take this observation a step further and argue for the importance of interrogating the ways in which discursive practices and institutions constitute gender, race, ethnicity, sexuality, and class as ideological categories. Such interrogations facilitate an examination of the ways that particular representations of women come to be accepted as legitimate scientific categories, as well as the roles these categories play in supporting or resisting unequal social relations among women, as well as between women and men.

Scholars working in this tradition are cognizant of the fact that both economics and feminism have their origins in Enlightenment conceptions of subjectivity, human rights, and political autonomy. Part and parcel of the Enlightenment tradition is the notion that the pursuit of scientific knowledge, as well as the rejection of tradition and superstition, will lead to social progress that will ultimately benefit all society. Poststructuralism, however, questions the notion that science is privileged knowledge, radically separate from power, and hence able to 'speak truth to power'. Instead, knowledge and power are always connected and hence the social good is a concept that easily serves the interests of the elite. Thus, feminist economics needs to theorize a multiplicity of oppressions and to examine the ways that subjectivities are produced and shaped by various, often contradictory, discourses, institutions, and the power relations inherent within them.

Gillian Hewitson's work provides a comprehensive treatment of poststructuralism in feminist economics (Hewitson 1999). She begins by articulating what is perhaps the key concept in poststructuralist analyses: a rejection of the referential or empiricist view of language. According to a referential view, language is a transparent, neutral medium in which words, signs, and symbols have meaning because they refer to, or represent, things in the external world. Poststructuralists reject this view and argue that language is best understood as a set of relationships and meaning is produced within those relationships. For example, 'the concept "tree" only has meaning through the differentiation of its sign from all other signs within the language system' (ibid., p. 13). Language is a structure, and meaning is constructed through difference rather than through naming. The early structuralists assumed that there was an origin, or source of meaning. The poststructuralists, however, reject this notion and argue that that there is no center or origin that fixes meaning. The implications of this are articulated in subtly different ways. Hewitson's analyses draws principally from the philosopher Jacques Derrida who argued that meaning is always deferred, it can never be complete or self present. '... meaning is always deferred, through the differentiation of the signs within the language structure, much like the endless deferral involved in the use of a dictionary' (ibid., p. 15).

According to this view, binary dualisms play a central role in creating meaning. The philosopher Jane Flax (1992) argues that since there is no unstable, or unchanging real, western philosophers impose an illusion of order on the world through binary oppositions. 'Order is imposed and maintained by displacing chaos into the less of each binary pair, for example culture/nature or male/female' (ibid., p. 453). She goes on to argue that once one sees that these are fictive categories then one can see that these dualisms imply that 'to be other, to be different than the defining one is to be inferior' (ibid., p. 453). Thus, to be woman is to be deficient, to be not man. Although the superior member of the dyad is also defined in opposition to the inferior, this opposition is not symmetrical. The superior member is the norm, the privileged, the ideal. Thus, for women to become 'equal' to men, they must become like men, they must fit into the universal, male subject position. The female body, however, does not always fit easily into this subject position.

Rethinking the mind/body dualism is central to feminist poststructuralism. The mind is the privileged member of the dyad and associated with reason, culture, and scientific knowledge, independent of and unadulterated by the body. This is the defining characteristic of the Cartesian knower, as discussed earlier, the isolated, passive recipient of knowledge, whose social location is completely irrelevant to knowing. Feminist epistemologists reject this conception in favor of one in which knowledge is constructed in knowledge communities and hence the social identity and context of knowers is significant. Knowledge claims are evaluated in the context of communities and the composition of such communities is relevant to such evaluations. This is the sense behind Tuana's (1992) claim that positing the community as the primary knower would resolve the tensions between feminist epistemologies. Feminist poststructuralism, however, goes even further than Nelson's (1990) post-Quinian position because it holds that that the discursive and material practices of science impinge on and affect the social objects being observed. The practices of knowledge production partially constitute what it is that researchers are trying to explain. Metaphors are not just descriptive, they are constitutive, and a referential view of language masks these constitutive effects. For economics, including feminist economics, this means that underlying processes of the economy are constituted through economic discourse. Moreover, for economics, the truth effects of the discourse depend upon the exclusion of the feminine (Hewitson 1999).

Hewitson analyses surrogate motherhood as an example. She examines the ways in which neoclassical economics constructs subject positions and relies on the exclusion of the feminine for its truth effects. The neoclassical account of surrogate motherhood is based on a womb-as-capital metaphor. This metaphor rewrites the pregnant woman's body 'to enable her to take up the masculine subject position of the contracting agent' (1999, p. 192), thus constructing another instantiation of the rational economic agent by denying the surrogate's status as mother. The woman as an embodied and sexed subject disappears and is replaced by the object of study, the contracting agent. The assumption that good science is merely a mirror of nature masks the productive work of the metaphor.

Although she does not identify herself as a poststructuralist, Susan Himmelweit's analysis of the ways that the concept of 'women's work' is constructed in both feminist and neoclassical economics demonstrates that metaphors are constitutive as well as descriptive (Himmelweit 1995). She argues that since women's work is derived from the notion of commodity-producing wage labor, it renders invisible those aspects of domestic activities and needs that do not fall neatly into a work/non-work dichotomy. One of the effects of this invisibility is that more and more of the needs and desires of workers and their families are being constructed in a form that has to be met through mass-produced consumer goods. Himmelweit works shows that the construction of 'women's work' is not a natural representation of such work, but rather is discursively constructed in ways that serve to further embed the satisfaction of human needs within the logic of the market.

Conclusion

Including gender as a category of analysis in economics, changing the questions economists ask, and the methods used to investigate them, leads to some interesting methodological issues and questions. What does it mean to do good science in this context? In answering this question, feminist economists enter into a variety of methodological debates in economic methodology and feminist epistemology. Questions about the linguistic turn in economics and the importance of rhetoric, the tensions between traditional empiricism and critical realism, and the challenges of poststructuralism all come to the fore. The challenges posed by poststructuralism are perhaps the most vexing.

Many feminist economists are wary of poststructuralism because they think it will get in the way of doing good empirical work that will lead to improvements in women's lives. Ironically, however, this stance precludes a critical examination of the category 'woman'. Such an examination is necessary because communities of poor women, women of color, and Third World women, continue to demonstrate a deep ambivalence toward feminism. In particular, liberal feminism, with its goal of sexual equality, seems to have little to offer. For the majority of the world's poor women, the oppressions created by racism, classism, and nationalism, can be far more devastating than gender oppression. Taking this seriously means that feminist economists need to theorize a multiplicity of oppressions and examine the ways that subjectivities are produced and shaped by various, often contradictory, discourses, institutions, and the power relations inherent within them.

At the same time, feminist economists work within the larger discourse of economics, and mainly in neoclassical economics. They need the analytical tools and vocabulary to work within that community. Moreover, as feminist *economists,* they share in the prestige of the discipline as a science, a prestige that is not to be taken lightly. So feminist empiricism remains the most fruitful way of characterizing the epistemological commitment of most feminist economists. How the tensions between poststructuralism and feminist empiricism are resolved in the future remains to be seen.

References
Albelda, Randy P., and Chris Tilly (1997), *Glass Ceilings and Bottomless Pits: Women's Work, Women's Poverty*, Cambridge, MA: South End Press.
Argawal, Bina (1997) '"Bargaining" and gender relations: within and beyond the household', *Feminist Economics*, **3** (1) 1–51.
Barker, Drucilla K. (1995), 'Economists, social reformers, and prophets: a feminist critique of economic efficiency,' *Feminist Economics*, **1** (3), 26–39.
Barker, Drucilla K. (2003), 'Emancipatory for whom? A comment on Tony Lawson and critical realism,' *Feminist Economics*, **9** (1), 103–08.
Benería, Lourdes (1992), 'Accounting for women's work: the progess of two decades', *World Development*, **20** (11), 1547–63.
Benería, Lourdes, and Gita Sen (1981), 'Accumulation, reproduction, and women's role in economic development: Boserup revisited', *Signs*, **7** (21), 279–98.
Bergmann, Barabara (1986), *The Economic Emergence of Women*, New York: Basic Books.
Berik, Günseli (1997), 'The need for crossing method boundaries in economics research', *Feminist Economics*, **3** (2), 121–26.
Blau, Francine D. and Marianne A. Ferber (1986), *The Economics of Women, Men and Work*, Upper Saddle River, NJ: Prentice-Hall.
Ferber, Marianne A., and Julie A. Nelson (1993), 'Introduction: the social construction of economics and the social construction of gender', in Marianne A. Ferber and Julie A. Nelson (eds), *Beyond Economic Man: Feminist Theory and Economics*, Chicago: University of Chicago Press, pp. 1–22.
Figart, Deborah M., Ellen Mutari and Marilyn Power (2002), *Living Wages, Equal Wages: Gender and Labor Market Policies in the United States*, London and New York: Routledge.
Flax, Jane (1992), 'The end of innocence', in Judith Butler and Joan Scott (eds), *Feminists Theorize the Political*, New York and London: Routledge, pp. 445–63.
Folbre, Nancy (1982), 'Exploitation comes home', *Cambridge Journal of Economics*, **4** (6), 317–29.

Folbre, Nancy (1995), 'Holding Hands at midnight: the paradox of caring labor', *Feminist Economics*, **1** (1), 73–92.
Folbre, Nancy (2001), *The Invisible Heart: Economics and Family Values,* New York: New Press.
Grapard, Ulla (1995), 'Robinson Crusoe: the quintessential economic man?', *Feminist Economics*, **1** (1), 33–52.
Grown, Caren, Diane Elson and Nilufer Cagatay (2000), 'Introduction', *World Development*, **28** (7), 1145–55.
Hands, D. Wade (2001), *Reflections Without Rules: Economic Methodology and Contemporary Science Theory*, Cambridge: Cambridge University Press.
Haraway, Donna (1990), 'A manifesto for cyborgs: science, technology and Socialist feminism in the 1980's', in Linda J. Nicholson (ed.), *Feminism/Postmodernism*, New York and London: Routledge, pp. 190–233.
Harding, Sandra (1986), *The Science Question in Feminism*, Ithaca, NY and London: Cornell University Press.
Harding, Sandra (1995), 'Can feminist thought make economics more objective?' *Feminist Economics*, **1** (1), 7–32.
Harding, Sandra (1999), 'The case for strategic realism: a response to Lawson', *Feminist Economics*, **5** (3), 127–35.
Harding, Sandra (2003), 'After objectivism vs. relativism', in Drucilla K. Barker and Edith Kuiper (eds), *Towards a Feminist Philosophy of Economics*, New York and London: Routledge, pp. 122–33.
Hartmann, Heidi (1981), 'The family as the locus of gender, class and political struggle: the example of housework', *Signs*, **6** (Spring), 365–94.
Hartsock, Nancy (1983), *Money, Sex and Power: Toward a Feminist Historical Materialism*, Boston, MA: Northeastern University Press.
Hewitson, Gillian J. (1999), *Feminist Economics: Interrogating the Masculinity of Rational Economic Man*, Cheltenham, UK and Northampton, MA, USA: Edward Elgar.
Himmelweit, Susan (1995), 'The discovery of "unpaid work"', *Feminist Economics*, **1** (2), 1–20.
Himmelweit, Susan, and Simon Mohun (1977), 'Domestic labor and capital', *Cambridge Journal of Economics*, **1** (1), 15–31.
Humphries, Jane (1995), 'Economics, gender and equal opportunities', in Jane Humphries and Jill Rubery (eds), *The Economics of Equal Opportunities*, Manchester: Manchester Equal Employment Opportunities Commission, pp. 55–86.
Jacobsen, Joyce (2003), 'Some implications of the feminist project in economics for empirical methodology', in Drucilla K. Barker and Edith Kuiper (eds), *Towards a Feminist Philosophy of Economics*, New York and London: Routledge, pp. 89–104.
Kuhn, Thomas (1962), *The Structure of Scientific Revolutions,* Chicago: University of Chicago Press.
Kuhn, Thomas (1977), *The Essential Tension*, Chicago: University of Chicago Press.
Lawson, Tony (1997), *Economics and Reality*, New York and London: Routledge.
Longino, Helen (1997), 'Cognitive and noncognitive values: rethinking the dichotomy', in Lynn Hankinson Nelson and Jack Nelson (eds), *Feminisms, Science, and the Philosophy of Science*, Dordrecht: Kluwer Academic Publishers, pp. 39–58.
Mäki, Uskali (1993), 'Two philosophies of the rhetoric of economics', in Willie Henderson, Tony Dudley-Evan and Roger Backhouse (eds), *Economics and Language (Economics as Social Theory)*, New York and London: Routledge, pp. 23–50.
McCloskey, Donald (1985), *The Rhetoric of Economics*, Madison, WI: University of Wisconsin Press.
Nelson, Julie A. (1993), 'The study of choice or the study of provisioning? Gender and the definition of economics', in M.A. Ferber and J.A. Nelson (eds), *Beyond Economic Man: Feminist Theory and Economics*, Chicago: University of Chicago Press, pp. 23–6.
Nelson, Julie, A. (1996), *Feminism, Objectivity, and Economics*, London: Routledge.
Nelson, Lynn Hankinson (1990), *Who Knows: From Quine to a Feminist Empiricism*, Philadelphia: Temple University Press.

Nelson, Lynn Hankinson and Jack Nelson (eds) (1997), *Feminisms, Science, and the Philosophy of Science*, London: Kluwer Academic Publishers.

Olmsted, Jennifer C. (1997) 'Telling Palestinian women's economics stories', *Feminist Economics*, **3** (2), 141–51.

Peter, Fabienne (2003a), 'Critical realism, feminist epistemology and the emancipatory potential of science', *Feminist Economics*, **9** (1), 93–101.

Peter Fabienne, (2003b), 'Foregrounding practices: feminist philosophy of economics beyond rhetoric and realism', in Drucilla K. Barker and Edith Kuiper (eds), *Towards a Feminist Philosophy of Economics*, New York and London: Routledge, pp. 105–21.

Quine, Willard V.O (1953), 'Two dogmas of empiricism', in *From a Logical Point of View*, 2nd edn, Cambridge, MA: Harvard University Press.

van Stavern, Irene (1997), 'Focus groups: contributing to a gender aware methodology', *Feminist Economics*, **3** (2), 131–37.

Strassman, Diana (1993a), 'Not a free market: the rhetoric of disciplinary authority in economics', in Marianne A. Ferber and Julie. A. Nelson (eds), *Beyond Economic Man: Feminist Theory and Economics*, Chicago: University of Chicago Press, pp. 54–68.

Strassman, Diana (1993b), 'The stories of economics and the power of the storyteller', *History of Political Economy*, **25** (1), 147–65.

Strober, Myra H. (1982), 'The MBA: same passport to success for women and men?', in Phyllis A. Wallace (ed.), *Women in the Workplace,* Boston, Auburn House, pp. 25–44.

Tuana, Nancy (1992), 'The radical future of feminist empiricism', *Hypatia*, **7** (1) 100–14.

Waller, William, and Linda R. Robertson (1990), 'Why Johnny (Ph.D., Economics) can't read: a rhetorical analysis of Thorstein Veblen and a response to Donald McCloskey's *Rhetoric of Economics*', *Journal of Economic Issues*, **24** (4), 1027–44.

Williams, Rhonda (1993), 'Race, deconstruction, and the emergent agenda of feminist economic theory', in Marianne A. Ferber and Julie A. Nelson (eds), *Beyond Economic Man: Feminist Theory and Economics*, Chicago: University of Chicago Press, pp. 144–53.

12 Rhetoric and postmodernism in economics

Robert F. Garnett, Jr.

Introduction

In the early 1960s, at the height of the Cold War, the scientific confidence of American economists seemed unshakable (Bernstein 1999; Morgan and Rutherford 1998; Stein 1996). College students were learning from Paul Samuelson's *Economics* (1964) that business cycles were a thing of the past. Professional economists were hearing similar pronouncements from leading theorists such as Samuelson's MIT colleague, Robert Solow:

> Most economists [now] feel that short-run macroeconomic theory is pretty well in hand. … The basic outlines of the dominant theory have not changed in years. All that is left is the trivial job of filling in the empty boxes, and that will not take more than 50 years of concentrated effort at maximum. (Solow, cited in Hahn and Brechling 1965, p. 146)

Samuelson and Solow were chief architects of this 'dominant theory,' a neoclassical-Keynesian synthesis that was hailed as the grand unification theory of modern economics, a marriage of neoclassical microeconomics and Keynesian macroeconomics that promised to bring final, scientific closure to lingering debates over the causes and implications of the Great Depression. The 1961 appointment of Solow and two other neoclassical-Keynesians to President Kennedy's Council of Economic Advisers and the famous success of their 1963 tax cut signaled the arrival of economics as a policy science. It also shifted arguments for American supremacy from the old-fashioned moralism of the McCarthy period to the progressive notion that U.S. economic engineers were better equipped than their Soviet counterparts to deliver sustained economic growth, at home and in the Third World. Circa 1965, economic science – and America itself – seemed poised for certain victory over the business cycle, poverty, Third World economic backwardness, and a host of other problems (Nelson 1991).

This confidence eroded quickly in the 1970s, however, as waves of political and economic turmoil revealed indisputable weaknesses in the neoclassical-Keynesian program. The public (including public officials) became disillusioned with its unfulfilled promises, especially in the realm of macroeconomic policy (Dean 1981; Heilbroner and Milberg 1995). Neoclassical-Keynesianism came under forceful attack by monetarist and new classical theorists as well as by critics outside the mainstream (institutionalists, Austrians, Marxians, post-Keynesians, neo-Ricardians, and others). These conflicts coincided with the political ascendance of Ronald Reagan and Margaret Thatcher and thus were overlaid with ideological tensions as well. These partisan differences were suppressed within official academic discourse as economists strained to preserve their image as ideologically neutral scientists. Yet in the public eye the intellectual and practical authority of economists was waning. Internally and externally, there was a growing sense of a discipline in disarray.

The dissolution of the neoclassical-Keynesian consensus led many economists to embrace some form of intellectual fundamentalism, turning inward and returning to first principles. This was clearly so among new classical economists (Lucas 1975 and 1976; Sargent and Wallace 1975). Returning to the first principles of individual self-interest maximization and logical-mathematical precision, the new classicals sought to rewrite economics from the ground up (Klamer 1983 and 2001). Their non-mainstream colleagues followed similar paths, returning to the first principles of dissident traditions in search of systematic alternatives to the failing orthodoxy (Kregel 1975; Eichner 1979; Dolan 1976; Steedman 1977; Desai 1979).

Rhetoric and postmodernism emerged as a different set of responses to the 1970s turmoil in professional economics. Broadly speaking, they arose as a critical response to the modernist philosophies of science embraced by the neoclassical-Keynesians and many of their critics. This led them to identify various forms of modernism in economics and to initiate what Arjo Klamer and Deirdre McCloskey (1988, p. 4) describe as a 'new conversation' about them. They were not untouched by the fundamentalist spirit. McCloskey, for instance, framed her rhetorical approach to economics as a return to the intellectual virtues of Adam Smith's Scottish Enlightenment liberalism (McCloskey 1985 [1998], pp. 191–92). Yet the interventions of McCloskey et al. were never simply a turn inward. They were more of a turn inside out, trying to reconnect economics to the world – to rebuild its moral and instrumental goodness – by reestablishing its identity as a liberal arts discipline. What has emerged from their efforts is an expansive array of new philosophical perspectives and dialogues, through which we are beginning to rethink the ends and means of economic science in our post-Cold War world. In this regard the most significant contributions of the rhetoric and postmodernism movement may yet lie before us.

Rhetoric vs. modernism
The issue of modernism was colorfully broached by McCloskey in her 1983 essay on 'The Rhetoric of Economics.'[1] McCloskey chastised economists for their unthinking allegiance to an illiberal and self-defeating philosophy

of science. She described this 'received view' as 'an amalgam of logical positivism, behaviorism, operationalism, and the hypothetico-deductive model of science' (McCloskey 1983, p. 484). She deemed it modernist (rather than simply positivist) '[t]o emphasize its pervasiveness in modern thinking well beyond science' (ibid., p. 484).[2] Its chief intellectual virtue is methodological uniformity, seeking to increase the quality and quantity of scientific knowledge by enforcing a single method of analysis, be it mathematical formalism, microfoundations, statistical significance, Austrian subjectivism, the institutionalist social value principle, Marxian value theory, or some other special code. For McCloskey, these ersatz philosophies of science arise from a narrow view of human knowledge and argument that is itself our principal problem.

McCloskey was quick to assure her colleagues that the abandonment of modernism did not entail an abandonment of economic science. The key to improving our science, she believed, was an increased ability to listen and speak to one another as scholars. And this requires not a more stringent adherence to a uniform Method but a renewed commitment to the intellectual virtues of the Scottish Enlightenment tradition from which modern economics itself emerged.[3] The adoption of a classical liberal ethos within the realm of academic discourse would give economists exactly what they need to reclaim their science from modernism, not the least of which is freedom from the totalitarian tendency of economic methodologists to try to 'legislate the knowable' based on a particular notion of science (McCloskey 1994, p. 306 and 1983, p. 515).

Modernism

McCloskey speaks of modernism – in general, not just in economics – in three related yet distinct ways. Her most common referent is twentieth-century modernism, marked by its narrow conception of science and rigid separation of science from the humanities. This modernism 'views science as axiomatic and mathematical, and takes the realm of science to be separate from the realm of form, value, beauty, goodness, and all things unmeasurable' (McCloskey 1998, p. 142). As McCloskey points out, this separation of science from the humanities gives rise to two related but opposed branches of twentieth-century modernism, '[o]ne artistic in origin and the other scientific' (ibid., p. 103). The 'literary modernism ... instanced by Woolf, Joyce, Picasso, and Stravinsky, attacked Science with a big-S' while the 'architectural' modernism of 'Le Corbusier, Mondrian, Bertrand Russell, and Paul A. Samuelson ... worshipped Science with a big-S' (McCloskey 2001, p. 103). For her purposes, however, the two are effectively one.

> The two modernisms ... come from the same intellectual culture. ... [Both] share an optimism about form, a distaste for the ungeneralizable, an obsession with provability,

a fascination with novelty, a celebration of the future, an affection for timeless axioms, a glorification of the individual, an aversion to ethical reasoning, a high value on the separation of fact from value, a belief in the theory that facts are independent of theory, and above all a strong feeling that reason and feeling are opposed realms (ibid., p. 103).[4]

In this broad sense, twentieth-century modernism is committed to the separation of what C.P. Snow called 'the two cultures' of science and the humanities (Klamer 1993, p. 235).

McCloskey situates this twentieth-century modernism within the broader category of Enlightenment modernism, the modernism of Descartes, Bacon, Kelvin, and the scientific revolution. 'Philosophically speaking, modernism is the program of Descartes, regnant in philosophy since the seventeenth century, to build knowledge on a foundation of radical doubt' (McCloskey 1998, 141). This concurs with Klamer's description of twentieth-century modernism as a 'return of Cartesianism,' an intellectual movement (or series of movements) epitomized by 'the Vienna Circle and its version of logical positivism . . . and, in the 1930s, the foundational analysis of mathematical economics' (Klamer 1993, p. 235).

Broader still is the modernism of Plato, the archetypal epistemological essentialist, whom McCloskey calls 'the first modernist' (McCloskey 2001, p. 115). This Platonic modernism is 'suspicious of reasonable persuasion' because it lacks the epistemic credentials of the search for Truth with a capital-T, knowledge that is 'free from doubt, free from metaphysics, morals, and personal conviction' (McCloskey 1998, p. 152). 'The modernisms of 1910 or of the Enlightenment or of the seventeenth century were recycled Plato, attempts to get underneath merely human persuasion to the bedrock of certitude' (McCloskey 2001, 115).[5]

In sum, McCloskey describes modernism as a recurring sense of finality and closure. 'In the form of the mistaken conviction that *Now* We Have It, modernisms keep being reinvented' (McCloskey 2001, p. 108). '[T]here have been as many modernisms as there have been spectacularly successful geniuses claiming transcendence' (ibid., p. 110).

McCloskey's objections to modernism in economics
McCloskey's critique of economic modernism begins with neoclassical-Keynesianism, 'the high modernism, for example, of Paul Samuelson's program' (McCloskey 2001, p. 102). She sees neoclassical-Keynesian economics as a prime example of the 'architectural' kind of modernism. 'Economists call it by various names, not all of them accurate: positive economics, scientific economics, rigor, serious work. In a word it is "Samuelsonian"' (ibid., p. 103). She offers two main objections to this conception of economic science.

First, as Bruno Latour famously puts it, we have never been modern (Latour 1988). The production of economic knowledge does not even remotely conform to the protocols of modernist methodology. 'Economists in fact argue on wider grounds and should' (McCloskey 1983, p. 482); and economists are hardly unique in this regard. 'If economists (or physicists) confined themselves to economic (or physical) propositions that literally conformed to such steps, they would have nothing to say' (McCloskey 1998, p. 150–51). As evidence, McCloskey cites several well-known episodes in the history of economics, most notably the Keynesian revolution.

> [T]he Keynesian revolution ... would not have happened under the modernist legislation for science. The Keynesian insights were not formulated as statistical propositions until the early 1950s, fifteen years after the bulk of younger economists had become persuaded that they were true. ... Modernist methodology would have stopped all of this cold in 1936: where was the evidence of an objective, controlled, and statistical kind? (ibid., p. 153).

Ex post 'rational reconstructions' notwithstanding, McCloskey concludes that 'the many official methodologies are apparently not the grounds for [economists'] scientific conviction' (McCloskey 1983, p. 482).

Second, modernist methodological prescriptions are impractical and illiberal in ways that should be obvious to contemporary descendants of Adam Smith.

> The greater objection to modernism in economics, though, is that modernism supports a rule-bound methodology. ... It claims that the philosopher of science can tell what makes for good, useful, fruitful, progressive science. ... The philosopher undertakes to second-guess the scientific community ... restricting the growth of the economic conversation to make it fit a philosopher's idea of the ultimate good. (McCloskey 1998, p. 156)[6]

Such rules are meant to enhance the growth of knowledge by providing clear criteria for distinguishing scientific from non-scientific propositions. Yet McCloskey argues that their likely effect is to *reduce* the growth of knowledge by encouraging scholars to embrace or reject arguments mechanically, without seriously engaging them. McCloskey finds it disturbing and odd and disturbing that a discipline founded on liberal principles would employ such illiberal methods to achieve its vision of scientific community. 'Something is awry with an appeal for an open intellectual society, an appeal defending itself on liberal grounds, that begins by demarcating certain ways of reasoning as forbidden and certain fields of study as meaningless' (ibid., p. 158).

In addition, such exclusionary practices reinforce an already cynical professional culture in which the pursuit and protection of specialized expertise often trumps the desire for learning. 'The maker of the rules for economic science has, of course, the noblest of intentions. Like the man from the government, he is here to help you' (McCloskey 1994, p. 20). 'In practice,' however, 'Methodology serves chiefly to demarcate Us from Them ... science from nonscience ... limiting conversation to people on our side of the demarcation line' (McCloskey 1998, p. 161).[7] '[My] attitude towards Methodology is similar to Adam Smith's attitude toward Mercantilism. Both Methodology and Mercantilism are attempts to blockade entry and acquire rents for the few already in possession. They sloganize about the public good, but violate it cynically, the better to stay in charge' (McCloskey 1994, p. 187). In this respect modernist methodologies tend to promote excessive specialization, i.e., specialization without trade. Continuing in the Smithian vein: 'Good economics knows that specialization is not in itself good. ... What is good about specialization is that it allows more consumption, through trade' (McCloskey 2000b, p. 158). 'If we actually read one another's work and let it affect our own, we are well and truly following the economic model of free trade. ... Most of the advances of science and scholarship have come from such trade' (ibid., p. 158).

Yet modernist methodologies inhibit such trade by equating science with Method and specialized expertise. Klamer notes here the parallels between modern economics and modern art. 'One characteristic of modernism, revealed in the disciplines of the arts as well as economics, is the conscious separation of [one's own] discipline from others. ... Thus they produce a highbrow culture, only to be fully understood by the initiated. ... [C]ommunication [turns] inward' (Klamer 2001, p. 89). This limits conversation and learning to those who already speak the same language. It also nurtures the specialist's distaste for listening and learning outside of his or her own small circle. McCloskey sees this as a common practice throughout the economics profession, among mainstream economists and their heterodox critics. 'The schools of [heterodox] economic thought have each their comical attachments to methodology' (McCloskey 1998, p. 161), taking seriously only those arguments that conform to their preferred methodological formula. In this regard 'they have been as narrow as thoroughgoing positivists' (ibid., p. 143). She also notes the general lack of respect paid to scholars in neighboring disciplines. 'Economists disdain learning. They want lawyers and political scientists and sociologists to pay attention to economics but will not listen in turn' (McCloskey 2000a, p. 149).

Despite these sharp words, McCloskey respects (as she herself once embraced) the professed aims of the high modernist movement in economics after World War II. She is mindful of the liberal motives that sparked the mid-century fervor for Truth and Method, arising from the historical experience of intellectual freedom fighters who clung to these ideals as 'a wall against irrational and authoritarian threats to inquiry' (McCloskey 1998, p. 169). Postwar U.S. economics was part of a 'grand crusade against fascism and totalitarianism' (Bernstein 1999,

p. 108). 'For the immigrants who lived through the interwar period in Europe – and some, like [Jacob] Marschak, who fled first Lenin and then Hitler – this hope of building a *wertfrei* social science, immune to propaganda of every kind, gave motivating force to the econometrics movement' (Leijonhufvud 1987, p. 181; cited in Redman 1994, p. 81; see also Hutchison 1938 [1960] and Popper 1945). 'The key figures shaping econometrics – Marschak, Joseph Schumpeter, and Tjalling Koopmans, among others – erected the new field with the spirit that science would guarantee a fair, objective, democratic world' (Redman 1994, p. 81). This compels McCloskey to emphasize that her criticism is directed not at mathematical and statistical methods themselves but the chauvinistic conversion of these tools into intellectual demarcation criteria, i.e., trade barriers. '[A]long with their new mathematical way of talking the economists adopted a crusading faith, a set of *philosophical* doctrines, that makes them prone now to fanaticism and intolerance' (McCloskey 1998, p. 140).

Rhetoric
McCloskey uses the term 'rhetoric' to highlight the conversational dimensions of economic science and to redirect economists' attention from the modernistic idols of Truth and Method to the interpersonal end and means of argument: persuasion. McCloskey's rhetoric is the study of how people persuade (McCloskey 1994, p. xiii). It is rhetoric in the sense of Aristotle ('the available means of nonviolent persuasion') rather than Plato ('mere ornament') (ibid., p. 287). This entails what she terms a small-m methodology (or 'anti-methodology') whose main tasks are to articulate the communal norms of good conversation, and to use these norms to illuminate the process of argumentation within our scholarly communities, to '[point] out what we actually do, what seems to persuade us, and why' (McCloskey 1998, p. 184) and to '[resist] the rigidity and pretension of rules' (ibid., p. 156).

A skilled and sensitive rhetor herself, McCloskey anticipates many of her readers' questions. First, she claims no originality for these ideas. The perspective she calls rhetoric borrows from the writings of the sophists, Cicero, scholastic philosophy, Hegel, the American pragmatists (McCloskey 1998, p. 183) and from contemporary philosophers of science such as Kuhn, Feyerabend, Toulmin, Lakatos, and Bloor who collectively have '[exploded] the myth of a single scientific method by means of detailed historical investigations into the origins and development of specific scientific theories' (Mirowski 1988, p. 121). But she is especially keen to highlight the classical liberal branch of the rhetorical tradition, the Adam Smith branch, which makes rhetoric native to economics (Heilbroner 1988) and connects economics to the larger 'conversation of humankind' (Oakeshott, cited in McCloskey 1994, p. 382).

Second, she does not claim that modern economics is wholly devoid of rhetorical virtues. Modern economics clearly endorses, if only tacitly, 'the goodness of community, solidarity, openness to ideas, educated public opinion, and a better conversation of humanity' (McCloskey 1994, p. 99).

> The word for it is *Sprachethik*, speech morality, the ethics of conversation ... liberalism incarnate: Don't lie; pay attention; don't sneer; cooperate; don't shout; let other people talk; be open-minded; explain yourself when asked; don't resort to violence or conspiracy in aid of your ideas. These are the rules adopted by the act of joining a good conversation (ibid., pp. 99–100).

McCloskey's concern is that these liberal virtues are frequently supressed *in the name of science* when groups of economists become zealously invested in particular definitions of 'serious work' (based on their own methodological, epistemological, or ideological preferences) and use them to exclude other economists' arguments from their conversations.

Finally, McCloskey's use of the term rhetoric should not be understood as a preference for literary matters over scientific ones. McCloskey's project is precisely to reunite these 'two cultures' – the sciences and the humanities – by demonstrating the quantitative and humanistic character of all sciences, especially the all-too-human science of economics.

With regard to epistemology, McCloskey embraces a pragmatic or hermeneutic notion of truth (small-t) as conjective knowledge, 'what we know together, by virtue of social discourse, scientific argument, shared language' (McCloskey 1994, p. 347). The difference between conjective truth and the objective Truth envisioned by modernist epistemologies is

> what divided Plato from Aristotle and after them much of the intellectual world, namely, the transcendental absolute as against the social character of truth. For 2500 years the followers of Plato have been trying to find a way to vault out of human society into a higher realm of forms, to find a procedure for deciding whether a proposition was True or False in the eyes of God. (McCloskey 1998, p. 292)

> The rhetorical view of knowledge denies that one can 'tell whether an assertion is persuasive by knowing from which side of the scientific/humanistic dichotomy it came ... You can tell whether it is persuasive only by thinking about it and talking about it with other thoughtful people. Not all regression analyses are more persuasive than all moral arguments; not all controlled experiments are more persuasive than all introspections. People should not discriminate against propositions on the basis of epistemological origin (ibid., p. 177).

From a rhetorical perspective, the conjectivity of intellectual standards operates no less in mathematics and other 'hard sciences' as in the social sciences and humanities.[8]

With regard to method, McCloskey's rhetoric becomes a dissertation on the social *process* of good economics, i.e., how we ought to govern ourselves as an intellectual community. Rhetoric assumes that good science is good conversation (McCloskey 1994, p. 100). In other words, 'it does not deal with Truth directly; it deals with conversation' (McCloskey 1998, p. 163). It provides 'procedural rather than end-state justice' (McCloskey 1994, p. 295). McCloskey envisions this process as a 'civilized conversation among equals' (McCloskey 2001, p. 107). She assumes that every economist should be free from the tyranny of Method, free to conduct research and produce arguments in accord with her own tastes and circumstances. Conversely, every economist should also accept the burden of respecting and facilitating this freedom in the academic lives of her colleagues. Rhetoric thus entails an ethical commitment to the disciplinary conversation itself, and to the anti-modern premise that there is no 'special set of terms in which all contributions to the conversation should be put' (Rorty 1979, p. 318, cited in Nelson 1991, p. 267) and 'no single, privileged "rational method" for deciding upon what is "true"' (Madison 1994, pp. 202–3).

While McCloskey is careful to distinguish her rhetoric from an 'anything goes' relativism, her vision of science bears a notable similarity to the methodological and epistemological anarchism of Paul Feyerabend (1975). As Boettke explains, 'McCloskey does advocate a sort of anarchism, but I believe it is not methodological anarchism (that is: anything goes and every argument is of equal value). Rather, McCloskey's anarchism is one of scientific organization. ... [I]t should be contrasted not with reason, but with the idea of centrally planned science' (Boettke 1994, p. 181). The idea of requiring all scholarly ideas to be produced and exchanged in accord with a particular Method is tantamount to a 'centrally planned science' inasmuch as it cedes to methodological legislators the power to decide which types of thinking are or are not intellectually acceptable – not unlike a government's imposition of a particular language or currency as the official medium of exchange. It reduces the scientist to a bureaucrat whose task 'is not to decide whether propositions are useful for understanding and for changing the world but to classify them into one or the other half, scientific or nonscientific, and to bring as many as possible into the scientific half' (McCloskey 1998, p. 176).

Rhetoric, in contrast, would allow the civic process of conversation itself to determine the form and value of arguments, resisting the notion that any single Method possesses intrinsic value. 'Rhetoric opposes intrinsicality, the foundationalism that makes people think they can lever the world from the blackboard or the lecture podium' (McCloskey 1994, p. 339). It's a free banking argument. The media and rules of exchange among scholars should be allowed to emerge from the intellectual marketplace itself. Those languages and evaluative criteria that prove valuable in exchange will flourish; those that prove less valuable will be altered or simply abandoned. 'What distinguishes good from bad in learned discourse ... is not the adoption of a particular methodology, but the earnest and intelligent attempt to contribute to a conversation' (McCloskey 1998, p. 162). Rhetoric envisions academic discourse as a common market, a polyglot network of scholarly communities and projects, regulated (at least potentially) by an invisible hand of truth.[9] No single Method ever guides a community of researchers anyway, says McCloskey. And none is needed as long as scholars are able to enact the virtues of good conversation. In a rhetorically virtuous world, '[t]here is no need for philosophical lawmaking or methodological regulation to keep the economy of intellect running just fine' (ibid., p. 28).

Consequences of rhetoric

McCloskey's hope is that '[a] rhetorical criticism of economics can perhaps make economics more modest, tolerant, and self-aware, and improve one of the conversations of humankind' (McCloskey 1998, p. 186). Rhetoric offers an alternative to the modernist extremes of hard-nosed Science and soft-hearted relativism, both of which inhibit conversation and learning. Rhetoric rejects these extremes in pursuit of a 'serious relativism ... admitting that we cannot achieve Truth but affirming that we can agree on truth [and demanding] . . . that we persuade each other' (McCloskey 1994, pp. 309–10). Individually and as a discipline, our intellectual progress depends on 'our ability to engage in continuous conversation, testing one another, discovering our hidden presuppositions, changing our minds because we have listened to the voices of our fellows' (A.O. Rorty, cited in McCloskey 1998, p. 163). Commitment to such a serious relativism would help economists 'to regain a scholarly life' (McCloskey 1994, p. 306), to 'know [better] why they agree or disagree, and [to] find it less easy to dismiss contrary arguments on merely methodological grounds' (McCloskey 1983, p. 482). Ruling out fewer arguments while listening more actively to our colleagues will do more to advance our worldly wisdom than strict adherence to any Method.

It is worth emphasizing that McCloskey is not a relativist. Her notion of rhetoric as a liberal arts ethos, 'a theory of democratic pluralism and of general education in a free society' (McCloskey 1994, p. 385), hardly precludes the criticism and weeding out of arguments within learning communities. 'The crucial point about the conversational view of intellectual life is that conversations overlap' (ibid., p. 100). '[T]he overlapping conversations provide the standards' (McCloskey 1998, p. 163). From this standpoint, 'the tolerance in rhetoric is not ... the thoughtless pluralism forced on the modernist by his lack of a way of debating values. ... To the contrary, it is a principled pluralism insisting that people defend their values openly' (McCloskey 1994, p. 385). Rhetoric is 'an invitation to leave the irrationality of an artificially narrowed range of argument and to move to the rationality of arguing like human beings' (McCloskey 1998, p. 168). It allows economists to profitably discuss the role of normative commitments in their scientific enterprise. 'At present, we allow it only secretly, a secrecy that poisons the economic conversation' (McCloskey 1994, p. 384). '[T]he Valley Girl madness of anything goes is in fact a consequence of ignoring rhetoric, not of recognizing it' (ibid., p. 255).

McCloskey sought to improve the economic conversation by encouraging mainstream and non-mainstream economists to recognize these 'overlapping conversations,' to gain new perspectives on their work by seeing themselves as part of an expansive network of learning communities. She sees this as a particularly liberating step for mainstream economists inasmuch as it offers them a better 'place to stand' outside of their discipline. 'A literary, humanistic, rhetorical approach to economics provides the economist with a place to stand outside the field. We need it, and think so, as we demonstrate in our frequent appeals to fancied rules of epistemology or scientific method. ... We economists cannot see what we are doing from inside economics itself' (McCloskey 1998, p. 283). It also encourages a pluralistic sense of one's own intellectual identity. For her own part, McCloskey has come to eschew the mechanical certainties of Cold War economic theory across the spectrum: left (Marxian anti-capitalism), right (Stiglerian laissez-faire), and center (neoclassical-Keynesian fine-tuning). Yet she continues to learn from the ongoing dialogue among these perspectives within her own mind.

> Rhetoric provides a place to stand from which to admire and criticize radically different metaphors of economic life, such as the Marxist metaphor of class struggle, which I clung to as an undergraduate, or the institutionalist metaphor of human geography, which I fell into naturally as an early graduate student, or, at length discovering the truth in my third year at Harvard graduate school, the Chicago-school metaphor of plebian little monads rushing about in search of rents. (McCloskey 1994, p. 384)

In addition, McCloskey's pluralistic vision of economics offers non-mainstream economists a better place to stand *within* the discipline by insisting that the economic conversation is one in which they can and should be heard. In this way, McCloskey registers a valuable break from the oppressive unity of Scientific Method (a single disciplinary conversation) and its radical counterpart, Kuhnian paradigmism (multiple but non-overlapping conversations).

From rhetoric to postmodernism

McCloskey was not the only economist seeking alternatives to modernism in the early 1980s. The emerging genre of anti- and postmodern economics was intellectually and ideologically quite diverse, ranging from the hermeneutic economics of Don Lavoie (1991) and Klamer to the social constructionist institutionalism of Warren Samuels (1990) and Philip Mirowski (1987) to the non-determinist Marxism of Stephen Resnick and Richard Wolff (1982), Jack Amariglio (1984), Antonio Callari (1981), and David Ruccio (1984).

By 1990, postmodernism had emerged as a shared label for these various projects.[10] The range of perspectives included under the postmodern umbrella extended well beyond McCloskey's rhetoric. For example, the postmodernism of the 'rethinking Marxism' group (Resnick/Wolff et al.) was largely inspired by the philosophical anti-humanism of the French post-structuralists Louis Althusser, Jean Francois Lyotard, and Michel Foucault all of whom equate modernism with the universalist presuppositions of Enlightenment humanism (Amariglio 1984, 1987, 1988; Callari 1981). Compare this to McCloskey's unreserved embrace of classical liberal humanism, and the breadth and heterogeneity of these 'postmodern' perspectives are strikingly clear.[11]

Notwithstanding their many differences, these dissenters from economic modernism were allied in their opposition to what McCloskey calls the 'mechanical, scientistic notion of what economists do' (McCloskey 1994, p. 343) as well as the equally mechanical (Samuelsonian) notion of how economic *agents* learn, think, and behave. They also shared a loosely libertarian resistance to 'those metanarratives, like liberalism and Marxism, that have held out the hope for total change in society and culture (and economy) through advocacy of particular principles and perspectives' (Cullenberg et al. 2001, p. 9). They could no longer take seriously 'the possibility of universal truth and beauty and in the value of monolithic methodologies' or 'the modernist conviction that intellectuals and artists can reform the world and shape a better future' (Klamer 2001, p. 85).

Even so, the initial conversations among these postmodern economists were markedly divided along party lines: a pro-capitalist Right (McCloskey and Lavoie) and a broadly anti-capitalist Left (Amariglio, Resnick/Wolff, Ruccio, Callari, and the Marxist-feminist economist Susan Feiner), with Klamer, Samuels, Mirowski, Diana Strassmann, and others floating somewhere in between. The community of postmodern economists in the early 1990s was therefore united in its opposition to modernist dogmatism yet also divided by fundamental disagreements about the nature and efficacy of free-market capitalism, and a parallel set of disagreements about McCloskey's hopeful vision of economics as an intellectual 'free market'.

One measure of these differences among economic postmodernists is their differing accounts of humanism, especially as it informs their criticisms of mainstream economics. For those on the postmodern 'right' and some on the 'left,' the main problem with mainstream neoclassicism is the poverty of humanism. Boettke (1994) argues that 'modernist economics forgets man' and urges that it be replaced with a more hermeneutical economics. Klamer expresses a similar view. 'We need an economics for human beings, not for godlike mathematicians. God sees the Truth; humans interpret' (Klamer and McCloskey 1989, p. 157). Likewise McCloskey: '[A] rhetorical approach to economics fits better with being human. This is not to say that the Method of Science is inhuman. The problem is that it is only one part of being human' (McCloskey 1994, p. 383).

For some on the postmodern 'left,' however, the problem with mainstream economics is not a lack of humanism but a surplus – essentialist notions of human nature and human society that serve to displace (by deeming secondary or temporary) antagonistic differences such as class, race, gender or ethnicity from the field of economic inquiry. In their view, the best way forward is to deconstruct and thus loosen the grip of humanism over contemporary economic discourse. This argument is forcefully advanced by Cullenberg, Amariglio, and Ruccio: 'Postmodern critique, then, should be distinguished from those forms of humanism (found in all sorts of heterodox schools of economic thought, including Marxism, feminism, institutionalism, and so forth) that seek to reinstall rather than end the primacy of a "lost" or missing human subjectivity in economic discourse' (Cullenberg et al. 2001, 34).[12]

Interestingly, however – in the very spirit of McCloskey's rhetoric – these differences have become sources of new conversations and mutual learning over the past decade, helping to redraw the philosophical lines among critics of economic modernism (Ruccio 1991).

Beyond capitalism/anti-capitalism

On the question of capitalism, Old Chicago McCloskey has become increasingly outspoken among her left-leaning postmodern colleagues. She laments the 'sad political fact' that 'most postmodernists are socialists,' and has endeavored to persuade her comrades that the democratic, anti-elitist ideals of postmodernism are the philosophical siblings of free-market capitalism and Scottish Enlightenment liberalism, not socialism or Marxism. '[Postmodernism] is mainly not leftwing. ... Postmodernism can be given an economic and classical liberal – I did not say 'conservative' or 'reactionary' – reading' (McCloskey 2001, p. 102). As an economic historian and rhetorician McCloskey sees a natural kinship between the virtues of rhetoric and market exchange. In recent work she characterizes these virtues as bourgeois, – and the vices of modernism as 'anti-bourgeois.'[13] From this perspective '[r]hetoric, the first postmodernism, was born with capitalism in the marketplaces of Greece' (ibid., 122).

McCloskey's arguments have drawn several critical responses within the postmodern literature. S. Charusheela applauds McCloskey's call for 'an integration of ethics and virtue into our discipline's methodology and discourse' and even more her suggestion that we 'return to an older tradition of political economy where culture and economy shape each other – culture providing the social glue that enables economic interaction, and economic interaction in turn shaping culture through the lived experience of interaction that marks economic participation in daily life' (Charusheela 2000, p. 46). At the same time, Charusheela objects to McCloskey's reductive theorization of the difference between capitalist and non-capitalist economies. She notes that McCloskey's identification of capitalism with market exchange precludes analysis of other forms and dimensions of capitalism. Further, Charusheela faults McCloskey for making the virtues of market capitalism practically a tautology, based on an 'a priori assignment of positives to markets' (ibid., p. 49). 'If capitalism is seen as synonymous with an ideal of free markets, there will always be some element outside markets to which bad things can be attributed. One attributes all good things to free markets, all bad things to "limits" on free markets, usually the state or non-Western, pre-modern culture' (ibid., p. 48).

Amariglio (2001) also questions McCloskey's coupling of postmodernism with capitalism. He challenges her 'identification of markets and exchange with capitalism,' pointing out that 'many Marxists would have serious misgivings' about such a broad, exchange-focused definition.' He also questions McCloskey's neglect of the working classes in her 'metanarrative of a world historical battle between the bourgeoisie and the aristocracy' (Amariglio 2001, p. 138) and her Hayek-like tendency to reduce feudalism, communism, and every other form of non-capitalism to authoritarian serfdom. Finally, and related: Amariglia criticizes McCloskey's pre-Foucauldian inattention to forms of power and coercion other than those exercised by a centralized state.

One striking revelation in this exchange is the degree to which McCloskey's 'postmodern liberalism' is framed by the ideological polarities of a Cold War modernism she otherwise seeks to escape. Her normative arguments for capitalism invoke a blunt dichotomy between postmodern and modern that is surprisingly similar to those drawn between First World and Second World circa 1960: totalitarianism/freedom, communism/capitalism, aristocratic elitism/ bourgeois virtue, Bentham/Hayek, positive liberty/negative liberty, modern/ postmodern.

With respect to liberty, for example, McCloskey claims that the 'Enlightenment project' harbors an uneasy mixture of scientism and liberalism. 'In a sentence: being unreasonably rational will eventually enslave us to rules' (McCloskey 2001, p. 110). Yet she describes the elements of this mixture as if they were oil and water, with no talk of complementarity. She identifies modernism with social engineering, a Benthamite quest for 'positive freedom' (ibid., pp. 117–18), and postmodernism with the 'freedom to be left alone' and faith in the self-regulating civility of the bourgeoisie. Such dichotomous thinking is odd for any postmodern liberal. It seems especially odd for McCloskey in view of her abiding ties to American pragmatism, a tradition defined by its efforts to overcome dichotomous thinking and to cultivate complementarities between positive and negative freedoms (Dewey 1939 [1979], for example).

Nevertheless, this unfolding dialogue between McCloskey and her critics is no longer simply a Cold War collision of rival systems (market vs. plan, West vs. East, liberalism vs. Marxism).[14] What is emerging instead is a new conversation about the forms and meanings of economic (in)justice and freedom in which many participants seem to share Don Lavoie's sentiment that 'it is time for these more liberal elements of the left and right sides of the old political spectrum to transcend the confines of these obsolete ideologies and work together to articulate a new vision of the free society' (Lavoie 1994, p. 283).

This new sensibility is further illustrated in a series of recent works by postmodern Marxist economists in which the central dualisms of Cold War Marxism (e.g., markets/planning) are reconceived in highly nuanced and surprising ways.[15] For example, Amariglio and Ruccio pointedly reopen the question of 'market versus plan' by criticizing the modernist Marxian tendency to overemphasize the disorderliness of capitalism and the negative consequences of this disorder and the related tendency to define socialism or communism as the transcendent opposite of this disorder, thus exaggerating 'the orderly nature of socialism, especially planning' and the positive consequences of such order (Amariglio and Ruccio 1994, 21).

DeMartino (2003) extends this argument to the normative domain. He carefully recasts Marxian demands for class justice within Amartya Sen's framework of capabilities equality, highlighting a 'positive freedom' Marxism that differs radically from the totalitarianism of official Soviet Marxism-Leninism.[16] As if to underscore this difference, DeMartino stresses the importance of 'normative open-mindedness,' urging Marxists to retain 'an unapologetic concern for class justice' along with an equally principled respect for other justice claims and normative concerns, 'to anticipate and even welcome the need to negotiate among competing normative principles' (DeMartino 2003, p. 23).

Burczak takes up this challenge in a series of recent papers where he uses Sen and the neglected work of David Ellerman (1991) to make a normative case for market socialism that is mindful of Marxian class justice as well as Hayekian ethical and epistemological arguments against centralized planning (Burczak 1996/97, 2001, 2002, 2003). Burczak's work is noteworthy in its openness to the possibility that tensions between different dimensions of economic freedom or justice might be embraced as difficult but productive, as complements rather than substitutes. He suggests, for example, that Hayekian negative liberty requires Senian positive liberty in order to achieve its highest aspirations, and vice versa (Burczak 2003).

In all, these discussions are helping to advance economic discourse by widening our senses of liberalism and Marxism as heterogeneous and overlapping traditions (not self-contained, rival systems), and sowing the seeds of new alliances and learning communities in which economists of different traditions can more effectively listen and speak to one another and thus advance the conversation, the science, of economics.

Beyond neoclassicism/anti-neoclassicism

With regard to economics as a discipline, the dialogue among McCloskey and her postmodern colleagues is also evolving in fruitful new directions. McCloskey has always rankled her critics with her sunny assessment of the merits and meritocracy of contemporary economics. 'Economics in its modern and mathematical form has grown into a brilliantly successful science. Unquestionably, it has' (McCloskey 1994, p. xi). 'Economics will not change much in substance when economists recognize that the [modernist] economic emperor has positively no clothes. He is the same fellow whether philosophically naked or clothed, in reasonably good health aside from his sartorial delusion' (McCloskey 1983, p. 482). 'The [rhetorical] cure would merely recognize the good health of economics, disguised now under the neurotic inhibitions of an artificial methodology of Science' (ibid., p. 515). On the heels of her claim that 'postmodernism aspires to a civilized conversation among equals' (McCloskey 2001, p. 107) and in view of her tendency to focus much more on the requirements for 'civility' than 'equality,' McCloskey seems to view the current institutional structure of the discipline as more or less consistent with requirements for 'free speech.'

Her fellow postmodernists are much less sanguine about the openness and efficacy of the current conversation. Many see McCloskey's assessment as a naïve if not self-serving oblivion to discriminatory hierarchies of power and prestige within the profession. They bristle at her Chicago School presumption that all participants in the marketplace of ideas are equally free to speak (Folbre and Hartmann 1988; Resnick and Wolff 1988; Strassmann 1993a and 1993b; Charusheela forthcoming). Many also criticize McCloskey for 'attacking the style but not the substance' of mainstream neoclassicism (Amariglio 1988; Heilbroner 1988; Mirowski 1988; Boettke 1994; Feiner 1994). They accuse her of intellectual inconsistency on this score: embracing a post-Cartesian view of *economist's* knowledge yet failing to criticize received economic theories of human behavior and interaction whose epistemological underpinnings are thoroughly Cartesian. Mirowski goes as far as to describe McCloskey's 'rhetoric' as a 'methodological justification of neoclassical economics' (Mirowski 1988, p. 122). Boettke is more charitable but registers the same complaint: 'McCloskey is far too favorable to the existing body of neoclassical thought and [her] own methodology points to a more critical approach' (Boettke 1994, p. 180).

McCloskey has responded with impassioned efforts to convince her critics that postmodern rhetoric and neoclassical economics *do* make sense together, and that the professional standing of non-mainstream groups would be better served if they were to embrace a persuasion-oriented, rhetorical approach.

On the first point, McCloskey takes a broad view of the neoclassical tradition, refusing to equate it with Walrasian general equilibrium theory or any other 'straw man.' She acknowledges the scientific limitations of the tradition yet insists upon its enduring usefulness. On the second point, she maintains that rhetoric is steadfastly pluralist doctrine that neither precludes nor advocates any particular theoretical approach. 'Rhetoric is consistent with any number of beliefs about the economy, between which one can toggle' (McCloskey 1994, p. 395).

> The openness of rhetoric gives voice to minority opinions. To this extent rhetoric is hostile to the mainstream ... But rhetoric is not intrinsically hostile to the mainstream. Rhetorical alertness can be used to force the dominant groups to face up to institutionalism or Marxism or feminism or Austrianism, as they should. But nothing inside the rhetoric itself implies one or the other view (ibid., p. 394).

In other words, she urges heterodox groups not to respond to the mercantilist modernism of the mainstream by erecting their own protectionist paradigm barriers but rather by embracing the virtues of rhetoric and intellectual free trade.[17] She believes that the most effective antidote to the dysfunctional hierarchies within the economics profession is 'a catholic rhetoric that encourages neoclassicals, Marxists, institutionalists, Austrians, and the other students of mankind in the ordinary business of life to gain more persuasive knowledge' (ibid., p. 178).

Over time, this clash of perspectives has generated a new awareness – on all sides – of the meaning and importance of intellectual freedom in the marketplace of economic ideas. Significant mutual learning has clearly occurred. McCloskey's reassertion of the differences between 'old Chicago' and 'Samuelsonian/modern' economics and her willingness to form alliances with scholars outside her own tradition have helped many heterodox economists to gain a more nuanced understanding of neoclassicism and of economic discourse generally. At the same time, McCloskey seems to have become more cognizant of institutional power structures within the discipline. For example, she has become a vocal critic of labor market discrimination against non-mainstream economists (McCloskey 1994, p. 360). She also has modified her position on heterodox schools of thought, suggesting that heterodox 'schools' play a positive role in the promotion of pluralism in economics by serving as incubators for rhetorical virtues on which the intellectual progressiveness of the economic conversation ultimately depends.

Case in point: the new pluralist ethos among heterodox economists

The recent international movement for greater intellectual pluralism in economic education, research, and policy formation is one arena in which these rhetorical/ postmodern ideas have begun to make a visible impact. These demands have arisen from numerous sites, most notably the French students and faculty associated with the Post-Autistic Economics movement ('Open Letter' 2000 and 'Petition' 2000) as well as from students at Cambridge University ('Opening Up Economics' 2001) and an international gathering of economists at the University of Missouri at Kansas City ('Kansas City Proposal' 2001). Meanwhile the Association for Heterodox Economics, the International Confederation of Associations for Pluralism in Economics, the European Association for Evolutionary Political Economy, and other umbrella organizations are taking unprecedented steps to bring various schools of heterodox economic thought together in an atmosphere 'where pluralism, not division, exists' (Lee 2002, p. 41). Many economics journals and publishers are making similar efforts. In short, the intellectual atmosphere and identity of non-mainstream (heterodox) economics appears to be shifting from the radical paradigmism of the 1970s and 80s (the quest for a single alternative to mainstream economics) to a resurgent and principled pluralism.[18]

These demands for greater pluralism are in many ways ethical demands, seeking greater intellectual freedom for economic scholars and students. This argument is most forcefully stated by the Cambridge 27. They charge that mainstream monism 'is harmful to students who are taught the "tools" of mainstream economics' but not 'their domain of applicability' or 'the existence and status of competing theories.' They also argue that this intellectual monism is harmful to economic science inasmuch as 'progress towards a deeper understanding of many important aspects of economic life is being held back.' 'Many economists therefore face a choice between using what they consider inappropriate methods to answer economic questions, or to adopt what they consider the best methods for the question at hand knowing that their work is unlikely to receive a hearing from economists.' '[W]e are not arguing against the mainstream approach per se, but against the fact that its dominance is taken for granted in the profession. ... Pluralism as a default implies that alternative economic work is not simply tolerated, but that the material and social conditions for its flourishing are met, to the same extent as is currently the case for mainstream economics. This is what we mean when we refer to an "opening up" of economics' (Cambridge 27, 2001).[19]

Still, despite generating fresh bursts of action and solidarity, this pro-pluralist campaign has also drawn bitter criticism from other corners of the heterodox movement. Unrepentant modernists like Paul Davidson (longtime editor of the *Journal of Post Keynesian Economics*) see pluralism as a self-defeating strategy for non-mainstream economists. He points to the recent removal of heterodox faculty from the economics Ph.D. program at the University of Notre Dame as painful evidence in support of his view that 'Until heterodox economists unite behind a single "general theory", they are going to be losers' (Davidson 2003a). Davidson believes that the best way to enhance the institutional power and voice of non-mainstream economists is not 'pluralism for pluralism's sake' (Davidson 2003c) but the development of a new paradigm, 'a single axiomatic foundation that provides the most general theory case, i.e., Keynes's *General Theory*' (Davidson 2002).

> [T]he problem with the 'heterodox' tent is that it is a logical tower of Babel. Thus the mainstream sees heterodox [economists] as ... people who do not deserve to be heard in proper academic circles because they clearly possess fundamental logical

inconsistencies in their approaches. Until they can get their house in order, why pay any attention? (Davidson 2002)

In Davidson's view, those who see cause for optimism in the recent surge of pluralistic solidarity among heterodox economists are engaged in dangerously wishful thinking.

> You cannot beat a rigid orthodoxy who despise non-pure bred Aryans (heterodox economists) with a 'let's all share the tent guys and gals' philosophy. As the Allies found out when dealing with Hitler, it takes an 'unconditional surrender' approach and stronger [in this case, stronger logical] forces to win what – whether you like it or not – the other side has declared to be a war of annihilation. (Davidson 2003b)

From a different angle, John Davis (2003) and Esther-Mirjam Sent (forthcoming) question the philosophical consistency of heterodox economists' demands for pluralism. Davis claims that heterodox economics is generally non-pluralist (monist, exclusionary, intolerant) at the level of ontology (Davis 2003, p. 17), e.g., when they argue 'not that their own theoretical approaches are *also* correct – a theoretical pluralist view – but rather that neoclassical economics is mistaken and misguided in its most basic assumptions, and that their own approaches remedy the deficiencies of neoclassicism – a theoretical monist view' (Davis 1997, p. 209; original emphasis). Sent maintains, similarly, that 'upon closer scrutiny, heterodox economists frequently are monists about theories' (Sent 2003, p. 19). Davis finds heterodox arguments for pluralism to be well-intentioned and useful but philosophically ad hoc, ungrounded in the traditions and principles of heterodox economics itself.

> Of course it is all fair and good for [heterodox economists] to press on a non-theoretical, purely practical basis for openness, non-discrimination, and for a 'free market' in ideas. ... These are ideals that ought to be defended across all of the humanities and sciences ... But this sort of program does not stem directly from the particular content of heterodox economics. It stems from a commitment to social values of long-standing that operate across the humanities and sciences and indeed in society generally. Only, it seems, were these ideals and values to become shared across heterodoxy and the mainstream, would there then be hope for a wider pluralism in economics. (Davis 2003, 17)[20]

Here I believe the postmodern 'McCloskey and critics' conversation about nature of economic pluralism points a very helpful way forward, by suggesting the possibility – and practical value – of an 'egalitarian' pluralism, a radical pluralism (pace McCloskey and postmodernism) that does not require economists to adopt a shared method of analysis, method of proof, or conception of reality augmented by a Senian capabilities approach, yielding an Aristotelian/liberal reconceptualization of economic science. The defining aim of this 'capabilities and conversation' approach would be to improve academic economics as a scientific (learning and teaching) community by enhancing the intellectual freedoms of all economists, heterodox and orthodox, as well as those of our many stakeholders who rely on our scholarship and teaching as an intellectual resource (students, policymakers, citizens, civic leaders, business leaders, and so on).

Sen of course speaks of economic rather than intellectual development. But the Aristotelian/liberal basis of his argument – his claim that Aristotle and Adam Smith both emphasize 'the central (intrinsic) value of freedom itself' (Sen 1999, p. 28)[21] and the related premise that wealth is not valuable in itself but as a 'general-purpose means for having more freedom to lead the kind of lives we have reason to value' (ibid., p. 14) – is easily extended to the intellectual realm.

The key premises of a capabilities approach in this context would be that human freedom is 'the primary end and as the principal means' of intellectual progress (ibid., p. xii); that the value of knowledge (truth, intellectual progress) lies in 'the substantive freedoms it helps us to achieve' (ibid., p. 14); and that '[intellectual] development consists of the removal of various types of unfreedoms that leave people with little choice and little opportunity of exercising their reasoned agency' (ibid., p. xii). A minimal definition of a good academic discipline (excluding the capabilities of stakeholders) would therefore be one in which all members are substantively free to achieve such vital ends as literacy (the ability to read, think, and speak effectively within her own discipline), or the ability to choose and move freely among alternative theoretical traditions, or the ability to participate with dignity in the public [professional] life of her community.

In terms of academic economics, this suggests that the removal of intellectual unfreedoms such as those described by the post-autistic petitioners ought to be regarded as basic prerequisites for 'good science.'[22] Here too Sen's capabilities approach offers a useful complement to McCloskey's rhetoric by stressing the multiple dimensions of freedom, not just the individual freedom to act (what Sen calls the 'process' aspect of freedom) but also the 'opportunity' aspect: the complex set of social/institutional conditions that enable or impede individual action. Both are pivotal to the process of intellectual development. Hence, Sen argues, 'we have to see individual freedom as a social commitment,' meaning that the expansion of individual freedom requires a commitment to change/modify social arrangements in order to expand the opportunities available to individuals. In other words, if all individuals are to enjoy to the substantive (not merely formal) freedom to lead choiceworthy intellectual lives, the community must assume the burden (subject to constraints, of course) of providing the resources to permit individuals to develop these essential ends. On this view, each academic community must be held to a normative standard:

Do prevailing institutional arrangements enable all members of the community to lead good intellectual lives, if they so choose? If not, then the community has an obligation, in the name of justice – and arguably also in the name of science – to design and implement policies that enhance the capability of people to achieve the essential intellectual functions (Burczak 2003, p. 6).

This combination of liberal and Aristotelian notions of science yields a complex notion of 'intellectual development as freedom,' arguably similar to Adam's Smith view of the moral and institutional requirements for a free society (Evensky 1993). In other words, as Sen and McCloskey each make abundantly clear, these ideas are native to our disciplinary discourse. Their principles stand on the same ground as the eighteenth-century Scottish Enlightenment liberalism from which modern economics itself emerged. This gives non-mainstream economists a much better place to stand when advocating changes to current disciplinary practices by allowing them (us), to embrace pluralism not just as a temporary means of 'crisis management' but as a genuine normative commitment, a commitment derived from the intellectual foundations of economics itself, that is, from our commitment to the intrinsic and instrumental value of human freedom (including intellectual freedom) itself.

Conclusion

The breadth and influence of rhetoric and postmodernism in economics have grown considerably since 1990.[23] What has emerged is far more than a flowering of McCloskey's project. It is a diverse set of overlapping conversations that has brought a new spirit of pluralism to economics and opened up several promising avenues for economic theory and policy beyond the grand designs of Cold War liberalism and Marxism.

McCloskey will claim only modest success for her *Rhetoric of Economics* (1983, 1985, 1998). 'I think the first edition and my later writings made a space in economics for thinking about the conversation' (McCloskey 1985 [1998], p. 189). She never made as much of an impact on mainstream economists as she would have liked. But she certainly gave heart and voice to many (libertarian, Marxists, and feminist economists, and scholars in several neighboring fields) who knew economics to be a liberal arts subject that is far broader than its modernist self-image.

Among the least persuaded have been the economic methodologists. Many found it hard to embrace McCloskey's program, in part because Donald's initial intervention rode roughshod over their field of expertise, jumping straight over their heads to declare an end to all talk of Method. These unrelieved hostilities continue to inspire inflated claims and counterclaims about the 'pomo.' Roger Backhouse, for example, characterizes postmodernism as an utterly relativistic view of knowledge that provides no absolute criteria by which to demonstrate the scientific inadequacy of mainstream neoclassicism (or any other dubious research program) and thus grants to each discourse community the unassailable right to 'create its own truth' (Backhouse 1997). He therefore dismisses it as a toothless and conservative approach to economic methodology and epistemology. 'The conservatism of [postmodernism] is emphasized by noting that it can be used to defend astrology or any other body of beliefs that is held by an identifiable community' (ibid., p. 24).

This may be a fair reading of the early Kuhn or certain radical strands of postmodernism. But it misses completely the openness and heterogeneity of 'intellectual community' envisioned by McCloskey, and the way in which her notion of rhetoric stands foursquare against the mercantilist tendency for paradigm communities to become autarkic and disconnected from the public spaces of academic debate. Rhetoric (or postmodernism *a la* McCloskey) is not the cause but rather the antidote for this kind of intellectual isolationism.

Far from bringing the quest for progress in economic science to a nihilistic end, rhetoric and postmodernism are helping to renew our professional enterprise by constructively rethinking the achievements and atrocities of twentieth-century economic modernism. The history of centrally planned socialism and communism surely rank near the top of this list but they are followed closely by the checkered legacies of socially engineered 'free enterprise'. After the fall of the Berlin Wall and numerous failed attempts to create free-market capitalism from the top down, we may now be in a better position to appreciate the postmodern wisdom of Czech President Václav Havel's statement to the World Economic Forum in 1992:

> The Fall of Communism can be regarded as a sign that modern thought – based on the premise that the world is objectively knowable, and that the knowledge so obtained can be absolutely generalized – has come to a final crisis … a signal that the era of arrogant, absolutist reason is drawing to a close and that it is high time to draw conclusions from that fact. (Havel 1992a)

Havel's postmodern point is that the statist hubris of Soviet central planners and Keynesian demand managers is but one face of economic modernism. Equally dangerous, in his view, is the utopian and authoritarian dogmatism of free-market economists. 'The cult of "systemically pure" market economics can be as dangerous as Marxist ideology because it comes from the same mental position' (Havel 1992b, p. 114).

Deirdre McCloskey's colorful campaign to save economics from itself bears more than a passing resemblance to John Maynard Keynes's well-known efforts to rescue liberal capitalism in the 1930s. Both were responding to an acute sense of economic, political, and intellectual crisis. As Dow observes:

> In [Keynes's] case it was the result of disillusionment about the inevitability of progress brought by the experience of the First World War and the shifting disposition

of economic and political power. ... [E]conomics at the turn of the 20th century was in the throes of mimicking classical mechanics in an attempt to portray economics as a science rather than a moral science. ... Keynes [however] came to economics from philosophy, and a concern to establish the basis for action in belief under uncertainty. Like Smith, Keynes appreciated the importance of rhetoric as a vehicle for persuasion in the absence of demonstrable propositions. (Dow 2001, pp. 72–3)

It may also be important to note that McCloskey's intervention, like Keynes's, was infused with a strong sense of national identity, and was undertaken at a time when her nation's identity was shifting (culturally, economically, and politically) from unchallenged hegemon to one nation among others.

The new conversations initiated by McCloskey et al. may become more important in the years to come as Cold War generations of economists retire from the field. More than Deirdre may know (and probably more than Donald would ever have imagined), her writings and commitment to pluralism are helping to persuade many heterodox economists to surrender the illusory guarantees of big-S Science and the bunker mentality of 'my paradigm, right or wrong' in exchange for a liberal pluralism that offers them and their ideas a better chance to flourish in the economic conversations of the twenty-first century. One day she may inspire even more to join the pluralist fold if her explorations of Christian feminism and Smithian moral sentiments should cause her to rethink her 3"x5"-card anti-socialism. But this will be a story, let us hope, for another day.

Rhetoric and postmodernism have already helped to shift the economic conversation from Cold War certainties to post-Cold War uncertainties; and therein lie a wealth of new opportunities for all of us to talk seriously about what is to be done.

Acknowledgement

I would like to thank Joe Blosser, Neil Browne, Ted Burczak, John Davis, Sheila Dow, Steve Horwitz, Ed McNertney, Judith Mehta, Dave Prychitko, Jochen Runde, and Warren Samuels for valuable comments on an earlier draft, and especially Yecenia Camarillo for what must have seemed like (and were) endless months of patience, love, and encouragement.

Notes

1. Ziliak describes McCloskey's rhetorical critique of economics as the tough but loving criticism of a lifelong partner (Ziliak 2001).
2. Klamer (1993) explores the connections between this economic positivism and the larger intellectual culture of modernism.
3. The reflexive style of McCloskey's critique may have been inspired by Coase's suggestion that methodological issues be seen as economic issues (Coase 1982 [1994]).
4. See also Amariglio (1990) and Klamer (1993).
5. This formulation follows closely the epistemological arguments of Richard Rorty who urges philosophers to reorient their discussions of truth from the Platonic question of 'how to

commune with the mind of God' to the Socratic one of 'how to improve the production and exchange of ideas among mere mortals' (McCloskey 1994, p. 84). See also Davis (1990).

6. For example, the economic methodologist Mark Blaug writes, 'What methodology can do is to provide criteria for the acceptance and rejection of research programs, setting standards that will help us to discriminate between wheat and chaff' (Blaug 1980, p. 264). This precisely illustrates McCloskey's complaint: 'The unanswerable question the Popperian philosophers want to go on posing is how we can demarcate good from bad argument forever and ever' (McCloskey 1994, p. 266).

7. McCloskey describes this type of elitism as 'sneering': The main purpose of sneering is to protect the sneerer from having to learn anything new. ... If one can simply sneer at neoclassical economics (or Marxist economics or institutional economics or whatever), then one does not have to follow the Maxim of Presumed Seriousness. ... The sneer is an assertion of rank. The economist sneers loftily at the sociologist, asserting rank and a fully finished education (McCloskey 1994, p. 349).

8. According to the philosophers of mathematics Philip Davis and Reuben Hersh, 'the line between complete and incomplete [mathematical] proof is always somewhat fuzzy, and often controversial' (1981, p. 34). 'The daily experience of mathematicians ... shows that mathematical truth, like other kinds of truth, is fallible, corrigible, tentative, and evolving, as is every other kind of human knowledge' (ibid., p. 406).

9. Of course McCloskey is not the first to suggest this metaphor. But coming from an avowed Chicago School economist, it remains a noteworthy feature of McCloskey's story. This continues to provoke complaints from McCloskey's critics, about which more below.

10. There is no reference to postmodernism in the published proceedings of the 1986 conference on the Rhetoric of Economics organized by Klamer and McCloskey (Klamer et al. 1988). This underscores the differences – intellectual as well as temporal – between McCloskey's rhetoric project and what later emerged as economic postmodernism.

11. The term postmodernism seems to have prevailed over other possible candidates (such as post-structuralism or deconstructionism) as a conscious compromise between McCloskey's rhetorical critique of modernism and the Marxist/post-structuralist heritage of Amariglio et al. From the beginning this created some unease about the label, even among its proponents (Klamer and McCloskey 1989). In a recent essay, Klamer argues that postmodern has never been an apt label for McCloskey's views or his own:

> McCloskey's case calls for alternative labels. ... The label I prefer is neo-traditionalist ... It makes one suspicious of radical programs, yet at the same time makes one susceptible to change. It makes one oppose any form of fundamentalism including the fundamentalist adherence to what was. Neo-traditionalism cuts through modernist dualisms, 20th-century ideological oppositions; it encapsulates modernist elements together with postmodernist sensibilities and then some more, such as interest in, and concern for, the traditions that frame our lives. (Klamer 2001, pp. 80–81)

12. These critical perspectives within the 'rethinking Marxism' school owe a special debt to the British post-Marxists Antony Cutler, Barry Hindess, Paul Hirst, and Athar Hussain whose path-breaking arguments in *Marx's 'Capital' and Capitalism Today* (1977) brought the philosophical anti-humanism of Althusser and Foucault to bear on the basic concepts, methods, and epistemology of Marxian economics. Their arguments became a catalyst for the emergence of the anti-essentialist Marxism that has come to characterize the RM school.

13. 'The anti-bourgeois character of modernism in all of its forms testifies to a lordly tendency among intellectuals to spurn persuasion. Intellectuals make up modernisms, and want them to be exclusive and regulated. Modernism is proudly, even obnoxiously, elitist' (McCloskey 2001, p. 112).

14. See especially the Austrian/Marxian dialogue on capitalism and justice published recently in *Rethinking Marxism* (Burczak 1998; Prychitko 1998; Boettke 1998; Cullenberg 1998) and the even broader discussion among free-market, feminist, postcolonial, and Marxist perspectives in McCloskey (2000c), Spivak (2000), and Charusheela (2000).

15. These works include Cullenberg (1992), Amariglio and Ruccio (1994), Gibson-Graham (1996), Wolff and Resnick (1996), Gibson-Graham et al. (2001), DeMartino (2000, 2003), and Burczak (1996/97, 2001, 2002, 2003).
16. DeMartino's argument stands in contrast to the views of Andrej Walicki (1988), Isaiah Berlin (1958) and others, *pace* McCloskey, who see Marxian notions of freedom and justice as little more than the coercive paternalism commonly associated with the totalitarianism of the former USSR and other putatively Marxist states.
17. 'An economics that does not recognize its own rhetoric can avoid facing the arguments of opponents indefinitely. That is how things have gone so far, one "paradigm" (Thomas Kuhn cringes) ignoring another' (McCloskey 1994, p. 387).
18. As John King notes, 'eminent practitioners of several varieties of heterodox economic theory' increasingly acknowledge that there is no 'single correct alternative to neoclassical economics' (King 2002, p. 84).
19. This parallels Sheila Dow's argument that a vigorous pluralism also serves to protect the rights of intellectual minorities (and thus sustains intellectual diversity) within discourse communities. This promotes better science (and scientists) in the long run by maintaining a diverse array of frameworks from which new ideas can be generated and preventing any one perspective from becoming an uncontested orthodoxy (Dow 1990, p. 155).
20. Mäki (1999) also suggests a possible inconsistency between the economics and meta-economics of non-mainstream thinkers.
21. In the words of Sir John Hicks: 'The liberal, or non-interference, principles of the classical (Smithian and Ricardian) economists were not, in the first place, economic principles; they were an application to economics of principles that were thought to apply to a much wider field. The contention that economic freedom made for economic efficiency was no more than a secondary support' (cited in Sen 1999, p. 28).
22. Economists are surprisingly disinclined to associate 'good science' with intellectual freedom, perhaps because our received (modernist) images of science and pedagogy are so heavily steeped in the values and techniques of central planning.
23. An excellent sampling of these works is Cullenberg et al. (2001).

References

Althusser, Louis, and E. Balibar (1970), *Reading Capital*, translated by B. Brewster, London: New Left Books.
Amariglio, Jack (1984), 'Economic history and the theory of primitive socio-economic development', unpublished Ph.D. thesis, Department of Economics, University of Massachusetts, Amherst.
Amariglio, Jack (1987), 'Marxism against economic science: Althusser's legacy', *Research in Political Economy* **10**, 159–94.
Amariglio, Jack (1988), 'The body, economic discourse, and power: an economist's introduction to Foucault', *History of Political Economy*, **20** (4), 583–613.
Amariglio, Jack (1990), 'Economics as a postmodern discourse', in Warren J. Samuels (ed.), *Economics as Discourse*, Boston, MA: Kluwer Academic Publishers, pp. 15–46.
Amariglio, Jack (2001), 'Writing in thirds', in Stephen Cullenberg, Jack Amariglio and David F. Ruccio (eds), *Postmodernism, Economics and Knowledge*, New York: Routledge, pp. 129–42.
Amariglio, Jack A. and David F. Ruccio (1994), 'Postmodernism, Marxism, and the critique of modern economic thought', *Rethinking Marxism* **7** (3), 7–35.
Backhouse, Roger E. (1997), *Truth and Progress in Economic Knowledge*, Cheltenham, UK and Lyme USA: Edward Elgar.
Berlin, I. (1958), *Two Concepts of Liberty*, Oxford: Clarendon Press.
Bernstein, M. A. (1999), 'Economic knowledge, professional authority, and the state', in Robert Garnett, Jr. (ed.), *What Do Economists Know?*, London: Routledge, pp. 103–23.
Blaug, Mark (1980), *The Methodology of Economics*, Cambridge: Cambridge University Press.
Boettke, Peter J. (1994), 'Storytelling and the human sciences', in Peter J. Boettke and David L. Prychitko (eds), *The Market Process: Essays in Contemporary Austrian Economics*, Aldershot, UK and Brookfield, US: Edward Elgar, pp. 179–86.

Boettke, Peter J. (1998), 'Rethinking ourselves: negotiating values in the political economy of post-Communism', *Rethinking Marxism* **10** (2), 85–95.

Boettke, Peter J. and David L. Prychitko (eds), (1994), *The Market Process: Essays in Contemporary Austrian Economics*, Aldershot, UK and Brookfield US: Edward Elgar.

Burczak, Theodore (1996/97), 'Socialism after Hayek', *Rethinking Marxism*, **9** (3), 1–18.

Burczak, Theodore (1998), 'Appropriation, responsibility, and agreement', *Rethinking Marxism*, **10** (2), 96–105.

Burczak, Theodore (2001), 'Ellerman's labor theory of property and the injustice of capitalist exploitation', *Review of Social Economy*, **59** (2), 161–83.

Burczak, Theodore (2002), 'A critique of Kirzner's finders-keepers defense of profit', *Review of Austrian Economics*, **15** (1), 75–90.

Burczak, Theodore (2003), 'The Nussbaum-Sen capability theory of social justice and Hayekian knowledge problems', paper presented at the ICAPE conference on The Future of Heterodox Economics, University of Missouri at Kansas City.

Callari, A. (1981), 'The classicals' analysis of capitalism', unpublished Ph.D. thesis, Department of Economics, University of Massachusetts, Amherst.

Cambridge 27 (2001), 'Opening up economics', *Post-Autistic Economics Newsletter*, 7 (July), article 1.

Charusheela, S. (2000), 'History, love, and politics', *Rethinking Marxism*, **12** (4), 45–61.

Charusheela, S. (forthcoming), 'Postcolonial thought, postmodernism, and economics: questions of ontology and ethics', in E. Zein-Elabdin and S. Charusheela, (eds), *Postcolonialism Meets Economics*, London: Routledge.

Coase, Ronald H. (1982 [1994]), 'How should economists choose?' in R.H. Coase, *Essays on Economics and Economists*, Chicago: University of Chicago Press, pp. 15–33.

Colander, David (2000), 'The death of neoclassical economics', *Journal of the History of Economic Thought*, **22** (2), 127–43.

Craver, Earlene, and A. Leijonhufvud (1987), 'Economics in America: the Continental influence', *History of Political Economy*, **19** (2), 173–82.

Cullenberg, Stephen (1992), 'Socialism's burden: toward a thin definition of socialism', *Rethinking Marxism*, **5** (2), 64–83.

Cullenberg, S. Stephen (1998), 'Exploitation, appropriation, and exclusion: locating capitalist injustice', *Rethinking Marxism*, **10** (2), 66–75.

Cullenberg, Stephen, Jack Amariglio and David F. Ruccio (2001), 'Introduction' in Stephen Cullenberg, Jack Amariglio and David F. Ruccio (eds), *Postmodernism, Economics, and Knowledge*, New York: Routledge, pp. 3–37.

Cullenberg, Stephen, Jack Amariglio and David F. Ruccio (eds) (2001), *Postmodernism, Economics, and Knowledge*, New York: Routledge.

Cutler, A., B. Hindess, P. Hirst and A. Hussain (1977), *Marx's 'Capital' and Capitalism Today*, vol. 1, London: Routledge and Kegan Paul.

Davidson, P. (2002), Message to post-Keynesian thought listserv www.csf.colorado.edu/pkt, August 23.

Davidson, P. (2003a), Message to post-Keynesian thought listserv www.csf.colorado.edu/pkt, March 5.

Davidson, P. (2003b), Message to post-Keynesian thought listserv www.csf.colorado.edu/pkt, March 6.

Davidson, P. (2003c), Message to post-Keynesian thought listserv www.csf.colorado.edu/pkt, March 9.

Davis, John B. (1990), 'Rorty's contribution to McCloskey's understanding of conversation as the methodology of economics', in W.J. Samuels, (ed.), *Research in the History of Economic Thought and Methodology*, vol. 7, Greenwich, CT: JAI Press, pp. 73–85.

Davis, John B. (1997), 'Comment', in Andrea Salanti, and Ernesto Screpanti, (eds), *Pluralism in Economics*, Cheltenham, UK and Lyme USA: Edward Elgar, pp. 207–11.

Davis, John B. (2003), 'Heterodox economics, the fragmentation of the mainstream, and embedded individual analysis', paper presented at the ICAPE conference on the Future of Heterodox Economics, University of Missouri at Kansas City.

Davis, P.J. and R. Hersh (1981), *The Mathematical Experience*, Boston, MA: Houghton Mifflin.

Dean, J.W. (1981), 'The dissolution of the Keynesian consensus', in D. Bell and I. Kristol (eds), *The Crisis in Economic Theory*, New York: Basic Books, pp. 19–34.

DeMartino, G.F. (2000), *Global Economy, Global Justice: Theoretical Objections and Policy Alternatives to Neoliberalism*, London: Routledge.

DeMartino, G.F. (2003), 'Realizing class justice', *Rethinking Marxism*, **15** (1), 1–32.

Desai, M. (1979), *Marxian Economics*, Oxford: Basil Blackwell.

Dewey, John (1939 [1979]), *Freedom and Culture*, New York: Paragon Books.

Dolan, E.G. (1976), 'Austrian economics as extraordinary science', in E.G. Dolan, (ed.), *The Foundations of Modern Austrian Economics*, Kansas City: Sheed and Ward, pp. 3–18.

Dow, Sheila C. (1990), 'Beyond dualism', *Cambridge Journal of Economics*, **14** (2), 143–57.

Dow, Sheila C. (2001), 'Modernism and Postmodernism: A Dialectical Analysis', in Stephen Cullenberg, Jack Amariglio and David F. Ruccio (eds), *Postmodernism, Economics and Knowledge*, New York: Routledge, pp. 71–6.

Eichner, A. (1979), *A Guide to Post-Keynesian Economics*, White Plains, NY: M.E. Sharpe.

Ellerman, D.P. (1991), 'Myth and metaphor in orthodox economics', *Journal of Post Keynesian Economics*, **13** (4), 545–64.

Evensky, J. (1993), 'Ethics and the Invisible Hand', *Journal of Economic Perspectives*, **7** (2), 197–205.

Feiner, S.F. (1994), 'A portrait of *Homo economicus* as a young man', in M. Woodmansee and M. Osteen (eds), *The New Economic Criticism*, London: Routledge, pp. 193–209.

Feyerabend, Paul (1975), *Against Method*, London: Verso.

Folbre, Nancy, and H. Hartmann (1988), 'The rhetoric of self-interest: ideology of gender in economic theory', in Arjo Klamer, D.N. McCloskey and Robert M. Solow (eds), *The Consequences of Economic Rhetoric*, Cambridge: Cambrdge University Press, pp. 184–206.

Foucault, Michel (1973), *The Order of Things: An Archaeology of the Human Sciences*, New York: Vintage.

Friedman, J. (1989), 'The new consensus: I. the Fukuyama thesis', *Critical Review*, **3** (3 and 4), 373–410.

Garnett, Robert (1994), 'Value, man, and markets in modern economic discourse', unpublished Ph.D. thesis, Department of Economics: University of Massachusetts, Amherst.

Gibson-Graham, J.K. (1996), *The End of Capitalism (As We Knew It), A Feminist Critique of Political Economy*, Oxford: Blackwell.

Gibson-Graham, J.K., S. Resnick and R. Wolff (eds) (2001), *Representing Class: Essays in Postmodern Marxism*, Durham: Duke University Press.

Hahn, F.H., and F.P.R. Brechling (eds), (1965), *The Theory of Interest Rates*, London: Macmillan.

Havel, Vaclav (1992a), 'The end of the modern era', *New York Times*, Sunday, March 1.

Havel, Vaclav (1992b), *Summer Meditations*, translated by P. Wilson, New York: Alfred A. Knopf.

Heilbroner, Robert L. (1988), 'Rhetoric and ideology', in Arjo Klamer, D.N. McCloskey and Robert M. Solow (eds), *The Consequences of Economic Rhetoric*, Cambridge: Cambrdge University Press, pp. 38–46.

Heilbroner, Robert, and W. Milberg (1995), *The Crisis of Vision in Modern Economic Thought*, Cambridge: Cambridge University Press.

Hutchison, Terence W. (1938 [1960]), *The Significance and Basic Postulates of Economic Theory*, 2nd edn, New York: Kelley.

King, J. E. (2002), 'Three arguments for pluralism', *Journal of Australian Political Economy*, **50** (December), 82–8.

Klamer, Arjo (1983), *Conversations with Economists*, Totowa, NJ: Rowman and Allanheld.

Klamer, Arjo (1993), 'Modernism in economics: an interpretation beyond physics', in Neil de Marchi, (ed.), *Non-Natural Science: Reflecting on the Enterprise of 'More Heat than Light'*, Durham: Duke University Press, pp. 223–48.

Klamer, Arjo (2001), 'Late modernism and the loss of character in economics', in Stephen Cullenberg, Jack Amariglio and David F. Ruccio (eds), *Postmodernism, Economics and Knowledge*, New York: Routledge pp. 77–101.

Klamer, Arjo, and D.N. McCloskey (1988), 'Economics in the human conversation', in Arjo Klamer, D.N. McCloskey and Robert M. Solow (eds), *The Consequences of Economic Rhetoric*, Cambridge: Cambrdge University Press, 3–20.

Klamer, Arjo, and D.N. McCloskey (1989), 'The rhetoric of disagreement', *Rethinking Marxism*, **2** (Fall), 140–61.

Klamer, Arjo, D.N. McCloskey and Robert M. Solow (eds) (1988), *The Consequences of Economic Rhetoric*, Cambridge: Cambridge University Press.

Kregel, J. (1975), *The Reconstruction of Political Economy: An Introduction to Post-Keynesian Economics*, London: Macmillan.

Kuhn, Thomas S. (1970), *The Structure of Scientific Revolutions*. 2nd edn, Chicago: University of Chicago Press.

Latour, Bruno (1988), *We Have Never Been Modern*, translated by C. Porter, Cambridge, MA: Harvard University Press.

Latour, Bruno (1993), *We Have Never Been Modern*, translated by C. Porter, Cambridge, MA: Harvard University Press.

Lavoie, Don (ed.), (1991), *Hermeneutics and Economics*, London: Routledge.

Lavoie, Don (1994), 'A political philosophy for the market process', in Peter J. Boettke and David L. Prychitko (eds), *The Market Process: Essays in Contemporary Austrian Economics*, Aldershot, UK and Brookfield, US: Edward Elgar, pp. 274–86.

Lee, F.S. (2002), 'The Association for Heterodox Economics: past, present, and future', *Journal of Australian Political Economy*, **50** (December), 29–43.

Lucas, Robert E., Jr. (1975), 'An equilibrium model of the business cycle', *Journal of Political Economy*, **83** (December), 1113–44.

Lucas, Robert E., Jr. (1976), 'Economic policy evaluation: a critique', *Journal of Monetary Economics*, **1** (April), 19–46.

Lyotard, Jean-François (1984), *The Postmodern Condition: A Report on Knowledge*, translated by G. Bennington and B. Massumi, Minneapolis: University of Minnesota Press.

Madison, G.B. (1994), 'Hermeneutical integrity: a guide for the perplexed', in Peter J. Boettke and David L. Prychitko (eds), *The Market Process: Essays in Contemporary Austrian Economics*, Aldershot, UK and Brookfield, US: Edward Elgar, pp. 201–11.

Mäki, Uskali (1999), 'Science as a free market: a reflexivity test in an economics of economics', *Perspectives on Science*, **7** (4), 486–509.

McCloskey, D.N. (1983), 'The rhetoric of economics', *Journal of Economic Literature*, **31** (June), 434–61.

McCloskey, D.N. (1994), *Knowledge and Persuasion in Economics*, Cambridge: Cambridge University Press.

McCloskey, D.N. (1985 [1998]). *The Rhetoric of Economics*, 2nd edn, Madison: University of Wisconsin Press.

McCloskey, D.N. (2000a), 'Kelly Green golf shoes and the intellectual range from m to n', in D.M. McCloskey, *How to be Human * *Though an Economist*, Ann Arbor: University of Michigan Press, pp. 481–517.

McCloskey, D.N. (2000b), 'The Invisible college and the death of learning', in D.M. McCloskey, *How to be Human* *Though an Economist*, Ann Arbor: University of Michigan Press, pp. 155–60.

McCloskey, D. N. (2000c), 'Postmodern market feminism', *Rethinking Marxism*, **12** (4), 27–37.

McCloskey, D.N. (2001), 'The genealogy of postmodernism: an economist's guide', in Stephen Cullenberg, Jack Amariglio and David F. Ruccio (eds), *Postmodernism, Economics and Knowledge*, New York: Routledge, pp. 102–28.

Mirowski, Philip (1987), 'The philosophical bases of institutionalist economics', *Journal of Economic Issues* 21 (September), 1001–38.

Mirowski, Philip (1988), 'Rhetoric, mathematics, and the nature of neoclassical economic theory', in Arjo Klamer, D.N. McCloskey and Robert M. Solow (eds), *The Consequences of Economic Rhetoric*, Cambridge: Cambrdge University Press, pp. 117–45.

Morgan, Mary, and M. Rutherford (1998), 'American economics: the character of the transformation', In Mary Morgan and M. Rutherford (eds), *From Interwar Pluralism to Postwar Neoclassicism*, Durham, NC: Duke University Press, pp. 1–26.

Nelson, R.H. (1991), *Reaching for Heaven on Earth: The Theological Meaning of Economics*, Lanham, MD: Rowman and Littlefield.

Post-Autistic Economics Newsletter (2000), 'Open letter from economics students to professors and others responsible for the teaching of this discipline', 2 (October), article 3.

Post-Autistic Economics Newsletter (2000), 'Petition for a debate on the teaching of economics', 2 (October), article 4.

Post-Autistic Economics Newsletter (2001), 'The Kansas City proposal: an international open letter (to all economics departments)', 8 (September), article 1.

Popper, K. (1945), *The Open Society and its Enemies*, London: Routledge.

Prychitko, D. (1998), 'Hayekian socialism: rethinking Burczak, Ellerman, and Kirzner', *Rethinking Marxism* **10** (2), 75–85.

Redman, D.A. (1994), 'Karl Popper's theory of science and econometrics: the rise and fall of social engineering', *Journal of Economic Issues,* 28 (1), 67–99.

Resnick, S.A. and Wolff, R.D. (1982), 'Marxist epistemology: the critique of economic determinism', *Social Text* 6 (Fall), 31–72.

Resnick, S.A. and Wolff, R.D. (1987), *Knowledge and Class: A Marxian Critique of Political Economy*, Chicago: University of Chicago Press.

Resnick, S.A. and Wolff, R.D. (1988), 'Marxian theory and the rhetorics of economics', in Arjo Klamer, D.N. McCloskey and Robert M. Solow (eds), *The Consequences of Economic Rhetoric*, Cambridge: Cambrdge University Press, pp. 47–63.

Rorty, Richard (1979), *Philosophy and the Mirror of Nature*, Princeton, NJ: Princeton University Press.

Ruccio, David F. (1984), 'Optimal planning theory and theories of socialist planning', unpublished Ph.D. thesis, Department of Economics, University of Massachusetts, Amherst.

Ruccio, David F. (1991), 'Postmodernism and economics', *Journal of Post Keynesian Economics*, **13** (4), 495–510.

Ruccio, David F., and Jack Amariglio (forthcoming), *Postmodern Moments in Modern Economics*, Princeton, NJ: Princeton University Press.

Samuels, Warren J. (1990), 'The self-referentiability of Thorstein Veblen's theory of the preconceptions of economic science', *Journal of Economic Issues*, **24** (3), 695–718.

Samuelson, Paul A. (1964), *Economics: An Introductory Analysis*, 6th edn, New York: McGraw-Hill.

Sargent, Thomas J., and N. Wallace (1975), 'Rational expectations, the optimal monetary instrument, and the optimal money supply rule', *Journal of Political Economy*, **83** (April), 241–55.

Sen, Amartya (1999), *Development as Freedom*, New York: Albert Knopf.

Sent, Esther-Mirjam (forthcoming), 'Pluralisms in economics', in S. Kellert, H. Longino, and K. Waters (eds), *Scientific Pluralism*, Minneapolis: University of Minnesota Press.

Spivak, G.C. (2000), 'Other things are never equal', *Rethinking Marxism*, **12** (4), 37–45.

Steedman, Ian (1977), *Marx After Sraffa*, London: New Left Books.

Stein, H. (1996), *The Fiscal Revolution in America*, 2nd revised edn, Washington, DC: AEI Press.

Strassmann, D. (1993a), 'Not a free market: the rhetoric of disciplinary authority in economics', in M.A. Ferber and J.A. Nelson (eds), *Beyond Economic Man: Feminist Theory and Economics*, Chicago: University of Chicago Press, pp. 54–68.

Strassmann, D. (1993b), 'The stories of economics and the power of the storyteller', *History of Political Economy*, 25 (1), 147–65.

Walicki, A. (1988), 'Karl Marx as a philosopher of freedom', *Critical Review*, **2** (4), 10–58.

Wolff, R.D. and Resnick, S.A. (1996), 'Markets, private property, Socialism and Communism', in C. Polychroniou and H.R. Targ (eds), *Marxism Today: Essays on Capitalism, Socialism and Strategies for Social Change*, Westport, CT and London: Praeger, pp. 119–42.

Ziliak, S.T. (2001), 'D.N. McCloskey and the rhetoric of a scientific economics', in S.T. Ziliak (ed.), *Measurement and Meaning in Economics: The Essential Deirdre McCloskey*, Cheltenham, UK and Northampton, MA, USA: Edward Elgar, pp. ix–xxvi.

13 Models in economics
Marcel Boumans

In general, I believe that one who claims to understand the principles of flight can reasonably be expected to be able to make a flying machine, and that understanding business cycles means the ability to make them too, in roughly the same sense. (Lucas 1981, p. 8)

Introduction

At the fifth European meeting of the *Econometric Society* held in Namur, Belgium, 1935, Jan Tinbergen (1903–1994) read a paper on 'A mathematical theory of business cycle policy'. As usual, a report of this meeting appeared in *Econometrica*, the society's journal. This time the report was written by Hans Staehle and published in 1937. The report noted that Tinbergen's paper consisted of three parts:

1. the presentation of a simplified business cycle 'mechanism',
2. an analysis of its various 'influencing coefficients' (*Beeinflussingskoeffizienten*), with a view to discovering those which might be modified by policy, and
3. an analysis of the conditions which would have to be satisfied in order to achieve the aims set by various types of policy. (Staehle 1937, p. 87)

The paper appeared as part of Tinbergen's article 'Quantitative Fragen der Konjunkturpolitik' in *Weltwirtschaftliches Archiv*, published in 1935. At the end of the article, there were summaries in three different languages, English, French and Spanish, in which the word 'mechanism' was replaced with 'scheme', 'schéma' and 'esquema' respectively. However, in the article itself, Tinbergen used the term '*Modell*'. This was perhaps the first time an economist used the term 'model' to denote a specific mathematical product of one's research. This cautious name-giving marked the beginning of a new practice in economics, today loosely called modeling.[1]

Up until then, the term 'model' had been used to denote a substantive analogy, as distinct from a formal analogy as denoted by the term 'scheme' (on this distinction, see Nagel 1961, p. 110). In substantive analogies, a system of elements possessing certain already familiar properties assumed to be related in known ways, is taken as a recipe for the construction of a theory for some second system. In formal analogies, the system that serves as the recipe is some familiar structure of mathematical relations. For example, in 1931 during the meeting of the Econometric Society at Lausanne, Ragnar Frisch used the term 'modèles mécaniques de "cycles"' (Staehle 1933, p. 83) to indicate that the pendulum is used as a substantive analogy to the business cycle. In the final section of his essay in the Cassel volume (1933), this model was explicated and designated as a 'mechanical analogy'. Frisch visualized the business cycle as a pendulum above which a receptacle filled with water is suspended. Water accumulating in the receptacle above the pendulum was seen as analogous to Schumpeterian innovations (Frisch 1933, pp. 203–5).

To see what the new practice of 'modeling' involved, let us first have a closer look at Tinbergen's article (1935). The 'model' was intended to be a macro-dynamic 'Darstellung'[2] of reality and was 'constructed' to investigate problems of business-cycle explanations and problems of business-cycle policy (Tinbergen 1935, pp. 370–71). The model was seen as a simplified representation of reality. The problem facing the economist was presented as finding the right degree of simplification in order to achieving an appropriate balance between approximating reality as close as possible while keeping the model manageable. Tinbergen recommended investigating a wide range of different models as the specific model discussed in the article could only provide incomplete answers.

The model consisted of 18 equations connecting 18 variables. Eight of these equations represented definitions, some of which were clarified by a scheme of economic circulation. The other ten equations expressed 'reactions' (Staehle 1937, p. 87) of some variables to others. Although these reaction equations were suggested by actual statistical enquiries, they were still abstract expressions. The parameter values were not yet measured but represented by symbols. The model was not as much a representation of a real economy, as it was a blueprint of a model of the Dutch economy consisting of 24 equations that Tinbergen presented to the Dutch Society of Economics and Statistics one year later (Tinbergen 1936a). This 1936 model was the very first macroeconometric model in the history of economics.[3]

A need for a methodology of models

Halfway through the 1930s, a new practice was born that was based on instruments called 'models'. This practice is characterized by building and applying empirical models, i.e. representations of (aspects of) the world. The aim of this chapter is to explore these kinds of representations. As a result, we will distance ourselves from various philosophical accounts focusing on theoretical models. These are often based on logicians' views on models and theories, emphasizing axioms and theory structure, and have little to do with the way empirical economists use models.[4] Even the most authoritarian axiomatizer of economics, John von Neumann, warned against too much 'de-empirization', as axiomatization was called by him: 'at a great distance from its empirical source, or after much "abstract" inbreeding, a mathematical subject is in danger of degeneration' (1961, p. 9). The model account explored here will take expressly the practice of empirical research as its exit road.

Our aim is to understand the practice of economic research, but we are not discussing so-called 'lower-case-m' methodology, that is to say, the study of methods: the practical techniques employed by economists in the execution of their day-to-day professional activities (see Hands 2001, p. 3). The aim is to redirect the focus of methodology to models. One should note that only till quite recently, economic methodology was mainly focused on theories. For example, Mark Blaug's *Methodology of Economics* (1980) does not have any reference to 'model' in the index, except one to a concrete one, namely the IS-LM model. In D. Wade Hands' book on economic methodology, *Reflection without Rules*, the index contains apart from references to structuralist and semantic views on theory-model distinctions only Mary Morgan's account of models.

Models as representations
The tradition that led to Tinbergen's use of the concept of a mathematical model is rooted in the work by James Clerk Maxwell (1831–1879). Tinbergen studied physics at the University of Leiden where Paul Ehrenfest (1880–1933) had a major influence on his early scientific development. Ehrenfest in his turn was initiated into both the substance and the spirit of theoretical physics by Ludwig Boltzmann (1844–1906). Throughout his scientific career, Boltzmann admired, developed, and expounded Maxwell's ideas. In Maxwell's work, a heuristic shift took place that was to lead to the new method of modern physics. It was this method that Tinbergen applied in economics (Boumans 1993).[5]

Maxwell's heuristics of using analogies
In his first paper on electromagnetism, 'On Faraday's lines of force' (1855 [1965]) (see Boltzmann 1892 [1974]; Klein 1970, p. 56), Maxwell set out the method he intended to use. He suggested that to study effectively the considerable body of results from previous investigations, these results have to be simplified and reduced to 'a form in which the mind can grasp them'. On the one hand they could take the form of 'a purely mathematical formula', but then one would 'entirely lose sight of the phenomena to be explained' (Maxwell 1855 [1965], p. 155). On the other hand, if they were to take the form of a 'physical hypothesis', that is, an assumption as to the real nature of the phenomena to be explained, this would mean that 'we see the phenomena only through a medium', making us 'liable to that blindness to facts and rashness in assumption which a partial explanation encourages' (ibid., pp. 155–6):

We must therefore discover some method of investigation which allows the mind at every step to lay hold of a clear physical conception, without being committed to any theory founded on the physical science from which that conception is borrowed, so that it is neither drawn aside from the subject in pursuit of analytical subtleties, nor carried beyond the truth by a favourite hypothesis. (Maxwell 1855 [1965], p. 156)

To obtain physical ideas without adopting a physical theory we have to exploit 'physical analogies', 'that partial similarity between the laws of one science and those of another which makes each of them illustrate the other' (ibid., 156). In other words, to the extent that two physical systems obey laws with the same mathematical form, the behavior of one system can be understood by studying the behavior of the other, better known, system. Moreover, this can be done without making any hypothesis about the real nature of the system under investigation. However, Maxwell stated clearly that a physical analogy, valuable as it might be, was not a substitute for 'a mature theory, in which physical facts will be physically explained' (ibid., p. 159).

In a second paper, 'On physical lines of force' (1861) [1965], he went further still and constructed a mechanism based on fluid vortices and friction rollers moving inside cells with elastic walls that served as a mechanical model for electromagnetism. It was the analysis of this mechanical model that brought Maxwell to the first formulation of the electromagnetic theory of light. It was not until his 'Dynamical theory of the electromagnetic field' (1865) [1965] that the formulae become more detached from the mechanical models. Maxwell still used mechanical analogies, but he no longer specified them in detail. Instead, he looked for the general mechanical assumptions that were most suitable to lead to phenomena that are analogous to those of electromagnetism. In a letter written to Peter Guthrie Tait, Maxwell contrasted his vortex and particle model with the later, more schematic, dynamical analogy. 'The former is built up to show that the phenomena (of electromagnetism) are such as can be explained by mechanism. The nature of the mechanism is to the true mechanism what an orrery is to the Solar System. The latter is built on Lagrange's Dynamical Equations and is not wise about vortices' (quoted in Klein 1970, p. 57).

In a later paper, 'On the mathematical classification of physical quantities' (1871 [1965]), Maxwell drew a distinction between a 'physical analogy' and a 'mathematical or formal analogy'. In the case of a formal analogy, 'we learn that a certain system of quantities in a new science stand to one another in the same mathematical relations as a certain other system in an old science, which has already been reduced to a mathematical form, and its problems solved by mathematicians' (ibid., pp. 257–8). We can speak of a physical analogy when, in addition to a mathematical analogy between two physical systems, we can identify the entities or properties of both systems. To avoid confusion about the shift in the meaning of the concept 'physical analogy', we follow

Nagel (see above) by referring to this later interpretation of physical analogy as 'substantive analogy'.

Hertz's requirements for images

Maxwell's success with a theory based on dynamical analogies stimulated a variety of reactions among his contemporaries. Heinrich Hertz (1857–1894) was one of these. As Janik and Toulmin (1973) wrote about Hertz:

> Hertz had been trying to determine the precise nature of Maxwell's theory, by considering the several different sets of equations used by Maxwell to express his theory, and thus to discern what sorts of things Maxwell was asserting about the deeper nature of electromagnetic phenomena. It occurred to Hertz that, in actual fact, Maxwell was saying nothing at all about the physical nature of these phenomena. His equations were logical formulas which enabled him to deal with the phenomena and to understand how they operated. (Janik and Toulmin 1973, p. 142)

Or as Hertz himself put it more succinctly:

> To the question, 'What is Maxwell's theory?' I know of no shorter or more definite answer than the following: – Maxwell's theory is Maxwell's system of equations. (Hertz 1893 [1962], p. 21)

For Hertz, representations of mechanical phenomena could only be understood in the sense of Maxwell's dynamical analogies, which is obvious in the section 'Dynamical models' of his last work, *The Principles of Mechanics Presented in a New Form* (1899) [1956]. First he gave a definition of a 'dynamical model':

> A material system is said to be a dynamical model of a second system when the connections of the first can be expressed by such coordinates as to satisfy the following conditions:
>
> 1. That the number of coordinates of the first system is equal to the number of the second.
> 2. That with a suitable arrangement of the coordinates for both systems the same equations of condition exist.
> 3. That by this arrangement of the coordinates the expression for the magnitude of a displacement agrees in both systems. (Hertz 1899 [1956], p. 175)

From this definition, Hertz inferred that 'In order to determine beforehand the course of the natural motion of a material system, it is sufficient to have a model of that system. The model may be much simpler than the system whose motion it represents' (ibid., p. 176). However:

> it is impossible to carry our knowledge of the connections of the natural systems further than is involved in specifying models of the actual systems. We can then, in fact, have no knowledge as to whether the systems which we consider in mechanics

agree in any other respect with the actual systems of nature which we intend to consider, than in this alone, – that the one set of systems are models of the other. (Hertz 1899 [1956], p. 177)

While the 'model' was still considered as something material, its relation to the system of inquiry was on a par with the images (*Bilder*) that are formed of a system.[6]

The relation of a dynamical model to the system of which it is regarded as the model, is precisely the same as the relation of the images which our mind forms of things to the things themselves. For if we regard the condition of the model as the representation of the condition of the system, then the consequents of this representation, which according to the laws of this representation must appear, are also the representation of the consequents which must proceed from the original object according to the laws of this original object. The agreement between mind and nature may therefore be likened to the agreement between two systems which are models of one another, and we can even account for this agreement by assuming that the mind is capable of making actual dynamical models of things, and of working with them. (Hertz 1899 [1956], p. 177)

Right in the beginning of the introduction of his *Principles of Mechanics*, Hertz formulated the three requirements that an image should fulfill:

> The images which we may form of things are not determined without ambiguity by the requirement that the consequents of the images must be the images of the consequents. Various images of the same objects are possible, and these images may differ in various respects. We should at once denote as inadmissible all images which implicitly contradict the laws of our thought. Hence we postulate in the first place that all our images shall be logically permissible – or, briefly, that they shall be permissible. We shall denote as incorrect any permissible images, if their essential relations contradict the relations of external things, i.e. if they do not satisfy our first fundamental requirement. Hence we postulate in the second place that our images shall be correct. But two permissible and correct images of the same external objects may yet differ in respect of appropriateness. Of two images of the same object that is the more appropriate which pictures more of the essential relations of the object, – the one which we may call the more distinct. Of two images of equal distinctness the more appropriate is the one which contains, in addition to the essential characteristics, the smaller number of superfluous or empty relations, – the simpler of the two. Empty relations cannot be altogether avoided: they enter into the images because they are simply images, – images produced by our mind and necessarily affected by the characteristics of its mode of portrayal. (Hertz 1899 [1956], p. 2)

In short, the three requirements that an image of a phenomenon should fulfill are: (1) 'logically permissible', that is logical consistency; (2) 'correctness', that there is correspondence between the relations of the representation and those of the phenomenon; and (3) 'appropriateness', that it contains the essential characteristics of the phenomenon (distinctness) as simply as possible. It is fairly straightforward to determine whether an image satisfies the first two requirements, but 'we cannot decide without ambiguity whether an image is appropriate or not; as to this differences of opinion may arise. One image may be more suitable for one purpose, another for another; only by gradually testing many images can we finally succeed in obtaining the most appropriate'. (ibid., p. 3) Appropriateness will appear as the crucial requirement for any satisfactory model building process. Every model is necessarily a simplified picture of a phenomenon under investigation, but this simplification should be such that the picture remains appropriate.

Boltzman's account of explanation

Ludwig Boltzmann placed great importance on Maxwell's concept of analogies, describing Maxwell as having been 'as much of a pioneer in epistemology as in theoretical physics' (Boltzmann 1912, p. 100).[7] The dynamical analogies were particular appealing to him. According to the historian Martin Klein, 'Boltzmann himself found the concept of a theory as an analogy or metaphor of reality a particular liberating one' (Klein 1970, p. 63):

> Most surprising and far-reaching analogies revealed themselves between apparently quite disparate natural processes. It seemed that nature had built the most various things on exactly the same pattern; or, in the dry words of the analyst, the same differential equations hold for the most various phenomena. (Boltzmann 1892 [1974], p. 9)

According to Boltzmann (1902b) [1974], p. 149), 'It is the ubiquitous task of science to explain the more complex in terms of the simpler; or, if preferred, to represent the complex by means of clear pictures borrowed from the sphere of the simpler phenomena'. Boltzmann's attitude towards the role of '*Bilder*' in scientific explanation was explicitly expressed in an essay 'On the development of the methods of theoretical physics' (1899a) [1974]. Referring to Hertz 'programme', Boltzmann stated that:

> [N]o theory can be objective, actually coinciding with nature, but rather that each theory is only a mental picture of phenomena, related to them as *sign* is to *designatum*. From this it follows that it cannot be our task to find an absolutely correct theory but rather a picture that is, as simple as possible and that represents phenomena as accurately as possible. One might even conceive of two quite different theories both equally simple and equally congruent with phenomena, which therefore in spite of their difference are equally correct. (Boltzmann 1899a [1974], pp. 90–91)

Although Boltzmann frequently referred to Hertz when discussing '*Bilder*' there is an important difference between the two men (*see* De Regt 1999, p. 116). Boltzmann rejected Hertz's demand that the pictures we construct must obey 'laws of thought' considered as 'indubitably correct': 'the sole and final decision as to whether the pictures are appropriate lies in the circumstance that they represent experience simply and appropriately throughout so that this in turn provides precisely the test for the correctness of those laws' (Boltzmann 1899b [1974], p. 105).

In physics, Boltzmann is better known as the man who founded 'statistical mechanics'.[8] Boltzmann developed his ideas on statistical mechanics in a series of long memoirs written over a number of years. His ideas provoked intense discussion and sharp controversy. There was much confusion about what he meant and how much of it had, or had not been, properly underpinned.[9] What was needed was an analysis and critique of the foundations of statistical mechanics. Ehrenfest was asked to provide such analysis and critique for the German *Encyclopedia of Mathematical Sciences* (*Encyklopädie der Mathematischen Wissenschaften*, Leipzig: Teubner, 1912). The resulting review article 'The conceptual foundations of the statistical approach in mechanics' (1912) [1990], was prepared in collaboration with his wife Tatiana Ehrenfest-Afanassjewa.

Ehrenfest's review also contained a discussion of J. Willard Gibbs's *Elementary Principles in Statistical Mechanics* (1902) [1960]. Gibbs (1839–1903) was more skeptical about the relation between the hypotheses and reality than Boltzmann:

Difficulties of this kind have deterred the author from attempting to explain the mysteries of nature, and have forced him to be contented with the more modest aim of deducing some of the more obvious propositions relating to the statistical branch of mechanics. Here, there can be no mistake in regard to the agreement of the hypotheses with the facts of nature, for nothing is assumed in that respect. (Gibbs 1902 [1960], p. x)

This was a position Ehrenfest would not defend. Ehrenfest described Gibbs's account of explanations as follows:

The kinetic 'explanations' become representations or mappings of some conceptual scheme ..., and correspondingly the two groups of hypotheses become more or less arbitrary assertions about the structure of this conceptual scheme. These assertions will be:

- About the structure of the gas model.
- About the selection of the group of motions.
- Freedom in the choice of these assertions seems to be restricted essentially by only one requirement: the scheme has to be self-consistent. (Ehrenfest 1912 [1990], pp. 43–4)

To Ehrenfest, the requirement of self-consistency was insufficient; he believed that statistical mechanics was 'in some sense, a "real" theory and no mere analogy' (Klein 1970, p. 136). If he had to choose between the requirements of 'logically permissible' and 'appropriateness', Ehrenfest would no doubt choose the latter.

Appropriateness vs. logical rigor

To see a model as an image implies that there is no unique view but that several perspectives or focuses are possible, depending on the model builder's purpose. Models are Hertzian images in the sense that they have to meet the following requirements: They must be *correct*, i.e. represent the relationships of the phenomenon at hand, *distinct* i.e. represent the essential phenomenological characteristics as far as possible, and *simple* i.e. need as few as possible empty relations. However, in the empirical tradition models do not have to be *logically permissible*, i.e. logically rigorous. Appropriateness, that is the combination of distinctness and simplicity, is far more important than logical rigor (Boumans 2001). Dealing with contradictory theoretical statements is not a matter of choosing between them but a matter of degree that should be settled by measurement. This strategy was exactly the method Tinbergen adopted in his work for the *League of Nations*, and which resulted in the second macro-econometric model in the history of economics (Tinbergen 1939):

> It is rather rare that of two opinions only one is correct, the other wrong. In most cases both form part of the truth. ... The two opinions, as a rule, do not exclude each other. Then the question arises in what 'degree each is correct'; or, how these two opinions have to be 'combined' to have the best picture of reality. (Tinbergen 1936b, pp. 1–2)

Contrary to Gibbs's tendency to require rigorous logic, in which self-consistency became more important than correspondence to reality, modeling arose in a tradition in which understanding means being able to deal with the representing mechanism. In a biographical sketch, Henri Bumstead noted that:

> Professor Gibbs was much inclined to the use of geometrical illustrations, which he employed as symbols and aids to the imagination, rather than the mechanical models which have served so many investigators; such models are seldom in complete correspondence with the phenomena they represent, and Professor Gibbs's tendency toward rigorous logic was such that the discrepancies apparently destroyed for him the usefulness of the model. Accordingly he usually had recourse to the geometrical representation of his equations, and this method he used with great ease and power. (Bumstead 1906 [1961], pp. xii–xiii)

The difference between a Boltzmannian and a Gibbsian epistemology leads to different methodologies: the first to modeling phenomena, the latter to axiomatization of theories.[10]

Intelligibility

In mathematics and physics, the term 'model' originally referred specifically to material objects (see e.g. Hertz's definition of a 'dynamical model' above), 'a representation in three dimensions of some projected or existing structure, or of some material object artificial or natural, showing the proportions and arrangement of its component parts', or 'an object or figure in clay, wax, or the like, and intended to be reproduced in a more durable material' (*Oxford English Dictionary*, 1933). Ludwig Boltzmann's entry for 'Model' in the *Encyclopaedia Britannica* (1902a [1974]) also indicates its material roots: 'a tangible representation, whether the size be equal, or greater, or smaller, of an object which is either in actual existence, or has to be constructed in fact or thought' (ibid., p. 213). To Boltzmann, models could only be material, a view that can also be found in his contribution to the *Katalog mathematischer und mathematisch-physikalischer Modelle, Apparate und Instrumente* (1892 [1974]).

At the beginning of the twentieth century, the term 'mathematical model' referred to a physical three-dimensional representation of a mathematical entity.[11] Usually the term 'scheme' was used to denote a non-material, mathematical representation. As we have seen, this shift in terminology from 'scheme' to 'model' gave name to a new practice of 'explicit mathematizing as technique' which matched with an empiric-oriented alternative to the logical view on mathematics (see also Alberts 1998, pp. 134–5).

So, although the term 'model' originally referred to a material object, it has now lost its physical substance in economics. Nevertheless, as Morrison and Morgan (1999) have shown, models still function *as if* they were material objects. Morrison and Morgan demonstrate that models function as 'instruments of investigation' helping us to learn more about theories and the real world because they are autonomous agents: that is to say, though they represent either some aspect of the world, or some aspect of a theory, they are partially independent of both theories and the real world. It is precisely this partial independency that enables us to learn something about the thing they represent:

> we do not learn much from looking at a model – we learn more from building the model and manipulating it. Just as one needs to use or observe the use of a hammer in order to really understand its function, similarly, models have to be used before they will give up their secrets. In this sense, they have the quality of a technology – the power of the model only becomes apparent in the context of its use. (Morrison and Morgan 1999, p. 12)

Morrison and Morgan's account of the understanding that is gained by building and using models fits into a longer tradition that started with what Galileo took to be intelligible and the concept of intelligibility that he developed. Machamer (1998) shows that Archimedean simple machines, such as the balance, the inclined plane, and the screw, combined with the experiences gained using them, constituted Galileo's concept of both theory and experiment:

> Intelligibility or having a true explanation for Galileo had to include having a mechanical model or representation of the phenomenon. In this sense, Galileo added something to the traditional criteria of mathematical description (from the mixed sciences) and observation (from astronomy) for constructing scientific objects (as some would say) or for having adequate explanation of the phenomena observed (as I would say). ... To get at the true cause, you must replicate or reproduce the effects by constructing an artificial device so that the effects can be seen. (Machamer 1998, p. 69)

This mode of scientific understanding was also emphasized by William Thomson (Lord Kelvin, 1824–1907). Thomson, who had an 'immense admiration for Maxwell's mechanical model of electromagnetic induction', saw a mechanical model in the sense of a substantive analogy:

> It seems to me that the test of 'Do we or do we not understand a particular subject in physics?' is, 'Can we make a mechanical model of it?' (Thomson 1884 [1987], p. 111)

In this tradition, understanding a phenomenon became the same as 'designing a model imitating the phenomenon; whence the nature of material things is to be understood by imagining a mechanism whose performance will represent and simulate the properties of the bodies' (Duhem 1954, p. 72).

A more recent, philosophically related view is Cartwright's 'simulacrum' account of models discussed in her *How the Laws of Physics Lie* (1983). Her account deals with the problem of bridging the gap between theory and phenomena in physics. Her aim is to argue against the facticity of fundamental laws, the idea that these picture the phenomena in an accurate way. For this we need models: 'To explain a phenomenon is to find a model that fits it into the basic framework of the theory and thus allows us to derive analogues for the messy and complicated phenomenological laws which are true of it' (Cartwright 1983, p. 152). The striving for too much realism in the models may be an obstacle to explaining the relevant phenomenon. For that reason she introduces an 'anti-realistic' account of models: models are simulacra, that is, 'the success of the model depends on how much and how precisely it can replicate what goes on' (ibid., p. 153).

In his paper, *'Bildtheorie* and scientific understanding', Henk De Regt (1999) shows how *Bilder* – images – fulfilled an explanatory task in Boltzmann's philosophy of science, or, in other words, how they functioned as tools for understanding. The kind of images Boltzmann preferred, as being most intelligible, were mechanical pictures. As De Regt (1999, pp. 121–2) argues, 'it is the practical success of mechanism – possibly linked with our familiarity with mechanical systems from daily experience – that has made it into a criterion for intelligibility in science':[12]

> What, then, is meant by having perfectly correct understanding of a mechanism? Everybody knows that the practical criterion for this consists in being able to handle it correctly. However, I go further and assert that this is the only tenable definition of understanding a mechanism. (Boltzmann 1902b [1974], p. 150)

In line with this Maxwell-Boltzmann tradition, Irving Fisher (1867–1947), one of the founders of modern economics, was convinced that understanding a certain mechanism or phenomenon demands visualization, 'for correct visual pictures usually yield the clearest concepts' (Fisher 1939, p. 311). Sometimes these pictures showed mechanical devices, because he believed that a 'student of economics thinks in terms of mechanics far more than geometry, and a mechanical illustration corresponds more fully to his antecedent notions than a graphical one' (Fisher 1892 [1925], p. 24). Fisher (1892 [1925]) used pictures of a hydrostatic mechanism to explain a three-good, three-consumer economy in his Ph.D. thesis.[13] He also used a mechanical balance to illustrate the equation of exchange and a hydraulic system 'to observe and trace' important variations and their effects in the *Purchasing Power of Money* (Fisher 1911 [1963], p. 108).[14] On other occasions he used geometrical illustrations to visualize properties of a system. For example, he gave a description of a three-dimensional construction of the properties of production factors in his 1939 paper 'A three-dimensional representation of the factors of production and their remuneration, marginally and residually' to help the students 'to see, literally to see with his eyes' (ibid., p. 311). He discussed a better method of graphical representation in his paper 'The "ratio" chart, for plotting statistics' (1917). There he recommended the ratio chart, in which only ratios are displayed and compared, because it 'simply utilizes the natural powers of the eye. Consequently, when one is once accustomed to it, it never misleads, but always pictures a multitude of ratio relations at a glance, with absolute fidelity and without the annoyance of reservations or corrections' (Fisher 1917, p. 600).

Gibbs may well have been influential in Fisher's efforts to use visualization. Gibbs' first two publications, 'Graphical methods in the thermodynamics of fluids' and 'A method of geometrical representation of the thermodynamic properties of substances by means of surfaces' (1873 [1961]) dealt explicitly with this issue. However, as we have seen, Gibbs was not a model builder. As Morgan (1999, p. 351) emphasizes 'it was Fisher who broke with the tradition of his teacher and developed constructions which we now recognize as "models" in his texts'. Though Gibbs saw geometrical illustrations as aids to the imagination, he could not see them as mode for understanding, nor as explanation. In opposition to this view, Fisher stressed the role of visualizations because they helped to understand a system or phenomenon. It connected the unknown to something familiar: to something we have experience of. Fisher made no principled distinction between geometry and mechanics, because geometry, too, was in his view 'consolidated experience' (Boumans 2001).

The appeal to simple and elegant models is that they are intelligible, that in their simplicity they provide a kind of understanding one at least could communicate to students or colleagues. Lucas (1988, p. 39) preferred to call them 'mechanics': 'a system of differential equations the solution to which imitates some of the main features of the economic behavior we observe in the world economy'. In my view it would be better to call them 'mechanisms', defined by Machamer et al. (2000, p. 3) as 'entities and activities organized such that they are productive of regular changes from start or set-up to finish or terminate conditions'. The understanding provided by a mechanistic explanation arises not from its correctness – whether the correspondence between the representation and phenomenon is correct -, but rather from an elucidative relation between the setup conditions and intermediate entities and activities and the termination condition of the phenomenon to be explained. 'Mechanism descriptions show *how possibly*, *how plausibly*, or *how actually* things work' (ibid., p. 21). A mechanism can be communicated to others without the need to mention or explain matters beyond that mechanism, even more so when they are simple machines that 'can be drawn or reproduced in a picture or recipe book. Such things can be seen or made by everyone and anyone' (Machamer 1998, p. 70).

A separate methodology of models

In modern economics, the dominant view is that quantitative expressions of our world are useful and that mathematical representations constitute – even better – knowledge about economic phenomena. This latter belief was explicitly voiced by Irving Fisher:

> The effort of the economist is to *see*, to picture the interplay of economic elements. The more clearly cut these elements appear in his vision, the better; the more elements he can grasp and hold in mind at once, the better. The economic world is a misty region. The first explorers used unaided vision. Mathematics is the lantern by which what before was dimly visible now looms up in firm, bold outlines. The old phantasmagoria disappear. We see better. We see also further. (Fisher 1892 [1925], p. 119)

This statement was made in the very last section of Fisher's Ph.D. thesis 'Mathematical investigations in the theory of value and prices', written in the last decade of the nineteenth century. When Fisher wrote his Ph.D., the belief that economic phenomena could be better understood through mathematics was not widely held. His work marked the beginning of a new era in which, bit by bit, economics became mathematicized. This process of mathematization took not place by means of translating verbally expressed theories, one by one, into mathematical language, but through the emergence of a new practice of economic research characterized by mathematical modeling.[15,16]

Models as instruments

To understand their specific function in economic research, models should be distinguished from economic theories. They are not theories about the world but pictures, images of the world used to gain some understanding of it. However, as mathematical representations, models should also be distinguished from pure formal objects. They should be seen, as the quote above says, as 'lanterns', as devices that help us to see the phenomena more clearly. Models are the economist's instruments of investigation, just as the microscope and the telescope are tools of the biologist and the astronomer. In a textbook on optical instruments, we find the following description:

> The primary function of a lens or lens system will usually be that of making a pictorial representation or record of some object or other, and this record will usually be much more suitable for the purpose for which it is required than the original object. (Bracey 1960, p. 15)

In the same way, models are used to function as optical instruments: to provide more suitable representations for a certain purpose than them. The main difference between models and material optical instruments is that models are both instrument and pictorial representation, camera and snapshot together.

Because mathematical models are used as though they are instruments, standard economic methodology, traditionally focused on theories, is not suitable. Standard accounts define models in terms of their logical or semantic connections with theories, and methodology is traditionally seen as a way to appraise theories. Instruments (models) are not theories and therefore should be assessed differently. A separate methodology needs to be developed that is able to assess how mathematical models function.

Despite that models function as material instruments, they cannot be assessed as such. The absence of materiality means that the physical methods used to test material instruments, such as control and insulation, cannot be applied to models.[17] This means that we cannot easily borrow from the philosophy of technology, which is geared to physical objects. Models, being 'quasi-material' objects belonging to a world in between the immaterial world of theoretical ideas and the material world of physical objects, require an alternative methodology.

How models are built

In several accounts of what models are and how they function a specific view dominates. This view contains the following characteristics. First, there is a clear-cut distinction between theories, models and data and second, empirical assessment takes place after the model is built. An exemplary account can be found in Hausman's *The Inexact and Separate Science of Economics* (1992). In his view, models are definitions of kinds of systems, and they make no empirical claims. Although he pays special attention to the practice of working with a model – i.e. conceptual exploration – he claims that even then no empirical assessment takes place. 'Insofar as one is only working with a model, one's efforts are purely conceptual or mathematical. One is only developing a complicated concept or definition' (Hausman 1992, p. 79). In Hausman's view, only theories make empirical claims and can be tested. Above that, he doesn't make clear where models, concepts and definitions come from. Even in Morgan's account 'Finding a satisfactory empirical model' (1988), which comes closest to mine and will be dealt with below, she mentions a 'fund' of empirical models of which the most satisfactory model can be selected.

Several studies of first-generation models (see Boumans 1999) have shown that these models are built by fitting together sets of data from disparate sources. A first-generation model is the first model that is built for a new problem. A problem is new when the phenomenon to be explained or described is new, or when one would like to apply a new technique.[18] To clarify the integration process, it is very helpful to compare model building with baking a cake without having a recipe. If you want to bake a cake and you do not have a recipe, how do you take the matter up? Of course you do not start blank, you have some knowledge about, for example, preparing cakes and you know the main ingredients: flour, fat, raising agent and sugar. You also know how a cake should look like and how it should taste. You start a trial and error process till the result is what you would like to call a cake: the color and taste are satisfactory.

Building a model with the purpose of solving a new problem is like baking a cake without a recipe. A comparable view is expressed by Clive Granger on model building in his study, *Empirical Modeling in Economics*:

> I think of a modeler as starting with some disparate pieces – some wood, a few bricks, some nails, and so forth – and attempting to build an object for which he (or she) has only a very inadequate plan, or theory. The modeler can look at related constructs and can use institutional information and will eventually arrive at an approximation of the object that they are trying to represent, perhaps after several attempts. (Granger 1999, pp. 6–7)

Others (e.g. Stehling 1993) compared model building with '*basteln*' – tinkering – to denote the 'art' of model building. The reason that I prefer the analogy of baking is that one of its characteristics is that in the end product you can no longer distinguish the separate ingredients; they become blended and homogeneous.

In a model, the ingredients are theoretical ideas, policy views, mathematical concepts and techniques, metaphors and analogies, stylized facts and empirical data. Integration takes place by translating the ingredients into a mathematical form and merging them into one framework. This idea of mathematics as homogenizer and harmonizer can be clarified by enlarging on the metaphor Morrison and Morgan (1999) use for the function of models, namely as mediator. The mathematical forms that are entered in a model are the result of painstaking negotiations. One could see it as a meeting at which various parties need to come to an agreement. They have little in common and are characterized more by their differences than their similarities, so they are highly suspicious of each other. An impartial mediator is needed to bring the parties involved closer together, step by step, carefully formalizing each result in the negotiations. The development and selection of appropriate formulations is part and parcel of the process and it cannot be determined beforehand.

The role of mathematics
As a result, the choice of the mathematical formalism ingredient is important. It determines the possibilities of the mathematical modeling. However, which formalism should be chosen is not obvious. However, the advantage of Archimedean simple machines is that they not only provide a mechanism to explain a phenomenon under investigation, but also they supply the mathematics to describe it. Maas (2001) presents us with an example of how the balance functions in the work of William Stanley Jevons (1835–1882), another founder of modern economics. Morgan (1999) and Boumans (2001) investigate how the balance provided the appropriate mechanism for developing the Quantity Theory of Money in the work of Irving Fisher. In the 1930s, the exemplar of a simple machine used to understand business cycles was the pendulum. For example, Tinbergen took harmonic oscillation – the mathematical representation of the pendulum – as a starting point for analysing the business cycle. Moreover, Frisch's classic Rocking Horse model of the business cycle (1933) was a pendulum (or rocking horse) hampered by friction but frequently hit by a stick (or water, see above) to maintain the cycle.

It is often assumed that mathematics is an efficient and transparent language. One of the most well-known supporters of this view is Paul Samuelson (1952), who took Gibbs's slogan 'Mathematics is a language' as the motto of his *Foundations of Economic Analysis* (1947) [1983]. Samuelson considers mathematics to be a transparent mode of communication and that it is this transparency that will stop people making the wrong deductive inferences. However, mathematics is not always transparent (neither, some would say, is language) and it does not necessarily function as a language. Moreover, mathematics is the stuff non-material models are made of and as such must be explored 'quasi-empirically'.[19] The selection of mathematical forms must be such that the disparate ingredients can be harmonized and homogenized into one effective model. Modeling is a process of committing oneself to how aspects of the economy should mathematically be represented and at the same time being constrained by the selected mathematical forms. Besides, not every element in the mathematical model necessarily has an economic meaning. To make the model workable, sometimes, elements of convenience or fiction have to be introduced. A similar view is developed by Nancy Cartwright (1983) in her simulacrum account of models, see above. To fulfill their bridge function between theory and phenomenon, the properties of convenience are introduced into the model to bring the objects modeled into the range of the theory. These properties of fiction play an important role in her argument that fundamental explanatory laws cannot be interpreted realistically.

Built-in justification
The role of mathematics as homogenizing and harmonizing material implies that the model-building process is the integration of several ingredients in such a way that the result – the model – meets certain a priori criteria of quality. And because empirical data and stylized facts belong to the set of ingredients that are integrated, justification is built in. Models built in this way are not appraised by ex post empirical testing. Such models are assessed by whether they satisfy their purpose, and, because in the model building process one works towards this goal, integration and justification are two sides of the same coin (Boumans 1999). A well-known sayings tells us that 'the proof of the pudding is in the eating', but if one prepares a pudding, tasting is an essential part of cooking.

This account of assessment is closely related to Mary Morgan's (1988) observation that econometricians of the 1930s were primarily concerned with finding 'satisfactory' empirical models. Assessing whether the models were satisfactory depended on the purpose of the models. Morgan presents five statements that cover the aims and criteria of the early econometricians:

1. To measure theoretical laws: Models must satisfy certain theoretical requirements (economic criteria).
2. To explain (or describe) the observed data: Models must fit observed data (statistical or historical criteria).
3. To be useful for policy: Models must allow the exploration of policy options or make predictions about future values.
4. To explore or develop theory: Models must expose unsuspected relationships or develop the detail of relationships.
5. To verify or reject theory: Models must be satisfactory or not over a range of economic, statistical, and other criteria.

(Morgan 1988, p. 205)

Morgan (see also Kim et al. 1995) presents these criteria of assessment as a form of quality control. If an empirical model exhibited a basic set of qualities, that is, satisfied some of the criteria listed above, it was considered satisfactory. Several practices in economics show that Morgan's observations can be summarized as: the integration of the various theoretical and empirical ingredients is deemed satisfactory when it meets a number of a priori criteria.

The integration of empirical facts into the model can be captured by the term 'calibration'. With respect to material instruments, calibration is a strategy for testing whether an instrument is working properly and the results produced with it are reliable (Franklin 1997, p. 31). With regard to models, it refers to the often used but mostly concealed 'adaptive strategy' of assessing models, in contrast to the official 'competitive strategy' (Hoover 1995). The competitive strategy is the received view of testing: 'Under the competitive strategy, theory proposes, estimation and testing disposes. In fine, alternative theories compete with one another for the support of the data' (Hoover 1995, p. 29). But 'economists do not practice what they preach' (Blaug 1980, p. xiii), they preach falsificationism but in fact they almost never practice it (see also Hands 2001, p. 277). Several case studies of empirical research practices show that practitioners actually carry out a more adaptive strategy:

> The adaptive strategy begins with an unrealistic model, in the sense of one that is an idealized and simplified product of the core theory. It sees how much mileage it can get out of that model. Only then does it add any complicating and more realistic feature. Unlike the competitive strategy, the aim is never to test and possibly reject the core theory, but to construct models that reproduce the economy more and more closely within the strict limits of the basic theory. (Hoover 1995, p. 29)

Conclusion

Probably, the first time the term 'model' was used in the sense of a mathematical output of empirical economic research was in 1935 by the Dutch economist Tinbergen. It was the result of a new type of economic research practice. The origins of this modeling practice can be traced in Maxwell's use of formal analogies and his views on their function in science. Hertz interpreted these analogies – 'images' – as a specific kind of idealizations: they should be logically consistent, empirically correct, appropriate and simple. The requirement of appropriateness entailed that the idealization should contain essential characteristics. What these essential characteristics are depends on the purpose of the model. Boltzmann followed Hertz's interpretation, with the essential distinction that unlike Hertz he did not require that the analogies should be based on logic but instead must represent experience.

The models discussed here in this chapter are understood as representatives of objects or systems in the world. The key philosophical question regarding the nature of these models is how they function as representations and how reliable the information is they provide. Margaret Morrison (1999) formulated this problem as follows.

> It seems not quite correct to say that models accurately describe physical systems since in many cases they not only embody an element of idealisation or abstraction, but frequently represent the world in ways that bear no similarity to physically realisable objects ... Hence, we need a reformulation of the philosophical question; more specifically, since models are sometimes deliberately based on characterizations we know to be false how can they provide us with information about the world. (Morrison 1999, p. 38)

The answer she (and Mary Morgan) gave is quite simple: models provide us information about the world by virtue of functioning as instruments of investigation. This answer, however, has far-reaching implications for the way models should be assessed. As we have seen, a methodology designed for models considered as instruments differs from a methodology for theories in various directions.

A separate methodology of models that does justice to the idea that models function as autonomous instruments of investigation has to reconsider and consequently redefine central methodological concepts: To see how model acquire reliability, testing of models has to be reevaluated in terms of calibration. While theoretical principles, or axioms if you like, have to form a consistent system, instruments are built on basis of a compromise of often incompatible theoretical and empirical requirements. Theories should be true, or at least not false, but models have only to fulfill their goal satisfactorily.

Notes

1. Qin (1993, p. 37) dates the 'creation' of this separate entity 'model' in econometrics in the same period. She explains this new creation by the conceptual separation of statistical laws from economic laws and the shift of use from mainly descriptive statistical tools to those of statistical inference. In her view, models were developed as an answer to the difficulties of measuring laws directly.
2. In German philosophy, there is a distinction between *Darstellung* and *Vorstellung*. While a *Vorstellung* is a passive mental image of a sense datum, a *Darstellung* is a consciously constructed scheme for knowing (see Janik and Toulmin 1973, pp. 139–40).
3. The original paper of 1936 is available in English under the title: 'An Economic Policy for 1936' in Tinbergen 1959. For the 1937 revised version, which concentrates on econometric aspects, see Tinbergen 1937.
4. Morgan 1998 provides a survey of the literature on models in philosophy and economics.
5. It is interesting to note that Morrison, who endorses a closely related account of how models function (see, for example, Morrison 1999), also takes Maxwell's ideas on analogies as a starting point in her various papers (1992a, 1992b, 1995) on the role and function of models in physics.
6. Apart from a difference in materiality, the meaning of 'image' and 'model' in Hertz's *Principles* are so close that Janik and Toulmin (1973, p. 283 note 45) decided to deviate from the standard English translation and to render the term '*Bild*' as 'model' and not as 'image'.
7. Boltzmann translated Maxwell's papers of 1855 (1965) and 1861 (1965) into German. This quotation is translated into English by the author.

8. But it was J. Willard Gibbs who gave the name 'statistical mechanics' to this new science in which the calculus of probabilities was applied to complex mechanical systems.
9. For detailed reconstruction of the arguments, see Klein (1970).
10. E. Roy Weintraub's (2002) uses this distinction between modeling phenomena and axiomatization to account for the two different routes of 'how economics became a mathematical science'.
11. Herbert Mehrtens (forthcoming) provides a detailed discussion of three-dimensional mathematical models.
12. Morgan and Boumans (forthcoming) discuss how A.W.H. Phillips built his famous hydraulic machine to get a grip on the macroeconomic thinking of his days. It is an engineering way of understanding, through the 'eyes and fingers', labeled by Eugene Ferguson as understanding through the 'mind's eye', 'the organ in which a lifetime of sensory information – visual, tactile, muscular, visceral, aural, olfactory, and gustatory – is stored, interconnected, and interrelated' (Ferguson 1992, p. 42).
13. The hydrostatic mechanism had also actually been constructed twice. Photographs of both these models were reproduced in Fisher (1925).
14. Mary Morgan (1999) provides a detailed account of how Fisher, in his *Purchasing Power of Money* (1911 [1963]), learned about the monetary system by building and using models.
15. See (Morgan 2002) for a similar account.
16. Considered as a historical claim, this is supported by Morgan's (2003) characterization of twentieth-century modern economics as an engineering science and the accompanying observation that 'during the 1930s, mathematics became attached to another tool – namely, "modeling" – to create a new style of scientific argument in economics' (p. 286); and by Solow's (1997) similar characterization of late twentieth-century economics not as formalistic, abstract, negligent of the real world, but as a model-building science obsessed with data.
17. This requirement of materiality for controllability (in the usual meaning of this term) has been discussed in (Boumans and Morgan 2001) and (Morgan 2003). Both essays also treat the kinds of controllability that are possible in the case of quasi-material or non-material experiments.
18. In 'normal' economic research practices, most models are of the *n*th generation. They are built by just slightly adapting one of the assumptions of an existing model. Their legitimacy depends on the success of the first generation model.
19. Note that mathematics is not equated with formal axiomatic abstractions, labeled by Lakatos (1976) as 'formalism'. Lakatos showed that mathematics grows as an informal, quasi-empirical discipline.

References

Alberts, Gerard (1998), *Jaren van Berekening. Toepassingsgerichte initiatieven in de Nederlandse wiskundebeoefening 1945–1960*, Amsterdam: Amsterdam University Press.

Blaug, Mark (1980), *The Methodology of Economics; or How Economists Explain*, Cambridge: Cambridge University Press.

Boltzmann, Ludwig (1892), 'Über die Methoden der theoretischen Physik', in Walter Dyck (ed.), *Katalog Mathematischer und Mathematisch-Physikalischer Modelle, Apparate und Instrumente*, München: Wolf, pp. 89–98. Reprinted as 'On the methods of theoretical physics', in Brian McGuinness (ed.) (1974), *Theoretical Physics and Philosophical Problems*, Dordrecht: Reidel, pp. 5–12.

Boltzmann, Ludwig (1899a), 'On the development of the methods of theoretical physics in recent times', in Brian McGuinness (ed.) (1974), *Theoretical Physics and Philosophical Problems*, Dordrecht: Reidel, pp. 77–100.

Boltzmann, Ludwig (1899b), 'On the fundamental principles and equations of mechanics', in Brian McGuinness (ed.) (1974), *Theoretical Physics and Philosophical Problems*, Dordrecht: Reidel, pp. 101–28.

Boltzmann, Ludwig (1902a), 'Model', in *Encyclopaedia Brittanica*, 10th edition, vol. 30, London: The Times Printing House, pp. 788–91. Reprinted in Brian McGuinness (ed.) (1974), *Theoretical Physics and Philosophical Problems*, Dordrecht: Reidel, pp. 213–20.

Boltzmann, Ludwig (1902b), 'On the principles of mechanics', in Brian McGuinness (ed.) (1974), *Theoretical Physics and Philosophical Problems*, Dordrecht: Reidel, pp. 129–52.

Boltzmann, Ludwig (1912), 'Anmerkungen', in L. Boltzmann (ed.), *Faradays Kraftlinien von J.C. Maxwell*, Leipzig: Engelmann, pp. 97–128.

Boumans, Marcel (1993), 'Paul Ehrenfest and Jan Tinbergen: a case of limited physics transfer', in Neil de Marchi (ed.), *Non-Natural Social Science: Reflecting on the Enterprise of More Heat than Light, History of Political Economy*, **25**, annual supplement, Durham, NC: Duke University Press, pp. 131–56.

Boumans, Marcel (1999), 'Built-in justification', in Mary S. Morgan and Margaret Morrison (eds), *Models as Mediators*, Cambridge: Cambridge University Press, pp. 66–96.

Boumans, Marcel (2001), 'Fisher's instrumental approach to index numbers', in Judy L. Klein and Mary S. Morgan (eds), *The Age of Economic Measurement, History of Political Economy*, **33**, annual supplement, 313–44, Durham, NC: Duke University Press.

Boumans, Marcel and Mary S. Morgan (2001), '*Ceteris Paribus* conditions: materiality and the applications of economic theories', *Journal of Economic Methodology*, **8** (1), 11–26.

Bracey, R.J (1960), *The Technique of Optical Instrument Design*, London: English University Press.

Bumstead, Henry Andrews ([1906] 1961), 'Biographical sketch', in Henry Andrews Bumstead and Ralph Gibbs Van Name (eds), *The Scientific Papers of J. Willard Gibbs*, New York: Dover, pp. xi–xxv.

Cartwright, Nancy (1983), *How the Laws of Physics Lie*, Oxford: Clarendon Press.

De Regt, Henk W. (1999), 'Ludwig Boltzmann's *Bildtheorie* and scientific understanding', *Synthese*, **119** (1–2), 113–34.

Duhem, Pierre (1954), *The Aim and Structure of Physical Theory*, translated by P.P. Wiener, Princeton, NJ: Princeton University Press.

Ehrenfest, Paul and Tatiana Ehrenfest (1912), 'Begriffliche Grundlagen der statistichen Auffassung in der Mechanik', in F. Klein and C. Müller (eds), *Encyklopädie der Mathematischen Wissenschaften* vol. 4:2:2 no. 6. Reprinted in English (1990) as *The Conceptual Foundations of the Statistical Approach in Mechanics*, translated by Michael J. Moravcsik, New York: Dover.

Ferguson, Eugene S. (1992), *Engineering and the Mind's Eye*, Cambridge, MA: MIT Press.

Fisher, Irving (1892 [1925]), *Mathematical Investigations in the Theory of Value and Prices*, New Haven, CT: Yale University Press.

Fisher, Irving (1911 [1963]), *The Purchasing Power of Money; Its Determination and Relation to Credit, Interest and Crises*, 2nd revised edn, New York: Kelley.

Fisher, Irving (1917), 'The "ratio" chart, for plotting statistics', *Quarterly Publications of the American Statistical Association*, **15**, 577–601.

Fisher, Irving (1939), 'A three-dimensional representation of the factors of production and their remuneration, marginally and residually', *Econometrica*, **7**, 304–11.

Franklin, Allan (1997), 'Calibration', *Perspectives on Science*, **5**, 31–80.

Frisch, Ragnar (1933), 'Propagation problems and impulse problems in dynamic economics', in *Economic Essays in Honour of Gustav Cassel*, London: Allen and Unwin, pp. 171–205.

Gibbs, J. Willard (1873 [1961]), *The Scientific Papers of J. Willard Gibbs*, edited by Henry Andrews Bumstead and Ralph Gibbs Van Name, New York: Dover.

Gibbs, J. Willard (1902 [1960]), *Elementary Principles in Statistical Mechanics. Developed with Special Reference to the Rational Foundation of Thermodynamics*, New York: Dover.

Granger, Clive W.J. (1999), *Empirical Modeling in Economics, Specification and Evaluation*, Cambridge: Cambridge University Press.

Hands, D. Wade (2001), *Reflection without Rules: Economic Methodology and Contemporary Science Theory*, Cambridge: Cambridge University Press.

Hausman, Daniel M. (1992), *The Inexact and Separate Science of Economics*, Cambridge: Cambridge University Press.

Hertz, Heinrich (1893 [1962]), *Electric Waves*, New York: Dover.

Hertz, Heinrich (1899 [1956]), *The Principles of Mechanics Presented in a New Form*, New York: Dover.

Hoover, Kevin D. (1995), 'Facts and artifacts: calibration and the empirical assessment of real-business-cycle models', *Oxford Economic Papers*, **47**, 24–44.

Janik, Allan, and Stephen Toulmin (1973), *Wittgenstein's Vienna*, New York: Simon and Schuster.

Kim, Jinbang, Neil de Marchi and Mary S. Morgan (1995), 'Empirical model particularities and belief in the natural rate hypothesis', *Journal of Econometrics*, **67** (1), 81–102.

Klein, Martin J. (1970), *Paul Ehrenfest. The Making of a Theoretical Physicist*, vol. 1, Amsterdam: North-Holland.

Lakatos, Imre (1976), *Proofs and Refutations: The Logic of Mathematical Discovery*, edited by John Worrall and Elie Zahar, New York: Cambridge University Press.

Lucas, Robert E. (1981), *Studies in Business-Cycle Theory*, Oxford: Basil Blackwell.

Lucas, Robert E. (1988), 'On the mechanics of economic development', *Journal of Monetary Economics*, **22**, 3–42.

Maas, Harro (2001), 'An instrument can make a science: Jevons's balancing acts in economics', in M.S. Morgan and J. Klein (eds), *New Age of Economic Measurement*, Durham, NC: Duke University Press, pp. 277–302.

Machamer, Peter (1998), 'Galileo's machines, his mathematics, and his experiments', in P. Machamer (ed.), *The Cambridge Companion to Galileo*, Cambridge: Cambridge University Press, pp. 53–79.

Machamer, Peter, Lindley Darden and Carl F. Craver (2000), 'Thinking about mechanisms', *Philosophy of Science*, **67**, 1–25.

Maxwell, James Clerk (1855), 'On Faraday's lines of force', in W.D. Niven (ed.) (1965), *The Scientific Papers of James Clerk Maxwell*, vol. I, New York: Dover, pp. 155–229.

Maxwell, James Clerk (1861), 'On physical lines of force', in W.D. Niven (ed.) (1965), *The Scientific Papers of James Clerk Maxwell*, vol. I, New York: Dover, pp. 451–513.

Maxwell, James Clerk (1865), 'A dynamical theory of the electromagnetic field', in W.D. Niven (ed.) (1965), *The Scientific Papers of James Clerk Maxwell*, vol. I, New York: Dover, pp. 526–97.

Maxwell, James Clerk (1871), 'On the mathematical classification of physical quantities', in W.D. Niven (ed.) (1965), *The Scientific Papers of James Clerk Maxwell*, vol. II, New York: Dover, pp. 257–66.

Mehrtens, Herbert (forthcoming), 'Mathematical models', in Soraya de Chadarevian and Nick Hopwood (eds), *Displaying the Third Dimension: Models in the Sciences, Technology, and Medicine*, Stanford, CA: Stanford University Press.

Morgan, Mary S. (1988), 'Finding a satisfactory empirical model', in Neil de Marchi (ed.), *The Popperian Legacy in Economics*, Cambridge: Cambridge University Press, pp. 199–211.

Morgan, Mary S. (1998), 'Models', in John B. Davis, D. Wade Hands and Uskali Mäki (eds), *The Handbook of Economic Methodology*, Cheltenham, UK and Lyme USA: Edward Elgar, pp. 316–21.

Morgan, Mary S. (1999), 'Learning from Models', in Mary S. Morgan and Margaret Morrison (eds), *Models as Mediators*, Cambridge: Cambridge University Press, pp. 347–88.

Morgan, Mary S. (2002), 'Seeing the world in models', unpublished working paper.

Morgan, Mary S. (2003), 'Economics', in Theodore M. Porter and Dorothy Ross (eds), *The Cambridge History of Science*, vol 7, *The Modern Social Sciences*, Cambridge: Cambridge University Press, pp. 275–305.

Morgan, Mary S. (2003), 'Experiments without material intervention: model experiments, virtual experiments and virtually experiments, in Hans Radder (ed.), *The Philosophy of Scientific Experimentation*, Pittsburgh: University of Pittsburgh Press, pp. 216–35.

Morgan, Mary S., and Marcel Boumans (forthcoming), 'The secrets hidden by two-dimensionality: the economy as a hydraulic machine', in Soraya de Chadarevian and Nick Hopwood (eds), *Displaying the Third Dimension: Models in the Sciences, Technology, and Medicine*, Stanford, CA: Stanford University Press.

Morrison, Margaret (1992a), 'Some complexities of experimental evidence', *PSA 1992*, volume 1, pp. 49–62.

Morrison, M. (1992b), 'A study in theory unification: the case of Maxwell's electromagnetic theory', *Studies in History and Philosophy of Science*, **23** (1), 103–45.

Morrison, M. (1995), 'Scientific conclusions and philosophical arguments: an inessential tension', in Jed Z. Buchwald (ed.), *Scientific Practice: Theories and Stories of Doing Physics*, Chicago: University of Chicago Press.

Morrison, M. (1999), 'Models as autonomous agents', in Mary S. Morgan and Margaret Morrison (eds), *Models as Mediators*, Cambridge: Cambridge University Press, pp. 38–65.

Morrison, Margaret, and Mary S. Morgan (1999), 'Models as mediating instruments', in Mary S. Morgan and Margaret Morrison (eds), *Models as Mediators*, Cambridge: Cambridge University Press, pp. 10–37.

Nagel, Ernest (1961), *The Structure of Science; Problems in the Logic of Scientific Explanation*, London: Routledge and Kegan Paul.

Neumann, John von (1961), 'The mathematician', in A.H. Taub (ed.), *John von Neumann, Collected Works*, Oxford: Pergamon Press, pp. 1–9.

Oxford English Dictionary (1933), Oxford: Clarendon Press.

Qin, Duo (1993), *The Formation of Econometrics: A Historical Perspective*, Oxford: Clarendon Press.

Samuelson, Paul A. (1952), 'Economic Theory and Mathematics – An Appraisal', *American Economic Review, Papers and Proceedings*, **42** (2), 56–66.

Samuelson, P.A. (1947 [1983]), *Foundations of Economic Analysis*, enlarged edn, Cambridge MA and London: Harvard University Press.

Solow, Robert M. (1997), 'How did economics get that way and what way did it get?', *Dædalus* **126** (1), 39–58.

Staehle, Hans (1933), 'La Réunion de la Sociéte d'Econometrie, Lausanne, Septembre, 1931', *Econometrica*, **1**, 73–86.

Staehle, H. (1937), 'Report of the fifth European meeting of the Econometric Society', *Econometrica* **5**, 87–102.

Stehling, Frank (1993), 'Wolfgang Eichhorn and the art of model building', in W. Erwin Diewert, Klaus Spremann and Frank Stehling (eds), *Mathematical Modelling in Economics; Essays in Honor of Wolfgang Eichhorn*, Berlin: Springer-Verlag, pp. vii–xi.

Thomson, William (1884 [1987]), 'Notes of lectures on molecular dynamics and the wave theory of light', in Robert Kargon and Peter Achinstein (eds), *Kelvin's Baltimore Lectures and Modern Theoretical Physics*, Cambridge, MA: MIT Press, pp. 7–255.

Tinbergen, Jan (1935), ,Quantitative Fragen der Konjunkturpolitik', *Weltwirtschaftliches Archiv*, **42**, 366–99.

Tinbergen, Jan (1936a), 'Kan hier te lande, al dan niet na overheidsingrijpen, een verbetering van de binnenlandse conjunctuur intreden, ook zonder verbetering van onze exportpositie?', in *Prae-adviezen voor de Vereeniging voor de Staathuishoudkunde en de Statistiek*, The Hague: Nijhoff, pp. 62–108.

Tinbergen, Jan (1936b), 'Memorandum on the continuation of the League's business cycle research in a statistical direction', archive of the League of Nations, Geneva.

Tinbergen, Jan (1937), *An Econometric Approach to Business Cycle Problems*, Paris: Hermann.

Tinbergen, Jan ([1936] 1959), 'An economic policy for 1936', in L.H. Klaassen, L.M. Koyck, and H.J. Witteveen (eds), *Jan Tinbergen – Selected Papers*, Amsterdam: North-Holland, pp. 37–84.

Tinbergen, Jan (1939), *Statistical Testing of Business-Cycle Theories*, Geneva: League of Nations.

Weintraub, E. Roy (2002), *How Economics Became a Mathematical Science*, Durham, NC, and London: Duke University Press.

14 Formalism

Peter Kesting and Arnis Vilks

Historically, formalism in economics is closely related to the use of mathematics. Logically, however, the connection between formalism and mathematics is subtle. On the one hand, mathematics can be – and often has been – used in economic reasoning in a relatively informal manner. Even within mathematics itself, ideas and arguments have for centuries been often discussed in a rather loose and non-formal way. On the other hand, it will be argued below that formalism does not necessarily entail the use of mathematics, or at any rate, that it does not necessitate the particular kind of mathematization characteristic of present-day mathematical economics.

Tentatively, and in a broad sense of the word, we take formalism to be an approach to theorizing that aims at making explicit the logical structure of any proposed theory. In this broad sense, formalism quite obviously does not require the use of mathematics, but it does require some notion of proof, deduction, or logical derivation. Of any assertion made in a theory, a formalist would indicate whether it is a derived one, and of any derived assertion he/she would indicate from where it can be derived.

Two more specific notions of formalism will be defined below – what we will call 'basic formalism', and the approach of present-day mathematical economics – which we will call 'set-theoretic formalism'.

Formalism in the broad sense has been followed in economic reasoning in varying degrees – more or less explicitly labeling underived statements as assumptions, postulates or axioms, and derived ones as theorems, propositions, or results. It is thus intimately linked to reasoning by means of models, as specifying a model involves specifying the model's assumptions, and reasoning within an economic model amounts to deriving assertions from the specified assumptions.

In the historical development of economic theory, the use of mathematics and the adoption of formalism have developed in an often amalgamated way, and by the middle of the twentieth century, a particular blend of formalism and mathematization emerged as the paradigmatic approach to economic theory. This kind of economics is most clearly exemplified by Debreu's *Theory of Value*.

Before we turn to a characterization of the specific notions of formalism, and to its relation to present-day mathematical economics, it is useful to briefly sketch the historical development of formalism that preceded Debreu.

A brief history of formalism in economic analysis

Formalism in the broad sense can be traced back to the early days of economic analysis. Since this time, formalistic reasoning developed from an outsider position to the predominant approach of economic analysis.

In the early days of economic analysis (from the beginnings to the 1860s), exponents of formalism were rare. For this period, formalism might in particular be associated with the name of Augustin Cournot, who most consistently applied mathematics to economic reasoning in his *Recherches sur les principes mathématiques de la théorie des richesses* (1838). As mathematical reasoning almost unavoidably follows formalism in the broad sense, the other mathematical economists of this period, such as William Whewell, A.J.E. Juvenal Dupuit and Hermann Heinrich Gossen, must also be seen as early formalists in economics.

However, the second important source of formalism is quite independent of any 'heavy' mathematical machinery – reasoning within 'formal' economic models, i.e. making inferences from explicitly stated assumptions. This approach had actually been taken before Cournot by Richard Cantillon, François Quesnay, David Ricardo, and most forcefully by Johann Heinrich von Thünen in his *Der isolierte Staat* (1826). In his *An Outline of the Science of Political Economy* (1836) Nassau William Senior explicitly stated postulates as the basis for the construction of an analytical apparatus.[1]

In this early period, the attitude of the economics profession towards formalism was very skeptical, if not hostile. It is true that Ricardo's work was generally recognized and accepted by contemporary economists, but he was heavily criticized for his method of isolation and abstraction, for which the phrase 'Ricardian vice' was coined (cf., for example, Schumpeter 1954, p. 473). Even more disapproving was the attitude towards mathematical economics. In the years following their publication, the works of Cournot and Gossen were almost completely ignored. In the preface of his *Recherches* Cournot expresses his perception of this negative attitude of the economic community by stating: 'With one accord they have set themselves against the use of mathematical forms, and it will doubtless be difficult to overcome today a prejudice which thinkers, like Smith and other modern writers, have contributed to strengthen' (p. I).

The employment of formalism received important, although hesitant, support from the neoclassical upheaval in the 1870s – with marginalism important concepts entered economic analysis that had an obvious mathematical expression in the differential calculus.

With the formulation of the system of general equilibrium in his pioneering *Eléments d'économie politique pure* (first published in 1874), Leon Walras adopted formalism in a most fruitful and elegant way. However, it took a long time until Walras' book developed its deep influence on economic reasoning. In the preface to the fourth edition of his *Elements* (1900) Walras complained:

'As for those economists who did not know any mathematics, who do not even know what is meant by mathematics and yet have taken the stand that mathematics cannot possibly serve to elucidate economic principles, let them go their way repeating that "human liberty will never allow itself to be cast into equations" or that "mathematics ignores frictions which are everything in social sciences" and other equally forceful and flowery phrases' (1874 [1954] p. 47). In fact, the general attitude towards mathematics was hostile for a long time even within the neoclassical period.

Marshall also argued within 'formal' models, but, unlike Walras, mostly refrained from an extensive use of mathematics – in his *Principles of Economics* (1890) he just underpinned his verbal argumentation by mathematical analysis in an appendix. Generally speaking, a similar approach was taken by most of the other leading 'formalistic' economists of this time, such as William Stanley Jevons, Knut Wicksell, Vilfredo Pareto, Irving Fisher and Francis Ysidro Edgeworth. This renunciation of an extensive use of mathematics may well have been a precondition for a broader acceptance of the writings of these economists.

Whether explicitly mathematical or not – in the neoclassical period, formalism was far from being generally accepted in the economics community. Especially in the beginning of this period, formalistic economists and inquiries were definitely a minority. Moreover, there was continuous opposition against formalism. Outstanding critics came from the German Historical School that firmly rejected formalism (cf., for example, Schmoller 1883).

It was not before the middle of the twentieth century that formalism received general acceptance in the economics community. Especially with his *Foundations of Economic Analysis* (1947) Paul A. Samuelson set a standard for economic reasoning within formal models. Together with Samuelson a generation of formalistic economists entered the profession – Roy F. Harrod, John R. Hicks, John von Neumann, Oskar Morgenstern and many others (in a recent publication, Mark Blaug (2003, p. 145), characterizes this 'profound intellectual transformation of economics in the years after World War II' as a 'formalist revolution').

While the understanding and the technique of reasoning in terms of models had been improved decisively by the middle of the twentieth century, and the use of mathematics had become standard, formalism in economics was thoroughly reshaped through the work of Gerard Debreu. In his *Theory of Value: An Axiomatic Analysis of Economic Equilibrium* (1959) he most explicitly adopts an methodological approach originating from the Bourbaki school in mathematics. This approach, which we call set-theoretic formalism, has since become a paradigmatic standard for formalistic reasoning within economic analysis. Before we turn to set-theoretic formalism, which today can be seen as the predominant approach of mathematical economics, we first describe an alternative version of formalism which emphasizes the aspect of 'explicitness' without necessarily requiring mathematization.

Basic formalism

A rather extreme, but conceptually very helpful version of formalism can be defined as the methodological requirement to set up any theory as a formal system. Before we explain the notion of formal system, which is a very fundamental one in modern logic and mathematics, it should be mentioned that terminology varies considerably – formal systems are sometimes also called 'axiomatic theories', 'calculi', 'deductive systems', or just 'formalisms'.

It should also be pointed out immediately that the extreme version of formalism is not actually followed in most present-day mathematics. However, one can safely say that most present-day mathematicians – or at any rate most of those mathematicians who care about foundations at all – would subscribe to some weakened version of it – one that only requires that 'in principle' it should be possible to set up mathematical theories as formal systems. The clause 'in principle' is meant to indicate that actual mathematical practice may – or even should – confine itself to the use of sketches or outlines of formal systems, as long as it is clear to the trained mathematician how one would have to proceed in order to transform the outline into a full-fledged formal system. We suggest the name 'basic formalism' for the methodological conviction that theories should 'in principle' be set up as formal systems.

A formal system $\mathcal{F}$ can be taken to consist of four types of ingredients:

1. The *alphabet* of $\mathcal{F}$, i.e. a list of all the elementary symbols (or undefined primitives) that may be used in $\mathcal{F}$; for instance, in propositional logic the alphabet could be taken to consist of the following six symbols: a, ', $\wedge$, $\neg$, (,).
2. The *formation rules* of $\mathcal{F}$, i.e. a list of rules that jointly define the 'sentences' or *formulas* of $\mathcal{F}$. (For emphasis, the formulas are often called the 'well-formed formulas'.) For instance, the formation rules of propositional logic can be taken to be the following three: (1) a, a', a'', etc. are formulas; (2) $(A \wedge B)$ is a formula, provided that A and B are; (3) $\neg A$ is a formula, if A is. One can then, for instance, determine 'recursively' that the 'meaningful' expression $(a \wedge \neg (a' \wedge \neg a''))$ is a formula of propositional logic, while $aa(\wedge' a \neg$ is merely a string of symbols that cannot be called a formula according to (1) through (3).
3. The *axioms* of $\mathcal{F}$, i.e. a set of (well-formed) formulas of $\mathcal{F}$. While the ancient understanding of axioms was that they neither can be proved nor need to be proved, being 'self-evident' and thus a 'firm basis' for the theoretical edifice erected on the axioms, modern formalists would refuse to characterize axioms as 'self-evident'. Rather, the axioms of $\mathcal{F}$ are simply seen as those

sentences which $\mathcal{F}$ asserts without proving them from other, more basic, assertions of $\mathcal{F}$. However, the axioms which are actually used in formal expositions of mathematics are definitely not arbitrary formulas 'plucked from the air' just for the sake of defining some formal system. At least some of them, such as $\neg(a \wedge \neg a)$, do look 'self-evident' if anything does. We will come back to the status of the axioms of mathematics below.

4. The *rules of inference* of $\mathcal{F}$ (sometimes called transformation rules). These are rules that allow one to generate a formula from others in a particular, specified way. An important example is the so-called 'modus ponens': From a formula A and another one of the form $\neg(A \wedge \neg B)$, one may 'generate' or 'infer' the formula B.

For any formal system $\mathcal{F}$, i.e. for any specification of alphabet, formation rules, axioms, and rules of inference, one can define the notion of 'proof in $\mathcal{F}$': A proof is a finite sequence of formulas such that every element of the sequence is either an axiom or is generated from previous elements of the sequence by means of a rule of inference. If $A_1, A_2, ..., A_n$ is a proof in $\mathcal{F}$, it is also called a proof of A_n in $\mathcal{F}$.

One can see that basic formalism is in fact nothing else but a more elaborate version of what we called formalism in the broad sense. Its aim is indeed to make explicit the logical structure of theoretical reasoning – it requires the theoretician to 'lay all cards on the table'. Although it has developed from an analysis of mathematical reasoning, and is rarely followed outside logic and mathematics, it is clear and worth noting that basic formalism does not require mathematization.

It was mentioned above that most present-day mathematicians adhere to basic formalism. However, almost all of present-day mathematics is built on a *particular* formal system (or rather, on some version of a narrow set of essentially equivalent formal systems). To wit, almost all of present-day mathematics is derived from set theory, and set theory can be set up as a particular formal system. The program of showing in detail that all the essential parts of mathematics can in fact be thought of as theorems in a formal system known as *Zermelo–Fraenkel* set theory, has been carried out by the famous group of mathematicians who wrote under the collective pseudonym of *Nicholas Bourbaki* (1954, 1968; cf. also Vilks 1995).

Set-theoretic formalism

In actual practice, most mathematicians hardly ever go back to the axiomatics of set theory. Instead, set theory is typically *taken for granted* as the foundation of mathematics, and the fact that it can be set up as a formal system places mathematics based on set theory within some version of basic formalism. However, the fact that set theory has come to be seen as the universal foundation of mathematics, has given rise to a methodological standard that is sometimes called informal axiomatization. It consists of beginning the exposition of some piece of mathematics by presenting the definition of some set-theoretic predicate.

For instance, an exposition of probability theory typically begins with the definition of 'probability space' : The triple $(\Omega, \mathscr{F}, P)$ is said to be a probability space, if Ω is a set, $\mathscr{F}$ is a sigma-algebra in Ω, and P is a mapping from $\mathscr{F}$ to the real numbers such that (a) $P(E) \geq 0$ for all $E \in \mathscr{F}$, (b) $P(\Omega)=1$, and (c) $P(E_1 \cup E_2 \cup \ldots)=P(E_1)+P(E_2)+\ldots$ for every sequence of disjoint sets E_1, E_2, ... from $\mathscr{F}$.

All the notions appearing in such an 'informal axiomatization of probability', such as triple, sigma-algebra, mapping, real numbers, etc., are ultimately themselves defined in terms of the basic alphabet of set theory, and in proving theorems about probability spaces one is allowed to use only what can ultimately be proved from the axioms of Zermelo–Fraenkel set theory.

In order to distinguish this approach from basic formalism, we call it set-theoretic formalism. Whereas basic formalism just aims at making all undefined terms and unproved assertions explicit, set-theoretic formalism is firmly wedded to one particular set of primitives and one particular set of axioms – the ones of set theory (including standard predicate logic). Set theoretic formalism demands we use only notions which can ultimately be defined in terms of the basic set-theoretic notions, and asserts only what can be proved from the axioms of set theory. By taking set theory for granted, this version of formalism actually distracts attention from the axioms and primitives of set theory – thereby allowing the mathematician to focus on the 'more interesting' derived notions and theorems.

For a discussion of formalism in economics, it can hardly be over-emphasized that it is much more the set-theoretic variant that shapes present day 'formal' economic theory. It is the work of Gerard Debreu – actually a student of one of the members of the Bourbaki group – which brings out this approach most clearly. In his methodologically paradigmatic *Theory of Value* (1959, p. 2), Debreu explicitly mentions that 'the logical foundations of set theory are taken for granted', and the central definitions that follow are exactly analogous to the above example of a probability space (p. 75):

> An economy E is defined by: for each $i=1,\ldots,m$ a non-empty subset X_i of $\mathbb{R}^\ell$ completely preordered by $\leq_i$; for each $j=1,\ldots,n$ a non-empty subset Y_j of $\mathbb{R}^\ell$; a point ω of $\mathbb{R}^\ell$. A state of E is an $(m+n)$-tuple of points in $\mathbb{R}^\ell$.'

Again, all the notions used in these definitions of 'economy' and 'state of an economy' are ones that are defined in terms of set-theoretic notions; moreover, all the theorems that are proved about economies are ultimately derived from nothing else than the basic axioms of set theory. To be sure, Debreu limits this approach to what he calls 'the theory in the strict sense', and adds interpretations which are not meant to belong to 'theory in the strict sense'. Given, however, that the Theory of Value is usually considered to be a piece of economic theory, it is remarkable that the 'strict' core of it is, logically speaking, nothing else than part of set-theoretic mathematics.

The unquestioned acceptance of set theory in economics

Another remarkable thing about set-theoretic formalism in economics is that the adequacy of the particular formal system that it relies upon is hardly ever considered worthy of discussion by its adherents. From the point of view of basic formalism one could very well consider the use of undefined notions and axioms not used in set-theory, but fundamental for economics, in addition to and on a par with set-theory. It has been argued elsewhere (Vilks 1991a, 1992) that notions such as 'action', 'preference' or 'feasibility' might well be considered as specific primitive notions of economics, and that some very basic principles of economics, notably a weak principle of rationality, can serve as axioms that regulate the use of the primitives in much the same way as the axioms of set-theory regulate the use of mathematical primitives.

Conversely, some of the basic axioms of the Zermelo–Fraenkel system that are taken for granted in standard mathematics, and thereby remain somewhat hidden in the set-theoretic version of formalism, are by no means unproblematic when it comes to formal theories of so-called 'propositional attitudes'. An individual agent's attitudes towards propositions – such as his/her knowledge or belief in particular propositions – figure prominently in many economic arguments, but are known to pose problems when treated by means of the 'extensional' language of mathematics. These problems are mainly due to the fact that an agent's attitude towards a proposition very often depends on how the proposition is expressed or 'framed'. To indicate the kind of difficulties that arise, consider the axiom of substitutivity which belongs to the typically unquestioned core of set-theoretic mathematics. It states that equal objects must have exactly the same properties, and can be formally expressed as $(X=Y) \Rightarrow (P(X) \Leftrightarrow P(Y))$, where $P(.)$ stands for an arbitrary predicate. As long as the predicate $P(.)$ is a standard mathematical one, this axiom does in fact seem pretty convincing. However, it has little plausibility when the predicate $P(.)$ is meant, for instance, to denote somebody's knowledge: While $823543=7^7$, and thus the two statements '$823543<900000$', and '$7^7<900000$' are mathematically equivalent, one can well know the obvious fact that $823543<900000$, but fail to know that $7^7<900000$ (cf. Vilks 1995).

It seems fair to say that Bourbaki-style mathematics with its set-theoretic foundations is treated by the overwhelming majority of mathematical economists as a reliable basis of economic theorizing, one that is valid or adequate quite independently of the context or subject to which it is applied. The adequacy of set theory for economic theorizing can be seen as belonging to the mathematical economists' disciplinary matrix in the sense of Thomas Kuhn (1970), or to the hard core of their research program, if Lakatos' (1970) analysis and terminology is preferred. The fact that discussions of this adequacy are strikingly absent from the scholarly discourse of mathematical economists, and the belief in set theory thus rather belongs to the *tacit* shared beliefs of mathematical economists only confirms this assessment: The 'hard core' of a research program or the 'disciplinary matrix' of a scientific community are not, as a rule, regarded as legitimate objects of doubt or discussion by the members of the community.

To be sure, given that most of present-day mathematics is in fact derived from set theory, asking for a discussion of the adequacy of set theory is tantamount to questioning the adequacy of mathematics. This is not a task that can be attempted head-on within the present chapter, either, but a couple of remarks seem to be in order. Obviously, there are no indications whatsoever that mundane mathematics such as arithmetic or even the differential calculus should be regarded as misleading in their typical economic applications. If an exploration of alternatives to standard mathematics is called for, it is only with respect to the subtler problems of economic theory – such as, for instance, the analysis of epistemic foundations of game theory (cf. Aumann 1999), where standard set theory may turn out not to be the most adequate theoretical framework. Given that economic theorists have in fact begun to address questions where standard informal set theory is not without alternatives, the question seems to belong on the agenda whether modifications of standard set theory might prove more adequate than the Zermelo–Fraenkel system.

At any rate, it is worth noting that physicists such as the Nobel Prize winner Eugene Wigner (1960) have posed the analogous question for the natural sciences quite some time ago, and there has been some informed debate about why mathematics seems so impressively useful in, for instance, physics (cf. Mickens 1990). Acccording to Wigner, 'the enormous usefulness of mathematics in the natural sciences is something bordering on the mysterious'. However, given that mathematics as we know it today has developed in close interaction with the development of the natural sciences (cf., for example, Kline 1980), and the success of the natural sciences has throughout been a success of natural science *plus* mathematics, the acceptance of mathematics by natural scientists seems to be much less of a mystery than its largely unquestioned acceptance by mathematical economists. After all, the usefulness of the natural sciences in solving problems that are regarded as important by society as a whole, is hardly matched by anything comparable in the case of mathematical economics.

In view of the above discussion, the plea seems justified that formal economic theory should pay close attention to its unproven assumptions *including* the ones that currently tend to be smuggled in by set-theoretic formalism. After all, it is basic formalism itself – or for that matter, formalism in the broad sense – that insists on making the unproven assertions explicit, so that their importance for the derived assertions can be better assessed, and alternative theoretical systems can be more readily compared.

Formal economics and the real world

Criticism of formalism in economics has often focused on the relation between formal models and economic reality. According to standard wisdom, a formal model and reality can be connected by giving an interpretation of the formalism. In fact, it was again Debreu in his *Theory of Value* (1959, p. x) who emphasized the dichotomy between 'the theory in the strict sense' on the one hand, and 'the informal discussion of interpretations' on the other hand.

At first sight, the relation between a formal model and reality seems to be straightforward. A formal model in the set-theoretic approach may be identified with a certain set of (formal) assumptions about the basic, set-theoretically defined notion.[2] In the case of Debreu's Theory of Value, for instance, a particular model would consist of a particular set of assumptions about an 'economy' (γ $(X_i), (Y_j), \omega$)), including, for instance, statements such as 'X_i is closed and convex', or '$Y_j \in 0$'. (It is worth noting that, in set-theoretic formalism, such assumptions are never *asserted* by the theory in the strict sense; rather they would appear as antecedent conditions in theorems of the form 'if assumptions $A_1, A_2, \ldots, A_n$ hold, then the economy has the property P'.) An interpretation of the model is then typically seen as assigning a real-world counterpart to each ingredient of the formally defined 'economy'. For instance, Y_j may be interpreted as the set of those production plans which are technically possible for the j-th producer. Once an interpretation has been specified, the interpreted model seems to consist of statements which are no longer purely mathematical statements, but statements about economic reality. Likewise, any statement that can be logically derived from the formal model, seems to carry 'real' economic content once the interpretation has been fixed. As the derivation itself, being 'merely formal', is believed to be valid for any interpretation whatsoever, the interpreted conclusions should hold true whenever the interpreted assumptions do.

However, two questions arise. First of all, there are, in general, many different interpretations of one and the same formal model. This is actually often regarded as a strength of the formal approach. To quote Debreu (1959, p. x) once again: 'It … makes possible immediate extensions of [the] analysis without modification of the theory by simple reinterpretation of concepts.' However, interpretations can also be more or less specific. For instance, one may either leave the phrase 'the j-th producer' unexplained, or one could actually name a specific, real-world firm as the interpretation of 'the j-th producer'. The fact that 'the realm of interpretations' is considered to be clearly outside the formal theory, seems to allow much freedom in filling in or leaving out details about what is actually meant by a 'specific' interpretation. As many concepts that appear in formal economic models do not have an obvious real-world 'counterpart', to which one could point, as it were, empirical specificity of an intended interpretation will typically require a more or less subtle 'operationalization', the use of proxies, techniques of statistical estimation, etc. A good deal of such a detailed empirical interpretation will itself require some degree of formalization. Very often, however, 'interpretations' of a formal model are given in relatively loose terms only, leaving any historical details unspecified.

In fact, the precise notion of interpretation of a formal economic model has received surprisingly little attention in the literature. A noteworthy definition has been suggested by Rubinstein (1991), who states that 'an interpretation is a mapping which links a formal theory with everyday language'. However, in this definition the notion of 'mapping' cannot really be understood in its usual mathematical sense. This would require that both the domain and the range of the mapping be sets, but in formal Zermelo–Fraenkel set theory, words of everyday language just do not appear. From the point of view of basic formalism, one could, of course, include words or phrases of everyday language – such as 'the j-th producer' – in a suitable formal system, and then use axioms which link these 'everyday language' words with the 'artificial' symbols of the required mathematics (cf. Vilks 1991b). However, this would include the interpretation itself within the formal system. It would also require a formal extension of Zermelo–Fraenkel set theory, and is thus not feasible within set-theoretic formalism. Clearly, the words of everyday language included in such a formal system would cease to 'carry' their everyday meaning to the extent that it cannot be reflected by suitable axioms. At any rate, the seemingly sharp distinction between 'formal theory' and its 'interpretations' is not at all that sharp from the point of view of basic formalism, which would actually demand to state explicitly any intended connection between artificial symbols and ordinary words, and to treat these 'interpretative' axioms with the same degree of circumspection and precision as standard mathematics.

A second question about the standard view of interpretation arises from the fact that formal models are often interpreted in a way that make some or even most of its assumptions obviously false. Examples would be perfectly competitive markets, perfect divisibility of all goods, a continuum of agents, and many others, which are used as explicit assumptions again and again in many models, but are not even intended to be literally true or reflect economic reality. One may legitimately ask what kind of knowledge can be gained from formal models which are based on assumptions which are obviously wrong even according to the intended interpretation.

We think there are two quite different answers that can be given to this question. (1) Formal economic models can be regarded as simplified representations of economic reality, or (2) as instruments for training the economists analytical abilities and perception of economic structures and mechanisms.

Formal models as simplified representations of economic reality

The first view of formal models is by far the more popular one, and corresponds to the very common analogy according to which formal economic models are like maps of economic reality. They are not meant to give a completely detailed and accurate picture of reality, but instead emphasize the important aspects of the world, and omit or even misrepresent the unimportant ones. According to this point of view, it is not required that formal economic models build on 'true' or even 'evident' assumptions. Instead they should represent the 'essential' aspects of the modeled portion of economic reality and, thus, provide a basis for understanding reality and for guiding economic decisions.

This view of the use of formal models obviously poses the problem of how to assess whether a particular formal models really captures the important aspects of the real economy, and describes them in an adequate way – rather than emphasizing unimportant things and giving a misleading picture of reality.

Today probably the most popular answer to this questions is the one given in the 1950s by Milton Friedman. 'Viewed as a body of substantive hypotheses, theory is to be judged by its prediction power for the class of phenomena which it is intended to explain' (Friedman 1953, p. 8). If the conclusion drawn from an (interpreted) formal economic model can be confirmed by empirical investigations, there is still no evidence that it is true in an epistemological sense. But empirical confirmation is a sufficient fundament to accept a theory pragmatically and use it 'as if' it was true. If, however, predictions of the model are contradicted by empirical investigations, the model has to be rejected, or at least treated with some critical distance. Friedman emphasized that an empirical confirmation is only demanded for the conclusions of a model, and not for its assumptions, because only its conclusions are used for forecasting purposes: '... a theory cannot be tested by the "realism" of its assumptions' (ibid., p. 23).

Friedman's methodological point of view has been much discussed, and we refrain from attempting an assessment of this discussion. However, we are convinced that mechanical procedures of empirical testing do not provide adequate grounds for judging the correctness or usefulness of a formal economic model. Quite apart from the logical fact that any assumption trivially implies itself, and the distinction between assumptions and conclusions is not as unproblematic as Friedman suggests, there are a lot of reasons why an empirical test of only those conclusions which 'the model is intended to explain', does not necessarily allow one to judge the adequacy of the model itself. Among these are that many variables of economic models cannot be measured directly and have to be represented by proxies in empirical investigations. As long as the relation between the proxy and the intended variable is not clearly specified, the empirical investigation may cast little light on the model itself. Also, empirical tests typically establish only correlations instead of causalities. Moreover, qualitative and structural changes in economies can affect the explanatory power of economic models – an empirical confirmation of a formal economic model *in the past* need not be a reliable indication of its correctness or usefulness *in the future*.

Against this background, Friedman's approach seems inadequate to us. To be sure, there is certainly a grain of truth in viewing economic models as simplified maps of reality. However, we would rather agree with Solow's view that useful economic models should be regarded as 'illuminating parables'. According to Solow the value of formal economic models lies less in giving reliable representations of economic reality than in providing concepts, pointing out logical structures, and thus helping a decision-maker to understand economical processes. Formal models can help to separate the important from the unimportant and to manage the complexity of economic reality. Yet the conclusions from formal economic models should always be treated carefully and with a critical distance, or, as Solow puts it: 'There are always aspects of economic life that are left out of any simplified model. There will therefore be problems on which it throws no light at all; worse yet, there may be problems on which it appears to throw light, but on which it actually propagates error' (Solow 1970, p. 1). Obviously, this does not provide clear criteria to distinguish 'light' from 'error', either, but unlike Friedman, Solow argues that the correctness and usefulness of a formal economic model has to be judged more subtly than just by means of empirical testing.

Formal models as training instruments
In fact, it seems appropriate to go one step further. It seems to us that formal economic models can very well be useful without being simplified representations or 'maps' of economic reality. Instead, much of the value of formal models derives from their role in improving the economist's intuition for phenomena and mechanisms that have some importance in economic reality – even if they are constantly counteracted by various other tendencies and mechanisms. Dealing with formal economic models, especially during academic education, trains the perception and analytical skills of young economists. This training especially concern the economist's skills to discover and to anticipate economic phenomena and mechanisms, and to take them into consideration for the assessment of real situations in a way which would be unavailable to the untrained 'common sense'.

Unlike the older philosophies of science which identified science mostly with systems of explicit statements or theories, Thomas Kuhn has argued in detail that the role of scientific socialization is not so much to teach true statements, but rather to impart to students the skills that a competent scientist is expected to have. He also emphasized that these skills normally consist of 'tacit knowledge' that cannot in general be expressed by a system of explicit statements. It seems to us that these findings of Kuhn can be applied to the role of formal models within economic analysis. Dealing with formal models trains the economist's ability to form a judgment about phenomena and processes which may occur in complex systems of interacting individuals. Thus, the value of formal economic models consists not so much in any specific statements about economic reality they might make, but rather in the effect that a the study of formal economic models has on the economist's ability to understand.

Understood in this way, the usefulness of formal economic models cannot be judged immediately in terms of their accordance with economic reality. However, if the function of economic models consist in building up 'tacit knowledge', and the economical ability to judge, it has to be admitted that, for the time being, their epistemologic status remains somewhat unclear. Of course, it has to be conceded that dealing with absurd models can also guide intuition in a wrong direction. Moreover, there are neither convincing criteria for the selection of the formal economic models an economist should deal with, nor for the way and the extent of advisable work with them.

Our general conclusion is that the relation between formal economic models and economic reality is far from being simple or fully understood. It also remains an open question, whether there are 'economic laws' and what their epistemological status might be. Are they only the means to develop 'tacit knowledge', or rather 'roughly right' statements about economic reality that can provide a reliable basis for economic decisions? How does one distinguish suitable from less suitable models? This somewhat unclear status not only makes a critical assessment of particular formal models difficult, but it also provides an starting point for a critical assessment of formalism in economics.

A critical reflection of formalism in economics
While set-theoretic formalism poses its specific problems that we discussed above, basic formalism and formalism in the broad sense seem to be pretty healthy methodological attitudes. Formalization does not aim at any particular content of an argument, but only at making any arguments explicit. Thus, it demands nothing else than clarification of theoretical reasoning, and can thus help to resolve scientific controversies.

However, some doubts about the advisability of formalization may result from the unclear epistemological status of formal arguments that was pointed out above. These doubts are intensified by the fact that formalization of economic arguments is not 'for free' ; formalization requires – sometimes considerable – amounts of energy which might alternatively be used to study economic phenomena more closely but informally. Moreover, formalized economic arguments tend to become complex and thus difficult to handle. This often complicates communication and discussion of economic arguments, and restricts it to a somewhat narrow scientific community. Another consequence of the technical difficulties of formalization is that in many cases relevant aspects of a problem have to be 'assumed away' in order to succeed with formalization. Consequently, formal models typically allow one to analyse only isolated and very limited aspects of economic reality.

Clearly, formalization of an argument always comes at a cost. As in mathematics itself, it seems advisable to weigh costs and benefits of formalization in every particular case of economic reasoning in order to find something like an 'optimal degree' of formalization. Quite obviously, this optimal degree of formalization will often be quite moderate. Only a small part of economic analysis is formalized à la Debreu. Instead, many economists employ mathematical methods rather in an informal way and refrain from making explicit every part of their analysis.

In fact, there are some potential dangers that have to be kept in mind when assessing the role of formalism in economics (a recent critique of formalism, somewhat similar in its arguments, but different in its conclusions can be found in Blaug, 1998, and 2003).

First of all, when economic reasoning is used as a basis for policy decisions or recommendations, formal economic models should be treated with the same critical distance as informal arguments – in particular when their epistemological status is doubtful. There is sometimes the tendency to take results of formal economic models at face value and treat them as 'economic laws' without recognizing that they are based on assumptions which are hardly ever all beyond reasonable doubt. Admittedly, this is not a criticism of formalism as such, but rather of an ill-understood use of formal models.

A more immanent danger of formalism is that formalists in economics often tend to select, analyse, and thereby to emphasize those questions that are easily accessible by a formal treatment. Conversely, problems which do not lend themselves easily to a formal treatment, may tend to be ignored. Predominance of formalism may thus lead to a distorted understanding of economic reality, and guide economists' intuitions in a wrong or biased direction.

A further problem with formalism in economics is that formalists often tend to confine themselves to the realm of the 'theory in the strict sense', and thus avoid the uncomfortable questions of interpretation. To some extent, this is certainly just a – completely legitimate – result of scholarly division of labor, but in extreme cases the refinements and variations of formal models with no regard to interpretations looks very much like *l'art pour l'art*. In particular, when the reputation connected to mathematically advanced research is much higher than what can be expected from other kinds of research, younger scholars have incentives to neglect the ill-defined or messy problems in order to excel by means of mathematical virtuosity.

To sum up, formalism in economics is like strong medicine. Diseases such as ill-conceived or fallacious economic arguments can hardly be overcome without it. Applied wisely, it strengthens economic understanding and intuition. But as it also has negative side effects, too much of it may be harmful – and may distort one's perception of reality, and make arguments unnecessarily complicated. It may also impair one's appetite for other healthy diet, and – in particular for the young and bright ones – it can easily become addictive.

Notes

1. Extended bibliographies of early exponents of formalism – mathematical as well as non-mathematical – can be found in the third edition of Jevons, *Theory of Political Economy* (1888) and in an appendix of the English edition of Cournot's *Elements* (1st edn 1897, by Irving Fisher).
2. It is worth noting that we follow the economists' usage by identifying a model with a set of assumptions. This is quite different from the usage in formal logic and mathematics, where models of a certain set of axioms are typically defined to be the (set-theoretic) objects satisfying the axioms.

References

Aumann, Robert J. (1999), 'Interactive epistemology I: Knowledge', *Journal of Game Theory*, **28**, 263–300.

Blaug, Mark (1998), 'Disturbing currents in modern economics', *Challenge*, **41** (3), 11–38.

Blaug, Mark (2003) 'The formalist revolution of the 1950s', *Journal of the History of Economic Thought*, **25**, 145–56.

Bourbaki, Nicholas (1954), *Elements de Mathematique XX Les Structures Fondamentales de l'Analyse. Livre I: Theorie Des Ensembles*, Paris: Hermann and Cie Editeurs.

Bourbaki, Nicholas (1968), *Elements of Mathematics: Theory of Sets*, Reading: Addison-Wesley.

Cournot, Augustin (1838), *Recherches sur les principes mathématiques de la théorie des richesses*, Paris, Hachette. Reprinted in English (1897), translated by N.T. Bacon, New York and London: Macmillan.

Debreu, Gerard (1959), *Theory of Value: An Axiomatic Analysis of Economic Equilibrium*, New Haven, CT and London, Yale University Press.

Friedman, Milton (1953), 'The methodology of positive economics', in: *Essays in Positive Economics*, Chicago: University of Chicago Press, pp. 3–43.

Gossen, Hermann Heinrich (1854), *Entwicklung der Gesetze des menschalichen Verkehrs und der daraus fliessenden Regeln für menschliches Handeln*, Braunschweig: F. Vieweg Sohn.

Jevons, William St. (1888), *Theory of Political Economy*, 3rd edn, London: Macmillan.

Kline, Morris (1980), *Mathematics: The Loss of Certaincy*, Oxford: Oxford University Press.

Kuhn, Thomas S. (1970), *The Structure of Scientific Revolutions*, 2nd edn, Chicago: Chicago University Press.

Lakatos, Imre (1970), 'Falsification and the methodology of scientific research programmes', in Imre Lakatos and A. Musgrave (eds), *Criticism and the Growth of Knowledge*, Cambridge: Cambridge University Press.

Marshall, Alfred (1890), *Principles of Economics*, London: Macmillan and Company.

Mickens, Ronald E. (1990), *Mathematics and Science*, Teaneck, NJ: World Scientific Publishing Co.

Rubinstein, Ariel (1991), 'Comments on the interpretation of game theory', *Econometrica*, **59**, 909–24.

Samuelson, Paul A. (1947), *Foundations of Economic Analysis*, Cambridge, MA: Harvard University Press.

Schmoller, Gustav (1883), ‚Zur Methode der Staats- und Social-Wissenschaften', Jahrbuch für Gesetzgebung, *Verwaltung und Volkswirtschaft im Deutschen Reich*, 7.

Schumpeter, Jospeh A. (1954), *History of Economic Analysis*, New York: Oxford University Press.

Senior, William. N. (1836), *An Outline of the Science of Political Economy*, London, Clover and Sons.

Solow, Robert M. (1970), *Growth Theory: An Exposition*, Oxford: Clarendon Press.

Thünen, Johan H. von (1826), *Der isolierte Staat in Beziehung auf Landwirthschaft und Nationalökonomie, oder Untersuchungen über den Einfluß, den die Getreidepreise, der Reichtum des Bodens und die Abgaben auf den Ackerbau ausüben*, Part I, Hamburg.

Vilks, Arnis (1991a), *Neoklassik, Gleichgewicht und Realität. Eine Untersuchung über die Grundlagen der Wirtschaftstheorie*, Heidelberg: Physica.

Vilks, Arnis (1991b), 'On metaphilosophy and methodology in economics', *Methodus*, **3**, 90–94.

Vilks, Arnis (1992), 'A set of axioms for neoclassical economics and the methodological status of the equilibrium concept', *Economics and Philosophy*, 8, 51–82.

Vilks, Arnis (1995), 'On mathematics and mathematical economics', *Greek Economic Review*, **17**, 177–204.

Walras, Leon (1874), *Éléments d'économie politique pure, ou théorie de la richesse social*, Lausanne, Paris and Basle. Reprinted in English (1954), translated by W. Jaffé London: Allen and Unwin.

Wigner, Eugene (1960), 'The unreasonable effectiveness of mathematics', *Communications on Pure and Applied Mathematics*, **13**, 1–14.

15 Methodological individualism and economics

Harold Kincaid

Individualism is a broad concept that resonates throughout economics. My goal here is to first sort out the many different ideas at work and then to make some progress in assessing them.

Two initial clarifications are in order. First, individualism has both normative and descriptive components. No doubt in practice these two components are often fused and no doubt the normative concepts help motivate the descriptive. The root intuition behind normative individualism--that justice and dessert are honored so long as social arrangements result from free human choices--is powerful and surely inspires the methodological thought that economics should explain via the choices of individuals. Nonetheless, the normative and methodological claims are logically independent. It is the latter that are explicitly involved in economic explanations and are my prime target.

Second, on my view the different theses of methodological individualism turn ultimately on empirical issues, often in quite specific ways. Consequently assessing individualism cannot be done completely without invoking specific issues in economics itself. These empirical issues will emerge naturally as we spell out different individualist claims.

The chapter proceeds as follows. Section I clarifies various individualist theses and their interrelations. Sections II, III, IV and V then assess in detail individualism as a claim about ontology, reduction, explanation, and research strategies respectively.

Theses

There are various colloquial slogans that express the general individualist position. Society is nothing but individuals. Only individuals are actors in the social world. Nothing comes about except through the actions of individuals. Any social explanation can be reduced to an individualist one. The best explanations are those in terms of individuals. No social explanation is adequate without individualist mechanisms. And so on. This section discusses just what these claims come to and how they interrelate.

These claims can usefully be put into five categories as assertions about ontology, reduction, explanation, mechanisms, and heuristics. Ontological claims concern the kinds of things that exist. Reductionism asserts that one theory can do all the explanatory work of another. Claims concerning explanation assert that accounts in terms of individuals have some fundamental role. Theses about mechanisms make individualist processes underlying social phenomena central in some way. Finally, heuristic theses see the search for individualist theories as the best way for social science to progress.

Thus put, methodological individualism makes assertions about the social sciences in general. As we shall see in the sections that follow, most of these theses have a more specific economic counterpart. Claims about reducing the social become claims about reducing the macroeconomic. Claims about the need for individualist mechanisms become demands for rational choice explanations of equilibrium behavior. These and other economic instantiations will be discussed below. Though at the abstract level the types of theses and arguments about individualism are common across the social sciences, it is the specific embodiments in discipline-specific disputes that is essential, because the empirical issues involved need not have a uniform resolution across domains.

There are at least three different ontological versions of individualism with some currency. Sometimes the claim is made that there is no such thing as society (or social entities). This eliminativist view is logically stronger than the second ontological claim that society is composed of and does not exist over and above individuals, for the latter thesis admits that social entities exist. A further ontological claim is that the facts about individuals are basic in that once all the facts about individuals are set, then so too are the facts about social entities. In the philosophical jargon, social facts 'supervene' on individual facts.

Reductionism makes a claim about the relation between theories. The root notion is that a theory expressed entirely in terms of individuals can do all the work of any well-confirmed theory couched in terms of social entities – just as it has been shown in physics that statistical mechanics captures everything that thermodynamics explains. Exactly how we should understand the phrases 'can' and 'capture' will be detailed later.

Claims about explanation are more slippery. Reference to individuals might be either necessary or sufficient to explain and might be required for full explanation versus any explanation whatsoever. Somewhat orthogonally, we might ask which explanation best explains. Out of these dimensions come the following interesting claims: (1) No social explanation is adequate without reference to individuals, (2) social phenomena can be fully explained in individualist terms, and (3) individualist theories provide the best explanation.

As a claim about mechanisms, individualism might be given either an evidential or explanatory reading (or both). The evidential thesis would be that:

- No claim about social entities is well confirmed without individualist mechanisms.

- But even if we rejected this claim and thought that confirmation of, say, causal relations between social entities was possible without mechanisms, we might still think that explanations without mechanisms are inadequate. So the explanatory version is:
- Social theories cannot explain (or explain fully) without citing individualist mechanisms.
- This thesis parallels earlier ones about explanation with the further requirement that reference be to individualist *mechanisms*, not just individuals.

A final important but ill-defined individualist thesis is about scientific progress. Methodological individualism, the thought is, promotes scientific success. This thesis is ill-defined in part because, as we have just seen, 'methodological individualism' is many different theses. It is also ill-defined because 'scientific progress' is ambivalent: progress in prediction, explanation, theory development, etc. can vary independently.

There are numerous connections between these theses, both logical and otherwise. For example, if reference to individuals is necessary to explain at all, for example, then it is necessary to fully explain (assuming some explication of that notion). We will discuss these various connections as we proceed.

Ontological claims

There are three basic ontological variants of individualism: the claim that only individuals exist, that social entities are composed of individuals, and that social entities do not act independently of individuals. These claims have distinctive import as they are spelled out in different ways and in different specific disciplines.

The eliminativist claim that 'there is no such thing as society, only individuals' (Thatcher 1987) has its advocates, some obviously influential. It is of a piece with other eliminativist claims in the history of science – that there are no vital forces, no phlogiston, no aether.

However, the parallel with these developments is forced. Rejecting vital forces did not mean denying that organelles, cells, and organisms exist. Instead, biologists denied that these entities were independent of the properties of molecules. So long as anti-reductionists in the social science are willing to allow some similar constraint, a similar position is open to them.

That brings us to the claims that society is composed of and does not act independently of individuals. The first claim seems trivially true. However, it is less obvious than it looks, since some inanimate material objects should perhaps be included as part of society as well. As we will see momentarily, this raises non-trivial issues when it comes to economics.

The second claim that social entities do not act independently likewise has more bite than its apparent triviality suggests. Here a concept from the philosophical discussion of physicalism is useful, viz. the notion of supervenience or determination (Hellman and Thompson 1975). Some philosophers of mind, for example, claim that once all the physical facts are set, then so are all the mental facts. In the terms of the trade, mental facts supervene on physical facts or the physical facts determine the mental.

Talk of 'facts' gets clearer if we specify particular theories and their basic categories. Then determination and supervenience hold respectively that the facts about A determine the facts about B in that once all the truths in the theory of A are set, then so are the truths of the theory about B or, in other words, the B truths are fixed by the A truths.

So the more precise version of this claim is that the truths of some individualist theory fix the truths of some social theory. Put in these terms, the individualist thesis is both more precise, more clearly empirical, and thus no longer trivial. Do the truths of sociobiology or social psychology fix what truths there might be about social entities? These are substantive empirical claims.

In their economic guise these theses are equally substantive. Consider first the claim that society or social entities are composed of individuals. Arguably they are not solely so composed, for there are material objects that should be included, something obvious in a discipline that is about the production and distribution of goods. But deciding what those physical entities are and how they should be conceived is a substantive economic issue. Is a subset of these goods 'capital'? What is that exactly? These substantive economic issues need not be settled in an individualist friendly way. If 'capital' is defined via the labor theory of value, for example, then the social entities populating Marx's economics are invoked. So the truism that society is composed of individuals does not on its own commit us to a strong form of individualism.

Moreover, even the claim that society is partly composed of individuals is more controversial than it would seem because of recent developments in philosophy of mind, cognitive science, and evolutionary game theory. The substantial self existing prior to the social realm has been replaced by 'embedded selves' (Clark 1998) constructed out of social interactions; the real atoms are subpersonal strategies that approximate neoclassical maximizers in ways that traditional individuals do not. This picture is further supported by the central place of evolutionary game theory, where it is strategies that are the basic individuals, not individual agents. This 'Dennettian' future for economics has been developed in path-breaking work by Ross (forthcoming), with similar ideas suggested by Mirowski (2001) (though not directly motivated by Dennett).

Similar questions arise for the claim that social entities do not act independently of individuals. This determination claim has multiple instantiations in economics and once again contentious issues are involved. The issues are those associated with the microfoundations literature as well as debates over aggregation (Weintraub 1979; Jannsen 1993).

At least the following questions are at issue in these debates:

- Do the preferences, assets, strategies, and knowledge of individuals determine or fix the facts about market equilibrium?
- Do the microeconomic facts determine or fix the macroeconomic facts?

These two questions are distinct because microeconomics typically is not entirely or often not at all about individual human beings. For it often treats firms and households as fundamental entities. But firms and households are social entities – aggregates of individuals with social structure. So even if it is true that the microeconomic facts fix the macroeconomic facts, that does not directly instantiate the individualist program. At most it might make it more likely in that the 'size' of the relevant social entities is 'closer' to individuals.

There are two good reasons to think that the first determination thesis is questionable. The literature on aggregation problems raises a first batch of doubts. For example, it is only under restrictive conditions that we can expect individual downward sloping demand curves to guarantee downward sloping demand curves for markets as a whole and the same seems true for other market level aggregates (Deaton and Muellbauer 1980).

The second set of doubts comes from the equilibrium requirement. Standard neoclassical market theory is a theory of equilibrium behavior. The question is whether the facts about individuals determine that an equilibrium exists. In Walrasian general equilibrium accounts the auctioneer (in conjunction with a host of other assumptions) ensures equilibrium exists. But if we move to more realistic mechanisms things are much murkier. Game theory results suggest that multiple equilibria are likely and that agents may need rather amazing abilities – like the ability to determine what is a subgame perfect Bayesian equilibrium – to find them. Investigations of learning and evolutionary mechanism show that it is far from inevitable that these processes will result in equilibrium either (Samuelson 1998).

There are two individualist responses here. First we might deny that individualism requires that 'the laws of economics are the same in the case of individuals and of nations' (Jevons 1879, p. 16). Then the aggregation problem loses its bite. Second, we might deny that equilibrium outcomes are required for individualism, eliminating the second problem.

These replies illustrate my earlier claim that the individualism debate turns on specific substantive issues in economics. While individualism can be defended by such replies, they provide a hollow victory for many current advocates of individualism. Walrasian and neoclassical approaches are often praised for and defended on the grounds of their individualism. But these replies would support individualism by giving up key tenets of these traditions.

What of the second version of determination – that microeconomic facts fix the macroeconomic? The obstacles are similar. We can only derive macroeconomic implications from choice-theoretic constraints at the microeconomic level if very restrictive, i.e. unrealistic, aggregation conditions are imposed (Jannssen 1993; Martel 1996). Moreover, those restraints typically involve assuming equilibrium outcomes. If macroeconomic phenomena are disequilibrium phenomena, then even successful aggregation would not be enough to ensure that the macroeconomic facts are fixed by the microeconomic – since equilibrium is assumed in the one and is denied in the other.

Reduction

Individualism is often put as a thesis about theory reduction. In this section I outline what theory reduction requires, look at and reject various conceptual arguments for the reducibility of social theories to individualist ones, and then argue that the issues are empirical in nature, with the evidence primarily supporting the anti-reductionist view.

As traditionally conceived in the philosophy of science (Nagel 1961), theory reduction is about deriving the laws of one domain from those of another. Since different theories have different vocabularies, derivation first requires some way to equate terms in the reduced theory with those of the reducing theory. Equivalent linguistic meaning, however, is too demanding a requirement – the concept of temperature does not simply mean 'average kinetic energy,' even though thermodynamics perhaps has been reduced to statistical mechanics. A weaker relation that will suffice for reduction is law-like coextensionality between every term to be reduced and some reducing term. In simpler terms, we want a constant one-to-one relation between cases where the reduced term applies and some reducing term holds. Once we have these 'bridge laws' as they are called, then we have a reduction if we can derive the laws of the reduced theory from the reducing. In the temperature case, that means taking molecular definitions of temperature, pressure and volume and Newton's laws of motion and then deriving the gas laws.

There is good reason to think these requirements – of bridge laws and derivability – are not sufficient for reduction. The root idea behind reduction is that one theory can explain everything that another can. But a long series of counterexamples (see Salmon 1989) shows that derivation from a law does not ensure explanation, contra the hypothetical deductive account of explanation. For example, it follows from 'No men who take birth control pills get pregnant' that some particular man does not do so, but we have not explained why. In the case of reduction, this weakness surfaces in alleged reductions that presuppose rather than eliminate the explanations to be reduced. For example, suppose I succeed in deducing parts of psychology from neuroscience. No interesting reduction will be forthcoming if my neuroscience describes neural states in terms like 'recognizes,' 'compares,' 'awareness level,' and so forth, because these are psychological states themselves. So reduction requires translation and derivation in a way that does not presuppose the theory to be reduced.

However, it is asking too much to demand that we *exactly* derive a theory or that we do so *in complete detail*. Since we are generally seeking to reduce a less fundamental theory to a more fundamental one, we should expect that the reduced theory is only captured approximately where it is in fact inaccurate. So reduction can involve correction. It is also too much to ask for a full derivation to be supplied. Instead what is needed is a demonstration that it is in principle possible.

So individualism as a reductionist thesis claims that a social theory – 'social' in that it refers to social entities such as corporations, states, etc. – can in principle be reduced to a theory referring only to individuals. In its most extreme form, individuals would only be described 'non-relationally' – without reference to essentially relational terms like 'more powerful than.' This view – a form of atomism – is not generally defended by methodological individualists. I will assume from here on that methodological individualism is the less drastic view that does allow relations.

To show that individualism as a reductionist thesis is false, it is strictly speaking only necessary to provide one compelling case where the requirements for reduction cannot be provided. But a more convincing case would provide reasons to think the failure was wide in scope. Individualism similarly gains support by providing actual cases of reduction and reasons to think them repeatable in other areas.

Both individualists and holists (my name for those who reject individualism) have tried to show that either reducibility *must* be possible or that it *never could be* on roughly conceptual, a priori grounds. Both sides seem misguided in that they claim more for philosophical argumentation that it can provide.

Holists argue that societies display 'downward causation': the nature of individuals is influenced by the larger social entities of which they are a part. Therefore reduction is impossible. Such arguments are uncompelling. Presumably if a social process influences an individual it does so via the actions of other individuals – social entities do not act on their own. So the individualist can simply reply that apparent cases of downward causation are likewise candidates for theory reduction.

On the other side a very common conceptual argument in favor of methodological individualism is that since society is composed of individuals and does nothing without them, explanations in terms of social entities must be reducible to explanation in terms of individuals (Watkins 1973, p. 179; Collins 1981, p. 989; Mathien 1988, p. 11). The conclusion does not follow. Seeing why will set up a more useful framework for thinking about reductionist versions of individualism.

Reduction, we said earlier, requires (1) one-to-one mappings from each social term to some individual terms such that we can derive social explanations from individualist ones (2) without invoking social explanations in the process. That suggests three possible obstacles to reduction: the one-to-one mapping may fail in either direction and the proposed reduction may presuppose social theory. To be more precise, the potential obstacles are:

- *Multiple realizations*: social terms may pick out entities or processes that can be brought about by many diverse different individual behaviors. If that happens our one-to-one mapping is defeated – that a given social term is instantiated does not entail that any particular description of individuals holds.
- *Context sensitivity*: types of individual behavior described in individualist theory might bring about different social entities or processes in different social situations. Then our one-to-one mapping is defeated because the individual description entails no unique social description.
- *Presupposing social information*: in the process of giving individualist explanations we may presuppose facts or explanations invoking social entities or processes.

Now return to the claim that social theory must be reducible because society is made of individuals and cannot act without them. That ontological fact tells us nothing about the expressive ability of our theories or how their explanations work. Society can be fully composed of individuals and yet the categories of social theory might not match up with individualist ones in the way that reduction requires. Social theory might capture causal patterns and types of events that individualist language does not. The ontological facts, in short, do not prevent the potential obstacles to reduction from being real.

The moral to draw is that individualism in its reductionist form is an empirical issue. In the broadest sense the empirical issue is whether the multiple realizations, context sensitivity and presupposing problems are real. How are we to decide that question? Three possibilities are: provide general considerations about social phenomena or social theories that makes those problems likely or unlikely, look at cases of alleged reductions, or look at apparently successful social theories and argue that they are or are not reducible.

Considerations of all three types can be advanced, I believe, to show that individualism as the thesis that all social theories are reducible, fails. However, doing so would involve details beyond the scope of a review and is moreover something I have attempted elsewhere (Kincaid 1996, 1997).

Evaluating reductionism in the economic context is a more tractable problem because we can deal with specific theories. We have already raised doubts about reducibility in our discussion of ontological versions of individualism. There I surveyed some of the microfoundations literature bearing on the question whether aggregate phenomena supervene on individual economic behavior. I argued that the relevant microfoundations were not forthcoming and thus to that extent did not support the supervenience claim. However, reducibility requires supervenience – it is the micro to macro side of the biconditional bridge law that reduction requires. So those problems for the ontological claims are equally doubts about reduction.

The doubts do not end there, however. There is good reason to think that the multiple realizations and presupposing information problems are real in economics.

Macro level kinds in economics are natural candidates for multiple realizations in individual behavior. A standard aggregate phenomenon of microeconomics – downward sloping market behavior – is a case in point. The early work of Becker (1976) and more recent work of Hildenbrand (1983, 1994) makes a strong case that the downward sloping market demand curve can result from diverse sets of individual behavior. Random preference differences along a budget line can produce aggregate downward sloping market curves, as can other kinds of preference distributions (see Martel 1996). So the aggregate market supply and demand laws can be realized by different sets of individual behavior.

We have two good economic reasons for thinking that firm behavior as well might be multiply realized in individual behavior. First, assume that economic selection actually works to bring about profit maximizing behavior. Selection mechanisms only 'care' about the property being selected for: if there are two equally good ways to organize individuals in a profitable firm, then selection will not 'see' the individual behavior in question. So we should not be surprised if profit seeking was brought about by different sets of individual behavior if we think it exists due to economic selection.

Further evidence comes from recent attempts to explain firm behavior in individualist terms. The problem is an embarrassment of riches. Typical firm characteristics – long-term employment relations, internal labor markets, and hierarchical structure, for example – have been tackled in various ways with the rational maximizing under constraints approach. A large variety of mechanisms – for example, transaction costs, inducements not to shirk, the threat of outside takeovers, markets for managers and directors among others – can produce the traits of typical capitalist firm (Kincaid 1995). This gives us reason to believe that there are multiple plausible economic mechanisms that could realize aggregate firm behavior.

The above evidence comes from microeconomics, albeit the aggregate part of it. 'Larger' macroeconomic aggregates ought likewise be open to multiple realizations. Macroeconomics describes markets at their greatest aggregation. The question thus is whether different combinations of less aggregative behavior (e.g. sectors) or of individual and corporate behavior might bring aggregates with the same economic properties. If so, the multiple realizations problem is real.

The third problem for reduction surfaces when the reducing theory presupposes the facts, categories or explanations of the theory to be reduced. There are many instances where alleged individualist explanations of aggregate economic behavior seem to do just that. Rather than simply listing examples, consider two general tools of economics: identifying equilibrium behavior in markets of rational self-seeking agents and equilibrium outcomes in games. Both presuppose rather than explain many facts about social entities and social structure.

Market analyses take the preferences of individuals and their assets as given. This is already to presuppose rather than explain much about norms and institutions. Equilibrium is often gotten by the auctioneer device, a stand in for institutional factors that allow markets to work. Assuming a distribution of assets is itself to presuppose that property rights already exist and are defined. Moves to incorporate expectations arguably must likewise assume defined macrostates about which individuals have beliefs (Colander 1996).

In game theory, similar assumptions are at work. The players, strategies, and payoffs are given. That is again to assume rather than explain facts about institutions, norms, and so on. Furthermore, many games have multiple equilibria. Narrowing down those equilibria to one often presupposes unexplained social facts. For example, the notion of 'focal points' relies on already shared norms. In the refinements literature unique equilibria are sometimes derived by assuming homogeneous priors in Bayesian games, thus presuming the institutional structure that produced the consensus (Jannsen 1993). Evolutionary and learning accounts may produce no unique equilibrium, but even when they do, social institutions are lurking in the environment that does the selecting (Jannsen 1993).

I note in concluding this section that none of these arguments show individualism in its reductionist guise misguided anywhere and always in economics. Because reduction is an empirical issue, no such global pronouncements are possible.

Explanation and mechanism
When doubts about individualism as a reductionist thesis arise, it is natural to think that we may have missed the target. Theory reduction is a rather specific doctrine. Maybe individualism can be formulated more plausibly as a thesis about explanation in some other sense?

One non-starter in this vein is the claim that all social phenomena can be fully explained in individualist terms even if the relevant theories cannot be reduced. This version is a non-starter because if we can provide full explanations, then we can provide reductions. Explanation is done by theories. If an individualist account explains all that can be explained, then it captures the explanations of social theory. But if it captures those explanations, then we can derive those explanations from individualist theory. However, that is theory reduction all over again.

There is another common way of construing individualism as a claim about explanation – viz. to assert that individualist theories are the *best* explanation. This claim is generally of dubious sense and implausible when it is not.

'Explanation' is often left undefined. Since that invites confusion, let's take the best explanation to be the most accurate account of the causes. However, for one theory to better explain than another, they must compete. But holist and individualist theories are at different levels. Theories at different levels may be compatible accounts of causal processes, as presumably molecular and organismic biology are.

To show that individualist and holist theories compete, we need some way to translate them into common coinage so that they are about the same things. One route to translation – reduction – we have already argued is generally implausible. Forgoing the type identities of reduction means looking at cases – looking at particular aggregate variables in particular circumstances and identifying the individual behavior realizing it.

Given these conditions, the apparent conflict between individualist and holist theories may often be only that. Suppose that someone claims that a neoclassical account of the distribution of income in terms of the marginal productivity of labor is superior to a sociological explanation invoking power and norms. There seems to be competition between explanations here, but is it inevitable? If we ask what kind of individual behavior realizes norms and power, we may find that facts about preferences, the prior distribution of assets, relative scarcity, and other factors that underlie supply and demand curves are involved. But these are variables seemingly compatible with the marginal productivity account. Only if the individualist claimed that marginal productivity alone determined income would the two theories be competing explanations. While some hasty textbook writers may find themselves asserting such a slogan, it is incoherent (see Hausman 1981).

Seeing the individualism/holism issue as about best explanation is encouraged by a common practice in economics and the social sciences more generally. I have in mind comparing theories in the form of regression equations against a data set to determine which 'explains most', i.e. which has the highest R^2. But R^2 is a measure of predictive power, not explanatory adequacy. Moreover, it makes sense to compare such equations only if we know that the variables in question are independent. But they well may not be in the individualism/holism case, since one set realizes the other.

Another important explanatory version of individualism asserts that mechanisms are necessary for all social explanations and that the mechanisms must be based in individual behavior. This demand seemingly motivates much of the 'microfoundations' literature in economics.

It is not plausible to think that there is any general methodological demand for mechanisms for good scientific theories. Note first that the demand for mechanisms is ambiguous: is the claim that mechanisms are needed for good *explanations*? Or are they needed to have sufficient *evidence*? Is the mechanism behind the hypothesis that A causes B some further cause C between A and B – a horizontal mechanism – or is it what realizes or makes up A – a vertical mechanism? And what is 'the' mechanism? Since causes can be described at different levels of aggregation and different levels of detail, 'the' mechanism is no more sensical than 'the' cause generally is. At best we can talk about 'a' mechanism.

In none of these diverse senses are mechanisms a *sine qua non* for scientific virtue. We can know that the throwing of the rock broke the window without knowing the molecular details of the rock's structure or of the rock/glass interaction. Citing the thrown rock likewise provides a good causal explanation without such details. Modern physics is full of macro explanations that are well confirmed and explanatory without providing lower level detail. Darwin explained evolution by natural selection without knowing about DNA. And so on.

Of course mechanisms can play an important role. Whether they do so depends on at least three questions: How well confirmed is the theory at the macrolevel? What does the theory presuppose about mechanisms at some specified level? How well confirmed is the theory at that level? When a theory at the macrolevel is relatively poorly confirmed, when it makes specific assumptions about mechanisms, and where our understanding of the mechanisms is good, then asking for mechanisms is indeed important. When the opposite is the case, the demand for 'macromechanisms' (Colander 1996) will be equally plausible.

A final preliminary point: even when mechanisms are central, the question remains open whether they should be *individualist* mechanisms. It may be that a macrolevel theory presupposes some strong claims about mechanisms, but the mechanisms are not ones involving individuals but instead social groups. We might want to see the mechanism producing equilibrium outcomes when our results depend essentially on the equilibrium requirement, yet the mechanism might be economic selection of *firms*.

Once these points are granted, their application to economics again requires a careful look at specific theories. The one general thing we can say is that a theory in economics gains no automatic support simply because it alleges individualist mechanisms. If the theory of the mechanism is highly implausible and macroeconomic claims presuppose no very specific individual level process, then individualist mechanisms should count for little. In this case pointing to individualist mechanisms as fundamental is grandstanding, not making a serious argument.

I won't pretend to carefully survey all the instances where the demand for individualist mechanisms has been invoked in economics. I want to rather point to some relevant areas and considerations.

Sometimes the microfoundations literature asks that macroeconomic claims be shown compatible with general equilibrium theory or perhaps, less demandingly, with rational maximizing behavior. Given our general framework for thinking about mechanisms, there are several points to make about these requirements. Strong market clearing and rationality assumptions (i.e. rational expectations) or ad hoc fixed price mechanisms both fall into the category of weakly confirmed theories of mechanisms that should be minimal constraints on macroeconomic theorizing. Nor are we forced to pick between the two. Learning and expectations might reasonably be demanded of macroeconomic theories without requiring hyperrationality or systematic stupidity. If macroeconomics needs individualist foundations, it does not follow that rational expectations or fixed price models exhaust the alternatives.

A second, related point: what goes under the guise of 'individualist' foundations in the microfoundations literature is sometimes anything but that. Models with 'representative agents' which treat aggregates of consumers or producers as if they were single individuals is individualism only in name. It is like trying to give a neurological account of brain processes by calling each major area of the brain a 'neuron' and giving them the properties of single neurons.

Turning from macroeconomics, individualist mechanisms might also be desirable in microeconomics, since the latter generally refers to households and firms, which are social entities. Recent work in the economics of the household and in the theory of the firm is motivated in part by such considerations. Again the key issues revolve around the three questions identified above and attention to specific accounts is called for.

At stake are both what traits of firms and households we want to capture and what sort of individualist account should be constraining, if any. One project would be to derive the behavioral assumptions of GET – profit maximizing, well-defined household utility functions, etc. – from individual behavior. Another would be to derive observed empirical behavior of firms and households from individual behavior. The theory of individual behavior might be the standard rational choice account or some other, more psychologically based bounded rationality model.

There is unlikely to be any simple and uniform answer to the question as to whether mechanisms are needed in these areas, because we are dealing with different and independent claims. It might be argued that GET does not make strong assumptions about individualist mechanisms in that profit maximizing can come about via economic selection on firms. Yet well-defined household utility functions can appeal to no such process and thus the need for mechanisms is more pressing. So in each case we are juggling three variables – plausibility of macrotheory, plausibility of microtheory, and the extent which the former presupposes specific facts about the domain of the latter. A detailed assessment of these various issues would be taking a position on a variety of substantive topics in multiple areas in economics and is beyond the scope of this chapter.

Heuristics

We come now to the last batch of individualist claims – those about heuristics. Here individualism is recommended as a route to scientific progress, a tool for discovery. Just as reductionism in the natural sciences has been at the heart of scientific method, so too should it be in the social sciences. The social sciences and economics in particular will advance best by seeking individualist explanations. This is a common rationale.

We have already discussed many different versions of individualism. Thus the advice to 'seek individualist explanations' cannot be just one recommendation. 'Seek reductions' is a significantly different strategy than 'seek individualist mechanisms,' for example. In principle there is a heuristic for each formulation discussed earlier.

Whatever heuristic is at issue, evaluating it is no easy business. We first have the problem of defining scientific progress and second the difficulties involved in finding evidence that any particular research strategy actually causes the virtue in question. Scientific research is a complex social phenomenon and it is no easier to identify its purposes and causes than it is for any other complex social phenomenon.

Assessing heuristics is further complicated by the fact that the same strategy can have different effects in different contexts. In fact, heuristics can sometimes promote their opposite: Newton's inductivism produced a theory confirmed by deductions from first principles.

These qualifications aside, we can venture some reasonable hypotheses. Following the precept 'seek reductions' is likely to lead to error. Focusing on individual detail when aggregate processes are multiply realized is likely to see diversity where there is unity. Focusing on individual detail when the aggregate effect is context sensitive may produce false generalizations. Ignoring higher level institutional detail can lead to ignoring important variables.

These difficulties refer to features of reduction in general. Thus it is not surprising that the history of science does not unequivocally support reductionism as the route to scientific progress. Vitalism dominated nineteenth-century biology, but arguably promoted progress because it allowed scientists to focus on biological phenomena in their own right (Coleman 1971). Reductionist strategies may have thwarted progress in evolutionary biology for reasons like those described above (Wimsatt 1980).

Weaker individualist heuristics may be more plausible. 'Seek individualist mechanisms' is perfectly compatible with giving the social or aggregate an essential place. When (1) a macrotheory makes specific presuppositions about mechanisms, (2) we have relatively well-confirmed theory at the individual level, and (3) there is reason to believe that the mechanisms involved are relatively universal, then seeking mechanisms no doubt may be a fruitful strategy.

There is again no reason to think that these criteria must be met everywhere or nowhere in economics. Thus assessing this individualist heuristic calls for careful case-by-case analyses.

Conclusion: philosophical morals

I end my discussion by drawing a philosophical moral from the debate over individualism. We have seen that individualism is many different theses and that at every turn evaluating them quickly gets us involved in quite specific substantive issues in economics. To even formulate various individualist theses, even apparently trivial ones such as 'society does not act independently of individuals,' we were led to talk about the relation between specific economic claims or theories. What seemed trivially true, when probed, was not so trivial after all but instead a contestable economic claim. Appeals to individualist virtues in various debates turned out on further scrutiny not to be appeals to some abstract theoretical virtue but a very specific proposal in economic theory.

The philosophical lesson I draw is that methodological virtues and disputes cannot be settled in the abstract nor can they decide empirical controversies in the abstract. Methodological virtues and methodological assessment are of a piece with concrete empirical inquiry.

This view of philosophy of science – as continuous with science itself – ought to come as no surprise, given the influential attacks of Quine some 50 years ago on the analytic/synthetic distinction and the resulting picture of knowledge as a web of belief, where everything is in principle revisable. Yet old habits die hard, and in practice many arguments in philosophy of science and in the sciences themselves still proceed as if they could be settled on perfectly general conceptual, a priori grounds. Seeing just how wrong that is in the case of the individualism debate is a useful reminder in practice of Quine's points in theory.

References

Becker, Gary (1976), 'Irrational behavior and economic theory', in *The Economic Approach to Human Behavior*, Chicago: University of Chicago Press.

Clark, Andy (1998), *Being There*, Cambridge, MA: MIT Press.

Colander, David (1996), 'The macrofoundations of micro', in D. Colander (ed.), *Beyond Microfoundations: Post Walrasian Macroeconomics*, Cambridge: Cambridge University Press.

Coleman, William (1971), *Biology in the Nineteenth Century*, Cambridge: Cambridge University Press.

Collins, Randall (1981), 'On the microfoundations of macrosociology', *American Journal of Sociology*, **86**, 984–1014.
Deaton, Angus, and John Muellbauer (1980), *Economics and Consumer Behaviour*, Cambridge: Cambridge University Press.
Hausman, Daniel M. (1981), *Capital, Profits and Prices*, New York: Columbia University Press.
Hellman, Geoffrey, and F.W. Thompson (1975), 'Physicalism: ontology, determination, and reduction', *Journal of Philosophy*, **72**, 551–64.
Hildenbrand, Werner (1983), 'On the law of demand', *Econometrica*, **51**, 997–1019.
Hildenbrand, Werner (1994), *Market Demand*, Princeton, NJ: Princeton University Press.
Janssen, Maarten (1993), *Microfoundations: A Critical Inquiry*, London: Routledge.
Jevons, William S. (1879), *The Theory of Political Economy*, London:Macmillian.
Kincaid, Harold (1995), 'Optimality arguments and the theory of the firm', in D. Little, (ed.) *On the Reliability of Economic Models*, Dordrecht: Kluwer.
Kincaid, Harold (1996), *Philosophical Foundations of the Social Sciences*, Cambridge: Cambridge University Press.
Kincaid, Harold (1997), *Individualism and the Unity of Science*, Lanham, MD: Rowman and Littlefield.
Martel, Robert (1996), 'Heterogeneity, aggregation, and a meaningful macoreconomics', in D. Colander (ed.), *Beyond Microfoundations: Post Walrasian Macroeconomics*, Cambridge: Cambridge University Press, pp. 127–45.
Mathien, Thomas (1988), 'Network analysis and methodological individualism', *Philosophy of Social Science*,**18**, 1–20.
Mirowski, Philip (2001), *Machine Dreams*, Cambridge: Cambridge University Press.
Nagel, Ernest (1961), *The Structure of Science*, London: Routledge and Kegan Paul.
Ross, Don (forthcoming), *Economic Theory and Cognitive Science,* vol. 1, *Microexplanation*, Cambridge, MA: MIT Press/Bradford.
Salmon, Wesley (1989), *Four Decades of Scientific Explanation*, Minneapolis: University of Minnesota Press.
Samuelson, Larry (1998), *Evolutionary Games and Equilibrium Selection*, Cambridge: Cambridge University Press.
Sklar, Lawrence (1993), *Physics and Chance*, Cambridge: Cambridge University Press.
Thatcher, Margaret (1987), 'Aids, Education and the Year 2000', *Woman's Own*, 3 October, 8–10.
Watkins, John (1973), 'Methodological individualism: a reply', in J.O'Neill (ed.), *Modes of Individualism and Collectivism*, London: Heinemann, pp. 179–85.
Weintraub, Roy E. (1979), *Microfoundations: The Compatibility of Microeconomics and Macroeconomics*, Cambridge: Cambridge University Press.
Wimsatt, William (1980), 'Reductionist research strategies and their biases in the units of selection controversy', in T. Nickels (ed.), *Scientific Discovery*, Boston, MA: D. Reidel, pp. 213–59.

PART III

SOCIAL ONTOLOGY
AND THE ONTOLOGY
OF ECONOMICS

16 Philosophical under-labouring in the context of modern economics: aiming at truth and usefulness in the meanest of ways

Tony Lawson

There are various competing ideas about how philosophical or methodological analysis can and does relate to a substantive discipline such as economics. Here I focus on just one conception, that which underpins the broadly philosophical project known as critical realism in economics. The conception I have in mind is philosophy as under-labourer for knowledge or science. And the aim of economists contributing specifically to the philosophical project of critical realism has been to under-labour for a (more fruitful) science or discipline of economics.

My objective is to elaborate on the idea of the philosopher as under-labourer. I want to indicate, in particular, how under-labouring can usefully proceed in the context of modern economics, and indeed has done so in this specific realist project. I also intend to suggest that philosophy so understood fulfils what is an urgent need at this juncture.

The under-labourer conception

The interpretation of philosophy in question derives from Locke. It is found, almost as an aside, in the 'Epistle to the Reader' of his *An Essay Concerning Human Understanding*:

> The commonwealth of learning is not at this time without master-builders, whose mighty designs, in advancing the sciences, will leave lasting monuments to the admiration of posterity; but everyone must not hope to be a *Boyle* or a *Sydenham*; and in an age that produces such masters as the great *Huygenius* and the incomparable Mr. *Newton*, with some others of that strain, it is ambition enough to be employed as the under-labourer in clearing ground a little, and removing some of the rubbish that lies in the way to knowledge. (Locke, 1690 [1985], pp. xlii, xliii)

As this extract makes clear, under-labouring for science is not the same as doing science. It is important to realise this. One of the many criticisms levelled at critical realist contributions, even by a few relatively sympathetic heterodox economists, is that they do not go far enough in developing alternative theoretical and policy positions. This criticism, however, overlooks the under-labouring role that has consistently been accepted for the project (see, for example, Lawson et al., 1996; Lawson 1997a, 2003). Doing substantive theory is simply not the task of critical realism.

Nor is it the task of the philosopher as under-labourer to identify sets of rules for scientists and others to follow. I am aware that not all methodologists accept this. Some, indeed, do sometimes treat philosophers as 'master-builders', who seek to instruct on how economics must be done. Indeed, many econometric texts and courses are like this, insisting on definite procedures or strategies for practice (for example 'falsificationist criteria of Popper must be used'). But methodological injunctions of this kind are no part of the under-labourer conception of philosophy.

My own suspicion is that there are few, if any, valid context-independent rules for science, and that those who attempt to lay down such rules for economics are being rather *un*helpful. But if there were valid universal rules to govern scientific practice, the activity of elaborating them would be more akin to instructing in the more basic techniques and skills of housebuilding, rather than ground clearing. The latter is an activity that happens before most of the paraphernalia of housebuilding even begins to be brought in. In fact, once the ground has been cleared, the builder may find that there exist possibilities or constraints that direct the building project in previously unimagined ways. And so I believe it is in science.

Now some may suppose that if such under-labouring on behalf of science, including economics, was once necessary, this is no longer so. That is, some observers may suppose that in this post-Enlightenment epoch, the entire scientific ground has long since been cleared of its rubbish. Perhaps Locke even faced such a reaction in his own time, at least in connection with natural science. After all, he was suggesting that philosophy had a useful role still to play in the face of the then recent scientific achievements of Boyle, Sydenham, Huygenius, Newton and others. Such was the astonishing nature of some of these achievements that many may have felt that science was in need of help from no activity other than itself. Certainly Locke appears to have anticipated such a response, for he is quite defensive about setting out on his under-labouring endeavour:

> It will probably be censured as a great piece of vanity or insolence in me, to pretend to instruct this our knowing age: it amounting to little less, when I own that I publish this *Essay* with hopes it may be useful to others. (p. xiii)

Censure of this sort is well known in modern times of course, particularly in economics. Very often, the practices of methodologists are dismissed as presumptuous and/or unnecessary. For example, the question of whether economists should do methodology was fairly recently raised in the discussion columns of the *Newsletter* of the *Royal Economic Society* (see for example Backhouse 1992; Hahn 1992a, 1992b). This discussion was subsequently brought to an end with the reproduction of the following extract from Irving Fisher's December 1932 Presidential Address to the *American Statistical Association*:

> It has long seemed to me that students of the social sciences, especially sociology and economics, have spent too much time in discussing what they call methodology. I have usually felt that the man who essays to tell the rest of us how to solve knotty problems would be more convincing if first he proved his alleged method by solving a few himself. Apparently those would-be authorities who are forever telling others how to get results do not get any important results themselves. (Fisher 1933)

Notice that this observation misses the point of the methodologist as under-labourer. At least it does so if the 'knotty problems' Fisher has in mind concern specific substantive issues, or if he imagines that methodology is restricted to giving dictates rather than offering supportive insight. But it is clear that the spirit of the piece, whatever its target, is of the sort that Locke was anticipating.

Aware of the possibility of negative reactions, but not wanting to claim false modesty by pretending his contribution was less useful than he hoped and anticipated it to be, Locke interpreted the nature of his contribution as modestly or unassumingly as he could without undermining his assessment of its worth:

> I shall always have the satisfaction to have aimed sincerely at truth and usefulness, though in one of the meanest ways. (p. xiii)

Why is his way of seeking knowledge one of the 'meanest'? Three hundred years ago the term signified something that is less than noble, unimposing or undistinguished. Here Locke was clearly comparing his role to that of the (noble) 'master-builders' of science whose 'mighty designs', he anticipated, would leave 'lasting monuments to the admiration of posterity'. Locke was interpreting the contributions of scientists as being superior to his own, but doing so in a manner that did not undermine the worth of his own contribution.

Perhaps Locke's is also a strategy for modern-day methodologists concerned with philosophy as under-labouring, particularly in the context of economics. If it will help deflect criticism of those who expect philosophy to deliver on the field of substantive theorising or science such a description will serve a useful purpose. I, for one, am happy for philosophy as under-labouring to be regarded as a mean way of pursuing truth and usefulness. To so describe it, of course, does not render it without value or inefficacious. Indeed at this moment in time I believe a strategy of under-labouring, in the context of modern economics, promises to be more worthwhile and efficacious than most, at least if an explanatory successful economics is the ultimate goal.

Why do I suggest this? Locke was aware that, despite the then recent successful contributions of Newton and others, (natural) science could always benefit from philosophy. He was worried, though, that the successes of science would engender a philosophical complacency. My own view is that modern economics has not come close to achieving explanatory successes sufficient to encourage a spirit of philosophical complacency. The reason for this is not that economists cannot make significant contributions (in my own assessment Smith, Marx, Veblen, Hayek and Keynes are amongst those who have done so previously, but that nowadays, at least within academic faculties of economics, the 'rubbish that lies in the way to knowledge' has become piled so high that (successful) economic science is (momentarily) well nigh impossible without a good deal of the litter first being cleared away. If under-labouring or ground clearing was ambition enough for Locke in his day, I believe it is an ambition bordering almost on necessity for any modern-day social theorist concerned that there be a fruitful academic discipline of economics.

Ways of philosophical under-labouring
How do we begin to clear the ground? There will always be many ways of proceeding depending, of course, on the nature of the perceived 'rubbish'. In modern times a real housing site may be covered in weeds or brambles. But equally it may have parts of old cars strewn across it. The nature of the problem bears on the sorts of ways it may be solved, on the sorts of ground clearing strategies that could be useful. So the first task is to identify the nature of the 'rubbish' that is to be cleared away. It is essential always to recognise that the concrete details of the situation will bear on the procedures most usefully adopted. Even so, at an abstract level, it does appear possible to distinguish broad orientations that philosophising as ground-clearing might take. Let me briefly consider three such possibilities.

One approach starts from the recognition that our commonsense or everyday thinking includes inconsistencies as well as unreflected-upon assumptions, biases, superstitions and prejudices, which do not withstand close scrutiny. These, however, may bear significantly in the process of science (like much else). Kant argued that it is a function of philosophy to analyse concepts and ideas that are already given but confused. The aim of philosophy, on this conception, is to free up science and other knowledge activities by exposing, criticising and explaining the unsustainable assumptions, inconsistencies and confusions these may contain.

A second approach seeks to inform the scientist of the nature of scientific (and other) contributions to knowledge, and epistemic states of affairs, both within economics and across the disciplines. It is to help the researchers understand where they stand in the wider field of knowledge-producing activities, and to help make them aware of potentialities they might explore. I recognise that this second approach can easily collapse into one in which the philosopher becomes a dictator rather than an under-labourer. For, the activity of pointing to ways of proceeding that have proven successful in some domains, all too easily slides into the generalisation that such procedures are everywhere appropriate, so that economists too must utilise them. But this step or 'slide', though easy to make, is unnecessary. On the approach I am here discussing the orientation to most if not all procedures prior to specific analyses is modal rather than injunctive.

A third approach is to seek to employ philosophy in the form of logic and argument to dissect and better understand the methods which economists or, more generally, scientists do, or could, use, and thereby to refine the methods on offer and/or to clarify their conditions of usage.

No doubt there are other ways of philosophical under-labouring. But these three roles, broadly the *demystifying*, *informing*, and *method-facilitating* functions, should give something of an indication of what is possible. And all three (perhaps especially the first) are found to play a part in the realist project to which I been referring.

The context of modern economics
If, as I have argued, specific methods of philosophical under-labouring cannot be determined prior to understanding the nature of the 'rubbish' that needs clearing away, a parallel insight holds for science. That is, it is not possible to determine the scientific method that it is appropriate to employ for a given task (in a particular context) without knowing the nature of the task. And to know the nature of any scientific task it is always essential to have an insight into (i.e. to seek to determine) the nature of the material that is to be investigated. Marx once observed that 'in the analysis of economic forms neither microscopes nor chemical reagents are of assistance' (*Capital* 1887 [1974], vol I, p. 90). His point, of course, was that the nature of the subject matter in question is such that the noted tools are not appropriate to its investigation. But the point being illustrated is a general one. The properties of material studied always make a difference to how we can and cannot know it.

Now if there is one feature that provides the greatest obstacle in the path of economics achieving its potential as an explanatory endeavour, it is precisely a failure to recognise the point just emphasised. Modern economics mostly proceeds from the idea that the methods of the discipline can be determined independently of considering the nature of its subject matter. I do not mean by this that modern economists experiment with various methods seeking to 'select' those that turn out to be most appropriate to the material being investigated. Rather certain methods are insisted upon and treated as more or less universally applicable, without much, if any, consideration of context of analysis. Indeed, even what counts as economics is defined in terms of method. And, of course, the method (or set of methods) that so many regard as defining of economics is that of mathematical-deductivist modelling. Consider the recent observations of Richard Lipsey:

> to get an article published in most of today's top rank economic journals, you must provide a mathematical model, even if it adds nothing to your verbal analysis. I have been at seminars where the presenter was asked after a few minutes, 'Where is your model?'. When he answered 'I have not got one as I do not need one, or cannot yet develop one, to consider my problem' the response was to turn off and figuratively, if not literally, to walk out. (Lipsey 2001, p. 184)

I believe it is the orientation of the discipline captured by this (common) experience that constitutes the primary source of 'rubbish that lies in the way to knowledge' in modern economics. The 'rubbish' in question, I hasten to emphasise, is not (of course) the practices of mathematical modelling per se. Rather it is the dogma that nothing (or almost nothing) else counts. It is the presumption, which is more or less an edict, that without a model a contributor does not deserve serious attention. It is the rejection of methodological pluralism. It is the idea that, whatever the context, deductivist formalism counts before all else. If this, then, is indeed the dominant form of modern economic 'rubbish' the question is how best to clear it away?

There are no doubt many ways of seeking to reorient the economics discipline. But the strategy that I have considered likely to be as effective as any consists in the following basic steps:

1. To remind/inform that there is indeed a generalised problem of modern economics.
2. To remind/inform that modern economics is indeed dominated by a project that supposes that the mathematisation of economics is the top priority
3. To demonstrate that the scenario identified as (2) explains the problems identified under (1)
4. To demonstrate that there are alternative ways of proceeding that at least carry the promise of greater explanatory success than has so far been achieved.

If steps (1) and (2) constitute under-labouring primarily under its *informing* role, and step (3) represents it mostly under its *demystifying* function, step (4) expresses it under its *informing*, *demystifying* and *method-facilitating* capacities, as I shall briefly indicate.

Starting with step (1) there are many economists who deny that economics does not perform especially well as an explanatory discipline. But as Kirman (1999, p. 14) notes such denials do not withstand critical examination. Still many are yet to fully appreciate just how bad things are. Clearly there must be many strategies of persuasion. My own has been twofold. First I have detailed numerous problem situations including those where the theory and practice of modern economics are highly inconsistent (see Lawson 1997a, Ch. 1). Second I have drawn on the self-reflections of mainstream (mathematical) economists themselves. Heterodox economists have long been aware of the subject's poor showing. But my hope has been that others will take more notice if they realise that this unfortunate state of affairs is acknowledged by leading mainstream economists themselves. And many do. Consider, for example, the following reflections by Rubinstein:

> The issue of interpreting economic theory is … the most serious problem now facing economic theorists. The feeling among many of us can be summarized as follows. Economic theory should deal with the real world. It is not a branch of abstract mathematics even though it utilises mathematical tools. Since it is about the real world, people expect the theory to prove useful in achieving practical goals. But economic theory has not delivered the goods. Predictions from economic theory are not nearly as accurate as those offered by the natural sciences, and the link between economic theory and practical problems… is tenuous at best. (Rubinstein, 1995, p. 12)

This mainstream 'theorist' continues:

> Economic theory lacks a consensus as to its purpose and interpretation. Again and again, we find ourselves asking the question 'where does it lead?' (Rubinstein, 1995, p. 12)

Turning to the second step, the use of mathematics is now so extensive that I doubt any economist will question the claim that modern economics is dominated by a project that supposes that mathematisation of the subject is the top priority. The problem here is more that the acceptance of formalistic methods is so widespread that economists can hardly be encouraged even to contemplate the idea that this reliance so exclusively on formalism might be unhelpful. I suspect, indeed, that many agree with Frank Hahn that the idea that there could be a problem with the emphasis on mathematics in modern economics is 'a view surely not worth discussing' (Hahn 1985, p. 18). Such sentiments bring to mind the following advice from Whitehead:

> When you are criticising the philosophy of an epoch do not chiefly direct your attention to those intellectual positions which its exponents feel it necessary explicitly to defend. There will be some fundamental assumptions which adherents of all the variant systems within the epoch unconsciously presuppose. Such assumptions appear so obvious that people do not know what they are assuming because no other way of putting things has ever occurred to them. With these assumptions a certain limited number of types of philosophic systems are possible, and this group of systems constitutes the philosophy of the epoch. (1926, p. 61)

I think this observation applies very aptly to the reliance on methods of mathematics in modern economics.

The most interesting steps, though, are (3) and (4). I have observed that economists turn to (mathematical) method without any concern for the subject matter of the discipline. By suggesting this is a problem, I am implying that it is possible that the formalistic methods of economists are being applied to materials for which they are not appropriate. This brings me to the subject of *ontology*, a topic with which has been a primary concern within the project of critical realism. Indeed I believe that ontological analysis constitutes just the sort of philosophical under-labouring which economics at this time most needs.

Ontology
By ontology I mean enquiry into (or a theory of) the nature of being or existence. It is an endeavour concerned with determining the broad nature, including the structure, of reality. Here I am especially concerned with the nature of *social* reality, with the question of social being.

To see how ontology can make a difference it is important to consider two of the roles that can be accepted for ontological analysis. First we must recognise that specific methods and criteria of analysis are appropriate to the illumination of *some* kinds of objects or materials *but not others*. This is the matter I have already stressed, that the properties of material studied will always make a difference to how we can and cannot know it. It is a failure to recognise this point that is a fundamental problem of the discipline. One role for ontological enquiry, then, is to determine the (usually implicit) conceptions of the nature and structure of reality presupposed by the use of any specific set of research practices and procedures. Equivalently, it can identify conditions under which specific procedures are relevant and likely to bear fruit.

A second, equally fundamental, role for ontology is the elaboration of as complete and encompassing as possible a conception of the broad nature and structure of (a relevant domain of) reality as appears feasible. The aim is to derive a general conception that seems to include all actual developments as special configurations. Put differently, a central objective is to provide a categorical grammar for expressing all the particular types of realisation in specific contexts.

Now the results achieved by ontology in each of these roles can be used in numerous ways. But of particular interest at this juncture is a recognition that the results achieved in these two roles can be used to especially good effect in combination. For if, by employing ontology in its second role, we can achieve a general framework, this can reveal the particularity of many scientific and practical ontologies revealed by employing ontology in its former role. In other words, applying ontology in both of the roles discussed allows us to compare the ontological presuppositions of specific methods with our best account of the nature of social reality. The application of ontological insight in this fashion can reveal in particular both the error, and the non-necessity, of universalising any highly specific approach or stance a priori. Ontology, so fashioned, can identify the error of treating special cases as though they are universal or ubiquitous.

Now, as I say, it is my assessment that the problems of modern economics largely stem from its failure to match its methods to the nature of its subject matter. Indeed, modern economics provides a very clear example of a rather narrow way of doing research being unthinkingly and erroneously universalised a priori, with unfortunate consequences. For as we shall see below it is fairly easy to establish that the sorts of formalistic methods everywhere advocated by modern mainstream economists are in fact only rarely appropriate to the analysis of social material, given its nature. In other words, it is easy to show that these methods that are universalised a priori are so erroneously. This, I argue, is why the modern discipline of economics is in such disarray. The theories formulated by economists are necessarily restricted so as to conform to the world view presupposed by their formalistic methods. Because this latter world view is found to characterise very little of human society, it is not surprising that mainstream theories are found hardly to advance understanding in most of the contexts for which they are constructed.

The persistence of this mismatch of method and material for analysis is really only comprehensible in the context of a continuing failure to address ontological issues in any very explicit and sustained fashion. This is why I urge that an ontological turn is especially of value at this point. A turn to ontology will not determine precisely how economists will proceed. But it can help. And urging it, and specifically demonstrating its benefits, and deriving insights on possibilities for economic practice, constitutes the form of philosophical under-labouring I have thought most useful at this point in time.

The mathematical-deductivism of modern economics

Note, to begin, that the sorts of formalistic methods that economists wield mostly require, for their application, the existence (or positing) of event regularities; they presuppose the occurrence of closed systems. Mainstream economics is a form of *deductivism*. By deductivism I just mean any form of explanatory endeavour that assumes or posits or constructs regularities (deterministic or stochastic) connecting actualities such as events or states of affairs.

Of course, the fact that formalistic modelling methods require the identification or construction of event regularities is well recognised by mainstream economists (see, for example, Allais, 1992). But the ontological preconditions of these methods do not end there. The dependency of mathematical-deductivist methods on closed systems in turn more or less necessitates, and certainly encourages, formulations couched in terms of (1) isolated (2) atoms. The metaphorical reference to atoms here is not intended to convey anything about size. Rather the reference is to items which exercise their own separate, independent and invariable (and so predictable) effects (relative to, or as a function of, initial conditions).

Deductivist theorising of the sort pursued in modern economics ultimately has to be couched in terms of such 'atoms' just to ensure that under given conditions x the same (predictable or deducible) outcome y always follows. If any agent in the theory could do other than some given y in specific conditions x – either because the agent is intrinsically structured and can just act differently each time x occurs, or because the agent's action possibilities are affected by whatever else is going on – the individuals of the analysis could not be said to be atomic and deductive inference could never be guaranteed.

Atomism, then, is essential, if closures of the sort economists usually require are to be assured. However, even in the noted scenarios, the assumption of atomism is not yet sufficient to ensure closure and facilitate deductivist explanation/ and prediction. For even with an atomistic ontology, the total effect on an outcome of interest may be changed to almost any extent if all the other accompanying causes are different. That is why, in concrete economic analyses, the (atomistic) individuals tend to be treated as part of an assumed-to-be isolated and self-contained set or system.

Notice I am not the first to make such observations. Even if, for example, Keynes never used the term 'ontology' and Veblen only occasionally referred to metaphysics, both identified the implicit presuppositions of dominant methods or relevant proposals of their time. Keynes first of all noticed that an atomistic ontology was an implicit presupposition of the inductive methods of natural science. Thus he wrote in his *A Treatise on Probability*:

> The kind of fundamental assumption about the character of material laws, on which scientists appear commonly to act, seems to me to be much less simple than the bare principle of uniformity. They appear to assume something much more like what mathematicians call the principle of the superposition of small effects, or, as I prefer to call it, in this connection, the *atomic* character of natural law. The system of the material universe must consist, if this kind of assumption is warranted, of bodies which we may term (without any implication as to their size being conveyed thereby) *legal atoms*, such that each of them exercises its own separate, independent, and invariable effect, a change of the total state being compounded of a number of separate changes each of which is solely due to a separate portion of the preceding state. We do not have an invariable relation between particular bodies, but nevertheless each has on the others its own separate and invariable effect, which does not change with changing circumstances, although, of course, the total effect may be changed to almost any extent if all the other accompanying causes are different. Each atom can, according to this theory, be treated as a separate cause and does not enter into different organic combinations in each of which it is regulated by different laws. (1973a, pp. 276, 277)

Note that in drawing attention to this assumption of atomic character of natural law, Keynes is simultaneously raising the logical possibility that not all natural phenomena need be atomic:

> The scientist wishes, in fact, to assume that the occurrence of a phenomenon which has appeared as part of a more complex phenomenon, may be *some* reason for expecting it to be associated on another occasion with part of the same complex. Yet if different wholes were subject to laws *quâ* wholes and not simply on account of and in proportion to the differences of their parts, knowledge of a part could not lead, it would seem, even to presumptive or probable knowledge as to its association with other parts. Given, on the other hand, a number of legally atomic units and the laws connecting them, it would be possible to deduce their effects *pro tanto* without an exhaustive knowledge of all the coexisting circumstances. (1973a, pp. 277, 278)

And as I have indicated elsewhere (Lawson 1997d, 2003) Keynes realised the same implicit ontology of atomism was required for certain (econometric) methods being proposed in the context of 1930s economics. But 40 years earlier Veblen also recognised these atomist presuppositions, even if he did associate them with a form of dominant Austrian economics. Thus Veblen wrote of the implicit presuppositions concerning the nature of the (usually 'hedonistic') human agent:

> The hedonistic conception of man is that of a lightening calculator of pleasures and pains, who oscillates like a homogeneous globule of desire of happiness under the impulse of stimuli that shift him about the area, but leave him intact. He has neither antecedent nor consequent. He is an isolated, definitive human datum, in stable equilibrium except for the buffets of the impinging forces that displace him in one direction or another. Self-imposed in elemental space, he spins symmetrically about his own spiritual axis until the parallelogram of forces bears down upon him, where upon he follows the line of the resultant. When the force of the impact is spent, he comes to rest, a self-contained globule of desire as before. Spiritually, the hedonistic man is not a prime mover. He is not the seat of a process of living, except in the sense that he is subject to series of permutations enforced upon him by circumstances external and alien to him. (Veblen 1898, pp. 73, 74)

I have not yet indicated precisely why I am suggesting the modern mainstream tradition fares so poorly as an explanatory endeavour. I have merely indicated that if the methods of mathematical deductivist modelling (as employed in modern economics) are insisted upon as universally valid for the social realm, a presupposition (and requirement for guaranteed success) is that the social realm everywhere comprises (closed) systems of isolated atoms (and noted that the likes of Veblen and Keynes saw this as well).

Now it is immediately clear, I think, that these latter conditions *need* not characterise the social realm. I have elsewhere argued, indeed, that the noted conditions for closure may actually be rather rare in the social realm. I draw this conclusion on the basis of the (a posteriori derived) theory of social ontology, a conception of the nature of the material of social reality, defended elsewhere. I do not have the space here to derive this social ontology. But let me say something of its method of derivation, and of the sorts of results that are achieved.

Transcendental argument

The point of departure adopted is to suppose that all scientific and other practices, *whether or not successful on their own terms,* are *intelligible*, that they have explanations. This might be called the *principle of intelligibility* (Lawson 2003). According to it, there are conditions that render practices actually carried out (and their results) *possible*. Thus, one strand of my strategy has just been to seek to explain (aspects of) certain human actions, to identify their conditions of possibility. Or, more precisely, my strategy has been to explain various *generalised* features of experience including human actions, and so to uncover generalised insights regarding the structure or nature of reality. This of course, is precisely an exercise in ontology.

The principle of intelligibility, that is the initiating presumption that human social activity is intelligible, should not be especially contentious. We all grant it. It is difficult, for example, to imagine anyone bothering to attempt to read and understand these lines that supposes or claims otherwise.

In addition premises of the sorts of (ontological) analyses to which I refer usually express certain fairly generalised features of experience. The form of reasoning that takes us from widespread features of experience (including here conceptions of generalised human practices, or of aspects of them) to their grounds or conditions of possibility, is the *transcendental argument*. The transcendental argument (or transcendental 'deduction') is thus clearly a special case of the *retroductive argument*, where the latter moves from conceptions of specific phenomena at any one level to hypotheses about their underlying conditions or causes (see Lawson 1997a, Ch. 2; or Lawson 2003, Ch. 4).

Any results achieved by way of transcendental reasoning are clearly conditional. They are contingent upon the human practices selected as premises and our conceptions of them, as well as upon the adequacy of the transcendental argument employed.

Moreover it is clear that philosophy so conceived, i.e., as method turning centrally upon the transcendental argument, considers the *same world* as the sciences, and indeed serves, in its insights, to complement the latter's results. However, it proceeds on the basis of pure reason (albeit exercising it always on the basis of *a posteriori* conceptions of historically rooted practices) and produces (fallible) knowledge of the necessary conditions of the production of knowledge.

Specific strategies

Contributors to critical realism have made use of transcendental arguments in many different ways. It is true, for example, that, when initiating an explanatory endeavour, some have adopted premises concerning the practices of natural science. I do not deny that I myself have made use of insights achieved in such exercises. Specifically, I have sought to uncover essential features of successful natural-scientific practice, and I have questioned the extent to which it is feasible to undertake similar practices in researching the social realm. Alternatively put, I have examined the extent to which *naturalism* is possible, where naturalism is the thesis that the study of social phenomena can be scientific in the sense of natural science. But it is important to understand how and why. This involves under-labouring under the *informing* role noted earlier.

The 'how', or manner in which the issue of naturalism has been pursued, has in no way involved imposing a conception of natural scientific practice onto the social realm. Rather, as I say, I have merely questioned the extent, if any, to which naturalism is possible. Thus the position on naturalism taken is an answer to this question. And determining an answer presupposes an independent analysis of social ontology; it is something determined only *after* a theory of social ontology, or other insights into the social realm, have been independently uncovered (see for example, Lawson 1997b).

The 'why', or reason for my having pursued the question of naturalism, is, in part at least, because I have regarded a re-examination of it to be strategically important at this point in time (see Lawson 1997b). Currently, the discipline of economics is a state of some disarray and, at the institutional level, dominated by a mainstream tradition distinguished by its insistence that economics mostly reduces to the application of methods of formalistic-deductivist modelling. Now this emphasis is often considered justified just because the methods in question are regarded as essential components of all science. In other words, naturalism is (1) already on the agenda, (2) asserted to be true by mainstream economists, and (3) interpreted in terms of the application of methods of mathematico-deductivist modelling. As I say, I reject the idea that naturalism, however interpreted, can be merely asserted as correct. But the mainstream assessment of natural science is, in any case, erroneous. It has thus seemed to me important to reveal this. For it removes one further barrier to a more informed and open discussion.

A theory of social ontology

However, although it has been helpful, this strategy has not been strictly necessary for the project. The only way to derive a social ontology is to look to the social realm directly, and to transcendentally infer the social conditions of human practices directly. I cannot do this here, and refer the reader to Lawson (1997a, 2003). However I can briefly summarise some of the results obtained.

By *social reality* or the social realm I mean that domain of all phenomena whose existence depends at least in part on us. Thus, it includes items like social relations that depend on us entirely, but also others like technological objects, where I take technology to be that domain of phenomena with a material content but social form.

Now if social reality depends on transformative human agency, its state of being must be intrinsically dynamic or *processual*. Think of a language system. Its existence is a condition of our communicating via speech acts, etc. And through the sum total of these speech acts the language system is continuously being reproduced and, under some of its aspects at least, transformed. A language system, then, is intrinsically dynamic, its mode of being a continual process of becoming. But this is ultimately true of all aspects of social reality, including many aspects of ourselves including our personal and social identities. The social world turns on human practice.

The social realm is also highly *internally related*. Aspects or items are said to be internally related when they are what they are, or can do what they do, in virtue of the relation to others in which they stand. Obvious examples are employer and employee, teacher and student, landlord/lady and tenant or parent and offspring. In each case you cannot have the one without the other. In fact, in the social realm it is found that it is social *positions* that are significantly internally related. It is the position I hold as a university lecturer that is internally related to the positions of students. Each year different individuals slot into the position of students and accept the obligations, privileges and tasks determined by the relation. Ultimately we all slot into a very large number of different and changing positions, each making a difference to what we can do. The social realm, then, is highly internally related or 'organic'.

The social realm is also found to be *structured* (it does not reduce to human practices and other actualities but includes underlying structures and processes of the sort just noted and [their] powers and tendencies). And the stuff of the social realm is found, in addition, to include *value* and *meaning* and to be *polyvalent* (for example absences are real), and so forth.

This broad perspective, as I say, is elaborated and defended in Lawson (1997a, 2003). But I doubt that, once reflected upon, the conception is especially contentious. Nor in its basic emphasis on organicism or internal-relationality is it especially novel, as we have already seen. However, it should be clear that if the perspective defended is at all correct, it is prima facie quite conceivable that the atomistic and closure preconceptions of mainstream economics may hold not very often at all.

Notice, though, that even once this ontology is accepted, the possibility of social closures (of the causal sequence sort see Lawson 2003) such as pursued by modern mainstream economists, cannot be ruled out a priori. Certainly, there is nothing in the ontological conception sketched above which rules out entirely the possibility of regularities of social events. But the conception sustained does render the practice of universalising a priori the sorts of mathematical-deductivist methods economists wield somewhat risky if not foolhardy, requiring or presupposing, as it does, that social event regularities of the relevant sort are ubiquitous. And to the point, if the social ontology sketched above does not altogether rule out the possibility of social event regularities occurring here and there, it does provide a rather compelling explanation of the a posteriori rather generalised lack of (or at best limited) successes with mathematical-deductivist or closed-systems explanatory methods to date.

Actually the ontological conception I defend is more explanatorily powerful still. For not only does it explain the widespread continued explanatory failures of much of modern economics over the last fifty years or so, but also it can account for both (1) the prima facie puzzling phenomenon that mainstream economists everywhere, in a *manner* quite unlike researchers in other disciplines, suppose that (acknowledged) fictionalising is always *necessary*, and (2) the types of conditions that prevail when mathematical methods in economics achieve such (limited) successes as are experienced. However I do not have space to explore this further here (see especially, Lawson 2003).

Implications of ontology
There are many ways other ways ontology can under-labour for economics. In this it can reveal methodological errors and dangers, as well as help clarify and give directionality to research practice. Let me briefly elaborate.

Errors and dangers
Ontology can reveal errors of, or dangers for, research practice by (amongst other things) disclosing various outcomes or configurations as but special cases of the range of outcomes or configurations possible, and thereby revealing the risks involved in universalising them a priori. For example, the ontological conception sustained above reveals social reality to be characterised by depth (or structure), openness and internal relationality, amongst other things. These insights respectively help guard against treating (1) actualities, such as the course of events (or features lying at any one level of reality), as though they are the sole constituents of the world, (2) particular conjunctions of events as though necessarily recurrent, or (3) features of reality that are rather abstract as though they are concrete (for an elaboration of these claims see especially Lawson 2003).

Clarification
Ontology can play an important clarifying role by providing a categorical grammar against which more substantive social theoretical conceptions and distinctions can sometimes be better understood. For example, all social systems

and collectivities can be recognised as ensembles of networked, internally-related, positions (in process) with associated rules and practices. This applies to the state, schools, hospitals, trade unions, the household, and so forth. Sub-distinctions can be made. A social system can be recognised as a structured process of interaction; an institution, as already noted, as a social system/structure (or even a form of behaviour) that is relatively enduring and perceived as such; a collectivity as an internally-related set of social positions along with their occupants, and so forth (see Lawson 1997a, pp. 165–6).

The basic categories elaborated also provide the framework for a theory of *situated rationality* (Lawson 1997a, Ch. 13, 1997c). Various real interests, as well as possibilities for action, depend upon the internally-related positions in which individuals are situated. Of course, we all stand in a large number of (evolving and relationally defined) positions (as parents, children, immigrants, indigenous, old, young, teachers, etc., etc.). Hence there exist possibilities of conflicting, as well as unrecognised, individual, in addition to collective or shared, (evolving) interests (and intentions).

This conception, then, also provides the basis for a meaningful theory of distribution. In particular it allows an analysis of the determinants of resources to positions, as well as of positions to people.

More generally, a conception such as that sustained encourages and informs a reconsideration of the many categories of social theorising taken for granted in modern economics. The list includes not only the already noted categories of institutions, systems, rationality, but also other equally central to economics such as money, markets, uncertainty, order and numerous others.[1]

Also, by examining a contributor's ontological preconceptions it is often possible to throw further light on the nature and/or meanings of their substantive claims and contributions, especially where the latter are found to be otherwise open to a large number of seemingly ill-grounded interpretations.[2] And so on.

Directionality

Let me turn to consider some of the numerous ways a conception of ontology, and in particular the conception defended here, may impart directionality to social research. In doing so I am turning to step (4) of the argument, and primarily considering methodology under its *methodology-facilitating* role.

Most clearly because the social world is found to be structured (it is irreducible to such actualities as events and practices) it follows that *actualism* is a mistake, that social research will need to concern itself not only with correlating, or otherwise describing, surface actualities, but also, and seemingly primarily, with identifying the latter's underlying conditions. Indeed social research has, as a proper and compelling object, the explaining of surface phenomena in terms of its underlying conditions. If patterns in surface social phenomena have scientific value it is in some part through their providing access to the structural conditions in virtue of which the former are possible. Of course, structural conditions in turn have their own conditions, so that the process of seeking to explain phenomena at one level in terms of causes at a deeper one may be without limit.

Further, to the extent that social phenomena not only depend upon transformative human agency and so are processual but also are highly internally related, it is prima facie rather unlikely they are manipulable in any useful or meaningful way by experimental researchers and others. Social research, in consequence, will typically need to be backward looking, being concerned to render intelligible what has already occurred, rather than interventionist/experimentalist and so predictionist. Certainly it would be rather risky to insist only on (learning and teaching) methods that presuppose that parts of social reality can be treated as isolatable and stable chunks.

It follows that the current excessive concentration (of skills, university research methods courses, etc.) on methods of deductivist (macro-, micro- and econometric) modelling is likely short-sighted indeed, that methods relevant to open systems in process will prove fruitful at least as often. Now I am aware in this regard that some researchers worry that in social explanatory endeavour there is no alternative to using methods that presuppose that the social world is, and will continue to be, everywhere closed. To meet this concern, I outline a general approach appropriate to open systems analysis in Chapter 4 of Lawson, 2003. This, though, does not (and could not) derive from the critical realist conception directly. It is merely a conception for which there is reason to expect more than a degree of social theoretical success given the perspective on the nature of the subject matter of the discipline uncovered.

Finally, it is easy to see that an ontological conception such as critical realism can carry implications for matters of ethics and so for projects of a practical or policy sort. For example, because all human beings are both shaped by the evolving relations (to others) in which they stand as well as being differently (or uniquely) positioned, it follows that all actions, because they are potentially other-affecting, bear a moral aspect. Further, any policy programmes formulated without attention to differences, that presume homogeneity of human populations, are likely to be question-begging from the outset. Certainly, programmes of action that ignore their likely impact on the wider community are immediately seen as potentially deficient. Eventually, of course, such considerations point to questions of power, democracy and legitimacy. They raise questions of who should be taking decisions in a world of different identities where most of us are likely in some way (differentially) affected by actions taken by others. And indeed they invite a questioning of whether anything less than the whole of humanity (and possibly much more) can constitute a relevant unit of focus in the shaping of emancipatory projects and actions.

Some final qualificatory remarks

Let me finish by sounding some notes of caution. I have argued that it makes sense to treat the contribution of at least some methodologists or philosophers to economics as engaged in activities of under-labouring. The aim is to aid, not supplant or instruct, the economic theorist. But I do not want to suggest that all methodologists always approach their task in this mean spirit. Many, I accept, presume to achieve more. But it does not follow that all do. And the project of critical realism in particular has been concerned with under-labouring, especially in the context of economics (for an early discussion of philosophy as under-labourer in the economics context, see Clive Lawson et al. 1996).

Second, there is nothing to prevent those who contribute to such an under-labouring project also being involved in substantive theorising and policy analysis. But it does mean that such activities must be distinguished from those of philosophy. This applies as much to the results of critical realism as to those of any other. Any derivation of substantive theoretical results, reliance on specific methods and/or support for concrete policy proposals, requires that the ontological conception sustained be augmented by specific empirical claims, as I have often stressed.

It is quite legitimate (and not uncommon) for those accepting the broad framework of critical realism to disagree over additional empirical claims, with different individual contributors thus arriving at contrasting substantive, methodological or political orientations for specific contexts (see Clive Lawson et al. 1996). The point is that although critical realism makes a difference to the sorts of approaches or frameworks adopted and so paths taken, it is never by itself determining of substantive positions reached. There is not a position on substantive theory, policy, or practice, even in a particular context, that warrants being distinguished as *the* critical realist position (see Lawson 1996, pp. 417–19).

Third, as far as I know, in recent years the only set of contributions that have been consistently described as under-labouring endeavour, certainly within economics, have been those systematised as critical realism. But I do not wish to imply that other methodological contributions are not effectively of this under-labouring sort. Indeed I would characterise the orientation adopted by various other contributors under this head (for example, Cartwright and Dupré), though in some cases adopting very different concerns. The emphasis of Hand's recent book, significantly bearing the title *Reflection Without Rules*, is also upon methodology of the non-injunctive sort. Perhaps the more this under-labouring aspect is spelt out (if I am correctly interpreting these other contributions here), the less fearful of methodology, substantively oriented economists will be.

Finally, I must emphasise that an under-labouring contribution, including one such as my own which concentrates on ontology, is (just like any other type of contribution to knowledge) inevitably fallible and partial and, in some aspects at least, doubtless transient. I believe this is well recognised by those contributing to the project of critical realism with the consequence that such individuals are continually endeavouring to extend the project's insights and rectify inadequacies. Indeed, the overview sketched above must be seen as unavoidably partial even within this realist project. Hopefully, though, the outline here provided succeeds in giving a sufficient feel for the sorts of results maintained and the manner of their attainment. I do not wish to prioritise the role of philosophy, even of ontology. I do think explicit and sustained ontological analysis, or its results, can be invaluable, and at this juncture, given the state of the modern discipline, probably essential. But as I say, ontology is itself a situated, limited, fallible (and of course always culturally conditioned) process, producing results that are likely to be transient, at least partially. I thus urge a rounded approach to theorising in economics. I advocate only that developments in ontology and those in method and substantive theorising evolve in tandem, with each informing or otherwise enriching the others, where possible. A division of labour is vital. There is plenty of scope for highly differentiated research; variety, as always, is fundamental. In emphasising the need and worth of philosophy in its under-labourer capacity I am, I suppose, revealing my own meanest of dispositions. But I readily accept there is point to such mean endeavour only as long as there is simultaneously a wider concern with the pursuit of economics as substantive science. The objective, indeed, is in some part to contribute to clearing the ground so that a few more specifically *economist* scientists might produce 'mighty designs', that, 'leave lasting monuments to the admiration of posterity'.

Notes

1. The list includes, in fact, money (Ingham, 1996), the firm and region (Lawson, C. 1999a, 2003), institutions (Lawson 1997a); transactions (Pratten 1997), the individual (Davis, 2003, 2004) social order (Fleetwood 1995, 1996), collective learning (Lawson, C. 2000), causality (Fleetwood 2001; Lewis 2000a; Runde 1998a), tendencies, (Pratten 1998; Lawson 1989, 1997a, 1998), markets (O'Neil 1998), households (Ruwanpura 2002), consciousness (Faulkner 2002), timeful theorising (Rotheim 2002); uncertainty (Dunn 2000, 2001); macroeconomics (Smithin forthcoming), space (Sayer 2000), probabilities (Runde 1996, 1998b, 2001), trust (Reed 2001), technology (Lawson, C. forthcoming), metaphor (Lewis 1996, 2000b).

2. For example, through examining the relevant author's ontological preconceptions it has proven possible to give support to (contested) assessments that Commons did hold a theoretical perspective (see Lawson, C. 1994, 1995, 1996, 1999b); that Hayek's position changed significantly over time (Lawson 1994; Fleetwood 1995); that Keynes' rejection of econometrics was not a superficial response based on ignorance of the topic (Lawson 1997d); that Veblen did favour an evolutionary economics and not merely because making economics evolutionary would render it up-to-date (Lawson 2003); that neither Smith nor even Newton adopted 'Newtonian' methodology, and Smith's contribution is hardly in the mould of, or a precursor of, general equilibrium theory (Montes 2002, 2003); that Popper was ultimately not a 'Popperian' (Runde 1996); that Marx's theory (of capitalist tendencies) is not a deterministic theory (Brown et al. 2002; Collier 1989), and so on.

References

Allais, Maurice (1992), 'The economic science of today and global disequilibrium', in Mario Baldassari et al., *Global Disequilibrium in the World Economy*, Basingstoke: Macmillan.

Backhouse, Roger (1992), 'Should we ignore methodology?', *Royal Economic Society Newsletter*, **78**, 4–5.

Brown, Andrew, Stephen Fleetwood, and Michael Roberts (eds) (2002), *Critical Realism and Marxism*, London and New York: Routledge.

Collier, Andrew (1989), *Scientific Realism and Socialist Thought*, Hemel Hempstead: Harvester Wheatsheaf.

Davis, John B. (2003), *The Theory of the Individual in Economics*, London and New York: Routledge.

Davis, John B. (2004), 'The agency–structure model and the embedded individual in heterodox economics', in Paul Lewis (ed), *Transforming Economics: Perspective on the Critical Realist Project*, London and New York: Routledge.

Dunn, Stephen P. (2000), 'Wither post Keynesianism', *Journal of Post Keynesian Economics*, **22** (3) Spring, 343–64.

Dunn, Stephen P. (2001), 'Bounded rationality is not fundamental uncertainty: a Post Keynesian Perspective', *Journal of Post Keynesian Economics*, **23** (4) Summer, 567–88.

Faulkner, Philip (2002), 'Some problems with the conception of the human subject in critical realism', *Cambridge Journal of Economics*, **26** (6), 739–53.

Fisher, Irving (1933), 'Statistics in the service of economics', *Journal of the American Statistical Association*, **28**, 1–13.

Fleetwood, Stephen (1995), *Hayek's Political Economy: The Socio-Economics of Order*, London: Routledge.

Fleetwood, Stephen (1996), 'Order without equilibrium: a critical realist interpretation of Hayek's notion of spontaneous order', *Cambridge Journal of Economics*, **20** (6), 729–47.

Fleetwood, Stephen (2001), 'Causal laws, functional relations and tendencies', *Review of Political Economy*, **13**, (2), 201–20, reprinted in P. Downward (ed.) (forthcoming) *Applied Economics and the Critical Realist Critique*, Routledge: London.

Hahn, Frank H. (1985), 'In praise of economic theory', the 1984 Jevons Memorial Fund Lecture, London: University College.

Hahn, Frank H. (1992a), 'Reflections', *Royal Economics Society Newsletter*, **77**.

Hahn, Frank H. (1992b), 'Answer to Backhouse: Yes', *Royal Economic Society Newsletter*, **78** (5), 12.

Hands, Wade (2001), *Reflection Without Rules: Economic Methodology and Contemporary Science Theory*, Cambridge: Cambridge University Press.

Ingham, Geoffrey (1996), 'Money is a social relation', *Review of Social Economy*, **LIV**, Winter, pp. 507–30, reprinted in Stephen Fleetwood (ed.) (1999), *Critical Realism in Economics: Development and Debate*, London: Routledge, pp. 103–22.

Keynes, John M. (1973a), *The Collected Writings of John Maynard Keynes*, vol. VIII, *A Treatise on Probability*, London and Basingstoke: The Macmillan Press for the Royal Economic Society.

Keynes, John M. (1973b), *The Collected Writings of John Maynard Keynes*, vol. XIV, *The General Theory and After: Part II Defence and Development*, London and Basingstoke: The Macmillan Press for the Royal Economic Society.

Kirman, Alan (1999), 'The future of economic theory', in Alan Kirman and Louis-André Gérard-Varet (eds), *Economics Beyond the Millenium*, Oxford: Oxford University Press, pp. 8–23.

Lawson, Clive (1994), 'The transformational model of social activity and economic analysis: a reinterpretation of the work of J.R. Commons', *Review of Political Economy*, **6** (2), 186–204.

Lawson, Clive (1995), 'Realism and Institutionalism: John R. Commons, Carl Menger and Economics with Institutions', PhD dissertation, Cambridge.

Lawson, Clive (1996), 'Holism and collectivism in Commons', *Journal of Economic Issues*, **30** (4) (December), 967–85.

Lawson, Clive (1999a), 'Towards a competence theory of the region', *Cambridge Journal of Economics*, **23** (2), 151–61.

Lawson, Clive (1999b), 'Commons' contribution to political economy', in Philip O'Hara (ed.) *Encyclopedia of Political Economy*, London: Routledge, pp. 120–23.

Lawson, Clive (2000), 'Collective learning and epistemologically significant moments', in David Keeble and Frank Wilkinson, (eds), *High-Technology Clusters Networking and Collective Learning in Europe*, Aldershot: Ashgate, pp. 182–99.

Lawson, Clive (2003), 'Technical consultancies and regional competencies', in Charles Dannreuther and Wilfred Dolfsma (eds) *Globalisation, Social Capital and Inequality*, Cheltenham, UK and Northampton, MA, USA: Edward Elgar, pp. 75–92.

Lawson, Clive (forthcoming), 'A Transformational Conception of Technology', mimeo: Gonville and Caius College, Cambridge.

Lawson, Clive, Mark Peacock and Steve Pratten (1996), 'Realism, underlabouring and institutions', *Cambridge Journal of Economics*, **20** (1) January, 137–51.

Lawson, Tony (1989), 'Abstraction, tendencies and stylised facts: a realist approach to economic analysis', *Cambridge Journal of Economics*, **13** (1), 59–78, reprinted in Tony Lawson, Gabriel Palma, and John Sender (eds) (1989), *Kaldor's Political Economy*, London and San Diego: Academic Press, also reprinted in Paul Ekins and Manfred Max-Neef, (eds) (1992), *Real-Life Economics: Understanding Wealth Creation*, London: Routledge.

Lawson, Tony (1994), 'Hayek and realism: a case of continuous transformation', in Maria Colonna, Harold Haggemann and Omar F. Hamouda (eds), *Capitalism, Socialism and Knowledge: The Economics of F.A. Hayek*, Cheltenham: Edward Elgar.

Lawson, Tony (1997a), *Economics and Reality*, London: Routledge

Lawson, Tony (1997b), 'Critical Issues in economics as realist social theory', *Ekonomia*, (special issue on critical realism), **1** (2), 75–117, reprinted in Stephen Fleetwood (ed.) (1999), *Critical Realism in Economics: Development and Debate*, London: Routledge.

Lawson, Tony (1997c), 'Situated rationality', *Journal of Economic Methodology*, **4** (1), 101–25.

Lawson, Tony (1997d), 'Horses for courses', in Philip Arestis, Gabriel Palma and Malcolm Sawyer (eds), *Markets, Unemployment and Economic Policy: Essays in honour of Geoffrey Harcourt, vol. 2*, London and New York: Routledge, pp. 1–15.

Lawson, Tony (1998), 'Tendencies', in John Davis, Wade Hands and Uskali Mäki (eds), *The Edward Elgar Companion to Economic Methodology*, Cheltenham, UK and Lyme USA: Edward Elgar.

Lawson, Tony (2003), *Reorienting Economics*, London and New York: Routledge.

Leontief, Wassily (1982), letter in *Science*, **217**, 104–7.

Lewis, Paul (1996), 'Metaphor and critical realism', *Review of Social Economy*, **LIV** (4), 487–506, reprinted in Stephen Fleetwood (ed.) (1999), *Critical Realism in Economics: Development and Debate*, London: Routledge.

Lewis, Paul (2000a), 'Realism, causality and the problem of social structure', *Journal for The Theory of Social Behaviour*, **30**, 249–68.

Lewis, Paul (2000b), 'Does metaphor have a place in a realist methodology of economics?', Cambridge: mimeo.

Lewis, Paul (ed.) (forthcoming), *Transforming Economics: Perspectives on the Critical Realist Project*, London and New York : Routledge.

Lipsey, Richard, G. (2001), 'Successes and failures in the transformation of economics', *Journal Of Economic Methodology*, **8** (2), 169–202.

Locke, J. (1690 [1985]), 'An essay concerning human understanding', in an abridgment selected by J. Yolton (ed.), London and Melbourne: Dent.

Marx, Karl (1887 [1974]), *Capital*, vol. 1, Frederick Engles (ed.), London: Lawrence and Wishart.

Montes, Leonides (2002), 'Phiosophical and Methodological Underpinnings of Adam Smith's Political Economy. A Critical Reconstruction of some Central Components', Ph.D. dissertation, Cambridge University.

Montes, Leonides (2003), 'Smith and Newton: some methodological issues concerning general equilibrium theory', *Cambridge Journal of Economics*, **27**, 723–47.

O'Neill, John (1998), *The Market: Ethics, Knowledge and Politics*, London: Routledge.

Pratten, Stephen (1997), 'The nature of transaction cost economics', *Journal of Economic Issues*, **31**, 781–803.

Pratten, Stephen (1998), 'Marshall on tendencies, equilibrium and the statical method', *History of Political Economy*, **30** (1), 121–62.

Reed, Mike J (2001), 'Organisation, trust and control: a realist analysis', *Organisational Studies*, **22** (2), 201–28.

Rotheim, Roy J (2002), 'Timeful theories, timeful theorists', in P. Arestis, M. Desai and S. Dow (eds), *Methodology, Microeconomics and Keynes, Essays in Honour of Victoria Chick*, volume 2, London: Routledge.

Rubinstein, Ariel (1995), 'John Nash: the master of economic modelling', *Scandinavian Journal of Economics*, **97** (1), 9–13.

Runde, Jochen (1996), 'On Popper, probabilities and propensities', *Review of Social Economy*, **54**, 465–85, reprinted in Stephen Fleetwood (ed.) (1999), *Critical Realism in Economics: Development and Debate*, London: Routledge, pp. 63–82.

Runde, Jochen (1998a), 'Assessing causal economic explanations', *Oxford Economic Papers*, **50**, 151–72.

Runde, Jochen (1998b), 'Probability, uncertainty and long-term expectations', in Philip O'Hara, (ed.), *Encyclopedia of Political Economy*, London: Routledge, pp. 1189–92.

Runde, Jochen (2001), 'Chances and choices: notes on probability and belief in economic theory', in Uskali Mäki (ed.), *The Economic Worldview*, Cambridge: Cambridge University Press, pp. 132–53. Revised and extended version of a paper that originally appeared in *The Monist* **78**, (1995), 132–53.

Ruwampura, Kanchana (2002), 'Social transformations in East Sri Lanka: a feminist economic reading of female headship, ethnicity, gender relations and political economy', Ph.D. thesis, Cambridge University.

Sayer, Andrew (2000), *Realism and Social Science*, London: Sage.

Smithin, John (forthcoming), 'Macroeconomic theory, critical realism and capitalism', in Paul Lewis (ed),*Transforming Economics: Perspective on the Critical Realist Project*, London and New York: Routledge.

Veblen, Thorstein B. (1898), 'Why is economics not an evolutionary science?', *Quarterly Journal of Economics*, **XII**, July, reprinted (1919) in *The Place of Science in Modern Civilization and other essays*, Viking Press, republished (1990) with a new introduction by Warren J. Samuels by Transaction Publishers.

Whitehead, Alfred N. (1926), *Science and the Modern World*, Cambridge: Cambridge University Press.

17 The conflict between formalism and realisticness in modern economics: the case of the new institutional economics

Stephen Pratten

Introduction

Fictions abound in modern economics. The types of assumptions upon which the models of modern mainstream economics are typically based – human agents as possessing perfect foresight or always rational (optimising) in their behaviour, identical, living in two commodity worlds, operating within two-firm, or entirely isolated, economies, etc. – are plainly false and widely recognised as such. Often these fictions are given an 'instrumentalist' justification whereby models are understood as merely a basis for generating predictions. From this instrumentalist perspective the issue of how these models express or relate to reality, over and above the question of predictive success, is of little concern. Proponents of critical realism[1] argue that these fictions are not chosen because they are desired at all, but are an unavoidable consequence of using methods that are largely inappropriate to social analysis. The sorts of formalistic modelling methods used by economists presuppose for their relevance that the world is closed in a certain sense. At the same time the social world is found to be largely open. As a consequence the worlds expressed in the formalistic models appear to have little if any connection with the sort of world in which we do or could live.

The insistence always on maintaining a framework within which deductive, usually formal mathematical, procedures can proceed severely restricts the kinds of assumptions that can be made. There is often a tension between the acceptance of formal methods as in some sense indispensable to, or defining of, economic analysis and the desire to be more realistic. However genuine the intent to be more realistic, as long as revisions are carried out within the context of an a priori commitment to formalistic modelling, they seem always likely in the end to be compromised. There exists a fundamental mismatch between the kind of ontology that would render coherent the preoccupation with formalistic modelling and our best ontological theories of social reality. For those economists for whom the task is primarily that of illuminating social reality any appreciation of the possibility of such a disconnection between formalism and social reality is accompanied by difficult questions of interpretation and strategy. Some seem to retreat from the project of illuminating social reality altogether choosing instead to pursue the programme of mathematising economics on pragmatic grounds. Others express the hope that persevering with mathematical modelling will eventually deliver some kind of relevant re-engagement and a narrowing of the gap between modern economic theory and reality. A few merely express bewilderment as to how best to interpret the present state of affairs.

This paper shows how this tension plays out in the context of the New Institutional Economics (NIE).[2] NIE provides a particularly useful illustration of the tension between an a priori commitment to formalism and realisticness since (a) proponents of NIE recognise that mainstream economics is unrealistic (and even provide a partial explanation of how this has come about), (b) consciously set out to be more realistic, yet (c) ultimately seek to retain/prioritise formalistic methods.[3] A prominent motivation for the NIE project is the artificiality of mainstream economics and the desire to push the discipline toward greater relevance and realisticness. The accusation levelled against the mainstream is that certain essentially methodological constraints have led to either the total neglect, or misrepresentation, of significant social institutions. The argument is precisely that modern economic theory has become detached from reality. At times NIE appears to recognise the need and current importance of explicit reflection on ontological matters. Alongside this fundamental, if underdeveloped, critique of the mainstream exists a quite different orientation. In characterising the development of the NIE and in differentiating it from alternative perspectives on organisations and institutions a claim often forwarded is that NIE shares with mainstream economics an emphasis on formalism and the need to adequately *operationalise* arguments. Here a continuity at the level of method is emphasised as a way of highlighting the distinctive contribution of the NIE. The a priori privileging of formalistic methods characteristic of mainstream economics is retained even as it is recognised that there remains some way to go before the NIE project is fully formalised. This chapter argues that the NIE attempt to move toward a more relevant and realistic institutional economics is compromised by a reductionism implied by the retained commitment to the explanatory approaches adopted from mainstream economics and accepted as appropriate.[4]

Mathematical formalism in economics: presuppositions and consequences

The mainstream persists in its insistence that formal modelling methods[5] should be universally applied, almost always without making any assessment of their suitability for investigating social material. It is simply taken for granted that such techniques are appropriate for, or perhaps more accurately essential to or defining of, economics. This attitude reflects a characteristic neglect of ontology. By contrast the arguments developed by proponents of critical realism imply that caution is required. A realist orientation recommends that when considering the prospects for and likely consequences of pursuing mathematical modelling in economics, it is necessary to be sensitive to the special features of the relevant subject matter. It is important to carefully identify what formal mathematical methods require for their efficacy and then to evaluate the relevance of such presuppositions in the context in which they are being applied.

Those contributing to critical realism argue that the sorts of formalistic methods used by economists presuppose that the social world is everywhere closed when, in contrast, it seems to be quintessentially open. A closed system is one within which regularities of the form 'whenever event or state of affairs *x* then event or state of affairs *y*' obtain. These regularities can be deterministic or take a probabilistic form. They are the sort of connections achieved, via human intervention, in well controlled experiments. By presupposing formalistic mathematical methods to be always appropriate mainstream economists assume that something at least approximating these sorts of conditions hold in the social realm. The difficulty for the modelling approach is that the social realm is of a nature that such conditions are rarely found.

It appears, then, that most social systems are open rather than closed. That is to say, they are subject not only to changes within the system but also to unpredictable influences from outside the system. To produce an event regularity in a well-controlled experiment (which is the site for most scientifically interesting event regularities) the experimenter has to identify a *stable* mechanism and effectively *isolate* it. The mechanism has to be isolated in order to prevent other interfering countervailing factors disrupting the regularity. The (isolated) mechanism has to be intrinsically stable so that when it is triggered (conditions *x*) predictable effects (outcomes *y*) always follow. However, the purpose of the experiment is not the production of an event regularity per se, but the empirical identification of the stable mechanism which has been experimentally isolated. In fact the results achieved can be applied outside the experiment precisely because they relate to the underlying mechanism not the event regularity corresponding to its empirical identification.

For social event regularities to hold there would need to be analogues to the isolated stable mechanisms of the controlled experiment. There would need to be some guarantee that the individuals depicted within the models would respond passively, that is in a stable predictable way, to the triggering conditions and further that the systems under examination were effectively isolated. That individual agents are invariably characterised in the models of modern economics as atomistic and depicted as acting within isolated environments can be seen as following on from its commitment to formalism. This sort of reductionist theorising is a necessary adjunct to, or requirement of, formalistic modelling. Yet the constitution of social reality is found to be quite different from what would be required in order to generate social event regularities. For example, it is easily demonstrated that social reality is, in fact, mostly far from atomistic or amenable to meaningful isolation being highly internally related, open and of the nature of a process.[6] If the social world is acknowledged to be typically open then the a priori commitment to methods which presuppose closure explains not only the prevalence but also the sorts of known-to-be-false assumptions about human nature and the social conditions within which agents act that modellers are forced to make. The modelling programme encourages the adoption of assumptions that are unrealistic in the sense that we have every reason to suppose that they lie outside the bounds of real possibility. As Lawson notes 'it is not that we could really be omniscient or always act rationally (in the sense of optimising), if only we could be bothered or choose to' (Lawson 2001b: 76).[7] Moreover these fictions are not chosen arbitrarily. Far from any old fiction sufficing, they typically take a form which facilitates the favoured modelling procedures.

None of this implies that science is not possible in the social realm. The analysis of experiments referred to above reveals that even in controlled experiments, when tight correlations are sometimes produced, the goal is not the production of these correlations per se, but the empirical identification of underlying mechanisms. Science is not a matter of seeking correlations at the level of actual events but is primarily concerned with identifying their underlying causes. Science moves typically from phenomena at one level to their causes lying at a different, deeper level. Although the opportunities for meaningful experiments, and so scientifically interesting correlations, have been found to be rather limited in the social realm,[8] it is still possible to identify the underlying causes of surface phenomena. In social science, according to this perspective, the event analogies are human activities and the primary aim is to identify and understand the social structures that render possible such activities as occur. Social structure is taken to be an emergent realm of causal powers. The emergent social realm sustains human agency but also depends upon it. That is, it is a realm of phenomena dependent upon human agents and their interactions but with powers irreducible to them (although capable of acting back on [making a difference to] human agents and their interactions).[9]

This realist orientation allows us to further clarify and assess attempted defences of formalism within economics. By way of illustration I shall briefly consider one recent exercise of this sort. A typical stance is merely to assert that formalism is necessary whatever the consequences and that there is no other viable way of proceeding. Dasgupta (2002) in responding to claims that the gap between economic theory and reality is ever increasing appears at times to adopt such a position:

> Economics is a quantitative subject. When the Chancellor of the Exchequer asks his expert advisers to tell him of the fiscal advantages and disadvantages of an increase in the tax on petrol, he does not want a philosophical discourse, nor a lecture on what

Marx would have thought about the matter. He wants to know how much revenue he would be able to raise, what effects its imposition would have on other sectors of the economy, what it would mean to the lives of different categories of people, and if the Minister of Environment is within earshot, he will also ask if it would reduce carbon emissions. *So mathematical modelling is essential and is here to stay.* But mathematical modelling of volition is inevitably, a repugnant exercise, because it seems to demean the human experience. ... But in order to make progress, we have to simplify in suitable ways. In many applications, individual choice as modelled by the economist, is a grotesque caricature of ourselves. Those who find mathematical modelling unsatisfactory think they would avoid such compromises if they were to go the literary route. So they take refuge in such aphorisms as that 'it is better to be vaguely right than precisely wrong'. What this misses however is that you won't even know if you are vaguely right if you operate within a framework in which you cannot be precisely wrong: there is no way to controvert a vague statement. (Dasgupta 2002, p. 81, emphasis added)

Dasgupta is clear in his view that a reliance on mathematical modelling is essential to the project of contemporary mainstream economics. Further, he appears to be suggesting that this insistence upon working with formalistic models is likely to be associated with the positing of theoretical entities that may be so unrealistic as to border on grotesque caricature. The centrality of mathematical modelling and related positing of transparently fictitious entities is not defended by reference to their relevance to, or appropriateness for, the nature of the material under investigation. Moreover, there is no suggestion that economists have been overly successful in forecasting and, of course, it would be difficult to legitimately forward any such claim. Dasgupta's defence of the privileged role of formalistic modelling in economics therefore reduces to its potential to facilitate the possibility of responding to requests for predictions and that there is no alternative. While the former seems a limited basis upon which to rest any kind of defence the latter would seem rather premature, at least if adopted prior to a sustained investigation into the nature of social material and the methods appropriate to its analysis.

A different strategy is to suggest that the models are, after all, becoming more relevant. Dasgupta at times seems to adopt this position in claiming that, in fact, rather than increasing, the gap between formal economic models and reality is narrowing. Here he draws on personal reflections on the trajectory of economics over the last thirty years or so. The 1960s are portrayed as a period where 'theory' was thoroughly separated from more concrete applied work. Today, in contrast, he suggests that the leading economics journals are dominated by work on problems of an 'applied-theoretic' kind where the focus is upon 'small, sharp questions'.[10] However, others who are equally committed to developing the mainstream project contest this interpretation of the recent development of economics. For example, Rubinstein in his tribute to Nash's contribution to game theory, suggests not only that there is a gap between formalistic modelling and reality but that the extent of this gap is significant and constitutes a pressing challenge to advocates of orthodox economic theory:

> The issue of interpreting economic theory is, in my opinion, the most serious problem now facing economic theorists. The feeling among many of us can be summarised as follows. Economic theory should deal with the real world. It is not a branch of abstract mathematics even though it utilises mathematical tools. Since it is about the real world, people expect the theory to prove useful in achieving practical goals. *But economic theory has not delivered the goods. Predictions from economic theory are not nearly as accurate as those by natural sciences, and the link between economic theory and practical problems such as how to bargain, is tenuous at best.* Although I have never heard an economist seriously claim that the Nash bargaining solution is a good predictor of bargaining in real markets, this solution is a standard tool in modelling interactions among negotiators. Economic theory lacks a consensus as to its purpose and interpretation. Again and again, we find ourselves asking the question 'where does this lead.' (Rubinstein 1995, p. 12, emphasis added)

Notwithstanding such interpretative disputes, the more fundamental issue relates to what any such narrowing of the gap between formal economic models and reality could mean. Given that Dasgupta apparently acknowledges that formalistic economic modelling involves the positing of fictitious entities – which cannot be defended in terms of relevance but only in terms of analytical tractability and the absence of a suitable alternative – a closing of the gap can relate only to some knowingly fictitious model being in some sense confronted with data. While the value of such exercises is unclear, they do little to counter the central criticism that methods that presuppose that closed systems obtain are being insisted upon as ways of analysing a seemingly open social world. In attempting to establish his argument that modern mainstream economics is, after all, in touch with reality Dasgupta reports that 90 perc ent of the articles published in the *American Economic Review* over a five-year period were either 'applied theory' – meaning 'a piece of theoretical analysis that tries to explain some observed fact, or which analyses the implications of particular types of policies' (2002, p. 79) or experimental and/or empirical economics. As Lawson notes:

> If economic data record phenomena generated within an open and highly internally related social system, and economists uncritically insist on analysing them using methods which presuppose that they record phenomena generated in closed and atomistic systems, claims to be in touch with reality just because data are involved are not well founded. Similarly, if the whole framework of theoretical modelling is inevitably, and known to be largely false, it is not obvious that there is any relevance or insight to be found in any policy conclusions drawn from it. (Lawson 2001b, p. 79)[11]

It is important to emphasise at this point that a realist orientation does not rule out the productive use of formal mathematical techniques in the social realm in an a priori way. For otherwise we would merely be replacing one form of dogmatism with another. Rather, what is recommended is caution. The stipulation from a realist orientation is that procedures and techniques should be tailored to the chosen object of study. Humphreys (2002) recent survey of mathematical modelling in the social sciences expresses this cautionary attitude well. He acknowledges that 'mathematical models can appear sophisticated when they are merely sophistical; they can produce the illusion of knowledge in situations where none is to be had; they can produce guilded absurdities; they possess the ever-present danger that mechanical computations will replace intelligent inference; and many of the assumptions behind the models either fail to be satisfied in practice, or only the flimsiest of justifications can be given for them' (Humphreys 2002, p. 167). Despite all the dangers and difficulties he concludes that formal modelling can yet play a significant if limited role: 'Modelling in the social sciences requires modest goals and recognition of the special features of its subject matter. Nevertheless, much can be gained by intelligently borrowing existing formal methods from other areas and reconstructing them so that they correctly apply to the social domain' (Humphreys 2002, p. 182).[12]

Relevance and realisticness in the new institutional economics
Leading proponents of the NIE programme identify the gap between modern economic theory and reality as a problem, provide some partial explanation as to its existence and forward the NIE as a response to it. In doing so they often appear to adopt something close to a realist orientation and a correspondingly cautious attitude toward the formalisation of economics in general and the NIE in particular.

In his address to the International Society of New Institutional Economics, Coase suggests that 'we are a society with a mission and that mission is to transform economics. When I speak of economics, I have in mind mainstream economics as expounded in countries in the West and particularly what is called microeconomics or price theory. Our mission is to replace the current analysis with something better, the New Institutional Economics' (Coase 1999b, p. 1). For Coase the discipline is in urgent need of substantial transformation and he suggests that there may currently be support for such a programme of reorientation precisely because of the growing recognition of the inadequacies of mainstream economics:

> If we have some sort of illness or disease or problem, you get along with it, you accept it, and then it gets so bad that you feel you ought to do something about it. Now I think that in economics people are now beginning to think that things have got so bad that one ought to do something about it, and therefore those people who have always wanted to do something about it have a more sympathetic audience than in the past. I think that is the present situation. You get lots of statements to the effect that what economists are doing is not particularly useful. (Coase 1999a, p. 8)

Why is this reorientation felt to be necessary? Coase is clear as to what he regards as problematic about the state of modern economics: that there is both a glaring neglect of obviously important social institutions and a broader disengagement of economics from real world phenomena and problems. In his view, mainstream economics has traditionally failed to consider significant aspects of the economic realm. Specifically with regard the firm, Coase argues that:

> The firm in modern economic theory is an organization which transforms inputs into outputs. Why firms exist, what determines the number of firms, what determines what firms do (the inputs a firm buys and the output it sells) are not questions of interest to most economists. The firm in economic theory … is a 'shadowy figure' (Coase 1988, p. 5–6)

Not only are significant features of the firm neglected but the market too is barely addressed within mainstream economics. Coase notes that while economists claim to study the working of the market 'in modern economic theory the market itself has an even more shadowy role than the firm' (Coase 1988, p. 7). He writes: 'when economists do speak of market structure it has nothing to do with the market as an institution but refers to such things as the number of firms, product differentiation and the like, the influence of social institutions which facilitate exchange being completely ignored' (Coase 1988, p. 8). For Coase both the firm and the market within mainstream theory 'appear by name but they lack any substance' (1994, p. 4–5).[13]

Coase is critical not only of the neglect of institutions but more generally of the trajectory of modern economics. Coase repeatedly refers to the artificial or fictional nature of much economic theorising: 'when economists find that they are unable to analyse what is happening in the real world, they invent an imaginary world which they are capable of handling' (Coase 1988, p. 8). This feature of modern economics has meant it has become devoid of policy relevance:

> Until comparatively recently economists tended to devise their proposals for economic reform by comparing what is actually done with what would happen in an ideal state. Such a procedure is pointless. We can carry out the operations required to bring about the ideal state on a blackboard but they have no counterpart in real life. In the real world, to influence economic policy, we set up or abolish an agency, amend the law, change the personnel and so on; we work through institutions. The choice in economic policy is a choice of institutions. And what matters is the effect that a modification in these institutions will actually make in the real world. … What should characterise modern institutional economics, and does to a considerable extent, is that the problems tackled are those thrown up by the real world. (Coase 1984, pp. 230–31)

Coase is equally clear as to how this situation is to be rectified. He insists that 'realism in our assumptions is needed if our theories are ever to help us understand why the system works in the way it does. Realism in assumptions forces us to analyse the world that exists, not some imaginary world that does not' (Coase 1994, p. 18). Coase here seems to be explicitly advocating the adoption of a realist orientation. That is, he is suggesting that our understanding of social reality should inform the assumptions adopted and more generally serve to fashion the methods of economic analysis. As such he is opposing the long-standing neglect of explicit ontological analysis that is so characteristic of modern economics. More specifically, he appears to be suggesting that a regard for issues of existence or ontology can underpin an anti-realist position with regard to specific perspectives (much mainstream theory) or items. This is an attitude he adopts explicitly when considering the assumption of the agent as a rational utility maximiser 'Most economists make the assumption that man is a rational utility maximiser. This seems to me both unnecessary and misleading. I have said that in modern institutional economics we should start with real institutions. Let us also start with man as he is' (Coase 1984, p. 231).

Williamson also sometimes appears sensitive to this need for ontological elaboration. Drawing on Simon, Williamson argues that 'nothing is more fundamental in setting our research agenda and informing our research method than our view of the nature of the human beings whose behavior we are studying' (Williamson 1996, p. 48). He repeatedly expresses the desire to explore the attributes of human agents relevant to the study of organisations and claims that NIE displays greater sensitivity than narrowly orthodox approaches regarding the need to elaborate and draw on a more compelling and accurate account of the human agent. For example, Williamson writes that:

> Many economists treat behavioral assumptions as unimportant. This reflects a widely held opinion that the realism of the assumptions is unimportant and that the fruitfulness of a theory turns on its implications. But whereas transaction cost economics is prepared to be judged (comparatively) by the refutable implications which this approach uniquely affords, it also maintains that the behavioral assumptions are important. (Williamson 1989a, p. 138)

This concern with the realisticness of behavioral assumptions is reflected in Williamson's rejection of orthodox accounts of hyper-rationality and use and development of notions of bounded rationality. According to Williamson, once the orthodox portrayal of the perpetually calculating and optimising human agent is abandoned a whole series of fundamental problems in economic organisation are opened up for examination. Williamson suggests that his discussion of opportunism also reflects his concern for developing a realistic account of the human agent within NIE.[14] If Williamson has shown a concern with the realisticness of the account of the human agent underpinning NIE, he has also become increasingly eager to differentiate between different types or levels of social institution. Moreover, he stresses that institutions are part of an evolving social process and that 'process issues' need to be examined when analysing economic organisations: 'The study of governance goes beyond structure and incentives and control instruments to include an examination of process. This is an area in which economists have been loath to enter ... I am persuaded that the self-conscious study of process has already played a vital role in the development of transaction cost economics ... and that additional study of process is sorely needed if core issues are to be exposed' (Williamson 1988, p. 163).

In trying to account for the neglect of institutions within orthodox economics and more generally the gap between modern economics and reality both Coase and Williamson point to methodological practices they associate with the mainstream. Coase suggests that this kind of retreat is, in part, a result of the increasingly 'abstract' nature of economic theory:

> The concentration on the determination of prices has led to a narrowing of focus which has had as a result the neglect of other aspects of the economic system. ... This neglect of other aspects of the system has been made easier by another feature of modern economic theory – the growing abstraction of the analysis, which does not seem to call for a detailed knowledge of the actual economic system, or at any rate, has managed to proceed without it. ... What is studied is a system which lives in the minds of economists but not on earth. I have called the result 'blackboard economics'. (Coase 1994, pp. 4–5)[15]

Although referring to abstraction what Coase is critical of here is clearly the way in which mainstream economists proceed by assuming as a starting point a transparently fictitious world that is totally different from the one in which we live or could possibly live. Coase insists that he is not against abstraction per se. He suggests that 'The right degree of abstraction depends on the problem that is being analysed' (Coase 1993, p. 97) and writes:

> It is of course true that our assumption should not be completely realistic. There are factors we leave out because we do not know how to handle them. There are factors we leave out because we do not feel the benefits of a more comprehensive theory would be worth the costs involved in including them. Their inclusion might greatly complicate the analysis without giving us greater understanding about what is going on. Again assumptions about other factors do not need to be realistic because they are completely irrelevant. ... There are good reasons why the assumptions of one's theories should not be completely realistic, but this does not mean that we should lose touch with reality. (1994, p. 18)

Coase recognises that abstraction is as essential to economics as it is to all science. He also appears to be deploying a traditional notion of abstraction as meaning focusing upon certain aspects of something to the momentary neglect of others. Abstraction, so understood, indicates that an analysis is necessarily partial, what it does not imply is that analysis necessitates a reliance on claims or conceptions we already believe to be fictitious. What Coase (1993, p. 97) objects to is 'mindless abstraction or the kind of abstraction which does not help us to understand the working of the economic system'. Coase in distinguishing between good (the right degree of) and bad (or mindless) abstraction recognises that any such assessment requires insight into the nature of the object.[16]

NIE authors suggest that the failure of orthodox theory to address obviously significant social institutions arises as a result of its reliance on fictitious assumptions. At times this is directly linked to the priority placed on mathematising economic theory:

> It is ... widely agreed that if mechanism B, not mechanism A, is thought to be generating the phenomena of interest, the intellectually respectable thing to do is to build theory B. ... The heavy emphasis on the development of mathematical economics during the past thirty years, however has often favoured theory A constructions. Transactional frictions, which do not yield easily to formal analysis, have been relatively neglected in the process. Although this may have been necessary, as a transitional measure, to reach the present level of refinement of economic theory, it has sometimes been at the expense of being artificial. (Williamson, 1975, p. 248)

Coase too suggests that an a priori commitment to the development of formal mathematical theory may have proceeded without sufficient regard to the nature of the material being investigated. When reviewing Marshall's method Coase attempts to clarify what Marshall found objectionable about the use of mathematics. Coase suggests that Marshall's worry was that the use of mathematics was likely to be a diversion. Reflecting on the contemporary scene he then notes:

> In these days, when the mathematical method rides triumphant in economics, one may ask whether Marshall's fears were well founded. Have we been tempted to embark on 'long chains of reasoning' without adequate supporting data? Do we neglect factors difficult to put into mathematical form? Do we concern ourselves not with the puzzles presented by the real economic world but with the puzzles presented by other economists' analysis? It is not, of course, possible to indict the whole economics profession – and much good work is done nowadays and some of this work is carried out with mathematical methods. Furthermore I feel sure that Marshall would have agreed that this was so. But it would be hard to deny that the extensive use of mathematics has encouraged the tendencies that he thought would be its probable consequence. Marshall's thought was that the extensive use of mathematics would lead us away from what he considered to be 'constructive work'. I very much doubt that what has happened in recent years would have led him to change his mind. (Coase 1994, p. 175)

Now, Coase certainly does not rule out the productive use of mathematics in economics. In fact he seems to remain rather optimistic in this regard. What Coase does insist upon is for a sensitivity to be maintained regarding the match between the methods used and material studied. Turning to the framework he developed in his famous article on 'The nature of the firm', he writes that: 'It will not have escaped the notice of some readers that this analytical scheme can be put into mathematical form. This should give us hope but only if this analytical power is used to enlighten us about the real rather than an imaginary world' (Coase 1991, p. 73). In expressing a preference for formal mathematical techniques Coase at the same time insists that their deployment makes sense only in a context where the nature of the object is capable of being illuminated by them.

To the extent that the NIE involves the adoption of a realist orientation it would seem to imply a significant methodological re-orientation. The emphasis on the adoption of realistic assumptions, the detailed analysis of institutions and the comparison of real world alternatives is seen as an important means of overcoming certain deep-seated methodological problems associated with modern economics, and specifically its damaging preoccupation with obviously fictitious states. Coase writes:

> Economics has been becoming more and more abstract, less and less related to what goes on in the real world. In fact, economists have devoted themselves to studying imaginary systems, and they don't distinguish between the imaginary system and the real world. That's what modern economics has been and continues to be. All the prestige goes to people who produce the most abstract results about an economic system that doesn't exist. (Coase 1997, p. 45)

Coase's aim 'is to bring into existence an economic theory which is solidly based' (Coase 1993, p. 97). Williamson suggests that within Transaction Cost Economics the 'fictions of firms as production functions, comprehensive contracting and efficacious court ordering all vanish' (Williamson 1993d, p. 50).

A retained reductionism within the new institutional economics

Coase, and to some degree Williamson, suggest that certain core methodological characteristics of mainstream theory have led to the neglect of social institutions, encouraged a gap between economic theory and social reality and limited the relevance of economics at the level of policy. There is within the NIE a recognition of the importance of ontological elaboration and the partial adoption of a realist orientation. Indeed NIE seems to be an extremely fertile area for ontological elaboration that extends to identifying the computational limitations of human agents, characterising the social world as a complex evolving process and acknowledging the multi-layered nature of social institutions. Yet it cannot be claimed that the NIE proceeds very far with these tasks of ontological elaboration and clarification. The move toward a more realistic account of the human agent, an adequate delineation and definition of distinct institutional levels and accommodation of change and process remain only partially carried through. Numerous commentators have noted that despite the significance attached by Williamson to re-examining the behavioral assumptions of economics he, in fact, adopts a rather thin form of bounded rationality.[17] When considering the relationship between the institutions of governance and the broader institutional environment he conceives of the latter merely as a locus of shift parameters. Williamson suggests changes in the institutional environment induce alterations in the costs of governance and therefore it is useful to consider how 'equilibrium distributions of transactions will change in response to disturbances in the institutional environment' (Williamson 1991a, p. 287).[18] Process issues are emphasised as key and yet it remains unclear how they relate to the emphasis given to the efficiency of organisational forms also regarded as central to the project. At times Williamson acknowledges that the 'entire institutional environment (laws, rules, conventions, norms, etc.) within which the institutions of governance are embedded is the product of history. And although the social conditioning that operates within governance structures ... is reflexive and often intentional, this too has accidental and temporal features' (1993c, p. 140). Yet NIE has repeatedly been criticised for its excessive functionalism.[19]

While the NIE attempts to move toward a more relevant and realistic institutional economics, it does not shrug off inherited notions of what counts as theory or what represents the appropriate pursuit of rigorous economics. In relying on conventional understandings the NIE is ultimately compromised by a reductionism implied by a retained commitment to the approaches adopted from mainstream economics and accepted as appropriate. Despite NIE authors sometimes expressing a concern regarding the blanket application of mathematical modelling strategies, Williamson nonetheless insists that the move toward ever greater levels of formalism is a natural progression which the development of the NIE conforms to and that the compromises which modelling necessitate in terms of fictional assumptions are after all inevitable.

Williamson claims that the NIE has progressed through a series of stages involving the gradual formalisation of the approach. The contribution of more recent transaction cost economics TCE authors is, in part, to have reframed Coase's arguments in such a way as to allow for more formal presentation.[20] Williamson writes: 'the transaction cost treatment of vertical integration has proceeded in a series of stages. The first and most critical was the statement of the general verbal argument ... this was then given a geometric interpretation ... was thereafter recast in a more general mathematical way ... and has since been developed more rigorously in the context of comparative incomplete contracting' (Williamson 1991b, p. 96). He traces the delayed impact of Coase's work to its lack of formalism and the associated failure to operationalise[21] the framework sufficiently:

> Coase has been misunderstood because he did not make his argument as accessible as it might be, and because the operational content of transaction costs is obscure. Coase eschews geometry or mathematics ... and instead uses ponderous arithmetic examples to explain his theories. Although this does not prevent Coase from recognising and discussing the nuances present in those theories, many readers would benefit from arguments once conceptualised, translated into a more formal language ... Coase ... makes no such efforts and does not acknowledge efforts at translation that have been done by others. A chronic problem with Coase's work has been that the concept of transaction cost is vague. ... Although Coase evidently acknowledges the need for operationalization, he has yet to address himself to this in a systematic way. (Williamson 1989b, p. 229)[22]

In all these reflections Williamson equates formalisation with progress.

Williamson further argues that formalisation and operational adequacy are central to identifying the contribution of the NIE. The NIE approach adds more than merely a focus on institutions, it is recognised that this would be far from novel. The NIE provides a framework that, while addressing institutional issues, responds to a felt need to develop arguments taking a certain recognisable form. A contrast is often drawn in this context with the old institutional economics. Williamson suggests that the NIE retains a commitment to rigorous analysis whereas the old institutional economics falls into mere description abandoning any hope of a systematic study of institutions:

> The New Institutional Economics turns on two propositions: institutions (1) matter and (2) are susceptible to analysis. ... Both the older and the newer approaches to institutional economics are in agreement on the first of these. Where they differ is with respect to the second. Thus whereas the older institutional economics made little effort to operationalize the argument that institutions matter, the New Institutional Economics insists that reconceptualisation and operationalization proceed in tandem. Indeed, but for this commitment to operationalization it is doubtful that institutional economics would have been awarded a new life. (Williamson 1990, pp. 8–9)

For Williamson, in order for an argument to count as systematic analysis it seems it must conform to a particular form, a stipulation the old institutionalists and others fail to meet.[23]

From this angle the NIE seems not, in the end, to constitute a fundamental move away from orthodox economics but its extension to issues that have long been ignored or only partially addressed. Williamson sees the significance of NIE as relating primarily to the provision of a new substantive research agenda and he quotes with approval Arrow's remark that: 'the new institutional economics ... does not consist primarily of giving new answers to the traditional questions of economics – resource allocation and degree of utilisation. Rather it consists of answering new questions, why economic institutions have emerged the way they did and not otherwise' (Arrow quoted in Williamson 1990, p. 3). What is significant here is that in providing a new agenda for research it is suggested that no fundamental methodological break from orthodoxy is required. On the contrary it is emphasised that NIE adopts standard economic methods to tackle institutional questions. By doing so it is suggested that a systematic study of social institutions is made possible. Even Coase at times appears to adopt this position, he writes:

> What distinguishes the modern institutional economists is not that they speak about institutions … nor that they have introduced a new economic theory, although they may have modified the existing theory in various ways, but that they use standard economic theory to analyse the working of these institutions and to discover the part they play in the operation of the economy. (Coase 1984, p. 230)

It is recognised that this prioritisation of operational adequacy and formalism carry implications for the realisticness of assumptions. For example, Williamson acknowledges that he only partially adopts Simon's analysis of bounded rationality.[24] Williamson's reluctance to explore further Simon's analysis of bounded rationality and link it to satisficing is not on the grounds that it is an inadequate account of the human agent. On the contrary, while Williamson appears persuaded that Simon has moved toward a more accurate characterisation, he claims that such sophistication comes at a cost:

> One possible objection to the use of maximisation/marginal analysis is that 'Parsimony recommends that we prefer the postulate that men are reasonable to the postulate that they are supremely rational, when either of the two assumptions will do our work of inference as well as the other'. … But while one might agree with Simon that satisficing is more reasonable than maximising the analytical toolbox out of which satisficing works is compared with maximising approaches incomplete and very cumbersome. Thus if one reaches the same outcome through the satisficing postulate as through maximising and if the latter is much easier to implement, then economists can be thought of as analytical satisfiers: they use a short cut form of analysis that is simple to implement. Albeit at the expense of realism in assumptions, maximisation gets the job done. (Williamson 1993c, p. 123)[25]

Satisficing then represents for Williamson a more adequate account of the agent, but this heightened realisticness, he suggests has to be weighed against the fact that it is very cumbersome and fails to conform to standard modes of analysis. Williamson conceives of his own discussion of bounded rationality as representing a sensible middle ground between the more realistic but less operational approaches represented by Simon and the more operationally satisfactory but less realistic narrowly orthodox approaches.[26] In his discussion of bounded rationality Williamson acknowledges that realisticness and mainstream theory are counterposed, or as he puts it, 'Reasonableness and tractability are in tension' (Williamson 2001, p. 7). Williamson's expressed interest in deploying a realistic account of the human agent can only be taken so far when faced by the retention of an a priori insistence on formalistic modelling.

It seems that for Williamson the supposed gains from formalism in terms of greater precision are likely to outweigh any losses at the level of the realisticness of assumptions. Here he is content to defer to Simon as an authority. He quotes Simon's assessment:

> 'Mathematics has become the dominant language of the natural sciences not because it is quantitative – a common delusion – but primarily because it permits clear and rigorous reasoning about phenomena too complex to be handled in words. This advantage of mathematics over cruder languages should prove to be of even greater significance in the social sciences, which deal with phenomena of the greatest complexity'. He [Simon] thereafter argues that the primitive state of the art of fully formal modelling notwithstanding, formal models are to be preferred to the 'legerdemain [of verbal reasoning] that consists of introducing a host of implicit and unacknowledged assumptions at each stage of the verbal argument. The poverty of mathematics is an honest poverty that does not parade imaginary riches before the world'. (Simon quoted in Williamson 2003, pp. 934)

Ultimately, these familiar references to complexity and greater precision miss the most telling point being advanced by those, like Coase, who recommend caution with respect to the application of formal mathematical modelling procedures within modern economics. It can be acknowledged that the physical sciences have successfully modelled enormously complex phenomena using abstraction and simplification to reduce the number of variables considered. But this has been made possible by the nature of the material being investigated. As Humphreys notes:

> The already sparse nature of some ... physical systems, the presence of dominant influences swamping smaller effects, and the separability of various influences, has resulted in quite accurate physical models being developed on the basis of a small number of mechanisms. Sparse systems with dominant, separable influences are, unfortunately, uncommon in the social sciences outside the laboratory. (Humphreys 2002: 168)

To insist upon the use of formalistic modelling procedures within economics is to assume that there exist counterparts in the social realm to such systems that are similarly amenable to formal modelling. From a realist perspective it is precisely the legitimacy of such an assumption that needs to be examined. It is, of course, possible that some who reject the compromises which modelling necessitates introduce implicit and unacknowledged assumptions at every stage of their analyses. But this is typical, neither of the best nor the majority of those who adopt non-formalistic approaches. Precision cannot be viewed as the preserve of those who insist on putting it before all else. Moreover, even if one were to concede that within formal models an attempt is made to specify initial (typically highly artificial) assumptions the prior presumption that such models are of relevance, or likely to have legitimate application, in the social realm is itself founded on a set of usually implicit and unstated assumptions about the nature of the social world. The problem with the modelling approach that most worries those adopting the kind of realist orientation outlined above is its seemingly inevitable irrelevance. The problem is precisely the (unnecessary) compromise to which Williamson refers between tractability and relevance.

If Coase's comments on the fictional or imaginary nature of much economic theorising and cautious attitude toward the formalistic trajectory of economics points in the direction of a realist orientation, the emphasis on methodological continuity with orthodox economics and the priority placed on adding operational content seems to imply the retention of the dogmatic a priori commitment to the modelling procedures so characteristic of modern economics (albeit with certain assumptions modified, the substantive focus shifted and only a limited formalism achieved). It is perhaps not surprising given these countervailing tendencies within the NIE that a sense of unease is often expressed regarding a move toward greater formalism even by those who equate it with progress. Williamson has recently expressed some disappointment with the project of formalising the NIE and even suggested that what may be needed is a 'new mathematics' in order to engage the 'issues posed by the economics of organisation' (Williamson 2003, p. 31).

Concluding remarks

Formal economic modelling invariably involves the use of assumptions which, when taken as descriptive statements, are simply fictions and known to be so. Yet many economists who express a desire to shift economics toward greater realisticness simultaneously remain tied to the idea that formalistic modelling is essential to progress in economics. To the extent that an a priori commitment to formalistic mathematical modelling is made without a careful evaluation of the extent to which such methods are appropriate to the material under investigation the disengagement of economic theory from reality seems a likely consequence. If a commitment to formalistic modelling comes first then severe restrictions are placed on the kind of assumptions that can be admitted. While concern may be expressed as to the plausibility of conventional assumptions any move toward greater realisticness in terms of, for example, the portrayal of the human agent or the account of social structures and institutions is likely in the end to be compromised by a need to retain conceptions which are tractable in the sense of facilitating the favoured modelling strategies. A realist orientation argues for greater caution suggesting that where possible no a priori stance be adopted concerning the appropriateness of formalistic modelling methods.

The argument developed within this chapter is that NIE provides a useful illustration of the tension between formalism and realisticness in modern economics. This type of analysis may clarify both the connections and distinctions between the NIE and mainstream theory and help to identify differing streams within the NIE itself. NIE authors characteristically criticise mainstream economics on the basis that it fails to account for significant social institutions and more generally has focused increasingly on irrelevant imaginary worlds. Yet the NIE itself is seen as conforming to a path of development in which it has been formulated in increasingly formal terms. The problem here is that NIE as a programme of research is being pulled in rather different directions. To the extent that the NIE retains an a priori commitment to formalism it would seem to share much in common with the mainstream and perhaps would be best interpreted as one further expression of it. Variety at a substantive level has after all long been recognised as a feature of the mainstream project. Williamson, in fact, anticipates that insights from NIE will be 'absorbed within the corpus of "extended" neoclassical analysis' and suggests that the 'capacity of neoclassical economics to expand its boundaries is quite remarkable in this respect' (Williamson 1989a, p. 178). In contrast, to the extent that a more thoroughgoing realist orientation is adopted (something that Coase perhaps more systematically argues for) the appropriateness of applying formal methods would need to be assessed in relation to our understanding of the constitution of social reality. Mainstream economics fails to engage in any such exercise and were the NIE to break away from this kind of ontological neglect then a more substantial breach with mainstream economics may be implied.

Acknowledgements
An earlier version of this chapter was presented at the Cambridge Workshop on Realism and Economics and I thank the participants for their reactions and encouragement. For helpful comments and criticisms on an earlier draft I would like to thank John Davis, Tony Lawson, Alan Shipman, Jochen Runde and Gregor Zwirn.

Notes
1. For an extended outline and defense of critical realism in economics see T. Lawson (1997); for a brief outline of certain key themes, T. Lawson (2001a); and for discussion, elaboration and criticism, Fleetwood (1999).
2. The New Institutional Economics is a broad set of perspectives. In this chapter the focus is primarily on the contributions of Coase and Williamson. While these contributions do not exhaust the NIE they are recognised as being especially influential and representative of important trajectories within the wider project.
3. Uskali Mäki (1994) emphasises the importance of distinguishing between realisticness as a family of properties of theories and their constituent elements and realism as a theory of scientific theories i.e., as a family of philosophical doctrines. In this chapter the argument is that the criticisms of orthodox theory set out by NIE point to both an advocacy of greater realisticness and the partial adoption of a broader realist orientation at the level of a theory of scientific theories. This is an interpretation that Mäki (1998) has himself called for with regard Coase. An additional component to the argument developed here is that alongside this realist orientation within the NIE there also exists the acceptance of conceptions of what counts as

appropriate theory carried over from mainstream economics which sit uncomfortably with advocacy of greater realisticness and realism.

4. The NIE can be seen as just one illustration of a much broader pattern of development within economics. A central contribution of critical realist interventions within economics has been to draw attention to, and highlight the persistence of, tensions within the discipline between relevance on the one hand, and deductivist, usually formalistic mathematical, method on the other. This tension has been found to manifest itself in numerous ways, not least the number of cases in which the initial project, wider vision or pre-theoretical insights that an author started out with turn out to be incompatible with, and often excluded by, their retained (deductivist) method. With regard Marshall, for example, I have argued that his failure to complete volume 2 of the *Principles*, a failure widely discussed and puzzled over in the history of thought literature, can be explained in terms of his desire to maintain realistic claims (drawing on metaphors from biology) in the face of his largely unquestioned acceptance of a broadly deductivist framework (Pratten 1998). Meanwhile Mario Da Graca Moura (2002) has shown how the widely observed tensions and inconsistencies in Schumpeter's thought are similarly rendered intelligible. Just as Schumpeter's visionary developmental framework presupposes an open and structured world so his contradictory equilibrium approach can be seen as driven by the retention of a deductivist method. Others have similarly explained tensions in the writings of, for example, Hayek (Fleetwood 1995; T. Lawson 1994) and Paul Davidson (Runde 1993 and Lewis and Runde 1999). Those contributing to critical realism argue that the identification of such tensions should not be taken to imply that inconsistencies between vision and method are in any way inevitable or compulsory. Rather the argument is that the prominence of these kinds of tensions reflect the persistence and harmful effects of retaining an a priori commitment to a particular set of methods quite independently of any evaluation of their appropriateness to the material under investigation.

5. For a detailed discussion of formalism in economics and its interpretation see T. Lawson (1997: especially Ch. 9; 2001b).

6. For an elaboration of the social metaphysics, or theory of social reality, associated with critical realism see T. Lawson (1997: chs 12 and 13) and also Archer (1995, 2000).

7. Following Lawson, the term 'unrealistic assumptions' is used within this chapter in a restricted sense. Lawson suggests that it is appropriate to include 'really possible counterfactuals as part of the real, and interpret propositions as unrealistic (or held to be) false which make claims that we have every reason to suppose lie outside the bounds of real possibility' (2001b, p. 76). Mäki uses the phrase in a broader manner for example he notes that 'A concept, statement or theory is often regarded as unrealistic if it is partial, if it isolates only selected aspects of objects for representation' (1994, p. 243). The more restricted sense is preferred here as it helps to differentiate between traditional conceptions of abstraction and the processes of idealisation and isolation typical of modern mainstream economics (see note 16 below).

8. Of course it is open to social investigators to try and make the conditions more like those of an experiment. In recent years there has been a growing interest in attempting to do just this within experimental economics.

9. A challenge for proponents of critical realism has been to identify methods that are appropriate for open as well as closed systems. Some have elaborated upon the method of contrast explanation as relevant here in the sense that it requires only the ex posteriori availability of surprising contrasts.

10. See Kreps (1997) for a similar reading of the development of modern mainstream economics.

11. A realist orientation also raises questions about claims that there exists a fundamental distinction to be drawn between formalism and modelling in orthodox economics. Solow (1997) suggests that model-building and formalist approaches to economics are altogether different sorts of activity. He claims that 'Formalist economics starts with a small number of assumptions about the behavior of individual economic agents, and a few more about their interactions with each other, and goes on to study what can then be said about the resulting economic system'. He claims that 'Modern mainstream economics is not all that formal'. Rather, he argues, 'A model is a deliberately simplified representation of a much more complicated situation ... The idea is to focus on one or two causal or conditioning factors, exclude everything else, and

hope to understand how just these aspects of reality work and interact ... modern mainstream economics consists of little else but examples of this process' (Solow 1997, p. 43). To the extent that the formalist programme is conceived of as a project concerned with illuminating social reality at all it can be seen as making the same kinds of assumptions that underpin the modelling exercises. Both require the absence of internal instability with regard the mechanism focused upon and its effective isolation from interfering factors.

12. T. Lawson (2001b) sets out a similarly cautionary stance, albeit one which is even less optimistic about the likely prospects for formal modelling in the social realm.

13. Williamson similarly deplores the way in which mainstream economics neglects social institutions and ignores organizational issues: 'orthodoxy holds that the allocation of economic activity between firms and markets is a datum; firms are production functions; markets are signaling devices; contracting is accomplished through an auctioneer; and disputes are disregarded because of the presumed efficiency of court adjudication. The economic purposes served by organizational variety do not arise' (1986, p. 171). According to Williamson the very costs of running the economic system are not taken sufficiently into account within traditional economic theory and as a consequence institutional themes are effectively suppressed.

14. Here it is recognised that agents are prepared to conceal or misrepresent facts, skirt rules, exploit loopholes, or otherwise capitalise on strategic advantages.

15. For a detailed discussion of Coase's criticisms of mainstream economics and his characterisation of 'blackboard economics' see Mäki (1998).

16. In considering Coase's distinction between appropriate abstraction and mindless abstraction it is useful to differentiate between abstraction and processes of idealization and isolation (see T. Lawson 1997, pp. 234–5 and Runde 1998). Lawson notes that 'Abstraction, meaning looking at something in a "one sided" manner, is indispensable in science. Its object is to individuate some component or aspect of a concrete entity in order better to understand the latter. And it is essential to recognise that this entails understanding the aspect in question within the relationships in which it stands, relationships which may be essential to its existence and/or mode of activity' (1997, p. 236). But to dismiss what passes for abstraction in modern economics as mindless or arbitrary is perhaps to miss its significance: 'in mainstream economics the term abstraction stands in as rhetoric for the pretence that economic phenomena are, after all generated under conditions equivalent to those achieved through experimental control' (1997, p. 235). Lawson suggests that these moves should be referred to as processes of idealisation or isolation and seen as distinct from the more traditional notion of abstraction.

17. See, for example, Douglas (1990), Foss (2001) and Pagano (1999).

18. More specifically Williamson suggests that 'changes in the condition of the environment are ... factored in – by adjusting transaction-specific governance in cost effective ways. In effect, institutional environments that provide general purpose safeguards relieve the need for added transaction-specific supports. Accordingly, transactions that are viable in an institutional environment that provides strong safeguards may be nonviable in institutional environments that are weak – because it is not cost effective for parties to craft transaction-specific governance in the latter circumstances' (Williamson 1993b, p. 476).

19. It does indeed seem to be the case that NIE authors do rely on functionlist forms of explanation. Coase notes 'In "The Nature of the Firm" I suggested that in a competitive system there would be an optimum of planning since a firm, that little planned society, could only continue to exist if it performed its coordination function at a lower cost than would be incurred if coordination were achieved by means of market transactions and also at a lower cost than this same function could be performed by another firm. To have an efficient economic system it is necessary not only to have markets but also areas of planning within organisations of the appropriate size. What this mix should be we find as a result of competition' (Coase 1994, p. 8). Williamson acknowledges that his argument 'relies in a general, background way on the efficiency of competition to perform a sort between more and less efficient modes and to shift resources in favour of the former. This seems plausible, especially if the relevant outcomes are those that appear over intervals of five and ten years rather than in the very near term. This intuition would nevertheless benefit from more fully developed theory of the selection process' (Williamson 1988, p. 174). For criticisms of the form of functionalism found within NIE see Granovetter (1985), Dow (1987) and Hodgson (1996). Foss clearly identifies the problem when he states:

'while an ontology that recognises the open endedness of the economic universe is necessary to Williamson's theorising, he has not gone very far down that road of process that would be implied by such an ontology' (Foss 1994, p. 56).

20. Williamson's own work is often seen as especially important in ensuring that NIE adopted an appropriate form of analysis. For example, Joskow writes 'it is [Williamson's] *Markets and Hierarchies* that put structure on this perspective. It provided the foundation for a theory of institutional choice and design that had the prospect of yielding clear causal relationships between transactional characteristics and institutional arrangements. This in turn began to give us a theoretical framework that could be subjected to empirical verification' (1991, p. 119).

21. For Williamson economising on transaction costs is mainly responsible for the choice of one form of organisation or governance structure over another. Operationalising this efficiency argument for Williamson means in essence detailing the concept of the transaction sufficiently to allow the appropriate or efficient governance structure to be read off from a description of the observable circumstances surrounding the transaction. Masten suggests that the crucial 'methodological advance in transaction cost reasoning came with Williamson's insight that the key to generating refutable hypotheses about organizational form lay in (i) identifying how the properties that distinguish organizational alternatives from one another influence the costs associated with organizing under each, and (ii) relating the incidence of those costs to observable dimensions of the transaction in a discriminating fashion' (Masten 1996, p. 45, see also Williamson 1989b, pp. 229–30). The various governance structures have distinct sets of properties, while transaction costs vary in systematic ways depending on the observable characteristics of the transactions in question. Competition is postulated as performing some sort of selection, generating in the process efficient organisational outcomes. This operationalisation procedure it is claimed allows transaction cost economics (TCE) to identify certain deeply rooted regularities existing between features specific to the transaction and carefully catalogued aspects of alternative governance structures. According to Williamson, it is this that represents the key contribution made by TCE and he notes: 'What has hitherto been regarded as a set of diverse and anomalous contracting practices has been shown [by TCE] to be variations on a common theme: economizing on transaction costs. Although the details differ, the underlying regularities are the same' (Williamson 1986, p. 199). Williamson in further clarifying what operationalisation requires places particular emphasis on the role of prediction, insisting that 'transaction cost economics must be assessed partly by its capacity to yield new or deeper predictive results' (Williamson 1986, p. 189). The objective appears to be to identify regularities between transactional characteristics and governance structures, thereby, in Williamson's words 'yielding a predictive theory of organisation' (Williamson 1986, p. 178). He compares the role that prediction performs within TCE with its relative neglect elsewhere: 'Sociologists can respond, with cause that there is more to the study of economic organisations than efficiency. The real challenge, however, is to demonstrate that the sociological viewpoint adds predictive content and in other respects deepens our understanding of complex organisations. Put differently, it would be unfortunate if sociologists were mainly to get caught up in methodological critique and did not develop the refutable implications that their viewpoint distinctly affords' (Williamson 1988, p. 183).

22. Elsewhere Williamson suggests: 'That the state of transaction cost economics in 1972 was approximately where Coase had left it in 1937 is largely attributable to the failure, for thirty five years, to operationalise this important concept. That this flat trajectory has been supplanted by exponential growth during the past fifteen years is because recent students of transaction cost economics have insisted that this approach meet the test of refutable implications' (Williamson 1991b, p. 90).

23. NIE authors have been particularly concerned with distancing their approach from Old Institutionalism. Coase, for instance, claims that the Old Institutionalism in economics 'led to nothing … the American institutionalists were not theoretical but anti-theoretical, particularly where classical economics was concerned. Without a theory, they had nothing to pass on except a mass of descriptive material waiting for a theory or a fire' (Coase 1984, p. 230). For a detailed discussion and evaluation of the relationship between Coase's approach and that of the Old Institutionalists see Medema (1996). For a reassessment of Commons' variant of Institutional Economics which challenges the assertion that the Old Institutionlists were anti or

non theoretical see C. Lawson (1994). While the focus has often been on the Old Institutional Economics corresponding reservations can be found concerning other competing approaches. Thus Williamson, comparing transaction cost economics with 'power' approaches, writes: 'power sorely requires, but has not received, a comparable effort at operationalization. The power approach to economic organisation will not qualify as a serious rival until this condition is remedied' (Williamson 1989c, p. 29). Similarly, with respect to evolutionary perspectives, he notes that 'the evolutionary approach is greatly in need of operationalisation' (Williamson 1989c, p. 33). With regard the competence perspective within Strategic Management, Williamson notes that 'The concept of competence is also important and it too has acquired a tautological reputation. … Its obvious importance and intuitive appeal notwithstanding a relentless commitment to the operationalization of competence is needed lest the study of competence experience the fate of American Legal Realism and run itself "into the sand"' (Williamson 1999, p. 1093). In all these cases the notion of operationalisation appears to be acting as some sort of filter essentially defining what is acceptable.

24. Bounded rationality tends to enter Williamson's framework as a constraint on the possibility of complete contracting. He even claims that the notion of bounded rationality implies that the relevance of an economising perspective is extended: 'An immediate ramification of bounded rationality is that impossibly complex forms of economic organization (such as complete contingent claims contracting) are infeasible. Standing alone, that is a negative result. But there is more to it than that. If mind is a scarce resource then economising on bounded rationality is warranted. This expands, rather than reduces, the range of issues to which the economic approach can be applied. Among other things, the "conscious, deliberate, purposeful" use of organization as a means by which to economize on bounded rationality is made endogenous' (Williamson 1993b, p. 458). In Simon's original version of bounded rationality the boundedness of rationality is linked to satisficing where rational agents let decisions beyond a certain range of interest take care of themselves, or rather be taken care of by relying on organisational and environmental cues in order to get by or function competently.

25. In similar fashion, comparing Simon's approach with Stigler's analysis of information, Williamson notes: 'In Stigler's case the search criterion is that of expected net gain, which involves optimisation. The search procedure described by Simon involves the replacement of the goal of maximising with the goal of satisficing, of finding a course of action that is "good enough". Satisficing is cumbersome and we must ask whether the added cost (of non standard and more complicated modes of analysis) justify the benefit (realism of cognitive assumptions). Judging from the influence of these two articles (Stigler massive; Simon limited) and from the negative verdict on the utility of the satisficing approach … the answer would appear to be negative' (1993e, p. 111).

26. Thus he writes that his 'approach straddles the methodological dispute that separates maximisers and satisfiers. Thus it relies on economizing arguments (which disciplines the analysis and appeals to maximisers) but substitutes comparative institutional for optimising procedures (which is more in the spirit of satisficing)' (Williamson 1981, p. 574).

References

Archer, M. (1995), *Realist Social Theory: the Morphogenetic Approach*, Cambridge: Cambridge University Press.
Archer, M. (2000), *Being Human: the Problem of Agency*, Cambridge: Cambridge University Press.
Coase, R.H. (1964), 'The regulated industries: discussion', *American Economic Review*, **54**, pp. 194–97.
Coase, R.H. (1984), 'The new institutional economics', *Journal of Institutional and Theoretical Economics*, **140** (1), 229–31.
Coase, R.H. (1988), *The Firm, The Market and the Law*, Chicago: University of Chicago Press.
Coase, R.H. (1991), 'The nature of the firm: influence' in O.E. Williamson and S. Winter (eds), *The Nature of the Firm: Origins, Evolution and Development*, Oxford: Oxford University Press, pp. 61–74.

Coase, R.H. (1993), 'Coase on Posner on Coase', *Journal of Institutional and Theoretical Economics*, **149** (1), 96–8.
Coase, R.H. (1994), *Essays on Economics and Economists*, Chicago: University of Chicago Press.
Coase, R.H. (1997), 'Looking for results: interview with T.W. Hazlett', *Reason*, January, p. 40–46.
Coase, R.H. (1999a), 'Interview with Ronald Coase', *Newsletter of the International Society for New Institutional Economics*, **2** (1), 3–10.
Coase, R.H. (1999b), 'The task of the society', opening address to the annual conference of the International Society for New Institutional Economics, 17 September, *Newsletter of the International Society for New Institutional Economics*, **2** (2), 3–6.
Dasgupta, P. (2002), 'Modern economics and its critics' in U. Mäki, (ed.), *Fact and Fiction in Economics: Models, Realism and Social Construction*, Cambridge: Cambridge University Press, pp. 57–89.
Douglas, M. (1990), 'Converging on autonomy: anthropology and institutional economics', in O.E. Williamson, (ed.), *Organisation Theory: From Chester Barnard to the Present and Beyond*, Oxford: Oxford University Press.
Dow, G.K. (1987), 'The function of authority in transaction cost economics', *Journal of Economic Behavior and Organization*, **8**, 13–38.
Dugger, W.M. (1983), 'The transaction cost analysis of Oliver E. Williamson', *Journal of Economic Issues*, **17** (1), 95–114.
Fleetwood, S. (1995), *Hayek's Political Economy*, London: Routledge.
Fleetwood, S. (1999), *Critical Realism in Economics*, London: Routledge.
Foss, N.J. (1994), 'Two Coasian traditions', *Review of Political Economy*, **6** (1), 37–61.
Foss, N.J. (2001), 'From "thin to thick" bounded rationality in the economics of organization: an explorative discussion', LINK working paper, Copenhagen Business School.
Granovetter, M. (1985), 'Economic action and social structure', *American Journal of Sociology*, **91** (3), 481–510.
Hodgson, G.M. (1989), 'Institutional economic theory: the old versus the new', *Review of Political Economy*, **1** (3), 249–69.
Hodgson, G.M. (1993), 'Institutional Economics, surveying the "old" and the "new"' *Metroeconomica*, **44** (1), 1–28.
Hodgson, G.M. (1996), 'Organizational form and economic evolution: a critique of the Williamsonian hypothesis', in U. Pagano and R. Rowthorn, *Democracy and Efficiency in the Economic Enterprise*, London: Routledge, pp. 98–115.
Humphreys, P. (2002), 'Mathematical modelling in the social sciences', in S. Turner and P. Roth (eds), *The Blackwell Guide to the Philosophy of the Social Sciences*, Oxford: Blackwell, pp. 166–84.
Joskow, P. (1991), 'Asset specificity and the structure of vertical relationships: empirical evidence', in O.E. Williamson and S. Winter (eds), *The Nature of the Firm: Origins, Evolution and Development*, Oxford: Oxford University Press, pp. 117–37.
Kreps, D. (1997), 'Economics – the current position', *Daedalus*, **126** (1), 59–85.
Lawson, C. (1994), 'The transformation model of social activity and economic analysis: a reinterpretation of the work of J.R. Commons', *Review of Political Economy*, **6** (2), 186–204.
Lawson, T. (1994), 'Hayek and Realism: a case of continuing transformation', in M. Colonna, H. Hageman and O.F. Hamouda (eds), *Capitalism, Socialism and Knowledge: the Economics of F. A. Hayek, vol II*, Aldershot, UK and Brookfield US: Edward Elgar, pp. 131–59.
Lawson, T. (1997), *Economics and Reality*, London: Routledge.
Lawson, T. (2001a), 'Economics and explanation', *Revue Internationale de Philosophie*, 217, 371–93.
Lawson, T. (2001b), 'Mathematical formalism in economics: what really is the problem?', in P. Arestis and S. Dow (eds), *Methodology, Microeconomics and Keynes, Festschrift for Vicky Chick*, London: Taylor and Francis.
Lawson, T. (2003), *Reorienting Economics*, London: Routledge.
Lewis, P. and J. Runde (1999), 'A critical realist perspective on Paul Davidson's methodological writings on – and rhetorical strategy for – Post Keynesian economics', *Journal of Post Keynesian Economics*, **22**, 35–56.

Mäki, U. (1994), 'Reorienting the assumptions issue', in R. Backhouse, (ed.), *New Directions in Economic Methodology*, London: Routledge, pp. 236–56.

Mäki, U. (1998), 'Is Coase a realist?', *Philosophy of the Social Sciences*, **28** (1), 5–31.

Masten, S.E. (1996), 'Empirical research in transaction cost economies: challenges, progress, directions', in J. Groenewegen (ed.), *Transaction Cost Economics and Beyond*, Dordrecht: Kluwer, pp. 43–64.

Medema, S. (1996), 'Ronald Coase and American institutionalism', *Research in the History of Economic Thought and Methodology*, **14**, 51–92.

Moura, M. da Graca (2002), 'Metatheory as the key to understanding: Schumpeter after Shionoya', *Cambridge Journal of Economics*, **26** (6), 805–21.

Pagano, U. (1999), Bounded rationality, institutionalism and the diversity of economic institutions, working paper, University of Siena.

Pratten, S. (1997), 'The nature of transaction cost economics', *Journal of Economic Issues*, **XXXI** (3), 781–803.

Pratten, S. (1998), 'Marshall on tendencies, equilibrium and the statical method', *History of Political Economy*, **30** (1), 121–63.

Rubinstein, A. (1995), 'John Nash: the master of economic modelling', *Scandinavian Journal of Economics*, **97** (1), 9–13.

Runde, J. (1993), 'Paul Davidson and the Austrians: reply to Paul Davidson', *Critical Review*, **7** (2–3), 381–97.

Runde, J. (1998), 'Abstraction, idealization and economic theory', in P. Arestis, G. Palma and M. Sawyer (eds), *Markets, Unemployment and Economic Policy: Essays in Honour of Geoff Harcourt*, vol. II, London: Routledge, pp. 16–29.

Solow, R.M. (1997), 'How did economics get that way and what way did it get', *Daedalus*, **126** (1), 39–58.

Williamson, O.E. (1975), *Markets and Hierarchies*, New York: Free Press.

Williamson, O.E. (1981), 'The economics of organization: the transaction cost approach', *American Journal of Sociology*, **87** (3), 548–77.

Williamson, O.E. (1985), *The Economic Institutions of Captialism*, New York: Free Press.

Williamson, O.E. (1986), 'The economics of governance: framework and implications', in R. Langlois (ed.), *Economics as a Process: Essays in the New Institutional Economics*, Cambridge: Cambridge University Press, pp. 171–200.

Williamson, O.E. (1988), 'The economics and sociology of organization: promoting a dialogue', in G. Farkus and P. England (eds), *Industries, Firms and Jobs*, New York: Plenum, pp. 159–85.

Williamson, O.E. (1989a), 'Transaction cost economics' in R. Schmaensee and R.D. Willig (eds), *Handbook of Industrial Organization*, Amsterdam: North Holland, pp. 135–82.

Williamson, O.E. (1989b), 'Review of Ronald Coase's *The Firm, The Market and the Law*', *California Law Review*, **77**, 223–31.

Williamson, O.E. (1989c), 'Internal economic organization' in O.E. Williamson, S. Sjorstrand and J. Jahnson (eds), *Perspectives on the Economics of Organisation*, Lund: Lund University Press, pp. 9–48.

Williamson, O.E. (1990), 'The firm as a nexus of treaties: an introduction', in M. Aoki, B. Gustafsson and O.E. Williamson (eds), *The Firm as a Nexus of Treaties*, London: Sage, pp. 1–25.

Williamson, O.E. (1991a), 'Comparative economic organisation: the analysis of discrete structural alternatives', *Administrative Science Quarterly*, **36**, 269–96.

Williamson, O.E. (1991b), 'The logic of economic organization', in O.E. Williamson and S. Winter (eds), *The Nature of the Firm: Origins, Evolution and Development*, Oxford: Oxford University Press, pp. 90–116.

Williamson, O.E. (1993a), 'Opportunism and its critics', *Managerial and Decision Economics*, **14**, 97–107.

Williamson, O.E. (1993b), 'Calculativeness, trust and economic organization', *Journal of Law and Economics*, **36**, April, 453–86.

Williamson, O.E. (1993c), 'Transaction cost economics and organization theory', *Industrial and Corporate Change*, **2** (2), 107–56.

Williamson, O.E. (1993d), 'The evolving science of organisation', *Journal of Institutional and Theoretical Economics*, **149**, (1), 36–63.

Williamson, O.E. (1993e), 'Transaction cost economics meets posnerian law and economics', *Journal of Institutional and Theoretical Economics*, **149** (1), 99–118.

Williamson, O.E. (1996), 'Economic organisation: the case for candor', *Academy of Mangement Review*, **21** (1), 48–57.

Williamson, O.E. (1999), 'Strategy research: governance and competence perspectives' *Strategic Management Journal*, **20**, 1087–108.

Williamson, O.E. (2001), 'Herbert Simon and the theory of the firm', mimeo, University of California.

Williamson, O.E. (2003), 'Examining economic organisation through the lens of contract', *Industrial and Corporate Change*, **12** (4), 917–42.

18 Structure and agency in economic analysis: the case of Austrian economics and the material embeddedness of socio-economic life

Paul A. Lewis

Introduction

The relationship between human agency and social structure is one of the most important, and highly contested, topics in social theory, raising fundamental issues about the nature of socio-economic reality and the manner in which socio-economic events of interest are best analysed. Within economics the structure–agency relationship is a major source of contention between orthodox and heterodox schools of thought. Heterodox economists have long challenged the orthodox model of man, criticising it both on the grounds that it excludes genuine human choice and also because its conception of people as atomistic beings whose attributes are given independently of their social context fails to do justice to the way in which economic activity is embedded in networks of social relations.

However, if there is something approaching a consensus among heterodox economists on the shortcoming of homo economicus, there is far less agreement about the account of the relationship between structure and agency which is to take its place. Two of the suggested alternatives will be examined below. Although both are drawn from heterodox economics, they differ in their precise provenance within heterodox thought. The first, which is discussed in Section II below, is taken from a school of substantive heterodox economic thought, namely Austrian economics. Members of the radical subjectivist wing of the Austrian school have recently extolled the virtues of portraying people as social beings, embedded within networks of shared meanings and interpretive traditions, on the grounds that doing so will facilitate a more profound understanding of how market economies generate social order. The second alternative has its origins, not in substantive economic thought, but in the methodology of economics and, more specifically, in an approach to economic methodology known as critical realism. The hallmark of critical realism is its emphasis on the ontological commitments of economic theories, that is, on what they presuppose about the nature of the socio-economic world. More specifically, critical realism is overtly prescriptive in orientation, arguing that substantive social research is most likely to be successful if it employs tools that are tailored to suit the nature of the socio-economic material under investigation. To this end, as Section III outlines, proponents of critical realism deploy philosophical arguments in order to construct an account of the ontology of socio-economic life, which is then used to characterise the methods that are most likely to bear fruit in social research. Prominent within their portrayal of the nature of socio-economic reality is, of course, an account of the relationship between social structure and human agency, the so-called transformational model of social activity. While there is a good deal of common ground between the latter and the model of the structure–agency relationship developed by radical subjectivist Austrians, there remain some significant differences between the two, the highlighting of which reveals potentially significant shortcomings in the Austrian approach (Section IV). The final section of the chapter summarises the argument and draws out some of the implications that shifting towards something like the transformational model of social activity would have for radical subjectivism.

The Austrian school, the evolution of subjectivism and the role of shared meanings in socio-economic analysis

The hallmark of the Austrian school of economics is its emphasis on the principle of subjectivism, that is, the idea that the driving force of socio-economic life lies not in objective states of affairs per se but in what they mean to people:

> Economics is not about things and tangible material objects; it is about men, their meanings and actions. Goods, commodities, wealth and all the other notions of conduct are not elements of nature; they are elements of human meaning and conduct. He who wants to deal with them must not look at the external world; he must search for them in the meaning of acting men. (Mises 1949 [1966], p. 92)

Austrians take the fact that the objects of economic analysis can be defined only in relation to human purposes to indicate that the discipline of economics (properly conceived) is centrally concerned with the questions of how people understand their world and how their interpretations lead them to act. The analysis of the socio-economic world, if it is to be fruitful, must always start with the subjective meanings that individuals attach to their actions and surroundings. More specifically, Austrians describe themselves as being committed to a variant of methodological individualism according to which socio-economic phenomena of interest are to be (causally) explained as the (often unintended) consequences of the subjectively meaningful, purposive actions of individual economic actors (Mayer 1932 [1994]; Hayek 1982 [1993], pp. 35–54; Cowan and Rizzo, 1996).

The Austrian school's understanding of subjectivism has been far from static. Lachmann (1990 [1994], pp. 243–6) distinguishes three stages in the evolution of subjectivism. The principle of subjectivism has its origins in the marginal revolution in the 1870s as a 'subjectivism of wants', the idea behind which is that different people have different tastes and so attribute different values to the same object. The second stage of subjectivism, the development of which was most closely associated with the work of Ludwig von Mises, involves the extension of the principle of subjectivism to encompass the fact that people's actions are driven by their subjective interpretations of their circumstances and so are not rigidly determined by the latter (O'Driscoll and Rizzo, 1996, pp. 1–2). This variant of the principle of subjectivism suggests that because the external circumstances which influence the outcome of any one individual's conduct include the creative and so often unpredictable behaviour of their fellow human beings, people must act in the face of (radical) uncertainty in the sense that they do not have even a probabilistic knowledge of the best means of achieving their desired ends (Mises 1949, [1966], pp. 105–18). This 'subjectivism of means and ends', as Lachmann (1990 [1994], p. 246) calls it, implies that faced with such uncertainty, people may pursue similar ends in dissimilar ways, acting on the basis of different (subjective) ideas about the best way to further a particular goal.

More recently, however, Ludwig Lachmann argued that the principle of subjectivism should be extended still further, on the grounds that uncertainty renders problematical not just people's choice of means but also the ends towards which their activity is directed. To see why, note that if uncertainty renders people unaware even of the existence (let alone the likely magnitude) of some of the factors that influence the consequences of their actions, then the question arises of how purposive conduct is possible at all. Lachmann, following Shackle, answers by maintaining that people deal with their ignorance of the future, and so manage to act in a purposeful, goal-driven fashion, by using their imagination to envisage desirable future scenarios and then deciding which actions might bring them about:

> Economic choice does not consist in comparing the items in a list, known to be complete, of given fully specified rival and certainly attainable results. It consists in first creating, by conjecture and reasoned imagination on the basis of mere suggestion offered by visible or recorded circumstance, the things on which hope can be fixed. These things, at the time when they are available for choice, are thoughts and even figments. (Shackle, 1972 [1992], p. 96, quoted in Lachmann 1990 [1994], p. 246)[1]

In other words, for Lachmann (as for Shackle), far from being 'given' unproblematically, the ends which people seek are actually a creative product of their imaginations, implying that subjectivism embraces not only peoples' choice of means but also the ends they strive to achieve. In a world of radical uncertainty, people must continuously reflect upon their goals, assessing whether in the light of the unforeseen changes in circumstances that accompany the passage of time the ends initially selected are still worth pursuing or whether other objectives (perhaps not formerly envisaged) have now become worthy of attention. In this way, Lachmann advocates the extension of the principle of subjectivism to encompass people's goals and the expectations of the future which inform them, a third, radical stage for which Lachmann coins the phrase 'the subjectivism of active minds' (Lachmann 1982, pp. 36–39, pp. 45–48, 1990 [1994], p. 246).

However, while the Austrian school has from its very inception marked its own 'progress' by its application of the principle of subjectivism to broader and broader swathes of socio-economic life,[2] Lachmann's extension of subjectivism to encompass people's goals and expectations has not been received with unqualified enthusiasm by all members of the Austrian school. On the contrary, some Austrians have argued that the subjectivism of active minds, far from being (as Lachmann viewed it) the 'highest' stage of subjectivism to which all others were merely the prelude, is a step too far, nihilistically undermining any attempt to tackle one of the most fundamental and important tasks in economics, namely that of explaining how a decentralised market economy is able systematically to generate an orderly allocation of resources.

To see why, note first of all that the successful coordination of socio-economic activity requires that people base their actions on plans which are mutually compatible in the sense that the one person's actions do not completely disrupt the plans of the others (Hayek 1937 [1948]). This in turn requires that each person is able (to an extent at least) to foresee and so orient his actions towards the behaviour of those of his fellows on whose conduct the fruition of his own project depends. And for that to occur, different people's plans must be informed by similar expectations about the future, for if people have widely divergent expectations, it is impossible for them all to be correct and thus impossible for all their plans to be implemented successfully (Vaughn 1994, p. 151; O'Driscoll and Rizzo 1996, pp. 80–81). The problem with the subjectivism of active minds, Lachmann's critics contend, is that it makes this conformity of expectations look highly improbable (to say the least). For if expectations are the spontaneous constructs of people's creative imaginations, and are so insubstantially founded upon objective facts that we live in a kaleidic world in which there is a wide variety of (often volatile) beliefs about the likely course of future events (Shackle 1972 [1992], pp. 76–79, 183, 428; Lachmann 1976 [1994]), then it is hard to see how the commonality of expectations required for plan coordination can be achieved. And, according to the critics, the absence of an account of how the requisite convergence of expectations is brought about effectively (and nihilistically) sabotages attempts to show that there is a systematic tendency for the price mechanism to induce consistency among individuals' decisions and thereby produce an orderly allocation of resources.

Of course, Austrians have long argued that people's actions are coordinated by price signals (Hayek 1945 [1948]).[3] However, invoking the informational role of prices does not by itself dispose of the difficulties that the subjectivism of active minds creates for attempts to explain how market economies generate orderly outcomes, for by themselves prices do not provide sufficient information to determine uniquely what it is optimal for people to do. While market prices do indeed convey information about the relative scarcities of goods and the intentions of other people, they do not do so unambiguously. People have to interpret relative prices in order to divine their meaning, basing their actions on what they believe the prevailing prices signify both about the current scarcity of goods and also concerning the conditions that will obtain in the future when people's projects are under way and (hopefully) coming to fruition (Lachmann 1956 [1978], pp. 20–22, 1986, pp. 19, 43–58).[4] The problem, of course, is that as soon as it is acknowledged that people must exercise their judgement in interpreting and establishing the significance of prices, the subjectivism of active minds re-enters the arena and the scope for a divergence of expectations to undermine the possibility of orderly socio-economic activity arises once again. For if there is not a mechanical link between prices and people's interpretations thereof, so that a given configuration of relative prices may be interpreted in different (possibly quite idiosyncratic) ways by different people and may therefore give rise to a variety of (subjective) expectations of the future (Lachmann 1970, p. 41, 1976 [1994], pp. 236–37), then we are returned to a kaleidic world in which, once again, it is difficult to see how the convergence of expectations required for the coordination of socio-economic activity can be systematically achieved.

Recent contributors to the Austrian tradition have argued that the key to explaining how the requisite convergence of expectations is brought about, and thus to rebutting the charge of nihilism, lies in a reappraisal of the account of the relationship between human agency and social structure which informs Austrian economic theory. More specifically, they contend that a satisfactory account of how market economies generate an orderly allocation of resources requires Austrians to eschew the atomistic model of man with which their approach has often been associated in favour of an account which portrays people, not as isolated Robinson Crusoes, but rather as social beings who are embedded in networks of shared meanings and traditions of interpretation.[5]

To understand the rationale for this claim, note first of all that according to contemporary Austrians such as Lavoie (1991a, p. 482, 1991b, p. 48, 1994a, pp. 57–58), Prychitko (1994b, pp. 264–71) and Horwitz (1995, pp. 261–65), the atomistic model of man as a solitary Robinson Crusoe reflects the legacy of the Cartesian and Enlightenment ideal of the detached observer who can free herself from the biases, prejudices and preconceptions of traditional modes of thought in order to gain a pure, unadulterated understanding of the world.

This Cartesian perspective would suggest that people attempt to solve the epistemological problem of acquiring knowledge of each others' future actions (Mises 1957 [1985], p. 311) by interpreting events and forming expectations that are objectively correct, unadulterated by the social, cultural and historical context in which those people are situated. However, once it is recognised that any attempt to understand the world must employ some theoretical scheme or other (Lavoie 1990c, pp. 2, 6), then it becomes apparent that by locating the source of meaning in socio-economic life in the unfettered imagination of the sovereign Cartesian ego, acting in complete isolation from shared interpretive frameworks, the atomistic approach runs of the risk of lapsing into a form of solipsism according to which each person's interpretations and expectations are purely private and subjective, bearing little relation to those of other people. And if people's expectations are merely a matter of personal opinion, and therefore potentially idiosyncratic and arbitrary, then (as we have seen) it is extremely difficult to see how they can overlap enough to facilitate a significant degree of coordination of economic activity (Addleson 1995, pp. 73–74, 88; Boettke et al. 2002, pp. 8–13).

This diagnosis suggests that the remedy to the problem of nihilism consists, not in a rejection of the subjectivism of active minds, but rather in acknowledging that far from being isolated Cartesian egos the minds in question are thoroughly social in nature (Lavoie 1991b, pp. 48). Building on the ideas of Lachmann (1970, 1990),[6] and drawing also on the philosophical writings of Paul Ricoeur (1971, 1981) and (especially) Hans-Georg Gadamer (1975 [1993]), the current generation of radical subjectivists has argued along those lines that the key to overturning the charge of nihilism lies in replacing the atomistic model of man as an isolated Robinson Crusoe with a portrayal of people as social beings whose attributes and behaviour are profoundly shaped by the social, cultural and historical context in which they are embedded (Granovetter, 1985). The Austrians who subscribe to this approach describe themselves as adopting a 'sophisticated' version of individualism that occupies the middle ground between an under-socialised, Cartesian conception of man as a solitary island and the opposite extreme of an over-socialised account which portrays people as the puppets of deterministic social forces (Boettke 1989a, pp. 76–77, 1990b, pp. 15–22, 1998a, pp. 58–65; Boettke and Storr 2002, pp. 162–76; Prychitko 1994b, p. 268; Vaughn 1994, pp. 130, 132–3). We can elaborate on this by noting that the current generation of radical subjectivists follow Gadamer (1975 [1993], pp. 262, 265–77, 304) in conceptualising people as finite or historically situated beings who, in virtue of being born and raised in a culture that pre-exists them, are 'thrown' into a socio-economic world that is not of their own making and that, more specifically, has already been interpreted according to the 'prejudices' – the traditional, historically given shared interpretive frameworks and conceptual schemes – of their predecessors (Boettke 1989b, p. 195 n. 7;

Kibbe 1994, p. 104; Addleson 1995, p. 83). One important consequence of the fact that people are brought up in such a pre-interpreted world is that their thinking is shaped by the intellectual traditions they inherit from the past: '[H]istory does not belong to us; we belong to it. Long before we understand ourselves through the process of self-examination, we understand ourselves in a self-evident way in the family, society and state in which we live' (Gadamer 1975 [1993], p. 276).

Hence, according to Gadamer, the way in which people think is thoroughly conditioned by the legacy of the past or 'effective history' (Gadamer 1975 [1993], pp. 300–302).[7] Significantly, contrary to the Cartesian and Enlightenment belief that such traditions are simply impediments to understanding, and therefore inimical to reason, Gadamer argues that the intellectual tools bequeathed by past generations are in actual fact indispensable for current thought, because it is only by means of the prejudices and preconceptions embedded in tradition that the present generation of people can even begin to conceptualise the world or, indeed, themselves (Gadamer 1975 [1993], pp. 270–83, 360–61).[8]

For Gadamer and modern radical subjectivists, then, it is peoples' location within a common tradition of thought that enables them to understand and successfully to negotiate their world (Bernstein 1983, pp. 128–30; Ebeling 1986, p. 47; Lavoie 1987, pp. 581–82, 585–88, 1990c, pp. 2, 6; Boettke 1989b, p. 185). In particular, the existence of historically given, shared norms of interpretation is of paramount importance for the generation of orderly outcomes in decentralised market economies. For in interpreting the significance of prices, say, people are able to avoid a purely subjective (and so potentially arbitrary and idiosyncratic) interpretation, with all the attendant dangers of solipsism, by drawing on the traditional conceptual frameworks that they share with other members of their society. These widely accepted interpretive schemes act as 'points of orientation' (Lachmann 1970, p. 38) the use of which enables people to reach common or intersubjectively agreed interpretations of the meaning and significance of prices and other relevant phenomena, thereby helping them to form expectations which are similar enough to facilitate the formation of mutually compatible plans (Ebeling 1986, pp. 47–52, 1990, pp. 186–90; Boettke 1990b, pp. 20–21; Kibbe 1994, p. 104; Boettke et al. 2002, p. 24).

As contemporary radical subjectivist Austrians such as Lavoie (1991b, p. 48) and Boettke et al. (2002, pp. 11–16) view matters, the apparent inability of radical subjectivism to explain how market economies generate orderly outcomes, far from being an inevitable consequence of subjectivism of active minds, is actually an artefact of the Cartesian model of man, a 'pseudo-problem' created by a failure to appreciate fully the significance of the fact that people are social beings. This line of reasoning suggests that the principle of subjectivism ought to be reinterpreted in order to make clear that the meanings to which Austrians accord so much attention issue not from the unfettered actions of isolated individual minds but rather from the engagement of social minds with shared interpretive frameworks. On this view, far from being private psychological phenomena, hidden in the recesses of people's minds, meanings are both intersubjectively agreed and also publicly available in shared traditions (Lavoie 1991a, p. 482, 1994a, p. 57; Madison 1994, p. 42; Addleson 1995, p. 72; Boettke et al. 2002, pp. 8–15). And once it is acknowledged that the basis of all knowledge lies not in the pure reason of the isolated (subjective) mind but rather in shared interpretive traditions, then the solipsistic isolation of Robinson Crusoe can be avoided and the convergence of expectations required for the coordination of economic activity explained (Lavoie 1994a, p. 57).

While Gadamer and those Austrians who draw on his writings set great store by the influence that tradition exerts on current behaviour, they are conscious of the need to avoid two dangers: first, that of reifying tradition by treating it as something which exists independently of people's actions; and, second, that of exaggerating the impact of tradition to such an extent that it is thought to dictate people's actions, reducing them to the status of mere cultural dupes who are incapable of a creative response to their circumstances (Boettke 1998a, pp. 58–61; Boettke and Storr 2002, pp. 170, 173, 175). In the first place, reification is avoided because it is readily acknowledged that while people are born and raised in a world of pre-existing traditions, the latter's continued existence depends upon the current generation's activities. 'Even the most genuine and solid tradition does not persist by nature because of the inertia of what once existed', Gadamer (1975 [1993], p. 281) writes. 'It needs to be affirmed, embraced, cultivated. It is, essentially, preservation, and it is active in all historical change.' On this view, tradition not only informs and shapes current socio-economic activity but is itself continuously being remade (either reproduced or transformed) by the latter (Gadamer 1983, p. 130; Ebeling 1987, p. 56; Addleson 1995, p. 94). Second, and relatedly, both Gadamer and the Austrians emphasise that recognising the importance of tradition need not preclude a role for creative human agency. While, as we have seen, the force of tradition constrains the wilfulness of purely subjective interpretations, people are not puppets whose interpretations and actions are determined by the traditions in which they stand. On the contrary, both Gadamer and the Austrians argue that the interpretive frameworks handed down from the past can never be used just as they stand but must always be modified to fit the concrete circumstances of the current generation. Gadamer (1975 [1993], pp. 324–30) argues that the legal process exemplifies this moment of 'application'. The law is not simply mechanically applied in order to determine the outcome of a particular case. Rather, judges must exercise their discretion in deciding precisely how the law bears upon the particularities of each case, sometimes going beyond (and thus transforming) established legal precedents in doing so. For Gadamer, then, people do not slavishly adhere to tradition, allowing it to dictate their interpretations of events. Rather, they actively appropriate it in order to establish its precise relevance to their own particular circumstances. Consequently, the meanings which emerge from this process, far from being dictated either by the interpreter's subjective imagination or by tradition alone, are the joint product of the interplay – the 'fusion of horizons', the 'conversation' or the 'dialogue', to use Gadamer's (1975 [1993], pp. 306–07, 362–89) metaphors – between the two. Understanding, Gadamer (1975 [1993], p. 293) argues, 'is neither subjective nor objective' but rather involves 'the interplay of the movement of tradition and the movement of the interpreter'. In a similar vein, modern radical subjectivists such as Ebeling (1986, pp. 50–52, 1990, p. 188–9) and Boettke (1989a, p. 84 n. 1, 1990b, p. 21) contend that people's attempts to assess the meaning of prices are informed (but not determined) by traditional interpretive frameworks. And, like Gadamer, they do so in recognition of the fact that individual people must appropriate the interpretive frameworks for themselves, applying them in the light of their 'knowledge of the particular circumstances of time and place' in order to reach a reasoned assessment of the course of future events (Hayek 1945 [1948], p. 80).

What this suggests is that both Gadamer and the radical subjectivist Austrians seek a middle way between determinism and voluntarism, according to which historically given traditions channel people's interpretations narrowly enough to enable them to form reliable expectations of each other's actions but so not so rigidly that the creativity of the human imagination is altogether excluded from the interpretive process. Pre-existing traditions both facilitate and constrain current human understanding and socio-economic activity, while current agency leads in turn either to the reproduction or transformation of those traditions. Put slightly differently, traditions and people are mutually constitutive, with the former being both an ever-present condition for the possibility of socio-economic activity and also a continually reproduced outcome of the latter. According to this perspective, social science deals with a pre-interpreted world, where the creation and reproduction of meaning-frames is an (ontological) condition of that which it seeks to analyse, namely human conduct. (Lavoie 1987, p. 588, 1991b, pp. 48–49, 1993, p. 105, 1994a, p. 58; Boettke 1998a, pp. 59, 62; Boettke and Storr 2002, p. 171).[9]

The upshot is a portrayal of socio-economic life as a process, set in historical time and involving a dialectical interaction between pre-existing traditions, hammered out in the course of past history, and current agency (Lavoie, 1987, p. 585; Madison, 1990b, pp. 42–43). At the heart of this account is a model of man as an interpretive being who constantly draws upon the conceptual frameworks bequeathed by previous generations in order to understand both himself and others (Palmer 1987, pp. 92–95, 97; Addleson 1995, pp. 90–93, 117; Prychitko 1997a, p. 210). More specifically, as we have already noted, these encounters between people and traditions are understood to take the form of a 'conversation' or 'dialogue' between the two. Indeed, on this approach, the notion of a dialogue or conversation provides the paradigm for all socio-economic activity. For instance, the market process is conceptualised as a discourse in which entrepreneurs attempt both to understand and anticipate the desires of customers (whether they be consumers searching for novel consumption goods or producers seeking new and improved production techniques) and also to persuade them (and potential backers) of the merits of the entrepreneurs' interpretations of the possibility of new products and production techniques. Just as a good conversation is an open-ended process that yields meanings which go beyond those originally intended by the interlocutors, so too is the market an open-ended process which produces a spontaneous order that transcends the original intentions of the participants (Lavoie 1987, pp. 582, 601–02, 1990b, pp. 74, 77–78, 1991b, p. 49–51, 1995, pp. 392–97; Horwitz 1992; Palmer 1987, pp. 101–04, 1990, pp. 303–04; Madison 1998, pp. 138–42).[10] And the aim of discipline of economics, on this view, is to construct an 'economics of meaning' (Lavoie 1994b, p. 9, 1997, p. 223; Boettke et al. 2002, p. 3) which explains how the interplay or 'tacking back and forth' (Boettke 1989a, p. 77, 1989b, p. 185, 1998a, p. 62; Horwitz, 1999, pp. 1–5) between people's purposive activities and the traditions which provide the context for those actions causes changes in prices, outputs, methods of production and so forth, and thereby generates an orderly allocation of resources (Lavoie 1994a, p. 56; Boettke et al. 2002, p. 25).

Critical realism and the transformational model of social activity
The heart of the critical realist ontology of socio-economic life consists in an account of the relationship between social structure and human agency. Proponents of critical realism share with modern radical subjectivists a concern to avoid the polar extremes of *voluntarism* (according to which social structure is ontologically reducible to human agency, being created *ex nihilo* by the latter) and *determinism* (which portrays people's actions as being determined by, and so ontologically reducible to, social structure). In contrast to such extremes positions, critical realists argue that human intentional agency and social structure are recursively related – each is both a precondition for and a consequence of the other – so that, as one radical subjectivist has put it (in words that critical realists would wholeheartedly endorse), socio-economic life is the result of a 'mutually dependent process in which both the individual and his social context are informing and informed by each other' (Kibbe 1994, p. 104). More specifically, critical realism proposes a *transformational model of social activity* according to which social structure and purposive human agency interact with one another over (historical) time, with people continuously drawing upon (pre-existing) social structures in order to act, and with

their behaviour leading (subsequently) either to the reproduction or the transformation of those structures.[11]

The starting point for the argument by which critical realists justify their commitment to this transformational model of the structure–agency relationship lies in their belief that the interplay between structure and agency occurs in historical time. Advocates of critical realism agree with radical subjectivists that people are 'thrown' into the world in the sense that at any particular moment in time they face pre-existing social structures – 'relics of the ... efforts of former generations' (Lachmann 1970, p. 68) – which are the product of actions undertaken, not the present, but in the past. The fact that antecedent social structures pre-exist current agency implies that the former are not simply the voluntaristic creation of the latter: 'We constantly operate in a world that, in some fundamental sense, we have not created. We are born into a world of pre-existing social structures and meanings' (Horwitz 1999, p. 3). The structures in question are inherited *involuntarily* by the current generation, confronting the latter as something that is 'ready made' and which, as a result, is ontologically distinct from their current beliefs and actions (Layder 1997, pp. 9–10, 19–23, 108; Sayer 2000, pp. 18, 35, 58–61). Critical realists accordingly divide the socio-economic world into three ontologically distinct realms: the *actual* (actual events and states of affairs, including people's actions and practices); the *empirical* (our sensory experiences of those events and states); and a domain of underlying social structures, which (as we shall see in due course) facilitate and constrain the activities of economic agents. Of course, while critical realists claim that there exist historically given social structures which are objective in the sense that they ontologically distinct from the current activities of agents, they do not reify those structures by denying their ultimate dependence on human agency. Critical realists readily acknowledge that while the structures which exist at a particular moment in time are the product of actions undertaken in the past, their *continued* existence depends upon *current* human agency. However, because current human agency takes place within the context formed by these ontologically irreducible social structures, and because (as we shall see) human agency is possible only in virtue of the fact that people can draw upon them, the relationship between social structure and human agency is best thought of as one in which current agency reproduces or transforms (pre-existing) social structure rather than (voluntaristically) creates it out of nothing.

The dependency of the continued existence of social structure on current agency is one aspect of the recursive relation between social structure and human agency. The second aspect concerns the fact that current agency is possible only because of the existence of ontologically distinct social structures. Consistent with the current generation of radical subjectivists, critical realists maintain that pre-existing social structures are of paramount importance in facilitating current socio-economic activity, in particular by helping to ensure that people have some idea of the consequences of their actions. The argument by which critical realists attempt to justify this conclusion begins with the claim, accepted by radical subjectivists such as Shackle (1966, pp. 74, 107) and O'Driscoll and Rizzo (1996, p. 76), that purposeful human action is possible only if people have some idea about how to achieve their goals. But whence comes the knowledge that informs people's decisions? For critical realists, the ex posteriori observation that generations of econometricians have had little success in finding enduring event-regularities (that is, patterns of the form, 'Whenever events or state of affairs x, then event or state of affairs y') in the socio-economic world indicates that the objects of such knowledge must be non-empirical (Lawson 1997, pp. 30–31, 70, 1998, pp. 357–60).[12] More specifically, critical realists argue that people's actions are informed and guided by their understanding of (non-empirical) social structures (social rules and institutions). For example, the legal system is a social institution that, by making it possible for people to enter into and to enforce contracts, enables them to secure a degree of control over their future income and expenditure (in the case of households) and revenues and costs (in the case of firms), thereby providing them with a measure of assurance about the future. While such contracts do not tie the future down completely, and so do not give rise to stable event regularities (there always remains the possibility, sometimes realised, that one of the parties will unexpectedly renege on their contractual commitments), in conjunction with the broader network of institutions and rules that constitute the legal system they can provide people with enough confidence in the consequences of their actions to facilitate intentional agency. Of course, the legal system and the contracts it underpins do not only facilitate action; they also constrain it. For example, contracts must be drawn up in particular ways if they are to be legally binding, and any party whose contracts fail to satisfy the relevant legal requirements will be unsuccessful in their attempts to use contracts to provide a measure of security in their future (Runde 1993, pp. 388–93; Lawson 1998, pp. 357–62; McKenna and Zannoni 2001; cf Boettke and Prychitko 1998, p. xxi).

Overall, then, adherents of critical realism (like radical subjectivists) contend that socio-economic life is best conceptualised as an intrinsically dynamic *process* of interaction between preformed social structures and current human agency. While historically given social structures are an indispensable condition for the possibility of purposeful activity, it is only through such activity that social structures of any sort endure. Social structures should never be regarded as permanently fixed – they should never be reified – because, given their dependency on (potentially creative and so transformative) human agency, the possibility of change is always present. Hence, both society in general, and specific social institutions such as the market, must be understood as inherently dynamic processes in which change arises not only because of exogenous shocks but is also endogenously generated as an integral part of social life (Lawson 1997, pp. 34–5, 170–71, 187–8; Layder 1997, pp. 81–2). The model of explanation to which this critical realist account gives rise resembles that adopted by Austrians in holding that explaining some socio-economic phenomenon of interest consists in giving an abstract, usually discursive and always fallible account of its causes. On this view, socio-economic phenomena are to be explained as the outcome of the causal interplay over historical time between (antecedent) social structure and (subsequent) human agency. More specifically, according to critical realists, the initial stage of an explanation involves the identification of the practices responsible for the phenomenon under investigation, after which it is necessary to uncover the social structures which make those practices possible, along with any unconscious psychological factors which motivate them (Lawson 1997, pp. 56–8, 191–271).

Critical realism, Austrian economics and the material embeddedness of socioeconomic activity

The previous section suggests that critical realists and radical subjectivists have a good deal in common. Both Austrians and critical realists seek to avoid the extremes of voluntarism and determinism, favouring an account of the structure-agency relationship that portrays socio-economic actors as socially embedded creatures whose (often creative) actions are both constrained and enabled by the social context in which they are situated (Boettke 1989a, pp. 76–77, 1990a, pp. 13–14, 18–22; Boettke and Storr 2002, pp. 7–9, 18, 21–23). However, fault lines become apparent when the question of the precise location of this middle ground is considered. The vantage point provided by critical realism suggests that while the sophisticated form of methodological individualism adopted by radical subjectivists constitutes a significant advance compared to approaches which treat people as atomistic Robinson Crusoes, it is insufficiently elaborate to do justice to the full richness of the social context in which current socio-economic activity is embedded, most notably because it fails to do justice to the material dimension of social structure.

Critical realists argue that the past's legacy to the present encompasses not just traditional interpretive frameworks and webs of intersubjectively agreed meanings but also features such as the distribution of vested interests and resources which are material or 'transsubjective' (Forstater 1997, pp. 161, 164–5, 2001, pp. 214–5) in the sense that they are ontologically distinct from and irreducible to (inherited) shared meanings and conceptual schemes. A critical realist interpretation of the structure–agency relationship suggests that historically given social structures influence current activity not only by providing conceptual frameworks but also because at any given point in time antecedent social structures embody a particular distribution of vested interests and resources. Depending on their location within the nexus of social structures, people are endowed both with the incentive to pursue particular objectives and also (usually) with (at least some of) the resources required to do so. And because these historically given endowments of incentives and resources are the result of actions undertaken in the past, then (like the structures which embody them) they constitute an ontologically irreducible influence on current behaviour (Lewis 2000, pp. 258–60).

The importance of acknowledging the existence of a distinct material dimension to social structure is driven home by the shortcomings of approaches that confine their attention to intersubjective meanings. Recall that such approaches are predicated on the idea that socio-economic life is best conceptualised as a discursive construct, analogous to a 'dialogue', a 'conversation' or a 'text'. However, exclusive reliance on the conversational analogy forecloses the possibility of addressing satisfactorily a number of potentially important issues. First, if it is indeed the case (as radical subjectivists contend) that the economy can fruitfully be viewed as a conversation in which economic agents attempt to persuade one another of the merits of their interpretation of events, whose voice will be heard in such conversations? Put slightly differently, if meanings are intersubjectively agreed, *whose* interpretations are to count in the negotiations through which agreement over those shared meanings is reached? A second, related question centres on why people are motivated to resist or support efforts to portray events, institutions, and so on in a particular light. Critical realists argue that attempts to answer these questions without referring to material aspects of social structure are unlikely to be convincing. A satisfactory explanation of why different people wish to promote different interpretations may well hinge on understanding how doing so furthers their interests (as bequeathed to them by pre-existing social structures). In a similar vein, explaining why some people (but not others) have access to the dialogues in which shared meaning are established, and also why some of the interlocutors have a greater influence on the outcome than others, is likely to refer to the way in which people's location in the nexus of social structures gives (or denies) them the resources (wealth, power, status, access to positions of authority, and the like) to impose their preferred meanings on others. If it is indeed the case, as this line of reasoning suggests, that answering such questions requires consideration of the distribution of incentives and resources embodied in antecedent social structure, then it is hard to see how they can be satisfactorily dealt with by an approach which view socio-economic life solely as a discursive construction (Fay 1996, pp. 57–63).

According to critical realists, then, the material aspects of socio-economic life are irreducible to people's interpretations thereof. The context within which negotiations over shared meanings take place includes material social structures that condition (without determining) both the interpretations that people strive to promote and also their capacity to do so. On this view, the allocation of resources generated as the outcome of the market process is shaped and channelled, not just by intersubjectively agreed meanings and interpretive frameworks, but also by the distribution of material resources (money, power and the like) embedded in inherited social structures. The latter pre-structure the way in which people interact with one another, influencing (though not determining) whose preferences count and what weight they will carry, and so condition the precise nature of the spontaneous order which emerges as the outcome of the market process (Lawson 1997, pp. 165, 171; Layder 1997, p. 168). And if it is indeed the case that at any given moment in time the process by which order emerges in the socio-economic world is itself structured by the distribution of vested interests and resources embedded in (pre-existing) social structures, then accounts which neglect such material, social structural considerations ignore factors which may have a significant impact on the course of socio-economic life and which are therefore potentially of great explanatory importance (Layder 1997, pp. 190–202, 246–51; Reed 1998, pp. 207–12).[13]

Conclusion

There is a considerable amount of common ground between radical subjectivists Austrians and critical realists. Critical realists acknowledge that because socio-economic reality depends on the meaning that people attach to their actions, social research must investigate people's interpretations if a satisfactory understanding of socio-economic life is to be had. There must always be an interpretive or hermeneutic moment in social science. However, in conceptualising the socio-economic world as an intersubjective fabric spun from shared meanings that persist or change as people negotiate interpretations of events and states of affairs, the radical subjectivists run the risk of failing to do justice to the importance of the non-discursive (material) aspects of social structures. Just as Austrians like Boettke (1997, p. 25, 1998b, pp. 175, 182) argue that socio-economic reality is not completely reducible to quantitative data – for instance, meanings cannot be measured or counted but rather must be interpreted and understood – so critical realists argue in a similar vein that while intersubjectively agreed meanings are partially constitutive of socio-economic life, they do not exhaust the latter. And if socio-economic reality is only partly discursively constructed, then (as we have seen) approaches like radical subjectivism which conceptualise it solely in terms of conversational or textual analogies are likely to ignore potentially significant factors (Outhwaite 1985, p. 37; Sayer 2000, pp. 6, 17–20).[14]

To draw out the significance of this line of reasoning for the structure-agency debate, let us consider its implications for the notions of constraint and empowerment in social theory. If critical realists are correct in thinking that socio-economic life is shot through with conflicts and power struggles over whose interpretations are hegemonic, so that many meanings are contested, then simply wishing that a particular interpretation of events is common currency is unlikely to be enough to bring it about. On the contrary, whether one person's interpretation becomes widely held is likely to depend not just on his rhetorical skills but also on whether he possesses the material resources to bring conversations to his desired conclusion simply by imposing his meanings on others. On this view, a person's capacity to influence the course of socio-economic life is conditioned not just by her powers of persuasion but also by her command over material resources, and to neglect the significance of the latter is to lapse into a form of voluntarism which exaggerates the importance of human agency (in this case, people's rhetorical skills) in relation to historically given social structures (Sayer 1992, pp. 33–35, 83, 111–12, 2000, pp. 25–26, 45; Layder 1997, pp. 191–202, 239; Lewis 2000, pp. 262–63).

In reaching this conclusion, critical realists are of course acutely conscious of the need to avoid the opposite extreme of reducing human subjectivity to pre-existent material circumstances. It is noteworthy in this regard that the transformational model of social activity does not suggest that social structures act behind the backs of agents or that people are the mere carriers of social structure. On the contrary, as we have seen, critical realists argue that social structures influence the course of socio-economic affairs only by the way they condition people's choice of action, not by acting autonomously (behind people's backs). Consequently, critical realists can speak of the impact that pre-existing material circumstances exert on socio-economic events without denying either the mediating role of people's interpretations (and hence the necessity of a hermeneutic moment in social science[15]) or the possibility that people may respond to their circumstances in an innovative way, and therefore without making any deterministic claims about the connection between people's material circumstances and their actions.

Presented thus, there seems to be little in the critical realist approach to which radical subjectivists would strenuously object. However, accepting something like the transformational model of social activity would have the important consequence of calling into question Austrians' long-standing commitment to methodological individualism. For in conceptualising socio-life as the product of the interplay between social structure and human agency, the transformational model is most accurately described as sponsoring a form of methodological *interactionism* than is quite distinct even from the most sophisticated varieties of methodological *individualism*. However, such a terminological change seems a small price to pay for a richer explanatory possibilities opened up by the interactionist approach.

Acknowledgements

I am very grateful to the editors, to members of the Austrian Economics Colloquium at New York University, and to participants in a seminar at Lancaster University, especially Steve Fleetwood, for comments on earlier versions of this chapter. Any remaining deficiencies are solely my responsibility.

Notes

1. As Lachmann (1976 [1994], p. 230) famously put it, '[T]he future is to all of us unknowable, though not unimaginable.'
2. Indeed, an Austrian reading of the history of economic thought yields the conclusion, famously expressed by Hayek, that subjectivism has been the primary engine of progress in the discipline of economics: '[I]t is probably no exaggeration to say that every important advance in economic theory during the last hundred years was a further step in the consistent application of subjectivism' (Hayek 1952 [1979], p. 52).
3. More specifically, Boettke (1990a, pp. 130–31) distinguishes three ways in which prices convey knowledge: first, prices guide people's decisions ex ante by informing them of the relative scarcities of goods; second, calculations of profit and loss facilitated by prices indicate ex post the success or otherwise of those decisions; and third, discrepancies between market prices may alert entrepreneurs to the existence of opportunities for profit of which they were ignorant hitherto.
4. Indeed, the claim that prices provide sufficient information uniquely to determine the optimal course of action for (rational) people to pursue is also regarded as suspect by Austrians on the grounds it effectively denies the possibility of genuine choice. For, given that Austrians contend that real choice requires that people could always have decided to pursue a different course of action than they actually selected, any approach which models them as having no option but to behave in a specific way amounts to a form of situational determinism (Latsis 1972, 1976) that leaves little scope for anything worthy of being described as 'choice' (Shackle 1972 [1992], pp. 122–23, 221; Lachmann 1978 [1994], pp. 221–25; Kirzner 2000, pp. 8, 55–65).
5. Prominent contributions to this line of thinking, many of whose authors either are or have been associated with George Mason University, include Addleson (1995), Boettke (1989a, 1989b, 1990b, 1990c, 1998a), Boettke et al. (2002), Ebeling (1986, 1987, 1990), Horwitz (1992, 1994, 1995, 1998, 1999), Lavoie (1986, 1987, 1990a, 1990b, 1990c, 1991a, 1991b, 1993, 1994a, 1994b), Madison (1989, 1990a, 1990b, 1994, 1998), Prychitko (1989–90 [1995], 1994a, 1994b) and the essays collected in Lavoie (ed.), (1990d) and Prychitko (ed.), (1995).
6. The success of Lachmann's own attempts to create an alternative to equilibrium analysis that avoids solipsism and nihilism are a matter of some debate in contemporary, radical subjectivist Austrian circles. See, for example, Vaughn (1994, pp. 155–61, 171), Lavoie (1994b, 1997) and Prychitko (1994a, 1997a, 1997b).
7. As Mises (1949 [1966], pp. 43, 46) puts it: 'As a thinking and acting being man emerges from his prehuman existence already as a social being. … Inheritance and environment direct a man's actions. They suggest to him both the ends and the means. He lives not simply as man in abstracto; he lives as a son of his family, his people, and his age; as a member of a definite social group; as a practitioner of a certain vocation; as a follower of definite religious, metaphysical, philosophical ideas; as a partisan in many feuds and controversies. He does not himself create his ideas and standards of value; he borrows them from other people. His ideology is what his environment enjoins upon him. Only very few men have the gift of thinking new and original ideas and of changing the traditional body of creeds and doctrines'.
8. For more on this, and other, aspects of Gadamer's thought, see Bernstein (1983), Warnke (1987) and the essays collected in Dostal (2002).
9. As Gadamer (1975 [1993], p. 293) puts it: 'Tradition is not simply a precondition; rather, we produce it ourselves inasmuch as we understand, participate in the evolution of the tradition and hence determine it ourselves. Thus the circle of understanding … describes an ontological structural element in understanding.'
10. For a similar view, see McCloskey (1994, pp. 313, 367–78).
11. For overviews of the transformational model of social activity, see Archer (1995) and Lawson (1997, pp. 30–32, 56–58, 157–73). For applications to economics, see Pratten (1993) and Fleetwood (1995, 1996).
12. Critical realists argue that the principal explanation for the absence of stable event regularities in the socio-economic realm lies in the fact, also emphasised by radical subjectivists like Shackle (1972 [1992], pp. 122–23, 365) and Lachmann (1978 [1994], pp. 221–25), that the creativity of active minds implies that a people's actions are not simply a determinate or single-exit response to their circumstances. On the contrary, the possibility of genuine choice

entails that if in any given circumstances (*x*) a person chose to do a particular action (*y*), then (s)he could have chosen to undertake some other course of action (not-*y*). But if that is indeed the case, then the exercise of genuine choice would appear to be preclude the widespread existence of stable event regularities in socio-economic life (Lawson 1997, pp. 8–11).

13. For a case study, see Campbell (1998 [2001]).

14. The radical subjectivists' failure to distinguish adequately between the socio-economic world and people's interpretations of it is an example of what critical realists term 'the anthropic fallacy', that is the idea that the nature of socio-economic reality can be conceptualised entirely in terms of some property of human beings. In this case, the fallacy consists in reducing (ontological) statements about the nature of socio-economic reality to (anthropocentric) statements about people's discourse or conversations, leading (as we have seen) to the neglect of the material context within which those dialogues take place and meanings are negotiated (Outhwaite 1985, p. 37; Sofianou 1995, pp. 376–78; Lawson 1997, pp. 34, 282).

15. See Lawson (1997, pp. 34–5, 200–201, 223–5) and Sayer (2000, pp. 17–18).

References

Addleson, M. (1995), *Equilibrium Versus Understanding: Towards the Restoration of Economics as Social Theory*, London and New York: Routledge.

Archer, M.S. (1995), *Realist Social Theory: The Morphogenetic Approach*, Cambridge: Cambridge University Press.

Bernstein, R.J. (1983), *Beyond Objectivism and Relativism*, Oxford: Basil Blackwell.

Boettke, Peter J. (1989a), 'Evolution and economics: Austrians as institutionalists', *Research in the History of Economic Thought and Methodology*, **6**, 73–89.

Boettke, Peter J. (1989b), 'Austrian institutionalism: a reply', *Research in the History of Economic Thought and Methodology*, **6**, 181–202.

Boettke, Peter J. (1990a), *The Political Economy of Soviet Socialism: The Formative Years, 1918–1928*, Boston, MA: Kluwer Academic Press.

Boettke, Peter J. (1990b), 'Individuals and institutions', *Critical Review*, **4**, 10–26.

Boettke, Peter J. (1990c), 'Interpretative reasoning and the study of social life', in David L. Prychitko (ed.) (1995), *Individuals, Institutions, Interpretations: Hermeneutics Applied to Economics*, Aldershot: Avebury.

Boettke, Peter J. (ed.), (1994), *The Elgar Companion to Austrian Economics*, Aldershot, UK and Brookfield US: Edward Elgar, pp. 59–80.

Boettke, Peter J. (1997), 'Where did economics go wrong? modern economics as a flight from reality', *Critical Review*, **11**, 11–64.

Boettke, Peter J. (1998a), 'Rational choice and human agency in economics and sociology: exploring the Weber–Austrian connection', in H. Giersch (ed.), *Merits and Limits of Markets*, Berlin: Springer-Verlag, pp. 53–81.

Boettke, Peter J. (1998b), 'Formalism and contemporary economics: a reply to Hausman, Heilbroner and Mayer', *Critical Review*, **12**, 173–86.

Boettke, Peter J., and David L. Prychitko (eds), (1994), *The Market Process: Essays in Contemporary Austrian Economics*, Aldershot: Edward Elgar.

Boettke, Peter J., and David L. Prychitko (1998), 'Introduction: varieties of market process theory', in P.J. Boettke and D.L. Prychitko (eds), *Market Process Theories,* vol. I, *Classical and Neoclassical*, Cheltenham: Edward Elgar.

Boettke, Peter J., and V.H. Storr (2002), 'Post-classical political economy: polity, society and economy in Weber, Mises and Hayek', *American Journal of Economics and Sociology*, **61**, 161–91.

Boettke, Peter J., Don Lavoie and V.H. Storr (2002), 'The subjectivist methodology of Austrian Economics and Dewey's theory of inquiry', George Mason University Department of Economics working papers in economics no. WPE 02.01.

Campbell, J.L. (1998 [2001]), 'Institutional analysis and the role of ideas in political economy', *Theory and Society*, **27**, 377–409, reprinted in J.L. Campbell and O.K. Pedersen (eds), (2001), *The Rise of Neoliberalism and Institutional Analysis*, Princeton, NJ and Oxford: Princeton University Press.

Cowan, R., and M.J. Rizzo (1996), 'The geneti–causal tradition and modern economic theory', *Kyklos*, **49**, 273–317.

Dostal, R.J. (ed), (2002), *The Cambridge Companion to Gadamer*, Cambridge: Cambridge University Press.

Ebeling, Richard M. (1986), 'Towards a hermeneutical economics: expectations, prices, and the role of interpretation in a theory of the market process', in Israel M. Kirzner (ed.), *Subjectivism, Intelligibility and Economic Understanding: Essays in Honor of Ludwig M. Lachmann on his Eightieth Birthday*, New York: New York University Press, pp. 39–55.

Ebeling, Richard M. (1987), 'Cooperation in anonymity', *Critical Review*, **1**, 50–61.

Ebeling, Richard M. (1990), 'What is a price? explanation and understanding', in Don Lavoie (ed.), *Economics and Hermeneutics*, London and New York: Routledge, pp. 177–94.

Fay, B. (1996), *Contemporary Philosophy of Social Science*, Oxford: Blackwell Publishers.

Fleetwood, S. (1995), *Hayek's Political Economy: The Socio-Economics of Order*, London and New York: Routledge.

Fleetwood, S. (1996), 'Order without equilibrium: a critical realist interpretation of Hayek's notion of spontaneous order', *Cambridge Journal of Economics*, **20**, 729–47.

Forstater, M. (1997), 'Adolph Lowe and the Austrians', *Advances in Austrian Economics*, **4**, 157–73.

Forstater, M. (2001), 'Phenomenological and interpretive-structural approaches to economics and sociology: Schutzian themes in Adolph Lowe's Political Economics', *Review of Austrian Economics*, 14, 209–18.

Gadamer, Hans-Georg (1975 [1993]), *Truth and Method*, 2nd, revised edn, translated by J. Weinsheimer and D.G. Marshall, London: Sheed and Ward.

Gadamer, Hans-Georg (1983), *Reason in the Age of Science*, translated by F.G. Lawrence, Cambridge, MA: MIT Press.

Granovetter, Mark (1985), 'Economic action and social structure: the problem of embeddedness', *American Journal of Economics and Sociology*, **91**, 481–510.

Hayek, Friedrich A. (1937), 'Economics and knowledge', in Hayek (1948), pp. 33–56.

Hayek, Friedrich A. (1945), 'The Use of Knowledge in Society', in Hayek (1948), pp. 77–91.

Hayek, Friedrich A. (1948), *Individualism and Economic Order*, Chicago: University of Chicago Press.

Hayek, Friedrich A. (1952 [1979]), *The Counter-Revolution of Science Studies on the Abuse of Reason*, 2nd edn, Indianapolis: Liberty Fund.

Hayek, Friedrich A. (1982 [1993]), *Law, Legislation and Liberty: A New Statement of the Liberal Principles of Justice and Political Economy*, London: Routledge.

Horwitz, Steven (1992), 'Monetary exchange as an extra-linguistic social communication process', *Review of Social Economy*, **50**, 193–214.

Horwitz, Steven (1994), 'Subjectivism, institutions and capital: comment on Mongiovi and Lewin', *Advances in Austrian Economics*, **1**, 279–88.

Horwitz, Steven (1995), 'Feminist economics: an Austrian perspective', *Journal of Economic Methodology*, **2**, 259–79.

Horwitz, Steven (1998), 'Hierarchical metaphors in Austrian institutionalism: a friendly subjectivist caveat', in R. Koppl and G. Mongiovi (eds), *Subjectivism and Economic Analysis: Essays in Memory of Ludwig M. Lachmann*, London and New York: Routledge.

Horwitz, Steven (1999), 'Money and the interpretive turn: some considerations', *mimeo*, St. Lawrence University.

Kibbe, M.B. (1994), 'Mind, historical time and the value of money: a tale of two methods', in Peter J. Boettke and David L. Prychitko (eds), *The Market Process: Essays in Contemporary Austrian Economics*, Aldershot, UK and Brookfield, US: Edward Elgar, pp. 96–112.

Kirzner, Israel M. (ed.), (1986), *Subjectivism, Intelligibility and Economic Understanding: Essays in Honour of Ludwig M. Lachmann on his Eightieth Birthday*, New York: New York University Press.

Kirzner, Israel M. (2000), *The Driving Force of the Market: Essays in Austrian Economics*, London and New York: Routledge.

Lachmann, Ludwig M. (1956 [1978]), *Capital and its Structure*, Kansas City: Sheed, Andrews and McMeel.

Lachmann, Ludwig M. (1970), *The Legacy of Max Weber*, London: Heinnemann.

Lachmann, Ludwig M. (1976 [1994]), 'From Mises to Shackle: an essay on Austrian economics and the kaleidic society', in Don Lavoie (ed.), *Economics and Hermeneutics*, London and New York: Routledge, pp. 229–40.

Lachmann, Ludwig M. (1978 [1994]), 'Vicissitudes of subjectivism and the dilemma of the theory of choice', in Don Lavoie (ed.), *Economics and Hermeneutics*, London and New York: Routledge.

Lachmann, Ludwig M. (1982), 'Ludwig von Mises and the extension of subjectivism', in I. Kirzner (ed.), *Method, Process and Austrian Economics: Essays in Honour of Ludwig von Mises*, Lexington, MA: D.C. Heath.

Lachmann, Ludwig M. (1986), *The Market as an Economic Process*, Oxford: Basil Blackwell.

Lachmann, Ludwig M. (1990), 'Austrian economics: a hermeneutic approach', in Don Lavoie (ed.) (1990d), pp. 134–46.

Lachmann, Ludwig M. (1990 [1994]), 'G.L.S. Shackle's place in the history of subjectivist thought', in Don Lavoie (ed.), *Economics and Hermeneutics*, London and New York: Routledge..

Latsis, S. J. (1972), 'Situational determinism in economics', *British Journal for the Philosophy of Science*, **23**, 207–45.

Latsis, S.J. (1976), 'A research programme in economics', in S.J. Latsis (ed.), *Method and Appraisal in Economics*, Cambridge: Cambridge University Press.

Lavoie, Don (1986), 'Euclideanism versus hermeneutics: a reinterpretation of Misesian apriorism', in Israel M. Kirzner (ed.), *Subjectivism, Intelligibility and Economic Understanding: Essays in Honor of Ludwig M. Lachmann on his Eightieth Birthday*, New York: New York University Press, pp. 192–210.

Lavoie, Don (1987), 'The accounting of interpretations and the interpretation of accounts: the communicative function of 'the language of business'', *Accounting, Organizations and Society*, **12**, 579–604.

Lavoie, Don (1990a), 'Understanding differently: hermeneutics and the spontaneous order of communicative processes', annual supplement to *History of Political Economy*, **22**, 359–77.

Lavoie, Don (1990b), 'Computation, incentives, and discovery: the cognitive function of markets in market socialism', *Annals of the American Academy of Political and Social Science*, **507**, 72–9.

Lavoie, Don (1990c), 'Introduction', in Don Lavoie (ed.), *Economics and Hermeneutics*, London and New York: Routledge, pp. 1–5.

Lavoie, Don (ed.), (1990d), *Economics and Hermeneutics*, London and New York: Routledge.

Lavoie, Don (1991a), 'The Progress of subjectivism', in M. Blaug and N. de Marchi (eds), *Appraising Economic Theories: Studies in the Methodology of Research Programmes*, Aldershot, UK and Brookfield US: Edward Elgar.

Lavoie, Don (1991b), 'The discovery and interpretation of profit opportunities: culture and the Kirznerian entrepreneur', in B. Berger (ed.), *The Culture of Entrepreneurship*, San Francisco: Institute for Contemporary Studies Press, pp. 33–51.

Lavoie, Don (1993), 'Democracy, markets, and the legal order: notes on the nature of politics in a radically liberal society', in E.F. Paul, F.D. Miller, Jr., and J. Paul (eds), *Liberalism and the Economic Order*, Cambridge: Cambridge University Press, pp. 103–20.

Lavoie, Don (1994a), 'The interpretive turn', in Boettke (ed.), (1994).

Lavoie, Don (1994b), 'Introduction: expectations and the meaning of institutions', in Don Lavoie (ed.), *Economics and Hermeneutics*, London and New York: Routledge, pp. 1–19.

Lavoie, Don (ed.), (1994c), *Expectations and the Meaning of Institutions: Essays in Economics by Ludwig Lachmann*, London and New York: Routledge.

Lavoie, Don (1995), 'The "objectivity" of scholarship and the ideal of the university', *Advances in Austrian Economics*, **5B**, 371–403.

Lavoie, Don (1997), 'On regrouping the intellectual capital structure of Lachmann's economics', *Advances in Austrian Economics*, **4**, 219–26.

Lawson, Tony (1997), *Economics and Reality*, London and New York: Routledge.

Lawson, Tony (1998), 'Clarifying and developing the economics and reality project: closed and open systems, deductivism, prediction, and teaching', *Review of Social Economy*, **56**, 356–75.

Layder, D. (1997), *Modern Social Theory: Key Debates and New Directions*, London: UCL Press.
Lewis, Paul A. (2000), 'Realism, causality and the problem of social structure', *Journal for the Theory of Social Behaviour*, **30**, 249–68.
Madison, G.B. (1989), 'Hayek and the Interpretive Turn', *Critical Review*, **3**, 169–85.
Madison, G.B. (1990a), 'How individualistic is methodological individualism?' *Critical Review*, **4**, 41–60.
Madison, G.B. (1990b), 'Getting beyond objectivism: the philosophical hermeneutics of Gadamer and Ricoeur', in Don Lavoie (ed.), *Economics and Hermeneutics*, London and New York: Routledge, pp. 34–58.
Madison, G.B. (1994), 'Phenomenology and economics', in Boettke (ed), (1994) Aldershot, UK and Brookfield US, pp. 38–47.
Madison, G.B. (1998), *The Political Economy of Civil Society and Human Rights*, London and New York: Routledge.
Mayer, H. (1932 [1994]), 'The cognitive value of functional theories of price', in I.M. Kirzner (ed.), *Classics in Austrian Economics: A Sampling in the History of a Tradition*, vol. II, *The Interwar Period*, London: William Pickering.
McCloskey, D.N. (1994), *Knowledge and Persuasion in Economics*, Cambridge: Cambridge University Press.
McKenna, E.J. and D.C. Zannoni (2001), 'Post Keynesian economics and nihilism', *Journal of Post Keynesian Economics*, **23** (Winter) 331–47.
Mises, Ludwig von (1949 [1966]), *Human Action: A Treatise on Economics*, 3rd, revised edn, Chicago: Contemporary Books.
Mises, Ludwig von (1957 [1985]), *Theory and History: An Interpretation of Social and Economic Evolution*, Auburn, AL: Ludwig von Mises Institute.
O'Driscoll, Gerald, and Mario J. Rizzo (1996), *The Economics of Time and Ignorance*, 2nd edn, London and New York: Routledge.
Outhwaite, W.B. (1985), 'Hans-Georg Gadamer', in Q. Skinner (ed.), *The Return of Grand Theory in the Human Sciences*, Cambridge: Cambridge University Press, pp. 21–39.
Palmer, Tony G. (1987), 'Gadamer's hermeneutics and social theory', *Critical Review*, **1**, 91–108.
Palmer, Tony G. (1990), 'The hermeneutical view of freedom: implications of Gadamerian understanding for economic policy', in Don Lavoie (ed.), *Economics and Hermeneutics*, London and New York: Routledge, pp. 299–318.
Pratten, Steven (1993), 'Structure, agency and Marx's analysis of the labour process', *Review of Political Economy*, **5**, 403–26.
Prychitko, David L. ([1989–90] 1995), 'Methodological individualism and the Austrian School', in David L. Prychitko (ed), *Individuals, Institutions, Interpretations: Hermeneutics Applied to Economics*, Aldershot: Avebury, pp. 9–18.
Prychitko, David L. (1994a), 'Ludwig Lachmann and the interpretive turn in economics: a critical inquiry into the hermeneutics of the plan', *Advances in Austrian Economics*, **1**, 303–19.
Prychitko, David L. (1994b), 'Socialism as Cartesian legacy: the radical element within F.A. Hayek's *The Fatal Conceit*', in Peter J. Boettke and David L. Prychitko (eds), *The Market Process: Essays in Contemporary Austrian Economics*, Aldershot, UK and Brookfield, US: Edward Elgar, 261–73.
Prychitko, David L. (ed.), (1995), *Individuals, Institutions, Interpretations: Hermeneutics Applied to Economics*, Aldershot: Avebury.
Prychitko, David L. (1997a), 'Lachmann's plan, and its lesson: comment on Lavoie', *Advances in Austrian Economics*, **4**, 209–17.
Prychitko, David L. (1997b), 'The dangers that court hermeneutics: rejoinder to Lavoie', *Advances in Austrian Economics*, **4**, 227–29.
Reed, M. (1998), 'Organizational analysis as discourse analysis: a critique', in D. Grant, T. Keenoy and C. Oswick (eds), *Discourse and Organization*, London and Thousand Oaks, CA: Sage Publications, pp. 193–213.
Ricoeur, Paul (1971), 'The model of the text: meaningful action considered as a text', *Social Research*, **38**, 529–62.

Ricoeur, Paul (1981), 'What is a text? explanation and understanding', in P. Ricoeur, *Hermeneutics and the Human Sciences*, Translated by J.B. Thompson, Cambridge: Cambridge University Press.

Runde, Jochen H. (1993), 'Paul Davidson and the Austrians: reply to Davidson', *Critical Review*, **7**, 381–97.

Sayer, A. (1992), *Method in Social Science: A Realist Approach*, 2nd edn, London and New York: Routledge.

Sayer, A. (2000), Realism *and Social Science*, London: Sage.

Shackle, G.L.S. (1966), *The Nature of Economic Thought: Selected Papers 1955–1964*, Cambridge: Cambridge University Press.

Shackle, G.L.S. (1972 [1992]), *Epistemics and Economics: A Critique of Economic Doctrines*, New Brunswick, NJ and London: Transaction Publishers.

Sofianou, Evanthia (1995), 'Post-modernism and the notion of rationality in economics', *Cambridge Journal of Economics*, **19**, 373–89.

Vaughn, Karen I. (1994), *Austrian Economics in America: The Migration of a Tradition*, Cambridge: Cambridge University Press.

Warnke, G. (1987), *Gadamer: Hermeneutics, Tradition and Reason*, Cambridge: Polity Press.

19 Collective intentionality, complex economic behavior, and valuation

John B. Davis

'We think, therefore we are.' (Shaftesbury, 1900 [1963], vol. 2, p. 275)

In this chapter I depart from the standard view of the individual in economics as an atomistic being to consider the individual as a socially embedded being. There are of course many different ways of understanding individuals as socially embedded; the conception I employ, however, is based on collective intentionality analysis, particularly as formulated by Raimo Tuomela. There is an advantage to economic analysis in doing this. Whereas other views of social embeddedness are holistic, and reason mostly in terms of social entities, collective intentionality analysis is explicitly an account of individuals, albeit in a particular kind of social setting. This makes it possible to compare the understanding of economic behavior that emerges from a collective intentionality analysis of individuals with the understanding of economic behavior associated with the standard rationality view of individuals as atomistic beings. Further, as an account of individuals, collective intentionality analysis also offers a way of understanding the seemingly paradoxical idea that individuals can be socially embedded and yet remain distinct beings. The basic idea derives from our understanding of first person plural intentions, or we-intentions. Only individuals form such intentions, just as only individuals form first person singular intentions, or I-intentions, but we-intentions effectively embed *social relationships in individuals*. This contrasts with holist accounts of social embeddedness that rather run the risk of eliminating individuals when they embed *individuals in social relationships*. Collective intentionality analysis thus allows us to both talk about socially embedded individuals specifically as individuals, and compare their behavior to that of atomistic individuals. Finally, since individuals form both kinds of intentions, combining accounts of behavior understood in collective intentionality terms – what I characterize as deontologically rational behavior – with accounts of behavior understood in instrumentally rational terms, offers foundations for a complete account of individual economic behavior. I suggest that economic behavior in such accounts should be considered complex.

Determining the extent to which individuals are deontologically rational rather than instrumentally rational in economic life seems to be in part an empirical question of the extent to which individuals are active in social settings in which they express themselves in we-intention terms. In the discussion here, I restrict my attention to smaller, relatively cohesive, institutionally well-structured social settings – social groups – on the assumption that shared intentions are more likely to have specific consequences for individual behavior in these sorts of circumstances than in larger, more diffuse, loosely organized social settings.[1] My argument for this assumption is *not* that smaller social groups more effectively monitor or discipline individual action – this would reduce deontologically rational to instrumentally rational behavior – but rather that smaller groups have stronger prospects of producing determinate outcomes, and this reinforces individuals' commitment to their shared intentions. Compare, for example, the need an individual feels in a place of employment to act upon relatively well-defined intentions shared with other employees ('we need do our respective jobs to meet our production deadline') versus the lesser need an individual feels in larger, more loosely organized social settings to act upon vague intentions that may only be weakly shared by others ('we need to do something about inflation'). Focusing on mid-sized social groups, then, essentially operationalizes collective intentionality analysis for economics by emphasizing the kinds of behavioral consequences that have been the subject of atomistic individual rationality analysis.

Section 1 briefly discusses social groups. Section 2 then reviews Tuomela's contribution to collective intentionality analysis. In section 3 I turn to how the socially embedded individual conception explained in collective intentionality terms involves a view of individual economic behavior distinct from that involved in standard rationality theory. A different view of normative reasoning associated with a collective intentionality analysis of the socially embedded individual conception in discussed in Section 4. Finally, section 5 offers concluding remarks.

Social groups

Social groups that are relatively cohesive and well-structured have been extensively investigated in sociology, anthropology, and social psychology. A social group may be characterized as (1) a plurality of individuals tied to one another by (2) some principle of membership that implies (3) a system of individual rights and obligations. A social group is not the same thing as a social category (such as income class, ethnicity, gender, etc.), which researchers employ to classify or group individuals according to a set of characteristics which the researcher selects. Groups, rather, are collections of individuals whose shared characteristics derive from their interaction with one another. Of the characteristics of social groups surveyed in the recent literature, I emphasize the following as particularly relevant to the analysis of mid-sized social groups in economic life: that individuals engage in repeated interaction, that they define themselves as members of a group, that they are defined by others as belonging to the group, that they share and observe group rules and norms, and that they participate in a set of interlocking roles that are central to how the group functions (Cartwright and Zander 1968, p. 48).

One advantage of construing groups in these terms is that it is allows us to say that groups need not operate on a face-to-face basis. Much sociological, anthropological, philosophical, and social psychological research focuses on small groups that do exhibit regular face-to-face contact. Indeed, in the limit a relationship between two people can be seen as a kind of group if those individuals see themselves as being in some type of repeated interaction with one another and observe rules and norms which determine roles for them in the relationship. Margaret Gilbert uses as one of her main examples the idea of two people 'taking a walk together' (Gilbert, 1989). Were 'taking a walk together' a regular interaction between two individuals, on the understanding here they would constitute a group. More long-lasting relationships of all kinds between two individuals, then, would also qualify as instances of groups. In economic life, however, groups are generally seen as being larger, somewhat more impersonal, and not infrequently involve limited or even no face-to-face contact (firms, unions, cartels, governments, etc.), and this is the sort of case I focus upon in order to concentrate on individuals' social embeddedness. The two-person limiting case kind of group, however, would still be worth investigating in economics to explain recurring market interactions between individuals, where trust relationships are better modeled along the lines of group behavior than in standard atomistic individual terms. But I do not address this sort of case here, in order to avoid needing to include sympathy or empathy as elements or factors in the analysis.

Tuomela's analysis
The philosophical literature on collective or shared intentionality distinguishes we-intentions corresponding to use of 'we' language from I-intentions corresponding to use of 'I' language. We-intentions are explained as a structure of mutually reinforcing, reciprocal attitudes shared by individuals in a social group. Important contributors have been Bratman (1993, 1999), Gilbert (1989, 1996), Searle (1990, 1995), and Tuomela (1991, 1995). Others, such as Etizioni (1988), have also distinguished 'I' and 'we' thinking, without employing the idea that shared intentionality can be described as a structure of mutually reinforcing, reciprocal attitudes. An advantage of Tuomela's work is its specifically individual focus. Though he sometimes informally refers to intentions being shared, he also emphasizes that this is not meant to literally imply that we-intentions exist in society apart from individual we-intentions. Rather, a we-intention is defined as an individual's attribution of an intention to the members of a group to which the individual belongs, based on that individual both having that we-intention and also believing that we-intention is held by other individuals in the same group. That is, I can only use 'we' language that pertains to you and

I, if I think that you would similarly apply it to you and I. Thus, expressing we-intentions is a matter of whether there exists a set *reciprocal* attitudes, not whether there is an actual *sharing of* attitudes. Indeed, in the limit an individual could have a we-intention that no other individuals have, if that individual were simply mistaken about others' we-intentions. Thus, a we-intention is not a supra-individual group intention separate from the attributions individuals make to groups, and when people use expressions such as, 'the intentions of the group', this is just a shorthand device for referring to a collection of individual we-intentions on the part of individuals in the group.

Tuomela's analysis of what he regards as the 'standard case' is as follows. An individual expressing a we-intention assumes that it is mutually believed that the we-intention is held by other group members. Consider the case in which an individual's we-intention is rooted in an attitude ('fear'), which the individual believes other group members also attribute to the group. For an individual A who is a member of a group G, 'A we-fears that X if A fears that X and believes that it is feared in G that X and that it is mutually believed in G that X is feared in G' (Tuomela 1995, p. 38). 'X is mutually believed' if not only do I believe others believe X, but they also believe that I believe X.[2] On this basis, A might suppose that 'group G has some intention' reflecting 'G's fear of X' (say, whether the group will avoid some danger). Of course A can only surmise that others in G have the same fear and also that the fear of X is mutually believed by members of the group. The strongest case using the idea that X is 'mutually believed' (a shared belief) would involve saying that the fear that X is iteratively believed by everyone. But Tuomela allows 'mutual' to have strong and weak interpretations, because groups themselves have strong and weak criteria for supposing their members share a belief, attitude, or intention. The main point is that we-attitudes are a group attitude not in the sense that a group over and above its members has an attitude towards something, but in the sense that individuals 'generally' in a group have some such attitude that they express in 'we' terms. Thus saying that they 'generally' have a we-attitude depends not just on the mutual belief condition, but on both conditions which when combined provide us with a reason to suppose that individual members of a group are justified in saying what they (that is, 'we') intend.[3]

Tuomela uses this framework to distinguish between rules and norms, and I refer the reader to his work for a fuller account. Rules are the product of an explicit or implicit agreement brought about by some authority, and used to determine a distribution of tasks and activities to individuals. Rules may be formal and written, such as laws, statutes, regulations, charters, bylaws, etc., or they may be informal agreements between individuals, sometimes orally established and sometimes silently agreed to. In contrast, in the case of norms a network of mutual beliefs substitutes for actual agreements between individuals in determining distributions of tasks and activities across individuals. As with we-intentions generally, mutual beliefs are beliefs reciprocally established between individuals, such that each believes that others have the same belief, and each also believes that others think the same about the others, and so on in a structure of reinforcing, mutually held beliefs.

Rules and norms are both understood to have motivational force, meaning that they constitute reasons for action on the part of the individuals who accept them. Indeed rules and norms are typically framed as 'ought' principles, and impose requirements on individuals as members of groups in the form of specific prescriptions for individual action. Formally, individual A feels obliged to do X, because A is a member of the group with a we-intention whose consequence is a rule or norm to the effect, 'we believe members of the group should do X.' But rules and norms are different in virtue of the different means by which they enforce a distribution of tasks and activities among individuals (Tuomela 1995, pp. 22–24). The prescriptive force of rules derives from there being sanctions that apply, whether formal/legal or informal, to those individuals who do not observe them. In contrast to rules, sanctioning with norms takes the form of approval or disapproval on the part of others. Because norms are internalized by individuals, in that they themselves accept them as reasons for acting, individuals apply others' potential disapproval to themselves, as when feeling shame or embarrassment.

In Tuomela's framework, then, it can be said that rules are the basis for institutions, and norms are the basis for social values. While it is true that many institutions also involve norms, as relatively settled social arrangements, institutions generally place greater reliance on rules. In contrast, since social values are rarely rooted in agreements, even informally, they usually place little weight on rules. Rather, social values reflect systems of mutual belief about individuals' interaction with one another. Thus when individuals create and/or change institutions, they adopt new rules, and produce new we-attitudes that define group action within an institutional framework that can be characterized in terms of agreements and corresponding sanctions. When individuals develop and/or influence social values, they adopt new norms, and produce new we-attitudes that define group action within a social value framework based on their mutual beliefs and systems of approval and disapproval. In both frameworks, rules/institutions and norms/social values, we-intentions are the foundation for understanding group action. Individuals thus influence institutions and social values as members of groups, and group action is the intermediate link between individual action and supra-individual institutions and social values missing from mainstream accounts of individuals' influence on institutions and social values.

Finally, it is important to emphasize that rules and norms can create different types of obligations – sometimes implicitly, sometimes explicitly – for individuals in terms of how different tasks, rights, and positions apply to different individuals in groups. Tuomela characterizes an individual's position within a particular group in terms of that individual's tasks and rights within that group. An individual's tasks and rights are then further distinguished according to whether they flow from rules or norms operating within the group, that is, whether they are rule-based tasks and rights or norm-based tasks and rights. In contrast, across groups, individuals' social positions are understood in terms of the whole array of actions that individuals are required and permitted to do across various economic and social settings. These social positions assign individuals a variety of different tasks whose performance is in each instance protected by rights, where these tasks–rights combinations may themselves exist within established modes of implementation that are also understood in tasks–rights terms. The overall framework thus explains individual rights and duties within and across groups in terms of tasks–rights pairs that ultimately have we-attitudes in groups as their foundation.

A revised view of individual economic behavior

The behavior of atomistic individuals is understood in instrumentally rational terms, because individual objective functions are defined solely in terms of individuals' own preferences. With no basis for action other than their own preferences, and putting aside that they might act out of habit or behave irrationally, atomistic individuals can do nothing other than seek to satisfy their own preferences. In contrast, when we treat individuals as socially embedded, we no longer say that individuals act only on their own preferences, because they also act in accordance with those rules and norms which function as 'ought' principles – what I have termed a deontologically rational or perhaps a rationally principled type of behavior. But proponents of the atomistic individual conception understand rule-following and norm-observance in instrumentally rational terms. Are 'ought' principles operating in social groups then better explained in instrumentally rational terms? Is instrumental rationality a sufficient explanation of individual behavior? There seem to be three objections to saying that something other than instrumentally rational behavior is involved here. I respond to each objection.

First objection

One way in which to argue that observing rules and norms which have the force of 'ought' principles is still fully within the compass of instrumentally rationality, is to maintain that the individual becomes subject to constraints additional to those usually assumed in standard constrained optimization analysis, namely, constraints associated with group membership. Though these additional 'social group' constraints further narrow individuals' choice sets, individuals would still maximize preferences, suggesting that socially embedded individuals are not significantly different from atomistic individuals. This argument, however, ignores what is involved in saying that individuals observe rules and norms on account of their sharing intentions with others regarding those rules and norms. Shared intentions are those intentions which individuals ascribe to the groups of which they are members. But as intentions, they must stem from individual objective functions rather than constitute constraints on those objective functions. That is, shared intentions are like our ordinary intentions in expressing what individuals *choose* to do rather than what they are *limited* to doing. It is true that individuals in groups are more constrained in their behavior as compared to when they act outside of groups. But this type of constraint has an intended aspect, and is consequently different from the usual sort of constraint that is entirely external to the individual.

Second objection
A second argument for explaining shared intentions in instrumentally rational terms accepts that shared intentions stem from individual objective functions, but argues that they express individual we-preferences, just as ordinary individual intentions express an individual's own preferences (or I-preferences). We-preferences have been analysed by Sugden, and characterized as team preferences (Sugden 2000; also cf. Bacharach 1999). Sugden explicitly rejects collective intentionality analysis as developed by Tuomela, Gilbert, and others, on the grounds that it assumes individuals are bound by obligations or 'ought' principles, which he regards as inconsistent with an account of instrumentally rational behavior (Sugden 2000, pp. 189–90). To preserve the latter, he reasons, the former has to go. This implies that rules and norms are things that members of teams prefer to observe rather than believe they ought to observe. Moreover, if we-intentions are really the product of we-preferences, then it seems that it is no longer necessary to say that individuals in teams (or groups) need to be treated as socially embedded, since the obligations or 'ought' principles they observe are what they prefer. Sugden essentially draws this conclusion when he argues that the 'existence' question regarding whether teams and other groups exist (and therefore can act as agents) is independent of the theory of instrumental rationality enlarged to include we-preferences. Were groups thought to be agents over and above their members, there clearly would be a stronger case for saying that their obligations and 'ought' principles were not always preferred by their members.

Sugden's argument, accordingly, depends on supposing that we-preferences do not really impose obligations or 'ought' principles on individuals. Why is it, then, that Tuomela and other proponents of collective intentionality analysis claim that this is a necessary dimension of we-intentions? The answer lies in their analysis of shared intentions as sets of reciprocal attitudes across individuals in groups. Though shared intentions are indeed individual intentions, unlike team preferences, which represent only what an individual independently prefers for the team, an individual's shared intention is one element in a set of reciprocal attitudes. Thus, when individuals ascribe intentions to groups of which they are members, this represents not what they prefer to ascribe to the group, but rather what they believe to be the group's intention based on what they believe that they and other group members believe to be the group's intention. On this view, shared intentions imply 'ought' principles, because individuals share an intention over which they have very limited influence. Indeed, this combination of sharing an intention and having it stand over oneself helps explain the particular quality of 'ought' principles as binding precepts that individuals nonetheless embrace. Preferences, by comparison, have but one master, namely, the individual.

It is true that team preferences do have a shared aspect to them. But absent a set of feedback connections between individuals, such as Tuomela describes for shared intentions, the shared nature of team preferences is simply the result of an accidental alignment of individuals' we-preferences about teams of which they are members. Team members may happen to share preferences about the teams they are on. Yet if these preferences regarding the team begin to diverge, there is nothing in the interaction between individuals that brings about an adjustment in individuals' preferences regarding the team. Indeed, there are many examples of teams in the real world which operate on the basis of Sugden's team preferences, and as a result break down, simply because individuals are driven by what they prefer rather than by what they believe obligates them. The problem, basically, is that, with we-preferences, just as with ordinary individual preferences, *de gustibus non est disputandum*. That is, individuals retain their atomistic status, and the 'teams' of which they are members do not exist as teams in the customary sense of the term.

Third objection
These conclusions, however, suggests a third argument regarding how instrumental rationality might be sustained vis-à-vis collective intentionality analysis. Suppose that we treat rules and norms as conventions understood as coordination equilibria (Lewis 1969). Then using evolutionary game theory, individuals can be seen as instrumentally rational players who seek the best possible response to one another's individual strategies (a Nash equilibrium), and rules and norms can be explained as endogenously determined sets of reciprocal expectations. This would allow for a feedback/adjustment process, as operates in collective intentionality theory, but it would not explain this process in terms of 'ought' principles. Rather, following Hume's view of conventions, individuals find it in their *interest* to conform to rules and norms to which they expect others will conform. There are different ways of explaining why individuals would find this in their interest. Hume relied on sentiments of approval and disapproval, and indeed used this as the basis for his theory of justice. Since a system of justice implies 'ought' obligations, this game theoretic/instrumental

rationality framework can also be argued to explain the 'ought' content of rules and norms, whether in moral or pragmatic terms. But in contrast to collective intentionality analysis, 'ought' principles in this instance derive from what individuals find to be in their interest.

In collective intentionality analysis, 'ought' principles derive from shared intentions, and shared intentions are explained in terms of individuals' use of first person plural 'we' language. Barring cases of deceit, first person plural 'we' language cannot be explained in terms of first person singular 'I' language, unless one denies elemental differences in human language, and engages in a reductionist sort of reasoning that has no support among linguists. In collective intentionality analysis, the reason that shared intention implies 'ought' principles is that they require a commitment on the part of the individual absent in the case of ordinary intentions that can be expressed in first person singular terms. Thus it seems clear that 'ought' principles that derive from collective intentionality analysis are not reducible to 'ought' principles that might emerge from a Humean framework. But this does not imply that the latter involves an unacceptable account of 'ought' principles, or that this account should be eliminated to produce one of 'ought' principles cast exclusively in shared intention and commitment terms. Rather it seems that both reductionist arguments should be rejected, because neither goes through, and because both are part of the view that thinking about individuals and society can be explained in terms of two inalterably opposed intellectual traditions: methodological individualism and methodological holism. Indeed, both accounts of 'ought' principles arguably have real world foundations. Just as there are teams that operate (often poorly) in terms of individual we-preferences, so there are 'ought' principles based on instrumentally rational behavior. Just as there are social groups that operate (usually more successfully) in terms of we-intentions, so there are 'ought' principles based on individual commitment.

My position is that individual behavior is complex in being rooted in both types of intentions. The challenge economists consequently face is in determining both the mix of types of behavior associated with different kinds of intentions, and in properly ascribing each kind of behavior to the correct real-world circumstances. Much mainstream economics, because of its adherence to the atomistic conception of the individual, imperialistically imposes instrumental rationality arguments on social settings where it does not apply. In using the wrong explanation in the wrong circumstances, mainstream economists impose 'thin' institutional explanations that overlook how the functioning of some social groups and institutional structures depends upon 'ought' principles stronger than can be explained in instrumentally rational terms. The holist economics tradition, in contrast, has at times been equally imperialistic, though in reverse direction, in using social whole-type explanations in circumstances for which they do not apply. These 'thick' institutional explanations overlook the extent to which individuals are relatively free of shared intentional experience, as well as individuals' need for navigating across social structures.

I do not attempt here to set forth a specific account of individual economic behavior as complex. There are a variety of different ways in which the two can be related.[4] But consider an example. Suppose an employee in a business is assigned a set of rule and norm-based tasks associated with doing a particular job. If one rule is to invoice customers by the end of the month, and the norm for how this is to be done is to include in the invoice a complete description of all purchases made by those customers, the individual assigned these tasks is likely still free to perform them in a variety of ways (inquire as to customer satisfaction, pursue follow-up orders, institute new record-keeping practices, etc.). How well individuals do their assigned jobs, then, can be a matter of the extent to which they also act on their own preferences regarding the way a job is best done. They consequently act in an instrumentally rational way when already behaving in a rationally principled manner.

Normative reasoning and the conception of the individual as socially embedded

Deontologically rational behavior need not be normative in raising explicitly ethical issues, but it can be. Moreover, a specifically normative deontologically rational behavior might take on a variety of value forms according to the range of values operating in social groups. Thus in contrast to the more narrow normative framework standardly associated with instrumentally rationality analysis, valuation in collective intentionality analysis is complex and multi-dimensional. Following Amartya Sen, we might refer to this enlarged normative framework as a 'deontic-value inclusive consequentialist' framework (Sen 2001, p. 64). As he explains it,

> It is neither that 'the good' comes first, and then 'rights and duties', nor that rights and duties congeal first followed by the good, but that they are linked concepts that demand simultaneous consideration. While considerations of freedoms, rights and duties are not the only ones that matter (for example, well-being does too), they are nevertheless *part* of the contentions that we have reason to take into account in deciding on what would best or acceptable to do. The issue surely is *simultaneity*. (Sen 2001, p. 61, emphasis in original)

Here I address how normative values might arise and operate not just in social groups but in organizations and institutions generally, or, as it has recently been expressed, whether we may treat '*values as partly endogenous to the economic system, and economic systems and their performance as partly functions of people's values*' (Ben-Ner and Putterman 1998, p. xvii; emphasis in original). I begin by contrasting the standard view of how normative values operate in organizations made up of atomistic individuals. Essentially following Hume, the standard account attempts to explain how conventions that lack a normative character in themselves can nonetheless come to acquire the status of moral norms.

'Moral' sentiments in organizations and institutions

Hume took a system of justice to be a set of conventions that arise when individuals come to expect one another to behave in regular and predictable ways (Hume 1739 [1888]). Individuals abide by a system of justice, because they find it in their interest to conform to its rules when they expect others to conform to them as well. The idea that such rules are 'conventional' comes from supposing that there are different possible rules of justice, and those that actually come about reflect a history of contingent interactions between people. Nothing a priori moral underlies actual systems of justice, making them for Hume not 'partly' but entirely 'endogenous to the economic system.' But why, then, should such rules be thought normative in nature? Why should they be thought to be anything more than simply persistent regularities in social behavior akin to other regularities that have no one believes have normative content? Hume's view, based on eighteenth-century Scottish-school psychology of sympathy, was that conformity with such regularities evokes sentiments of approval, and failing to conform with them evokes sentiments of disapproval. When these sentiments become widely shared and become attached to an idea of the general good, he believed they may then be characterized as a *moral* approval and disapproval. A system of justice, then, is ultimately nothing more than a relatively settled set of conventional expectations between individuals chiefly concerned with their own interest that is reinforced by sentiments of approval and disapproval.

This conception has been modified and redeveloped in recent years by Lewis and Sugden. For Lewis, conventions are coordination equilibria (Lewis 1969). Coordination equilibria can be explained in game-theoretic terms with players acting on individual strategies to achieve a common expectation regarding which individual strategies offer the best reply to one another (that is, they are Nash equilibria). Hume's psychology of sympathy is replaced by the characterization of individuals in terms of strategies, but any norms that emerge are still conventional and entirely endogenous to the economic system. Sugden similarly explains conventions in terms of individuals' expectations of one another conforming to regularities in behavior, but adds a concern individuals are said to have over incurring others' resentment as an emotion underlying conformity to conventions (Sugden 1986, 1989). When this emotion operates widely to reinforce individuals' adherence to conventions, Sugden suggests that *normative* expectations obtain among them (Sugden 1998). But against this it might be said that the emotion of resentment deserves the label 'normative' as much as Hume's approval and disapproval deserves the label 'moral.' Sugden argues in reply that this criticism misses the point behind providing a Humean *naturalistic* analysis of values. 'In such an analysis, the definition of a moral sentiment has to be naturalistic; one cannot then object that some of the sentiments allowed by the definition are not "really" moral' (Sudgen, 1998, p. 84).

In my view, such a response is question-begging. The claim that 'moral sentiments' are just that, namely, somehow 'moral', needs a stronger defense than the suggestion that it should be possible to explain moral values naturalistically, and that therefore there must exist such things as 'moral' sentiments. Indeed, making this sort of argument seems to involve exactly what G.E. Moore famously labeled the 'naturalistic fallacy' (Moore 1903). Note also, that the program of producing a naturalistic account of normative values is closely associated with the aim of producing a positivist interpretation of moral life. Sudgen is explicit about this connection, asserting that economists 'trained in a positivist tradition' must seek to explain normative values without 'assuming the existence of moral facts' (Sugden 1998, p. 76). A moral fact is a fact about something being right or wrong, good or bad, etc. For example, one might say it is a fact – specifically a moral fact – that it is wrong to needlessly harm another person. To deny that moral facts exist is to say there is nothing in society or nature that can be described in normative terms as a matter of fact. Normative values, rather, are subjective judgments, and must accordingly be explained in terms of some sort of 'moral' sensibility people exercise and impose on the world. Two obvious problems arise with this sort of approach. First, the idea that human society can or should be described naturalistically is highly questionable, and has not surprisingly, long been contested in the history of social science. Sugden and others in this tradition generally do not explain why a natural science approach to social science might be plausible, and I am skeptical that any good arguments exist on this score. Second, this approach creates a very strong problem for making the transition from 'is' to 'ought' (thus Moore's naturalistic fallacy). Sugden addresses this problem by simply insisting on a re-definition of 'moral' in naturalistic terms. Whether this is a reasonable re-definition of 'moral', however, depends on whether the account of moral behavior that emerges on these terms captures what we ordinarily think is bound up with the normative.

What is it, then, that is most characteristic of the normative domain? We can begin to answer this question by emphasizing the implied content of the moral 'ought.' When 'ought' appears in an expression in a normative way, it indicates the presence of a moral obligation. If individuals do something because they believe they morally ought to, they do so out of a sense of moral obligation operating upon them. There are many ways of understanding what this sense of 'ought' involves, but following Kant (1785 [1948]), I take the minimum essential idea to be a matter of doing something because it is required irrespective of one's inclinations or desires. But then the idea of acting out of a sense of obligation is not what is involved in acting on a 'moral' sentiment. If one is motivated to respect a norm or convention, because one fears others' resentment or disapproval for failing to do so, it is not a sense of obligation but an inclination that operates as one's motivation. Rather fear of others' resentment or disapproval has *replaced* acting out of a sense of obligation. The closest Sugden comes to referring to a sense of obligation, then, is when he argues that one of the virtues of his analysis is that it 'allows us to consider cases in which normative expectations and self-interest pull in opposite directions … cases in which individuals follow conventions even though this is contrary to self-interest' (Sugden 1998, p. 83). But this is not evidence of acting out of a sense of obligation, since one might well be inclined to observe a convention that was contrary to self-interest.

Thus if we take the idea of acting out of a sense of obligation to underlie what is involved in moral 'ought' thinking, a naturalistic, moral sentiments type of approach does not capture what we ordinarily think is bound up with the normative. This gives us good reason to conclude that the Lewis–Sugden type development of Hume regarding how values operate in organizations and institutions as conventions is not an account of distinctively *normative* expectations. This in turn suggests that a naturalistic approach probably cannot explain how normative values arise and operate in organizations and institutions. Thus, since the Humean tradition derives from its starting point in the notion that individuals are naturalistically described as isolated from one another, and generally acting in their own interest, let us rather begin at a different starting point by describing individuals as embedded in social groups in the collective intentionality sense, and then ask how normative values might arise and operate in organizations and institutions. Two questions can be addressed. (1) Does this alternative strategy enable us to talk about what is most characteristic of the normative domain, namely, a sense of obligation that individuals have when they use 'ought' language? (2) Does this strategy provide us an account of the variety and range of different types of relationships between normative values in social life along the lines of Sen's 'deontic-value inclusive consequentialist' framework?

Question 1: Moral obligation in organizations and institutions?
The first question can be answered by explaining what must be involved in saying that socially embedded individuals, understood in a collective intentionality sense, have we-intentions as well as I-intentions. The Humean framework, by taking individuals as fundamentally isolated from one another, operates exclusively with I-intentions. As previously argued, the use of 'we' language generally creates obligations for individuals – and not just in the moral sense. The collective intentionality framework, particularly as developed by Tuomela, shares with the Lewis–Sugden account of convention the idea that individual expectations are established within a system of reciprocal expectations between individuals. But Tuomela's account is different in that individual expectations have as their object reciprocal sets of we-intentions rather than have as their object the I-intentions implicitly involved in the Humean framework. We-

intentions, as previously argued, create obligations for individuals, because the successful use of 'we' by an individual needs to conform to how others use that same 'we.' Outside of a requirement of using language correctly, this obligation does not exist for the use of 'I.' Of course some obligations which individuals recognize are pragmatic, and consequently do not have moral content. But on the interpretation here collective intentionality analysis is not naturalistic, and certainly not motivated by positivistic aims. Thus it is as reasonable to suppose that moral facts exist as to suppose that they do not. From this it follows that some of the obligations individuals observe are indeed moral in nature. Though the dividing line between pragmatic and moral obligations may often be difficult to draw, and though it may change over time, it seems there are many clear cases of each, and thus fair to say that individuals who form we-intentions and use 'we' language often operate under a sense of moral obligation.

So a collective intentionality framework, by operating with a conception of socially embedded individuals rather than atomistic ones, makes it possible to include a sense of moral obligation alongside individual inclination as a form of individual motivation. Turning to the second question above, then, what does the collective intentionality framework and the conception of individuals as socially embedded tell us about the range and variety of normative values in social life and the relationships between them?

Question 2: An expanded normative domain?
The emphasis on moral obligation thus far has rested on looking at moral obligation as something that particular individuals recognize. But a fuller characterization of the concept needs to see these obligations not just from the point of view of the individuals who have them, but also from the point of view of the individuals to whom they may apply. This suggests a concept of moral obligation which relies on an 'externalist' conception of the individual, where this is a matter of understanding individuals in terms of their relations to one another, in contrast to a concept of moral obligation which relies on an 'internalist' conception of the individual, where this is a matter of understanding individuals in terms of properties that apply to them independently of their relations to one another (Davis, 2003). An example of the latter is the Pareto efficiency standard, which employs an 'internalist' conception of the individual to explain normative recommendations that judge states of affairs according to whether one person is better off *ceteris paribus* all other individuals.

Externalist-individual normative concepts, it can be argued, just because they emphasize relationships between individuals, generally require that we give attention to a range of normative concepts that go beyond whatever particular normative concepts (say, regarding what is good) might constitute a particular individual's moral view. Thus to give any kind of detailed explanation of the moral obligations that one has to others, one typically also needs to have an understanding of others' and one's own rights. But systems of rights are themselves generally embedded in broad social commitments to such ideals as freedom, equality, fairness, human dignity, community, justice, etc. Thus employing an externalist-individual type of normative concept typically commits one to examining an entire range of accompanying normative concerns. This also means that the connections between different normative concerns cannot generally be mapped out with any high degree of precision, making moral questions complex and often ultimately undecidable.

The idea of an expanded normative domain may be linked to a collective intentionality understanding of individuals' social embeddedness in terms of their involvements in social groups in the following way. Social groups generally have goals that help define them. Thus their members' we-intentions often concern a consequentialist type of moral reasoning, as when something is regarded as right on account of its helping bring about some outcome desired by the group. But this sort of consequentialist moral reasoning, when it is expressed in we-intention terms, also has independent concepts of moral obligation associated with it. Thus a particular individual using 'we' language in regard to what potential good consequences a group wants to bring about operates both with an idea that what is right is a matter of bringing about the relevant outcome, and also the idea that what is right is a matter of observing obligations upon oneself understood in we-intentions terms. This latter sense of right may draw in turn upon other ideals such as justice, equality, and dignity. This is one way of talking about a 'deontic-value inclusive consequential reasoning,' in which, '[i]t is neither that "the good" comes first, and then "rights and duties", nor that rights and duties congeal first followed by the good, but that they are linked concepts that demand simultaneous consideration' (Sen 2001, p.437).

Concluding remarks

This chapter does not attempt to explain how instrumentally rational and deontologically rational economic behavior are coordinated. It does suggest, however, that this may in part depend upon the extent to which individuals are active in social group settings in which their behavior has an economic character, that is, where production, exchange, and consumption activities are engaged in. The standard view on the part of proponents of the atomistic individual conception is that behavior in groups can always in principle be decomposed into the behavior of instrumentally rational individuals. But this view has not stood up to scrutiny (cf. Kincaid, 1996), and in any case such arguments beg the central issue here, namely, that individuals act on we-intentions as well as on I-intentions. Thus the need to explain behavior as complex remains on the agenda. In closing I merely suggest a set of considerations that could figure in the way in which this issue might be addressed.

One possible view is that one of the two spheres somehow determines the boundaries of the other. Thus social groups might establish certain domains of activity in which individuals would act in an instrumentally rational fashion. As in the example at the end of the third section, the practices in a business firm, or in a department of one, might be to collectively delegate to particular individuals the responsibility of acting as they would find rational, subject to their observing the boundaries placed on that domain of activity by the group. Alternatively, instrumentally rational individuals might delegate domains of activity in which group considerations were regarded as primary. For example, were heads of households instrumentally rational in the market, they might nonetheless treat the household as a sphere in which customary relationships reflecting we-intentions would prevail. But this general model – one sphere determining the boundaries of the other – also suggests another model in which behavior in one sphere invades the boundaries and undermines the behavior of the other. For example, individuals may express we-intentions deceitfully, and act in ways that are contrary to them. Alternatively, groups may seek to impose rules and norms on individuals where mutual beliefs are absent.

One reason that instrumental rationality theory has been attractive in economics is that having a single model of analysis makes possible a high degree of logical and mathematical determinacy in economic explanation. But the consequences of achieving this precision are that certain types of behavior go unexplained, and possibly that the activity of individuals that is meant to be explained is misrepresented. Collective intentionality analysis constitutes one framework in which these risks might be avoided. The implication of this chapter is that a larger framework including that analysis which presupposes that economic behavior is complex is more likely to offer a more adequate account of economic behavior on both counts.

Acknowledgements
Thanks for comments on a previous version of this chapter go to Jelle de Boer, Alain Marciano, Jochen Runde, John Searle and Raimo Tuomela. Errors are my own alone. This chapter also appears in *Protosociology*, vol. 18 (2003).

Notes
1. A similar argument regarding the economic consequences of social proximity was made by Adam Smith, though he relied on sympathy rather than shared intentions as the underlying motive force.
2. Gilbert explains 'we' language in a similar way: 'A person X's full-blooded use of "we" in "Shall we do A?" with respect to Y, Z, and himself, is appropriate if and only if it expresses his recognition of the fact that he and the others are jointly ready to share in doing A in relevant circumstances' (1989, p. 199). Gilbert holds that individuals use of 'we' language constitutes a 'plural subject' (1989, pp. 199ff).
3. Tuomela draws on an account of mutual belief that has become fairly standard among philosophers which relies on the idea of a hierarchical set of beliefs iterated across individuals (Tuomela 1995, pp. 41ff). See Shwayder (1965, p. 257) and Lewis (1969, pp. 52ff) for early formulations.

4. For one example of how such an explanation might be produced, see Minkler (1999), where a 'commitment function' is added to a standard utility function representation of individual behavior. The individual is said to engage in a two-step iterative procedure with the first step corresponding to a response to group requirements and the second step corresponding to an instrumentally rational maximization of utility.

References

Bacharach, M. (1999), 'Interactive team reasoning: a contribution to the theory of cooperation', *Research in Economics*, **53**, 117–47.

Ben-Ner, A., and L. Putterman (1998), 'Values and institutions in economic analysis', in A. Ben-Ner and L. Putterman (eds), *Economics, Values, and Organization*, Cambridge: Cambridge University Press, pp. 3–69.

Bratman, M. (1993), 'Shared intention', *Ethics*, **104**, 97–113.

Bratman, M. (1999), *Faces of Intention*, Cambridge: Cambridge University Press.

Cartwright, D., and A. Zander (1968), *Group Dynamics Research and Theory*, New York: Harper and Row.

Davis, J. (2003), *The Theory of the Individual in Economics: Identity and Value*, London: Routledge.

Etzioni, Armitai (1988), *The Moral Dimension: Toward A New Economics*, New York: Free Press.

Gilbert, Margaret (1989), *On Social Facts*, London: Routledge.

Gilbert, Margaret (1996), *Living Together: Rationality, Sociality, and Obligation*, Lanham, MD: Rowman and Littlefield.

Hume, David (1739 [1888]), *A Treatise of Human Nature*, edited by L. Selby-Bigge, Oxford: Clarendon Press.

Kant, Immanuel (1785 [1948]), *Groundwork of the Metaphysic of Morals*, translated by H. Paton, New York: Harper and Row.

Kincaid, H. (1996), *Philosophical Foundation of the Social Services: Analysing Controversies in Social Research*, Cambridge: Cambridge University Press.

Lewis, D. (1969), *Convention: A Philosophical Study*, Cambridge, MA: Harvard University Press.

Minkler, L. (1999), 'The problem with utility: toward a non-consequentialist/utility theory synthesis', *Review of Social Economy*, **52** (1), 4–24.

Moore, G. (1903), *Principia Ethica*, Cambridge: Cambridge University Press.

Searle, John (1990), 'Collective intentions and actions', in P. Cohen, J. Morgan and M.E. Pollack (eds), *Intentions in Communication*, Cambridge, MA: MIT Press.

Searle, John (1995), *The Construction of Social Reality*, New York: Free Press.

Sen, Armatya (2001), 'Symposium on Amartya Sen's Philosophy: 4 Reply', *Economics and Philosophy*, **17** (1), 51–66.

Shaftesbury, A. (1900 [1963]), *Characteristics of Men, Manners, Opinions, Times*, edited by J. Robertson, reprint edn, Gloucester, MA: Peter Smith.

Shwayder, D. (1965), *The Stratification of Behaviour*, London: Routledge.

Sugden, Robert (1986), *The Economics of Rights, Co-operation and Welfare*, Oxford: Blackwell.

Sugden, Robert (1989), 'Spontaneous order', *Journal of Economic Perspectives*, **3**, 85–97.

Sugden, Robert (1998), 'Normative expectations', in A. Ben-Ner and L. Putterman (eds), *Economics, Values, and Organization*, Cambridge: Cambridge University Press, pp. 73–100.

Sugden, Robert (2000), 'Team preferences', *Economics and Philosophy*, **16** (2), 175–204.

Tuomela, R. (1991), 'We will do it: an analysis of group intentions', *Philosophy and Phenomenological Research*, **51**, 249–77.

Tuomela, R. (1995), *The Importance of Us: A Philosophical Study of Basic Social Notions*, Stanford, CA: Stanford University Press.

20 Descartes' legacy: intersubjective reality, intrasubjective theory

Edward Fullbrook

The idea of intersubjectivity is the hypothesis that human consciousnesses are constitutionally interdependent, that, as unique human personalities, we form and reform ourselves, not in isolation, but rather in relation to and under the influence of other human subjects and institutions. Neither now nor in other recent eras is this a view likely to provoke wide controversy. So it is markedly strange that intersubjectivity, under any name, did not figure significantly in modern philosophy until the last century, did not, until recently, mediate in social theory between holistic and radically individualistic explanations, and to this day remains axiomatically banished from a mainstream economics founded on subjective value theory.[1]

The origins of this banishment seem incompletely understood. Much has been written about how the desire to model economics after classical mechanics required the assumption of economic agents whose individual identities, like Newton's atoms, are unchanging and, most especially, impervious to mutual influence (Mirowski 1989; Fullbrook 1996, 1997). But from where did this unlikely idea about human beings come? And why, when it runs contrary to all known experience, have so many intelligent and educated people found it plausible? Does a philosophically grounded intersubjective alternative exist? Finding the answers to these questions is a prerequisite for advancing economics beyond the reign of the neoclassical model of homo economicus. This chapter looks for answers in the histories of modern philosophy and social theory and their relations to economics. What follows is divided into three sections. The first explores the tradition of Western intrasubjective philosophy, the second traces the development of intersubjective philosophy and social theory, and the third, in the light of the first two, considers the strange case of economics.

Intrasubjective philosophy
Prior to the Enlightenment, most people enjoyed religious certainty regarding their notion of self and of their place in the world. But from the sixteenth century onward, secularized conceptions undermined religious ones, depriving the latter of their self-evident status, and so destroying the certainty regarding self that had been a common birthright in the West for centuries. René Descartes (1596–

1650) began his famous metaphysical deliberations (*Discourse on Method*, 1637; *Mediations*, 1641) at this historical crossroads. Plagued by existential despair – he felt that even his own existence fell within 'the sphere of the doubtful' – the French philosopher resolved to overcome it by rediscovering – he knew not yet where – certainty.

For this quest Descartes invented a method which he explains as follows: 'I thought it necessary ... to reject as if utterly false anything in which I could discover the least grounds for doubt, so that I could find out if I was left with anything at all which was absolutely indubitable' (*Discourse on Method*, part IV).

Descartes counted as doubtable anything revealed by our senses, because sometimes they deceive us (as when a straight stick looks bent in water), 'how do I know that He [an all-powerful God] has not brought it to pass that there is no earth, no heaven, no extended body, no magnitude, no place, and that nevertheless they seem to me to exist just exactly as I now see them' (First Meditation, p. 18).

Descartes concluded that he did not and could not know these things for certain. Furthermore, this uncertainty and his methodological doubt extended to the existence of his own body: 'I shall consider myself as having no hands, no eyes, no flesh, no blood, nor any senses, yet falsely believing myself to possess all these things ... (First Meditation, translated by Haldane and Ross, p. 19).

Having a body, Descartes concluded, was not part of his essential nature. In the end only his existence as an incorporeal thinking being withstood his programme of radical doubt. 'I am thinking, therefore I exist.' On the basis of this alleged disembodied subjective certainty, together with an argument for a perfect God, Descartes sought to re-establish 'objective' knowledge. That he succeeded is debatable. What is not is that his presumption of subjective certainty became the foundation of modern philosophy.

Descartes may only have been seeking a way beyond an existential and epistemological impasse. But his solution offered a new conception of the human self, one that, in the centuries that followed, permeated, defined and structured intellectual pursuits including philosophy, social theory and economics, and, through these, shaped the thinking of the general populations of western societies. By conceiving himself as disembodied, Descartes not only found the metaphysical certainty that he desired, but also initiated the idea of a thinker/observer who is completely detached, existing independently of time, place and other human beings, and therefore, like God, totally objective. 'I am a substance', he wrote in A *Discourse on Method* (Part IV), 'the whole nature or essence of which is to think, and which for its existence does not need any place or depend on any material thing.' This phantom of perfect self-consciousness and independence was reified by succeeding generations to become the intellectual ideal of western society, an ideal that academics came increasingly to believe they had attained.

British empiricism, contrary sometimes to popular belief, founded itself on Descartes' notion of a completely autonomous self, separate from place, time, materiality and society, and therefore self-identical over time. True, John Locke (1632–1704) broke with Rationalism by declaring that all our ideas were derived from experience (*An Essay Concerning Human Understanding*, 1690). But he saw knowledge as a product of reason working out the connections between those ideas, and he insisted upon Descartes' phantom as the agent who carries out this process of reason. Locke made a distinction between 'person' and 'man', and, by extension, between personal identity and a man's identity. The identity of a man, he wrote, is 'participation of the same continued life, by constantly fleeting particles of matter, in succession vitally united to the same organized body' (*An Essay Concerning Human Understanding* II. xxvii, 6). But the identity of a person is that of 'a thinking intelligent being, that has reason, and reflection, and can consider itself as itself, the same thinking thing in different times and places' (II. xxvii. 9). Locke's thinker is not his concept of 'man' but rather his Cartesian concept of 'person', who, out of ideas, creates knowledge independently of time, place and society, and who became for British philosophers, no less than for Continentals, their imaginary, ideal persona.

At times the Scottish philosopher David Hume (1711–1777) courted scandal by rejecting the notion that we know ourselves as simple, unified beings who are self-identical from one time to another. He offered his famous metaphor of the theatre and suggested that each of us 'is nothing but a bundle or collection of different perceptions, which succeed each other with an inconceivable rapidity, and are in a perpetual flux and movement' (*A Treatise of Human Nature*, 1739–40, Book I, section VI). But this outlook, so unflattering to members of his profession, failed to seduce them. Indeed, following the appearance of Immanuel Kant's *Critique of Pure Reason* (1781), Hume's unassuming assessment of the nature of a philosopher's self disappeared from sight. By identifying Descartes' disembodied God-like self with philosophers in particular, Kant offered his colleagues a view of themselves that too few since have been able to resist. He sought to show that philosophical knowledge can transcend the bounds of experience, and this required him to center the putative power of transcendence with philosophers themselves.

Through the centuries the inward-looking line of thought begun by Descartes became a worldly and pervasive force in society. The Cartesian view of human reality, both on the Continent and in Britain, shaped the way we think, especially the way we theorize, about all aspects of social and personal existence, including, as we shall see, the economic. Descartes' disembodiment of the thinker created a conceptually unbridgeable gap between the observer and the observed, the knower and the known, the subject and the object, thereby ascribing to each individual two separate planes of existence, an inside and an outside: one where we are the observer, the knower and the subject, the other where we are the observed, the known and the object of thought and perception. Under this dualism the body came to be thought of as a mere capsule, with windows called sense organs, in which human consciousness, cut off from the immediacy of the world around it and forever secure from the possibility of intersubjectivity, lived. This led to the tradition of thinking of the 'nature' of human beings abstractly, as outside and beyond society, thereby erasing the complex and ongoing development of human agents.

In some spheres the categorical denial of intersubjectivity continued through the twentieth century. Indeed, with the advent of the analytical movement, Descartes' disembodied philosopher reached new heights of godliness. Bertrand Russell, in *The Problems of Philosophy* (1912), effectively the movement's manifesto, first sets out the agenda, then calls for the development of philosophers capable of realizing it. The job specifications do not fit everyone. For recruits, Russell wants only intellects capable of 'true philosophic contemplation' who:

> will see as God might see, without a *here* and *now*, without hopes and fears, without the trammels of customary beliefs and traditional prejudices, calmly, dispassionately, in the sole and exclusive desire of knowledge – knowledge as impersonal, as purely contemplative, as it is possible for man to attain. Hence also the free intellect will value more the abstract and universal knowledge into which the accidents of private history do not enter, than the knowledge brought by the senses, and dependent, as such knowledge must be, upon an exclusive and personal point of view and a body whose sense-organs distort as much as they reveal. (Russell 1912 [1967], p. 93)

Faith in this atemporal, disembodied and, therefore, intrasubjective self, both as an ultimate unit of analysis and as constituting the accredited performing philosopher, underwrites the analytical tradition. It is especially conspicuous in the tradition's considerations of 'rationality', as when John Rawls reveals the foundational presuppositions of his celebrated *A Theory of Justice* (1971):

> The essential point is that we need an argument showing which principles, if any, free and equal rational persons would choose … My suggestion is that we think of the original position as the point of view from which noumenal selves see the world … The description of the original position interprets the point of view of the noumenal selves, … (Rawls 1971, pp. 255–6)

For philosophers, this notion that some individuals possess the means to 'see as God might see', to attain 'the original position' so that their point of view should then outweigh and invalidate all others holds a powerful attraction, capable of seducing the best minds, even Bertrand Russell's.

Intersubjective philosophy and social theory
At the beginning of the nineteenth century, Georg Hegel (1770–1831) rebelled against the abstract universalism of the Enlightenment by turning the Cartesian

subjective self inside out. He argued that history displays a determinate direction and process of development, powered by an evolving collective Mind of which individual minds are but the finite and historically determined parts. Hegel's works include brilliant analyses of how individual consciousnesses depend on recognition from others and of how they are socially constructed, and also of how reason is a changing structure of consciousness rather than an eternal archetype. In the main, however, Hegel's philosophy dissolves subjectivity into a collective whole. Under his system, individual subjects are not so much 'inter' related as 'sub' related to an historical, all-transcending and largely determinate totality. This, as explanation, reverses the direction of causation. Just as the atomistic Cartesian self underpins methodological individualism, the 'Hegelian self', and its related notion of an all-encompassing whole, provides the ontological foundation of methodological holism. For the realm of human affairs, Hegel, in effect, reversed the putative direction of causality between the whole and the parts.

Intersubjective philosophy, which, in its modern form, emerged only in the last century, occupies the ambiguous middle-ground between these Cartesian and Hegelian extremes. It conceives of the individual as neither wholly autonomous nor wholly dependent, as neither wholly closed nor wholly open. This intrinsic conceptual ambiguity of the intersubjective project accounts in part for its failure to develop as a well-defined philosophical movement. Unlike its atomistic and holistic rivals, intersubjective philosophy, including its social theory offshoots, does not have categorical certainty at its command with which to frame pontifical pronouncements. Even its origins, though recent, are obscure and a little confusing.

Although the phenomenological movement, as founded by the German philosopher Edmund Husserl (1859–1938) at the beginning of the last century, is generally recognized as the watershed in the growth of the intersubjective approach to philosophy, the crucial philosophical moves that made it possible date from the late 1900s. The first involved dusting off an old idea, one common to the Scholastics of the Middle Ages. Philosophers had not always believed that consciousness was a container in which a person could, like Descartes, find their virgin self lurking in some obscure interior corner, or, like homo economicus, observe their inner self to discover the data needed to construct their consumer preference map. Descartes' sharp separation of body and mind led inevitably to the distinction between external and inner perception (or Locke's 'sensation' and 'reflection') which, in turn, required the notion of consciousness as a space where things exist through time and can be inventoried and measured by some further entity that is never named. Today this seventeenth-century notion of consciousness remains, alas, the sole version of the truth in most of the world's economics departments. But in 1870s Vienna a very different notion of consciousness was advanced, one that conceives of consciousness not as a repository but as a relation. This is Franz Brentano's theory of intentionality (1874).

Brentano's theory states that consciousness is always consciousness *of* something. Instead of regarding consciousness as a kind of receptacle holding perceptions, sense data and images, Brentano taught – and his students included Franz Kafka, Carl Stumpf, Sigmund Freud, Alexius Meinong, Christain von Ehrenfels, Edmund Husserl, Bertrand Russell, G.E. Moore, Max Scheler and Martin Heidegger – that consciousness is a *relation* that human beings have to objects, material and immaterial, including those real, imagined and remembered (Honderich 1995, p. 104). Every moment of consciousness has something *of which* it is conscious. Brentano's conception of consciousness as a relation that a being has to other beings and kinds of being, rather than a separate area of being, renders nonsensical attempts to look inwards for the self or ego or, indeed, for consumer preferences. Instead this view implies that the self – or selves – is, like everything else known in the world, merely an object *of* consciousness and thus, given the flow of consciousness, continually open to reconstruction.

Brentano's principle of intentionality has a further dimension disruptive of the traditional metaphysical order. It maintains that it is the objects themselves – the Coca Cola bottle, the bowl of chili, the juicy red apple – which figure in acts of consciousness. This view contravenes philosophy's empirical tradition, as well as the Cartesian branch of the continental tradition, which, as in Hume's theatre analogy, tends to regard consciousness as an indirect and passive experience of the world. It is indirect because it holds that when one looks at the red apple, the actual apple is not the object of consciousness, but rather a likeness or picture of the apple which appears *in* one's consciousness. Thus, this view regards perception as only indirectly of things in the world. The principle of intentionality changes all that. The redness and juiciness of the apple are no longer 'sensations' but rather what is sensed; they are properties of the apple which consciousness intends, rather than elements of consciousness representative of those properties. Under this way of thinking, the world is seen as something through which a consciousness moves and intervenes, and interacts and transmutes with other consciousnesses and their creations.

The other great demolisher of the Cartesian myth of a stable, coherent, disembodied and atomistic self, and the person whom Edmund Husserl credited as 'the father of phenomenology', was Henri Bergson. Whereas Brentano focused on the nature of consciousness vis-à-vis the world, Bergson explored its and the self's relation to time and to the body. Today Bergson appears as a paradoxical figure in the history of philosophy. Although little read in the last sixty years (notwithstanding his current revival), he has had immense influence, having been widely read, discussed and digested by other philosophers in his own lifetime (1859–1941).

Bergson's ontological world differed fundamentally from his predecessors. His philosophical interest was in Becoming rather than Being and in concrete particulars rather than in abstract and universal forms. These philosophical predilections made for great and productive mischief when applied to the notion of the human subject. Although Bergson conceived of the self as unified, he attributed this property not to the existence of a continuing essence, but to an evolving life-history that could accommodate change in all aspects of one's personal identity. He emphasized the openness of the human subject, its developmental nature and its possibility of indeterminate – that is, real – choice. By working on the plane of living reality, Bergson deconstructed the stable and determinant self so loved by philosophers.

But Bergson's demolition of the Cartesian self went much further. He also escaped from the traditional mind/body dualism, and did so without resorting to reductive materialism. The following brief passage, in which the perceptions and actions referred to are his own, encapsulates his central innovation: 'thus perceptions are born and actions made ready. *My body* is that which stands out as the center of the perceptions; *my personality* is the being to which these actions must be referred' ((1896) 1991, p. 47).

Rather than regarding his body as something distinct from his self or 'personality', his body *is* him in so far as he is an active person. His body is the 'center' of the perceptions on the basis of which he chooses his bodily actions which, in turn, refer back to his self. His body, far from belonging to a distinct realm of being, is central to and inseparable from how he experiences himself and how he chooses himself. In short, his self is embodied. This placement of the subject visibly and vulnerably in-the-world, when coupled with the intentionality principle, gave rise to the notion of intersubjectivity.

Edmund Husserl brought together these advances by Brentano and Bergson and made 'intersubjectivity' part of the philosopher's lexicon. He recognized that for each of us the phenomenological status of the world is a reality shared with other human subjects. We are each integrally linked or embedded in this social reality, and the linkage is dynamic and diverse. Let me elaborate.

The mind's embodiment means that the self exists 'out there' as a natural and social entity, intersubjectively permeable and therefore only partially under our control. Daily existence brings us in contact with the Other, both individual and collective others who apprehend our bodies from perspectives different from our own. Thus, to comprehend one's self as a worldly subject/object one needs to adopt the multifarious and shifting perspectives of others. Furthermore, all our social acts (and very few of our acts are not social) take place in preexisting and ever-changing fields of intersubjective meaning. Events are, wrote Husserl, 'experienced by each perceiving subject in a preconstituted intersubjective field of experience, events in which several human subjects participate' (quoted in Petit 1999, p. 233). Our experiences, including those formative and reformative of our individual selves, take place *inside intersubjective structures* – genders, races, languages, legends, histories, governments, fashions, genres, games, news, professions, families, romances, friendships, etc., etc. – which we, as autonomous individuals, may modify but which are ontological prior to each of our individual subjectivities, selves, preferences, etc. Nor do the complications of intersubjectivity for the constitution of our selves stop here. Our social embeddedness is kaleidoscopic. In the coming and going of everyday life, as well as in the pursuit of ambitions, we enter and leave, and simultaneously inhabit different intersubjective fields, micro and macro, and with diverse and changing sets of people, which exercise their different influences on who we are. Finally, the view that intersubjective consciousness is built into selfhood, that intersubjectivity is an integral aspect of the self as subject, means that the we-dimension is ontologically fundamental to human reality.

This broadly intersubjective conception of the human being, *the intersubjective self*, that emerged in twentieth-century philosophy carries us a very long way from Descartes' notion of consciousness as a private and impenetrable walled-off sphere, wherein resides a pristine self that commands the certainty of definition and constancy through time to support the God-like vision of Russell, the linguistic atomism of the early Wittgenstein, the noumenal self of Rawls and the well-defined and stable preferences of the neoclassical economist.

The intersubjective alternative to the Enlightenment's Cartesian subject moved philosophy out of the realm of pure logic and pure thought by linking it to the physical, social and cultural worlds, including the general flux of experience. As always with revolutions, this one had unintended and unanticipated consequences, the most important being that it provided the first adequate philosophical grounding for social theory. It was no longer necessary for philosophical-grounded non-holistic social theory to regard human 'nature' as outside or before society or a-historical and static. Instead the human subject was now conceived of as intrinsically ambiguous and variable, each individual uniquely situated or embedded in an ever-changing intersubjective world, partly self-defined, partly defined by their history of particular situations. According to intersubjective philosophy, writes Mark Poster:

> Not only did the individual inject meaning into the world, but the world injected meaning into the individual, so that the individual was immediately social. Defined both by others and by himself, he was out there in the world, perceiving and being perceived through his body. (Poster 1975, p. 148)

Of course, all this is only commonsense. But, as I have shown, it is a way of seeing the human world that completely contradicts the philosophical tradition set in motion by the Enlightenment. The *intersubjective self* stands far removed from the idea of the single and unified self or subject presupposed by analytical philosophy and neoclassical economics. Under the new way of thinking, one's view of oneself is neither more real than nor exempt from the influence of the views that others hold of oneself. Rather than being a simple and given unity, or even a unity formed on the basis of logical entailment, one's self is a synthesis requiring management, upkeep, investment, friends, perhaps even therapy.

Through phenomenology, the post-Cartesian and post-Hegelian upsurge established the irreducibility of intersubjective consciousness, and thereby the joint interdependence of the 'I' and the 'We', of the individual and society, of the event and history, rather than the dependence of one on the other that theretofore had in the main characterized social philosophy and social theory. This re-conceptualization of the human being was potentially momentous to the human sciences, including economics. This is because every study of human behavior bases itself, explicitly or implicitly, on some conception or model of the human being, which then determines the scope, nature and often the conclusions of its inquiry. Intellectuals did not take long to see that the intersubjective perspective had the effect of opening up new frontiers of the phenomenal world to investigation and perhaps even to understanding. From the 1930s on, the influence of the intersubjective conceptual foundation spread through social thought in numerous directions. These included French Existentialism (especially Simone de Beauvoir, Maurice Merleau-Ponty, and Jean-Paul Sartre), European and American sociology, (first Max Scheler, Karl Mannheim and Alfred Schutz, later Norbert Elias, Erving Goffman, Maurice Natanson, Thomas Luckmann, Perter Berger and Pierre Bourdieu), ethnomethodology (Harold Garfinkel), psychiatry (R.D. Laing), the many-faceted Frankfurt School (especially Walter Benjamin, Max Horkheimer, Erich Fromm and Jürgen Habermas), and, of course, the later work of Ludwig Wittgenstein and his followers, which showed that intersubjective, not intrasubjective, experience is the foundation of language.

This account of the development of intersubjective social theory remains radically incomplete. There is another side, one pioneered by women and people of colour that is no less important, although traditionally, alas, omitted from accounts such as this one. Both atomistic and holistic social theories leave oppressed social/cultural groups out in the cold. Atomistic theory tells the oppressed that their predicament is their own fault, and holistic theory that it is due to macro forces beyond their influence. So for such groups to launch, prior to the developments described above, liberation movements grounded in social theory, they themselves had to intellectually pioneer a way though the intersubjective middle, one that included both upward and downward causation (social structures shaped by individuals and vice versa), one that emphasized the social construction of individuals but also taught them both how to collectively reconstruct themselves as individuals and how to band together to manipulate and change macro forces and structures.

Whereas today academic social theory is predominately concerned with traditional white male reality – social class, socio-economic status and occupational ranking – it used to be exclusively so. But for social theorists who belonged to oppressed groups and who in consequence usually found themselves outside the academy, oppression was the central issue. It fell to them to theorize the relations between the races and between the sexes. Indeed, it was these men and women who linked social theory to questions of human emancipation and developed the intersubjective social analysis, especially intersubjective identity theory, that broke down the traditional 'division between conceptions of the person and conceptions of people in society' [Elias 1978, p. 129], and that increasingly underpins today's academic sociology.

Olympe de Gouges in France (*The Declaration of the Rights of Woman and the Female Citizen*, 1791) and Mary Wollstonecraft in England (*A Vindication of the Rights of Woman* 1792) argued that women were socially constructed according to cultural notions of 'feminine' and that these structures could and should be changed. De Gouges paid the ultimate price for her cultural heresy and died on the guillotine. But her and Wollstonecraft's ideas were amplified at the women's rights convention held at Seneca Falls, New York, USA in 1848. Symbiotically, this important event coincided with the rise of the American anti-slavery movement. In 1845 Frederick Douglass, escaped slave and intellectual, published his influential autobiography with its narrative structured around the idea that observable differences between the races and the identities of their members are socially and economically constructed rather than natural or innate or intrasubjective. By the end of the nineteenth century these intersubjective ideas were central to a growing body of African-American social thought, most notably in the work of the sociologist W.E.B. Du Bois. In 1903 Du Bois, who had studied under William James at Harvard and later at the University of Berlin, published *The Souls of Black Folk*. It includes a short passage that has been quoted hundreds if not thousands of times and that I am going to quote again because it has been so influential in the development of contemporary social theory. The African-American, writes Du Bois, lives in:

> a world which yields him no true self-consciousness, but only lets him see himself through the revelation of the other world. It is a peculiar sensation this double consciousness, this sense of always looking at one's self though the eyes of others, of measuring one's soul by the tape of a world that looks on in amused contempt and pity. One ever feels his twoness, – an American, A Negro; two souls, two thoughts, two unreconciled strivings; two warring ideals in one dark body. (Du Bois 1903 [1965], pp. 214–15)

Here, in a few words, Du Bois harnesses together a formidable and formative team of intersubjective concepts: the self permeated by the social world, the social construction of race, the social embeddedness of the individual self, embeddedness in contradictory positions resulting in multiple selves or identities, the subject–object dichotomy in social relations, embodiment and, of course, the Other.

But what does this have to do with economics? Well, consider Du Bois's next paragraph where he applies some of these concepts to understanding a situation of 'two unreconciled strivings':

> The history of the American Negro is the history of strife, – this longing to attain self-conscious manhood, to merge his double self into a better and true self. In this merging he wishes neither of the older selves to be lost. He would not Africanize America, for America has too much to teach the world and Africa. He would not bleach his Negro soul in a flood of white Americanism, for he knows that Negro blood has a message for the world. He simply wishes to make it possible for a man to be both a Negro and an American, without being cursed and spit upon by his fellows, without having the doors of Opportunity closed roughly in his face. (ibid., p. 215)

But our perceptions of economic phenomena have become so conditioned by neoclassicism that the penny may still not have dropped. So consider yet another passage, this one first published in 2002 and whose author and source I will for the moment withhold:

> dispossessed races and classes face a Hobbesian choice. One possibility is to choose an identity that adapts to the dominant culture. But such an identity is adopted with the knowledge that full acceptance by members of the dominant culture is unlikely. Such a choice is also likely to be psychologically costly to oneself since it involves being someone 'different'; family and friends, who are also outside the dominant culture are likely also to have negative attitudes toward a maverick who has adopted it. Thus individuals are likely to feel that they can never fully 'pass'.

In the paragraph following this passage its author cites Du Bois's *The Souls of Black Folk*, but, unfortunately, without suggesting any direct indebtedness. The author is George Akerlof, winner in 2001 of what is popularly known as the Nobel Prize for Economics, and the passage quoted is from the paper he delivered when accepting the prize (Akerlof 2002, p. 427).

Economics

Akerlof has sought to show the role that intersubjectively determined group identities play in the distribution of income and in the shaping of economic agents. This project deserves every possible encouragement, but it is very far from being based on a new idea. A central thesis of Simone de Beauvoir's *The Second Sex* and of the materialist school of feminism (Christine Delphy, Colette Guillaumin, Monique Wittig, Ann Oakley, and so on) is that gender derives in large part from economic relations, especially divisions of labor by sex, not only between occupations, but also between paid and unpaid labor. This feminist argument is an application of the older and more general hypothesis that situations of work, including training for them, entail intersubjective effects that radically shape and reshape individual and groups of workers. A century of neoclassical hegemony seems to have erased from the profession's memory the fact that this hypothesis stood at the origins of modern economics and was fundamental to Adam Smith's 'principle of division of labour'. It is worth quoting Smith at length, if only to show that economists, in the beginning, neither denied intersubjective reality nor were maliciously disposed toward the great majority of humankind:

> The difference of natural talents in different men is, in reality, much less than we are aware of; and the very different genius which appears to distinguish men of different professions, when grown up to maturity, is not upon many occasions so much the cause as the effect of the division of labour. The difference between the most dissimilar characters, between a philosopher [economist] and a common street porter, for example, seems to arise not so much from nature as from habit, custom, and education. When they came into the world, and for the first six or eight years of their existence, they were perhaps very much alike, and neither their parents nor play-fellows could perceive any remarkable difference. About that age, or soon after, they come to be employed in very different occupations. The difference of talents comes then to be taken notice of, and widens by degrees, till at last the vanity of the philosopher is willing to acknowledge scarce any resemblance. (Smith, 1776, Book One, Chapter III, 1979, p. 120)

It seems to have gone almost unnoticed that neoclassical economics turned Smith's principle of division of labour upside down. Instead of the division of labour accounting for differences between individuals, the neoclassicists claim that the differences are already there and account for the kinds of jobs and positions in the work hierarchy that individuals and groups (e.g. races) occupy. The market, so goes their account, tends toward realizing the maximum efficient use of scarce resources, including their optimal development. Of course, it is not claimed that this story holds true in every case, but in the vast majority. This is neoclassicism's central message: the 'free' market system by and large deploys resources, especially human ones, in a manner that best develops and utilizes their capacity to generate output and then pays them the value of their marginal product. According to neoclassicism, the economic differences between adults are not, as Smith argued, due mainly to the way the market, for whatever reasons, discriminates between similarly endowed individuals, but rather to 'the difference of natural talents'.

This fundamental disagreement between Smith and the neoclassicists stems from the even more fundamental one which this chapter has been at pains to illuminate. In offering his principle of the division of labour, Smith assumes, like Du Bois and Beauvoir, that individual identities, and hence the differences between them, are primarily endogenous to the socio-economic process, that is, they are intersubjectively determined. He is not, of course, denying the existence of inherited differences, but rather accepting the fact that the human being is in large part a socio-economic creature, not only in its behaviour but also in its making and remaking. The neoclassicists, on the other hand, have postulated their axioms in the tradition of high Cartesianism. The economic agent is assumed – and the whole logical superstructure of the neoclassical enterprise stands on this Cartesian assumption – to enter into economic relations with other economic agents without being changed by them. Without this assumption, all of neoclassical economics' additive functions across populations of agents are non-existent.

Neoclassicism's hypothetical exogenizing of the economic agent resulted in changes in economics infinitely more fundamental than its abandonment of the labour theory of value. First, it effectively walled-off the greater part of the realm of economic phenomena from scholarly and scientific enquiry. In the name of axiomatic certainty, which it mistook for science, economics turned its back on some awkward but central empirical realities. Second, this cognitive disaster led to a moral one. Its turning its back on all economic phenomena that are not *intra*subjective, that do not conform to its Cartesian metaphysic, gave rise to a spurious naturalism and the unarticulated but culturally powerful line of racism and sexism that it logically entails (Fullbrook 2001). As George Akerlof gently puts it, 'Neoclassical theory suggests that poverty is the reflection of low initial endowments of human and nonhuman capital' (Akerlof 2002, p. 412). Poverty, as we all know, is not distributed evenly between races and sexes. So, when it is said that poverty reflects the 'low initial endowments' of the people suffering it, a statement is being made about natural differences between races and sexes.

Although the inculcation of such views in the young is deplorable, the impetus behind the creation of neoclassical economics 130 years ago seems to have been entirely innocent. It grew out of the marriage of two exceptionally powerful but rigidly limited strands of thought, the doctrine of the Cartesian or intrasubjective self, with which this chapter has been preoccupied, and the doctrine of Newtonian atomism, whose importance to the neoclassical project has been widely recognized. But significantly the union of the seventeenth century's most important metaphysical ideas did not take place for nearly 200 years. By then, the 1870s, the hegemony of both doctrines in their respective fields was waning. The challenge to the Cartesian self in philosophy and social theory already has been noted. Meanwhile, the development of thermodynamics and Maxwell's magnetic theory meant that the atomistic reductionism of classical mechanics no longer reigned on the frontiers of physics. But not so in the public imagination. Here mechanics was still king, and science was science only to the extent that it mimicked the Newtonian model. William Stanley Jevons (1835–1882), co-founder of neoclassical economics, was not only drawing on his general training in the natural sciences, but also playing to the public galleries when in the preface to *The Theory of Political Economy* (1871) he wrote:

> But as all the physical sciences have their basis more or less obviously in the general principles of mechanics, so all branches and divisions of economic science must be pervaded by certain general principles. It is to the investigation of such principles – to the tracing out of *the mechanics of self-interest and utility*, that this essay has been devoted. The establishment of such a theory is a necessary preliminary to any definite drafting of the superstructure of the aggregate science. (emphasis added) (Jevons 1970, p. 50)

Marie Léon Walras (1834–1910) begins and proceeds in the same vain in his *Elements of Pure Economics* (1874–1877) Alluding to the role of force and velocity in mechanics, he says:

> Similarly, … this pure theory of economics is a science which resembles the physico-mathematical sciences in every respect. This assertion is new and will seem strange; but I have just proved it to be true . (Walras 1984, p. 71)

Walras does not have just any mathematics in mind, but rather that of classical mechanics. In applying a mathematics to an empirical domain, the key question for the real scientist is always whether or not the structures described by the former are isomorphic to those found in the latter.

Today the question might never violate the thought processes of an economist trained in a priorism. But for Walras, trained as a mining engineer, this question would have been at the forefont of his mind. It is the 'proof' of an isomorphism between the differential calculus of classical mechanics and the economic phenomena of the marketplace (and thus also between economic and mechanical phenomena, i.e., Jevon's 'mechanics of self-interest and utility') that Walras sets out to demonstrate at the beginning of his treatise. As he well understood, everything that follows in his book depends on this 'proof'. Of what does it consist?

Well, of course, nothing empirical. Like Descartes, but in the name of science rather than of philosophy, Walras chooses to proceed definitionally, slicing up the universe into realms and assigning them the properties that will yield him his desired 'results'. We may, he says, 'divide the facts of our universe into two categories': '*natural* phenomena' and '*human* phenomena', whose essential difference, he proclaims, is that whereas the former result from 'blind and ineluctable forces', the latter result from human will which is 'self-conscious and independent' (Walras 1984, p. 61) By 'human will' Walras means the wills of individuals. This is the crucial Cartesian point. It is these wills, as Walras repeats numerous times, which are proclaimed *independent* and thus intrasubjective. But whereas Descartes devised this arrangement to relieve his philosopher's existential angst, Walras needs it to launch economics as 'a physico-mathematical science like mechanics' (Walras 1984, p. 71). This Cartesian self is mandatory if economic relations between human personalities are to be imagined as isomorphic to those between Newtonian bodies, that is, interacting but without altering their individual identities. A scientifically legitimate application of the mathematics of classical mechanics to economic phenomena requires this property of atomism. Without it, the individual supply and demand functions are not additive, thereby leaving the market or aggregate supply and demand functions undefined and, indeed, putting market analysis beyond the scope of the theory. But the neoclassical project's dependence on Cartesianism extends further. It also requires, as Walras emphasizes (pp. 61–2), Descartes' notion of self-consciousness: 'nothing is more easily or manifestly perceptible to me than my own mind' [Descartes 1641 [1970], p. 75). Post-Freud, no aspect of Cartesianism appears sillier and more untrue than this one. Nonetheless, neoclassical economics requires the crystalline self-knowledge of the Cartesian self in order to generate its putative functions. Having purged itself of the intersubjective dimension, it has only the self-knowledge of subjects hermetically sealed from influence from other subjects and their institutions to which to appeal for its hypothetical data for its 'mechanics of self-interest and utility', for its 'physico-mathematical science'.

In constructing his 'proof', Walras sketched an ontology that guaranteed, as he justly emphasized, the purity of his product. By eliminating the intersubjective, Walras created a make-believe world in which the social dimension of economic agency was decreed from existence. This sociopathic ontology has now dominated economics for over a century. In his back-of-the-envelope style, Walras explicitly defined its basic categories. It divides the entities of the universe 'into two great classes: *persons* and *things*. Whoever is not conscious of itself and not master of itself is a thing' (Walras 1984, p. 62). It 'divide[s] the facts of our universe into two categories': '*natural* phenomena' and '*human* phenomena' (p. 61). The latter is the product of human wills that are 'self-conscious and independent' (p. 61). The 'realm of human phenomena' consists of two and only two categories: 'human actions in respect to natural forces', e.g. mining, and 'relations between persons and persons' (p. 63) whose wills or subjective identities are independent of one another.

As we have seen, in the beginning modern economics did not duck the complexities of economic reality. I do not know when and where its intersubjective tradition began, only that in Adam Smith it was in good heart. And the neoclassical project need not have changed that. Neoclassicism is neither a useless nor an inherently intolerant, anti-scientific undertaking. Pretending that economic agents are radically different from how they are offers one point of view, even if a narrow one, from which to study economic reality. But the pseudo-science and fundamentalism that was already salient in Walras and Jevons became dominant in neoclassicism and has continued to be so down to the present day. Instead of contributing to a body of knowledge, neoclassical economics became a mandatory viewpoint, insisting that in matters economic it offered the only way to the truth. The result has been 'a triumph of ideology over science' (Stiglitz 2002b).

In the century since economics' autistic turning, many economists have tried, with varying degrees of influence, to effect its rehabilitation. Caroline Foley was the first off the mark. In 1893 she published in *The Economic Journal* a long and elegantly argued article titled 'Fashion' (Foley 1893; Fullbrook 1998), which not only called for the re-expansion of economics' conceptual framework so as to include intersubjective demand phenomena, but also pointed out that rising standards of living cause consumer demands to become ever less closely tied to biological needs so that intersubjective factors enter increasingly into demand determination. Late the following year Thorstein Veblen not only took up Foley's challenge but also her approach when he published 'The economic theory of woman's dress', launching in his middle-age the line of intersubjective analysis for which he is celebrated (Veblen 1894). The whole institutionalist school to which Veblen's work gave rise was committed to considering economic agents as social beings. In the United States in the 1920s the Institutionalists briefly threatened the neoclassical hegemony before rapidly losing ground. Keynes's *General Theory* (1936), as well as some more traditional business cycle theories, turned on aggregate intersubjective effects, and with the post-war rise of Keynesianism it appeared that economics might, not just on the margins but in the main, escape from its Cartesian prison. But once again it was not to be. Led by John Hicks and Paul Samuelson, the neoclassicists marketed an emasculated Keynesian analysis, one without intersubjective agents, and succeeded in turning back the clock. Even John Kenneth Galbraith, whose work added much to the intersubjective tradition, could not reverse or even halt the retrogression. By the end of the 1980s any economist expressing professional concern with the intersubjective dimension of economic reality risked being assigned to the outer reaches of heterogeneity.

But what about the rise of game theory? One might say that because game theory is explicitly about direct interactions between individuals, it is about intersubjectivity. Such reasoning, however, misses the central thrust of this chapter. Classical mechanics is also explicitly about interactions between individuals and how their interactions change their behaviour. The criterion for intersubjectivity methodology is not whether or not interactions take place between human individuals but rather whether those interactions are conceptualized as sometimes changing those individuals' subjective characteristics.

Does game theory conceptualize human agents as intersubjective? In the main, no. It describes how in game-like situations agents choose strategies *given exogenously fixed* utility functions which represent the agents' subjectivities. (This is true even of Lewis 1969.) But what about 'evolutionary' game theory (e.g. Samuelson, 2002)? Despite its name, this appears to be a dead-end for intersubjective analysis. A byproduct of evolutionary biology, where the 'players' are species and genes, its novel feature is that it treats players as hard-wired with particular strategies and therefore without the freedom to change, not only their ends, but also their strategic means.

A more promising route for bringing game theory to bear on some subset of intersubjective economic phenomena is Thomas Schelling's (1960) 'coordination game' approach. André Orléan (2003), seeking to understand 'the inter-subjective and self-referential dynamics' (p. 179) of stock markets, has used it to achieve what is in effect a formalization of Keynes's famous beauty contest parable (1936). Drawing on Shiller (1991), Orléan shows how a group belief can emerge autonomously relative to the beliefs of the group's individual members and them become part of those individuals' belief systems.

But there is much more to understanding the role of intersubjectivity in economic reality than formalization, let alone game theory, can reveal. Recent years have witnessed, despite the surge in neoclassical fundamentalism, new beginnings and growing respectability for intersubjective economics. And the new interest is diverse, not only geographically but also in terms of research programmes and topics: in France the French Intersubjectivists (Aglictta and Orléan 2002; Dupuy 1989, 1991, 2002; Levy 2002; Orléan 1989, 1990, 1992, 1998; Thévenot 2002), in the UK the Critical Realists (Fleetwood 1996; Lawson 1997, 1999; Lewis and Runde 2002), in the US hybrid offshoots of Critical Realism (Davis 2002), in France, the US and the UK Feminist Economics (Delphy 1984; Delphy and Leonard 1992; Feiner 1994, Nelson 1995; Barker and Feiner 2003); in Switzerland and elsewhere Experimental Economics (Fehr and Falk 2002; Fehr and Schmidt 1999), in the UK and US a new wave of Institutional Economics (Hodgson 1998, 2002; Mayhew 2002), as well as dispersed and assorted independents (Ackerman 2002; Akerlof 2002; Dow 1990; Fullbrook 2001, 2002, Hargreaves Heap 2002; Kaul 2002; Ormerod 2002; Rizvi 2002; Sofianou 1995; Stiglitz 2002a; Wynarczyk 2002). Will these and other developments lead to freeing economics from Descartes' legacy, enabling it to reconnect with Adam Smith's tradition?

Note
1. There is of course also 'intersubjectivity' in the modern epistemological and procedural sense of the testing of hypothesizes.

References
Ackerman, Frank (2002), 'Flaws in the foundation: consumer behavior and general equilibrium theory', in Edward Fullbrook (ed), *Intersubjectivity in Economics: Agents and Structures*, London and New York: Routledge, pp. 56–70.

Aglietta, Michel, and André Orléan (2002) *La Monnaie entre violence et confiance*, Paris: Odile Jacob.

Akerlof, George (2002), 'Behavioral macroeconomics and macroeconomic behavior', *American Economic Review*, June 2002, **92** (3), 411–33.

Barker, Drucilla K. and Susan Feiner (2004), *Liberating Economics: Feminist Perspectives on Families, Work and Globalization*, Ann Arbor MI: University of Michigan Press.

Bergson, Henri (1896 [1991]), *Matter and Memory*, translated by N.M. Paul and W.S. Palmer, New York: Zone Books.

Brentano, Franz (1874 [1995]), *Psychology from an Empirical Standpoint*, translated by Linda L. McAlister and D.B. Terrell, London: Routledge.

Davis, John B. (2002), 'Collective intentionality and individual behavior', in Edward Fullbrook (ed.), *Intersubjectivity in Economics: Agents and Structures*, London and New York: Routledge, pp. 11–27.

Delphy, Christine (1984), *Close to Home*, London: Hutchinson.

Delphy, Christine, and Diana Leonard (1992), *Familiar Exploitation: A New Analysis of Marriage in Contemporary Western Society*, Oxford: Polity Press.

Descartes, René (1637 [1965]), *A Discourse on Method*, translated by E.S. Haldane and G.R.T. Ross, New York: Washington Square Press.

Descartes, René (1641 [1970]), 'Meditations on first philosophy', translated by E. Anscombe and P.T. Geach in *Descartes Philosophical Writings*, London: Open University.

Dow, Sheila C. (1990), 'Beyond dualism', *Cambridge Journal of Economics*, **14** (2), 143–57.

Du Bois, W.E.B. (1903 [1965]), *The Souls of Black Folk*, in *Three Negro Classics*, New York: Avon.

Dupuy, Jean-Pierre (1989), 'Convention et common knowledge', *Revue économique*, 2 March, 361–400.

Dupuy, Jean-Pierre (1991), *La Panique*, Paris: Les empêcheurs de penser en round.

Dupuy, Jean-Pierre (2002), 'Market, imitation and tradition: Hayek vs. Keynes', in Edward Fullbrook (ed.) *Intersubjectivity in Economics: Agents and Structures*, London and New York: Routledge, pp. 139–58.

Elias, Norbert (1978), *What Is Sociology?*, London: Hutchinson.

Fehr, Ernst, and Armin Falk (2002), 'Reciprocal fairness, cooperation and limits to competition', in Edward Fullbrook (ed.), *Intersubjectivity in Economics: Agents and Structures*, London and New York: Routledge, pp. 28–55.

Fehr, Ernst, and K. Schmidt (1999), 'A theory of fairness, competition and cooperation', *Quarterly Journal of Economics*, **144**, 817–51.

Feiner, Susan (ed.) (1994), *Race and Gender in the American Economy: Views Across the Spectrum*, New York: Prentice-Hall.

Fleetwood, Steve (1996), 'Order without equilibrium: a critical realist interpretation of Hayek's notion of spontaneous order', *Cambridge Journal of Economics*, **20** (6), November, pp. 729–48.

Foley, Caroline A. (1893), 'Fashion', *Economic Journal*, **3**, September, 458–74.

Fullbrook, Edward (1996), 'Consumer metaphysics: the neoclassicists versus the intersubjectivists', *Archives of Economic History*, **vii**, (1), 53–74.

Fullbrook, Edward (1997), 'Post-modernising homo economicus', in Steven Earnshaw (ed.), *Just Postmodernism*, Amsterdam and Atlanta: Rodopi, pp. 67–87.

Fullbrook, Edward (1998), 'Caroline Foley and the theory of intersubjective demand', *Journal of Economic Issues*, **XXXII** (3), 709–31.

Fullbrook, Edward (2001), 'Conceptual displacement: from the natural to the social', *Review of Political Economy*, **LIX** (3), 285–96.

Fullbrook, Edward (2002), 'An intersubjective theory of value', in Edward Fullbrook (ed.), *Intersubjectivity in Economics: Agents and Structures*, London and New York: Routledge, pp. 273–99.

de Gouges, Olympe (1791 [1989]), *The Declaration of the Rights of Woman and the Female Citizen*, Pythia.

Hargreaves Heap, Shaun P. (2002), "Everybody is talking about it': intersubjectivity and the television industry', in Edward Fullbrook (ed.), *Intersubjectivity in Economics: Agents and Structures*, London and New York: Routledge, pp. 123–38.

Hodgson, Geoffrey M. (1998), 'The approach of institutional economics', *Journal of Economic Literature*, **XXXVI**, March, 166–92.

Hodgson, Geoffrey M. (2002), 'Reconstitutive downward causation: social structure and the development of individual agency', in Edward Fullbrook (ed), *Intersubjectivity in Economics: Agents and Structures*, London and New York: Routledge, pp. 159–80.

Honderich, Ted (ed.) (1995), *The Oxford Companion to Philosophy*, Oxford: Oxford University Press, 1995.

Hume, David (1739–40 [1978]), *A Treatise of Human Nature*, Oxford: Oxford University Press.

Jevons, William Stanley (1871 [1970]), *The Theory of Political Economy*, Harmondsworth England: Pelican.

Kant, Immanuel (1781 [2003]), *Critique of Pure Reason*, translated by Norman Kemp Smith, London: Palgrave Mcmillan.

Kaul, Nitasha (2002), 'A critical 'post to critical realism', *Cambridge Journal of Economics*, **26** (6), 709–26.

Keynes, John Maynard (1936), *The General Theory of Employment, Interest and Money*, London: Macmillan.

Lawson, Tony (1997), *Economics and Reality*, London: Routledge.

Lawson, Tony (1999), 'What has realism got to do with it?', *Economics and Philosophy*, **15**, 269–82.

Levy, Thierry (2002), 'The theory of conventions and a new theory of the firm', in Edward Fullbrook (ed.), *Intersubjectivity in Economics: Agents and Structures*, London and New York: Routledge, pp. 254–72.

Lewis, David (1969), *Convention*, Cambridge, MA: Harvard University Press.

Lewis, Paul, and Jochen Runde (2002), 'Intersubjectivity in the socio-economic world: a critical realist perspective', in Edward Fullbrook (ed.), *Intersubjectivity in Economics: Agents and Structures*, London and New York: Routledge, pp. 198–215.

Locke, John (1690 [1993]), *An Essay Concerning Human Understanding*, London: Dent.

Mayhew, Anne (2002), 'All consumption is conspicuous', in Edward Fullbrook (ed.), *Intersubjectivity in Economics: Agents and Structures*, London and New York: Routledge, pp. 43–55.

Mirowski, Philip (1989), *More Heat Than Light*, New York: Cambridge University Press.

Nelson, Julie A. (1995), *Feminism, Objectivity and Economics*, London: Routledge.

Orléan, André (1989), 'Pour une approche cognitive des conventions économiques', *Revue économique*, **2** March, 241–72.

Orléan, André (1990), 'Le role des influences interpersonnelles dans la formation des cours boursieers', *Revue économique*, **5**, September, 839–68.

Orléan, André (1992), 'Contagion des opinions et founctionnement des marchés financiers', *Revue économique*, **4**, July, 685–98.

Orléan, André (1998), 'La monnaie autoréférentielle: réflexions sur les évolutions monétaires contemporaines', in Michel Aglietta and André Orléan (eds), *La Monnaie souveraine*, Paris: Odile Jacob, pp. 359–86.

Orléan, André (2003), 'What is a collective belief', in P. Bourgine and J.-P. Nadal (eds), *Cognitive Economics*, Berlin: Springer-Verlag, pp. 171–84.

Ormerod, Paul (2002), 'Social networks and information', in Edward Fullbrook (ed.), *Intersubjectivity in Economics: Agents and Structures*, London and New York: Routledge, pp. 216–30.

Petit, Jean-Luc (1999), 'Constitution by movement: Husserl in light of recent neurobiological findings', in Jean Petitot, Francisco J. Varela, Bernard Pachard and Jean-Michel Roy (eds), *Naturalizing Phenomenology: Issues in Contemporary Phenomenology and Cognitive Science*, Stanford, CA: Stanford University Press, pp. 220–44.

Poster, Mark (1975), *Existential Marxism in Postwar France*, Princeton, NJ: Princeton University Press.

Rawls, John (1971), *A Theory of Justice*, Cambridge, MA: Harvard University Press.

Rizvi, S. Abu Turab (2002), 'Adam Smith's sympathy: towards a normative economics', in Edward
Fullbrook (ed.), *Intersubjectivity in Economics: Agents and Structures*, London and New York:
Routledge, pp. 241–53

Russell, Bertrand (1912 [1967]), *The Problems of Philosophy*, Oxford: Oxford University Press.

Samuelson, Larry (2002), 'Evolution and game theory', *Journal of Economic Perspectives*, **16**
(2) Spring, 47–66.

Schelling, Thomas (1960 [1977]), *The Strategy of Conflict*, Oxford: Oxford University Press.

Shiller, R. (1991), *Market Volatility*, Cambridge, MA: Massachusetts Institute of Technology
Press.

Smith, Adam (1776 [1979]), *The Wealth of Nations*, Harmondsworth: Pelican.

Sofianou, Evanthia (1995), 'Post-modernism and the notion of rationality in economics', *Cambridge
Journal of Economics*, **19** (2), 373–90.

Stiglitz, Joseph E. (2002a), 'Information and the change in the paradigm in economics', *American
Economic Review*, **92** (3), 460–501.

Stiglitz, Joseph E. (2002b), 'There is no invisible hand', *The Guardian*, 20 December 2002.

Thévenot, Laurent (2002), 'Conventions of co-ordination and the framing of uncertainty', in Edward
Fullbrook (ed.), *Intersubjectivity in Economics: Agents and Structures*, London and New York:
Routledge, pp. 181–97.

Veblen, Thorstein (1894 [1934]), 'The economic theory of woman's dress', *Popular Science
Monthly*, December, pp. 198–205, reprinted in L.A. Ardzroomi (ed.), *Essays in Our Changing
Order*, New York: Viking Press.

Walras, Léon (1874–77, [1984]), *Elements of Pure Economics: or the Theory of Social Wealth*,
translated by William Jaffé, Philadelphia: Orion Editons.

Wollstonecraft, Mary (1792 [1992]), *A Vindication of the Rights of Woman and the Female Citizen*,
London: Penguin Books.

Wynarczyk, Peter (2002), 'The economics of criminal participation: radical subjectivist and
intersubjectivist critiques', in Edward Fullbrook (ed.), *Intersubjectivity in Economics: Agents
and Structures*, London and New York: Routledge, pp. 105–21.

21 Information, knowledge and modelling economic agency

*Philip Faulkner and Jochen Runde**

Introduction

The relationship between the information available to economic actors and what they are presumed to know, and then how and in what form this knowledge informs their actions, raises some of the most difficult questions in economics. This chapter concentrates on how the relationship between information and knowledge is treated in mainstream microeconomic theory. Our aim is to establish that even in models that relax the standard assumption that actors have 'perfect' knowledge, this typically amounts to no more than introducing small 'black spots' into the otherwise unlimitedly sharp and comprehensive knowledge that they are assumed to have of their model 'world'. We then identify some different ways in which this approach, while useful in some respects, fails to address some important aspects of the relationship between information and knowledge as they arise in actual economic situations.

Our argument begins with a brief account of what we mean by information and knowledge. The paper then splits into two halves. The first explores the mainstream economics perspective on information and knowledge by way of a detailed examination of a representative game theoretic model. The second considers three aspects of the relationship between information and knowledge that are largely neglected on the mainstream approach: non-probabilistic forms of uncertainty and ignorance, the subjectivity of knowledge, and tacit knowledge. We here touch on themes related to the treatment of rational agency in economics that also arise in other chapters in this volume, particularly those of Frey and Benz, Hargreaves Heap, Lewis and Fullbrook, but focusing exclusively on the nature and extent of the knowledge that can be attributed to economic factors.

Information and knowledge

Let us begin with what we mean by information and knowledge and what we see as the connection between them. By information we mean any kind of datum, potentially accessible to us via personal experience or indirectly via the report of others, the apprehension of which could be a source of knowledge. By

* This chapter is a descendant of work that first appeared in Philip Faulkner's 2003 Cambridge PhD dissertation.

datum we mean a fact, for example that something exists, has occurred, and so on.[1] While the particular things we choose to isolate as facts, and how we see, assess and state them, always depend on us to some extent, whether or not our statements can indeed be regarded as statements of fact will depend on how accurately they express what it is that they are referring to. When we refer to information in what follows, then, we mean properties of, or facts about, the world under consideration.

By knowledge we mean the beliefs and capabilities that we acquire and develop from exposure to information of different kinds. Now beliefs and capabilities are different things and it is important that they be kept apart. Let us begin with beliefs. The key issue that arises here is how good our beliefs have to be in order to count as knowledge. Clearly not any belief will do. In the philosophical literature it is often assumed that true belief is a necessary condition for knowledge. Some philosophers go even further and argue that justification, when added to true belief, is a necessary and sufficient condition for knowledge.[2]

As will become evident below, mainstream microeconomic theory tends to equate knowledge with true belief. Further, and as we shall also show below, it usually assumes that actors' beliefs map onto their model 'worlds' in a one-to-one way, thereby collapsing the distinction between information and knowledge. The trouble, of course, is that our beliefs don't correspond to the world in a simple one-to-one way. For the content of our beliefs is dependent in part on more or less contingent descriptions, which are affected by our attitudes, interests, biases and ways of seeing things. And even where they are accurate in some respects, our beliefs are usually partial and often fragmentary. If my watch is running three minutes fast, for example, my beliefs about the time will only be approximately true at best, and yet still be good enough to avoid any disruption in my schedule.

There is no easy way around these complications. If we set the standard for what counts as knowledge too high, we will exclude many of the beliefs that serve us very well. By the same token, if we set the standard too low we run the risk of including beliefs that verge on the plain false. Indeed, even the idea of a standard is questionable in this context, since it suggests that there is some absolute criterion by which we could adjudicate between that which is knowledge and that which is not. Better, perhaps, to recognise that what counts as knowledge itself depends on context. That way we could say that we have knowledge of the time for most purposes even when our watch is three minutes fast, although our beliefs wouldn't qualify as knowledge if we were estimating how long we have to escape a time bomb that is about to explode. For the purposes of what follows, then, we shall regard beliefs as knowledge when they are (approximately) true relative to the context in which they play a part.[3]

We also mentioned that knowledge could take the form of capabilities rather than beliefs. What we were referring to here is knowledge on which economic actors draw, but which is not of the propositional form to which the predicates true or false might apply (knowledge that), but of the subconscious, tacit variety (knowledge how). Tacit knowledge is also something that is acquired through exposure to information via example, observing the behaviour of others, and so on, as well as being the product of mimesis, practice and repetition. We shall defer further discussion of tacit knowledge until later in this chapter, where we consider the impact of its neglect in standard mainstream models of the sort we discuss in the next two sections.

A game of complete information

In this section and the next we consider the treatment of information and knowledge in mainstream microeconomic theory. We do so using the example of a one-shot Cournot duopoly game, first under conditions of what game theorists call 'complete information' and then, in the next section, under conditions of 'incomplete information'.[4] We have chosen this example, partly because it is simple and compact enough to be considered in full, but mainly because it is highly representative of the kind of analytical approach widely adopted in contemporary economics. Our aim in this section is to demonstrate the conventional assumption that actors' knowledge of the contents of their 'model world' corresponds exactly to the formal expression of that world. That is, knowledge and information in these models coincide perfectly. In the section that follows, we argue that even in models that explicitly recognise that information and knowledge are not coextensive, this amounts only to introducing small 'black spots' into the otherwise perfect knowledge attributed to the actors concerned.

A game is one of complete information if the structure of the game (the moves, the payoffs, and so on) is common knowledge to all of the players.[5] The particular game we shall consider here involves two firms, A and B, in competition as the sole suppliers of a homogenous good. The firms simultaneously choose their preferred output (q_A and q_B), each knowing that total demand for the good is characterised by the inverse demand function:

$$P(Q) = a - Q,$$

where $Q = q_A + q_B$ in equilibrium. The firms employ identical technologies, such that the total cost to firm i of producing a quantity q_i is:

$$C(q_i) = cq_i.$$

We assume that $a > Q$ in equilibrium (such that the market clears at a strictly positive price) and that $c < a$. The structure of the game is assumed to be common knowledge, something we return to after we have reviewed the solution to the game.

The standard game-theoretic solution to the one-shot Cournot game with complete information is the Nash equilibrium. This involves determining a pair of strategies, one for each firm, such that each firm is maximising its payoff given the strategy being played by the other. Strategies for each firm are simply quantities, and payoffs the firms' profits. Expressed as a function of the strategies chosen by each firm, profits for firm i given firm j's output are:

$$\pi_i(q_i, q_j) = q_i[P(q_i + q_j) - c] = q_i[a - (q_i + q_j) - c].$$

The strategy pair $(q_A{}^*, q_B{}^*)$ is a Nash equilibrium if, for each firm i, $q_i{}^*$ solves the maximisation problem:

$$\max \pi_i(q_i, q_j{}^*) = \max q_i[a - (q_i + q_j{}^*) - c].$$

The first-order condition for this problem, which is both necessary and sufficient given the assumptions we have made about demand and technology is:

$$q_i = \tfrac{1}{2}(a - q_j{}^* - c).$$

This means that for the strategy pair $(q_A{}^*, q_B{}^*)$ to be a Nash equilibrium, the firms' quantity choices must satisfy:

$$q_A{}^* = \tfrac{1}{2}(a - q_B{}^* - c)$$
$$q_B{}^* = \tfrac{1}{2}(a - q_A{}^* - c)$$

Simultaneously solving this pair of equations yields the Nash equilibrium pair of strategies:

$$q_A{}^* = q_B{}^* = \tfrac{1}{3}(a - c)$$

The model having been set up and solved, our interest now is in the assumptions about information and knowledge that the model makes.[6] Remember that we defined information as any datum, the apprehension of which could be a source of knowledge. In the context of the 'model world' we have just considered, then, information consists exactly of no more and no less than the formal statement of the model:

1. The Players
The players consist of two firms that:

- produce a single, identical product;
- are fully described by their identical cost functions; and
- are rational in the sense that they are single-minded in their goal of profit maximisation and perfect reasoners in the sense that they do not make any slips or other mistakes of reasoning, choose consistently, and are able to deduce the full logical consequences of all the knowledge that is attributed to them.

2. The Environment
The environment consists of

- the demand conditions for the good being produced, that is, the inverse demand function; and
- the restrictions that $a > Q$ in equilibrium and $c < a$.

The entities, properties and restrictions listed above exhaust the 'world' of the Cournot game. Considering now what the two players are assumed to know about their world, we said earlier that the game is one of 'complete information' in the terminology of game theory, meaning that the structure of the game is common knowledge to both players. This means, in the first place, that both firms know not only their own characteristics, but also those of their competitor and the market they are operating in. Knowing, here, amounts to a perfect one-to-one correspondence between actors' beliefs about each aspect of their model world and the formal expression of those aspects. That is to say, actors are assumed to know their world in terms of exactly the same mathematical expressions in which it is written down (i.e. there are no ambiguities, misinterpretations, and so on, which it is of course one of the purposes of formal analysis to ensure). The model we have reviewed is thus very much in accordance with the so-called 'perfect knowledge' assumption of standard neoclassical theory.[7] In the second place, it means that what each firm is assumed to know about the other firm's knowledge takes a particular form. Specifically, not only does Firm A know everything about the world it operates in, it also knows that Firm B knows everything about its world, and that Firm B knows that Firm A knows everything, and so on. The same applies with respect to Firm B's knowledge of what Firm A knows.

It will be apparent that the assumption of complete information is a demanding one, and the last thirty years or so have seen a great deal of work in economic theory aimed at investigating the consequences of relaxing it (see Stiglitz's (1994) review of the so-called 'information theoretic' approach to economic analysis). We shall attempt to convey the flavour of this approach and the modelling strategy it adopts, by introducing a restriction on the knowledge of one of the firms in the Cournot game.

A game of incomplete information

We now assume that both firms know everything about their 'world' that they knew before, *except* that firm A does not know firm B's costs (perhaps because B has developed new technology or is a recent entrant into the market). The game becomes one of incomplete information in the terminology of game theory, since the structure of the game is no longer common knowledge to both firms. As will become apparent, this version of the game breaks with the assumption of a one-to-one correspondence between information and knowledge in the game of complete information considered in the preceding section.

How does the introduction of incomplete information change the game theoretic analysis of the Cournot duopoly? In order for game theory to get going, some specific form must be given to Firm A's ignorance of Firm B's costs, so that in turn some form can be given to A's knowledge of the payoffs it faces. The standard move here, originally suggested by Harsanyi (1967), is to suppose that while firm A does not know Firm B's true costs, it does know that Firm B is one of a given set of possible 'types' of firm, where each type is distinguished by its costs. For example, in the simple case we will consider here, Firm B is one of only two possible types, either 'low' cost or 'high' cost. The crucial assumption here is that the contents of Firm A's beliefs with respect to Firm B's type can be expressed probabilistically. For in this way Firm A's payoffs (profits) can be constructed in terms of expected profits conditional on Firm's B's type.

If we now consider the solution to our one-shot Cournot game with asymmetric information, the only change to the model is that Firm A knows that Firm B's marginal costs are c_H with probability p and c_L with probability $(1 - p)$. This is common knowledge, as is the fact that Firm B knows both its costs and those of Firm A. The rest of the model is as before. The two firms compete by simultaneously choosing their desired level of output, knowing that the price they will receive for each unit of output is given by the inverse demand function:

$$P(Q) = a - Q.$$

The solution concept applicable to static games of incomplete information is the Bayesian Nash equilibrium, which requires a strategy to be specified for each possible type of player.[8] Given that Firm A's cost function is:

$$C_A(q_A) = cq_A,$$

and Firm B's cost function:

$$C_B(q_B) = c_H q_B \text{ with probability } p$$

$$C_B(q_B) = c_L q_B \text{ with probability } (1 - p).$$

we can determine the maximisation problem that each type of firm faces.[9] Let $q_B{}^*(c_H)$ and $q_B{}^*(c_L)$ denote Firm B's quantity choices as a function of its cost, and let $q_A{}^*$ denote firm A's quantity choice.

If firm B's cost is high, it chooses $q_B{}^*(c_H)$ to solve:

$$\max \; [(a - q_A{}^* - q_B) - c_H]q_B.$$

If firm B's cost is low, it chooses $q_B{}^*(c_L)$ to solve:

$$\max \; [(a - q_A{}^* - q_B) - c_L]q_B.$$

Firm A knows that firm B's cost is high with probability p and should anticipate that firm B's quantity choice will be $q_B{}^*(c_H)$ or $q_B{}^*(c_L)$, depending on its costs. Thus firm A chooses $q_A{}^*$ to solve:

$$\max \; p[(a - q_A - q_B{}^*(c_H)) - c]q_A + (1 - p)[(a - q_A - q_B{}^*(c_L)) - c]q_A$$

so as to maximise expected profit. The first-order conditions for these three optimisation problems are:

$$q_B{}^*(c_H) = \tfrac{1}{2}(a - q_A{}^* - c_H)$$
$$q_B{}^*(c_L) = \tfrac{1}{2}(a - q_A{}^* - c_L)$$
$$q_A{}^* = \tfrac{1}{2}(a - c - p q_B{}^*(c_H) - (1 - p)q_B{}^*(c_L))$$

Assuming that the two firms' costs are not too different – if they are, then the high-cost firm produces nothing – these first-order conditions characterise the solutions to the earlier maximisation problems. Solving the first-order conditions gives:

$$q_B{}^*(c_H) = \tfrac{1}{3}(a - 2c_H + c) + \tfrac{1}{6}(1 - p)(c_H - c_L)$$
$$q_B{}^*(c_L) = \tfrac{1}{3}(a - 2c_L + c) - \tfrac{1}{6}p(c_H - c_L)$$
$$q_A{}^* = \tfrac{1}{3}(a - 2c + pc_H + (1 - p)c_L)$$

which corresponds to the Bayesian Nash equilibrium of the game. Comparing the solution of this Cournot game with incomplete information, to the earlier Cournot game with complete information, we can say that a 'high-cost' ('low-cost') type Firm *B* produces more (less) in equilibrium when Firm *A* is ignorant of Firm *B*'s type as compared with the complete information case, since Firm *B* knows that Firm *A* is maximising expected, rather than actual, profit.

As before, we wish to examine the information and knowledge contained in the game. To save repetition however, let us focus on what has changed now that we have introduced an asymmetry into what the firms know. In terms of the information in the model, we simply observe that for whatever reason, Firm *A* conceives of there being two possible cost-types of Firm *B* and attaches a certain probability to the likelihood of each. The set of types and the probability distribution are information according to our definition, as is the fact that Firm *A* is an *expected* profit maximiser.

Let us now consider the knowledge that the game presumes firms to possess. Firm *B* continues to have full knowledge, in the sense that its knowledge corresponds exactly with the information in the game. On the other hand the scenario was designed to allow for Firm *A*'s knowledge to be limited in some respect. It is now clear how the game theoretic analysis of such situations restricts the limitations we can impose on a player's knowledge. Although we started with the assumption that Firm *A* was ignorant of Firm *B*'s costs, in solving the game we have that Firm *A* is far from ignorant. Rather, Firm *A* knows accurately the set of possible cost-types of Firm *B* and the probability distribution with which nature draws the particular type.[10] It is for this reason that we say that Firm *A* merely suffers from a 'black spot' in its knowledge of Firm *B*'s costs, so as to highlight the particular structure that game-theoretic analysis imposes on the knowledge (and ignorance) of the two firms.

This kind of approach is widely employed in the economics of information, namely to begin with a world in which all information is transparent and available to the actors concerned (one-to-one relationship between information and knowledge) and then to study what happens when there is some perturbation, namely when one or more of the actors involved suffers a 'black spot' (and where the usual move is to replace knowledge of a certain outcome or state of affairs with certain knowledge of a list of possible outcomes or states of affairs with their associated probabilities). While models of this kind are illuminating in some respects, they gloss over the differences between information and knowledge and, accordingly, the ways in which these differences may matter for the way that we think about economic phenomena. Our claim then is that such a modelling approach necessarily limits the mainstream microeconomic analysis of imperfect knowledge. We now move on to discuss some important aspects of economic agency that are neglected or obscured on the mainstream approach.

Uncertainty and ignorance

The first feature of the mainstream approach to information and knowledge that we consider concerns its treatment of uncertainty and its neglect of a certain kind of ignorance. This will require us to look in a little more detail at the model of the economic actor most widely used in mainstream analyses of decision-making under uncertainty, the expected utility (EU) model. Originally devised with non-strategic 'games' against nature in mind (e.g. Savage 1954), the EU model reduces the actor's decision problem to the following basic components: (1) a set of feasible 'acts' a_i ($i = 1, 2, ..., m$), (2) a set of exhaustive and mutually exclusive 'states of the world' s_j ($j = 1, 2, ..., n$) and (3) a set of consequences, one for every act/state pair, c_{ij}. According to the EU hypothesis, and subject to certain postulates of 'rational choice' such as the Savage Axioms, a cardinal utility $U(a_i)$ may be attached to each act. The argument then proceeds in two stages. In the first, numerical indicators of utility $u_i = u(c_{ij})$ are assigned to each consequence.[11] Then, in the second, and given the probabilities representing the actor's beliefs about the states of nature p_j ($j = 1, 2, ..., n$), the expected utility of each act is expressed as the mathematical expectation of the utility of the consequences:

$$U\left(a_i\right) = \sum_{j=1}^{n} p_j u\left(c_{ij}\right)$$

The decision rule associated with the EU model is to select that act which offers an expected utility that is at least as high as that of any other act.

While the EU model dominates mainstream analyses of decision-making under uncertainty, such a simple model is inevitably a highly stylised representation of actual human behaviour.[12] Here we restrict ourselves to commenting on the conception of uncertainty associated with the EU model, in particular considering the extent to which it captures the nature and severity of the kinds of uncertainties decisions-makers actually face in their day-to-day lives. We shall concentrate on two points that are often raised in this respect: the particular way that the EU model represents uncertainty and its neglect of an important form of ignorance.

Uncertainty in the EU model arises from the decision-maker not knowing which of the possible states of the world will be realised (except in degenerate cases where the probability of some state is 1) and, hence, which consequence will actually follow from each act under consideration. This uncertainty is quantified by way of a classical probability distribution defined over the set of states, with questions concerning the nature and source of these probabilities typically ignored by this approach. In many EU models the probabilities in question are simply assumed to correspond to objective frequencies, while in other cases, where objective frequencies are not available, theorists fall back on a subjectivist or 'Bayesian' conception of probability. On the subjectivist view, rational actors are simply assumed to have numerically definite personal probabilities about random events at the back of their minds at all times, which they update in a Bayesian fashion.

While some of the decision-situations we encounter in day-to-day life clearly are of the sort that involves obvious (or at least calculable) objective frequencies, such situations are actually rather rare. Much more common is the case in which people do not have access to such probabilities and are forced to fall back on their own judgements. The difficulty here, expressed by authors sympathetic to the views on uncertainty in economic life expressed by Keynes (1973) and Knight (1921), is the implausibility of the assumption that decision-makers always act 'as-if' they have numerically definite probabilities at the back of their minds in such situations (see McCann in this volume and Runde 2001 for a survey and discussion of some of the issues involved). Contrary to the EU model, people are often found to violate this assumption, even in straightforward and transparent situations.[13] Furthermore, many important aspects of economic behaviour may be the consequence of people not being able to form precise probability estimates in the way assumed on the EU approach. There are numerous examples here, including convention-following on stock markets (Bibow et al. 2003; Dequech 1999); rule-following, habits and behavioural routines (Cyert and March 1992; Hodgson 1997; Vanberg 1994); and the incompleteness, rigidity and long-term nature of wage contracts (Mukerji 1998; Williamson 1985).

The second issue we want to raise relating to the EU model concerns the assumption that actors always know the full set of mutually exclusive possible states of the world relevant to their decision problems.[14,15] As will again be familiar enough from ordinary experience, it is often very difficult to fulfil this requirement. There are three main reasons for this. First, even if the decision-maker has a reasonably good idea of what the range of possible eventualities might be, there remains an unavoidable element of arbitrariness in the framing of decision problems, in deciding where the boundary is between one state and the next, and so on (see the discussion of the 'Background' below). Second, coming up with a full list of possible outcomes in a decision problem often requires more in the way of attention and imagination than many decision-makers have. And third, it has been suggested that actors may sometimes be unable to come up with the full set of eventualities, not for epistemic reasons, but because these eventualities may not even exist as possibilities at the time of decision (Shackle 1972).

Considered together, the kind of non-quantifiable uncertainties and ignorance described above are both cause and consequence of the indeterminacy that characterises much of economic life. They are a cause because, in the absence of sharp probabilities and well-defined states, actors are forced to rely on conjectures about what the consequences of their action might be. As these conjectures are the product of the imagination, and as the imagination is not bound by what went on before, they represent an important source of novelty in human affairs when acted upon (Shackle 1972). They are the consequence of indeterminacy, because it is precisely because actors in an open world do not have full knowledge that they are driven to fall back on them. Now of course indeterminacies are common also in the sharply defined worlds of game theory, indeed sometimes even in the most simple of games.[16] But the possibilities in these models are always pre-specified and therefore limited, and hence offer no scope for vague probabilities, novelty and surprise (unless it is one of the actors doing something 'irrational' like choosing a dominated strategy, behaviour that is ruled out by assumption). And this in turn means that these models, and more specifically the standard assumptions about information and knowledge that they embody, do not have the resources to accommodate economic phenomena in which vague probabilities, novelty and surprise are important: previously unimagined moves by firms in a competitive environment, the notion of entrepreneurial 'alertness' associated with the Austrian conception of the market process, and so on.

The subjectivity of knowledge

An important characteristic of mainstream models of the sort we reviewed earlier is that the actors within them know their world as, and in exactly the same mathematical terms in which, it is written down by the economist, save of course where one or more of the actors suffer some or other 'black spot'. With this exception, actors in these models are endowed with a God's-eye view of their world, there being effectively a one-to-one relation between that world as it is and what they know about it.

One thing that this conception ignores is that the knowledge we have of our circumstances is in general highly subjective, being dependent on our intentions and desires, past experiences and knowledge, geographical and temporal location, physical and emotional state, and so on. While the 'black spot' manoeuvre could be interpreted as a first step towards acknowledging this subjectivity, since it at least allows actors' knowledge in these models to differ, the nature, causes and effects of the subjectivity of knowledge do not significantly contribute to mainstream analyses.[17] Now the range of possible issues we might consider here is vast. As such we intend to focus on one important factor in the subjectivity of knowledge, that is, the structured nature of conscious experience.[18] To this end we draw on the philosopher John Searle's (1983, 1992, 1995, 1999, 2001) work on consciousness and intentionality. While not uncontroversial in some quarters, we regard Searle's work as providing a clear and what is to us a commonsensical account on which to base our discussion.

Searle's account of the structured nature of conscious experience starts from the idea that many conscious mental states are intentional,[19] by which is meant that they are intrinsically about, or directed towards, something or someone. Thus you may intend to purchase a share, remember that you purchased a share, wish that you had purchased a share, and so on. Intending, remembering and wishing are all intentional states by virtue of the fact that they are necessarily directed at something, in this case the purchase of a share. All intentional states have what Searle calls conditions of satisfaction, namely the conditions that must be met for an intention to be fulfilled, a belief to be true, and so on. Thus the condition of satisfaction of your belief that you will buy a share is that you do in fact do so.

By virtue of intrinsically referring to, or being about, other things, intentional states are seen as crucial by Searle in mediating the minds' causal relations with the external world. One aspect of this is the mechanism by which intentional mental states function causally in behaviour, what Searle terms the mechanism of intentional causation. The central proposition here is that many intentional states influence behaviour by virtue of their contents being consciously scrutinised so as to establish their conditions of satisfaction. For example, a desire functions causally as a result of being consciously examined to determine what actions must be carried out in order for it to be fulfilled.

Searle then notes that in general, intentional states never function in isolation. Instead they depend firstly on a network of other intentional states. The desire to purchase shares in a particular company only functions causally in association with my knowing where that company is listed and how many shares I can afford to buy. But the functioning of intentional states also depends on non-intentional capabilities or what Searle terms an actor's Background: a reservoir of non-intentional 'capacities, abilities, tendencies, habits, dispositions, taken-for-granted presuppositions and "know-how" generally' (Searle 1999, pp. 107–08). In contrast to intentional states, Background capacities operate without conscious intervention or reflection. As Searle would have it then, conscious intentionality consists of thought processes that work in the way they do relative to a Background of unthought capacities, skills and know-how.

Rather than prove the existence of the Background, Searle instead prefers to demonstrate his thesis by the accretion of examples. His favourite ones are linguistic in nature, and specifically deal with how the Backgound enables linguistic interpretation. Consider the three statements:

- John flew into Heathrow,
- John flew into his opponent,
- John flew into a rage.

While each sentence shares the same basic form, 'X flew into Y', what we understand by 'flew into' in each case clearly differs. To be told that John flew into a rage does not lead us to imagine him arriving at Heathrow. Nor do we imagine him flying into his opponent when we are told that he will be arriving at Heathrow. Instead, we correctly determine the meaning of each sentence without any conscious act of interpretation. Searle proposes that this ability is one instance of our Background abilities.

The functioning of the Background is not restricted to fixing the semantic content of sentences. Searle maintains that all intentional states only function against a set of non-intentional Background skills. While the determination of the conditions of satisfaction of an intentional state firstly requires other intentional states, the process of drawing consciously on additional intentional states does not, and cannot, go on forever. At some point the process of intentional causation always 'bottoms out' on non-intentional, non-conscious, Background capacities that contribute to the determination of the intentional states conditions of satisfaction but that require no conscious intervention.

Turning now to the structured nature of conscious experience, Searle argues that all intentional mental states possess 'aspectual shape' (Searle 1992, pp. 156–7), which refers to the fact that whenever we perceive or think about something, we necessarily do so under particular aspects and not others. But to experience something *as* something, that is experience something under a certain aspect, we must already be familiar with the set of categories under which we experience that aspect. Thus our ability to recognise a piece of paper as a banknote presupposes that we already have the category of 'banknote'. The same goes for most of the objects and events that fill our everyday life, which we recognise immediately and without apparent effort. Searle regards the knowledge of, and ability to apply, such categories as a Background ability.

The structuring of consciousness by the Background is not limited to individual objects or momentary events. The Background also conditions our experiences in a dynamic way, by providing perceptual and linguistic categories that extend over sequences of events and which allow us to structure those sequences into comprehensible narrative shapes (Searle 1995, pp. 134–5). These 'dramatic' categories allow us to form what Searle calls 'scenarios of expectations', our taken-for-granted conceptions of how certain kinds of situations typically unfold, such as our negotiating to purchase a used car or our paying for a meal at a restaurant. Thus we become accustomed to and take for granted certain courses of events following on from each other.

That the structuring of conscious experience is a significant cause of the subjectivity of knowledge follows from the fact that many of the categories we draw on are learned rather than innate. Consequently these categories are a function of the social and cultural environment in which we have grown up and the way in which these past experiences have shaped our Background. Now once we recognise that each of us interprets or structures the information we receive in different ways, a range of phenomena become possible that the mainstream approach excludes by virtue of assuming a strict one-to-one relationship between information and knowledge.

Perhaps the simplest illustration of the kind of effect we have in mind here is provided by the example of two actors who may have quite different experiences of the same event. For instance suppose the event concerned is a controversial incident at a football match or the latest announcement made by a publicly quoted company. In the first case an actor's view of the event will in part depend on the football team that they support; while in the second the knowledge derived from the company's statement is likely to depend on whether an actor holds a short or long position in the company concerned.

Insights of this kind have recently begun to attract the attention of some economists, albeit those from outside of the mainstream. The notion that individuals engage in mental accounting (Thaler 1980, 1999), that is operate a set of rules by which they organise, evaluate and keep track of their financial activities, or that individuals implement a set of basic editing operations when faced with simple gambles (Kahneman and Tversky 1979, Kahneman 2000) prior to evaluating the available alternatives, incorporates the idea that the set of rules that people implement is partly subjective and that their knowledge of these rules and implementation of them is in part a tacit, Background operation. The related finding that individuals tend to be susceptible to 'framing effects', being unconsciously influenced by the presentation of a decision-situation (Tversky and Kahneman 1981, 1986; Camerer 2000; Shafir et al. 1997) also appears to presuppose an account of conscious experience similar to that we have pursued in this section (Faulkner 2002).

Tacit knowledge
The final characteristic of the mainstream modelling approach that we wish to highlight is that the actors within these models are assumed to form comprehensive, conscious representations of their decision-situations and, on the basis of these representations, to deliberate consciously (and perfectly) about the best way to proceed in those situations. The associated conception of knowledge is of that which resides in propositional form, that is, a form suited to the direct application of discursive reasoning. Indeed, as we showed above, this is exactly the form in which knowledge is 'given' to the economic actors in the models concerned.

We recognise that we are adopting a very literal interpretation of microeconomic models here, as descriptions of what real economic actors do. This is certainly not the only way such models can be interpreted.[20] But it is a natural interpretation, particularly in the case of game theory, much of which purports to model situations faced by real economic actors and where the analysis consists in attempting to reconstruct the discursive reasoning of those actors about what constitutes their best course of action in the light of their expectations about what the other actors will do. Certainly it would be hard to make sense of much of the economics of asymmetric information were the actors it considers not assumed to be deliberating consciously about what to do in the situations in which they find themselves. For the very point of such work is to investigate how rational deliberators respond when they have (slightly) less than perfect knowledge to work with.

The key point that we would like to make in this section is that economists' obsession with formal rational choice models, and the exclusive appeal to conscious, propositional knowledge that this entails, has led to a neglect of tacit knowledge in mainstream economics. By tacit knowledge we mean knowledge embodied in many of the skills, capacities and dispositions that human actors routinely draw on without conscious reflection.[21] In contrast to propositional knowledge, which operates at the foreground of the mind and tends to be readily codifiable and communicable, tacit knowledge is often difficult to express and need not be consciously thought about when enacted. In our view mainstream rational choice theory deflects attention from, first, the extent to which human behaviour relies on tacit rather than conscious functioning, and second, the fact that conscious, propositional knowledge always functions in conjunction with tacit knowledge. We shall consider these points in turn, beginning with the idea that human behaviour is driven by non-conscious skills, routines and habits as much as it is by conscious beliefs and desires. The point is quite widely recognised in non-mainstream contributions (e.g. Ambrosini 2003; Hayek 1948; Hodgson 1988; Lawson 1997; Nelson and Winter 1982; Nonaka and Takeuchi 1995) but rather than attempting to review this literature, we shall instead focus in some detail on one particular example, that of heuristic-based judgement.

The idea that actors frequently employ heuristics, or simple rules of thumb, to guide their behaviour first emerges in economics in Simon's work on satisficing (Simon 1956). More recently the idea of heuristic-based judgement has received considerable attention in behavioural finance as an explanation for the persistent biases observed in individuals' probability estimates (Camerer 1995; Kahneman et al. 1982; Kahneman and Tversky 1973; Plous 1993; Rabin 1998; Shefrin 2000; Warneryd 2001).[22] One such heuristic is availability, according to which actors' judgements about the likelihood of an event are influenced by the ease with which instances of that type of event can be brought to mind. Investors, for example, assessing the likelihood of bankruptcy in a particular company are likely to be influenced by the number of similar company failures that they can recall.

Now the reason for introducing the idea of heuristic-based judgement here is that such heuristics function tacitly and, as such, exemplify a number of points about tacit knowledge in general. Taking the example of availability, the tacit nature of the heuristic lies in the fact that, rather than consciously deciding to focus only on information concerning how easy it is to recall or imagine possible instances of some class of event, the actor's conscious mind is 'automatically' focused on information relating to availability. In effect then heuristics and tacit knowledge in general, serve to economise on the conscious effort required of an actor, by concentrating the conscious mind on only certain important, rather than all, aspects of the situation being considered.

The benefit to heuristic-guided judgement comes from the fact that the more complicated the actor's environment, the better the actor is likely to perform by following a heuristic rather than by consciously reasoning in accordance with the Savage axioms or some such. The reason for this lies in the boundedness of human mental capacities. Suppose that an actor has complete information on which to make a judgement. Given limited computational power (be this for lack of time or ability) an actor may make more accurate judgements on average by being predisposed towards focusing only on information concerning availability rather than performing an incomplete or inaccurate Bayesian calculation, attempting but failing to correctly incorporate all information.[23] The situation becomes even more favourable towards the heuristic-guided actor when complete information is not freely available. For, before any calculation, actors must decide how much effort to put into searching for information. The heuristic-guided actor immediately focuses on availability, whereas the Bayesian actor must decide in which direction to search by comparing the costs of search relative to its (unknown) benefits.

Against the advantages associated with economising on conscious effort, the disadvantages to tacit knowledge follow from the elimination of complete conscious reflection. Again our example of heuristic-guided judgement demonstrates the point. The disadvantage to relying on heuristics is that the resulting judgements will tend to be biased. The availability heuristic, for instance, is susceptible to the fact that factors other than frequency and probability affect the ease with which instances of an event can be brought to mind. The likelihood of events which have received widespread media attention, or that are particularly salient to an individual by virtue of past experiences, is likely to be consistently overstated by an individual forming judgements in accordance with availability.

Our example of judgemental heuristics also suggests a number of observations about tacit knowledge and rational choice models. First, and as they are usually presented, the actors in these models would gain nothing from employing heuristics since they face no computational constraints. Indeed with the costs (if any) to acquiring information known and unlimited conscious computational abilities, actors have no need for any type of tacit knowledge since they would gain nothing by restricting their conscious effort. Therefore mainstream economists neglect of tacit knowledge is at least understandable given the (admittedly unrealistic) assumptions of their models.

A more sophisticated variant of rational choice model (Heiner 1983) acknowledges the possible utility to actors of adhering to simple rules, by portraying rule-following as an actor's rational response to their own cognitive limitations. In effect these models simply increase the number of constraints faced by an actor to include search and processing costs, with the result that a (boundedly) rational actor may choose to adopt a heuristic. The problem with this approach remains the fact all knowledge in these models is propositional and all functioning, intentionalistic. Yet if an actor is to be guided by a heuristic he must do so unthinkingly in each decision-situation, which requires an account of tacit functioning. So while it is appropriate to identify heuristics as being beneficial to an actor because they enable conscious effort to be automatically directed, these models must also recognise heuristics as functioning tacitly in order for them to perform this function.

The second theme we pursue in this section concerns the role of tacit knowledge in the functioning of propositional knowledge. Here we again refer to John Searle's work on intentionality to illustrate our arguments. Earlier we introduced the notion that many conscious mental states, including those here conceived of as propositional knowledge, are intentional and that these states function causally in behaviour in accordance with the mechanism of intentional causation. According to this mechanism, an intentional state functions causally by virtue of being consciously scrutinised. Now we wish to make two points in relation to the idea of intentional causation. The first is that mainstream rational choice models deal with an idealised form of intentional causation (Runde 2001), since if we accept that these models portray an actor consciously choosing a preferred course of action given their wants and beliefs then that actor is behaving intentionalistically. Our second point here is that these models eliminate the role Searle attributes to the Background in the functioning of intentional states.

As we discussed earlier, Searle finds that rather than functioning in isolation, intentional states always function in conjunction with a Network of other intentional states and a Background of non-intentional capacities. In effect the Background, which consists of non-conscious capacities, skills and know-how, provides the backdrop against which all intentionalistic functioning, including rational decision-making, takes place. In the case of my desire to purchase a quantity of shares in a particular company, a considerable amount of tacit knowledge concerning the conduct of share transactions is implicated in the functioning of my desire, just as is my propositional knowledge concerning the particular market on which that share is listed. By ignoring the role of tacit knowledge in the functioning of propositional knowledge, the mainstream approach draws our attention away from the importance in purposeful, intentionalistic, behaviour of the things that we typically have tacit knowledge of, such as the rules and structures that influence our social interactions (Lawson 1997), the complex technical skills that we draw on (Nelson and Winter 1982) or the habits we develop (Hodgson 1988).

Conclusion

The shift in mainstream microeconomics since the 1970s, towards explicitly modelling imperfections and asymmetries in the knowledge of economic actors, represents a clear and significant advance from the point of view of the mainstream project. In recognising that actors are often less than perfectly knowledgeable about their economic environment and that they may be disadvantaged in what they know relative to other actors, mainstream analyses of many areas of economic activity have changed dramatically (on which, see Stiglitz 2000). Yet our analysis in this chapter suggests that as a move towards fully incorporating the complexities of human knowledge into economic analysis, the information theoretic revolution is only (and can only be) partially successful.

We have highlighted three particular areas of economic agency that, while apparently central to the issue of information and knowledge, are neglected by the mainstream approach. First of all we drew attention to features of the expected utility model that at once overestimate people's capacities to arrive at numerically definite probabilities, and underestimate the role of novelty and surprise in economic behaviour. We then showed that the subjectivity and context-dependence that characterise much of what people know about their decision situation, is excluded from mainstream models by virtue of the one-to-one relationship between information and knowledge imposed by these models. Finally we argued that by restricting all knowledge to be of an intentional form (beliefs and preferences), the role that tacit knowledge plays in behaviour is suppressed. In each instance we have sought to indicate how the particular aspect of human agency under consideration matters to the economic analysis of the phenomenon in question, and consequently how its neglect by the mainstream necessarily limits the usefulness of this approach to information and knowledge.

Notes
1. Some accounts draw a distinction between information and data, where information consists of data that has already been systematised in some way. We do not make this distinction here.
2. On debates in philosophy concerning the notion of justification involved here, see Zagzebski (1999) and Hands (2001, pp. 141–54).
3. Within epistemology such a position is known as contextualism, on which see DeRose (1999).
4. Our exposition of the Cournot model in this section and the next follows Gibbons (1992).
5. A proposition is common knowledge in some social system if everyone in that systems knows it, every knows that everyone knows it, everyone knows that everyone knows that everyone knows it, and so on.

6. On the meaning and significance of the Nash solution, see Gibbons (1992, p. 17), and Gravelle and Rees (1992, pp. 301–4.)

7. Notwithstanding that the game is one of 'imperfect information' in the terminology of game theory, since both of the two firms move simultaneously without knowing and being unable to deduce the level of output the other firm will choose. Common knowledge of the game, then, even in conjunction with common knowledge of rationality, is not enough to ensure that the firm will play their Nash strategies (although being perfect reasoners they will know that if they do not play their Nash strategies they will not be in equilibrium). But this is a wider problem that need not detain us here.

8. The reason for this need not detain us greatly. Essentially a Bayesian Nash equilibrium still requires that each player play their best response to the strategies played by their opponents. Since not all players know the type of their opponents with certainty, strategies for some players will be conditional on the strategies of all possible types of each of their opponents. Therefore for the equilibrium to consist of best response strategies by each player, some (or all) players' strategies must specify a plan for each of their possible types, since otherwise we cannot know whether or not all players are playing their best response. In our example, if the solution concept were not to specify a plan for each possible type of Firm B then we could not determine whether or not Firm A is playing its best response to Firm B's plan, since Firm A's profits (and so optimal choice) depend on the plans of both low and high cost-type Firm B's.

9. With $c_L < c_H$.

10. In addition to which it remains the case that what each firm knows is also assumed to be common knowledge.

11. The procedure involves comparisons between sure consequences on the one hand and pairs of random consequences on the other, and yields a (von Neumann–Morgenstern) utility function that is unique up to origin and scale. An equivalent procedure, applied in the reverse, may be used to quantify an actor's beliefs about the realisation of states as subjective probabilities.

12. One illustration of which is the vast literature that documents discrepancies between actual human behaviour and that predicted by the EU model, on which see Arrow et al. (1996) and Camerer (1995).

13. The standard reference here being Ellsberg (1961), who provides some simple choices that tend to elicit behaviour in conflict with the idea that peoples' choices are always 'as if' guided by numerically definite subjective probabilities. There are two main theoretical approaches to accommodating such choices. One is to assume that people do not always have unique probabilities in mind, but sets of them, the so-called 'multiple prior' approach (Bewley 1986; Epstein and Wang 1994; Gärdenfors and Sahlin 1982; Gilboa and Schmeidler 1989, 1993; Kelsey 1993, 1994; Kelsey and Quiggin 1992; Kyburg 1990; Levi 1986). The other replaces the Bayesian prior with a non-additive measure or capacity (Kahneman and Tversky 1979, 1992; Dow and Werlang 1992a, 1992b, 1993; Gilboa 1987; Schmeidler 1989). Neither of these two approaches commands anything like the assent commanded by the EU model.

14. In game theory, at least in games of incomplete information that employ the Harsanyi transformation to convert the game into one of imperfect information, the states of nature consist of the possible types of each player. And as we saw in the case of the Cournot game, the full set of possible states of nature and associated probabilities are common knowledge to all players, a practice that is not unproblematic due to possible difficulties with the use of Bayesian rationality (i.e. the Savage axioms) in the context of strategic interaction (see Mariotti 1995, 1997).

15. In principle the EU model need not require an actor to know correctly the full set of possible states of the world, merely that he have some conception of the possible states and that he acts on the basis of this conception. Yet this is not the way models of this sort usually proceed, since all actors are assumed to have the same, correct, conception of the set of possible states.

16. The game of Heads and Tails is a good example. This game involves two players independently choosing Heads or Tails, where both of them know they will receive a prize if they both make the same choice and nothing otherwise. This game has two Nash equilibria in pure strategies (Heads, Heads) and (Tails, Tails), but there is nothing in the formal structure of the game to give the players a reason to choose either Heads or Tails.

17.   Among non-mainstream economists, these issues frequently arise in debates surrounding the subjectivism of Austrian economists such as Menger, von Mises, Hayek, Knight and Shackle. Horwitz (1994) and Kirzner (1995) provide two helpful recent accounts of Austrian subjectivism.
18.   A closely related perspective is supported by work on perceptual schema and cognitive framing in cognitive theory (e.g. Bruner 1973, Lloyd 1972) and recent work in psychology (Clark 1997; Cosmides and Tooby 1994b; Margolis 1994; Plotkin 1994), which emphasises the role that context plays in human reasoning.
19.   But not all. For instance, one may have conscious feelings of anxiety that have no specific focus or target.
20.   Some economists argue that formal economic models should never be seen as claiming any more than that economic actors act 'as if' they actually deliberate consciously about what to do, and that such models should be assessed primarily in terms of their predictive rather than descriptive adequacy (Friedman 1953). Others argue that formal rational choice models should be seen as normative, as indicating what rational actors should do in a particular situation.
21.   Within philosophy, writers who emphasise this type of knowledge include Bourdieu (1990), Polanyi (1967), Reber (1993), Ryle (1949) and Searle (1992). Smith (1988) provides a useful introduction to many of the central issues in this literature.
22.   An important, and in some ways competing, perspective on heuristics is also gaining ground in economics. Influenced heavily by evolutionary psychology (e.g. Cosmides and Tooby 1994a, 1996), this approach emphasises the fact that deviations from perfectly rational judgement in particular experimental settings need not imply general deficiencies in actors' underlying abilities (Gigerenzer 1991, 1994). Rather, the experimental findings of the 'heuristics and biases' programme may simply reflect the sensitivity of such abilities to the way in which actors are presented with information. A second feature of this approach is an evolutionary account of heuristics, according to which these reflect specialised, inherited, computational devices designed to solve the 'adaptive' problems encountered by human beings over the course of their evolutionary history (Gigerenzer and Todd 2000). For an interesting perspective on the scale of the differences between these two approaches, see Samuels et al. (1999) and Samuels et al. (2002).
23.   Such a situation might be termed the curse of information, since an actor presented with all relevant information may make worse judgements on average than an actor who only has available to him a subset of this information. A related but distinct phenomena is the curse of knowledge (Camerer et al. 1989; Camerer 1995) in which better informed actors in asymmetric information models such as the earlier Cournot game are unable to accurately imagine being in the position of the less well-informed actors because the extra knowledge cannot be ignored.

References

Ambrosini, V. (2003), *Tacit and Ambiguous Resources as Sources of Competitive Advantage*, Basingstoke: Palgrave Macmillan.
Arrow, Kenneth, Enrico Colombatto and C. Schmidt (1996), *The Rational Foundations of Economic Behaviour*, IEA Conference vol. 114, London: Macmillan.
Bewley, T. (1986), 'Knightian decision theory: part 1', Cowles Foundation discussion paper no. 807.
Bibow, J., Paul Lewis and Jochen Runde (2003), 'On convention: Keynes, Lewis and the French School', in Jochen Runde and S. Mizuhara (eds), *The Philosophy of Keynes Economics: Probability, Uncertainty and Convention*, London: Routledge.
Bourdieu, Pierre (1990), *The Logic of Practice*, translated by Richard Nice, Cambridge: Polity Press.
Bruner, J. (1973), *Beyond the Information Given*, Boston, MA: Martinus Nijhoff.
Camerer, C.F. (1995), 'Individual decision making', in J. Kagel and A. Roth (eds), *The Handbook of Experimental Economics*, Princeton, NJ: Princeton University Press, pp. 587–703.
Camerer, C.F. (2000), 'Prospect Theory in the wild: evidence from the field', in Daniel Kahneman and Amos Tversky (eds), *Choices, Values and Frames*, Cambridge: Cambridge University Press, pp. 288–300.

Camerer, C.F., G. Loewenstein and M. Weber (1989), 'The curse of knowledge in economic settings: an experimental analysis', *Journal of Political Economy*, **97**, 1232–54.

Clark, A. (1997), *Being There: Putting the Brain, Body and World Together Again*, Cambridge, MA: MIT Press.

Cosmides, Leda, and John Tooby (1994a), 'Better than rational: evolutionary psychology and the invisible hand', *American Economic Review*, **84** (2), 327–32.

Cosmides, Leda, and John Tooby (1994b), 'Beyond intuition and instinct blindness: toward an evolutionarily rigorous cognitive science', *Cognition*, April–June, 41–77.

Cosmides, Leda, and John Tooby (1996), 'Are humans good intuitive statisticians after all? Rethinking some conclusions from the literature on judgment under uncertainty', *Cognition*, **58** (1), 1–73.

Cyert, R.M., and J.G. March (1992), *A Behavioural Theory of the Firm*, 2nd edn, Oxford: Blackwell.

DeRose, K. (1999), 'Contextualism: an explanation and defense', in J. Greco and E. Sosa (eds), *The Blackwell Guide to Epistemology*, Oxford: Blackwell.

Dequech, David (1999), 'On some arguments for the rationality of conventional behaviour under uncertainty – concepts, applicability and criticisms', in Claudio Sardoni and Peter Kriesler (eds), *Keynes, Post-Keynesianism and Political Economy: Essays in Honour of Geoff Harcourt*, vol. 3, London: Routledge, pp. 176–95.

Dow, J., and S.R. Werlang (1992a), 'Excess volatility of stock prices and knightian uncertainty', *European Economic Review*, **36**, 631–8.

Dow, J., and S.R. Werlang (1992b), 'Uncertainty aversion, risk aversion and the optimal choice of portfolio', *Econometrica*, **60**, 197–204.

Dow, J., and S.R. Werlang (1993), 'Nash equilibrium under Knightian uncertainty: breaking down backward induction', *Journal of Economic Theory*, **64**, 305–24.

Ellsberg, D. (1961), 'Risk, ambiguity and the Savage axioms', *Quarterly Journal of* Economics, **75**, 643–69.

Epstein, L.G., and Wang, T. (1994), 'Intertemporal asset pricing under Knightian uncertainty', *Econometrica*, **62**, 283–322.

Faulkner, Philip (2002), 'The human agent in behavioural finance: a Searlean perspective', *Journal of Economic Methodology*, **9**, 31–52.

Faulkner, Philip (2003), 'Three essays on rationality, intentionality and economic agency', PhD thesis, Cambridge University.

Friedman, Milton (1953), 'The methodology of positive economics', in *Essays in Positive Economics*, Chicago: University of Chicago Press, pp. 3–43.

Gärdenfors, P., and N.E Sahlin (1982), 'Unreliable probabilities, risk taking and decision making', *Synthèse*, **53**, 361–86.

Gibbons, R. (1992), *A Primer in Game Theory*, Hemel Hempstead: Harvester Wheatsheaf.

Gigerenzer, G. (1991), 'How to make cognitive illusions disappear: beyond "heuristics and biases"', *European Review of Social Psychology*, **2**, 83–115.

Gigerenzer, G. (1994), 'Why the distinction between single-event probabilities and frequencies is important for psychology (and vice versa)', in G. Wright and P. Ayton (eds), *Subjective Probability*, New York: John Wiley.

Gigerenzer, G., and P. Todd (2000), *Simple Heuristics That Make Us Smart*, New York and Oxford, Oxford University Press.

Gilboa, I. (1987), 'Expected utility theory with purely subjective non-additive probabilities', *Journal of Mathematical Economics*, **16**, 141–53.

Gilboa, I., and D. Schmeidler (1989), 'Maximin expected utility with a non-unique prior', *Journal of Mathematical Economics*, **18**, 141–53.

Gilboa, J., and D. Schmeidler (1993), 'Updating ambiguous beliefs', *Journal of Economic Theory*, **59**, 33–49.

Gravelle, H., and R. Rees (1992), *Microeconomics*, London: Longman.

Hands, Wade D. (2001), *Reflection Without Rules*, Cambridge: Cambridge University Press.

Harsanyi, John (1967), 'Games with incomplete information played by Bayesian players, Parts I II and III', *Management Science*, **14**, 159–82, 320–34, 486–502.

Hayek, Friedriech A. (1948), *Individualism and Economic Order*, Chicago: University of Chicago Press.

Heiner, R. (1983), 'The origin of predictable behaviour', *American Economic Review*, **73** (4), 560–95.

Hodgson, Geoffrey (1988), *Economics and Institutions*, Cambridge: Polity Press.

Hodgson, Geoffrey (1997), 'The ubiquity of habits and rules', *Cambridge Journal of Economics*, **21**, 663–84.

Hodgson, Geoffrey (1999), *Evolution and Institutions*, Aldershot, UK and Brookfield US: Edward Elgar Press.

Hogarth, R.M. (1987), 'Decision making under ambiguity', in R.M. Hogarth and M.W. Reder (eds), *Rational Choice: The Contrast Between Economics and Psychology*, Chicago: Chicago University Press, pp. 41–67.

Horwitz, Stephen (1994), 'Subjectivism', in P.J. Boettke (ed.), *The Elgar Companion to Austrian Economics*, Aldershot, UK and Brookfield US: Edward Elgar, pp. 17–22.

Kahneman, Daniel (2000), 'Preface', in Daniel Kahneman and Amos Tversky (eds), *Choices, Values and Frames*, Cambridge: Cambridge University Press, pp. ix–xvii.

Kahneman, Daniel, and Amos Tversky (1973), 'On the psychology of prediction', *Psychological Review*, **80**, 237–51.

Kahneman, Daniel, and Amos Tversky (1979), 'Prospect theory: an analysis of decision under risk', *Econometrica*, **47**, 263–91.

Kahneman, Daniel, and Amos Tversky (1992), 'Advances in prospect theory: cumulative representation of uncertainty', *Journal of Risk and Uncertainty*, **5**, 297–324.

Kahneman, Daniel, and Amos Tversky (1996), 'On the reality of cognitive illusions', *Psychological Review*, **103** (3), 582–91.

Kahneman, Daniel, Peter Solvic and Amos Tversky (1982), *Judgement under Uncertainty: Heuristics and Biases*, Cambridge: Cambridge University Press.

Kelsey, D. (1993), 'Choice under partial uncertainty', *International Economic Review*, **34**, 297–308.

Kelsey, D. (1994), 'Maxmin expected utility and weight of evidence', *Oxford Economic Papers*, **46**, 425–44.

Kelsey, D., and J. Quiggin (1992), 'Theories of choice under ignorance and uncertainty', *Journal of Economic Surveys*, **6**, 133–53.

Keynes, J.M. (1973), 'A treatise on probability', in *The Collected Writings of John Maynard Keynes*, vol. 8, London: Macmillan.

Kirzner, Israel (1995), 'The subjectivism of Austrian economics', in G. Meijer (ed.), *New Perspectives on Austrian Economics*, London and New York: Routledge, pp. 11–24.

Knight, Frank (1921), *Risk, Uncertainty and Profit*, Chicago: University of Chicago Press.

Kreps, David M. (1988), *Notes on the Theory of Choice*, Boulder, CO: Westview Press.

Kyburg, H.E. (1990), *Science and Reason*, New York: Oxford University Press.

Lawson, Tony (1997), *Economics and Reality*, London: Routledge.

Levi, I. (1986), 'The paradoxes of Allais and Ellsberg', *Economics and Philosophy*, **2**, 22–53.

Lloyd, B. (1972), *Perception and Cognition*, Harmondsworth: Penguin.

Lucas, Robert E. (1981), *Studies in Business Cycle Theory*, Cambridge, MA: MIT Press.

Margolis, H. (1994), *Paradigms and Barriers: How Habits of Mind Govern Scientific Beliefs*, Chicago: University of Chicago Press.

Mariotti, M. (1995), 'Is Bayesian rationality compatible with strategic rationality?', *Economic Journal*, **105**, 1099–109.

Mariotti, M. (1997), 'Decisions in games: why there should be a special exemption from Bayesian rationality', *Journal of Economic Methodology*, **4**, 43–60.

Mukerji, S. (1998), 'Ambiguity aversion and incompleteness of contractual form', *American Economic Review*, **88**, 1207–31.

Nagel, Thomas (1986), *The View from Nowhere*, New York: Oxford University Press.

Nelson, Stanley, and Sydney Winter (1982), *An Evolutionary Theory of Economic Change*, Cambridge, MA: Harvard University Press.

Nonaka, I., and H. Takeuchi (1995), *The Knowledge-Creating Company: How Japanese Companies Create the Dynamics of Innovation*, Oxford and New York: Oxford University Press.

Plotkin, H. (1994), *Darwin Machines and the Nature of Knowledge: Concerning Adaptations, Instinct and the Evolution of Intelligence*, Harmondsworth: Penguin.

Plous, S. (1993), *The Psychology of Judgment and Decision Making*, New York: McGraw-Hill.

Polanyi, Michael (1967), *The Tacit Dimension*, London: Routledge and Kegan Paul.

Rabin, Matthew (1998), 'Psychology and economics', *Journal of Economic Literature*, **36** (1), 11–46.

Reber, A. (1993), *Implicit Learning and Tacit Knowledge: An Essay on the Cognitive Unconscious*, Oxford and New York: Oxford University Press.

Runde, Jochen (2001), 'Chances and choices: notes on probability and belief in economic theory', in Uskali Mäki (ed.), *The Economic Worldview*, Cambridge: Cambridge University Press, pp. 132–53.

Runde, J. (2002) 'Filling in the background', *Journal of Economic Methodology*, **9**, 11–30.

Ryle, G. (1949), *The Concept of Mind*, New York: Barnes and Noble.

Samuels, R., S. Stich and P. Tremoulet (1999), 'Rethinking rationality: from bleak implications to Darwinian modules', in E. LePore and Z. Pylyshyn (eds), *What is Cognitive Science?*, Oxford: Basil Blackwell, pp. 74–120.

Samuels, R., S. Stich and M. Bishop (2002), 'Ending the rationality wars: how to make disputes about human rationality disappear', in R. Elio (ed.), *Common Sense, Reasoning and Rationality*, New York: Oxford University Press, pp. 236–68.

Savage, L.J. (1954), *The Foundations of Statistics*, New York: John Wiley.

Schmeidler, D. (1989), 'Subjective probability and expected utility without additivity', *Econometrica*, **57**, 571–87.

Searle, John R. (1983), *Intentionality: An Essay in the Philosophy of the Mind*, Cambridge: Cambridge University Press.

Searle, John R. (1992), *The Rediscovery of the Mind*, Cambridge, MA: MIT Press.

Searle, John R. (1995), *The Construction of Social Reality*, Harmondsworth: Allen Lane, Penguin Press.

Searle, John R. (1999), *Mind, Language and Society*, London: Weidenfeld and Nicolson.

Searle, John R. (2001), *Rationality in Action*, Cambridge, MA: MIT Press.

Shackle, G.L.S. (1972), *Epistemics and Economics: A Critique of Economic Doctrines*, Cambridge: Cambridge University Press.

Shafir, E., P. Diamond and A. Tversky (1997), 'Money illusion', *Quarterly Journal of Economics*, **112** (2), 341–74.

Shefrin, H. (2000), *Beyond Greed and Fear*, Boston: Harvard Business School Press.

Simon, Herbert A. (1956), 'Rational choice and the structure of the environment', *Psychological Review*, **63**, 129–38.

Smith, B. (1988), 'Knowing how vs. knowing that', in J. Nyiri and B. Smith (eds), *Practical Knowledge: Questions of a Theory of Traditions and Skills*, New York: Croom Helm.

Stiglitz, Joseph E. (1994), *Whither Socialism?*, Cambridge, MA: MIT Press.

Stiglitz, Joseph E. (2000), 'The contributions of the economics of information to twentieth century economics', *Quarterly Journal of Economics*, **115** (4), 1441–78.

Thaler, Richard (1980), 'Toward a positive theory of consumer choice', *Journal of Economic Behaviour and Organisation*, **1**, 39–60.

Thaler, Richard (1999), 'Mental accounting matters', *Journal of Behavioural Decision Making*, **12**, 183–206.

Tversky, Amos and Daniel Kahneman (1981), 'The framing of decisions and the psychology of choice', *Science*, **211**, (4481), 453–8.

Tversky, Amos, and Daniel Kahneman (1986), 'Rational choice and the framing of decisions', *Journal of Business*, **59** (4), 5251–78.

Vanberg, Victor J. (1994), *Rules and Choice in Economics*, London: Routledge.

Warneryd, K.-E. (2001), *Stock-Market Psychology*, Cheltenham, UK and Northampton, MA, USA: Edward Elgar.

Williamson, Oliver E. (1985), *The Economic Institutions of Capitalism*, New York: Free Press.

Zagzebski, L. (1999), 'What is knowledge', in J. Greco and E. Sosa (eds), *The Blackwell Guide to Epistemology*, Oxford: Blackwell, pp. 92–116.

22 Conceptions of probability
Charles R. McCann, Jr.

Introduction

Economic theory has from its earliest incarnations focused upon the intricacies of individual decision-making; economics (as catallactics) is primarily concerned with the choices and actions of individuals who have a necessarily imperfect apprehension of the consequences of their actions through an unpredictable future. The incorporation of probability in economics thus became manifest as the natural consequence of the very nature of individual decision-making. Many important early contributors to economics – A.A. Cournot, F.Y. Edgeworth, Alfred Marshall, W. Stanley Jevons, Ludwig von Mises, to name but a few – either wrote on the topic of probability itself, included digressions on the subject in their economic treatises, or employed probability arguments. Marshall, for example, became embroiled in a newspaper debate with Karl Pearson relating to the latter's statistical study of parental alcoholism;[1] Edgeworth made significant contributions to both probability and statistical theory.[2]

This chapter will address only certain philosophical aspects of probability. The focus will be on knowledge and belief, and the way in which probability theorists have attempted to model them. Probability as it is employed in statistics and econometrics will not be considered.

Knowledge and belief

Before discussing probability proper, it is necessary to clarify certain terms. The term 'knowledge' denotes certain belief. This is not to be construed as coincident with mere belief, feeling, or any other normative criterion, but is essentially a conclusion drawn from evidence *and limited to that evidence*. Belief alone – mere belief –is not a legitimate condition for knowledge; even 'true' belief cannot be so equated, since a true belief may be predicated on a false premise or a misapprehension. Bertrand Russell's definition, of knowledge as a true belief that 'is either intuitive or inferred (logically or psychologically) from intuitive knowledge from which it follows logically', goes a long way toward establishing the desired meaning (Russell 1912, p. 139). For the moment, we shall define 'knowledge' as certain belief that is demonstrable.

From this demonstrative knowledge, leading from true premises to a necessarily true conclusion, inferences may be derived through syllogistic reasoning. Such deduction is logical entailment: from p (the antecedent) and $p \supset q$ follows *q* (the consequent). Given that the premises are true, the conclusion then must, of necessity, also be true. The problem with deduction lies in its inherent limitations, namely, that the inferences derived, while certain, are nonetheless non-ampliative: the conclusions derived from the premises are themselves *contained in* the premises, and merely reaffirm what has been asserted (Salmon 1967, p. 8). No new knowledge can be gained. Even so, it must be acknowledged that non-ampliative inferences serve an important role in allowing us to acknowledge hidden structures, as they perform much the same role as an encyclopedia to which we refer as a means of ensuring consistency.

Knowledge is certain belief that is demonstrable. Any other 'belief', even if true, is, by contrast, not knowledge per se, but rather falls in the general category of 'opinion', or, for want of a better term, 'probable knowledge'. Knowledge proper allows one to draw conclusions the certainty of which is indisputable. For probable knowledge, the contingent nature of the conclusions argues against any such certainty. One cannot draw certain conclusions from given premises, which themselves are not beforehand stipulated as true and certain. (Of course, it may be the case that one cannot draw certain conclusions even if the premises are true and certain, if incomplete.)

In the consideration of probable knowledge, we can no longer rely on deductive reasoning. For this we require a form of inference capable of accommodating *contingent* knowledge. It is here that induction becomes important, for inductive inferences are accepted as valid *contingently*, not *conclusively*. Such inferences need not be truth-preserving, as they are non-demonstrative, and so the conclusions are established only with a degree of probability.

The import of induction is that, unlike deduction, it allows one to draw ampliative inferences, inferences that extend beyond the premises themselves to establish new knowledge. The question is thus, as Wesley Salmon argues, whether there can exist ampliative, truth-preserving inferences. For this to occur, for new knowledge beyond the stipulated premises to be forthcoming (and for induction to have as sound a basis as deduction), some a priori condition must be advanced as a demonstrative principle, such as, for example, the principle of the 'uniformity of nature'. If we could ascertain that, for the phenomena in question, the form and substance we perceive will continue into the future with no deviation or transformation, then we could derive conclusions that extend beyond the content of the premises, and these conclusions would be as valid as those derived through deduction. If this principle were a synthetic a priori – as it would have to be, since analytic arguments cannot extend beyond the content of the premises – then a demonstrative inference could be made ampliative (Salmon 1967, p. 9–10). If not, if the inference is non-demonstrative (i.e., if one denies the concept of synthetic *a priori* truths), we may nevertheless be content with the procedure so long as it performs the task to which we assign it (Ayer 1952, p. 50).

In the absence of such synthetic a priori truths, demonstrative inferences are not possible, and induction lacks any foundation. Inductive inferences then are valid only with *some* degree of probability, and therefore cannot lead to knowledge as defined above. Therefore, induction may be justified by considering it a form of *probabilistic reasoning*.

Preliminaries to probability

Before coming to a formal presentation of probability interpretations, we must first establish a set of axioms common to those interpretations that conform to numerical probability[3] and state some mathematical preliminaries that will serve as foundations. The axioms as listed are essential to the definition of a *probability measure*, and should not be taken as prerequisite to the elucidation of any specific *interpretation*. Additional axioms and supplementary propositions will be introduced as they become necessary.

Given *a* and *h*, where *a* is a hypothesis or conclusion and *h* is evidence or premises, $P(a|h)$ is established as a *conditional probability*. Let A = {*a*, *b*}, where *a* and *b* are any two hypotheses. The following axioms are stipulated and are for the most part self-explanatory:[4]

Axiom 1: there exists a unique value of $P(a|h)$, where such a value can be defined; probability is a single-valued function (property of existence)

Axiom 2: $0 \le P(a|h) \le 1$ (property of non-negativity)

Axiom 3: if *h* implies *a*, then $P(a|h) = 1$ (property of certainty)

Axiom 4: if *h* implies not-*a*, then $P(a|h) = 0$ (property of impossibility)

Axiom 5: $P[(a \cap b)|h] = P(a|h) \cdot P[b|(a \cap h)] = P(b|h) \cdot P[a|(b \cap h)]$ (the axiom of conjunction, or the product axiom)

Axom (5a), if *a* and *b* are independent propositions, then Axiom 5 becomes: $P[(a \cap b)|h] = P(a|h) \cdot P(b|h)$

Axiom 6: $P[(a \cup b)|h] = P(a|h) + P(b|h) - P[(a \cap b)|h]$ (the axiom of disjunction)

Axiom (6a) if *a* and *b* are disjoint (i.e., if $a \cap b = \varnothing$), then $P[(a \cap b)|h] = 0$, and the disjunction axiom becomes the axiom of addition, i.e., $P[(a \cup b)|h] = P(a|h) + P(b|h)$

It should be noted that (5a) and (6a) are postulates, not axioms, and hold only under given stipulations: independence for (5a) and mutual-exclusivity for (6a). While all of the axioms are valid universally, the postulates need not be so, as they hold only under the special conditions.

It also should be remembered that the above axioms are valid as stated, for a finite set of elements of $A = \{a_1, a_2, \ldots a_n\}$. We may then define a *probability measure* as a function satisfying (1), (2), (3), and (6a), i.e., it is a finite, non-negative, finitely-additive function. (More restrictively, it is a Lebesque measure $\forall\, a \in A$.) In conjunction with the above-listed axioms, we define the notions of partial and total order. A binary relation (i.e., one that holds between any two propositions or arguments) R on a set A is defined as a *partial order* if:[5]

1. for every $a \in A$, a R a (reflexivity)
   For every $a, b, c \in A$,
2. if a R b and b R c, then a R c (transitivity)
3. if a R b and b R a, then $a = b$ (antisymmetry)

If the set A is partially ordered, and if, for all $a, b \in A$, $a \neq b$, either a R b or b R a (i.e., the set is *connected*), then the set is *totally-ordered*. (Note that, under the conditions of the partial order, it may be possible that, for some $a, b \in A$, neither a R b nor b R a obtains, i.e., some a and b may be non-comparable). In what follows, and as is presupposed by (1)–(3) above, the relation R is taken to be the weak ordering '$\leq$'.

From the above-listed axioms, we can derive a form of Bayes' theorem.

From Axiom 5: $P[(a \cap b)|h] = P(b|h) \cdot P[a|(b \cap h)]$

It then follows that: $P[a|(b \cap h)] = P[(a \cap b)|h] / P(b|h)$

Now again by Axiom 5: $P[(a \cap b)|h] = P(a|h) \cdot P[b|(a \cap h)]$

Therefore: $P[a|(b \cap h)] = P(a|h) \cdot P[b|(a \cap h)] / P(b|h)$

Let the sample space be partitioned into k mutually-exclusive non-null subsets. Then, by definition:

$$P(b|h) = \bigcup_{i=1 \to k} P[(b \cap a_i)|h]$$

Now, by Axiom 6 and postulate (6a):

$$P(b|h) = \Sigma_{i=1 \to k} P[(b \cap a_i)|h] = \Sigma_{i=1 \to k} P(a_i|h) \cdot P[b|(a_i \cap h)]$$

(by Axiom 5). Finally, combining terms:

$$P[a|(b \cap h)] = \frac{P(a|h) \cdot P[b|(a \cap h)]}{\sum_{i=1 \to k} P(a_i|h) \cdot P[b|(a_i \cap h)]}$$

which is Bayes' theorem, a cornerstone of the theory of probability and of fundamental significance to the economic theory of decision-making under uncertainty.

Probability types
There is no lack of reference material on the theory of probability and its history in the various fields to which it has been applied. Isaac Todhunter (1865), John Maynard Keynes (1921), Ian Hacking (1975, 1990), Roy Weatherford (1982), and Stephen Stigler (1986) are but a few of the works treating the development of probability as a means through which we may confront the problems associated with incomplete knowledge and induction.

Rudolf Carnap (1950) provides a useful typology of approaches to the topic of probability, distinguishing between Probability$_1$ and Probability$_2$. Probability$_1$ is an objective, analytic concept, through which conclusions are derived relative to given evidence. This form of probability belongs to the field of inductive logic – the evidence is sentential, meaning that the empirical element enters through the evidentiary propositions, which are not themselves empirical. Probability$_1$ arguments are thus propositions (or sentences) that assert a 'partial logical implication' (Carnap 1950, p. 31).

Probability$_2$, by contrast, relates to properties, classes, kinds, types, etc. Statements of Probability$_2$ are empirical, as the arguments refer to long-run, relative frequencies, while the theorems upon which it is structured are analytic. Probability$_2$ is 'logicomathematical' (Carnap 1950, pp. 33–34).

The Carnap typology is quite useful in demonstrating the problem of the incorporation of new evidence. If a Probability$_2$ statement is shown to be invalid, i.e., if some additional evidence arises which fails to conform to the predictions made, then the statement is deemed false, and the new evidence may be incorporated so as to provide a better assessment. A Probability$_1$ statement, by contrast, is *defined* with respect to given evidence, and as a result, the new evidence cannot alter the conclusions derived from the previous evidence. The additional evidence necessitates the reconstruction of an entirely new Probability$_1$ statement, which replaces the former (Carnap 1950, p. 192).

Ian Hacking (1975) 'appropriates' Carnap's classification, labeling the categories epistemic and aleatory, referring to those interpretations involving degrees of belief (encompassing inductive probability) and those involving chance (e.g., games of chance, frequencies, and statistical calculation). Epistemic theories include those of Keynes and of Harold Jeffreys (1931) at the one extreme (representing logical interpretations), and Frank Ramsey (1926), Leonard Savage (1972), and Bruno de Finetti (1964) at the other (representing personalist, belief-based views). Aleatory theories include those of John Venn (1888), Richard von Mises (1941, 1957), and A.N. Kolmogorov (1950). (Hacking's distinction is not always as clear-cut as one may wish, for a particular probability interpretation may be regarded as both aleatory and epistemic, or belong to neither category.)

Finally, regarding the delimitation of approaches to probability, Salmon (1967) proposes five types – classical, subjective, frequency, logical, and personal – while Weatherford (1982) offers four (combining the subjective and the personal). Savage (1972) divides schools of probability into three, more explanatory categories – necessarian, personalist, and frequentist. Tony Lawson (1988) divides *economic* uses of probability into two types: those which identify probability as a *form* of knowledge (the epistemic), and those which identify it as an *object* of knowledge (the aleatory). Those advocating probability as a *form* of knowledge see probabilities as that 'which agents *possess*, or *attach* to particular propositions', while those advocating probability as an *object* of knowledge view 'probabilities as something to be *discovered*, *learned* about, and *known*' (Lawson 1988, p. 40).

Here we will review classical, frequency, necessarian (logical), and personalist interpretations, using Lawson's categories as a means of elucidating the notion of uncertainty.

Classical probability

The classical interpretation of probability is the oldest of the interpretations with which we shall deal. On this interpretation, probability is the ratio of favorable to possible types of occurrences in a sufficiently well-defined sequence of events, where each case is assumed *a priori* equally possible. The Principle of Equipossibility, as well as the Principle of Sufficient Reason (which refers to the lack of any rationale for preferring or differentiating one probability value over any other – if one cannot decide whether $P(a) > P(b)$, or $P(b) > P(a)$, then one can say only that $P(a) = P(b)$), are the principal propositions of the classical interpretation.

The most widely acknowledged and best-established work on the classical view is the 1820 *Philosophical Essay on Probabilities* by Pierre Simon Laplace. Truth is the basis of Classical or Laplacian probability. The universe of the Laplacian probabilist is closed and determinate, that is to say, the world of natural phenomena is reducible to deterministic laws, and these laws are objective and discoverable. The only barriers to the discovery of 'truth' are the ability and the constitution of the observer. Things are as they are of necessity; it is up to the individual to discern the underlying causal reality.

Classical probability is not therefore concerned with the actual structure of the universe, but with our *understanding* of that structure. Our inability to understand the workings of an essentially determinate order is a result of our own limited abilities of apprehension. The classical interpretation of probability, predicated on a mechanical view of nature, provided the 'scientific' foundation by which we may eventually 'know' that which we at present accept only as 'belief'.

Among the major achievements of the classical probability model is the presentation by Jacques Bernoulli, another of the great classical probabilists, of a limit theorem, a 'law of large numbers', by which the 'certainty' of a probability value is guaranteed in the limit; the probability that the observed (sample) relative frequency will equal the true or expected relative frequency, differing only by an arbitrarily small constant, approaches unity. Symbolically:

$$\text{Prob} \left[-\varepsilon \le (k/n - p) \le \varepsilon \right] \to 1,$$

where k/n is the observed frequency of occurrence of the event, p is the true frequency, and ε is an arbitrary constant.[6]

Bernoulli's theorem has been interpreted as suggesting an underlying order to what may otherwise appear as chance observations, although in fact it applies only to drawings from a single event-space, such as balls drawn from a single urn or tosses of a coin. To Laplace, this theorem is not applicable only to games of chance or other similar well-defined experimental situations, but is taken to be a general result, applicable to natural and social phenomena alike. Single events viewed in isolation take on a random character and may thus appear to have arisen by chance. A series of such events over a period of time, by contrast, possesses a regularity that gives the illusion of an order arising out of the chaos (see, for example, Venn 1888, p. 16). Such regularity is expressible through reference to natural laws. The universe is determinate, events are understandable as the outcomes of specific laws of nature, which are both necessary and immutable.

Probability as frequency
The reaction to the classical conception of probability was a theory ascribed to the British empirical school and known as the frequentist approach or frequency interpretation. While the frequency interpretation can be found in the work of Augustin Cournot (among others), John Venn is typically regarded as having established the framework upon which this approach rests, and Richard von Mises (1957) presents a refinement and clarification of the central issues. In his 1888 *Logic of Chance*, Venn identifies the central concept of 'series', defined as a sequence of events each of which possesses certain notable attributes. Probability does not attach to a *single* event, but only to events as part of a well-defined, extended (ideally infinite) sequence of *repeated* events. The series is *the* essential element of probability as frequency; probability is meaningful *only* in consideration of the presence of an attribute within a given extended series. Single events are analyzable *only* as part of a well-defined and homogeneous reference class. Unique, one-time occurrences belong to no identifiable series (although if we should take enough time and sift through enough observations, a series may eventually be identified). Probability is then the ratio of favorable

to possible cases in an empirical series, or, in another sense, is the limiting value of the 'relative frequency with which certain events or properties recur' within a sequence of observations, wherein the sequence is of infinite length (R. Mises 1957, p. 22). The superiority of the frequency conception of probability over the classical interpretation lies in abandoning reliance on the *a priori* condition of equipossibility.

Probability as frequency is applicable to a series that 'combines individual irregularity with aggregate regularity' (Venn 1888, p. 14). Venn distinguishes between 'natural uniformities' (empirically-observable series occurring in nature) and those uniformities arising from games of chance. The distinction revolves around the notion of stability: natural uniformities exhibit fluctuations, while the uniformities associated with games of chance are fixed (ibid., p. 16). Only the latter type of series is truly amenable to the frequency analysis, as chance itself provides an objective, homogeneous, stationary series (so that the game, if fair, shows an aggregate regularity). In empirically-observable series, by contrast, homogeneity and regularity may not obtain, as the environment is unstable. Too many unobservables and extraneous elements interfere to introduce 'noise' into the system, and this noise is a detriment to valid inference.

In referring to the use of probability in the analysis of human behavior, Venn notes that it is not always possible to measure the subjective degree of belief in a proposition due to the influence of such extraneous elements as emotion and surprise. These countervailing tendencies interfere with the maintenance of the necessary appropriate homogeneous reference class. In fact, one of the major problems with the frequency interpretation is in defining the appropriate reference class: A.J. Ayer (1961, pp. 369–70) insists upon narrowing the class by conjunction ($A \cap B \cap C \dots$), while Salmon (1967, pp. 91–93) insists on the broadest homogeneous reference class.

Statements of frequencies are regarded as true or false irrespective of whether they are believed to be so, and so are of a completely objective nature. The frequency interpretation is thus devoid of any reference to the degree of belief or knowledge concerning the outcome of a future event.

Yet subjective considerations must enter when the situation involves actual decision-making among alternatives. Objective frequencies alone are not sufficient to serve as a basis for action.

Necessarian (logical) probability

The logical or necessarian approach to probability is most closely associated with John Maynard Keynes' 1921 *Treatise on Probability*, and can be found as well in the works of Ludwig Wittgenstein (*Tractatus Logico-Philosophicus*, 1921) and Carnap (*Logical Foundations of Probability*, 1950). We shall concentrate attention here on Keynes' interpretation of the logical approach.

Keynesian probability is essentially a *relational* calculus. According to Keynes, arguments are either conclusive or inconclusive. Conclusive arguments are those of which a proposition (the conclusion) is entailed by the premises; this is the realm of pure knowledge as distinguished from mere belief. (Keynes regards knowledge as fundamental.) Inconclusive arguments are those in which a proposition stands in a relation of less than certainty to the premises, while still holding a claim to some *degree* of certainty. Belief – by which is meant 'rational belief', belief dependent upon evidence – is defined with respect to knowledge; rational belief in a proposition lies somewhere along a continuum extending from 'pure ignorance' to 'pure knowledge'. Only when rational belief is certain may it be regarded as knowledge (Keynes 1921 [1973], pp. 10–11).

All judgments of probability are relative to the knowledge of a given proposition. Let h represent the premises of an argument; h then is termed an *evidential proposition*. Let a represent the conclusions. Then we may assert that a stands in relation to h, i.e., a R h. (Technically, both a and h are propositional *functions*.) The evidential statements are then readily seen to be inseparable from the conclusions derived. Specify R as the relation of probability, P. Then a P h represents what Keynes terms the primitive, undefined, conditional probability relation.

The proposition a – the *primary proposition* – may be known directly, or indirectly through knowledge of the evidential propositions and knowledge of a certainty-relation between premise and conclusion. The primary proposition is a derivative of the evidentiary statement, the connecting link being the *secondary proposition*. Knowledge requires that one possess direct and certain apprehension of the proposition a or, failing that, that the proposition h be known with certainty and that a secondary proposition be known which states a certainty relation. The proposition a is known in this second instance with certainty, but this knowledge is indirect.

A degree of rational belief of less than certainty, by contrast, implies that either the secondary proposition is known and we have insufficient knowledge regarding the primary proposition, or the evidential proposition is known but the secondary proposition asserts a *probability* relation. While the *probability relation* itself does not depend upon the evidence, the *magnitude of this probability* does so depend. This Keynes terms knowledge *about* the proposition a; because in this case we deal not with knowledge but with belief, all we can assert is that $0 < P < 1$ (Keynes 1921 [1973], pp. 11–18).

Elaborating on the relation of probability to rational belief, Keynes further defines the conditional probability, $a \mid h$, as equal to α; α is, in other words, the degree of rational belief in the conclusion relative to evidence (Keynes 1921 [1973], p. 4). As h represents relevant knowledge, one will not entertain a degree of rational belief of less than α. Should it be the case that we have an alternative set of premises representing incomplete knowledge or partial evidence (we may not have access to all available evidence, or for some reason may neglect to incorporate it), the degree of rational belief resulting will differ from that based on more complete knowledge.[7]

How, then, are we to understand probability? For Keynes, probability is subjective in the sense that a proposition stands in relation to knowledge in varying degrees and is therefore knowledge-dependent; it is objective in that, once the evidence is given, the probability judgment is no longer in question. The objective component pertains to the probability relation itself. The subjective element enters through the premises with respect to which the conclusion is related with a degree of rational belief, as the premises will be contingent on the circumstances underlying the formation of this judgment.

There are thus three aspects to Keynesian probability: the logical relation, which is objective; the *knowledge* of this relation, which is subjective; and the knowledge of the central propositions or premises from which conclusions are derived with respect to the probability relation, which is also subjective (Keynes 1921 [1973], pp. 18–19). The objective aspect of Keynesian probability is defined solely with respect to the probability relation; the relation is objective, while the judgment is subjective.

Of central import to Keynes' *general* approach is the notion that probability cannot be restricted to a measurable function. Indeed, on this view it is only to a limited extent that it is possible to determine numerically definite probabilities at all (specifically, to ascertain when it is legitimate to apply the Principle of Indifference or when it is possible to make judgments of probability on the basis of a knowledge of frequencies, and when the conditions for determining the relevant frequencies are met). At the other end of the spectrum, probability in the most general sense (which is the way Keynes expresses it) allows for the possibility of unique events, i.e., it accommodates surprise in the sense of G.L.S. Shackle (1972).

Despite Keynes' critical attitude toward measurement, he does accept the possibility of comparison, such a comparison as may be achieved through a rank order of greater or less. Such an ordering, though, affords only an approximation, not an exact numerical series. Once the ordinal scale is constructed and probabilities ordered, then, one may obtain a close approximation.

Keynesian probability is therefore an order calculus. Yet only where a probability relation is known, and a unique and homogeneous reference class is identified, is an order possible. The axiom of transitivity, for instance, is valid only for such a unidimensional comparison. Any and all alternative series consisting of common (coincident) events are non-comparable. All that is certain with multiple, intersecting series is that probability lies somewhere between certainty and impossibility; along which continuum and in what relation to other values of probability are questions not readily answerable (Keynes 1921 [1973], pp. 32–38).

Keynes stipulates certain properties of ordered series as central to his system. These are (1) every probability lies between certainty and impossibility, and the whole forms an ordered series; (2) the series is not necessarily or even in most instances compact, since 'betweenness' is not a necessary property of a series (and so represents to a limited extent a departure from the above-listed axioms); (3) the same probability can belong to more than one series; and (4) if ABC and BCD are ordered series, where A < B < C, and B < C < D, then ABCD is also an ordered series. The consequence of these conditions is that each set of degrees of rational belief comprises an ordered series, ordered by the relation 'between'; all probabilities lie between 0 and 1 (designating impossibility and certainty, respectively); and if A lies between 0 and B (this being termed AB), then B > A and 0A and A1 are true for all probabilities (Keynes 1921 [1973], pp. 42–43).

Finally, we must address a point that is, in a sense, unique to Keynes. In making comparisons of probabilities, Keynes distinguishes between (1) situations in which the evidence is the same but the conclusions reached in respect of the evidence differ (a judgment of preference), and (2) situations in which the evidence differs, but the conclusions reached are the same (Keynes 1921 [1973], p. 58). The first type relates to a comparison between $x|h$ and $y|h$. Where the judgments are equivalent, i.e., where $x|h = y|h$, we find ourselves indifferent; should the equality not hold, we exhibit a preference for one over the other.

The second type is a judgment of the *relevance* of the premises themselves, and compares $x|h$ to $x|h_1h$. If additional evidence makes no difference to the conclusion, this evidence is termed irrelevant; otherwise, it is said to add *weight* to the conclusion. The notion of weight is of particular interest to Keynesian probability, since it relates conceptually to the degree of confidence one can express in a probability judgment as a guide to conduct: the greater the weight, the more intense the preference.[8]

Now we are in a position to connect belief and weight. While additional relevant evidence may increase or decrease the degree of *belief* in a given proposition (i.e., it is consistent with increased, decreased, or unchanged values of probability), it will *always* have the effect of increasing the *weight* of the argument (as it increases the degree of confidence in any conclusion drawn). Weight is a function of the *completeness* of the evidence, not its mass. As weight is increased, so Keynes suggests, the confidence level – the extent to which we might feel justified in relying on probability as a guide to conduct – is increased.

Personalistic probability
The personalistic theory of probability, sometimes also referred to as subjective probability, has its beginnings in the work of Emile Borel and Ramsey, and

was later refined by Savage. This concept of probability lies at the heart of current micro- and macroeconomic analysis as well as the game-theoretic analysis of choice.

Borel's 'A propos d'un traité de probabilités', published in the *Revue Philosophique* in 1924, is the pioneering statement of the principles of subjective probability. Here Borel differentiates between objective and subjective probabilities. Objective probabilities are those 'common to the judgments of all the best informed persons', and may also be termed event probabilities; these are the probabilities associated with the frequency approach. Subjective probabilities are those the value of which depends on the apprehensions of the individual; they are more on the order of opinion (Borel 1924 [1964], p. 50).

Borel's contribution lies in the establishment of a method whereby probability could be measured through the use of a betting method. Qualitative probability (degrees of rational belief) may be quantified through the use of an experimental mechanism which allows for a scale of comparison.

Ramsey offers an interpretation of probability similar to that of Borel, emphasizing the measurability of probability and the elicitation of probability values through the use of behavioristic experimentation. In his 'Truth and Probability' (1926), Ramsey sets to the task of developing 'a purely psychological method of measuring belief' (Ramsey 1926 [1990], p. 62). For Ramsey, all belief is measurable; it is of little use to distinguish between measurable and non-measurable components (risk and uncertainty) since, even were the distinction relevant, it is not important enough to disallow quantification of that segment of rational belief amenable to measurement. All that is required is consistency.

Ramsey did offer a solution to the measurement problem. His proposal identifies degree of belief with a measure of the individual's preparedness to *act* upon that belief, i.e., his willingness to accept a 'bet'. To account for the difficulty of measuring something as vague and indefinable as 'feelings', Ramsey concentrates on effects, meaning the *consequences* of action. Probability must then deal with 'belief *qua* basis of action' (Ramsey 1926 [1990] p. 67). For Ramsey, the problem with studying behavior by examining responses to a series of monetary bets, as had been suggested by Borel, was that this method was 'insufficiently general'. In its place he proposes one look at 'goods' and 'bads', and so offers a psychological experimental approach.

In devising his version of personalist or subjective probability, Ramsey discards the additivity and measurability assumptions in favor of an axiomatization based on the concept of an 'ethically-neutral' proposition, a proposition the truth or falsity of which is irrelevant to the individual (Ramsey 1926 [1990], p. 73). This proposition is given a value of $\frac{1}{2}$. In conjunction with the requisite set of axioms and theorems which specify relations between 'states', Ramsey could employ the concept of ethically-neutral propositions as a basis for measuring beliefs. Preference gives an ordering relation that is in a one-to-one correspondence with the real numbers. Measurability is accomplished with relatively few restrictions, and probability theory is placed on as logical a foundation as is mathematics. There is no need of a Principle of Indifference.[9]

Savage's *Foundations of Statistics* (1954; 2nd edn 1972) presents a form of personalism that extends the theories of Borel and Ramsey to account for decision-making as it concerns the relation of acts to consequences; this is not so much a theory of probability as it is a theory of expected utility. Savage's theory then relates to the theory of utility developed by John von Neumann and Oskar Morgenstern, to which we shall briefly turn.

In their *Theory of Games and Economic Behavior* (3rd edn, 1953), von Neumann and Morgenstern postulate an individual possessing complete information and a totally-ordered preference set. Since cardinality is the focus of von Neumann–Morgenstern utility theory (as opposed to the ordinalism inherent in the Keynesian probability approach), the frequency theory is essential to its elucidation. Cardinality requires that values be defined only up to a linear transformation. Uniqueness guarantees the existence of a numerical scale; the linear transformation is order-preserving, sign-preserving, and marginal utility-preserving, unlike the ordinal measure, which is only order- and sign-preserving. However, subjective probability cannot be completely discounted, as it may be incorporated into a theory of utility provided 'the two concepts (probability and preference) can be axiomatized together' (von Neumann and Morgenstern 1953, p. 19 n. 2). *If* the choices are *consistent*, i.e., if the decision-maker's ranking is complete and transitive, a cardinal index may be constructed as easily as if the probabilities were objective. This simultaneous axiomatization of utility and subjective probability is precisely that attempted by Savage; Savage needs only the weaker definition of monotonicity, but can retain cardinality.

The difference between the two utility concepts (Savage and von Neumann/Morgenstern) is inconsequential. The von Neumann–Morgenstern axioms refer to comparisons among *utilities*; the Savage axioms weigh comparisons among *acts*. For Savage, an act is a function attaching a consequence to each state of the world, and so an act is identified with its consequences; more strictly, an act is a function mapping states to consequences. It is this mapping which is central to Savage; the reliance on consequences leads to a preoccupation with risk as opposed to uncertainty and to a strict reliance on ordinal utility, which Savage classifies, after George Stigler (1950), as 'probability-less' theory (Savage 1972, p. 96).

In terms of axiomatization, Savage favors the more restrictive total ordering on the grounds of consistency; his definition requires only connectedness and transitivity, combined with irreflexivity (whereby either $a < b$ or $b < a$, but not both. The total order, being more restrictive, guarantees comparability.

Savage notes that the universe of propositions under consideration may be reduced in size and complexity by ignoring the non-fundamental distinctions between states, allowing elements of little or no possibility (of measure zero) to be considered as equally unlikely and therefore to be ignored for purposes of decision-making (Savage 1972, pp. 9–10). Nothing in the formal definition of a probability measure precludes elements of measure zero. However, Savage (as well as Paul Halmos (1944), and A.N. Kolmogorov (1950)) defines probability in such a way that any two subsets of an event set (an event being a set of states) are to be considered identical which difference has probability zero. The relevant σ-algebra is thus reduced by identifying elements of zero measure with the null class of elements, which by definition have probability zero. Savage needs only finite additivity for this obvious reason.

Probability in economics

Uncertainty vs. risk

Discussions of probability, especially in the economic context, seem almost of necessity to require some comment on the place of uncertainty. The term 'uncertainty' is somewhat ambiguous, and is often employed in two quite different ways: in reference to the manifest variability of the environment, and to our *apprehension* of that environment. In other words, there is a distinction between the occurrence or non-occurrence of an event, and our *belief* that the event will occur or has occurred. The former is ontological, the latter epistemic.

We may begin by reviewing the connection between probability, risk, and uncertainty. Following the presentation of Lawson (1988), we may distinguish probability types as either aleatory or epistemic, i.e., probability as an object of the environment, and probability as a form of knowledge, respectively. Risk and uncertainty denote the degree of commensurability. We have thus four categories: aleatory risk, epistemic risk, aleatory uncertainty, and epistemic uncertainty. *Aleatory risk* is descriptive of events that belong within the confines of the frequency interpretation; it refers to the intrinsic nature of chance events numerically measurable and representable as stationary, homogeneous series. *Epistemic risk* refers to beliefs and apprehensions of chance events that can be evaluated and internalized by the subjective application of the numerical probability calculus; we are aware that an event may transpire, and, further, we can arrive at a degree of belief as to its potential for occurrence. *Aleatory uncertainty* includes unique, empirical events for which a reference class may not exist; the event may have a 'facility' of occurrence, but has not done so in fact (or if it has, this is beyond our knowledge). *Epistemic uncertainty* takes account of the situations of which we are incapable of forming any belief or opinion; we simply have no reason to conclude that an event is possible let alone probable, for we have no mechanism for assigning a reference class. *Ignorance* is a final category of unknown probabilities, and connotes incommensurability as well as the lack of knowledge of the secondary proposition (also part of the Keynesian view of probability). We are ignorant if we not only cannot determine whether a reference class exists, but are equally uncertain about the *procedure* for determining this fact.

It must be noted that the aleatory category is only strictly defined with respect to risk. Aleatory means 'depending upon chance', while epistemic means 'the act of knowing'. Chance implies risk; uncertainty implies lack of knowledge. In the most general terms, uncertainty implies unknowability, and may best be understood within the context of belief. As noted above, in respect of Keynes' interpretation of probability, certainty is 'the highest degree of rational belief'. Lower orders of rational belief may be equated with '*degrees* of certainty', and may be amenable to analysis through the probability calculus; one may in fact argue (as Keynes does) that certainty is 'maximum probability' (Keynes 1921 [1973], pp. 15–16). Uncertainty (for Keynes, at least) relates to an inability to apprehend the probability *relation* (not indeed an inability to arrive at any specific probability *value*) – we have but a limited ability of perceiving the mechanism that allows us to form probability judgments, and so have no foundation upon which to make the necessary comparisons.

Continuing on, the terms epistemic risk and epistemic uncertainty denote those instances in which apprehension is limited by knowledge deficiencies, and those instances in which there is no mechanism by which we may arrive at a valuation of belief, respectively. Epistemic risk and epistemic uncertainty are most clearly identified with the economics of Keynes, which follows along the lines of his approach to probability. Similarly, aleatory risk and aleatory uncertainty denote those instances in which events are seriable and those instances of single, non-seriable occurrences, respectively. An approach that relies on aleatory risk and aleatory uncertainty is Frank Knight's 1921 *Risk, Uncertainty, and Profit*.

In sum, uncertainty is only truly defined epistemically. The world is not uncertain – uncertainty has no independent existence – and therefore one cannot perceive or confront uncertainty. Rather, there is generated, within individuals, *feelings* of uncertainty, so that we *are* in some circumstances uncertain. Events are unpredictable, the environment may be unstable and highly variable, but it is our *apprehension* of this environment that engenders uncertainty.

Having explicated various approaches to probability, we have now to conclude by showing very briefly the way in which these ideas have been incorporated into economic theory.

Keynesianism

While Keynes himself understood the distinction between epistemic and ontological uncertainty, and the importance of the former to an understanding of the decision process, those who identify themselves as Keynesians have not in general come to regard the distinction as significant, and so have for the most part ignored Keynesian necessarianism in favor of frequentism and personalism.

In seeking to retain the mathematical framework of probability – at least for the sake of tractability – New Keynesians and Post Keynesians, while purporting to construct models accounting for uncertainty, stipulate those very incongruities Keynes himself dismisses as inconsistent with epistemics. New Keynesians focus attention on informational differentials and the uncertainties engendered as a result of interdependencies among economic agents. Robert Gordon (1990) and Shaun Hargreaves Heap (1995) offer efficient summaries of this perspective. Perhaps the most prominent Post Keynesian commentator on the subject is Paul Davidson (1988), who distinguishes between ergodic and non-ergodic theory, concocting a binary environment of certainty (1) and uncertainty (0). One can then deny by definition the existence of a *continuum* of probability judgments ranging from the numerically definite to the vaguely comparative. If one assumes a stochastic environment, as neoclassical economists are alleged to do, ergodicity is merely a sufficient condition for convergence to equilibrium. If one assumes a non-ergodic environment, taken to be consistent with Keynes' own analysis, then the future cannot be predicted, probabilities cannot be calculated, and so contingent claims contracts take on central importance.

Other Keynesian presentations fare somewhat better with respect to the handling of uncertainty, but are also in some sense deficient. David Dequech (1997a, 1997b), for one, distinguishes between strong and weak uncertainty, but does so with respect to *information*, not with *belief* or to the *subjective apprehensions* of the individuals under consideration. There is here a confusion between weight and uncertainty.

Rational expectations
The rational expectations approach to economics is actually *predicated* on the notion that uncertainty *per se* is irrelevant. Here, following Savage and von Neumann and Morgenstern, the underlying probability space is restricted so as to include only *measurable* elements. Specifically, such models are typically constructed under the assumption that there exists a triple $(\Omega, \mathcal{T}, P)$, where Ω is a state-space, $\mathcal{T}$ is a σ-algebra of subsets of Ω, and P is a probability measure defined on $\mathcal{T}$. A random variable is a function $\theta: \Omega \rightarrow R$. (By definition, then, the random variable is measurable. To be more specific, θ is measurable if, when $B \in \mathcal{T}$, $\theta^{-1}(B) \in \mathcal{T}$.) Define a stationary stochastic process as a collection of random variables θ indexed over time: $\Theta = \{\theta_1, \theta_2, ..., \theta_T\}$, with the following properties:

(1) $E(\theta_t) = \mu$, $\forall$ t

(2) $\sigma(\theta_t, \theta_{t+r}) = E[(\theta_t - \mu)(\theta_{t+r} - \mu)]$, $\forall$ t, r

(3) $var(\theta_t) = \sigma_\theta^2$, $\forall$ t

where E is the expected-value operator.

The process is time-independent, and may be characterized completely by the first and second moments. Now, if: $P[\theta_{t+1}|\theta_0, \theta_1, ..., \theta_t] = P[\theta_{t+1}|\theta_t] \; \forall \; t$, then $\{\theta_t\}$ follows a Markov process. It is upon this foundation that the rational expectations model is constructed.

Despite claims of a Ramsey–Savage basis in accounting for uncertainty, the need for any such foundation is unclear; here, the logic of choice is not an issue, and non-comparability and non-measurability are irrelevant by assumption. As the new classical macroeconomists are primarily concerned with *prediction*, not with questions of knowledge or epistemology, the focus is on risk. To the extent that uncertainty is mentioned, it is of the Knightian variety.[10]

Efforts at reintroducing choice into new neoclassicism, such as those of Richard Cyert and Morris DeGroot (1974) and Robert Townsend (1978), have succeeded in adding Bayesian learning to the models, but continue to ignore fundamental uncertainty, while the model of David Cass and Karl Shell (1983) actually succeeds in incorporating the element of 'surprise' (although the 'shock' is objective and so the manifest uncertainty is ontological).

Austrianism
Economists working in the Austrian tradition may variously be regarded as necessarians or personalists, as questions of subjectivism, information, knowledge, and epistemic uncertainty are afforded central place. The focus on process combines with a concern with the shortcomings of measurement. In Austrianism, we see with Ludwig von Mises (1949), the brother of Richard, an explicit rejection of the conflation of probability with frequency (non-seriable events cannot be ignored), and with Friedrich Hayek (1937, 1945) an emphasis on process and learning (the logic of choice), which suggests an affinity with the Keynesian concept of weight. In addition, Shackle (1949–50, 1956), who straddles the Austrian and Keynesian traditions, emphasizes elements of uniqueness, surprise, possibility, openness, and epistemic uncertainty, as he rejects many of the postulates of frequentism.

Acknowledgements
I wish to thank John Davis, Alain Marciano, and Jochen Runde for many helpful comments on an earlier draft. Much of the material here follows McCann (1994).

Notes
1. These letters have been reprinted in Whitaker (1996). See in particular Letters 967, 971, 972.
2. For an appreciation of Edgeworth's contributions, see Stephen M. Stigler (1986).
3. A number of interpetations of probability do not conform to these axioms. For example, Axiom 1 does not hold with respect to those approaches that allow a place for vague or non-numerical probabilities.

4. See especially Russell (1948, pp. 345–6). See also Keynes (1921 [1973], Chs 12–15), which elaborates axioms, theorems, and definitions essential to the grounding of probability. Bernard Koopman (1940: 164–5) presents a slightly different set of axioms predicated on the partial order.
5. On the notion of order, see especially Kolmogorov and Fomin (1970, pp. 20–21) and Savage (1972, pp. 18, 21).
6. This is but one means of expressing the law of large numbers. On different 'laws' of large numbers, see Richard von Mises (1957).
7. On this, see especially Russell (1948, pp. 376–7) and Keynes (1921 [1973], Ch.1.).
8. On the weight of arguments, see especially Runde (1990, 1991).
9. Interestingly enough, in insisting that 'the laws of probability are laws of consistency, an extension to partial beliefs of formal logic, the logic of consistency', Ramsey actually accepts, after a fashion, the necessarianism of Keynes (Ramsey 1926 [1990], p. 78). He even goes so far as to acknowledge that 'the calculus of probabilities', as a branch of logic, is 'concerned simply to ensure that our beliefs are not self-contradictory' (ibid., p. 87), and even later argues that '[a] *probability-theory* is a set of numbers associated with pairs of propositions obeying the calculus of probabilities' (Ramsey 1929 [1990], p. 96; emphasis in original).
10. This is explicitly accepted by Robert Lucas. See Arjo Klamer (1984, p. 44). See also Stephen LeRoy and Larry Singell (1987) for a more thorough discussion of the Knightian dichotomy.

References

Ayer, Alfred Jules (1952), *Language, Truth, and Logic*, New York: Dover.
Ayer, Alfred Jules (1961), 'On the probability of particular events', *Revue Internationale de Philosophie*, **XV** (58), 366–75.
Borel, Emile (1924 [1964]), 'Apropos of a treatise on probability', in Henry E. Kyburg, Jr. and Howard E. Smokler (eds), *Studies in Subjective Probability*, New York: John Wiley.
Carnap, Rudolf (1950), *Logical Foundations of Probability*, Chicago: University of Chicago Press.
Cass, David, and Karl Shell (1983), 'Do sunspots matter?', *Journal of Political Economy*, **91** (2), 193–227.
Cyert, Richard and Morris DeGroot (1974), 'Rational expectations and Bayesian analysis', *Journal of Political Economy*, **82** (3), 521–36.
Davidson, Paul (1988), 'A technical definition of uncertainty and the long-run non-neutrality of money', *Cambridge Journal of Economics*, **12** (3), 329–37.
de Finetti, Bruno (1964), 'Foresight: its logical laws, its subjective sources', in H.E. Kyburg and H. Smokler (eds), *Studies in Subjective Probability*, New York: Wiley.
Dequech, David (1997a), 'Uncertainty in a strong sense: meaning and sources', *Economic Issues*, **2** (part 2), 21–43.
Dequech, David (1997b), 'A brief note on Keynes, unknown probabilities and uncertainty in a strong sense', *History of Economic Ideas*, **V** (2), 101–10.
Gordon, Robert (1990), 'What is the New-Keynesian Economics?' *Journal of Economic Literature*, **XXVIII** (3), 1115–71.
Hacking, Ian (1975), *The Emergence of Probability*, Cambridge: Cambridge University Press.
Hacking, Ian (1990), *The Taming of Chance*, Cambridge: Cambridge University Press.
Halmos, Paul R. (1944), 'The foundations of probability', *American Mathematical Monthly*, **51**, 493–510.
Hargreaves Heap, Shaun (1995), *The New Keynesian Macroeconomics*, Aldershot, UK and Brookfield US: Edward Elgar.
Hayek, Friedrich A. von (1937), 'Economics and knowledge', *Economica* (NS), **IV** (13), 33–54.
Hayek, Friedrich A. von (1945), 'The use of knowledge in society', *American Economic Review*, **XXXV** (4), 519–30.
Jeffreys, Harold (1931), *Theory of Probability*, Oxford: Clarendon Press.
Keynes, John Maynard (1921 [1973]), *Treatise on Probability*, vol.VIII of *The Collected Writings of John Maynard Keynes*, edited by D. Moggridge, New York: St. Martin's Press for the Royal Economic Society.
Klamer, Arjo (1984), *Conversations with Economists*, Totowa, NJ: Rowman and Allanheld.

Knight, Frank H. (1921), *Risk, Uncertainty, and Profit*, Boston: Houghton Mifflin.
Kolmogorov, A.N. (1950), *Foundations of the Theory of Probability*, translated by Nathan Morrison, New York: Chelsea.
Kolmogorov, A.N. and S.V. Fomin (1970), *Introductory Real Analysis*, New York: Dover.
Koopman, B.O. (1940 [1964]), 'The bases of probability', in Henry E. Kyburg, Jr. and Howard E. Smokler (eds), *Studies in Subjective Probability*, New York: John Wiley.
Laplace, Pierre Simon (1820 [1951]), *Philosophical Essay on Probabilities*, translated by F.W. Truscott and F.L. Emory, New York: Dover.
Lawson, Tony (1987), 'The relative/absolute nature of knowledge and economic analysis', *Economic Journal*, **97** (388) (December), 951–70.
Lawson, Tony (1988), 'Probability and uncertainty in economic analysis', *Journal of Post Keynesian Economics*, **XI** (1) (Fall), 38–65.
LeRoy, Stephen F. and Larry D. Singell, Jr. (1987), 'Knight on risk and uncertainty', *Journal of Political Economy*, **95** (2) (April), 394–406.
McCann, Charles R., Jr. (1994), *Probability Foundations of Economic Theory*, London: Routledge.
Mises, Ludwig von (1949), *Human Action*, New Haven, CT: Yale University Press.
Mises, Richard von (1941), 'On the foundations of probability and statistics', *Annals of Mathematical Statistics*, **12**, 191–205.
Mises, Richard von (1957), *Probability, Statistics and Truth*, 3rd edn, translated by Hilda Geiringer, New York: Dover.
von Neumann, John, and Oskar Morgenstern (1953), *Theory of Games and Economic Behavior*, 3rd edn, New York: John Wiley.
Ramsey, Frank P. (1926 [1990]), 'Truth and probability', in D.H. Mellor (ed.), *Philosophical Papers*, Cambridge: Cambridge University Press.
Ramsey, Frank P. (1929 [1990]), 'Probability and partial belief', in D.H. Mellor (ed.), *Philosophical Papers*, Cambridge: Cambridge University Press.
Runde, Jochen (1990), 'Keynesian uncertainty and the weight of arguments', *Economics and Philosophy*, **6** (2), 275–92.
Runde, Jochen (1991), 'Keynesian uncertainty and the instability of beliefs,' *Review of Political Economy*, **3** (2), 125–45.
Russell, Bertrand (1912), *The Problems of Philosophy*, Oxford: Oxford University Press.
Russell, Bertrand (1948), *Human Knowledge: Its Scope and Limits*, New York: Simon and Schuster.
Salmon, Wesley C. (1967), *The Foundations of Scientific Inference*, Pittsburgh: University of Pittsburgh Press.
Savage, Leonard J. (1972), *The Foundations of Statistics*, 2nd edn, New York: Dover.
Shackle, G.L.S. (1949–50), 'A non-additive measure of uncertainty', *Review of Economic Studies*, **17**, 70–74.
Shackle, G.L.S. (1956), 'Expectation and cardinality', *Economic Journal*, **66** (262), 211–19.
Shackle, G.L.S. (1972), *Epistemics and Economics: A Critique of Economic Doctrines*, Cambridge: Cambridge University Press.
Stigler, George J. (1950), 'The development of utility theory', *Journal of Political Economy*, Part I: **58** (3), 307–27; Part II: **58** (5), 373–96.
Stigler, Stephen M. (1986), *The History of Statistics: The Measurement of Uncertainty Before 1900*, Cambridge, MA: Belknap Press.
Todhunter, Isaac (1865 [1949]), *A History of the Mathematical Theory of Probability*, New York: Chelsea.
Townsend, Robert M. (1978), 'Market anticipations, rational expectations, and Bayesian analysis', *International Economic Review*, **19** (2), 481–94.
Venn, John (1888 [1962]), *The Logic of Chance*, 4th edn, New York: Chelsea.
Weatherford, Roy (1982), *Philosophical Foundations of Probability Theory*, London: Routledge and Kegan Paul.
Whitaker, John K. (1996), *The Correspondence of Alfred Marshall, Economist*, vol. III, *Towards the Close, 1903–1924*, Cambridge: Cambridge University Press for the Royal Economic Society.
Wittgenstein, Ludwig (1921 [1963]), *Tractatus Logico-Philosophicus*, translated by D.F. Pears and B.F. McGuinness, London: Routledge and Kegan Paul.

23 Money

Geoffrey Ingham

Introduction

In the late nineteenth and early twentieth centuries, the question of the nature of money played a central role in the methodological dispute (*Methodenstreit*) during which modern academic economics was formed (Hodgson 2001). As Schumpeter observed at the time, '[t]ere are only two theories of money which deserve the name ... the commodity theory and the claim theory. From their very nature they are incompatible' (quoted in Ellis 1934, p. 3). With the economic theorists' victory and subsequent hegemony, the commodity-exchange theory of money came to dominate the 'orthodox mainstream' conception of money (Smithin 1994; Goodhart 1998).

There are two slightly different variants of the commodity theory. On the one hand, as in common sense, money is regarded as a 'thing' that 'circulates' with a 'velocity'. Apart from other serious problems, this conception was anachronistic at the time of its classical statement in Fisher's 'quantity theory' (1907). By then, virtually all significant transactions were carried out by the book clearance of debits and credits in the banking giro, not by the circulation of 'money-stuff'. Moreover, a hundred years on in the era of 'e-money', the analytical structure of 'quantity theory', continues to inform orthodox economics.

On the other hand, it is also asserted that money is analytically unimportant, that money is no more than a 'neutral veil' over transactions in the 'real economy'. Neoclassical economics' most prestigious paradigm (general equilibrium theory) acknowledges that it has no place for money in its mathematical models (Hahn 1987, p. 1). In the Walrasian model, money exists only as a *numeraire* that in no way affects the determination of value in *commodity-exchange*. In this regard, it is important to note that the *numeraire* is not pure abstract value, but rather the symbolic representation of the value of an arbitrarily chosen commodity, or 'bundle' of commodities. As money is not held to play a vital role in the economy, this tradition has consequently shown little or no concern for the ontology of money – that is to say, its nature and conditions of existence.

During the *Methodenstreit*, an alternative to this commodity-exchange theory of money was advanced by the broad 'Historical School of Economics' and this has influenced, at least implicitly, contemporary sociological and heterodox economic thinking. Here, more emphasis is given to the abstract nature of monetary value and how this is socially and politically constructed. Money of account, in this view, defines the 'token' value of money as a 'claim' or a 'promise' of payment. Banished from academic economics and, as a result of economic theory's hegemony, neglected by modern sociology, this analysis was virtually lost to mainstream social science. It is claimed that Marxism avoided these errors (Fine and Lapavitsas 2000); but this tradition has itself been weakened by a conception of money as a 'mask' or 'veil' over an underlying 'reality' (Ingham 2001).[1]

Differences between the two conceptions are evident in the emphases that they give to money's 'functions'. By the late nineteenth century, the question of what money *is* had given way, in economic analysis, to an evasive functionalist definition, which remains the standard textbook approach. Money *is* what money *does*, and it is said to do three things. It is (1) a measure of value (unit, or money of account); (2) a medium of exchange and means of payment; (3) a store of value. From this deceptively simple starting point problems soon become apparent. Do *all* the functions have to be performed? Are they all of equal importance? If not, which is definitive? Mainstream economics has focused on money as a *medium of exchange*; the other functions are assumed to follow from it. The 'historical' alternative stresses the importance of *money of account* as a measure of *abstract* value – that is, purchasing power that is stored and transported through time. The distinction has a long pedigree.[2]

Economic orthodoxy: money in the 'real economy'
Modelling itself on the natural sciences, economics sought to establish deductive 'laws' based on the axioms of individual rational choice maximisation of utility and the associated equilibrium model of the perfectly competitive market (Hodgson 2001). This 'economy' comprises exchange ratios between commodities (object–object relations), established by individual acts of utility calculation (individual agent–object relations). Agent–agent, or social relations form no part of the model (Ganssmann 1988). The object–object and agent–object relations constitute what is known as the 'real' economy.

This 'real' economy is essentially a model of a simple 'natural' (moneyless) barter economy in which 'higgling' transforms myriad exchange ratios into a single price for a uniform good (for the classic description, see Schumpeter, 1954 [1994], p.277). Money is introduced into the model as a commodity that acts as a medium of exchange to facilitate the process – for example, cigarettes in prison. As a commodity, the medium of exchange can have an exchange ratio with other commodities. Or as a symbol, it can *directly* represent 'real' commodities. It is in this sense that money is a 'neutral veil' that has no efficacy other than to overcome the 'inconveniences of barter' which, in the late nineteenth century formulation, result from the absence of a 'double coincidence of 'wants'. Exchange with money is more efficient than barter, but analytically they are *structurally* identical. Consequently, orthodox economic theory is unable to uniquely specify money; it cannot analytically distinguish money from commodities (Clower 1984).

Menger's (1892) rational choice analysis of the evolution of money remains the basis for neoclassical explanations of money's existence (Dowd 2000; Klein and Selgin 2000). Money is the unintended consequence of individual economic rationality. In order to maximise their barter options, traders hold stocks of the most tradable commodities which, consequently, become *media of exchange* – beans, cigarettes, etc. Coinage is explained with the further conjecture that precious metals have additional advantageous properties – such as durability, divisibility, portability, etc. Metal is weighed and minted into uniform pieces and the commodity becomes money. In short, orthodox economic accounts of money are *commodity-exchange* theories. Both of money's 'historical' origins and 'logical' conditions of existence are explained as the outcome of a natural process of economic exchange (Ingham 2000a).

There are a number of serious problems with this analysis of money. First, the 'dematerialisation' of money broke the explanatory link between individual rationality and system benefits. 'Institutions such as money make for the common interest, and yet … conflict with the nearest and immediate interests of contracting individuals'. Why should the 'individual be ready to exchange his goods for little metal disks apparently useless as such, or for documents representing the latter'? (Menger quoted in Jones 1976, p. 757). Subsequently, neoclassical economics has tried to resolve the problem by showing that holding (non-commodity) money reduces transaction costs for the individual (Dowd 2000; Klein and Selgin 2000). But this in turn exposes the logical circularity of neoclassical economics' methodological individualism. It is only 'advantageous for any given agent to mediate his transactions by money *provided that all other agents do likewise*' (Hahn 1987, p. 26). To state the sociologically obvious: the advantages of money for the individual presuppose the existence of money as an institution.

Second, the 'barter→commodity→money' transition is not supported by the historical record (Ingham 2000a; Wray, 2000, 2004).

Third, the model of the natural barter economy with its 'neutral veil' of money is singularly inappropriate for understanding the capitalist monetary system. In the Commodity → Money → Commodity (C–M–C_1) sequence of the 'real' economy, money exists *only* as a *medium* for the gaining of utility through the *exchange* of commodities. It models the 'village fair' in which capitalist financing of production does not occur (Minsky 1986). In the early twentieth century, attempts were made to explain the fact of bank credit, within the framework of 'real' analysis. For example, Wicksell's 'natural' rate of interest in the 'pure credit economy' is a measure of the 'natural' propensities and productivity in the 'real' economy and not, for example, the power of bankers to set a 'money rate'. The 'natural rate of interest' is an extension of the 'neutral veil' concept insofar as money, in the last instance, can only reflect or express the 'real' (Smithin 2000, p. 6). In contrast, as Keynes stressed, capitalism involves a Money → Commodity → Money sequence (M–C–M$_1$) in which the money side is relatively autonomous. The act of bank lending *creates* money-capital to finance the future production of commodities (on Keynes, see Smithin 1994, p. 2).

However, the fundamental problem in economic orthodoxy, from which all the other difficulties stem, is the misunderstanding and neglect of *money of account*. Medium of exchange is taken to be the key function and it is assumed that all the others follow from it. The 'natural' market produces a transactions-cost efficient medium of exchange that becomes the standard of value and numerical money of account. Coins evolved from *weighing* pieces of precious metal that were cut from bars and, *after* standardisation, *counted*. Alternatively, a standard commodity or 'bundle' of commodities act as the *numeraire*. Without further assumptions, it is difficult to envisage how a money of account could emerge from myriad bilateral barter exchange ratios based upon subjective preferences. One hundred goods could yield 4950 exchange rates (Davies 1994, p. 15). How could discrete barter exchange ratios of, say, 3 chickens : 1 duck, or 6 ducks : 1 chicken, and so on, produce a single unit of account? The conventional economic answer that a 'duck standard' emerges 'spontaneously' involves a circular argument. A *single* 'duck standard' cannot be the equilibrium price of ducks established by supply and demand because, in the absence of a money of account, ducks would continue to have multiple and variable exchange values. A genuine 'market' which produces a single price for ducks requires a money of account – that is, a stable yardstick for measuring value. As opposed to the *commodity duck*, the *monetary duck* in any duck standard, would be an *abstract duck*. If the process of exchange could not have produced the abstract concept of money of account, how did it originate?

Monetarism
However, the analytical structure of the orthodox commodity theory has continued to inform mainstream economics. After the mid-twentieth century's Keynesian interlude, orthodox economic theory was restored in Friedman's 'monetarism'. Further problems soon became apparent (Smithin 1994, 1996). In 'monetarism' money is a 'thing' whose supply is 'exogenously' determined, quantifiable and controllable by the monetary authorities. *Ceteris paribus*, an increase in the supply of money will increase prices. However, it soon became apparent that it was not clear what should be counted as money – notes, coins, current bank accounts, savings accounts, etc. The issue is complex, but the concept of money as a quantifiable and controllable 'stock' produced policy incoherence in the continuous proliferation of measures of money – M_0, M_1, … M_{10} and so on (Guttman 1994). Moreover, by the 1990s, monetary aggregates

increased as inflation fell, in contradiction of the theory (Issing 2001). In practice, macro-monetary policy became focused almost exclusively on the control of 'endogenously' created bank credit-money through central banks' discount rates.

New Monetary Economics and the 'end of money'
Despite the demise of 'monetarism', the orthodox conception of money continues to guide analysis. For example, advanced communications and information technology has led to a revival of the conjecture that the Internet could become the basis for the actualisation of the model of the 'real' economy. New Monetary Economics asserts that computers could make Walras's economic model of barter–credit equilibrium a reality (Smithin 1994, 2000; OECD 2002). It is suggested that this 'end of money' would bring about the redundancy of central banking (King 1999). Pre-agreed algorithms would determine, according to the value of the transaction, which financial assets were sold by a purchaser. Computers would be able to verify *instantly* the creditworthiness of counter-parties. The unique role of central bank money as the means of final settlement would become redundant.[3]

Monetary policy as such would give way to the more 'technically neutral regulation' of the integrity of the computer systems that verify the creditworthiness of the counter-parties' assets (King 1999).

Strictly speaking, such a system would not be 'moneyless', but 'cashless'. In order to function, these barter–credit systems would only require an abstract money of account to overcome the temporal problem of Jevons's famous absence of a double coincidence of wants. The Walrasian model would be made real. The exclusive attention on medium of exchange as money's *essential* property implies that the question of money of account is unproblematic. However it is not. New Monetary Economics simply asserts that a *commodity standard*, based on the prices of a 'basket of commodities' could produce both a unit of account and benchmark standard of value. This would simply be a 'matter of public choice', and its regulation would be no more difficult than existing weights and measures inspection (King 1999).

However, such arguments rest on two basic errors. In the first place, economic value is not 'natural' like the relatively constant properties of, say, distance and weight. That is to say, economic value fluctuates in response to the distribution of social and economic power. Second, as we shall see, it is implausible that a money of account could emerge spontaneously in the process of exchange. Theoretical considerations and the historical record point to the fact that money of account has to be established by an 'authority'. Money of account is not the product of market exchange, rather it makes the 'market' possible (Keynes 1930; Ingham 1996, 2000a; Hoover 1996; Hicks 1989; Orléan 1998; Wray 2000).

Optimum currency areas
'Real' analysis with its conception of money as a neutral medium of exchange also underpins the notion of 'optimum currency areas' (Mundell 1961). Here it is argued that a process of transactions cost minimisation, based upon the economic profile of a region, will determine existence of single or multiple currencies. Factors such as openness, labour market flexibility, concentration of production, etc. are held to define a natural economic space for which a single money would be appropriate. The theory entirely lacks empirical support (Goodhart 1998). An alternative tradition insists that monetary space is 'sovereign' space which is logically anterior and historically prior to the 'economic' space (Aglietta and Orléan 1998; Ingham 2002).

Economic heterodoxy: money as abstract value and token credit
Heterodox monetary analysis has two sources. On the one hand, it can be traced to analyses of the credit-*money* that appeared in Western Europe in the sixteenth century. In this regard, it is important to note that this development did not simply involve the use of *credit* in the sense of *deferred payment*. Rather, these 'credits' were 'money' in that 'promises to pay' (IOUs), issued outside the sovereign mints, began to circulate as *means of payment*. Only later were they backed by precious metal in a hybrid bank credit/gold standard.[4] The general use of 'endogenously' generated *transferable* debt is specific to capitalism. 'Depersonalised' and hence readily transferable debt is used as means of payment to a third party: A's IOU held by B is used to pay C (Ingham 1999). After two thousand years during which coin and money were synonymous, this new money-form posed intellectual puzzles (Sherman 1997). Some of the answers departed from the Aristotelian commodity theories of money. They led to the idea that *all* money was *constituted* by *social relations* of credit and debt (Ingham 2000a, p. 23).

A second source of heterodox analysis accompanied the construction of the nineteenth century German state. Money's role in taxation and as the expression of national integrity and power were emphasised. Knapp's *State Theory of Money* (1905 [1973]), challenged economic explanations of money's properties in terms of the exchange value of its commodity form. By declaring what it accepts for the discharge of tax debt, *denominated in its own unit of account*, the state creates and establishes the 'validity' of money. Private bank notes become money when they are denominated in the state's money of account and accepted as payment of tax debts owed to the state and reissued in payment to the state's creditors (Knapp 1905 [1973], pp. 95, 143, 196). Money consists in a *reciprocal relationship*: states issue 'credits' to pay for their goods and services which, in turn, must be acquired for payment of taxes. Money is a 'token' that 'bears' units of *abstract* value. 'State theory' is also known as 'chartalism' (from 'charta', the Latin for token) and sometimes as monetary 'nominalism' (Ellis

1934). Both the claim/credit and state theory approaches are, at least implicitly, concerned with the essential properties of money and its social construction – that is to say, with money as an 'institutional fact' (Searle 1995).

In these approaches, money is generically an abstract or nominal claim or credit, regardless of its specific form. The state theory of money, especially, was anathema to the early twentieth proponents of the exchange theory of value (catallaxy). In objecting that states could not establish the purchasing power of money, the economic theorists misunderstood Knapp. In fact, his argument helps to resolve commodity theory's difficulty in trying to identify the 'moneyness' by its utility or exchange value alone. Economic theory cannot uniquely specify money – that is, distinguish money from other commodities. Following Knapp, money becomes a commodity with an exchange value only *after* it has been constituted as money by a social and political process. States establish the 'validity' of money by the 'proclamation' of the *nominal unit of abstract value* and the 'acceptation' of the tokens that correspond to it.

The Historical School's analysis influenced Simmel's sociological classic *The Philosophy of Money*, but after the sharp division of intellectual labour in the social sciences following the *Methodenstreit* its impact on the discipline was muted (Ingham 1998). However, it is a clear statement of the idea that money is constituted by social relations.

Simmel's The Philosophy of Money

Simmel rejected all economic theory that locates money's value in the substance of the 'money stuff'. The value of money does not derive from either the costs of its production, or supply and demand, or labour-value. Rather, Simmel developed the implicitly relativistic theory of value to be found in the Austrian subjectivist theory of exchange. 'Money is the value of things without the things themselves' (Simmel 1907 [1978], p. 121). Money is the *abstraction* of the 'distilled exchangeability of objects … the *relation* between things, a relation that persists in spite of the changes in the things themselves' (ibid., p. 124 emphasis in original). Following the 'nominalists' of the 'Historical School', Simmel asserts the logical primacy of the abstraction of money of account. Money is 'one of those normative ideas that obey the norms that they themselves represent' (ibid., p. 122). (See Orléan 1998: money is *autoreferentielle*. See also Searle 1996.)

Money is a form of 'sociation' and is structurally different from barter. 'When barter is replaced by money transactions a third factor is introduced between the two parties … the direct line of contact between them … moves to the relationship which each of them … has with the economic community that accepts the money' (Simmel 1907 [1978], p. 177). Simmel then endorses the credit theory of money: '[t]his is the core of the truth in the theory that money is only a claim upon society' (ibid., p. 177). Indeed, '[m]etallic money, which is usually regarded as the absolute opposite of credit money, contains in fact two presuppositions of credit which are particularly intertwined' (ibid., p. 178). First, the metallic substance cannot be normally tested in cash transactions and is, rather, verified by the secondary characteristics stamped on coins by the issuing authority. Second, people must *trust* that the tokens of value will retain their value. This may be based on objective probabilities; but this 'kind of trust is only a weak form of inductive knowledge' (ibid., p. 179). There can never be sufficient information for it to be the only basis for holding money.

However, having rejected essentialist and costs of production theories of intrinsic precious metallic value, Simmel is left with the problem of Austrian 'subjectivism' – how can myriad individual preferences produce a scale of inter-subjective values? 'Money as abstract value expresses nothing but the relativity of things that constitute value' (ibid., p. 121); but *at the same time*, it transcends the relativity of exchangeable values and 'as the stable pole, contrasts with the eternal movements, fluctuations of the objects with all others' (ibid., p. 121, emphasis added). But how does it do this? Simmel agrees with the Austrian economists that money expresses exchangeability, but sees that it cannot have been the *result of the process of exchange*. Rather, it 'can have developed only out of *previously existing values…*' (ibid., p. 119 emphasis added). But which might these have been? Simmel left no more than scattered clues.

Second, how is the abstract value of modern dematerialised money established and maintained? Precious metal is a means of maintaining confidence, but in an 'ideal world' money would be no more than 'its essential function', as a symbol of abstract value. Here, Simmel reverts to a thoroughly positivist economic conception of money. '[M]oney would then reach a neutral position which would be as little affected by the fluctuations in commodities as is the yardstick by the different lengths that it measures' (ibid., p. 191, emphasis added). Simmel accepts the economists' 'ideal world' in which the value of commodities is the result of the interplay of subjective preferences, mediated by the neutral symbol of money. But in both cases this 'ideal world' is not explained.

Keynes's concept of money

Together with the nineteenth century Banking School's 'credit theory', 'state theory' influenced Keynes's *A Treatise on Money* (1930). During his 'Babylonian madness' in the 1920s, Keynes studied the German Historical School's work on ancient Near Eastern money. During the third and second millennia BC, their economies were organised with a *money of account*, but payments were made in commodities, labour service, silver by weight, etc. (Ingham 2000a; Wray, 2004). 'Money of Account, namely that in which Debts and Prices and General Purchasing Power are expressed, is the primary concept of a Theory of Money'. Forms of money such as coins '*can only exist* in relation to a Money of Account' (Keynes, 1930, p. 3, emphasis added). In other words, the quality of 'moneyness' is conferred by the abstract measure of value that is imposed by the state when it writes the monetary 'dictionary' (Keynes 1930, pp. 4–5; 11–15). 'Money' existed for several thousand years before the first use of coinage around 700 BC.

Keynes also identified 'Acknowledgements of Debt' as forms of money (Keynes 1930, pp. 6–9). The chapter 'The "Creation" of Bank Money' provides a description of the creation of new deposits of money by the act of lending in a way that is relatively independent of the level of incoming deposits of savings. 'There is no limit to the amount of bank-money that banks can safely create provided that *they move forward in step*'. Bank chairmen believe that 'outside forces', over which they have no control, determine their decisions. '[Y]et the "outside forces" may be nothing but himself and his fellow chairmen, and certainly not his depositors' (Keynes 1930, pp. 26–27, original emphasis). The analysis points to *the socially constructed reality of the norms of banking practice*. Bank money is the result of the act of lending – that is to say, the social relation of debt constitutes money.[5] This analysis has been elaborated in the Post Keynesian concept of 'endogenous' money and other closely related theories.

'Endogenous' money

The theory of 'endogenous' is traceable to the writings of the nineteenth-century Banking School (Wray 1990; Smithin 1994). The modern use of the term is closely associated with Kaldor's Post Keynesian argument that, in a capitalist economy, money is the result of producers' *demand* for credit from the banking system (Rochon 1999, Ch. 3). Money is produced 'endogenously' in the normal course of the financing of capitalist production. There are three related essential propositions in the theory (Wray 1990, pp. 73–4). First, loans make deposits, second, deposits make reserves, and third, money demand induces money supply. As the demand for money is for productive investment, it is often argued that the 'monetarist' idea of an 'excessive' money supply that creates inflation does not make sense (Smithin 1994). In this regard, many Post Keynesian theories of 'endogenous money' imply a reversal of the direction of causation in the classical quantity theory of money – from right to left: P (prices) to M (quantity of money) rather than left to right as in Fisher's equation. Consequently, they favour a 'cost–push' theory in which inflation is primarily the result of precisely that factor which Fisher specifically ruled out in his original formulation – the wage demands of labour (see the references in Fischer 1996, pp. 200–203). Mainstream 'exogenous money' theorists acknowledge that the banking system creates credit-money, but insist that the central bank is able to exercise control over this process by its power to create the base money for the system (see Rochon 1999, p. 42). In contrast, Post Keynesians maintain that central banks are presented with a fait accompli by the commercial banks who meet any level of demand for loans that satisfies their creditworthiness criteria. Some Post Keynesians depart even more radically from economic orthodoxy and argue that 'fractional reserves' have no real impact on the creation of credit-money (see Rogers and Rymes 2000; Wray 1998). Rather, the central bank can, at best, influence the creation of money *indirectly* through its discount rate. In a most general sense, Post Keynesians reject the notion that there exists a 'stock' of money the supply of which is mediated by the central bank and commercial banks. Notwithstanding orthodox economic terminology, Post Keynesian analysis implies a sociological generalisation about the production of credit-money. This would require *empirical* analysis and not simply the statistical manipulation of macroeconomic variables. It implies that the 'supply' of money must be explained in the context of the social structure of the power relations in typical capitalist banking systems. This is more apparent in a continental European variant – the theory of the 'monetary circuit'.

The theory of the 'monetary circuit'
The French and Italian 'circuit' theory differs in important respects from most British and American Post Keynesian analysis (see especially, Graziani 1990; Parguez and Seccareccia 2000). The 'circuitists' tend to reject the treatment of money in *The General Theory* in favour of *A Treatise on Money* and Keynes's articles of the late 1930s (Rochon 1999, p. 9). They are more consistent in their endorsement of the credit theory of money: 'money is a debt which circulates freely' (Schmitt 1975, p. 106). And, most importantly, this conception of money has led to their focus on the actual structure of relationships that constitutes the capitalist 'monetary circuit'. Indeed, a number of these French and Italian writers entirely reject the analytical framework of the *supply and demand* for money.

The actual structure of the monetary circuit that they have in mind is based on the interpretation of bank lending, as found for example in the nineteenth-century Banking School and, in particular, the writing of Thomas Tooke where money is seen to move in two phases. In the first 'efflux' phase debts are issued by bank credit to allow private firms to start production. In the 'reflux phase' the debts are extinguished when firms reimburse the banks with the circulating debt that they have acquired through the sale of production. Money is *created* by bank credit and *destroyed* by the repayment of the debt from the profits of production at the end of the circuit. This approach differs from the orthodox economic methodology that also informs much Post Keynesian theory – for example, the attention to individual 'liquidity preference'. In contrast, 'circuit' analysis is explicitly sociological: money is a 'social reality within the system: a non commodity in a universe of commodities (de Vroey 1984, p. 383)

This 'social reality' may be seen as a 'three-way balance sheet relation' between the issuers of credit, the borrowers and those employed by the borrowers who spend it as 'money'. Graziani has outlined this social structure in more detail (Graziani 1990). It comprises the complex relationships between three 'macro-groups' in the economy: those between banks and firms; between firms and workers; and between the banks and the central bank. Most importantly, 'banks and firms must be considered as *two distinct kinds of agents* [which] cannot be aggregated into one single sector' (Graziani 1990, p. 11, emphasis added). In other words, following the early Keynes, Minksy and others, the money and production sides of the capitalist economy must be seen as relatively autonomous in both the short and long runs.

Modern neo-chartalism

The connection between Knapp and Keynes has recently been revived in an application of the 'state theory' to the problem of securing non-inflationary full employment (Wray 1998; 2000; Bell 2000, 2001). As yet its impact on academic economics beyond the heterodox fringe is limited. Its iconoclasm is evident in the charge, from a strong supporter of 'monetary circuit theory', that Wray's current 'chartalism' cannot be reconciled with his earlier Post Keynesianism, and that he is best described as a 'funny monetarist' (Rochon 1999, p. 298).

Wray integrates Lerner's theory of 'functional finance' with Knapp's fundamental proposition that the population works in order to earn the money to meet their tax obligations. Writing in the early days of the US's 'Keynesian' fiscal policy, Lerner argued that traditional doctrines of 'sound' government finance should be replaced with a level of spending in the economy that was 'neither greater nor less than that rate which at the current prices would buy all the goods that it is possible to produce' (Lerner 1943, p. 39 quoted in Wray 2000). The state should act as the 'employer of last resort' (Mosler 1997). Neo-chartalists correctly identify the state's role in social and economic structure of monetary creation, but, as economists, they tend to overlook that monetary policy is not simply a matter of 'functionality'. As Weber saw clearly, it is an outcome of social and political struggle.

Weber on money

Weber[6] upheld Knapp's distinction between the 'valuableness' and 'value' (1978: 193, see also pp. 78–79). But, in addition to money's 'formal validity' ('valuableness'), there must also exist 'the probability that it will be at some future time acceptable in exchange for specified or unspecified goods in price relationships which are capable of approximate estimate' (ibid., p. 169). In this emendation of 'state theory', Weber followed economic orthodoxy, and his critique of Knapp's analysis of inflation is based, to some extent, upon the commodity and quantity theories of money (ibid., p. 192, also pp. 180–184). Weber believed that the analysis of the price of goods – including the purchasing power of money – was more properly part of economics (ibid., p. 79). Nonetheless, he was unable to resist, mainly in footnotes, making incisive comments on the nature of economic theorising. *Economy and Society* contains the germs of a sociological recasting of a 'substantive theory of money' (ibid., p. 190).

Typically, Weber confronts *both* economic orthodoxy and its socialist critics (ibid., pp. 78–80, 107–109). Prices, which in conventional theory are the result of the interplay of supply and demand, are seen as the 'product of conflicts of interest [that] result from power constellations' in 'the struggle for economic existence'. Consequently, money is not economic theory's 'neutral veil' draped over exchange ratios of commodities. Rather, money 'is primarily a weapon in this struggle, and prices are expressions of this struggle; they are instruments in this struggle only as estimated quantifications of relative chances in this struggle' (ibid., p. 108).

The market may be a power struggle; but Weber offers no comfort to the socialists, who, following Marx, wished to remedy the inequality by issuing vouchers for an agreed 'quantity of socially useful labour'. In order to produce rational calculability, money has to be a weapon in the struggle for economic existence between 'the play of interests oriented only to profitability' (ibid., p. 183). The exchange of a socially agreed quantity of labour for specific goods would 'follow the rules of barter' (ibid., p. 80), and could not produce a measure of abstract value. Weber agreed with the Austrian theoretical economists in the 'socialist calculation' debate money can never be a 'harmless "voucher"' as its valuation is 'always in very complex ways dependent on its scarcity' (ibid., p. 79). Any equilibrium or price stability in equation of quantities of money and goods, in particular the interest rate, will be the expression of a *predictable balance of power*. Conversely, in this admittedly incomplete formulation, price instability in general is as much the result of the 'economic struggle for existence' as it is the product of an overabundance (inflation) or scarcity (deflation) of money. In short, socialism could not produce rational monetary calculation. Bureaucratic administration could never produce 'the "right"' volume or the '"right" type of money' because state bureaucracies are 'primarily oriented to the creation of purchasing power for certain interest groups' (including the state itself) – which would cause inflation (ibid., p. 183).

Fundamentals of a theory of money

Attention should focus on three questions. What is money? How is money produced? How does money obtain, retain, or lose its value?

What is money?

Mainstream economic theory's focus on money as an actual medium of exchange entails a 'category error' in which specific *forms* of money have been mistaken for the *generic* quality of 'moneyness'. This has resulted in long-standing confusion over closely related issues – for example, the distinction between money and credit, the so-called 'dematerialisation' of money, the advent of virtual 'post-modern' money, electronic money and the 'end of money' (Ingham 2002). Money is uniquely specified as a *measure of abstract value* and a *means of storing* and *transporting* this abstract value.

Monetary exchange consists in the calculation, exchange and transfer of debits and credits according to a money of account. Money cannot be created without the simultaneous creation of debt. For money to be money, it presupposes the existence of a debt measured in money of account elsewhere in the social system. The holder of money is owed goods.

> [M]oney is only a claim upon society. ... The liquidation of every private obligation by money means that the community now assumes this obligation to the creditor ... [M]etallic money is also a promise to pay and ... differs from the cheque with respect to the size of the group which vouches for its being accepted. The common relationship that the owner of money and the seller have to a social group – the claim of the former to a service and the trust of the latter that this claim will be honoured – provides the sociological constellation in which money transactions, as distinct from barter are accomplished'. (Simmel 1907 [1978], pp. 177, 174–9)

The traditional metaphor of a 'circulation' is inappropriate. Rather, vast dense networks of overlapping and interconnected bilateral credit-debit relationships constitute money. This is more obvious in the case of the 'clearing' of debits and credits in a bank giro, where money-stuff does not actually 'flow' from one account to another; but it applies equally to coins and notes which might be referred to as 'portable debt' (Gardiner 1993, p. 224). The essential point is that the debt is either transferable (bank giro) or portable (coin) because it is denominated in money of account. Money is constituted by the *continuation* of relations of credit–debt – hence the counterintuitive observation that money would disappear if all debts were paid (Bloch 1954).

This conceptualisation becomes clearer with consideration of the multiplicity and dissociation of money 'things' in relation to the abstraction of money. Money of account, means of payment for the unilateral discharge of debt, and any media of exchange need not be integrated in single form – as in coinage. Not all the media forms of modern money express the full integration – cash, plastic cards, cheques, magnetic traces in computer disks, and so on. The same point is clearly expressed in a study of money and national identity in early capitalism.

> By the 1830s, then, Britons could at different times and places have understood gold sovereigns, banknotes, or bills of exchange as the privileged local representatives of the pound ... the pound as an abstraction was constituted precisely by its capacity to assume these heterogeneous forms, since its existence as a national currency was determined by the mediations between them. (Rowlinson 1999, pp. 64–5)

How is money produced?

Different 'modes' of the production of money may be identified. These consist in social relations between issuers, issuer and users, and the technological means available for the storage and transportation of abstract value – from clay tablets, to coins, to pen and paper, to magnetic traces and so on. However, the fundamental question concerns the 'origins' of money of account; that is to say the abstract 'idea' of money. The production of money involves a social and political process by which money is assigned 'functions' and thereby constituted as an 'institutional fact' (Ingham 1996; Searle 1995). In other words, money is not produced in the course of economic exchange as the most tradable commodity that reduces transactions costs – as the economic mainstream maintains. To be sure, money has these 'functions', but they are only able to operate after the 'moneyness' of money has been assigned.

Money of account

'Unless the commodities used for exchange bear some relation to a fixed standard, we are dealing with barter [because] ... the parties in barter-exchange are comparing their *individual needs*, not *values in the abstract*' (Grierson 1977, pp. 16–19, emphasis added). For example, the tobacco used as a medium of exchange in seventeenth century Virginia only became money when its value was fixed at three shillings a pound (ibid., p. 17). The standard of value, determined by weight (the exchange value of money-stuff), is not the important issue. Rather 'countability' transforms the 'commodity' (*qua* convenient medium of exchange) into 'money'. This might be 'countable-useful' (slaves, cattle, furs) or 'countable-ornamental' (teeth, beads, shells) (Grierson 1977, p. 33, see also Hoover 1996).

As an alternative to the theory that a measure of abstract value could emerge from subjective preferences in barter, Grierson argues that it originated in a very early social institution for the settlement of disputes, later examples of which are known as *wergeld* (Grierson 1977, p. 19). *Wergeld* (worthpayment) sanctioned payment of damages and compensation for injury and insult according to a fixed scale of tariffs.

'The conditions under which these laws were put together would appear to satisfy, much better than the market mechanism, the pre-requisites for the establishment of a monetary system. The tariffs for damages were established in public assemblies, and. ... Since what is laid down consists of evaluations of injuries, not evaluation of commodities, the conceptual difficulty of devising a common measure for appraising unrelated objects is avoided' (ibid., p. 20–21). The punitive and compensatory tariffs expressed both the *utilitarian* and *moral* components of society (Ingham 1996). *Wergeld* symbolically represents society's two faces in prescribing recompense for both *injury* and *insult*. On the one hand, it accounted for the functional worth of the contribution of social roles to societal welfare by assigning a tariff to the loss or impairment of their individual incumbents; for example, young men of fighting age were worth more than old women and so on. On the other hand, such schemes of functional or utilitarian worth were embedded in norms and values that directly reflected the hierarchical status order of society. Compensation for the loss of a Russian nobleman's moustache, for example, was four times greater than for the loss of a finger (Grierson 1977, p. 20). *Wergeld* was the codification of the social values without which society would be left open to socially and economically debilitating blood feuds.

Standards of value

Once the concept of abstract monetary accounting (unit of account) was available to society, the next step was the development of a standard of value based on commodities, as occurred in the ancient Near Eastern empires in the period from 3000 to 1000 BC (Goldsmith 1987; Ch. 2; Keynes 1982, pp. 223–93; Wray, 2004). The Babylonian *shekel* was originally fixed at 1 *gur* (1.2 hectolitres of barley) and later at a more manageable 8.3 grams of silver. However, these societies were command economies with only very small trade sectors. The overwhelming majority of payments were rents and taxes to religious and secular authorities. There was no coinage and payment was made in commodities, labour services, or silver by weight (*shekel, mina, talent*) (Goldsmith 1987). The state not only fixed the standard, but also the prices of taxes, rents, and so on. Money has its 'logical origins' in money of account and its historical foundation in the 'chartal' money of early bureaucratic empires. It was not the spontaneous product of the market.

Coinage

The integration of all the attributes (unit of account, means of exchange/payment, store of value) in the form of coin came 2,000 years later in Lydia and Greece around 600 BC (Davies 1994). Centralised monarchical states and developments in metallurgy made it possible to embody money of account, standard/store of value, and means of payment/exchange in a single object. It is probable that the disintegration of the larger bureaucratic empires into smaller states was important in the development of coinage. Small unstable states were dependent on mercenary soldiers whom they paid in lumps of precious metal (Kraay 1964). As campaigning soldiers spent their lumps, they greatly expanded the scale and scope of market exchange. However, the fundamental money relation was taxation: '...there is no reason to suppose that [coinage] was ever issued by Rome for any other purpose than to enable the state to make payments ...Once issued coinage was demanded back by the state in payment of taxes' (Crawford 1970, p. 46).

Four aspects of coinage should be noted in relation to the commodity theory of money. First, the precious metal coins used for payment of taxes were almost invariably too large for daily use. This medium of exchange function was performed by *base metal tokens*. For example, Rome had the gold *aureus* and silver *denarius*, supplemented by the *sestertius* of copper, zinc and tin (Goldsmith 1987, p. 36). Second, coins frequently were not struck with a numerical signifier of their relationship to the money of account. (Further, only the silver penny of Charlemagne's abstract money of account of pounds, shillings, and pence was ever minted.) Monetary policy, usually from fiscal motives, involved, on the one hand, 'crying up' or 'crying down' the coinage – that is to say, changing its value in relation to the abstract money of account. On the other hand, it was important to ensure that bullion and nominal values of the precious metal did not diverge to the point where the coins went out of circulation to be melted down (Gresham's Law). Third, the 'token' character of coins is apparent in that debasement of the coinage, by reduction of its metallic content, had very little effect its purchasing power over considerable periods of time (Einaudi 1934; Wray 2000; Goldsmith 1987, p. 37). Fourth, as prices had already begun to rise sharply decades before the discovery of South American silver, it seems improbable that its importation was the cause of seventeenth-century inflation (Fischer 1996).

Capitalist credit money
Until late sixteenth-century Europe, credit networks were restricted to small mercantile sectors and did not developed into widely circulating 'private' money (Boyer-Xambeu et al. 1994). The issue of money remained the sovereign's prerogative. In capitalism, however, monetary sovereignty is shared between the state and the private banking system.

'The development of the law and practice of negotiable paper and of "created" deposits afford the best indication we have for dating the rise of capitalism' (Schumpeter 1954 [1994], p. 78). Money was freed from the physical constraints of territory and geology and could become an autonomous force of production (ibid., p. 318). But, this development cannot be explained in terms of the functional need for a more 'efficient' money in an economy whose dynamic lay elsewhere in 'real' factors such as technology, the division of labour, or capital-labour social relations of production (Ingham 1999). Modern forms of credit money were the result of particular geopolitical conditions and social structural changes in the reawakening of Europe after the collapse of the Roman Empire and its coinage system.

When minting of coin *(moneta reale)* resumed in the myriad political jurisdictions of fragmented medieval Europe, they were integrated by Charlemagne's abstract *moneta immagineria* (money of account) (Einaudi 1936 [1953], p. 230). The Holy Roman Empire was too weak to impose a centralised minted coinage, but it was able to provide a common money of account for taxation and ecclesiastical transfers. This dissociation of the two elements of money in provided one of the conditions for the emergence of merchants' private bank money, which was based on the bill of exchange (Bloch 1954). These bills, denominated in the *moneta immaginaria* (money of account), existed in an unstable relationship with myriad coinages. Eventually, the bills became detached from the commodities that they actually represented and, resting only on the banker's promise to pay, became means of payment. Thus, after a long struggle, money ceased to be the sovereign's monopoly.

With regard to 'state theory', it should be noted that the merchants' private bank-credit money only became widely accepted when the states joined the bank giros (Wray 1990). The fusion of state and bank credit money developed first in the Italian city-states during the fifteenth and sixteenth centuries, then spread to Holland and, most decisively, to England with the formation of the Bank of England in 1694. The widespread use of debt as a means of payment outside the networks of traders required the state to establish the legal depersonalisation and negotiability of debt by which the simple credit of the personal IOU, recorded in unit of account, could become credit money (Carruthers 1996, Ingham 1999). All subsequent developments have been extensions and refinements of this evolutionary leap in monetary practice. The hybridisation of precious metallic standard coinage with state and bank credit-money persisted until the twentieth century.

Modern money is constituted and sustained by the norms that govern two fundamental and reciprocal debtor creditor relations. Money consists in these social relations. First, to meet their expenses, states issue money, which is required, in turn, for the payment taxes. Second, the national debt, held by the state's creditors, comprises a base of 'high powered' money, held in the banking system. Norms for 'marching in step', as Keynes expressed it, specify how new money can be 'endogenously' created from this base (Wray 1990; Smithin 1994; Ingham 2000(b). Other forms of private or 'near' money exist in capitalist networks and local exchange trading schemes, but they remain subordinate to state money (Ingham 2002).

The value of money
For orthodox economic theory, the question of the value of money, as expressed by the price level, is a function of the relationship between the quantities of money and commodities. In the long run, the two quantities attain an equilibrium – that is, money is neutral. Short-run disequilibria between 'real' ('natural') prices and rising, inflationary 'nominal' prices will occur; but, according to the model, these will be self-correcting and money's neutrality will be reasserted – in the *long run*. A recent survey of mainstream literature by European Central Bank economists confirms the status of these assumptions: 'The one to one relationship between money and prices is one of the few *results* that have remained undisputed over time and across economists' (Issing 2001, pp. 9, 76–77. Emphasis added to indicate that this is not a 'result' of empirical research, but an axiom). However, it is also acknowledged that, first, 'a satisfactory and

agreed distinction between the long and short run is not available' (ibid., p. 8). Secondly, there is no satisfactory way of constructing empirically based models of these short run effects, nor of judging the relative merits of the models (ibid., p. 7, 21). Furthermore, as 'the different models carry highly different alleged implications for monetary policy' economic analysis would appear not to provide a secure basis for policy-making. Nonetheless, the search for a 'neutral rate of interest' is recommended, regardless of the fact that this is 'difficult to estimate and impossible to know with precision' (Blinder 1998, p. 50).

In other words, since the failure of 'monetarism', the relationship between orthodox economic theory and monetary policy has become incoherent. To be sure, it may be argued that monetary authorities are now in the business of shaping inflation 'expectations', but in the absence of a single definitive economic model available to all economic agents, then, this process cannot be of the kind modelled by Lucas and the rational expectations theorists. Rather, monetary authorities are 'players' in the Weberian struggle for economic existence in which money is a 'weapon'. Further analysis along these lines cannot be undertaken here beyond brief comments on the social bases of inflation/deflation and the rhetorical and ideological construction of the value of money.

The social bases of inflation/deflation

As we have noted, it makes at least equal sense to reverse the assumed left to right *causation* MV to PT in the quantity equation. In the 'struggle for economic existence', agents attempt to monetize their positions of power by raising their prices which, in turn, are met by the 'endogenous' creation of credit-money in the banking system. Monetary policy involves the attempt to restrict this process by central bank interest rate policy. Of course, this is recognised to some extent within orthodox economic analysis, but the social and political process involved is not *theorised*. The idea that inflation results from escalating claims has a long pedigree in Keynesian 'cost push'/'mark up' theory (Fischer 1997, pp. 232–4). During the hyperinflation of the 1970s, a promising sociology of inflation was developed (Hirsch and Goldthorpe 1978), but it waned as inflation fell.

In contrast, the 'economic' puzzle of Japan's protracted recession and deflation since 1990, for example, demands a similar analysis. As economic theory maintains, rational Japanese restrain consumption, in the expectation of continued price deflation, and the economy falls into Keynes's 'liquidity trap'. Only borrowing and spending can cure the 'debt deflation'. However, the recession has also created a level of insecurity that is a direct consequence of the *social structure* of the Japanese economy. In the post-war reconstruction, the provision of social welfare and security – especially lifelong employment – was assigned to the Japanese conglomerate corporations (*keiretsu*) and not so much the state as in the West. Eventually, the recession eroded the willingness and ability of the *keiretsu* to continue this role. Regardless of the important political dimensions of Japan's impasse, chronic insecurity resists all conventional economic policy measures to inflate the economy.

The social construction of abstract value

This constant tension between the expansion and contraction of value through the creation of debt and the possible disintegration of the standard of value through inflation is a central dynamic of capitalism. This is a socially constructed non-mechanical relation and institutions are required to keep the two forces in balance. 'The overriding problem is to find some means to maintain the working fiction of a monetary invariant through time, so that debt contracts (the ultimate locus of value creation) ... may be written in terms of the unit at different dates' (Mirowski 1991, p. 579). The effectiveness of money as the continuity of stable abstract value through time depends on a commitment to a course of action that is based on trust that others will continue to accept our money. But this trust needs to be explained.

Monetary space is form of *impersonal* trust (Schapiro 1987). In the face of radical uncertainty, self-fulfilling long-term trust is rooted in social and political legitimacy whereby potentially untrustworthy 'strangers' are able to participate personally in impersonal complex multilateral economic relationships. However the market is not in the business of trust building and the history of successful money is the history of successful states (Goodhart 1998). Conversely, chronically unsuccessful states fail to produce adequate money precisely because they are unable to forge and sustain the two main monetary relations with its citizens on politically acceptable terms– taxation and government debt. The recent histories of Argentina, Russia and Afghanistan provide compelling evidence for this generalisation.

Social conventions based on no more than either an equilibrium of competing interests or consensual agreement are fragile (Douglas 1986). Enduring social institutions such as money require a stronger foundation. 'There needs to be a analogy by which the formal structure of a crucial set of social relations is found in the physical world, or in the super-natural world, or in eternity, anywhere, so long as it is not seen as a socially contrived arrangement' (Douglas 1986, p. 48). If successfully enacted, ideological naturalisation conceals the social production and malleability of institutions. Until the twentieth century, the ideological naturalisation of money was achieved, and its social construction concealed, by the commodity form of money in the gold standard (see Carruthers (1996). With the abandonment of gold, however, the fiction of a universal, immutable, natural monetary standard became increasingly difficult to sustain. Nonetheless, the rhetoric of a 'natural' economic process persists in the theory that underpins monetary policy.

The production of a 'working fiction' of stable money now consists of (1) the attempt to control the price of debt through interest rates and (2) monitoring monetary policy's avoidance of a fall in the value of money. The creation of money by states must be seen to be non-inflationary with regard to accepted conventions derived from economic theory. Expert economists in independent central banks assess whether economic activity might force interest rates and employment above their 'natural' levels (Issing 2001). Economic *theory* plays a 'performative' role in the formation not only of expectations that define the situation, but also the social institutions that produce the money (on 'performativity' see Searle 1995). In other words, economic theory does not simply describe the process by which the value of money is attained, it is, rather, a constitutive part of it. Japan's current impasse is again instructive. As modern neo-Chartalists and 'functional finance' theorists argue, states can 'print' as much money as they wish, but despite the remote prospect of inflation, the Japanese monetary authorities continue to pursue orthodox conventions. These are aimed at reassuring creditors that their investments will not be eroded by inflation because monetary policy is aligned with the natural propensities of the economy as specified in economic *theory*.

Central banks establish their 'monetary credentials', according to this rhetoric, and through the buying and selling of currencies the global money markets deliver their verdicts the credibility of the 'working fictions'. The process has become increasingly formalised through the use of the hierarchies of credibility of sovereign debt produced by credit-rating agencies. Permanent monetary stability in a capitalist economy can only be considered to be theoretical possibility if orthodox economic theory's assumptions of neutrality and a natural tendency towards long-run economic equilibrium are accepted. But neither is helpful in explaining money as a social institution. As Weber argued in his interpretation of Austrian economics, all monetary systems, if they are to produce market prices and produce and store abstract value, are necessarily precarious and unstable. In his view formulation, the possibility of the formal rationality of monetary calculation lies in substantively non-rational economic conflict.

As constituted by 'real' social relations of debt, money is an autonomous and active element in economic life that has double-edged or contradictory effects. It is the means of creating expanded value in the form of commodities; but it is also the means of their destruction (Schumpeter 1912 [1934]; Minsky 1986). The attribution of real force and efficacy to money does not entail a metaphysical 'nominalism' or a form of 'money illusion'. This is so only if the economy is taken to comprise nothing of importance other than commodities and their 'real' relations. Rather, money is an expression of human society's capacity for self-transformation. Arguably, this most powerful of 'social technologies' is one over which we have, *inevitably*, a most insecure grasp.

Notes

1. The labour theory of value committed Marx, and his successors, to a version of the commodity theory of money, with all its attendant errors (Marx 1976, pp. 162, 186,188). Most important, this prevented Marx from realising that his theory of capital as a social relation applied also to money. In particular, he did not fully understand capitalist credit money (Ingham 1998). Like orthodox economics, the Marxist analysis of money has been disabled by the search for the value of money in the commodity (Fine and Lapavitsas 2000 and the critique in Ingham 2001). It has been unable to consider the proposition that *all* money consists in symbolic 'tokens' of *abstract* value that signify and are constituted by social relations of credit–debt. Later Marxist analyses of 'finance capital' have perpetuated the misunderstanding (Hilferding 1910 [1981], pp. 36, 376; see Henwood 1997). But Marx's distinctive departure from classical economics is to show that monetary relationships do not merely represent a *natural economic* reality, but also mask the latter's underlying reality of the *social relations* of production. These constitute the reality that appears in a monetised alienated form. For Marx there are *two* 'veils'. Behind money lie 'real' economic forces, as they do in somewhat different manner in the orthodox economics. In turn behind these economic forces lie the 'real' social relations, which also appear as monetary relations.
2. 'Imaginary' or 'ghost' money was contrasted with actual coin in the early medieval period (Einaudi 1936 [1953]; Wood 2002).
3. Note that it is implicitly assumed that states' taxation demands could be met in this way.
4. Early bank credit money is often seen as supporting the 'market' theory of money. But three facts should be borne in mind. First, the banks grew with support of states. Second, the bank issue of 'private' money was linked to a state's money of account. Third, early private bank money only flourished when it integrated with state money (Boyer-Xambeu et al. 1994; Wray 1990).
5. However, by the *General Theory of Employment, Interest and Money* (1936) Keynes's implicitly sociological analysis had given way to a more economically orthodox treatment in which investment must also be equal to *ex ante* savings (see Rogers and Rymes 2000). Nonetheless, Keynes's analysis broke with orthodoxy's preoccupation with the 'things' that function as *media of exchange*.
6. The enormous secondary literature on Weber's analysis of capitalism scarcely refers to his analysis of money. The chapters on money and banking in *General Economic History* have been almost completely ignored (Weber 1927 [1981]). This neglect is more puzzling in light of his lavish praise for Knapp's *State Theory of Money*. One would have expected scholars to have followed Weber's lead in exploring the 'permanently fundamental importance' of this 'magnificent work' (Weber 1978:184,169; also pp. 78–79).

References

Aglietta, Michel, and André Orléan (eds) (1998), *La Monnaie souveraine*, Paris: Odile Jacob.

Bell, S. (2000), 'Do taxes and bonds finance government spending', *Journal of Economic Issues*, **XXXIV** (3), 603–20.

Bell, S. (2001), 'The role of the state and the hierarchy of money', *Cambridge Journal of Economics*, **25**, 149–63.

Blinder, A. (1998), *Central Banking in Theory and Practice*, Cambridge, MA: MIT Press.

Bloch, Marc (1954), *Equisse d'une histoire monetaire de Europe*, Paris: Armand Colin.

Boyer-Xambeu, M.T., G. Deleplace and L. Gillard (1994), *Private Money and Public Currencies: The Sixteenth Century Challenge*, London: M.E. Sharpe.

Carruthers, B. (1996), *City of Capital*, Princeton, NJ: Princeton University Press.

Carruthers, B., and S. Babb (1996), 'The color of money and the nature of value: greenbacks and gold in Postbellum America', *American Journal of Sociology*, **101** (6), 1556–91.

Clower, Robert (1984), 'A reconsideration of the microfoundations of money' in D. Walker (ed), *Money and Markets: Essays by Robert Clower*, Cambridge: Cambridge University Press, pp. 81–9.

Cohen, B. (2001), 'Electronic money: new day or false dawn', *Review of International Political Economy*, **8** (2), 197–225.

Crawford, M. (1970), 'Money and exchange in the Roman world', *Journal of Roman Studies*, **60**, 40–48.

Davies, G. (1994), *A History of Money*, Cardiff: University of Wales Press.

de Vroey, Michel (1984), 'Inflation: a non-monetarist interpretation', *Cambridge Journal of Economics*, **8** (4), 381–99.

Dodd, N. (1994), *The Sociology of Money*, Cambridge: Polity Press.

Douglas, M. (1986), *How Institutions Think*, London: Routledge

Dowd, K. (2000), 'The invisible hand and the evolution of the monetary system', in J. Smithin (ed), *What is Money?*, London: Routledge, pp. 139–56.

Einaudi, Luigi (1936 [1953]), 'The theory of imaginary money from Charlemagne to the French Revolution', in F.C. Lane and J.C. Riemersma (eds), *Enterprise and Secular Change*, London: Allen and Unwin.

Ellis, H. (1934), *German Monetary Theory 1905–1933*, Cambridge, MA: Harvard University Press.

Fine, B. and Lapavitsas, C. (2000), 'Markets and money in social theory: what role for economics?', *Economy and Society*, **29** (3), 357–82.

Fischer, D. (1997), *The Great Wave: Price Revolutions and the Rhythm of History*, Oxford: Oxford University Press.

Fleetwood, Stephen (2000), 'A Marxist theory of commodity money revisited' in John Smithin (ed), *What is Money?*, London: Routledge, pp. 174–93.

Ganssmann, H. (1988), 'Money. A symbolically generalized medium of communication?', *Economy and Society*, **17**, 285–315.

Gardiner, G. (1993), *Towards True Monetarism*, London: Dulwich Press.

Giddens, Antony (1990), *The Consequences of Modernity*, Cambridge: Polity Press.

Goldsmith, R. (1987), *Pre-Modern Financial Systems*, Cambridge: Cambridge University Press.

Goodhart, C. (1998), 'The two concepts of money: implications for the analysis of optimal currency areas', *European Journal of Political Economy*, **14**, 407–32.

Graziani, A. (1990), 'The theory of the monetary circuit', *Economies et Societes*, **24** (7), 7–36.

Grierson, P. (1977), *The Origins of Money*, London: Athlone Press.

Guttman, R. (1994), *How Credit-Money Shapes the Economy*, New York: M. E. Sharpe.

Hahn, Frank (1987), 'Foundations of monetary theory', in M. de Cecco and J. Fitousi (eds), *Monetary Theory and Institutions*, London: Macmillan, pp. 21–43.

Hart, K. (2000), *The Memory Bank: Money in an Unequal World*, London: Profile Books.

Henwood, D. (1997), *Wall Street*, London: Verso.

Hicks, John R. (1989), *A Market Theory of Money*, Oxford: Oxford University Press.

Hirsch, F. and Goldthorpe, G. (eds) (1978), *The Political Economy of Inflation*, London: Martin Robertson.

Hodgson, Geoffrey (2001), *How Economics Forgot History*, London: Routledge.

Hoover, Kevin (1996), 'Some suggestions for complicating the theory of money', in S. Pressman (ed.), *Interactions in Political Economy*, London: Routledge, pp. 2004–16.

Hilferding, Rudolph (1910 [1981]), *Finance Capital*, London: Routledge and Kegan Paul.

Ingham, Geoffrey (1996), 'Money is a social relation', *Review of Social Economy*, **LIV** (4), 507–29.

Ingham, Geoffrey (1998), 'On the underdevelopment of the sociology of money', *Acta Sociologica*, **41**, 3–18.

Ingham, Geoffrey (1999), 'Capitalism, money and banking: a critique of recent historical sociology', *British Journal of Sociology*, **50** (1), 76–96.

Ingham, Geoffrey (2000a), '"Babylonian madness": on the sociological and historical "origins" of money', in John Smithin (ed), *What is Money?*, London: Routledge, pp. 16–41.

Ingham, Geoffrey (2000b), 'Class inequality and the social production of money' in R. Crompton, F. Devine, M. Savage and J. Scott (eds), *Renewing Class Analysis*, Oxford: Blackwell, pp. 66–86.

Ingham, Geoffrey (2001), 'Fundamentals of a theory of money: untangling Fine, Lapavitsas and Zelizer, *Economy and Society*, **30** (3), 304–23.

Ingham, Geoffrey (2002), 'New monetary spaces?' in Organisation for Economic Co-operation and Development, *The Future of Money*, Paris: OECD.

Issing, G. (2001), *Monetary Policy in the Euro Area*, Cambridge: Cambridge University Press.
Jones, R. (1976), 'The origin and development of media of exchange', *Journal of Political Economy*, **84** (4), 757–75.
Keynes, John M. (1930), *A Treatise on Money*, London: Macmillan.
Keynes, John M. (1936 [1973]), *The General theory of Employment, Interest and Money* in D. Moggeridge (ed.), *The Collected Writings of John Maynard Keynes*, vol. 7, Cambridge: Cambridge University Press.
Keynes, John M. (1982), *The Collected Writings of John Maynard Keynes*, vol. 28, D. Moggeridge (ed.), Cambridge: Cambridge University Press.
King, M. (1999), 'Challenges for monetary policy: new and old', *Bank of England Quarterly Bulletin*, **39**, 397–415.
Klein, P., and George Selgin (2000), 'Menger's theory of money: some empirical evidence', in John Smithin (ed), *What is Money?*, London: Routledge, pp. 217–51 2000.
Knapp, G. (1905 [1973]), *The State Theory of Money*, reprint, New York: Augustus M Kelley.
Kraay, C. (1964), 'Hoards, small change and the origin of coinage', *Journal of Hellenistic Studies*, **LXXXIV**, 76–91.
Lerner, A. (1943), 'Functional finance and the Federal debt', *Social Research*, **10**, 38–51.
Marx, Karl (1976), *Capital*, vol. I, Harmondsworth: Penguin.
Menger, Carl (1892), 'On the Origins of Money', *Economic Journal*, **2** (6), 239–55.
Minsky, Harold (1986), 'Money and crisis in Schumpeter and Keynes', in H.-J. Wagener and J. Drukker (eds), The *Economic Law of Motion of Modern Society*, Cambridge: Cambridge University Press, pp. 112–22.
Mirowski, Philip (1991), 'Post-modernism and the social theory of value', *Journal of Post-Keynesian Economics*, **13**, 565–82.
Mosler, W. (1997), 'Full employment and price stability', *Journal of Post-Keynesian Economics*, **20** (2), 167–82.
Mundell, Robert (1961), 'A theory of optimum currency areas', *American Economic Review*, **51**, 657–64.
Organisation for Economic Co-operation and Development (2002), *The Future of Money*, Paris: OECD.
Orléan, André (1998), 'La monnaie autoreferentielle: reflexions sur les evolutions monetaires contemporaines', in Michel Aglietta and André Orléan (eds), *La Monnaie souveraine*, Paris: Odile Jacob, pp. 359–85.
Parguez, A., and M. Seccareccia, (2000), 'The credit theory of money: the monetary circuit approach', in J. Smithin (ed.), *What is Money?*, London: Routledge, pp. 101–23.
Rochon, L.-P. (1999), *Credit, Money and Production: An Alternative Post-Keynesian Approach*, Cheltenham: Edward Elgar.
Rogers, C., and T. Rymes, (2000), 'The disappearance of Keynes's nascent theory of banking between the *Treatise* and the *General Theory*', in John Smithin (ed.), *What is Money?*, London: Routledge, pp. 257–69.
Rowlinson, M. (1999), '"The Scotch hate gold': British identity and paper money', in E. Gilbert and E. Helleiner (eds), *Nation-States and Money*, London: Routledge, pp. 47–67.
Schapiro, S. (1987), 'The social control of impersonal trust', *American Journal of Sociology*, **93** (3), 623–58.
Schmitt, R. (1975), *Monnaie, salaires et profits*, Paris: Presses Universitaires de France.
Schumpeter, Joseph (1912 [1934]), *The Theory of Economic Development*, Cambridge, MA: Harvard University Press.
Schumpeter, Joseph (1954 [1994]), *A History of Economic Analysis*, London: Routledge.
Searle, John (1995), *The Construction of Social Reality*, London: Penguin.
Sherman, S. (1997), 'Promises, promises: credit as a contested metaphor in early capitalist discourse', *Modern Philology*, **94**: 327–48.
Simmel, Georg (1907 [1978]) *The Philosophy of Money*, London: Routledge.
Smithin, John (1994), *Controversies in Monetary Economics*, Aldershot, UK and Brookfield, US: Edward Elgar.
Smithin, John (1996), *Macroeconomic Policy and the Future of Capitalism*, Cheltenham, UK and Brookfield, US: Edward Elgar.

Smithin, John (ed.) (2000), *What is Money?*, London: Routledge.

Weber, Max (1978), *Economy and Society*, Berkeley: University of California Press.

Weber, Max (1927 [1981]), *General Economic History*, New Brunswick, NJ: Transactions Publishers.

Wood, D. (2002), *Medieval Economic Thought*, Cambridge: Cambridge University Press.

Wray, R. (1990), *Money and Credit in Capitalist Economies*, Aldershot, UK and Brookfield, US: Edward Elgar.

Wray, R. (1998), *Understanding Modern Money*, Cheltenham, UK and Lyme, US: Edward Elgar.

Wray, R. (2000), 'Modern money', in John Smithin (ed.), *What is Money?*, London: Routledge, pp. 42–67.

Wray, R. (2004), *Credit and State Theories of Money: The Contributions of A. Mitchell Innes*, Cheltenham, UK and Northampton, US: Edward Elgar.

Index